THE HEBREW GODS

(BOOK 1)

REFLECTIONS ON THE JEWISH CONDITION

&

THE JEWISH TRADITION

In the Light of the Timeless Wisdom

Sarah Gihon

To the Ascended Master Sananda

Dedicated with reverence and love to Ascended Master Sananda to whom I am indebted for imparting the formerly hidden information around which this book was written.

'In something like historical times [Yahweh] was a being who played a part in creating one aspect of your reality on the Earth plane, setting in motion a particular phase of experience of what has become humanity's experience. There have been a number of different creations on this Planet, not just one creation'. (Ascended Master Sananda)

****

'Humanity has come from a number of different sources. There have been genetic inputs into the human race at different times in its history. The Jewish people was the recipient of a particular strand of DNA which contained particular types of information concerning the role to be played by those people who had this aspect of DNA within them. The safeguarding of this DNA strand took on the character of a goal: it offered the possibility of exerting a kind of stewardship over the rest of humanity'.
(Ascended Master Sananda)

COPYRIGHT 2008 by Sarah Gihon

Cover background image –

Credit to NASA/ESA & "The Hubble Heritage Team".

ISBN 978-1-84753-110-0

All rights reserved.

No part of this book may be reproduced, stored or transmitted in any form or by any means.

Published in the United States by LULU.com

iv

CONTENTS

INTRODUCTION THE PRIMEVAL GODS OF HUMANITY	Page x
PART ONE	Page 1
THE FATHER - YANG, COSMIC MASCULINE ENERGY (Sin & Retribution)	
CHAPTER 1 THE MYTH OF CREATION	Page 1
CHAPTER 2 DESTRUCTION – THE FATHER & SATAN PLOT THE DOWNFALL OF HUMANITY	Page 129
CHAPTER 3 ABRAHAM & THE FATHER – The Gods of Sumer accompany Abraham into exile	Page 146
CHAPTER 4 MOSES & THE FATHER – The Gods of Egypt escort IsRaEl out of exile	Page 182
CHAPTER 5 SOLOMON & THE GODDESS – the 'Sacred Feminine' enters the Temple	Page 283
CHAPTER 6 RESURGENCE OF THE GODDESS - THE MOTHER (Love & Redemption)	Page 333
CHAPTER 7 THE MYTH OF THE JEW	Page 386
CHAPTER 8 MATERIALISM OF THE OLD TESTAMENT	Page 449
PART TWO DRAMA OF MAN IN THE TEMPORAL WORLD	Page 459
BIBLIOGRAPHY	Page 637

SYNOPSIS

The Hebrew Gods written by Rabbi Moses de Vilna has lain hidden in the vaults of St Katherine Monastery at the foot of Mount Sinai. A group of friends set off on a journey of discovery to the biblical land of their ancestors in order to retrieve the manuscript and have it translated by a social scientist, Benzaccai. Benzaccai is under pressure from a strict religious faction to abandon the translation of the manuscript which contains a timeless knowledge that would render their ancient religious system obsolete. The sect stands for that which is archaic and unchanging. They are the 'people of the form'. Attached to the 'old Earth' point of view, caught up in the old paradigm, they are keeping their followers in a state of inertia and disempowerment. They diffuse the materialism of separateness, fear and authority to which people react, responsive to the subtle energies that stir up division and misunderstanding. In order to translate and safeguard the manuscript, Benzaccai goes into hiding. Concerned for his safety his friends trek the country looking for him as they retrieve the translated chapters he has entrusted a few dependable contacts with. During their travels they meet fascinating individuals who enrich their experience, stimulate their reflection and challenge their views. Below are some of the themes examined:

- Worship of time
- Worship of a temporal god
- Stellar origins of the god of the Book of Genesis
- The 'personality' of the temporal god
- Biological origins of the Jewish people
- Worship of the physical self
- Masculine/feminine polarity
- Soul/ego polarity
- Unity/duality
- The gods of Ancient Sumer reappear in the Old Testament
- Ancient Sumer, birthplace of the Jewish tradition
- The god of Ancient Sumer enlists the assistance of Abraham

- Moses & the god of Ancient Sumer
- Rise of Monotheism & patriarchal ascendancy
- The Ten Commandments examined and 'Revised'
- Solomon & the Goddess - the Sacred Feminine reappears
- The myth of the Jew - playing roles
- The Jew defines himself in biological terms
- Materialism of the Old Testament
- Ritualistic religion is of temporal man

Throughout *The Hebrew Gods* and its sequel *Twilight of the Hebrew Gods* we have used the word 'man' to mean both man and woman. For the sake of briefness we have also used 'his' and 'him' meaning also 'her'.

PREFACE

An 18th century manuscript *The Hebrew Gods*, written by a biblical scholar Rabbi Moses de Vilna, is discovered in a monastery which nests in the shadow of Mount Sinai. The text, inspired and informed by the Spiritual Wisdom of the East, contains disclosures of some significance for humanity at this time of accelerated change.

The Hebrew Gods focuses on two major issues: the Hebrew Tradition and the Jewish Condition.

What *The Hebrew Gods* sets out to present is an exhaustively researched synthesis of the Timeless Wisdom with academic research intended to be used as an exploratory tool in the search for the underlying meaning of the Old Testament and the nature of the Jewish condition.

The Hebrew Gods presents a critical evaluation of the ancient Hebrew world view in the light of the Wisdom of the Ages known to the mystical East.

The Hebrew Gods encourages the reader to adopt a questioning attitude to the past as it promotes a deeper insight into the Hebrew tradition and the Jewish condition until now shrouded in myth. It also suggests a novel way of forging a creative, innovative relationship with the Old Testament.

The text is divided into sections which can be read separately and independently of each other.

The Hebrew Gods explores the past, delves into the present and outlines some of the features of the future in the making.

The self and its 'gods' are dynamically illustrated in the archetypal Myths and symbolic biblical dramas. We are informed by the Masters that man contains the entire universe. In this light, cosmic events can be construed as psychological events and the cosmic battle between Good & Evil as the struggle between the unregenerate self and the Soul.

The physical world is entirely abstract and without 'actuality' apart from its linkage to consciousness'. (Eddington, physicist)

The objective world rises from the mind itself.' (Buddha)

INTRODUCTION
THE PRIMEVAL GODS OF HUMANITY

Jeremy, a channel to the Masters will be leading a series of inner journeys to the Stars which have influenced the evolution of humanity from time immemorial. He begins with an introduction: 'The course on Star Consciousness has for subtitle *'On Becoming a Universal Being'*. Impressive yet awesome for the faint-hearted. The idea of being 'universal' stretches our imagination and perception to infinity.

'Awesome it certainly is, interrupts Clara, the human race has, for aeons, been conditioned to feel cramped and rather insignificant, especially in the old religious systems of the world.

'That's right, pursues Jeremy, humanity has been conditioned to identify with physical reality. Identification with the body is also taken for granted. Few believe that they are anything other than their material selves. But all this is changing and science is playing a significant role in this transformation. When Einstein enounced his famous equation $E=MC^2$, he changed our perception of the world for ever. He proposed that energy and matter are interchangeable; one can change into the other. To illustrate this point let's consider the Big Bang that ignited the formation of the universe. Science tells us that a particle of energy exploded into matter birthing the universe, in other words energy generates matter. With the explosion of the nuclear bomb, it is the reverse scenario; a small quantity of matter releases a vast quantity of energy. Energy generates matter, matter releases energy.

'What are the implications of Einstein's theory, enquires the inquisitive Clara?

'As I understand it, replies Jeremy, the split between energy and matter is being proved to be illusory. As a result, the biblical presentation of this rift must be declared obsolete. The biblical tradition, bedrock of Western civilisation, hinges on this rupture. Refuted by Spiritual Law, it is now being disproved by science.

'This is another way of affirming the unity of the world, if energy can change into matter and matter into energy, one is the other, remarks Tara.

'This is my understanding too, we tend to think of the universe as 'other' than us, as separate from us and existing outside us, but this is not so, expands Jeremy. We are part of the universe; I heard an astro-physicist say 'all the atoms that make up our body were created the first seconds following the Big Bang'. We were contained in the first atom, we are that first atom, we are the universe! Billions of years ago one atom charged with immense energy exploded and the universe came into existence. The billions of stars and galaxies that make up the cosmos were contained in that single atom. By the way, the world was not created in six days, it has been expanding ever since, new stars are being birthed and old stars are dying.

'Nothing is static in the cosmos, nature loathes immobility, nothing stands still, interrupts Clara, except the stagnant conditions and solidified beliefs in which we find ourselves entrapped by a static tradition and an inert religious system.

'You have a point, continues Jeremy, the universe loathes static conditions, everything is in perpetual motion, the Logos himself evolves and changes. 'Figuratively the Father stands for the unchanging, immovable nature of the universe', said Sananda.

'Not the god of the Jews, exclaims Clara, this one is frozen in time and space! The Father stands still, and anyone who dared to suggest otherwise has met with untimely death and a painful death at that! Think of the Essene Master, think of Moses, think of Spinoza!

'One thing is certain, notes Jeremy, Spiritual Law and science meet at the point of realisation that energy precedes matter. Matter is energy vibrating at a certain frequency. One infinitesimal energy source unleashes the creation of matter. Unity fragments into diversity, primeval unity is ruptured. 'In the beginning was the Word, and the Word was with God and the Word was God'. We may interpret these enigmatic words in metaphysical terms or in the idiom of modern physics.

'After this necessary parenthesis, back to the stars, resumes Jeremy. At present powerful waves of light are beamed on to our Planet by the thirteen Star systems of our galaxy. The aim of this intervention? To empower us to establish once again connection with the Source. Part of this process is to come to know ourselves more fully as beings of light who carry within us the energy of many stars across the galaxy.

This internalised star energy can now be stimulated so that we know ourselves once more as universal beings, existing in many realms simultaneously.

'It makes sense, human beings as puppets on a string pulled by fate-controlling gods are in no position to claim their cosmic stature, inserts Levinson, they do not recognise their deathless nature, their cosmic origin.

'The stars are enabling us to reconnect with the universe, whispers Clara.

'The stars we will encounter in our inner journeys have completed their evolution. They also have an abiding interest in human evolution. They intervened long ago and are doing so once again. We shall visit stars which have a direct relevance to human progress, the unfolding of the cosmic Plan and the evolutionary path of our Planet, Sirius, the Pleiades, Arcturus, Orion and Lyra. You all are familiar with Sirius the brightest star in the sky and you may recall the deep regard the Egyptians had for that star, and well informed they were too! Sirius as expression of divinity, as star of Initiation holds a vision of humanity's highest purpose.

'The Egyptians are said to have positioned their pyramids to come into alignment with Orion and Sirius, I read a book about it, notes Johansson.

'I need to read this book, laughs Jeremy. We will reactivate our stellar connection transmitted through the Beings who live in association with them.

'Quite an historic moment, remarks Levinson deeply moved, a momentous event not just for us but also for the Planet. Humanity has long lost the memory of this connection except for the Egyptians who obtained it from Atlantis. The pyramids are said to be ancient knowledge encoded in stone.

'Fascinating, we will discuss this later, suggests Jeremy. These thirteen strands of star light are encoded to begin a process of transformation.

'Thirteen strands of light, echoes Clara hesitantly?

'Strands of light from the thirteen stars thread the energy matrix on which our human 'beingness' is woven. Science tells us that cosmic rays penetrate everything in their path, changing the molecular structure of all objects they pass through. The encoded stellar rays entering our energy field are changing our atomic structure. Because we interact with the Planet, as this light becomes available on Earth through our conscious participation, we also assist Earth on her path of evolution.

'I never thought of evolution as affecting the Planet, I tended to view it in isolation, remarks Johansson.

'Even the Bible acknowledges an intricate relationship between man and the Planet, continues Levinson feeling at home with the topic. The texts emphasise the responsibility man has toward the animal kingdom and to the Planet. You recall that in time of disasters, the deity blamed mankind for the physical upheavals. Physical disasters were thought to be the resultant of human action. Today the relationship between man's activity and environmental problems make the headlines. We have protocols to limit the emission of carbon dioxide which is depleting the ozone layer. We have agreements to prevent the destruction of the rain forest which influence weather patterns.

'If you all are ready, we can begin. Sananda will be giving his own introduction'. Calm is restored, all settle for the first meditation. Sananda now overshadows Jeremy whose voice rises in a beautiful, powerful tone, with a rich musicality: 'Welcome greets the Master; we are going to work with star light in order to assist this Planet on her path of growth. You will, through your awareness, connect with particular forms of light and bring them to this Planet for the soul of Earth to use. In this process you will also bring benefit to yourself, awakening aspects of your own energy. Then, you will have an opportunity to radiate those gifts of light outwards into the world around you, to the rest of humanity rather than directly to the Earth herself. The qualities of light you bring in affect the totality of who you are. It begins to open you up to enable you to release light which has become trapped in some aspects of your being. This is part of the process of becoming more radiant. Although you know yourselves as human beings and identify closely with that level of your being – and this is only natural – you are also truly universal beings, in some respect you might say that the universe itself is another of your bodies. You are connected to a greater or lesser extent to your universe. Your mind is a doorway to the entire universe. At present, in common with almost everyone on Earth, you use only a tiny bit of your mind; but the rest is available to you and so part of the way you access the remainder is by noticing thoughts that you have not noticed before, noticing the sensations you have not noticed before; just watching, being a watcher, an observer of your own mind, watching the way it happens, the way you sense things. In general, meditation is very useful, because meditation stills the hubbub of the mind, it gives you an opportunity to be quiet, to be still, to open to the inner world rather than focus on the outer world. And so meditation is the key that opens the inner world.

'Pretending can help as well, continues the Master. Use your imagination, some of the things you make up are real, your imagination is proving to you, finding ways to demonstrate to you what is really happening. Feel free about it and tell yourself, 'maybe I am making it up, may be not!' You do not want your imagination to run away with you, but you also want to give it some freedom, as it brings you new things, new insights. The outcome can be an important way of refining that ability. As a general rule, where you are imagining what is real you are led further on and further in. Conversely, there is not much energy behind that which is not real and so it tends to crawl away and disappear. You can also use the other part of your mind, the analytical, the rational part to analyse what your imagination is bringing to you and decide whether you like what your imagining has conjured up. You can combine the different aspects of your mind this way, the intuitive and the rational.

'We shall be working with the light, the primeval light that underpins all reality. You will be given a glimpse of the way in which the beings of the star Arcturus experience themselves. Each Arcturian knows himself as the entire universe. In order to manifest, he explores within himself the energy, the essence of the abstract quality or the object he wants to manifest. For example should he wish to create more freedom, he explores within himself the energy of freedom, he travels out to a space in his inner universe in search of a string, a note, a chord which resonates with the energy of freedom. If you wish to create or bring into manifestation an essence-quality or an object, you will be working with light to create that quality or bring that object into your life. You create your reality; you all are involved in reality creation. What you will be learning is to steer consciously this process of creation rather than be surprised and alarmed at what you attract in your lives. You state the object of your desire; you travel out in your universe to find the chord, the note that is the essence of that desire.

'The universe is within you as well as without you. The Universal Soul animates you and permeates all matter. So even as I speak to you, there is a part of you which is beginning to resonate with the quality of energy you associate with Orion, one of our inner destinations. Feel yourself beginning to see life through the eyes of your soul, feeling the constant presence of Love that is your soul. As your soul is releasing the bonds of time, you begin to know yourself as a being beyond time, knowing past, present and future. As you focus on the state of joy and love, feel your boundaries dissolve, so that you begin to expand to what feels your natural limits.

'The star system of Lyra has many connections with humanity. Some of your earthly ancestors made their way to your Planet from Lyra. There are still strong energy associations between you and Lyra. We are going to lead you on an inner journey to link up more closely with the qualities of light Lyra transmit to humanity, to Earth. The beings from Lyra who are waiting to greet you in joyous anticipation are your brothers and sisters, living in a different place, with a different life style.

'Like Lyra, Sirius has a long connection with Earth and with humanity. The beings of Sirius take a deep and abiding interest in your progress. You will construct a vehicle of light that will transport you to Sirius, a Merkhaba. In the inner realm you will be taken to a Temple of light, constructed out of light. This Temple has been built by the beings of Sirius to safeguard part of the inheritance of humanity; certain aspects or blueprints have been stored in that Temple.

'Now, move within, find that peaceful core, that centre within. Moving from outer reality, letting go of the outer world, relaxing, becoming centred. You may have a degree of awareness of beings around you, among them beings from Sirius. Beings from Sirius and other Lightworkers assist you in building a bubble of light within which you will travel, a Merkhaba. Sense a beautiful intricate geometry of lines, a structure of light forming around you'.

The meditation begins and unfolds at a gentle pace, as they travel into their inner universe. At the close of the meditation each one is asked in turn to recount their experiences during the inner journey. Tara seems to have difficulty returning to outer reality, and when she does she is crying. Attention focuses on her as she is invited to share her experience. She had a deeply moving and disconcerting encounter during the inner journey to Sirius. There is nothing new in this, for in all her meditations she encounters beings from other dimensions. This one is different; the being she meets has an urgent message for humanity and urges her to accept an assignment. Inexpressibly stirred by the encounter, she has difficulty in controlling her emotion. She relates the meeting: 'On returning from Sirius, Sananda asked us to direct the light we had brought back onto our chosen part of the globe. I directed it to the Middle East where it is much needed; there is so much conflict, pain and trouble there. At that moment a beautiful being approached me and said silently: 'Come with me, I want to show you a place you once knew and loved'. We flew to what I took to be a monastery, and then we headed for a subterranean corridor in what I sensed to be Israel. The being

xv

who guided me showed me an earthenware jar in which scrolls of parchment were hidden. 'You put the scrolls in this jar long ago, for safe keeping before you fled with your group, at a time when this country was under siege by the Romans.'

'The Essenes, exclaims Clara, you were an Essene too!

'Yes, I instantly knew I was a member of the spiritual community which lived on the shore of Lake Galilee, the Essenes. The being went on, 'They had links with Greece and were sensitively attuned to the Masters of Tibet. Their predicament was striking. The ruling class disowned them as heretics because of their cultural association with Greece. The Essenes considered themselves enlightened Hebrews, for they had gained a considerable insight into the Timeless Wisdom as embodied in Egyptian culture, in Greek thought and in the mysticism of India and Tibet. They had a direct spiritual bond with Shamballa over the Gobi Desert. The Essenes were men of the world who regarded themselves as citizens of the Planet, indeed as citizens of the universe, and they refused to be silenced by the intolerant priesthood. They were persecuted during Greek occupation, for they refused to fight against the Greek armies. This you already know deep within and you can access this information at will simply by moving within yourself.

'However, the recovery of these scrolls is only part of your assignment and of lesser importance at this moment. My message is altogether more urgent. Let me take you to someone who wishes to meet you'. We flew at great speed to a Desert bathed in gold light. A man standing alone held his hand out and smiled a luminous smile to greet me, 'I am Rabbi Moses, and you consented before this life to bring my manuscript to the attention of the world. Under the inspiration of Master Sanaka in India I wrote *The Hebrew Gods* for my community in Vilna. On my return to Vilna I decided to break the long journey and to make a detour in order to visit Safed and meet the scholars of Cabbala. Forces hostile to the progress of humanity interfered to obstruct the realisation of the Plan. The manuscript was stolen but found its way into the vaults of St Katherine Monastery at the foot of Mount Sinai where the priests gave me refuge when ill and alone I was unable to travel back to Europe, my final destination. My earthly life came to a close and the mission entrusted to me by my spiritual guide, the Master Sanaka unfinished'.

They listen intently as she concludes 'we were involved in that time period, we were all Essenes'. And we are going to meet more Essenes soon'. Deeply moved she continues, 'we were together then as we are now. The revelation contained in the manuscript is of concern to all humanity at this time of accelerated change. The time has come for us to find it and bring it to the attention of the world'. After a brief silence, 'I grasped in a flash of realisation what he expected of us'.

PART ONE

THE FATHER – YANG, COSMIC MASCULINE ENERGY
(Sin & Retribution)

'I would say that Judaism is seeking to connect with the Oneness of the Divine as an ever-present, unchanging state or Source-state'. (Master Sananda)

CHAPTER 1

THE MYTH OF CREATION

'And the Word said: Let Maya flourish and let deception rule'.

SINAI - ST KATHERINE MONASTERY

They drive through starkly magnificent territory on desolate roads deeper into uninhabited land. This austere, forbidding landscape of unspoilt and untouched bleakness seemed to have stood for ever, unperturbed by the passing of the ages, yet the erosion of time was visible. They had come to the mountain as if summoned by this mysterious and silent wilderness. Dominated by the bright reds and greys of the limestone and granite mountains, the colours, the light and the air were charged with wild beauty and a strange, inexplicable force. They stop to look at some unknown plants that offer a green contrast to the stark bareness of the mountains. They fall under the spell of this strange and magical land, allowing the spirit of the mountain to capture and ravish them. Leaving behind the coast, they head inland into dramatic mountainous terrain. The desert landscape has jagged peaks and ragged crests. They drive through a narrow pass in the mountains. Someone suggests they stop to take in this vast expense of desert, the beauty of it stirs something primeval in them. How can wilderness be so captivating, so uplifting, so enthralling? They emerge from the enchantment to resume their journey. They drive along the road until they reach Ain Hudra and the oasis. And what a pleasant and refreshing site it is! They interrupt their drive to enjoy the sharp contrast, the pleasant sight of intense green in the dazzling light. Continuing south through majestic, spellbinding scenery they head towards St Katherine village. Benzaccai points to a chapel dedicated to Aaron, on the site where the Golden Calf was fashioned and adored by the Hebrews tired of waiting for Moses' return from the mountain.

He sighs, 'who would, on arriving at this place, claim that we invented monotheism? At any moment we revert back to idol worship. Humanity has engaged in idolatrous worship since the dawn of time, since primitive humans separated from the herd and sensed something resembling individuality. They looked up to the sky and began to feel something greater and more powerful and they adored that something. This is what we have been doing ever since and our much revered mono-theism is no different, the label only has changed. This is the thing prehistoric man discovered and one which we eagerly snatched and clutched with both hands, in spite of Moses ' endeavours to civilise, discipline and renew us.

St Katherine Monastery huddles at the foot of Mount Sinai and in the setting sun the rocks and the roofs are all aglow with gold light. A tall wall surrounds the monastery with its elegant and delicate bell tower and Mount Sinai ascending behind it. And the verses come streaming out of the mouth of one who has abandoned the ancient beliefs; they are endowed with a new vigour, a new meaning, a new intensity:
'Yahweh called out to Moses from the Mount.
And Moses went up on the Mount,
And the cloud enveloped the Mount.
And the glory of Yahweh rested upon Mount Sinai,
Covered by the cloud, for six days;' quotes Levinson restraining his emotion, visibly moved by the Mountain that had such a profound impact on human history, a space connected with the history of the people he had left behind and with the history of the Planet herself. 'What happened at the foot of this bleak mountain has profoundly influenced the course of history. Uncertain as to the intent of this last remark, they remain silent, preferring not to invade this moment, so deeply moving for him.
'This is astonishing, the mountain and the desert are just as Moses saw them. I have a strange feeling of 'déjà vu'. This place looks familiar, remarks Clara.
At the gate, they are greeted by a monk, Father Nathaniel. They enter the complex, more a medieval town than a monastery. It reminds Clara of Mont St Michel, a medieval town with houses and church built on a rocky island. The Father takes them to the main building graced with arches where they are invited to share the evening meal. The food is plain but substantial, served with great simplicity and reverence on a large refectory table. The atmosphere is imbued with humility, dignity and reverence.

The food, consisting of freshly baked bread, potatoes, goat cheese and dates takes on a special quality, blessed by man, enhanced with a glow of spirituality. After the meal, they have an audience with the librarian who informs them that several manuscripts are hidden in a secret part of the library reserved to rare scripts of latent significance for mankind. The Father takes them to the vault and says laconically, 'the time may well be now, a guiding hand brought you here, I can only assume that God approves, peace be with you and with mankind'.

Moments later a religious delegation arrives at the gates of the monastery. Four bearded men dressed in black and in much agitation approach the gates making large gestures of discontent. They are furious and want the world to see and hear their anger which they find not only justified but admissible. On hearing of the turbulence, Father Nathaniel abandons his meal to hasten silently towards the entrance gates. He graciously invites the men to step inside the compound; courteous invitation they reject as impertinent. They are indignant at having to walk a desecrated soil, irked at being among monks whose presence they find abhorrent. The enduring tenets of their doctrine are holy & profane, pure & impure, Jews and non-Jews. The world is split in two irreconcilable segments. They permit no negotiation, tolerate no compromise. They belong with the pure, the unstained and will neither walk nor associate with the impure. Their world is uncomplicated, exactly and neatly carved up. They thrive on fragmentation, on rupture, on fracture deeply convinced that they are firmly anchored in the 'right' side of duality and in a state of perfect equilibrium. The many signs and symbols they detect as they glance from the open gates are truly execrable for they offend their monotheistic sensitivity. They are persuaded that they alone own the truth, that God is their god and that he rejoices in their behaviour. They look away in disgust, genuinely afraid of defilement. They will not stay a moment longer in a profane environment that might blemish the purity of their nature. They do not waste time in courteous overture and demand to see Benzaccai.

Benzaccai hurries to the gates, alarmed and apprehensive. 'How did they find out about the manuscript, he enquires? I am in for a lot of trouble, they will not let go of me, who told them? They are going to harass me until I give up and go away, he mutters in an agitated state.

'This will not happen, replies Jeremy calmly, we travelled all this way to unearth Rabbi Moses' manuscript and bring it to the attention of the world, not to be put off by a group who have a vested interest in keeping the world in ignorance. Remember our 'assignment Earth'; we incarnated to bring light, not to suppress it. They may insist on turning the clock back to the Dark Ages, we are here to throw open the doors they have kept shut. We are the workers of the Hierarchy, instrumental in bringing about the next phase of development, our function on Earth is to lift the vibrational frequency of Earth; they sense it and they are scared.

'Jeremy is right, takes up Levinson reassuringly, even if after what we have been through in this life, it is difficult to imagine that we are on a mission to lift the vibrations of the Planet! In my dark moments, I disbelieve. Go to them and climb over this hurdle, the first of many we are going to encounter, no doubt, the forces of opposition are not going to give up that easily!

'I agree, continues Clara, who like Levinson remembers vividly the bitter experiences of her early life entrapped in the same negative forces. They have kept an entire people cut off from the rest of mankind and if we show the slightest hesitation, they will throw us out of balance. What is at stake extends beyond our intellectual curiosity, or even our spiritual adventure, the implications are far-reaching. We all share the conviction that we came to Sinai on an assignment; we are engaged in world service. Furthermore, we planned this trip long before we incarnated. We must not give in to their fear and hostility. Ignorance is the enemy of light, and we are workers of light. Be like Joshua; break down the walls of Jericho!

A heated conversation ensues which the group observe with curiosity, amusement and concern, from a distance. Benzaccai is drawn into a furious polemic with men who see themselves as the only legitimate heirs and guardians to manuscripts or any objects found in the ground or above ground. They argue stormily that the world was created for the Children of Israel; they know the mind of God and are the only qualified people to make decision and take effective action. They dispute any academic claim to the study of the manuscript. The text is theirs and that is final! The manuscript is doomed.

'No impious Jews or impure Gentile is allowed to investigate; we alone have been given this right by God. It would an insult to the Holy One. The words 'blasphemous', 'defilement', 'desecration' and 'profanation' are banded around with increasing velocity, animosity and animation. The oldest man shouts in pious indignation that the manuscript belongs to them by right. Benzaccai visibly irritated refuses to be intimidated. After all, he too belongs to the people who invented the mental acrobatics of the 'pilpul'. The pilpul Talmudic polemic, fast moving argumentation pursued over trifling notions is a heated, subjective claim to understanding the mind of god and the way he wants things done! Benzaccai intends to take the argument as far as it goes, he is losing his calm. The pious indignation animating the rabbis is now being fanned with visible effervescence. Beaten, but not defeated, they leave in great haste and displeasure, 'You will hear from us, insists one of the men, wherever you go, look over your shoulder, we shall not be far behind'. On this note of threat they leave, much to the relief of the group.

Benzaccai turns to his friends who have been watching in amazement this contest of will punctuated by threatening gestures on the part of the rabbis. He is weary and embarrassed: 'I am sorry to put you through all this. This rabbi has been hampering all attempts made by archaeologists. The Holy Land is a gold mine for researchers; every inch of the ground holds a secret waiting to be discovered. He told me that he has been appointed by the Lord to make my life a misery', he adds in a weary tone. They are well represented in Parliament, the present administration rules without a firm majority and ministers need the support of the extreme religious Right. The problem is that they foster a climate of fear as they wave the Books in anger at the world. Not only are our neighbours object of their biblical wrath, we the liberal Jews are the enemy within.

Levinson confirms, 'I recently watched a report by a BBC correspondent in which he waves the spectre of civil war between opposing ideological factions within the Jewish people. It is unbelievable that after 2000 years of the most horrendous exile, we should engage in civil strife and find it defensible. It scared me, soon after reading an article in The Times in which your right wing representatives demanded segregation on the buses, reminiscent of the state of apartheid in South Africa, except that it is apartheid against Jewish women, their own people! Is madness in the air you breathe?

Clara intervenes, 'I also saw the 'Correspondent' programme in which the reporter concludes after gathering all the evidence that 'if the Jews did not have the Arabs to worry about, the situation already tense at home would degenerate into a civil war.

Benzaccai retorts, 'You know what happens, it is hard to believe for Europeans, but we are turning the clock back to the Dark Ages. The religious promoters lack a leader of substance, the age of the great scholars is long gone and lacking the direction of a competent mentor, they have turned to the doctrinaires who use dogma as a substitute for knowledge. They believe their religious leader to be inspired by god and they gather the words that fall from his mouth, like 'manna' from heaven, as if it were the word of god himself. He is adamant, we must not concede an inch of land to our neighbours, and we must fight to the last breath to retain the land that God gave to Moses, Joshua and the Children of Israel. Bu who does the fighting and the dying? Not them!

Jeremy asks hesitantly, 'did God give Canaan to the Hebrews?'

'Not after we fought hard for it, we got it by force, after a long siege which lasted years, replies Benzaccai, God did not show up during the fighting. In order to justify our actions, we must have good on our side, and we have no difficulty in finding good! Has not the universe been created for us, with the rest of humanity as mere accident? We must find a lesser race that will set us apart and entitle us to subdue them. When you want to dominate, the last thing you encourage is equality, you must create an imbalance, the scales must be tipped, with the finer race high and the lower race low.

'The Nazis invented an inferior and menacing enemy, the Jews, remarks pertinently Johansson, in order to guarantee the support of the masses. Mass destruction became legitimate, it had the mandate of the people and was state organised. The roots of tyranny for all times are plain to see.

'So long as we can convince the masses that the purity of the race demands it, or that god commands it, we will continue to manipulate the mind of the people and stagnate in the murky waters of the past, remarks Levinson. Refraining his impatience and irritation he adds, 'this manuscript is going to revolutionise the way we think about the Scriptures, it will ignite the readers to a new realisation. Their viewpoint will change, for if they do not adapt, they will disappear. Life is perpetual change; those who resist change choose not life but death. The Yeshiva of the 21st century will be unrecognisable, assuming that it survives the dramatic transformation taking place at this time as powerful waves of light are pouring on to the Planet, ushering in a metamorphosis. Humanity is evolving into the next dimension of being.

'How do you envision the modifications? Are changes possible, enquires Clara with fascination, she too is mobilising her energy and focusing her attention on the overthrow of the obsolete system.

'Crucial modifications are to come into effect. An amended syllabus will reflect the new world view, answers Benzaccai boldly. No longer will the Old Testament and its appendages be taught to the exclusion of all else. They will be placed in context and instead of approaching them from a theological perspective; they will be studied with the tool of the scientific method. The subjects will of necessity centre around the ancient texts of Sumer, Chaldea, Mesopotamia, India, Greece, and Egypt. Genesis can be traced back to Sumer and Mesopotamia, as do our mythological sources.

'We still adhere to the practices of the ancient Egyptians, believing them to be God-given - circumcision, dietary customs, the Shabbat and the immersion in water for purification. All these and others were retained by the Hebrew fleeing the pursuit of the Egyptians in the belief that they would preserve their well-being, prolong their life and ensure the healthful survival of their descendants. In order to imprint these in the psyche of their rebellious charge, the priesthood added a threatening note, 'these laws were given by god, observe them well, ignore them at your peril'.

'It is strange, remarks lucidly Jeremy, that the Hebrews, a persecuted people who finally abscond from their tormentors should escape enriched or burdened - depending on your viewpoint - with religious practices and more to the point, that this same people have hidden encoded in their most sacred texts, some of the profound esoteric beliefs of their persecutors!

'We borrowed much from Egypt, continues Levinson, yet unashamedly we condemn Egypt as 'the land of darkness'. Without Egypt we would not exist. Within the limits of our comprehension we borrowed from that luminous culture beliefs, practices and gods. Of course there was Moses himself, the Egyptian initiate with his profound grasp of Egyptian wisdom, his intimate knowledge of the direct role of Sirius in the creation of the Egyptian civilisation, Moses who knew how the beings from Sirius immortalised into stone the knowledge and wisdom of the lost continent of Atlantis. Our name which was granted to Jacob by the angel conceals the names of Egyptian gods!

'This will also be included in the syllabus of the school of the future. The cultural histories of Egypt, Sumer and Babylon, world mythologies, archaeology will be taught alongside the Jewish scriptures; they are inseparable and complementary stemming from the same sources. These sources stretch back to the beginning of time when the Sun-Gods left the divine throne and came to Earth to assist infant humanity. The student of the future will make an informed analytical appraisal of the Texts and a comparative critique of all ancient theological systems. The study of the Old Testament will be a scientific investigation blending history, archaeology, volcanology, oceanography, biology, genetics and any other informative avenue of knowledge. We have discarded all sources that could shed light.

Benzaccai is kidnapped by Bedouins

Time rushes by, they are oblivious of its passing, absorbed almost entranced by the issues under discussion. A new mental landscape is appearing before their very eyes and broadening out in all directions. Benzaccai informs his friends that he must return to the university that same day; he will not have supper with them. Late that evening he sets off in his car, as the sun is setting behind Mount Sinai majestic in its stark bleakness. An hour later, on the ground of the monastery with the Sinai peak rising before them, their quiet stroll is interrupted by a tumult of loud voices. Benumbed they watch in a detached almost trance-like state a group of men charge towards the entrance and run screaming through the main gates, up in arms, all talking at once as they rush in a tight formation toward the group, their arms waving in wild gestures. Something terrible has surely happened! Finally aroused, the friends run to the monk who had swiftly and quietly walked to the Bedouins and who is now making appeasing gestures, in an effort to pacify them.

'Do remain calm, implores Father Nathaniel, unperturbed. You have nothing to fear, I know these men, they bring their produce to the monastery and are quite friendly in spite of their liveliness. They are saying that Benzaccai was stopped by several Bedouins and taken away in a military vehicle. They did not recognise the Bedouins who might be soldiers disguised as Bedouins.

'Why should soldiers take away a perfectly innocent man and a reputable academic, it does not make sense, remarks Jeremy.

'I think it does, there must be many opposing factions which have no wish for the content of this book to be divulged. They may hate each other, but they are united on this one thing. Religious extremists and right wing activists may feel in some way threatened, replies Father Nathaniel. Open-mindedness is a rare occurrence in this world. Our order has a long history of impartiality and fairness, we live a secluded life and this has enabled us to remain free from entanglements, political and doctrinal.

'Impartiality, fairness, discernment, freedom, open-mindedness these are soul attributes, the qualities of energy of the Age of Aquarius, notes Tara. And we find them in this remote post, sheltering within this isolated community!

'If Benzaccai has been kidnapped by Bedouins, the manuscript has disappeared too, concludes Clara. This manuscript is of vital importance to us and to humanity. We have to find it.

'The forces of opposition did not take long to pass to the offensive, notes Tara. I had a strange dream last night, when I woke this morning, it had gone but the impression of doom remained. The forces hostile to the emancipation of mankind will place all manner of obstacles in our way that was the lingering mood the dream left behind. The Lords of Form never sleep; they thwart attempts by the forces of freedom to usher in the new awareness. They ostensibly stand in the way of the birth of man. We cannot stand and wait.

'We are not going to be intimidated by the 'opposition'. When I once said to the Master who was teaching me at the time that I felt heavy energies around me, he remarked with implacable objectivity, 'there is no good or bad energy, there is only energy'. When we qualify energies as 'negative' we fortify and vitalise them, we give them life because the things the mind concentrates on have a tendency to expand and thrive. Fighting 'evil' is futile, the more we fight evil the stronger it becomes. Cosmic law states, 'energy follows thought', the thing we think about becomes energised, dwelling on it simply intensifies it explains Jeremy reassuringly.

'Was it Shakespeare who said, 'There's nothing either good or bad, but thinking makes it so', quotes Clara? In the last analysis it is our imagination that decides what is good and what is evil. And in the prelude to Genesis, 'Let there be light', only light removes darkness.

'If fighting evil vitalises it, if thinking about it strengthens it, so what can we do, mutters Johansson nervously?

'Convert it, replies Jeremy! Attacking darkness is futile, this is the way of religion and religion has failed. Conversion of energy is what we cosmic workers have come to demonstrate. Only one thing destroys evil, its opposite, Love. Love is the creative power, the life force in the universe, the substance which creates and sustains. Love alone can destroy evil by transforming it. Not to every body's taste, I agree, but this is cosmic Law. We did not come to Earth to attack the forces opposed to the birth of man, we came with the mandate to convert, to transform, to transmute. In other words, to turn darkness into light.

'In this world hate has never yet dispelled hate. Only love dispels hate. This is the Law, said Buddha, quotes Tara. Religion is barking at the wrong tree.

'That's right, we are talking about energy conversion, says Jeremy.

'To redeem, says Johansson, somewhat uneasy at using the language of the past. He adds with a smile as if in apology, 'I no longer accept the authority of formal religion.

'To redeem. The language is the same, says Jeremy reassuringly. To redeem is to rescue. Redemption for us signifies the release of the light trapped in matter, the liberation of the Self captured in the materialism of form and dogma; it means emancipation from the tyranny of the self …

'… from the dictatorship of monotheism and its ally patriarchy. It stands for the liberation of the spirit, interrupts Clara.

The following night, unable to quell their anxiety in spite of the reassuring and encouraging presence of the monks and the calming influence of Jeremy, they decide to spend the night outside, in the inner precinct. The night is still, the stars sparkling like diamonds; the magical atmosphere of this mystical and barren location appeases them and as tension lessens, their anguish lessens too. As dawn is breaking, they decide to go to their rooms to snatch a few hours sleep in order to dispel the fatigue that compounds their malaise.

They fall asleep from exhaustion and worry, but are soon awaken by a loud disturbance coming from the gates. They leap out of bed and run to the window. At the gates, a group of Bedouins are arguing with a monk, and among them Benzaccai, looking weary, drawn and dishevelled. He is returned, unharmed; his capture by the Bedouins was unintended, a case of mistaken identity. When they realised their mistake, they apologised to him and treated him well before returning him safe and sound.

Threat of a terrorist attack on the monastery

Benzaccai arrives one morning in a state of great agitation. Out of breath, he mumbles, 'A rumour is spreading like wild fire on the university campus. A young man acting suspiciously was arrested by a security guard last night. On questioning he confessed to being an activist and a member of an extreme group sent to attack the university and other academic institutions including archaeological sites. He warns of an imminent retaliation.

Jeremy reassuringly suggests the obvious, 'Have you warned the police or the military authorities?

'Naturally, but we do not know if there are other activists hiding on campus. With a forced smile he adds 'we all look alike you know'.

'This fact is apparent to the world, except to you. To think that we are so closely related, yet determined to exterminate one another, says Levinson with a feeling of desolation he cannot conceal.

'I suggest we retire and meditate for a while. We must demonstrate what we preach, proposes Jeremy with confidence. If love destroys evil, let's put it into practice. We are going to meditate on love. We shall journey into the inner realm of the Heart, draw love from the Source within and send it out to the world. This is an effective form of service, this is world service.

'Let us see if we can find out more about this unsettling event and if we can avert any unpleasant outcome, suggests the practical Benzaccai. Benzaccai is not the contemplative type; he does not join in the meditation, preferring to get into the action to affect events the way he knows, in a dynamic military manner. He leaves in haste to return to the university. In the afternoon, news arrive that a terrorist plot had been detected by the Secret Services and the men responsible arrested. The terrorist plot against the monastery had been averted. Yet an air of unease, an ominous feeling prevails. Jeremy suggests a day of meditation in the monastery. Was the terrorist attack just postponed?

Rabbi Moses grapples with his Angel

Rabbi Moses narrates his story. 'One morning as we were absorbed in the contemplation of the sun rising in a glorious orange glow, my mentor said with unusual emotion 'I know of a Master who lives at the foot of the majestic mountains of the Himalayas in a monastery of great repute for its priceless library of ancient manuscripts written by the great Masters of long ago. The reputation of this Master has spread well beyond the land of India and its noble mountains and a request to send a delegation of our most distinguished elders has been granted. The monastery is also celebrated for advanced teachings in Buddhist philosophy, spiritual Law, medicine and the ancient literature of the East.

'He is Master of Buddhist knowledge?

'Yes, and much more beside. He has long since disregarded their beliefs, dogmas and rituals, but it is convenient for him to remain there.

'And for those around him.

'Indeed, his wisdom and luminous presence ennobles and empowers all those who approach him. He is one of those rare beings who have the ability to transform by their very presence. They do not have to utter a word, they just have to be present and the change occurs. Look at the sun, as it rises it dispels the darkness of the night; it is the same with such Masters. They awaken slumbering souls. Figuratively they raise the 'dead'. In such a presence you become truly alive.

'How does this happen, I enquire?

'The true Master knows how to hasten your awakening; he simply brings out what is already there. The Buddha light shines in you; it is dormant within you, waiting to be set alight. He is revered by all lamas throughout the land as a Bodhisattva. You see ... my Mentor hesitates.

'What should I see, I prompt respectfully.

'With a smile at my impatient curiosity, he replies: 'This is of crucial importance, learn that no Master can give you what you are looking for. The true Master points to the centre where that knowledge is: your being, the dwelling place of the Self. It is also the portal to the universe. It is within that he discovered Reality and he will urge you to search within to find the answer to your life question. You will leave without delay for India where you will meet the Master'. This is what my Mentor suggested in preparation for what was to come. A few days later, we parted; I was heading for a country I had discarded as a land of mysticism and idolatry. I was aroused with thrilling anticipation yet filled with foreboding. My Mentor gave me his blessing and sent me on my way with these enigmatic words: 'Go, Rabbi Moses, do not delay, the world is waiting'.

My small caravan comprised my guide and translator, two senior lamas and myself. I travelled light; I had shed the ancestral beliefs. I have to fight off the debilitating memories which continue to hurt me. It is the indignity, the chagrin that is the worst. I was intent on opening my mind to all that was new. For too long I had been entombed in one mode of thought and one style of living, having rejected all others. I now realised that my life had been lived in a prison cell of my own making. I was grieving, the sense of loss was crushing, yet I also was longing to know, to experience, to be!

'We bought two mules which did not deserve the reputation mules have. We soon were climbing a winding, narrow path up the mountain till we reached the trading town of Kalimpong in the Himalayas. We decided to change our mules for a pony and hire two porters. We curved our way up the steep mountain, not daring to look down, for fear of losing balance. We set up camp for the night and resumed our difficult and perilous trek early morning. The journey seemed endless. Towering snow-covered peaks were gleaming in the morning sunshine. Soon clouds swept over the sky and a mist enveloped the mountains. Through the veil of mist, standing alone and majestic was the mysterious Tibetan monastery, a centre of knowledge where the Timeless Wisdom was studied and taught. This mystical knowledge had been entrusted to the people of India in antiquity by great Masters of Wisdom. We were in the land of mysterious and profound knowledge I did not know existed, and I had studied the Kabala!

'Ganden Monastery that houses some 5,000 lamas, situated just beyond Lhasa is an impressive centre of learning. There they teach philosophy, mysticism, astrology, ancient Buddhist and Tibetan literature and metaphysics as well as the healing arts. As you imagine, there are superior scholars in Ganden. The monastery was positioned attractively on the mountainside, a magnificent structure that seem both imposing and yet precariously perched on the edge of the mountain. This was a daunting sight, how could such a massive building have been built on the mountain face? I stood for a while thrilled and apprehensive, wondering what this grand and noble place had in store for me. Why had my fate taken such a bizarre twist?

Here I was, a learned and once respected Rabbi who, dissatisfied with the old teachings had yearned for a new insight, for an injection of new life, a resurrection of the spirit. In my torment I turned to a new religious movement which promised to infuse a new life in the stale and dormant world I inhabited. Since childhood I had been troubled by a strange disquiet and a pervading anguish I could not explain. None of my masters could either, none of them was perplexed, and none was yearning since they had all the answers! I wanted to emulate them, convinced in my innocence, that their quiescence was a mark of their greatness. Or were they so bored that they took their unchanging boredom for virtuous contentment? Unable to understand my disquiet, they resorted to the age-old method of prayer, Psalms reading, repentance for sins I had not committed. They placed the blame squarely on my shoulders and shrewdly set out to make me feel an outcast, a freak. That was an astute twist; those who feel inadequate often shift the blame onto those they cannot understand. It is the fault of the pupil, never the teacher. My restlessness mingled with a sense of inadequacy and guilt. When the select few are given a mirror in which to view their unenlightened state, they hide behind a mask of indignation and horrified piety. My mind was a mystery to them, I could not be held captive in their intangible prison. It was sound to them, but wholly untenable to me.

After climbing the steep rock steps we came to the huge door which swung open effortlessly. We were expected; several lamas wrapped in draped gold and maroon robes moved toward us and greeted us graciously with refined oriental courtesy. They escorted us through large rooms and a labyrinth of corridors until we finally arrived at a door elegantly decorated and carved. A lama gently pulled a gold bell-sash. The door opened slowly, my heart pounding in breathless anticipation at the thought of meeting such a formidable being, my knees so weak I feared would not carry me. I am conducted in the august presence of the Master Sanaka whose reputation as a spiritual master, mystic, world thinker and philosopher was described with reverence by my Sufi Mentor. He was thought to be an enlightened Being. There is no going back; I am now in his dignified and somewhat intimidating presence. The whole room is filled with majesty and light. A joss-stick is releasing a pungent perfume with a delicate smoke. An oil-lamp is burning against the wall, casting a trembling shadow. He is standing, tall, slender in his saffron robe, with the dignity of an emperor. The quiet, almost stern expression gives way to a luminous smile, his eyes sparkle, his hand is held out and with great courtesy and warmth as if meeting a long lost brother:

'Welcome Rabbi Moses, do come in and be seated. It is a joy to greet you. You must be tired; the climb to the monastery is exhausting for someone not used to such dizzy heights, in the literal sense of the term, he adds with a twinkle of humour in his eyes. I was expecting you. Looking at me intently, 'you are just as I saw you'. This great man whose name echoes throughout the enlightened world is so accessible; there is a spontaneity about him I find captivating.

'You knew of my arrival, enquires Moses?

'Your Mentor visited me in meditation and told me of your quest.

'You have done away with language and writing, just as you have overcome the limitations of space and time I said boldly. Yet I know of miracles …

'Miracles to you because you have not studied cosmic Law: the nature of matter, energy and mind, as we have done for thousands of years. So you see, what is miracles to you are universal laws that we study and master. I have been expecting this moment for some time.

'I had a dream ....

'It was not a dream, I came to you in the inner world; you saw me. I travel effortlessly to visit those who invoke help, those who need me or those like you, I wish to visit.

'You knew I had need of you?

'I have been aware of you for some time, but you already know this; you have felt my influence around you for years.

'Yes I have but could not explain what I was feeling, and my religious teachers were unable to make sense of it, they urged me to pray and repent; it was too strange for them, too odd for me.

'Your teachers did the best they knew how, but do no expect men who devote their lives to explaining and enforcing rules, customs, habits and practices to understand a mind like yours! They are locked in the beliefs that the personality creates to explain the world.

'Their beliefs were god-given, mutters Moses, timid and awkward.

'The self generates ideas which it ascribes to its gods. It is in the nature of the self to do so. The self is a wonderful instrument that scrutinizes the world in an effort to explain its workings. The self is important, how else would we make sense of the world without it? It is a vital l outcome of evolution, not to be sneered at, but to be valued. Your teachers live in the domain of the visible, the solid, and the tangible. There is no requirement in their lives for liberating flights into the inner worlds, energising travels into other dimensions of being, inspiring journeys into the world of light. They live in the here-and-now.

'Is it wrong to live in the present; is it not what wisdom teaches?

'The present is all there is. The present I am referring to is time transcended. The here-and-now means 'solid' Earth, the Earth plane of existence to which they confine themselves because they forgot where they come from.

'They long for union with their god, I mumble'. My position was untenable, I had fled from them and now I was speaking in their defence, I was no longer the prosecutor, but the defence.

'This is difficult for you, he adds gently, sensing my unease. You are right, they long for union. They implore external powers to assist them when all the time, the God their decline to encounter is throbbing in their chest! In my disembodied travels I come across many sincere religious men who beat their chest in desperation, yearning passionately to unite with their god, yet experiencing only frustration and angst. 'Why are you forsaking me, O god of my fathers', they lament? And these sincere and often deeply spiritual men weep in sorrow as they plead. Unable to make sense of their god's indifference, they blame themselves over some imagined sinfulness.

'Why indeed is he forsaking them?

'Because he is not there! He is just where he has been since the dawn of time, just here (he points to Moses' chest). He is beating inside their chest. To arrive at this realisation requires a giant leap in awareness they are not yet prepared to make. A shift in perception: from the distant Father to the living God inside their chest.

'Why is it such a painful leap, why a leap in awareness? I ask emboldened.

'Because no matter how bad things are for your people, to battle, argue, invoke and haggle with an unreachable god is still better than to look inside yourselves to find the truth. All knowledge is inside you, nothing in the universe is external or forbidden, and you are the universe. All you have to do is access it. To do this implies a vast leap in consciousness. The reluctant belief in the unjust Father is still preferable to admitting that we are alone, that there is no one out there for us. Any hardship, it seems, is better than to grapple with life alone.

'What is the message I came all this way to hear, asks Moses unable to disguise his unease?

'You already found it, Moses, you have always known it and you are rediscovering it: it is time to claim your place among the evolved elements of humanity, time to embark on the Path of Return, time to abandon the stale dogmas that keep you stationary, time to wake up to who you truly are. We shall talk a great deal more about all these issues later.

His words had a significant effect on me, I realised that I was on the brink of a momentous realisation. He invited me to talk about my travels and the world I had left behind, he himself had travelled intensively.

'In the astral plane?

'No, in my body, he laughs, I travelled all over Europe and I can speak several European languages; that is why we can dispense with translators. I studied at the universities of Paris, Prague and Vienna. I spent twenty years in Europe, wonderful years which I remember with joy. My travels were part of an inclusive scholastic education. I was sent away to learn about other countries and cultures. I went to theatres and attended concerts, I read novels and poetry and I listened to music. Though I prefer the piano, I decided on learning the violin, it is easier to carry, he adds in jest. I love Bach and I still play, when my duties permit.

'I could barely conceal my surprise. Here was a Master who apart from being a realised Being was also proficient in worldly knowledge and he played the violin! This would have been anathema to the rabbis of Vilna who regarded all activities, other than biblical reading, profane.

As if reading my thoughts, 'All knowledge is important, think of the Sufis in medieval Europe, they were eminent scholars in all fields of human endeavour and they were mystics cultured in the Timeless Wisdom.

He explores me with kindness and intent. He seems to look into my soul. His look cuts into me with the sharp edge of reason as with the sharp grasp of intuition. His expression is a little disconcerting for it blends kindness with firmness. He fuses love and will. Never before have I witnessed such divergent qualities merging so perfectly and effortlessly in one man. I sense a transcending quality in his presence.

A thrill runs through me in response to his regal presence, I feel different in a manner I cannot explain. A wave of joy sweeps over me, my mind is expanding. The crippling limitations nurtured since childhood fade away, run off like water. For the first time since early childhood I feel limitless. I had forgotten those precious moments. Listening to Mozart, in secret because such profanity was illicit, gave me this magical feeling. There is something in Sanaka human yet unworldly which teases my curiosity. My initial anxiety slowly fades away, I become aware of a change gradually taking over and to which I can offer no resistance. Tears come to my eyes; the mental torment and emotional upheaval I had experienced over the past three years seem to gently melt away like snow under the kiss of the midday sun. Nothing seems to matter, the rejection, the loss, the betrayal, the aloneness, my whole shattered life! It is all receding into the distance while these elusive feelings continue to rise unhindered. I am floating, and this new found peace is penetrating the core of my being. My tortured mind in which thoughts crowd, jostle and struggle to torment me is arriving at a pause.

The questions that had troubled me with unrelenting tenacity no longer matter. I sensed, in the presence of this being who exudes peace, that they are unreal. How could that be? Was I dreaming? I am certain that my problems are real, yet my conviction is fading. I had been excommunicated and I lost my family. Everything that had made up my life, all recognisable landmarks had vaporised and I was left in a void. Yet in his presence I view my life in the light of truth. The disasters that had struck me did not originate in a malevolent world 'out there'. I had made them happen, I had precipitated these events. The truth hit me with such clarity that I felt faint. 'Do take a chair', I heard the Master say as if in a dream. I am unable to answer: I had caused my misfortunes; they had manifested in response to a hidden, personal call. I was in a far-away monastery in the luminous presence of this enigmatic Master. I was the maker of my life events. This thought hit me like a bolt of lightning.

We sat and drank tea enriched with rancid butter. The taste was peculiar; the harsh climate dictated that they supplement a frugal diet of rice and nuts with some butter in order to keep at bay the worse of the cold. Master Sanaka sipped the tea with concentration. He sensed my unexpressed question and answered it with a smile. 'This is the way of Buddhism, every action is important, nothing is trivial, we invest in our movements thought and intent. Buddhism is not just in the profound philosophical teachings of Buddha; it is in the smallest of actions. Now that you are reposed would you begin your story, I wish to hear it. This was the invitation I was waiting for.

'When I lost all, it was as if the earth had opened up to engulf me. I sank into despair and began a heroic struggle with god, arguing, questioning and despairing as no answer came. Like Job I was numbed with pain, unable to comprehend yet questioning. Nothing made sense anymore.

'I think that Job understood very well, that is why he never flinched, replies Sanaka. He accepted his tribulations with dignity because he knew that he had designed and implemented them. He rejected the idea of fate; he declined the notion of a malign god who persecutes man for his amusement. He knew that nothing ever happens to man without his consent. Man is not a puppet on a string that a bored deity shakes at his pleasure. He never lost belief in the intuitive knowing of his higher Self; he never lost touch with the wisdom of the universe. He was at peace with himself and with the world because he was in control at all times. You see, he adds with a smile, the legend of Job emanates from India.

Moses withdraws within, lost in thought. 'I never understood Job. I sank into despair not because I lost faith but because I lost control, I handed over my freedom, it was my being I had forsaken, I became a puppet in the hands of fate. Light at last! I thought I had lost my god but it is all fading away now I understand the true nature of what I lost. Reading my thoughts, Sanaka answers with a paradox, 'You lost god to find God. Remember the patriarchs, they too were cosmic servers, they too came to dispel illusion and spread the light of mind and they too battled with their god, as did Job. There is drama in this epic struggle, there is bravery too. It takes courage to recognise the limits of the gods you once endorsed. We must be quite clear on this: to admit to the limits of the gods you once worshipped is to admit to your own limits and this is painful. It takes courage to leave the redundant past behind and move on. As you let in the new, as you allow change, you gain a new grasp of your situation; you make a new evaluation of your old beliefs. A spirit of critical enquiry replaces the old acceptance. Your mind expands; nothing will ever obscure your horizon.

'Freedom finally attained in the strangest of ways, says Moses with lassitude, by letting go of what I once valued. All my life spirituality was synonymous with religious endeavour, and now as I reach the end of my life, I realise that the two are not related but that they even exclude each other! I have to learn from scratch like an infant who takes his first steps. This is truly daunting. I have so much unlearning to do, so much weeding to do, it may take me several life times to complete. When will the real learning begin?

'Only the weak surrender, worn down by fear and doubt. You are of the strong, you do not surrender. What increasingly matters now is integrity and self-knowledge. You will never again make do with unverified answers, untested by experience. Answers given by men, who make irrevocable pronouncements on crucial issues, are not for your uncompromising mind

This contrived conviction is no other than bored dissatisfaction, lethargic negligence. Things are never quite what they seem!

'But I lost my god and I feel peaceful. How can I feel peace! The excruciating pain I thought would never heal is fading.

'That is because you only lost your idea of god! It was not even your idea but the idea your ancestors implanted in the collective mind. You are losing an illusion and releasing the hold it had on you. It had become a reassuring habit, but habits paralyse the mind and the will.

'I do not even feel guilty at having forsaken my people.

'You lost the idea your people had formed of god, that idea has gripped you for ages. Knowing god is one thing and believing in god is quite another. You will soon differentiate between the two. Your ancestors fashioned a god conjured up from the faint memory they had of him, created around stories of his actions while he was on Earth, and on supposition and surmise as to who he was. It was guess work by generations who could not comprehend the might of that stellar being.

'In truth I lost only an idea, says Moses with relief.

'You already differentiate, smiles Sanaka, you lost a mirage, it has dissipated before your very eyes and now you are making contact with the cosmic force that does not require sacrifices and praise. You no longer need to engage in diligent study in order to grasp the elusive mind of the god of long ago. Do you realise that outside the Book, your ancient god ceases to exist? The god that dwells within you does not take its reality in a book but in the Heart.

'The world has followed in our footsteps, emulating our outlook, notes Moses.

'The world took from your tradition the idea of a transcendent god, it endorsed the authoritarian Father. But this seemingly 'unified' faith disintegrated into an all-exclusive faith. This tradition approved by the world was dismissive of universal truths. It is the opposite of freedom, equality, reason and tolerance, the principles that became the rallying goals of the Revolution. It has taken nearly 2000 years for these noble truths upheld by the enlightened Essenes and Greeks to re-emerge in Europe amid great opposition and hostility from established religion and the 'ancient regime'. The poets and musicians of that era did not write hymns to the Father but to the Cosmic Mind. Philosophers hailed freedom of thought and reason. From the concrete Father to the abstract Mind. What a leap in consciousness! They mused over the life force that fills the universe and understood it to be universal not sectarian, inclusive not exclusive, infinite rather than separative.

'You approve of the Revolution? I looked to the revolutionary thinkers for inspiration, I saw them as my intellectual mentors, adds Moses visibly relieved. Jacob too is an inspiration; I feel an affinity with his plight. He struggled with the visible and the invisible, grappled with the worldly and the unworldly, man and god.

'Your affinity for Jacob does not surprise me, smiles Sanaka, you follow in his footsteps. You are the Jacob of your generation.

'The story narrates that Jacob wrestled with the angel of Esau till day break, alone in the night, pursues Moses with animation, unable to halt the flow. And when the angel did not prevail, he touched Jacob's thigh out of joint. And the angel said, 'let me go, for the day breaks', but Jacob said, 'I will not let you go unless you bless me'. The angel accepts his defeat and recognises Jacob's superiority in this mythical struggle: 'Your name shall no longer be Jacob but Israel. For you have struggled with god and with men and you have prevailed', to which Jacob replies 'for I have seen God face to face and my life is preserved'.

'I sense the reason for your affinity with Jacob and his heroic struggle, smiles the Master with affectionate irony. It hints at a sound evaluation of your own life. Jacob is the mythological hero who struggles with men, angels and gods in order to find himself. He is tested to the limits. Like you he engages in a harrowing war against limiting beliefs. The greatest struggle the hero has to triumph over is his attachment to his group values and group beliefs. This is the ultimate test for the hero, indeed the ultimate test of any human being! What he held true before the encounter with the angel is no longer relevant. The fight is symbolic; it is old beliefs and ideas he grappled with and he has to shed if he is going to be the leader of a new nation. Bringer of a new age Jacob now knows that he is equal to men, angels and gods. The New Age is fast approaching and you are being called, like the heroic Jacob to take up your post and affirm your power. But Jacob is not to be revered as an epic hero, he is every man, each man has to assert his freedom, integrity and individuality. Each Jew is Jacob, that is the meaning of the new name he is given. This mythical battle must be re-enacted by each one of you.

'Does each man have to grapple with god and angels and to what end?

'In order not to fall into the kind of tragic predicament that has been the continued fate of your people. When you accept the past but do not question it then you head for disaster. Each and every man is presented with one vital question in any lifetime: 'Who am I'?

'We answered this question long ago.

'Indeed, but is this answer relevant today? The uncritical masses are defined by their physicality. They reply 'I am a Jew because of my mother's bloodline'. But is man simply his body, his bloodline, his group beliefs? Each one must endeavour to answer this one crucial question during his lifetime. As a group you have evaded that question.

In each incarnation you are confronted with the question: 'Who am I, shall I be an imitation of my father and his father before him? Am I going to cast myself in the old worn out mould? Shall I hide into the defunct past, too timorous to face up to reality or am I going to grapple with reality and do what Jacob did, fight angels, demons, gods and all external forces that collide with my purpose? If you refuse to question the truth of your beliefs you are an idol worshipper, you worship images, ideas and opinions unquestioningly. You no longer exercise your divine autonomy.

'This is relevant to my situation, if I may be bold enough to say so, remarks Moses. I clearly see the truth of what happened to me; the similarity of my situation with Jacob's is uncanny. The aloneness, the darkness, the abandonment, the betrayal, the night that heralds no dawn.

'Like Jacob you went through a painful initiation. You had to shed the old and make yourself available for the new, not only available but instrumental in bringing in the new. This normally takes place several times in any man's life; you may view this in terms of 'death and transfiguration'. At the end of the night, the angel bids farewell to Jacob, this symbolically suggests that Jacob, like you, emerges from the darkness into the light. Night is always followed by dawn. Excruciating it was, but giving birth to the Self is a painful experience. You see, the greatest disservice you do to yourself - and through you to mankind - is to give up who you are in order to serve a belief which has no relevance to the world, plays no role in your growth but is resolutely hostile to your emancipation and the emancipation of the Planet.

'Why the Planet, why mankind? I was agonising alone.

'So you think! No one is an island, what affects one individual concerns all living things and affects the life of the Planet. Mankind and Earth are one. The body of man is made of the body of Earth. Earth is truly Mother Earth and we abuse her at our peril. You parted with humanity and with the Mother. You have lived dangerously because you have lived unthinkingly. In future, when man begins to evaluate his actions, it will become plain for all to see. There is no hiding place. Actions, emotions and thoughts-forms remain in your astral body lifetime after lifetime until you decide to change them. But you prefer to ignore that you have involved Earth in that same karmic wheel of suffering, delusion and darkness. Mankind has put a thick fog around Earth, so the cycle of reincarnation, suffering, delusion and death is repeated. You are an integral part of humanity and of Earth; this fact will not go away.

'Why is the Planet involved in man's activity? Why is our deluded thinking affecting mankind and the Planet? What are the relationships?

'As I just explained, man is made of the body of Earth. Man and Earth are inseparable they are made of the same substance. To deny this intimate relationship is to deny one's very existence. Millions of years ago, Earth offered to assist the soul of man on its long path, and so she became intimately involved in the evolution of man. But it works both ways; man too is responsible for the evolution of Earth. Man acts in ways which affect humanity and the Planet because of this intimate relationship. There is no place to hide! With the rest of humanity you are caught up on the ever-turning wheel of rebirth, suffering, illusion and death.

'What of heaven, what of life after death?

'You may ask, Moses, what of heaven? Sadly 'heaven' is no other than the continuation of the Earth plane. Like Earth it is also the plane of illusion. After death man returns to the astral plane – you call heaven - where he is confronted with the same illusion. He is just as disappointed and disorientated and so he prepares to reincarnate in the hope that things will get better. And he comes back with his troubled emotions, persistent thought-forms, stubborn beliefs and he is caught up on the treadmill once again. Theologians have captured man on the Earth realms, ensnared him on the emotional plane of deception and the mental plane of illusion.

But Moses finds this new revelation too painful to bear. It is all becoming too much, he fears for his mental stability. He reverts back to his own torment, 'I was in a solitary struggle. I passed through disabling and disturbing phases from known god to unknown god.

'God is neither known nor unknown, it is your idea of god which fluctuates, and you had to grapple with this realisation in solitude. Like Jacob injured and despairing of life you had to answer your life question. In each incarnation man is confronted with the same question and he has to answer it, but theology often prevents him from doing so.

'Why, is it not the role of theology to explain and guide?

'That's what you think! In truth it does the very opposite, it gives the answer and forbids man to ask the question! So man plods through life limping, disabled, perplexed. If he asks pertinent questions on the meaning of life or his origins, he is branded a heretic and ostracised. So he gives up and blunders his way through yet another existence that resolves nothing. At the dawn of the Age of Pisces, our era, the decision-makers in Jerusalem decided that there would be no 'new' era. The long awaited for Messianic age would not happen. The light bringers were planting the seeds of sympathy, justice, equality, compassion, reconciliation, autonomy of the soul and freedom of expression. But the theologians declared that all this was not for them and most definitely not for their people! They wanted to hold on to the 'thou shall not', 'do & obey', 'vengeance is mine and 'an eye for an eye'. They sought to go on controlling from their graves the mind of their people.

'That is just what they have done, replies Moses.

'Do you know what happens after death, asks Sanaka?

'I no longer know anything, sighs Moses.

'There is neither Heaven nor Hell. The terrifying scenes the 'dead' behold, continues Sanaka, arise from their troubled minds, they knew no peace in this life, and they know no peace in the next. What they see as external events exist only in their tortured imagination, no one else can see. Earth plane and astral plane are entwined; both form the world of illusion. Each person sees reality in his own unique way, according to his beliefs, culture, karmic residue, attachments, emotions and thought-forms. At another level of meaning the angel Jacob grapples with is his own imagination, his own world of illusion.

Rabbi Moses' narrative story continues. 'The next morning Master Sanaka and I took a walk among the lovely wild flowers until we reached a quiet stream. A few yaks were resting by the water; sheep were grazing, tranquil scene I never associated with the forbidding peaks of the Himalayas.

'You know that travel in the fluid ether is made easier in this rarefied atmosphere? You have been given the rare opportunity to transform your life, smiles Sanaka sensing the mood; you might say that what happened before your arrival belongs to a previous lifetime.

'What I wish to know is why I have been singled out for this work?

'I urge you to let go of the lower octaves of the past and open yourself to the higher octaves of Now. No one sent you, no one selected you and no one chose you! Learn to accept this, you offered yourself for this work and the Masters of Shamballa who search Earth for awakening souls recognised in you a sincere seeker, suitable for the work of awakening humanity.

The dramatic struggle between the personality & the soul

'In the nature of the One, all dualities are absorbed and all differences lose their meaning'. (Master Djwahl Khul)

'Rabbi Moses, we are going to unravel the main themes of the Old Testament in the time you will spend with us at the monastery. It is not only crucial for your people, it is also important for the rest of the world. Much of it you arrived at by your own reflection and much springs from your higher Self released from its bondage when you let go of the chains of man-made beliefs. Some of it you will find startling and disquieting as the mists of the past are reluctant to lift and residues of group values and beliefs linger. Fragments of discarded dogmas, debris of archaic notions, decaying memories are still lurking deep in your mind. They will lift eventually like the stubborn night fog finally surrenders to the morning light.

Master Sanaka is not inviting a response from Rabbi Moses, so he continues uninterrupted. 'In the East we have no Creation story, no Fall, no long-standing conflict between man and woman, no ongoing discord between God and man, no dispute between man and Nature. Fear, the axis on which the Old Testament rotates is for us absent. There is a good reason for this; we were spared a divine revelation! Fear appears early, it runs through the myth of Adam and Eve, the fable of Cain and Abel, the legendary conflict between Isaac and Esau. Moses, my son, what do these allegories have in common?

'They come in pairs. Duality is evident in these battles between good and evil, light and darkness.

'Excellent, Rabbi Moses. Duality and fear run through the entire revealed texts, not surprisingly you are the living memory of both.

'Why is fear the axis, duality I understand but fear? Why does the entire revealed material hinge around fear? Why is fear both the driving and the obstructing force?

'Sound question Moses. Fear is the opposite of love. Fear appears with the Fall when unity splinters into duality.

'Unity splinters into duality and fear is the outcome?

'The Reality that underlies form we call the undifferentiated Oneness. Then duality appears on the stage of the world to be acted out and fear makes its entrance. The Old Testament plays out the drama of duality all the way in every page, every story and every character. Fear appears in part because duality you perceive as evil and this distorts your view of things. From then on all is evil: man, woman, Nature, Earth.

'The world of duality is not our invention, corrects Moses.

'You bow to it; we refuse to be bound by it! We see it for what it is a clever theatrical device, a learning tool; we are not deceived by it. We seek to transform it back into its pristine nature. We have been treading the Path in the full light of day, we are fully aware of what we are in essence. Why the Path? Because we identity with all life, with the cosmos and with the Infinite. Whereas you have identified with the world of form, appearances and phenomena, you have entrapped all generations. When you regard the world of form as real, you unwittingly identify with the transient, the perishable, and the fragmentary. The Path opens up into never imagined before states of consciousness, worlds and dimensions. For us the Path widens to include ever more, the path for you goes on shrinking as it excludes ever more.

'Is it fear that causes this shrinking?

'Fear has much to do with it; fear prevents you from leaving the imposed path, the path traced out for you. Dreams, aspirations, creative flights of imagination, intuitive insights are frowned upon, who knows they might just set you free! 'And the truth shall set you free'. The truth of your infinite, timeless, deathless nature might emerge and this is incompatible with the imposed path.

'We are the people of the 'yoke' sighs Moses. The 'yoke' is tight around our necks and we do not know where we are going in spite of bold assertions.

'That is one of the reasons why you adopted duality with such vigour, such conviction. The truth is that duality belongs to the world of appearances, the phenomenal world. Reality - the essence - underlies duality. We know in the East what we are, we are that essence. We refuse to be deceived by appearances; we penetrate to the core where oneness is, where we are that oneness. We look beyond form, beyond multiplicity and we find only unity. You refuse to see reality - the cosmic life force pulsating in all. The life force in you is the life force in the vegetable and animal kingdoms. And so where we see unity you see diversity where we sense oneness you affirm separation and division. These are some of the themes we will be exploring: Creation of the cosmos, time, space and matter and creation of man.

'The universe was created, it exists in duality, this is an undeniable fact. Time entered Creation with the word Berechit: 'In the Beginning God created heaven and earth' these are the words opening the Book of Genesis.

'The crux of the matter lies in the primordial division. Man became separated from his Self, the cosmic part of his nature. The myth of Adam and Eve tells of this separation. This is the starting point; the rest comes hurtling down with inevitability. As you aptly note, Berechit enters the stage. Berechit inaugurates time; eternity has broken up into time. Adam who formerly lived beyond time is now caught in time and controlled by it. Temporality enters the picture. What is so significant about time?

'Limitation, separation and ultimately death, replies Moses hesitant, for his learning which designated him as a biblical scholar back in Vilna seems now in the land of wisdom inadequate, flimsy. He would prefer to remain silent.

'Excellent, but there is something which concerns your people specifically.

Why is time so significant?

'Man at Creation enters the 3rd dimension: matter, space and time. He has now to grope his way, travel the Path across insurmountable hurdles.

'They are not insurmountable to us in the East, why are they insurmountable to you? Does this have to do with Berechit, 'in the Beginning'? In the beginning time and duality enter the human stage. Adam, symbolically the physical self, is working in the garden discussing plans with his god whereas Eve, symbolically the Self, is talking to the Serpent of Wisdom. Do you see something striking about this?

'Adam is now separated from his cosmic Self as he occupies himself with the affairs of the world.

'Indeed, Moses. Time has precipitated the separation of man from his cosmic element. Mortal man, Adam is now confronted with the problems and difficulties inherent in the physical world. What is perhaps more remarkable is that he converses with his god. What do you think the intention of the Cosmic Beings was when they sketched this text?

'Adam split from his higher Self needs his god to guide him through life, he has lost his direction and must somehow finds his way back to his primordial perfection, find the Path.

'I accept this but there is more. Adam, symbolically the lower self, converses with the god who tells him how to live within the confines of time, space and matter.

Remember that he is now dissociated from his Self, alone and forlorn, Eve has left him, rather he has left Eve. In other words Adam, the personality, has emerged and is creating its own world detached from cosmic reality.

'So if I understand, time appears with duality and both precipitate the personality break from the human Self and presumably from the cosmic Self.

'You presume right, smiles Sanaka. Sure enough time anchors man in selfhood. From then on it is downhill, the self begins to build a vast body of beliefs, attitudes, prejudices, dogmas, memories and phantasms. It begins to believe in its own existence and permanence. 'Berechit ...' in the beginning' opens Genesis. The starting point of the Hebrew's sense of self is rooted in this one word. Then comes the symbolic drama of the Self captured in time. No other people on the Planet are more aware of time; you divide time into holy time and profane time! No other group is more bound by time; equally no other group is more driven by the personality. The conflict between the personality and the Self is staged at the outset with the split between Adam and Eve. The conflict is taken a step further in the murderous quarrel between Cain and Abel. Further down the line a new act in the drama is played out between Isaac and Esau. Each time the struggle between personality and higher Self unfolds.

'In a mysterious way all this seems so familiar, notes Moses.

'It is. When you rip the web of beliefs woven by the personality of your ancestors you set your soul free. You are now your higher Self liberated from the ancestral yoke which is keeping others subdued and fastened to each other. You are no longer restricted, no longer bound and gagged. Adam working in a world empty of the Cosmic Presence fashions a god he can relate to.

'The Self needs no god, no rules, no direction, no morality, and no legality?

'The mortal self does! This is causing you pain because you learned at a tender age to esteem the personality and it will not leave you without putting up a fight. The path trodden by your group is that of the personality clamouring for more authority, solidity and legality. Your ancestors have written volumes upon volumes to convince themselves and their descendents of the sacredness and permanence of the personality, each generation has reinforced the belief in personality.

'Some of us believe that only the Hebrew is endowed with a soul.

'Some of you, laughs the Master, believe that you are endowed with several souls, while the rest of us mere mortals have none! Always you see the personality at work fashioning, structuring, fabricating, fantasising! Buddha dismissed all theology as 'a thicket of views', 'a puppet show of views'. It is a figment of the imagination, a construction by the personality to convince itself of its sacredness and everlasting quality. The god of personality builds castles in the air, 'I am made in the image of god, my god is the only god, my god chose me, I am the elect, I am holy and the rest of the world is unholy, I am a man, I have a mission and a purpose, the world rests on my shoulders, I am the saviour of humanity, I have a vast body of moral rules and legal laws to prove that I am special.'

'It is all so clear now, exclaims Moses. The personality split from the Source requires beliefs for reassurance. The entire edifice of beliefs, attachments, precepts and principles, prejudices and attitudes are cast on to a god existing 'out there', a god we can worship!

'And the light was …' laughs the Master. The many gods of the ancients did exist: they symbolised important moments in the growth and development of individuals from birth through to death and beyond.

'The meaning of the Old Testament, the message hidden by the Masters?

'The march of humanity through time is also the march of humanity given over to the worship of personality. The texts chart the journey of personality through time and space. Personality deified is concerned with maintaining the world of its own creation.

'This has been the curse of humanity since the Fall!

'Mankind was never abandoned entirely to its own folly! Time and again the Masters have incarnated to steer man on the Path. Redeemers came; it was the point of evolution of the people that determined how they were received. They came to Lemuria, Atlantis, Egypt and India and even in your own land where the cosmic Soul presented itself before the august assembly of the doctors of the law. There the Soul met with anger, disbelief, resentment and indignation. The sentinels of the personality mocked, heckled and cursed. The personality could not relinquish its status to the Soul. Better the long agony of the Christian exile, better suffering and pain, better death than the recognition of the soul in man!

'Why is it so difficult for us to acknowledge the perennial struggle between the personality and the Self?

'I should be asking you this question, chuckles the Master. It has to do with the willingness to let go of the past. All mythologies focus on the cycles of human life:

birth, childhood, adulthood, marriage, old age and death, the cycles of life in nature as in man are similar. The Old Testament like all ancient mythologies, maps out in allegorical form, the cycles of nature and the cycles of human life, but the similarities end there, whereas ancient cultures move on from one phase onto another in a progressive fashion, leaving behind the old to enter the new, you do the reverse. You have the same rites of passages and more rituals than any other groups, yet your rituals which should guide you on to your life journey arrest you in the past. Every phase of life implies a 'death' and an initiation, the 'death' of the old life and the initiation into a new life.

'You are saying Master that in spite of the elaborate rites of passage, in spite of celebrating the cycles of nature we remain static?

'This is the paradox. Adults attached to their parents experience stunted growth; think of the mythological character of Daphne who was unable to leave her father. Now the reasons why ancient mythologies - and the Old Testament is no exception - celebrate the various rites of passage is to encourage the young to move on, to grow and develop. You are absorbed in the past; therefore you are captive of the fantasies, beliefs, images and emotions of the childhood of humanity. With Berechit, enters time, with time history, with history the past. The past is hazardous if it is not understood and each generation has to relive the past; the past is rekindled, re-enacted. The past is not questioned and even less resolved and so it is passed on to the next generation which re-enacts it and solidifies it into stagnation. You have been doing this for thousands of years, sheltering under the wing of the god of childhood. And this applies not only to the people as a whole but to many individuals within it. This is indeed a cruel fate for not only are many individuals stuck in their own childhood they are also stuck in the childhood memories, images, fears and phantasms of the group.

'And we are proud of our loyalty to history and our attachment to permanence. We hold on to it believing it to be god-given.

'And so it is! Given by the god you have worshipped from time immemorial. The personality dwells in the past and it requires gods to sanction it.

'The present is all?

'The present is all, the present is eternity and as our Self we live in eternity. The personality and its gods wallow in the past and worship the past; they require temples, festivals, blood sacrifices, moral laws that generate fear, guilt, reward and punishment and much suffering. Most diseases spring from guilt, fear and shame. Groups like

30

individuals need healing. To heal is to bring the afflicted into the present and encourage them to live in it.

'The past is the source of suffering, pain and disease?

'That's right. For this you came to India. You will return to Vilna to heal: to bring them into the present, to encourage them to dispel the mists of the past that are keeping them in pain and in fear. The past is preventing them from experiencing reality, from knowing who they truly are.

Worship of Duality

'See the One in the many. As long as you see diversity you will go from death to death. Cease this wandering and embrace your Oneness'. (Upanishads)

Allegory of Creation: Adam and Eve

Rabbi Moses was recovering from his long journey to India and the illness that was precipitated by his excommunication. Master Sanaka had explained the reason behind his illness, 'You think that others are responsible for your illness and so they are. But things are more subtle, it all has to do with your state of mind. I am enouncing a cosmic Law here; man is receptive to thought-atmosphere. The mind of man responds to thought-influences, these may be directed at him or not, but he receives them when he makes himself vulnerable to their negative impact. Thoughts will hit you if you attract them.

'Are you saying, Master, that I am responsible for my illness?

'Sadly yes, I want you to grasp a fundamental Law: thoughts will hurt you if you attract them, if you place yourself in their path so to speak, if you intercept them. Thoughts fill the ether, those thoughts that are at our level we attract. The human mind is a magnet, like a magnet captures iron, so the mind captures thoughts. They hurt you because you let them. They knew that you would permit this intrusion, they sensed your vulnerability, your brokenness and they took the liberty to invade you. Human beings are extremely sensitive to the mood of others. Thought is all. 'With our thoughts we make the world' said Buddha. The universe came into being by the power of thought.

He was alone having lost all; his mind churning the same painful event the 'death sentence' by the respected scholars of his community and the betrayal that no amount of self-examination would diminish. He had to give up his studies, his work, even his

31

wife. Unable to endure hardship and humiliation, his wife had returned to her parents living him at once deserted by all. He had touched the lowest point of the descending curve. The pain would not subside, in spite of his efforts to analyse his new situation. 'There must be an unseen design, a hidden meaning to all this. Life could not be so unfair, so cruel'. He had lost the consolation of faith, he no longer believed in the god of his ancestors. God and men had betrayed him. When gods betray man, faith falls away. Faith is a fragile flower that does not endure harsh conditions.

Master Sanaka did not visit him for a few days, allowing Moses time to adjust to his new environment. The beauty, the peace of the majestic mountain range, the snow-capped peaks, the monastery itself, so large and populated, yet so isolated and remote, had a profoundly beneficial effect on his tortured mind and declining health. One day as he was taking a stroll within the monastery enclosure, he noticed that the light was translucent; the sun was illuminating the peaks. The despondency that had been his companion for so long lifted and he saw, he truly saw the peaks, the snow, the monastery, and the monks. They all came to life. Then suddenly, Master Sanaka appeared, he was standing before him, looking deep into his eyes, deep into his soul with his sparkling smile and enigmatic expression. Echoing the agonizing thoughts Moses had been stirring:

'Being betrayed by men is a serious affliction, but being betrayed by god looks more like an indiscretion. Sensing Moses' inner turmoil, 'When you place your reliance away from you, a crash is inescapable. Your centre is displaced; it is no longer in you, under your firm control, but out there at the whims of the outer world. There will always be people and situations that will influence you, simply because part of you is 'outside', exposed, vulnerable; and so your integrity is threatened. Your vulnerability is played upon, preyed upon by stronger personalities. You may come in contact with a more powerful force which will bend yours, a force made all the more potent by an unbending tradition, crystallised beliefs and hardened views. You could not submit, so you quit. Sanaka waits for Moses to ingest his words; he remains silent, looking away toward the white peaks, immersed in his own thoughts. Moses too remains silent; the pain he is experiencing is all absorbing.

Breaking the silence, Sanaka utters, 'The Master who brought a new awareness to the world understood that humanity, in order to survive had to rise to a higher consciousness; this implied accepting responsibility for oneself, learning self-reliance.

Early man was reliant on supernatural forces, and controlled by physical conditions. When man is wrapped up in physical reality, he is unaware of his own power. You had to rediscover this too.

'In order to rise to a higher consciousness I had to go through all of that?

'To rise to a new realization, you must 'die' to the lower consciousness. 'Except ye die, ye shall not live'. You must understand that you set yourself up as a laboratory to experiment with the energies you encountered and you did so in order to transmute them. Like all cosmic workers, you came to shed light in dark corners'. He moves away, leaving Moses to reflect, alone. After a pause, 'the survival of humanity depends on accepting responsibility. When you look outside for direction you are like a child who expects a present and who is distraught when the present does not arrive! It also depends on recognising the boundless world man carries within himself. Looking deep into the eyes of Moses, he asks with slow and deliberate intent the life-transforming question, stressing each word: ' When man knows himself to be the universe, is there a force in the cosmos qualified to give him that help?

Master Sanaka moves away as silently as he had appeared. Moses is unable to wrench himself from the spot, time passes. The sun has moved over the next line of mountain peak. 'How long have I been looking at the scenery, this place is uncanny, I am awake yet I feel dazed, as if under a spell. Time is playing tricks on me; it is either crushed or elongated. I have to get a hold of myself, if I am not to lose my mind, altogether'.

'This beauty is truly compelling, so intense that it seems to induce an altered state of consciousness, so magical that it seems to bend time. Master Sanaka has reappeared; he is standing by Moses, smiling his radiant smile. Unwilling to let go of the initiative and intent on fostering the element of surprise, he continues, 'Just like the first day of Creation, the world remains in its primordial unity and integrity, nothing can impair this primeval perfection. And so we are going to begin at the beginning, he chuckles.

'Master I was waiting for you to initiate the process, says Moses in a weary, faint voice. Shall we return to the monastery?

'No, we shall begin on this spot, can you think of a better place, smiles ironically the Master. 'And it begins .., but you know how it begins, you are a distinguished biblical scholar, I am not going to insult your intelligence with wearisome repetition, I guess you had more than your fair share of both. You may have endured an overload of repetitive narratives, which as you know, are no more than shells, until they are broken up to release the hidden kernel. The real meaning has eluded you, brooding over the shell, shaking your head in reverence, you have turned it over and over, never realising that a priceless gem lay unseen inside. You have been enthralled by the outer form, the shell.

So let's not waste any time; the narrative matters not so much as the underlying meaning. You will in time find that the verses are not quite what you thought they were. The form has always enticed you. Again I emphasise, it is the world of meaning behind the allegory I am aiming for. 'In the Beginning there was One Life, complete, self-sufficient, undivided, uninterrupted, unbroken. But the One decided to bring about separation, fragmentation, division and so the universe came into being. The primordial white light split into its seven component colours and the world as you see it is built on the seven Rays, just like the entire music of Bach is composed with the seven notes of the scale.

'Why the seven colours?

'Because when white light passes through a prism it splits into the seven visible colours of the spectrum. The cosmic Rays of Creation individualised came under the responsibility of the Masters. These Rays make up everything that exists including the personality of man and the nature of his soul, just as the seven notes of the scale make up all the music that has ever been composed or will be composed. The seven Rays like the seven notes are the building blocks of the world. This initial division and individualisation is encapsulated in a beautiful myth in which the Garden of Eden represents the universe of man. Think of the Tree of Life, it is the symbol of man himself, man growing and reaching out, giving fruit, creating life. And so at the outset, we are presented with a complex play of symbols to decipher. Trees are powerful symbols of the nature of man. The Garden of Eden is the symbolic representation of earthly man. The Tree of Knowledge and the Tree of Life - so powerful that they have preoccupied and inspired poets, artists, philosophers and theologians continue to exert a profound influence on humanity. This is the power of myth. Myths are inexhaustible, releasing new meanings in the appropriate language for each generation.

'Master would you shed light on the Tree of Knowledge, the authorised version has never satisfied me?

'Myths contain universal truth. Truth is encapsulated in this form because mythology transcends history, place and culture. The biblical myths are found in almost all world mythologies, they originate from the same source, the Masters of the Wisdom. I must emphasise this point, Hebrew myths are not fundamentally different from all other world myths, the form may differ, for instance instead of referring to the Moon-goddess as Ishtar, you personify her and call her Rebecca. The same applies to the Sun-god Hephaistos adored by many ancient cultures who you personify as Esau. In order to preserve the appearances of monotheism you disguise the elemental truth shared by all mythologies. The time will come when the ancient myths will be scientifically studied by the prominent academics of that generation who will uncover the world of meaning hidden behind the façade. You grappled with the outer form when the Initiates of the world were decoding the text with the key and compass they had learned in the Mysteries Schools. Attached to the story line you have confused yourselves and plunged generations into confusion. Myths have many facets and one reading of the Tree of Knowledge is man's misdirected perception of good and evil as implanted in religious imagination. The biblical scholar perceives evil as a force contrasting good, as a force in its own right. He discusses it with assertiveness because he believes it to be real.

'It seems real enough, the myths in Genesis support this, we see the effects of evil all around us, and it is plain for all to see.

'I must answer with a paradox. Evil is plain for all to see, yet evil is only a shadow, an absence of light. In a dark room you can see nothing, but as soon as you light candles, the darkness disappears. Darkness does not exist of itself. In believing it to be real you give it a force it does not have. Cosmic Law states that the thought we concentrate on becomes energised, it comes to life; this is the law behind thought forms. Persistent thoughts continually fed with mental energy become things; they can take shape and even lead a life of their own, because 'energy follows thought'. Evil has no existence, except in the mind that brings it to life.

'What is the nature of evil then?

'One definition is that evil is nothing, it has no reality but the reality you give it, it has no existence, but the existence you give it. In other words evil belongs to the world of matter. Only the lower self is aware of evil, the soul is not.

'Evil is an illusion constructed by the human mind, then?

'You could say that. The myth conceals important truth not exhausted at any one time. It is partially accessed by successive generations. Each one discovers a new facet, a new meaning, each one ventures in the myth deeper, still the myth has not yielded all of its secrets. And so it is with the oldest myth, the myth of Adam and Eve. You must realise that the Hierarchy clothed it in this form for specific reasons, the myth must remain many-faceted, it must retain its complexity and its flexibility. The Masters were not writing just a story. Today we are going to approach it from one angle, next time from another angle. Let us reflect on Eve, not as the eternal woman, the sacred feminine but as the soul in its moment of awakening, the birth of the soul in humanity. Mankind as Adam and Eve is just emerging from the state of unconsciousness that has lasted millions of years. Mankind is waking; the soul in humanity is being stirred. The soul had laid unconscious in the depth of matter, in bondage. Primitive man is searching, sensing that there is a finer aspect to him other than mere animal urge for survival. The opening scene of the mythological drama finds Eve doing just that. Eve demands knowledge; she wants to know who she is, what it is all about.

'The great myth of Creation is the story of the awakening of the soul in man?

'You sound surprised, Moses, what could be more momentous? It was important enough for the Masters to inscribe into the Book of Genesis. The moment when animal-man becomes human, when he becomes conscious, must be the most awesome moment in the history of the world.

'I always thought that Adam had been created perfect, noble and omniscient, nothing like your description of animal-man.

'Yours is the authorised version, smiles Sanaka, mine is not, and I was taught by the Masters not by men of another age. The soul is making a giant leap forward as it wakes up: it realises the presence of good and evil, it begins to grasp polarity. The soul in animal-man who lived a crude existence is now seeking knowledge of itself. The light is dim, barely visible; questions are forming in the mind of Eve, she looks out on the beautiful world around her and she wonders. She wants to know what she is doing in this 'Garden', she feels that she is part of the world. Who is she in relation to the world? The longing is real. Eve is not asking frivolous questions. The faint gleam of light is evoking a response. Someone is answering her questions. As Eve turns outward in search of answers, the Crown is beginning to vibrate. The fables we read to children tell of a princess who after being plunged into a long sleep finally is awakened by her prince. Eve, the soul is being roused from the density of matter with the discovery of good and evil and this realisation comes with the gift of freewill from the gods.

' Yahweh presents man with a choice and demands that he chooses good, he impresses on the mind of man that only good is acceptable.

'Indeed, the gods who tutor early man impress upon him the importance of good action and good intent. Would this be necessary if Adam was the illumined being your tradition trusts him to be? What would a god-like being do with the simple doctrine of good and evil?

'Awareness of good and evil is not the highest state man can aspire to?

'Knowledge of good and evil, smiles Sanaka is not the greatest achievement man is capable of. Perfected man overlooks appearances and blends differences: he recreates the primeval unity; he uncovers the one Reality that underlies all creation. Awakened man transcends duality. Awareness of duality is awareness of an illusion. Unquestioned acceptance of duality is a stumbling block; it is that which has thrown mankind into disarray. Biblical scholars have misinformed humanity just as they have deluded themselves. Man believes what he sees, not questioning the accuracy of his perception.

'So if duality is an illusion, why did the Masters impart it?

'They did not set out to trick you; they only gave the early history of man awakening after millions of years of unconsciousness. They disclosed facts, they allowed man to grow and evolve sufficiently to arrive at his own interpretation. It has taken the best part of 4000 years but it is gradually happening. The Masters inform, guide, teach and point the way but they do not enforce, they remain impartial and detached.

'Master why is Eve blundering, what is she really asking?

'Eve is probably thinking something like this, 'I am given freedom of choice, not only I am allowed to use it, I must use it!' Eve is awakening to a new reality: she has choice, like god she has the power of decision, she can influence events, and she can change the course of things for good or evil.

'What a giant leap! I never read the myth in this light. Eve is depicted as the woman mischievous, mindless, easily distracted and distracting, and so the tradition was born to ignore women, avoid their presence, prevent any contact or conversation with them. A man is not allowed to even sit next to his wife, lest he be distracted or corrupted by her.

'This is what happens when patriarchy gets hold of a good myth! Eve, the soul is receiving a faint, fleeting glimmer of a response that indicates her place in the world.

'When man begins to build fanciful notions around his identity and his place in the world, enquires Moses?

'The rabbis have done this for him, replies Sanaka with his radiant smile. They were not the first, other ancient civilisations did it; it was a case of emulating and borrowing. Custodians of the myth of Creation, you contemplate, discuss, debate and comment that first stirring of the soul when long ago animal-man became aware of his nascent humanity. They have done this for centuries and continue to do so. To this day they journey into the myth with the same reverence, the same awe, the same exhilarated gratitude for their god and with a chuckle, 'with the same contempt for Eve.

'Eve is seen as the eternal woman, unreliable and foolish.

'Regrettably so! Unity is ruptured in the Book of Genesis. Boundaries are first drawn by Adam as he pictures himself split from Eve: when he perceives himself divided into body and mind, conscious and unconscious, masculine and feminine. A modern approach to the myth is to picture Adam as the practical, realistic, pragmatic facet, the concrete mind. In this new context we have Adam the personality being confronted by Eve the soul; Adam does not understand what she embodies. He is fully engaged in the outer world, tending the 'garden' - the physical environment - whereas Eve is tuned into the inner world, reflecting, wondering. You see, to disclaim Eve is to disclaim the highest element in man. In repudiating Eve, the guardians of the Myth unwittingly repudiate their higher aspect - the feminine, the soul. In disowning the soul they have become prejudiced, dogmatic and narrow-minded.

'I recall that the more contemptuous of Eve they were, the more admired they were for their saintliness. I know now why I so disliked their attitude! Their disdain for Eve and the non-Jewish world was a measure of their spiritual status. They tended to over do it in order to appear more righteous.

'This happens, you recall the phrase 'When the Tao is lost, there is need for legality, morality, knowledge and much pretence'. To satisfy the needs of the lower mind you neglect the needs of the higher Mind; this initiates a mythological struggle between soul and personality. They neglect the request of the soul in order to satisfy the claim of the human mind which demands order, rule, law and obedience. The soul, fertile soil of infinite possibilities, of limitless potentialities is dismissed by those who decline the primordial qualities of unconditional loving kindness, sensitive understanding and unreserved service to mankind.

'Yet the study of the myth goes on in earnest. With Eve, they continue to fathom out their place in the scheme of things as they venture further in the voyage Eve embarked upon.

'A sound observation, Moses.

'The world was created for man, was it not?

'And this was taken literally, for man not for woman, for Adam not for Eve!

'Excluding the soul, enquires Moses tantalisingly?

'The world was created for Eve so that she may grapple with matter, its darkness and limitations and surmount it by gaining mastery over it. It is through renouncing the tyranny of the self, through resisting the downward pull of physicality; through overcoming the temptation of selfishness and sensuality that Eve can walk the path that leads back to the Tao. The path is paved with pain, temptations, fear, discouragement and despair. And so centuries ago, in troubled Jerusalem, the Masters appeared to demonstrate to the beleaguered people that the time was Now. 'We bring you good news, brothers, they said, we came from behind the veil to set you free. You no longer need to identify with Eve and go on the same journey she took all those aeons ago. The past holds you enthralled, let go of it. The story of Eve was to be understood as a phase in evolution, not to be taken literally not to be perpetuated as if it was real.

'It was not real, says Moses, a mist of sadness descending over him?

'A myth has unlimited potential but it is not real. The time had come to outgrow your limited vision, your partial realisation, let go of your constricted grasp, your narrow perception.

'They were urged to escape the mental prison, sighs Moses with a sorrow he barely disguises. There is no more solid prison than the mind.

'Time to dispel the mists of theology and disperse the fog of illusion, continues Sanaka. They explained that man was imprisoned in that primal state of awareness as he continued to identify with Eve awakening from her long sleep. Man was still condemning himself to retrace the steps Eve had taken as if in an entranced state. They explained that the personality had to make a giant leap. But beleaguered man, beset by doubt, threatened from all sides, rebelled. He jolted, he screamed in horror 'blasphemer'!

'Master I understand one facet of the myth where Eve emerging from unconsciousness learned to discriminate between good and evil. The two are interrelated, moral

39

realisation and spiritual awakening are simultaneous but how do you equate her awakening with the conditions faced by the leaders of Jerusalem 2000 years ago?

'Very wise of you, Moses! You just answered your question. Spiritual and moral awakening are simultaneous.

'If I may clarify a point, Master'. A brilliant smile urges him on, 'the priesthood in Jerusalem wanted to retain what Eve had achieved for all times. Like Eve they assumed that they knew their place in the great Plan, and they took charge of it, overriding the intention of the Hierarchy, the appointed guardians and interpreters of the universal Plan.

'Excellent, Moses, smiles Sanaka with visible joy. Like Eve they exercised their right to affect events, to influence evolution, to change the course of things. Eve had discovered free will and they insisted on expressing it.

'It is a tragic irony, notes Moses that in choosing to exercise their free will they embarked on a journey in which they abdicated their autonomy.

'Very perceptive Moses! They wanted to stand still and keep things exactly as they had always been. Their ancestral god wanted it that way; they dared not envision change without ratification from the deity. And, remember that Yahweh was no longer around. They did not know that the one God is Sanat Kumara, the Planetary Logos in 'whom we live, move, and take our being'. The new is often daunting.

'One of the foundation stones of Judaism is that nothing changes, all is in a perpetual state of stasis. The Law was given and so it is fixed, immovable, and unchangeable. There is a horror of change; it is seen as dissenting.

'The rabbis in their desire to keep things unchanged were unwittingly infringing the very law of life. They halted the natural life flow not realising in their obedient devotion that they were challenging the very purpose of Creation. Life is by definition fluid, moving, irrepressible. Cosmic life in all its manifold manifestations is never static. The divine is Life ever flowing.

'Were the Masters expecting too much, asks Moses?

'The Masters do not think so. They have been observing mankind since the beginning of time; they have educated, protected, guided and instructed mankind over millions of years. They are exquisitely sensitive to man's needs, hopes and progress, they scan minds and hearts, attentive parents who eagerly watch their child make his first steps. Their evaluation of man's capability and their assessment of his potentiality were exact.

'Yet the priesthood did not accept their evaluation, remarks Moses.

'Their estimation of themselves may have fallen short, or they genuinely felt that anything else would be deviant. The Masters were inviting them to resolve duality, rise to the soul and affirm the power of thought where man knows himself to be creator of his reality, master of his destiny.

'This was daunting, a bolt of lightning! No wonder they shouted 'blasphemy'.

'And you should know, replies Sanaka with faint irony. They were arrested at the point of evolution Eve had attained. There was no attempt at integrating opposites in order to transcend them, no attempt at bringing to a close the world of separation and suffering, Maya. No attempt at entering the Age of the Soul and embrace the unity that characterises soul nature. A disjunction resulted, a fracture that split the world in two: one group went on idolising every word, letter, sign and symbol as given in the Creation story, resolutely intent on perpetuating it unchanged, untouched.

'And we are still holding on to those early whisperings and wanderings. What is the nature of the 5th dimension they rejected?

'In the higher consciousness, soul and personality join and fuse in awareness that there is only One Life. Duality and pain vanish. Life is experienced through love, peace, beauty, knowledge and wisdom. The world witnessed the triumph of the personality, mortal man evading the inevitability of progress, avoiding the inescapability of his destiny, postponing his rise. In fairness to them, the rabbis saw themselves as custodians of the letter of the law they had to preserve at any cost; it was their responsibility to do so. But what of the spirit of the Law? Enough for now, back to the myth.

'Was the myth just a poetic way of telling us a truth?

'Understand, Rabbi Moses that the main protagonists are symbolic. There were no Adam and Eve as two distinct individuals. There was, millions of years ago, a primitive group of men and women who might qualify for the title. You must realise that the Hierarchy gave the Old Testament in a deliberately ambiguous form. The meaning was hidden for the most advanced individuals to fathom out. It was to be the task of the Initiates of all lands and all generations to unravel the inner secrets, decipher the hidden codes. The outer form hides from view the core; the form, the shell is only a veiled message unwisely thrown at the masses with visions of hell fire pouring out of the excitable imagination of enthusiasts who believe the allegory to convey the whole truth.

Imagine a child receiving a priceless diamond encased in a box; he likes the box so he throws away the diamond! After this introduction let us move on to the myth of Adam and Eve.

'Adam is not Adam, Eve is not Eve. The myth invites further investigation.

'Excellent, you have shed the old ways of reading, smiles Sanaka with humour. As you say, Adam is not Adam, he symbolises the body, matter, earthly, earthy man. Eve is not Eve; she stands for the spark that enters the body of matter. You may recall the phrase, 'the light shines in the darkness and the darkness comprehends it not', an allusion to the light of the soul implanted in the darkness of matter, Eve inhabiting the body Adam.

'In this case the Serpent is not the Serpent!

'Indeed, my son! The Serpent is perhaps the most intriguing and disconcerting character in the drama of early humanity emerging from unconsciousness. In all mythologies the Serpent evokes the life force, the living principle, the Kundalini. In the enlightened man, the Kundalini dormant at the base of the spine and coiled like a serpent is finally roused. The Kundalini is a ring of cosmic energy which, as it rises from the Root to the Crown, becomes a spiritual energy of unrivalled power.

'Vital energy becomes spiritual energy.

'There is only one energy in the world, cosmic energy. The Serpent hints at the true nature of man, he points to the latent power in man. Hebrew scholars who insist on seeing the Serpent as an evil force, have done humanity a great disservice, they declined the wisdom of the Hierarchy to insert their own misconception, their own fear.

'Master, we live in the world of duality, of division and separation, is this not certitude for all human beings living on the Planet?

'Not for all, replies Sanaka with the luminous smile which always softens the impact his words might have. Not for me, not for those who have awakened. In the inner worlds, there is no duality, only Reality, undivided, undifferentiated as it was before creation. You will discover this as you become more adept at meditation. You came to India in search of this primordial unity, which you searched diligently and painstakingly in your holy books. But unity is not in books, it is in you. What brought you to India was your uncompromising nature which would not settle for less, your unappeasable yearning for truth. But the truth is not in books, it is in you. It is this compelling force to know more of who you are, to discover your true nature that brought you to this monastery.

'What of the end?

'The end is the beginning. Except that it will be a beginning considerably enriched and far more beautiful, far more exhilarating. Long ago, the Nefilim turned natural man into a human being; they gave him simple rules of conduct that would distinguish him from the brute in the wild. In the following ages human beings as they evolved, have added more rules and opinions, ideas and principles; this was necessary to consolidate the gains made over aeons of evolution. At Sinai, the rules of conduct were given again to your ancestors with the same objective in mind: polish rough edges, refine coarse natures, expand consciousness and turn man into a decent human being, capable of discriminating between right and wrong, a social being able to function fairly in social groupings.

'Why give the rules again at Sinai?

'It was felt by the Hierarchy that to repeat them was necessary. All this was intended as the foundation on which to build the next platform of human evolution: from animal nature to moral conscience, from utilitarian brain to abstract mind, from reliance on external rules to self-determination, from dependency to freedom of decision, from subordination to authority to respect for autonomy. Buddha came to usher in this new awareness, to introduce mankind to the light of the Mind and plant the germ of reason. Then it was the turn of the Essenes to introduce a new awareness. Their task was to acquaint humanity with the light of the Soul, they explained that man was now able to rise above physicality and enter the next stage of his development.

'I knew them to be a messianic group, living apart, a non-conformist group, a thorn in the flesh of authority. They came to introduce the age of the Soul?

'That was their mandate; this mandate emanated from the highest authorities in Shamballa. Their mission was misinterpreted, they were perceived as a threat to the established order, a peril to the Talmudic institution the rabbis were erecting to preserve the past. You have to see this from their view point, they felt that the old order was about to disintegrate, a challenge they could not ignore. They fought back. Their view of the world had to prevail; they would not be intimidated by the dissenting ideas of a group of rebels. They were perceived as revolutionaries by the establishment and they were!

'So evolution was delayed because man got too attached to the past and was unable to make the leap in faith; faith in his own perfectibility, faith in his innate power.

'That's right; they lived in fear of the new, in fear of freedom.

'Better the god you know than the god you don't', but Moses' heart is heavy. 'Eve symbolises the soul, how can the soul stumble? The verse explicitly states that 'Adam was not deceived; it was Eve who was deceived'. How could the soul blunder?

'Good question. In the beginning the Source emitted fragments of himself, all of which were endowed with his characteristics: higher reason, autonomy, creativity, intuitive knowing, and sensitivity. The answer is, yes the soul can be deceived. Eve can delude herself, whereas Adam cannot. When the soul stumbles and falls, the body falls too. The soul is the only aspect of man capable of being misled: 'As a man thinks in his heart, so is he', reminds us the Master. Man is the result of his thinking rather than the victim of inherited traits. The quality of his thoughts determines his character and physical form, even his health. Man is sick not because of his body, but because of his thoughts. And when he stumbles from one incarnation into another, burdened by the same imagined limitations, weighed down by the same thought forms, he brings back with him the same outlook, the same tendencies and spreads around him the same misery.

'Change your thinking and you change your destiny.

'Indeed, this is something your people has found difficult to do. Any hint of change is abhorrence. But you have to realise that the individuals who incarnate in the Jewish condition are those who are inhibited by similar thought forms, shaped by a similar outlook and moulded in the same beliefs. They find in the Hebrew mode something they resonate with and they come down to experience again what they once knew, what they are familiar with.

'So even if we wanted to change our thinking mode, we are being thwarted by those who resonate with it and come back to Earth intent on preserving it. There is no way out of this predicament, says Moses with a note of despair.

'There is, but it is for humanity to come to a realisation of spiritual Law, among which the Law of Attraction which states 'likes attracts like'. All is of the mind. When human beings decide that they will never again reincarnate in complete ignorance, unconsciously driven by the combined laws of Karma, Reincarnation and Attraction, things will begin to change. Only humanity can save itself, only humanity can dissolve the old beliefs, only humanity can effect changes. Man is his own redeemer; no supernatural power can save him but himself, this was the message Buddha gave his disciples, 'You are your only Master, who else? Subdue yourself and discover your Master'.

'Man is his own redeemer, his own messiah.

'When you are not troubled with discriminations and attachments you will in no time or effort attain the spiritual way. The message is clear, do not look up to the gods for deliverance, there is no one 'out there' who can save you, your salvation is in your hands, so start without delay, because if you delay you will continue to be firmly locked on the wheel of rebirth, with a worsening karma.

'The pattern is complicated, individuals are attracted to the Jewish condition because they resonate confirming the Law of Attraction and this in turn exacerbates the existing Karmic burden they bring back with them in reincarnation!

Worship of the Fall

'Historically speaking there came a point where the comparatively small number of people living on the Planet at that time became aware of an incoming flow of energy … a 'dark energy', a slower, heavier vibration which they felt was part of their divine mission to accept, to come to an understanding of and to learn to integrate'.
(Master Sananda)

Adam and Eve - split between the self & the Soul

'There remains to present the ancient and noble myth of the human predicament in its alchemical form, smiles Sanaka with a twinkle in his eyes.

'I thought the myth had been explored from every angle.

'The great Myths are inexhaustible. They deliver a new message for each generation that is why the Masters chose this particular form to embody an ever-changing, ever-evolving insight into the human condition. Begin with 'Berechit', chuckles Sanaka.

'Adam and Eve represent the timeless attraction of opposites. The masculine and feminine principles are the universal principles at work in our lives, in all kingdoms of nature.

'Moses, you have an excellent grasp of the first allegory. There is something you overlook, yet you studied diligently the Myth for nearly half a century. Why insist on what is after all attraction of the genders?

'It goes beyond genders; in symbolic imagery it expresses the attraction of body and mind, matter and spirit.

'Quite right, my son. Attraction and what about repulsion? Think of the image of Buddha, behind him are Sun and Moon.

'Duality is found in man as in the universe, Sun and Moon are to the cosmos what Adam and Eve are to mankind.

'Indeed, you are getting there, chuckles Sanaka. Think of the creative force that draws man and woman together. The creative masculine energy - you call God - needed the cooperation of the feminine force in order to create the universe, this you read in the first verses of Genesis, 'And the spirit of God was over the Waters'. The 'birth' of the cosmos, like the birth of a child calls for the union of the masculine and feminine principles.

'Of necessity duality appears early in Creation, it has nothing to do with the wickedness of man', notes Moses invariably distressed by the subject. It never fails to remind him of his assiduous studies, of many sleepless nights spent exploring the sacred texts, all to nothing.

''Of necessity' is the key word. Duality is inseparable from Creation. With Creation there is a breaking up into multiplicity. The creative power - God as you know it - gave itself the challenge of incarnating into a universe in which primordial unity is broken.

'Is broken or appears to be broken?

'Excellent my son! Both really. Some of us refuse to see it broken and dedicate our lives to recover the primordial unity.

'I have given much anxious thought to this, notes Moses. I still fail to grasp why the universe came into being. For the love of man? I have rejected this opinion long ago with the whole bundle of beliefs which place man at the centre of Creation.

'That's right; the more man is caged in beliefs the more he enlarges his importance. Quite a paradox. Why the universe? The creative consciousness was seeking self-expression. He set out to explore his nature and the nature of the universe. When man is split from his own Self, that part of the cosmic Mind which joins him to the universe, he invents 'thickets of views', 'puppet shows of views' to give him importance and consolation.

'So the greater his sense of separation from his Self, the greater his sense of importance, notes Moses!

'As man succumbs to the beliefs and views of his group, the less insight he has. He lives an unconscious existence. His life is lived for him. He neither knows himself nor the world in which he lives. Remember the first verses of Genesis 'God created man in his image, in the image of God created he him; male and female created he them'.

'Of course I understand! There were no man and woman joined at the rib, this is just symbolic. Adam was both male and female, he was whole, undivided.

'Now you see! Adam was one with his own Self, aware of being unbroken from the greater Self. But then the Fall! The feminine moves out and there is separation, rupture between human self and cosmic Self. And one becomes two! Man splits himself between his mortal self and his spiritual Self. Duality is now in full swing. But union of man and woman can recreate primal unity.

'And Adam and Eve jeopardised all this by eating the fruit of knowledge? ''Jeopardise' is your perception of the great march of humanity toward enlightenment! The apple in the symbolic language of myth means something quite different. In ancient mythologies the apple is the sacred fruit of the Gods; the mysterious fruit which grants immortality.

'Immortality? Adam and Eve are cursed for eating the apple! They become mortals. I don't understand, replies a mystified Moses.

'Apple, the fruit of the Gods promotes death in the imagination of patriarchy which resists the knowledge that will liberate mankind from captivity. The apple of Wisdom grows in the Garden of Eden. The symbolic imagery of Genesis emerges from the arcane tradition of Egypt, Sumer, Mesopotamia and Chaldea.

'The Myth travelled from these arcane traditions but it lost its esoteric meaning in the transfer, retorts Moses in desperation. We have a sacred book drained of vital knowledge, filtered out of the agents of transformation. And I spent half a century delving into it?

Boundary-creating ability of the Jewish mind

Maya is irretrievably bound to time. It is encrusted in our biblical tradition and rooted in our psyche. Time is central to Old Testament mythology as are the laws of nature. "And the Word said: Let Maya flourish and let deception rule'.

With Maya flourishing and deception ruling boundaries spring up. Adam set out, on the order of his god, to organise the world. Docile servant he applies himself diligently to the task of mapping and indexing the world. Yahweh commands him to name all natural things; this implies that he must classify, categorise, class, map, brand, index, edit and file the various kingdoms in nature. Let us invite Ken Wilber to unravel the implications: '[Adam] had to learn to draw a mental boundary line between the various groups ... The great task Adam initiated was the construction of mental or symbolic dividing lines. Adam was the first to delineate nature, to mentally divide it up, mark it off, and diagram it. Adam was the first great map maker. Adam drew boundaries'. His legacy is stronger than ever: our lives are frittered away drawing boundaries in the social, academic, political, economic, geographic and religious domains. Boundaries are all around us and inside us. Quite apart from this oppressive narrowing down, this breaking up of the world into bits, there is a more insidious implication as Ken Wilber reflects, 'The exasperating fact which Adam learned was that every boundary line is also a potential battle line; so that just to draw a boundary is to prepare oneself for conflict'. The human ego Adam, under the insidious influence of the 'divine' ego, was initiating the divisions we believe to be real. This boundary-creating ability is universal and so well internalised that we cannot imagine a world other than the one we inherited.

Worship of Time

'People like us, who believe in physics, know that the distinction between past, present and future is only a stubborn, persistent illusion'. (Einstein)

Time, duality & selfhood

'Time, space and causation are like the glass through which the Absolute is seen ... In the Absolute there is neither time, space nor causation'. (Vivekananda)

'The Book of Genesis begins with the letter 'Beth' closed on three sides and opened into the text. Significant choice of letter! It visually illustrates that Creation is closed to Infinity. 'Beth' ushers in time. With the very first word of the first verse, Genesis demonstrates with one letter, that the world has entered Duality in earnest.
'An unlikely choice, comments Moses, the beginning should start with the first letter, 'aleph'. The choice of the letter 'beth' has been debated for centuries.
'This is one suggestion; you may challenge me on this. The Creation story as recounted in the Sumerian text introduces the 'personality' of Yahweh and the experiments he

engaged in, but it also inevitably brings in Duality. Endorsing the texts the Hebrews confirmed Duality. They gave approval to the world of forms, countersigned the fact of plurality.

'Was not the universe created around Duality, asks Moses, the letter 'beth' indicates this clearly.

'Yes, but the period that follows the Deluge inaugurates the reign of Duality in earnest. The opening verses usher in the religious importance of the Dualist myth. The rupture the myth illustrates turns into an enduring structure. It becomes the Hebrew 'heresy'.

'Why heresy, the Hebrews did not invent Duality, they ratified a fact.

'I leave you to formulate your own answer. In the beginning man's unity with the Whole is cracked, man's unity with the universe is shattered. It is this break that the myth embodies, man no longer knows his origin and he no longer remembers himself as the universal Self. He has lost his essential unity with the soul – the feminine aspect of himself– so now he perceives the soul as a stranger, one he does not recognise. The soul stands apart from him, challenging him. Where there was union there is now rupture and separation. He is no longer able to think from the viewpoint of a higher consciousness; he no longer has a clear vision of reality as an all-embracing picture, but only a fragmented one as if seen in a broken mirror. Man in his 'fallen' state sees the world from the stance of a lower consciousness.

Waiting a while to appreciate the effect his words have on Moses, Sanaka admits, 'man as a cosmic being is separated from his soul and doomed to begin a long march through time in order to repossess his higher consciousness, recover his lost unity. The theme of duality reverberates throughout the revealed Text. It is obvious in the allegory of Abel and Cain where good encounters evil, later it reappears in the story of Jacob and Esau again a reminder that good and evil - the forces of light and darkness - are the only reality in the world.

'The Hebrew heresy you refer to is the recognition of a reality. Duality appears in the world at the moment of Creation, as the Whole fractures into the many. Should they have denied reality?

'No, affirming it or denying it proceeds from the same attitude of mind. The Hebrew heresy builds a religious structure around desolate and forlorn man living now in a hostile universe. Human law, religious law, palpable affirmation of Duality, takes the place of what is lost. 'When the Tao is lost, there is need for legality, morality and much pretence'. It is a defensible heresy, for when confronted with his inescapable isolation, man understandably feels lost. What is left now is natural law, man's instinctive nature to curb and surmounts and that is the realm of religious legislation. The religious system fully recognises the 'fallen' state of man and proceeds to rebuild him, to restore him to his former state.

'Man faced with a catastrophic split fashions a world that gives him consolation and offers some meaning, does he not?

'Right, the restoration of man can only be achieved at a price – acceptance of Duality. The separation is very clear in his mind; the world is split in two distinct parts at odd with each other. They stand as opposites, body and soul, man and woman, matter and spirit. He no longer perceives unity under the complexity of forms. He must construct a large body of principles and precepts to explain the multiplicity and absolve it. Now in his 'fallen' state, broken like a branch from the main Tree of Life, man is judged incapable of taking charge of his destiny; incapable or regaining his primeval wholeness alone. So he must be harnessed to external forces that will do it for him. In his 'fallen' state man knows himself as mortal. Cosmic man was powerful. Mortal man is fragile and needs help from outside. In giving up his autonomy he abdicates to external forces: the law of man and the god of man. His refuge is the god of physical reality, the originator of created things, of Maya. He is caught up in the limitations of form and time. From now on he will have to make do with external, formalised teaching, having lost his inner Master. I note your enquiring brow, smiles Sanaka.

'Was not the Hebrew answer to the 'fallen' state of man a sound response? Your striking account forces me to reappraise that response. Confronted with such loss, man realises his diminished status and sets about to construct a moral and social system that will inform his life and lead him back to lost 'Paradise'

'Excellent Moses, my son; the religious method as an answer to the plight of 'fallen' man is presenting us with a striking paradox: man, in order to regain his former unity must submit to the god of nature, the historical 'Dualist' view. Adam's 'fall' precipitates him in the arms of the god of matter. The Dualists held that it was not God who created the world, but Satan. A dangerous temptation! If so, why submit to him?

One morning as Moses was leaving his room, he noticed an unusual activity, a humming sound reverberated through the monastery, monks were hastening, moving smoothly past. The immense quiet was disturbed. 'What is happening, asks Moses, are you preparing for a festival?

'No, replied the monk appointed to look after Moses, we are receiving a distinguished visitor. What makes this visit so special is that he seldom leaves his isolated monastery, but he has accepted to visit us on Master Sanaka's invitation. He is one of the great Masters who live in a remote part of Tibet, Shigatse, pure land of the enlightened ones in physical form. He seldom leaves Shigatse, except on rare occasions to visit the renowned monastery where he teaches. He is the Master Raja Chandrakirti. This is a great honour, a much appreciated gift. His presence will bring much merit to our brothers and sanctification to our monastery. He is going to leave strong imprints in our minds, imprints that will remain with us through future incarnations, we are increasing our merit. Moses repressed a smile, he thought looking at the enchanted expression on the monk's face, 'so much enthusiasm, so much naivety!' His amusement turned sour, 'is he different from me a few years ago, I too believed in fanciful notions, older than him I was feeding on fantasy tales of another age, designed to satisfy the simpler mind of ancient man'.

The following day, the much awaited Master arrived. All gathered on the grounds of the monastery, near the gate where he was due to make a grand entrance. Master Sanaka was standing by me, his eyes sparkling with a touch of humour or irony. 'It is indeed a great honour to greet such a noble being. Master Chandrakirti, who took his higher initiation years ago, has long transcended the limitations of the human condition. He could leave the Planet now, never to return, never to reincarnate, having fulfilled his goal, having attained liberation, but in Bodhisattva tradition he has made the solemn pledge to return to serve humanity until such time that each human being is enlightened. 'He may have a long time to wait, remarks Moses hastily.

'Not necessarily, smiled Sanaka. He is not waiting but actively engaged in the service of humanity; look around you, the abbots, the monks, the initiates, they all feel that the time is approaching. Seeing such an enlightened being is the experience of a life time. 'Shall I be able to meet him?

'Certainly, he is coming on my request and he already knows you. He will be conducting the meditations, he will also address the assembly and give talks, to all these you are invited and expected.

The following day, after the morning meal, Moses was invited to visit Master Chandrakirti. Daunted, he hastened to the Master's room. The door was opened by a monk and in the middle of the room stood this handsome Tibetan, a splendid being of aristocratic countenance. His features expressed infinite kindness; his noble appearance lit up the room and enveloped Moses, encircling him in an orb of love. Moses sensed the ring around him and a feeling of serenity came over him.

'It is a joy to greet you, Rabbi Moses, smiles Chandrakirti, please take a seat, I understand that you are studying with the Master Sanaka the opening chapters of Genesis and I have been requested to contribute my reflections to those of the enlightened Master. The story of Cain and Abel did puzzle me long ago, when I examined it.

'You examined the story of Cain and Abel?

'Yes, this was part of my scholastic assignment; I had to explore all ancient mythologies and religious beliefs in some depth. Attached to the ashram of the Master of the 6th Ray, I made the study of religious methods one of my main fields of research. Let us begin, this is a fascinating myth.

Cain & Abel – allegory of the self in temporality

'This story, begins Master Chandrakirti, like so many legendary fables, leaves the essential for us to decipher and each generation must attempt to offer a searching answer relevant to the time. It has not escaped your keen observation, Rabbi Moses, that the great biblical myths set the stage for a drama between two protagonists, Adam and Eve, Cain & Abel, Jacob & Esau.

'The legend of Job that other enigmatic character has only one actor on stage, notes Moses. Genesis pictures the world after the Fall, a world fragmented.

'Indeed, Rabbi Moses, more later. You wish to say more on the subject?

'Job occupies centre stage since he is not split, since he is integrated.

'Of course! The drama of Job is not that of Cain & Abel, it is not the drama of the self. It is the drama of man in his completeness seeking greater perfection. The Cain & Abel allegory, deadly conflict between twin brothers is a clear illustration of the cruelty of man to man, the selfish materialism of human nature, the alienation of man from man.

'With respect Master, Abel is the man of conscience.

'Certainly, pertinent observation. Yet it is Cain who emerges as the central character, the hero of the drama. At one level of meaning, Abel is mankind in its noble and true state; he has conscience, the highest principle in man. Whereas Cain symbolises mankind in its fallen state, lost in the darkness and concreteness of matter, for this reason the reader tends to either secretly identify with him or reject him. He emerges as more human, because he sees the world through the physical senses. Realistic, practical, his concrete mind sees things as they are, he is everyman. Abel, on the other hand is ethical, a day dreamer. In the 'real world' there is little room for Abel. The world is full of Cain.

'What is the reason that makes Cain behave as he does? It is more than just an ethical difference. The accepted view was and still is that the moment two men appear on the face of the Earth, one must eliminate the other and grab all for himself. This is the brutal but realistic view.

'It was presented to you as a moral conflict, because you are a moral people. You are right; there is more to it. After all, as you know morality is decided by group customs, it changes as times change. The tragedy of Cain transcends morality; it is of a spiritual kind. He is unaware of the true nature of man, he has forgotten his divinity and he denies the divinity in others. He does not conceive of his brother - in the philosophical sense of the word – as emanating from the same source. His brother is separate, a stranger, and a potential threat. He does not grasp the reality of the one humanity.

'He is humanity after the Fall: he has lost touch with his own Self and the cosmic Self.

'I accept this. He stands for the world of opposites and inevitably of conflict, a world in which he is free to intimidate his brother, free to deny him his rights and even free to kill him.

'Cain has taken freewill too far, he is victim of his own freedom. Any sensitive person who reads this story must feel sympathy for Cain.

'I agree, continues the Master, Cain is victim of his ignorance, the bond with his higher Self has been severed. He embodies the worship of materiality, hostility and ignorance of the meaning of life. He symbolises the lower nature of man illustrated in the three mental poisons denounced by Buddha as the blight of humanity: attachment, aversion and confusion. These have kept humanity chained to the wheel of rebirth for aeons.

'Abel is not really the victim, the real victim is Cain, discerns Moses. This is the allegory of man's nature. The myth of Adam and Eve is taken a step further. With Cain and Abel we are beholding not just the separation of Self and personality but the slaying of Self by personality - or of conscience by the grasping self. Nothing much has changed; mankind is still acting out the drama of Cain and Abel.

'Do you spot the implications for the world, asks the Master?

'It is clear now, for the first time, exclaims Moses! The allegory of Cain and Abel must have prayed heavily on the mind of religion-makers. If Cain is man after the Fall, then he must be curbed and controlled by society. He must be given bountiful dogmas, taboos, rituals; he must be kept fully absorbed. But to keep him compliant and 'doing', the rules must appear to emanate from a powerful god, an identifiable figure hovering over him, suitably frightening and repressive.

'This is only half of the story, smiles the Master.

'Of course, replies Moses, the official god is the umbrella under which the lesser gods find shelter. We invent our lesser gods as we travel through time: country, race, origins, religion, social groups and customs.

'Evolution is a slow process, concedes the Master. This reading of the myth of Cain and Abel is significant because it has a cosmic dimension. At another level of meaning, behind the mythological struggle lies a true life story hinted at. Taken from Sumer it is the recounting of the bitter dispute between the main protagonists of the Sumerian Scriptures. Of these two gods only one remains in the Old Testament.

'We need a break to assimilate the dialogue, says Levinson. The Old Testament is the most eloquent advocate of monotheism; we need to examine this issue further.

'Why this preoccupation with one god, one tradition, asks Jeremy, when the ancient world knew a plurality of gods, each expressing a different idea, each complementing the others? No religious rivalries, no wars of extinction in the name of a given god. And of course, no religious intolerance, no dogmatism 'my god is better than yours, you better believe it or else' kind of attitude. The same gods crossed borders and are found in all lands under different names, in most mythologies. In a sense, the recognition of the same gods across boundaries ensured a form of globalisation, a unification of a sort. It hinted at something fundamental: the quest for meaning and paradoxically the search for an essential unity. If all gods are equal then all men are equal.

'You overlook an important point, control, taunts Johansson. How do you regulate a plurality of gods, how do you manipulate people's variety of beliefs and how do you control people's actions? Monotheism is a large umbrella and is as much political as it is religious; it has to do with organisation and control. It is easier to control one god and one set of beliefs.

'My god is better than yours' means 'I am better than you', continues Levinson. This brings the worst out of humanity; I assert my superiority and your inferiority. I am the only one who counts; you do not, so I can eliminate you. This was State policy in Fascist Germany. Except that in Fascist Germany there was no god, only a diabolical ideology.

'That's right; gods were thoughts, emotions and beliefs. Today we no longer have gods; we have ideas or ideologies, inserts Jeremy.

'The dream of unity does not tolerate more than one god, remarks Clara.

'Selfishness in man is Cain, selfishness in society is Fascism, continues Johansson. In politics, selfishness defends the diminishment of man and even his destruction. In religion, selfishness advocates intolerance, fanaticism, dogmatism and wars. Do you spot the difference?

'What difference? The Hierarchy thought this allegory significant enough to be inserted in the Bible, says Clara. It set the tone for what has taken place in our history; the slaying of Moses by the mob, the persecution of the Essenes by the priesthood. Each event stands as a symbolic reminder of the ego grappling with the soul, realism slaying idealism, materialism slaying spirituality. 'Am I my brother's keeper' asks the brutal Cain? He personifies the ferocity and self-absorption of the human ego.

Cain denies the nature of life & the nature of the Divine

'I am pushing the myth to its limits, admits Johansson.

'Go ahead, I always stretch ideas to their limits and beyond, laughs Jeremy.

'As a son of a parson, I realise that religious man is in a jam, he is rooted in the Fall, like Cain, but he longs to be like Abel. He personifies the ego grappling with the soul, materialism slaying the divine in man, while longing to be readmitted in Paradise. The Prodigal Son, after his long meandering in the world, is returning home. He must try one more stunt: religious zeal, dogma and ritualism.

'As a son of a rabbi, I too realise that religious man is in a jam, echoes Levinson. He is indoctrinated into believing that he alone has the truth and that all others are lesser humans. He dismisses them as unimportant while elevating himself to great heights. Selfishness breeds separateness, purity, holiness, chosenness and a sense of mission.

'I agree, let's return for a moment to the beginning, suggests Johansson. To be 'in the image and likeness of God' is to accept in us the same divine qualities: empathy, acceptance, tolerance and resilience. It is to recognise that life is ever-renewed, ever-changing. Perhaps the most intriguing is that all life tends toward its own completion, its own perfected state. Perhaps this is the hidden meaning of Paradise, not a place but a completion. The seed grows to be a plant, the bud opens into a flower, and the acorn becomes a tree. Life strives to release the soul-germ concealed in it.

'It is the recognition that life, the same life animates all forms, from the bacteria to man, confirms Jeremy. The law of evolution states that the urge of life is to evolve.

'If all life is the same life-current pulsating under a diversity of forms, then truly, 'I am my brother's keeper', continues Levinson. This has to be understood in the wider sense, all creation is one life. No one is an island, each needs the other to realise its innate perfection.

'Each contains the others, man contains the mineral, vegetable and animal kingdoms; he evolved from all three. Man holds the entire world of nature in him. He claims to be superior and separate, folly, notes Jeremy!

'Indeed, it means that no one is empowered without empowering the others, continues Tara, an impassioned Buddhist. 'I am my brother's keeper'. The selfishness of Cain is pointless. Trapped in his ego he does not grasp the reality of the interdependence of all life. Buddha taught that selfishness is the root of all evil, the reason behind humanity's perpetual journey into darkness. Cain as the ego has to learn that fixation with the ego leads to disaster, the perpetual wheel of rebirth and the misery of accumulated karma.

'I am not a Buddhist, chuckles Jeremy, but you have convinced me!

'I agree, continues Johansson. Buddha denounced dogmas and gods, I see why. Religious men like your father Levinson and my father are more like Cain while yearning to be more like Abel. Caught up in the Fall, they yield to the clamours of the ego: their dogmas, intolerance and self-delusion attest to their fall. They believe that liberation must fall from the sky, confident of their own chosenness. In other words, each denies the fundamentals of life.

'Though not Buddhist, I agree takes up Benzaccai. From the scientific angle, natural man endowed with a concrete mind sees the world through his senses. The world appears solid and permanent and man feels powerless, he must protect himself in a hostile world; Cain is the opportunist, the pragmatist, concrete man in the 'real world'. We are dealing with a universal myth we are free to expand. Let's fantasise Abel as aware of the deception of the senses. Let's imagine that he is the Eastern mystic or the Quantum physicist; he understands that the world is not opaque and solid, when closely observed matter dissolves into energy and energy underpins all that exists, 'the field' Einstein speaks of. There is nothing but energy made form, the true nature of things is energy.

'Energy is the unified field that underpins all, echoes Jeremy.

'Form is emptiness, emptiness is form', quotes Tara.

'That's right, pursues Benzaccai, the same life-energy animates all the diverse forms we see around us, the same energy holds everything from the atom to the galaxies.

'In other words, there is only unity. Duality, form, diversity are all illusion of our senses, concludes Jeremy.

'But Cain does not grasp the unity of life, the reality of the one life force running through everything, continues Johansson. And so he shouts in anger 'Am I my brother's keeper?' This one phrase encapsulates the view of the vast majority, 'I am for me, we are separate, I have nothing to do with him, I am responsible for me alone; his life is his problem, not mine'. Cain is man after the Fall.

'He is also your religious father and my religious father, remarks Levinson. But there is yet another dimension to this allegory of the ego. Lower man, Cain symbolically kills Abel, the human spirit. Abel has no place in the 'real world'.

'This is tantalising, says Clara, this will excite some passion! Let's try to look at it from the perspective of the Hierarchy. They are painting a picture of the world after the Fall. It is an impartial picture in all its bleakness. The myth depicts the struggle between good and evil which the world has now inherited, the reality after the Fall. This is the 'real world' and so Abel has to be slain, at least symbolically.

'One might say, whispers Jeremy as in a dream, that the drama of Cain & Abel was played out for real 2000 years ago.

The double-headed Dragon

'Man has lost the sense of his cosmic origins. But his tie with the Source is not severed; a ray, a beam of light reaches upwards from the Heart to the Central Sun. He remains under the influence of his Self at all times, and so the unrelenting conflict that rages in him. The personality at war with the Self seeks to establish and consolidate its position; to this end it erects an intricate edifice of gods, precepts and laws. The forceful self creates sinfulness to justify the vast corpus of rules it fashions. Man in his primeval state knows no sin, no gods, no ethics and no legal code. The personality has now fashioned gods of clay. The double-headed Dragon is born; one of its head is 'god', the other 'sin'. God dictates that man be subservient and dependent, 'sin' demands that he obeys ethical and legal rules. Man is now a fragile thing bound and gagged, a cork tossed by the waves, a leaf torn from a tree and blown by the wind. He is now incarcerated in the prison of the law that the personality devises and implements. Divine, infinite, deathless man has now become a sinful wreck who must be rescued by external forces. Fallen, he must be redeemed from outside. This is truly the Fall!

Worship of a myth: the unchanging Father

Through your own growth God also grows. So that God is at once the unchanging Father and the Son, changing and evolving'. (Master Sananda)

'Who is the god who asks this central question to Cain, enquires Jeremy with a touch of scepticism? He sounds like an ethical god with a sense of social justice, is he the same god who orders the stoning of sinners? Who is the god, real or imagined who demands a moral response to life, who regards correct human relations as vital to the stability and survival of the group? He is a mystery to me.

'He is a mystery to his own people, continues Levinson. He springs from the fertile and anxious imagination of ancient man.

'Is he the one who decrees that all other gods be demoted or eliminated and who demands unconditional allegiance? The same god who demands that unbelievers be penalized, who incites the destruction of groups not committed to him, pursues Jeremy with uncharacteristic insistence.

'Propaganda makes persecution of other groups acceptable. The Old Testament draws attention to a new phenomenon, something almost unknown until then: separation between man and man, man and nature and man and his Self. Mankind is entering a new phase in the arrogant expression of the self. To slay in the name of god becomes the honourable thing to do, reflects Johansson.

'As mortal man pacifies his gods where is the silent observer, asks Jeremy?

'Getting more silent! Yet it is the objective observer within who mocks the many gods man is burdened with, replies Clara. I heard it so clearly then!

'When the Self is forsaken, a myriad of gods appear and in the mayhem they jostle for attention, inserts Benzaccai.

'Slaying in the name of god is justifiable to those with the Cain temperament, insists Tara. In Christendom the drama of Cain and Abel has been played out relentlessly on the stage of the diabolical Inquisition and the ghastly Crusades. In our 20th century Cain reappears in the strident nationalism and diabolical ideologies of selfishness. And what about the occupation of countries by Europeans who felt that they had the right to impose their views?

'There is more, think of the Cain syndrome in the zeal of the missionaries who went to Africa with book, bell and gun! Think of the ghastly slave trade! The Cain energy of selfishness and greed fought insanely before expiring on the battlefields of the world in the 20th century, expands Benzaccai.

'It has not expired yet, continues Johansson! Gods and ideologies are the self in its many manifestations. Each god demands satisfaction and so to slay to preserve received dogmas and inherited beliefs about the world becomes not only permissible but legitimate.

'All the time we appease our gods we nurture the self that much longer! What a sad reflection on the human condition, notes Clara!

Having interrupted the reading to reflect on the dialogue, they now return to Rabbi Moses' manuscript. 'I am going to read the rest of the dialogue, says Jeremy boldly, this story is yielding incredible insight, throwing a fascinating light on the human condition, I never suspected was there.

Jeremy reads on, 'One could go on probing the allegory of Cain and Abel, reviews Chandrakirti. It encapsulates the nature of the self; it exposes the delusion, cruelty and the length to which the self will go to force its will. There is yet another facet to this allegory which may not have escaped your attention. The tale hints at the hostility between the Sumerian twin deities, one of which became the principal god of your ancestors. At yet another level of meaning, the Fall becomes the new reality and early humanity is getting acquainted with the limiting factors of aloneness, division and isolation. With alienation comes the denial of responsibility for the 'other'. 'Am I my brother's keeper', questions the man of the Fall who keenly senses the need for self-preservation? Fear arouses hostility and unleashes chaos. Order in the world is lost; the 'real world' is now unpredictable, potentially threatening. Uncertainty holds sway.

'Where is man going to turn for his deliverance, he has nowhere to turn, asks Moses with anguish.

'The hidden message of the myth of Cain and Abel points to this insight. Man now divested of his higher Self, with diminished perception is constructing a terrifying reality. He has lost the security of group consciousness, he is aware of being alone and separate. He has lost Paradise. The goals of early man are now revised and built around the way he perceives himself and how the world appears to him. Cain's world is irrevocably changed; his goals are self-protection and selfish survival.

'Man needs certainty, I know I did, says Moses with a sigh of sadness.

'True, but remember the price you had to pay for that certainty. In the end it burst in your face because it was no certainty at all! Human effort for all its bravery ends up in disaster, because there is attachment to the ideas that man fashions and these ideas become as solid as rocks in his imagination.

'So we must live without any certainty, sighs Moses.

'That's right. In the world of illusion any certainty is a potential disaster. Your history is the illustration of this point, you are the living demonstration of the quest for certainty and it resultant collapse. The self to satisfy its need for certainty sets out to create ideas. The self seeks to explain and as it does it becomes enamoured with the ideas it creates, like Narcissus falling in love with his image reflected in the water.

'In spite of the tragic nature of the human condition, strangely there is exhilaration in the realisation. I never felt more alive, more liberated than when I was forced to confront this reality.

'There is dignity and courage in admitting the fact of impermanence and uncertainty. To deny this basic reality spells disaster. Man aware of his aloneness finds consolation not in external forces but in himself. We live in a world of illusion and any effort at creating certainty feeds that illusion and serves to prolong it. This is the central message of your troubled history; each generation has fed and preserved the illusion.

'And we embody this illusion for humanity to identify, laments Moses.

'If we dig deeper, we can discover yet another layer of meaning. With the Fall, man has forgotten the primordial wholeness, he feels alone in an unfriendly universe. He now rummages around for a powerful entity to serve in return for protection, or the promise of it. Ritualism is born. This is the world we inherited. Primordial oneness is broken up and differences appear.

'Where I come from, comments Moses, it is even more serious, it goes like this: how can a man love equally all men when all men are not equal, when the select few only have full human status and all the others are denied it? If the Jew alone has a soul how can other men forge a relationship with god? But this is the starting point to a handbook of illusion, if other men are denied a soul, then we are god's appointed guides and teachers, we must teach wretched humanity moral laws, decency and correct living, we are responsible for the conduct of mankind. We divide humanity into two unequal fragments.

'Precisely, Cain is humanity after the Fall; he has forgotten his primeval unity with all life. Now, for ancient man to say 'I am my brother's keeper' was and still is the height of spiritual achievement, the ultimate in moral attainment. But this is only half the story! The truly evolved man does not stop there, he utters with profound conviction, 'I am my brother and my brother is me. My brother and I are One'. This is the response of the enlightened being.

'I wonder if Abel would say that! For biblical man, 'you are you and I am me'.

'The enlightened ones do not see differences; they see only unity and oneness. The man of the Fall is no longer at home in the universe, no longer at ease with himself and his fellow men; he is apprehensive, defensive and hostile. He no longer knows serenity, good human relations or peace. We have two humanities at odds with each other.

The Elohim & Yahweh

'In the Book of Genesis, begins Johansson, the names Elohim and Yahweh are used randomly, or so it seems, to label the same deity. Though the Hierarchy gave two Creation stories, confusion set in. Unable to grasp the fact of their fundamental dissimilarity the biblical scribe fuses them into one, hence the confusion. And so throughout Genesis and in other books, Yahweh and Elohim are used interchangeably. Yet there is no common denominator between the two. The Elohim, first emanation of the Logos, get the mandate to create man. In stark contrast, Yahweh a galactic being comes to Earth with his own agenda. Explorer, conqueror and builder of civilisation, he is a manipulator of life, the genetic architect of prehistoric man.

'Modern researchers, continues Benzaccai, Sitchin in particular accounts for this; he suggests that when Elohim is mentioned in the texts, it is Enlil, Yahweh's brother who is hinted at rather than Yahweh himself. The lives, loves, conflicts, ambitions and dreams of domination of the Nefilim are chronicled in the ancient texts of Sumer. A detailed narrative sheds light on a period of prehistory which has remained unknown, yet one which laid the foundation for the Book of Genesis.

'Monotheism must triumph! In order to uphold the myth of monotheism, continues Johansson, events relating to the periods before and after the Deluge were removed, leaving the Book of Genesis in its condensed form, concise and 'accurate', yet lacking in factual information. It hints at it, but does not deliver. It is the task of our generation to make sense of it all. The world is still waiting for the meaning to emerge. Nothing was ever more debated about, no other book inspired more artists, poets, philosophers, theologians and musicians, no other text has had such profound impact nor made such an indelible impression on world civilisation yet so little significant information has been imparted.

Johansson is writing a thesis on 'Comparative Mythologies' with the aim of outlining the shared cultural features. 'But, the illusion of theism has been preserved at the expense of the truth, with the Bible writers grappling with the two sets of gods, fusing and blending them to give the appearance of unity.

''To give the appearance of unity', echoes Clara, it seems that they were in ignorance of the identity of either and when they read the two Creation events the stories become one.

'This makes sense, remarks Jeremy, I am no expert on the old Book for which I feel no inclination but this explanation is plausible.

'Elohim and Yahweh are also fused to designate Yahweh alone when 'Yahweh Elohim' speaks in Genesis, indicative of ignorance of the true nature and origin of either. Let's be clear on this, the Elohim are a group of divine Beings while Yahweh serves as spokesman for the Nefilim, a group of galactic visitors. Yet the writer almost certainly had access to the Sumerian Scriptures from which was borrowed the allegory of Creation.

'This is history revised to make a point, in this case to implant the illusion of monotheism and embed theology and mythology firmly in human consciousness, continues Johansson who is very much in his element.

'Think of the intellectual confusion, theological debates, philosophical theorising, verbal squabbling, disquieting uncertainty and prolonged anguish the 'revisionists' would have spared humanity, reflects Levinson. If only they had respected ancient texts and restated them in their entirety regardless of doctrines, opinions and dogmas.

'They had not arrived at the conception of intellectual integrity.

And Man adored gods

'Those, whose wisdom has been led away by desire, resort to other gods, engaged in rite, constrained by their own nature'. (Krishna)

'We now come to a review of the beings that make up the pantheon of the Hebrew gods, proposes Sanaka. You are acquainted with the ancient world and its many cults, if only because your ancestors denounced them vigorously and fought them equally vigorously. What may have escaped your attention is the true extent of Hebrew reliance on the many 'foreign' gods they adopted during their migrations. This is not surprising, today for instance, an educated Jew travelling through Austria, Prussia or Russia would inevitably come into contact with the intellectual life of those countries. The gods were to the ancient world what the humanities are to the modern world, the expression of that particular epoch.

'Master Sanaka, you speak of the gods as if they were an abstract field of study. They were abhorred by the rabbis and prophets. Idolatry was considered a form of religious degeneracy, of spiritual decadence, something to condemn and eradicate.

'Indeed, continues the Master, this is the uncompromising attitude of the scholars. But you have to recognise that the Old Testament is a compilation of two main renditions of the Hebrew history and of those the Yawist interpretation is the dominant one, just as you have two versions of the Creation of man. Let us start with El, a familiar figure to the Hebrews who encountered him when they invaded Canaan. El is 'master of time' and claims absolute power. The Hebrew god El, the god they carried with them in the Desert also claims absolute power.

'Why time?

'Humans have little of this precious commodity; any one who masters time must be a god. The Nefilim were deemed immortal, their lives extending over thousands of earth-years. Mortals wanted a share of 'immortality', but it was denied by the gods who insisted in retaining this unique advantage. But gods have companions and the consort of El was Ishtar. Do you recall Ishtar, the Moon-goddess? Complicated? No more so than the complex relationships among the royal families of Europe. The Nefilim were the very first 'royal' family on the Planet. They engaged in ruthless armed conflicts and romantic rivalry, these preserved in legends and myths. Not only did they deny man immortality, they also refused him knowledge 'lest he be like us'. They wanted to remain in absolute control of the Planet, mankind and time.

'Refusing immortality I understand, but why refuse knowledge?

'Because knowledge is power, the best way to control the masses is by keeping them in ignorance. All the despots in history have done it.

'Was not Ishtar the Esther of the story of Purim?

'Yes, the Purim story hints while masking it at the ever lingering presence of the Goddess. In the Purim version, it is the goddess Esther (Ishtar) who saves the people from annihilation. She was the beautiful Goddess of fertility worshipped by the Hebrews as 'the Queen of Heaven'. Centuries ago, the descendents of the Hebrews who had not left Egypt regarded the moon goddess, Ishtar as the consort of Yahweh.

'Who had not left Egypt? A Hebrew community in Egypt centuries ago? Did not all the Hebrews flee Egypt on the 'night of nights', on Passover night?

'Obviously not! Religious history is more concerned with symbolism than with facts. It must strike the imagination. It would seem that only a few migrated out of Egypt on that night, others join them in the following months and years. There was no 'night of nights'. The story conceals a profound symbolic meaning to be deciphered. Remember that the Hierarchy gave fables and myths for the more insightful to decipher. On the part of the biblical writer Exodus is a romanticised version of events, heroism had to be built into the story. It is not heroic for the 'chosen' people to disregard the cry for liberation, to ignore the exhortation to freedom! This tends to take place in all exiles. At the end of the Babylonian exile, only two out of the twelve Tribes did return to Israel, the other ten stayed behind and assimilated. Assimilation is a favoured option. These facts are secreted in some obscure texts.

'No 'night of nights', mumbles Moses!

'Is it too much for one day?

'Please do go on, urges Moses.

'Finally, let us turn to Satan, not a god but a terrible figure which haunts the Book of Genesis. The Creation narrative is found in most ancient mythologies, it is not the sole preserve of Genesis. In the Sumerian story of Creation, there is a dividing line between the forces of Light and the forces of Darkness. This gave rise to the doctrine of Dualism the Hebrews adopted during the Babylonian exile. Dualist doctrine endorses the presence of God and the Devil. The Hebrew mind is steeped in Dualism which crops up almost everywhere in the texts. Duality pervades the Old Testament: God & Satan, Adam& Eve, Cain & Abel, Jacob & Esau are but a few instances.

'Satan is an abstraction?

'Satan, the 'adversary' is the being who tempts Eve into disobedience, the same Satan who forges an alliance with Yahweh in order to put Job to the test; Satan the personification of evil. Satan is either the opponent or the ally of Yahweh according to the 'political' mood of the time.

'Master may we go back to the goddess?

'Am I going too far or too fast? You have a singular interest in the goddess. The goddess is fascinating and I promise you that when the time comes the Masters will invite you to Shamballa where you will be enveloped in the luminous presence of the Goddess.

'Why should the Masters invite me?

'They have been observing you and recording your progress, remember that you accepted this assignment with their sanction. Do you want to continue?

Please do, I long to know, I yearn to make up for lost time.

'Sacred marriage and temple prostitution were central to the cult of Ishtar; just as later they became features of temple life in Jerusalem. Elsewhere, temples were built to Yahweh and Ishtar, both worshipped by the Hebrews.

'Ritualistic prostitution in the Temple of Jerusalem?

'As in other temples of the ancient world, sex and religion were celebrated together. Goddess worship was the celebration of life; it recognised and accepted all facets of life. It is patriarchy - the masculine force - which separates, judges and condemns. The goddess is not moralistic, the goddess is life. Patriarchy is moralistic. With patriarchy there is a rupture between body and mind, matter and spirit. Patriarchy forbids the full expression of life. Yet life is divine physical or spiritual, it is the same life, the same elemental force, the distinction exists only in the minds of patriarchy.

'This aspect of our ... I can no longer pursue for I feel the incongruity of feeling part of a tradition I no longer regard as mine ... of Hebrew religious history tends to be played down, dismissed as a temporary aberration.

'It was not temporary nor was it an aberration. Ancient Hebrews believed in 'other gods'. The official god shored up by patriarchy, the god who plays the lead role in the Old Testament did not mobilise the loyalty nor arouse the adoration of the masses. The Hebrew deity known in Sumerian Scriptures as the 'god of the sea' instructed man in agriculture, crafts, architecture, law, literature, medicine and astronomy. He polished the crudeness of primitive man and refined his character by teaching him the arts and sciences. In Sumer the god who created man in his laboratory was also the god of civilisation. The Nefilim taught primitive man dietary and sexual hygiene implanted the notion of justice and gave rules for decent living. As man was becoming 'detached' from the Source, he was learning to become responsible for his actions. Free-will had entered the human stage.

'What a paradox. Yahweh demands absolute obedience but he also teaches primitive man to be moral and responsible for his actions. He wants man to be free and subservient?

'What is surprising about that? Freedom is very difficult to handle even for modern man; subservience on the other hand is something that the masses prefer for they like to be told what to do even if they bitterly rebel!

Atlantean origins of the Hebrew 'religion'

'The 'Fallen Angels' of antediluvian tradition married 'the daughters of men'. Sounds familiar?

'The Nefilim used Atlantis as their theatre of feat, asks Moses in awe?

'It looks that way. Now to the religion of the lower castes in Atlantis: they practiced a form of crude religion more like sorcery which later travelled to Europe, Africa and elsewhere. The lower castes were mutinous and intent on toppling the noble core of esoteric wisdom. You recall that the Masters of the Wisdom walked among men in Atlantis.

'Who were these lower castes?

'Their degraded beliefs aimed at the downfall of the legitimate order, the spiritual order. They practiced an earthy, primitive form of religion with distinctive traits. A salient feature is the agrarian or pastoral character of their festivals.

'Succoth, Passover, Yom Kippur, Simhah Torah, Rosh Hashanah they all fall in early autumn and early spring, exclaims Moses! The agrarian and pastoral character of our religion never struck me before!

'In all primitive rites there were blood sacrifices. In the Temple of Jerusalem animal sacrifices were offered at the time of the agrarian festivals. Archaic rites and ceremonies had a magical character, they sought to activate some hidden power in nature rather than express a genuine longing for the sacred.

'The ancient rites seem pagan and very much profane!

'Yet you practice them with intense enthusiasm to this day, you believe them to be God given! Another trait more disquieting, the rites have no moral code.

'That is why we had to descend into Egypt to learn moral principles!

'Your ancestors cursed Mother Earth yet you retain from the earthy religion of Atlantis a certain awe of the powers of Nature. Your rites revolve around natural cycles. The crude religion of Atlantis emphasised the cyclic support of the forces of Nature by certain seasonal sacrifices. So did you in the Temple.

'Our religion is very much universal; its basic features are to be found the world over in all primitive religions?

'The relics of the worship of Atlantis are to be found everywhere; they share a global belief in a covenant with the unseen forces of Nature. These natural forces are invoked to sustain the life of the tribe by the magical yield of crops and the fertility of the herds. Do not forget that your official god is a nature god, a fertility god. So it all fits together rather well.

'Nature rites are not a religion, remarks Moses pertinently.

'That's right. In time they took on the form of a religious system because the pundits adopted methods of organisation to ensure their continuation. I have to stress that this primitive nature-worship was not that of the nobler races of Atlantis, initiated into the Great Mysteries. The adepts of the Arcane Wisdom had nothing to do with crude nature-worship. Nature-worship does not make for a conscious life. Nature-worshippers are arrested in the world of time and matter; they are steeped in Maya, the

67

world of illusion. For as long as man is unaware of the 'sacred knowledge' known to the Masters of the Wisdom he remains unconscious of his true nature. The esoteric doctrine tells us that 'so long as [man] does not consciously acquiesce in it, he is on the same footing as the rest of insentient nature; he does not participate in the Divine Plan or enjoy the spiritual advantage which formerly he did enjoy ...'

'So this is what the Essenes came to do, rekindle our memory, awaken us to our true nature, our divine nature. We turned them away, we cursed them! And we have died, down the ages, to preserve the nature rites of the primitive races of Atlantis!

'In the temple of Poseidon a ceremony took place on Midsummer Day and over which the twelve kings of Atlantis presided. They concentrated a powerful ray of mental power upon the destructive forces of Earth, to render them inactive. Horns were sounded to accelerate the flight of the malign earth-forces. Once more the harmful powers had been exiled from the land and the masses were safe for yet another year. Finally the kings entered the temple to offer bulls in sacrifice to Poseidon.

'The magical twelve! The twelve Tribes, the twelve constellations, the twelve loaves of bread in the Temple! We blow the Shofar at Yom Kippur, at the end of the day when we are written again into the Book of Life and feel safe for yet another year! In the Temple of Jerusalem a scapegoat would carry our sins into the Desert to die!

'Barbaric! But the masses never change; they show the same credulity, ignorance and superstition in all time periods and all lands. Naturally these vain rituals were alien to the spiritual brotherhoods. Liberation is achieved not with pointless rituals and meaningless prayers but in the realisation that man and God are One: the individual spirit, man, is no other than the universal Spirit, God. In the words of Shankara, 'Liberation cannot be achieved except by the perception of the identity of the individual spirit with the Universal Spirit'. This is true spirituality; the rest is superstition and illusion.

'And we continue to act out the prehistoric rites performed before the Deluge by the crude masses which triggered the Deluge! Progress is slow. But the masses need reassurance; they want nothing to do with lofty ideas.

'That's right; the spiritual elites were concerned with the Great Mysteries of Being. The Mysteries sought to inform the initiate on the nature of God, the nature of the universe and the mystical union between man and God. The masses were content to know that bulls were being sacrificed in their names! They felt redeemed by the blood of innocent beasts. The idea of moral and spiritual progress seldom moves the masses, they prefer to trip up in 'the vain repetitions of the law that kills' since it dulls the mind and the senses. This is what the Essenes tried to change 2000 years ago in vain.

'But the bull, repeats Moses, we sacrificed bulls in the Temple!

'The crude religion of Atlantis was tied to the bull and its sacrifice. The masses make do with blood sacrifices and prescribed prayers. Man in whom dwells the Divine Presence, this great and noble being goaded by an ignorant priesthood has to make do with prayer, the crudest way to relate to the transcendental. The Bhaghavatam informs us, 'Materialistic-minded men who have no information of the Kingdom of God are mechanically engaged in the ritualistic discharge of prescribed duties and are inclined to satisfy the bygone forefathers and controlling demigods by performance of sacrifices ...'

'Egypt got the Great Mysteries and we got the superstition!

'And the world with you! The world is in the throes of darkness, ignorance, suffering, destruction and wars, legacy of the forces of materialism.

'The Messiah will restore the sacrifices in the new Temple!

'Do you really believe that Buddha Maitreya will restore pagan rites and blood sacrifices on the altar of the god Poseidon? You may wish to worship Poseidon under any other name but not with the approval of Maitreya! When the Master presented himself before the Sanhedrin ruling elite to announce, 'You are Gods', they resorted to violence. The crude practices indulged by the lower castes in Atlantis that led to the destruction of that continent were good enough for them.

The Nefilim: 'gods' of the Old Testament

Rabbi Moses makes no attempt at hiding his anguish when the time comes to discuss the Book of Creation with his Master. Master Sanaka, I have pondered over the first chapters of Genesis for most of my life, not satisfied with the answers given by the biblical scholars over the centuries. Would you throw some light on this most perplexing text?

Smiling Master Sanaka replies, 'the most perplexing ideas are often self-evident. We are bemused simply because we come to them with pre-conceived notions, instead of allowing the text to reveal its content. Now tell me what is troubling you and I assure you that you already know the answer, both in your conscious mind, you are a man of intellect and in your higher mind which has known the answer for always.

'In the opening verses Genesis narrates the extraordinary account of a visit to Earth by beings who came from some other region of the universe. They literally fell from the sky, or as the text states 'they were cast down'. Would you shed light on this?

'Certainly, Moses, the verses assert boldly, without any attempt at disguising it an event which has thrown generations of scholars into an agony of doubt because it undermines the long-held belief in the one god, the foundation stone of Hebrew faith.

'I no longer know what to make of these enigmatic verses:

'The sons of the gods

saw the daughters of man, that they were attractive;

and they took them for wives … ', quotes Moses.

'They are straightforward; trust your reason.

'Exactly what the text states, answers Moses, 'giants' came down from the sky, found human females attractive and took them. But who are these 'giants' who appear from nowhere and take liberties with humans? I was never able to find a satisfactory answer to my question, but I did manage to exasperate my teachers who decided that I was a trouble maker and that my perpetual questioning would drown me in the deep waters of heresy.

'And they were right, chuckles Sanaka with that ironic sparkle in his eyes

This text retells the Sumerian narrative of 'gods' descending to Earth, their interaction with mortals and the progeny born of these encounters. Greek mythology, the best known rendition of the Beginning, abounds in stories of gods mingling with mortals. Do go on.

'The text continues the narrative of the interaction between gods and humans:

'The Nefilim were upon the Earth

in those days and thereafter too,

when the sons of the gods

cohabited with the daughters of the Adam

and they bore children onto them'.

'The text could not be clearer, replies Sanaka, the Nefilim, a group of stellar beings come down to Earth, implant themselves on the Planet, establish a colony and their 'sons' begin to procreate with human females.

At this point Clara interrupts the reading, 'I have to barge in, the official translation of 'Nefilim' is 'giants'. The translators of the Sumerian text evaded the issue. They borrowed the tale from Sumer but when faced with the reality they backed down.

'What do you mean, asks Johansson briskly, disapproving of the outburst?

'I had to butt in, what I have to say is relevant, Clara adds looking at Johansson, it will shed more light. I am not being disrespectful of the manuscript but I have to elucidate this point in the light of recent research. Modern scholars are forcing us to re-evaluate the view which for so long has been an act of faith. The 'Nefilim' are visitors from our galaxy. Zachariah Sit chin's study of ancient Sumerian literature concludes that these 'gods' are physical beings who eat, speak, walk and get angry.' Slightly embarrassed at her outburst and the attention focussed on her, she pleads, 'please do continue reading the manuscript, I am as eager as you all are.

The reading resumes: 'One of the gods, Ea who came down from the sky was caught up in a merciless quarrel with his brother Enlil, explains Sanaka, each fighting the other in a bid to establish his dominion over Earth. Well, as you can see, power struggles are as old as the world, even the gods succumb to them! Ea occupies centre stage in your tradition; ambitious and innovative Ea set out to transform the land, build cities and dry up the marshes of southern Sumer. To carry out these vast projects he required an able labour force, for he already had the means and scientific knowledge. Unimpressed by the local pool of primitive humans, he set out to 'fashion' his own work force. Using scientific methods, he implanted the seed of the male who looked more intelligent into the womb of his sister-wife. This experiment was repeated over centuries to produce a human species that would be sufficiently intelligent to work for him.

'In some obscure Talmudic texts it is written that god when planning to create the Adam took a considerable time to get it right. He had to repeat the procedure several times. An inquisitive student I wondered how God could get things wrong. His failures challenged his absolute perfection.

'These hidden texts seem to convey information which should be taken very seriously, replies Sanaka. Genesis clearly states, at the risk of offending the loyal believers in the Father that Yahweh walked around the Garden Adam was tending and discussed work with him.

'He was physically present; it is not a story to be interpreted symbolically. This is what you are saying, Master?

71

'No, this is what you are saying, Rabbi Moses, but of course you always knew, you just did not give credit to your intuitive knowing or were you too frightened to know?'

'Too frightened, I guess, the text was speaking to me, but I closed my mind.

'The easy way out of the dilemma. The truth is almost always unsettling, because it challenges unquestioned beliefs. Mankind is attached to its beliefs and is prepared to kill and die to perpetuate them. Attachment is viewed by Buddha as one of humanity's deadly poisons. You know now that there is no saving lie. Each lie keeps you in captivity and keeps others in captivity with you. A lie kept in the secret of your heart affects not only you but mankind at large.

'Why should mankind be affected?

'Because mankind is one giant being, all of us make up humanity, what affects one affects the whole. Take your body for instance, if your foot is infected the whole of you suffers; the infection may spread to the entire body.

'The fear of truth kept me from reading the text intelligently.

'And what is so terrifying about the truth? The truth is feared so long as man feels small and insignificant. But when man figures out that nothing is greater than he is, he not only accepts the truth, he goes out of his way to hunt for it! An enlightened Greek stated, 'Man is the measure of all things'. There is nothing more liberating than the truth, but it comes at a price! When you begin to perceive the truth integrity and responsibility intrude in your life and there is no turning back. You have become a seeker after the truth, on his way to Initiation, a man who the Hierarchy will be observing and testing before they make use of you. Your physical self is weakening its hold and your cosmic Self is making its presence felt and will take over.

'Hassidic doctrine demands that we nullify our self.

'The subjugation of the self is indeed the task of the disciple and the Initiate, but nullification to what?

'Nullification to god, answers Moses. He turns pale for he now realises the true import of his answer. Nullification to Yahweh, what am I saying!

'What the disciple aims for is the 'sacrifice' of the self and its absorption into the soul. There is 'death', but death of the lower into an augmented life. There are many 'deaths', many stages of growth throughout life, but the final 'death' to which the disciple aspires is the death of the lower self and the 'birth' into the Self.

'The tiny stream joins the large river and the two as they fuse and unify flow to the sea, says Moses.

'And a very appropriate simile. The idea of nullification is sound but misapplied. Nullification to the deity is the capitulation of the slave to his despotic master. The tenet to 'nullify' oneself before the deity is a command to 'die' for the lower self, to 'die' in order to remain as we were, in a state of stasis, conscious only of the self and its beliefs, its loyalty, its dogmas, its speculations. It is a loss of real identity, surrender to the oppression of form. Where there is adhesion to form there is obstruction to the flow of life.

'Why a loss of identity, why obstruction of the flow of life, enquires Moses?

'The slave has no identity, the master has. Only the Self can be said to have a genuine identity. What we call identity amounts mostly to stating the obvious, the superficial, the ephemeral, 'I am this or that'. With identification with the self there is disruption of the flow of soul life and attachment to form. What is required is the erasing of form, not attachment to it!

'If I may sum up, renunciation of the lower self to the deity is renunciation of the self to itself? True renunciation occurs when we begin to identify with the collective, with the whole, when we look at the greater picture.

'Absolutely! Renunciation of the self to the greater whole is the recognition that man is one with the whole, one with the universe, one with the whole of Life. Ultimate affirmation of power! So to nullify to the soul is to 'die' to the lower self and rise into the greater life of the soul. Death with transfiguration.

'Truly illuminating, Master. This raises a new question, the deity instructs Abraham, 'be holy onto me', I accepted as true, all my educated life, that man in order to be 'holy' had to detach himself from mankind, to disengage from all that is not 'pure' or 'holy', to walk away. In other words to exclude himself, to remove himself.

'I was waiting for this question, you have not disappointed me, says Sanaka with his luminous smile. Holiness in its narrow sense is separation from the whole. As the whole includes not only humanity but also the Planet and the entire cosmos, your idea of holiness is a distortion. When the deity appoints Abraham to take charge of his civilisation on Earth, he insists, 'Be holy before me', in other words 'be separate, dissimilar, estranged'. There is no holiness in separation, in exclusion. There is holiness only within the whole, when man recognises that he is one in the wholeness of life.

Father & Son

'I would like to return to the theme of Creation, utters Sanaka one morning that the wind was blowing hard and snow was falling in a blizzard over the mountains. His gaze moving away from the mountains came to rest on his disciple, 'Moses, my son, inhale this pure air and know that you breathe in cosmic life; consciously breathe out and wrap Earth in a cloak of light.

'This I did. I wrapped Earth into a luminous glow of light and I did feel that it was doing some good. It certainly made a difference, a feeling of peace came over me, I was not evolving for myself alone, my progress was being channelled to encompass Earth and the whole of humanity. I was contributing something.

Smiling his luminous smile, 'It does feel good to help Earth and all the lower kingdoms; you are participating in the work of creation. You see creation did not happen once and for all, it is happening with each breath we take, each breath we direct to assist the world. All is mind. The whole of creation is mind. When you mindfully direct your breath to engage in creation, you become co-creator. You function as your true Self when you realise the brotherhood of man, the personality bathes in the light of the soul. Remember that the soul is light and is all-encompassing. Exclusion and separation are foreign to the soul. Separation lies outside the natural rhythm of life. Service to the whole of life is the primary concern of the soul.

'Where I come from there was a similar idea, but expressed differently. It was not known that 'the whole of creation is mind', but it was believed that the way to help the world was by applying scrupulously the myriad of rules and rituals. 'Torah and mitzvoth' echoed throughout the land. Service was promoted but for the other Jew only, it did not extend beyond.

'Learning and doing, repeats Sanaka. It is not a bad idea, except that your particular strand of learning has to do with the intellect and the intellect is the expression of the personality. The rituals are man-made, the product of human comprehension, an attempt at controlling external forces.

'Controlling?

'Controlling! Even for a group like yours living at the mercy of a deity. You seek to influence events by pacifying your god. The method is flawed but the saving factor is the intention to help, even if limited to your group. Group consciousness is central to your lives. Group consciousness - the brotherhood of man - also figures prominently in the agenda of the Hierarchy, but for them it includes, with you it excludes.

'If group consciousness is the goal of the Hierarchy, this is the way humanity is travelling and we are running against the flow, remarks Moses.

'This is why you were born Moses, the reason that brought you to this monastery. Your task is to awaken people to the new reality, spur them to let go of the exclusive Father and begin to think of the One humanity.

'The world of Genesis, the static world of the Father is ending?

'That was one view; it did not exhaust all possibilities. There are two differing views of Creation. In Genesis, creation is an event which determines the entire future of the world. The world is fixed. Man is locked in captivity in this unchanging world. 'God created the world in six days and rested on the seventh'. No more creation, no change is envisioned, the universe is static. But the world is in constant movement, stars birth and die, whole worlds are born and die, the universe is in constant change. Creation is happening now.

'Is this the meaning behind the allegory of the Father?

'The Father is indeed unchanging, stable, and immovable and Hebrew thought hinges around the idea of the stagnant, unyielding Father.

'I do not know of another view, sighs Moses. I come from a static world in which change is unknown, indeed unimaginable.

'Yet there is another. The second view makes the process of Creation active, creative and fluid. The world is not given for all time, not fixed, not determined but in the making, changing, evolving! Freedom which had disappeared in Genesis reappears when the Son enters the cosmic stage introducing the crucial and vital principle of evolution and with it freedom.

'Why freedom?

'Because if man is not predestined then he is free to act, free to change, free to evolve, nothing is preset for him, he is not a puppet on the strings of the gods, but an autonomous being who can shape his future. With change comes wholeness.

'Why wholeness?

'For the same reason. When man is free, his conscious actions will ultimately restore the primeval unity within himself and this will extend outside. Since the Fall man feels incomplete, divided, he believes himself alone in a hostile universe. He will seek to unite with the rest of the world. He will endeavour to bring about what is symbolically described as the Kingdom of God on Earth, even if he denies the existence of the inner worlds. He will have rediscovered the spiritual principles.

'So the idea of the Father is flawed; in promoting stagnancy it hinders the natural flow of evolution towards the resolution … towards the Beginning.

'It has jeopardised the progress and completion of the Plan.

'Wholeness lost at the time of Creation lives on in the imagination, it remains a dream for artists, musicians and prophets, a source of artistic and spiritual inspiration. Man feels alone in an alien universe with no means of making sense of his situation, unable to begin the return journey home. The Prodigal Son is lost. The Hebrews who insistently speak of unity – unity of god, unity of the people - paradoxically find themselves locked in a sealed universe, separate from the All, separate from the soul. This is the opposite of unity'.

'We have to interrupt the reading', butts in Jeremy who has spotted questioning looks. The issues are crucial; we must discuss them with Sananda. Any one keen to ask the questions, you Clara, he adds with a smile, he knows her eagerness.

'I will. The questions have been forming in my mind for a while'. They settle quietly, Jeremy closes his eyes. All are silent. A smile in her direction signals that Jeremy has made contact with Sananda and is ready to begin. Turning to Clara with an encouraging and amused smile, Sananda through Jeremy greets her and invites her to put her question.

Father & Son allegory

'Does the allegory of Father and Son refer to the whole course of evolution? When you, the Spiritual Hierarchy, gave the Old Testament at Sinai, was it your intention to impart the image of a static universe, which still prevails today among the Judeo-Christian orthodoxy in all countries?

'It can be said, answers Sananda, that God also evolves. This is a universe of change, of growth. Through your own growth, God also grows. So that God is at once the unchanging Father and Son, changing and evolving. While one does not see an allegory of evolution out of one vision of God, another grows more evolved. You have to bear in mind that both the Old and New Testaments have a historical context. They appeared at a specific time and in a specific location, at a time when rigidity of precept and practice was important to save mankind from itself. You can see the evolutionary process at work. I would recommend caution no to extrapolate a total view of the divine message.

'Is the expansion of the universe mirroring the expansion of divine Consciousness?

'There is a degree of illusion in affirming the expansion of the universe. It appears to scientists, with the prevailing theoretical approach that the universe is expanding. It is a part of the truth, for there are two other views of the cosmos, one which sees the universe stable, the other as coming together (not quite shrinking). It can be argued that the expanding universe theory is a reflection of human knowledge and of humanity's view of itself.

'Humanity, at the time the Old Testament was given, continues Sananda, was recovering from deep traumas and so a version of the universe which suggests stability, permanence and reliability was said to be the most helpful view of the universe at that moment in the history of humanity. Those recovering from deep traumas, need reassurance and certainty, but it is also important to give them the promise, the vision of a wonderful thing about to happen, something of great significance that will occur in future and bring a brand new vision, which holds a promise of great joy: the Son. The idea of evolution is not new, for the society of your era, this particular age of humanity. But the idea of the survival of the fittest posited by Darwin is new, the idea of evolution goes back a long way. The sense of the possibility of growing into a better state is intrinsic in humanity. Ever since the Fall, the desire to regain a lost paradise, to recover a lost innocence, to rediscover a lost greatness and return to the primeval integrity is inherent. Evolution is the path to redemption. This has been a motivating force in this age. The principle of growth is fundamental to the universe. An expanding universe is an illusion.

'Was humanity ever aware of its own greatness and power?

'Before what is known as the Fall, humanity had a fuller awareness of its nature. The period of awareness deficit ultimately amplifies awareness beyond the level of awareness previously attained and will add to greater consciousness. With the Fall mankind lost its own sense of greatness and power.

'With the allegory of the Son it is a new definition of the Divine that is presented to a troubled humanity and with it a new world view?

'Exactly.

'I suppose that the cycle of Initiations you are offering us now is directly related to this? If so can Initiation be divulged to all who wish to hear about it?

'Initiation is primarily experiential initiation. As things are, hearing or reading about Initiation does not do Initiation. There may come a time to participate by reading or writing. You may speak of your experience and the principles involved but at this stage it would only be describing.

'If there is light to give, it must be given to the majority who in the past was denied that light. Initiation was the privilege of the select few. I object to this view of selection and privilege. It is untenable in the 20th century and I am very much of the 20th century!

'This is the spirit of the age, replies the Master. Our purpose is to make this process available to as many as possible. It is not our intention to keep things secret. Our purpose is to make the signpost public. We do not wish these things to be hidden away.

'The Master Djwahl Khul speaks of an imminent new Revelation.

'You are participating in the Revelation rather than the Revelation coming to you from some outside agency, in the way you, as a group share experiences, reveal one another important truths. This is what you have been doing in this group. You are revelators of truth and receivers of revelation. It links up with the blueprint for humanity. It is fluid and occurring at present, in groups such as this one. You are doing it. There will be no formal revelation handed down'. The dialogue with Sananda comes to an end.

Opening his eyes and smiling Jeremy turns to Clara, 'no question? I feel a shudder when you ask a question, I immediately think 'O dear, Clara is questioning, how I am going to answer this one?'

'Praise or criticism? Besides, I don't ask you the questions. Alright you want grief I'll give you grief!

'I don't want any grief, please!

You'll get it anyway! Sananda was just saying that evolution is an uninterrupted feature of human life and history. He also said that revelation is a thing of the past. At various times when humanity was plunged into darkness, some Masters appear on the human stage to light up the way, fulfilling the promise made long ago by the Hierarchy that humanity would never be abandoned to itself. Krishna's pledge.

'The Masters were coming back to instruct mankind on evolution, reminding man that he is not just a body, but a deathless soul and that soul evolves through time, through countless rebirths, and that both Karma and Reincarnation are the two pillars of human evolution, replies Jeremy.

'In the past, and this prevailed among primitive societies, a return to spiritual sanity was associated with a reinforcing of religious ritual, says Johansson.

'This is particularly true of the Jewish people, at each crucial moment of their tortured history, someone appeared to harden their beliefs and thicken the 'thicket of views' and practices. They were reinforcing all that the Masters were trying to weed out, says Levinson.

'The Masters came to repeat some essential idea, to educate and to remind. Buddha discarded religious speculations and offered a rational appraisal of man's situation in the world. He rejected religious myths and stabbed at illusion with clinical precision. And with scientific rigor he showed man alone in the universe. He insisted that man is fully responsible for his own redemption. Buddha can be said to have taught mankind the principle of conscious evolution, as more recently Darwin demonstrated the principle of biological evolution, replies Jeremy.

'We are told that biological evolution is unconscious and uncontrolled whereas mental evolution is both conscious and controlled, inserts Levinson.

'So the age of the Masters incarnating to receive revelations from the top of mountains is over, notes Tara with relief.

'That's right, you heard Sananda. It is clear that the Hierarchy will not be sending any more Moses to lead mankind back to the light.

'We are to do it ourselves, reflects Clara. This is the spirit of the age. Mankind is capable of taking its own destiny into its own hands. The age of the prophets, religious leaders and revealers of truth is over. We are the revealers of truth, each one of us, we are creating our own truth and as we do we are inspiring humanity to create its own truth.

Genesis

One day after the early morning meditation, Master Sanaka unexpectedly turns to Moses and says, 'Just like the first day! Look at the majesty and radiance of the sun, the light that greets us each morning. The sun, that expression of the Divine, lights up the world and has been doing so to help mankind on its path of evolution. Worshipping the sun is natural to man; it is an act of gratitude for the life-giving, light-giving power of the sun.

'Not to us it is not, exclaims Moses!

'That is because you never recovered from periods of darkness when the sun failed to rise during the great cataclysms of the past. The Solar Logos is a being of absolute, unconditional love, like the universal Logos. Do narrate the story of the creation of man, Rabbi Moses, you are an authority on the subject, he adds with an encouraging smile and a touch of gentle irony. Surprised, Moses hesitates but intuitively knows that the Master is directing him sensibly and gently.

'Then God said, 'Let us make man in our image, in our likeness', quotes Moses uncertain as to where this is leading to.

'All the world myths recount tales of gods who came down from the sky to lead mankind on its path of growth. The beings who came from the stars took upon themselves to speed up the evolution of primitive man.

'Who were those beings and where did they come from?

'They came from the many stars that have guided the steps of humanity since the beginning of time, Sirius, Lyra, Orion, the Pleiades, among others. The Egyptian Pharaoh was believed to return to the stars after his death, hence the complicated burial rituals. A few ancient tribal societies still hold that their ancestors came from the stars and have built their religious life around this belief. The stellar beings were already highly advanced and looked upon early man with kind affection. They wanted to encourage man's progress.

Moses is eager to know and dreading to know at the same time. 'Your nervousness tells me that you already know, smiles Sanaka.

'Apart from the Nefilim other stellar beings visited Earth? What was their role?

'The Nefilim did not want humans to be aware of polarity, but there was a major snag: this universe was created to make polarity possible!

'We are presented with a dilemma at the outset, exclaims Moses impulsively.

'Precisely. On the one hand the cosmos comes into being to make polarity possible so that the Creator has the chance to learn in incarnation, through man. But a demigod arrives and attempts to conceal polarity.

'So man is not authorized to know polarity and through him it is the Creator who is refused the right to know polarity. This throws a new light on the myth.

'It does, smiles Sanaka. The Creator fashions a complex world in which he is presented with questions in order to formulate answers. Samsara – the created world - is divided in polar opposites and as you well know, he smiles with humour, rabbis are adroit at debate!

'We call it 'pilpul'. We do take pride in our ability to throw up questions and argue possible answers. The Talmud encourages such disputes. This is new: the Talmud is well rooted in Samsara, the world of polarity! What were the intentions of the Nefilim and other stellar beings towards mankind, were they moved by sympathy?

'Many of those beings were indeed moved by a genuine interest in the advancement of man but not all. Love is the greatest force in the universe and very widely spread, but not all star civilisations are moved by altruistic motives. Those who came with love came as light bearers.

'What about Yahweh, did he come as light bearer?

'It can be said that he changed native man into modern man as we know him today. Once the new man was fashioned according to his terms, he deleted knowledge of polarity. Newly conscious man was forbidden to know.

'I see now, exclaims Moses that is why Genesis speaks of the Tree of Knowledge of good and evil.

'Indeed, you see knowledge of polarity would have given man an advantage. Non-awareness of polarity makes man simple and naïve like a child. But there is a problem, as man is deprived of his birth right; the Creator is deprived of the very thing the universe was created for: the exploration of polarity! The demigod in one sweep dealt a mighty blow to the Divine both in transcendence and in immanence, in the universe and in man.

'So the opening verses of Genesis recount an aberration, realises Moses looking anew at a story he thought he knew well.

'Adam's ignorance of duality implies that he is lacking in awareness. No awareness, no questioning! It suggests that he does not question his god's actions, he submits to them. Man is forbidden to eat of the Tree of Knowledge for fear that he opens his eyes to reality. As he disobeys, he asserts his autonomy. More importantly, he is asserting his right to know, to explore, and to enlarge his horizon.

'And Eve has been cursed for her disobedience ever since, exclaims Moses! Eve was demonised because of her gesture of independence which is perceived as defiance, rebellion, sheer wickedness. In fairness to them, is it wrong to hark back to a lost Paradise?

'Yes, if it denies the unfolding of the Plan of Creation. Man is the Divine incarnate and mankind decided long ago to experience life on Earth in order to learn through polarity and surmount the challenges of Samsara. Pretending that polar opposites do not exist is not the same as fusing opposites into primal unity! The Rabbis lament a time when mankind was living before Samsara in a state of oneness. To deny is not to resolve. To understand is to resolve.

'To the rabbis, Adam's coming of age is a tragedy, they call it the Fall. Man fell from grace the moment he became aware of himself as an autonomous being. They believe that Torah will bring man back to his lost innocence.

'Moses, do go on quoting the first verses of Genesis, invites Sanaka.

'Then the Lord God said, 'Behold, the man has become like one of us, knowing good and evil. He must not be allowed to reach out his hand and take also from the Tree of Life and eat, and live forever'.

'Do comment, Moses.

'It is self-explanatory, man has disobeyed god's orders, he has eaten the 'fruit', he now knows polarity, his eyes are open to the reality of life on Earth, he is conscious of his situation and in a way he is like his god. But now that man is aware he wants immortality and the gods are worried.

'I agree, continues Sanaka, inevitably the human race has been perplexed as to the identity and intentions of the 'gods'. At the time of the great Flood, humans are abandoned to their fate. The 'gods' disappear. Yet a few 'gods' do help humans as is the case with Noah who is miraculously rescued. This conflicting behaviour on the part of the 'gods' leaves a profound imprint in human memory. These two facets of the gods are recorded deep in man's emotional being, and ever since humanity has hovered uneasily between hope and despair, belief and doubt, fear of desertion and hope of redemption. This inner struggle seems to have affected the Hebrews more, for they had a dim recollection of a bitter time when they were being 'fashioned' by their god for whom they retain to this day secret anger and fear.

'Is it this fear and anger that the Rabbis have attempted to bring under control in solidifying the Messianic hope, asks Moses?

'The deity may be despotic and unethical but in the mind of those who need him, he is the Holy One Bless He Be! In spite of their long history of suffering and rejection, they want to believe that he still loves his children! The stellar makers selected groups of earthlings who were similar in looks and endowed them with feeling of excellence. They gave them a mission. To the select few, 'the chosen ones' the gods promised a glorious future, enduring protection and a unique relationship. Children receive the physical and mental characteristics of their parents. If an earthly group was 'made' by an advanced non-human race, this explains why the Hebrews still carry an unshakable belief in their own excellence, in spite of their terrible fate which they interpret as a sign of their 'chosenness'.

Two stories of Creation - Yahweh & the Elohim

'Something does not quite gel, mumbles Benzaccai, I was a biblical student for many years and not by choice I have to say! As a child I learned about Creation and accepted it on faith. It never dawned on me to enquire why we were so focused on the creation of the material world, it was the hub of our study at the 'yeshiva'; we read it with reverence at the synagogue. Why be so preoccupied with the material world?

'I did ask this impertinent question, replies Clara, and made myself unpopular. No intelligent answer came my way. I got a look of disapproval and a stern reply of pious frustration. They counted on unquestioned consent; they made me feel defective. True believers do not question. They looked down on me from their towering spiritual height!

'They looked down with kind pity on all of us, kids from the slums, from their towering height like the gods of Mount Olympus pitying mortals. It did not strike me at the time how as 'redeemers' of the world we got stuck in the Creation story. We solidified with Creation. The Fall? Still immersed in it, we remain resolutely 'fallen'. The Flood? We are still sinking in it, we never reached the shore! We are like the Flying Dutchman cursed to sail for ever.

'So much human potential discredited in the name of a god, says Jeremy!

'What kind of god demands the squandering of human talent, mutters Tara!

'The god of Samsara frowns upon what makes us truly human, asserts Clara. He is the god of human sacrifice in one form or another. He must diminish man as if the world was not large enough for both.

'In contrast the universal Mind wishes us to evolve, grow, learn and understand the world and ourselves, reflects Jeremy. We were placed on Earth to expand our consciousness and enrich the universe.

'It is as if the world of Samsara - time, space and matter - is the only one. It is the only world we know, comments Levinson. We are entrapped in Samsara.

'Those who taught us, recalls Clara, devoured the verses avidly, mouthing them with sensuous reverence. Addiction to the allegory of Creation mirrored the fixation with pureness of food and purity of body.

'It has to do with matter and the flesh. Mind you, I have no objection to either, says Benzaccai in jest. What strikes me now is the insistence on the creation of matter. Where is the mind in all this?

'The mind is a relatively recent event, not developed in the biblical era, a time of physical upheaval, political turmoil, social strife, emotional devotion, irrational fervour and pious fury, replies Clara.

'God created our Solar System; this was the extent of biblical cosmology. It seems that the creation of sun and planets was all there was to concern oneself with, sums up Johansson, the biblical scholar.

'What of the twelve constellations, the twelve tribes of Israel and the twelve loaves of bread in the Temples of Babylon and Jerusalem, asks Levinson?

'It is not our fixation with the creation of matter which troubled me the most. Something else mystified me, reflects Clara, I could not quite grasp the approved version of the two Creations stories, sitting side by side and when I questioned they registered a threat. One even said to me 'with questions like these you will become a heretic'.

'That's exactly what you have become, laughs Jeremy!

'Jeremy I must put the question to Sananda, implores Clara.

'I think this can be arranged smiles Jeremy expecting the request. I knew you would not sit for long before asking'. They all sit quietly in anticipation of Sananda's arrival and contact. His eyes closed Jeremy smiles in the direction of Clara. It is an invitation from Sananda to put her question: 'Master Sananda, what was the intention of the Bible writers ... well ... that is you the Hierarchy, begins Clara hesitantly suddenly aware of the strangeness of the situation, when they offered' ... again she hesitates ... 'when you offered the two versions of the story of Creation: Creation by Yahweh and Creation by the Elohim.

'Yes, there are really two separate Creations, confirms Sananda. You could think of the Creation by Yahweh as being symbolic of the creation of the entire universe; that would be one possible interpretation. However, it is also the case that the being of that name can be seen as a distinct entity from the All That Is. In something like historical time, he was a being who played a part in creating one aspect of your reality on the Earth plane; setting in motion a particular phase of the experience of what has become humanity's experience. There have been a number of different creations on this Planet, not really just one creation. There was a prime and primal Creation that comes from the Source of All. However, overlaying this initial Creation, on a number of occasions, beings of great power have come to Earth and adapted, changed or recreated aspects of life. So the being you know as Yahweh could be seen as one of those beings distinct from the Source of All, a more localised force, a more specific force.

'If I may sum up, Master Sananda, Yahweh was a powerful entity, distinct from the Source, who came to Earth to adapt, change or recreate early man and begin a new phase in the history of humanity which is still unfolding. Humanity is still living under his influence. Yahweh is not the Source, but who are the Elohim?

'This is also the case with the Beings known as the Elohim who came in, having received their instructions from the Source of All. Formed out of the divine essence, they divided themselves into creators and created. You could see yourselves as the created and the Elohim as creators. But it is also true - though this may be difficult to understand - that you are the creators and they are the created! There is one Cosmic Energy which separates out - this is the world of polarity - to experience itself in these two separate ways, as creator and created. This is also, to a degree, true of the way in which Yahweh operated, though the situation is slightly different, there is more of a historical context.

'Was he a scientist who came to change things?

'That would be a way of describing him, yes you could use that description, and there would be much truth in it.

'Was he in part human or someone from a different civilisation?

'I would say at that point not human and from what you could describe as another civilisation - but perhaps not as your imagination might conceive of as civilisation -

wishing to explore certain aspects of his own power and to put forth aspects of that energy into human form, so that within humanity you will find aspects of that beingness. At a later date, looking back, you might say 'O well, Yahweh had elements of humanness'. But that would be putting the cart before the horse!

'Was his intention benevolent toward mankind, or did he come here to intervene or interfere with human evolution?

'That being, I would say, wished to explore certain ways of working with power. You may wish to draw your own conclusion, to decide whether they were benevolent or not. I would approach this from the perspective where all is well; all becomes well, all that happens works for the best. That would be my perspective. I would add that the way in which he chose to explore power is not wholly the way that perhaps you would choose to explore power! It would be possible and accurate to say that your change of viewpoint is at least in part due to the experience of power used in that way. It is another way of saying to you that ultimately all works out for the best.

'Is it not inherent to the Judeo-Christian tradition to see man as insignificant?

'Yes, indeed it has been one of the beliefs ....

'... Man must be broken; there is virtue in being 'broken', interrupts an animated Clara. 'God likes a broken heart' I was taught. Man must feel worthless, sinful and corrupt.

'Yes, it certainly has been one of the strands of those beliefs. I would not suggest that it is the totality of those religions but it has been a strong strand in both. You are quite right, but I would add that an important part of the process of evolution of both religions is to release those strands. Others may differ in their views they are free to do so, that is what I would say.

'In Genesis it is said that the Lord breathed life into man in order to animate the inert form of clay. This is a beautiful metaphor, is it life as we know it? What of the spirit? Did he have anything to do with the spirit of man?

'Let me suggest that you apply what we previously discussed to this situation. I talked about the underlying energy matrix which draws to it the human form. To turn that over, another way of looking at it in the story, God breathes life into clay. This is another way of saying that the spirit which is a portion of God, the spirit puts itself forth into the human form, it animates, and it brings to life the human form. The spirit leaves when the body dies or changes its form. It is all part of the same way of looking at things: the breathing in of life can be seen as the spirit choosing to move into the physical world. There can be particularities to this. There are beings in your universe who have learnt the skill of bringing life into physical form, that is to say they have learnt to work with the spirit, to align the spirit to physical form; they have become participants in the process. But ultimately, at the deepest level, in reality you create yourself, for you also are God. There are many different ways of looking at this issue. You may want to ask more about this.

'So 'the Lord breathed life into man' is a metaphor for life itself, for the spirit animating matter. It must be taken figuratively. The text emphasises Yahweh as sole creator of man. It may well be a metaphor, the text stresses that he breathes in life, but he is not the Source, how can he take upon himself to use or to hijack the spirit, life?

'Ultimately we all are created by the Source, but in order to enter particular types of experience, you may choose at soul level, to interact with other beings who are portions of the Source. So, while it is certainly true that you are brought forth as a spark of light from the Source of All, just as all beings are, in order to experience life on Earth, you may, at some point, come along to a being, let us call this being Yahweh, a powerful and evolved being. You come to this being in order to move into a form that has been prepared for you. Let us say this being has the capacity to create certain types of genetic make up, and you, as a being come along and think, 'it would be interesting to explore what it is like to live in that particular genetic matrix, that particular set up of genes, that particular type of physical form. I will make the choice to align my beingness with that form, therefore I will give my beingness temporarily to this being Yahweh. This being may align my energy using the skills that he has with this particular form that he has created'. However, the creation of the human form can be seen as the basic template which is over and beyond the creation of a single being, very widespread throughout the universe. We are looking at a lot of different layers here, and the truth you see depends on the layer you choose to pull out and examine. I hope this clarifies it a little bit'.

The encounter comes to a close leaving all in silent awe. A new facet has emerged that is unsettling. Before this life, while planning to come back in incarnation, they had to align their 'beingness' to the Jewish genetic form. Furthermore they had to entrust their 'beingness' temporarily to Yahweh for him to align to the Jewish form. Bewildering! This clearly shows that coming into Jewish incarnation is not as simple as they first thought. When incarnating into a Jewish body, a kind of scientific contract is drawn up between the individual and the master geneticist. And what if he had turned the application down?

'Sananda is explaining, begins Levinson to clarify things for himself, that the Source is the originator of the Elohim, and all conscious life in the universe including Yahweh and the Nefilim. By the way the Elohim <u>are</u> a group of Beings, a disquieting g idea for the diehard 'monotheists'! Though the Elohim are the creators of our beingness, we too are creators by virtue of the fact that we are part of the Source. At once created and creators. There is one Source and we are it! Nothing can exist outside that essence, by implications nothing can exist outside our essence! Existing within divine essence, we are the creative principle. Sananda also draws a parallel between the Elohim and Yahweh, not that they are in any way similar, but in the sense that Yahweh himself was created and in turn became creator.

'The Bible chroniclers got their facts mixed up, inserts Johansson, how could an issue so crucial for humanity as the origin of man by the Elohim be interpreted away in such a casual fashion? The biblical scribes transcribed the Sumerian Creation myth and subsequent generations of scholars kept it as it fitted neatly with the newly adopted idea of the 'one' god.

'What Sananda just said about giving one's beingness to Yahweh so that he aligns it with the Jewish form is bewildering to say the least, says Clara. I assumed that we are the product of our parents' genetic mix and that the Self returns into that new body.

'There is more to it than that, Sananda' s answer seems to confirm the deeply held belief that it is the Yahweh-force which creates us, each one of us, each time, ponders Levinson. The ancestral belief holds more truth than we could ever imagine. This certainly gives validity to the old beliefs. I shall have to adjust to this, it is a difficult one.

'He does not create the spark, rectifies Clara. But he does align it with the physical form. Our geneticists have not arrived at this yet.

'Sananda makes a clear distinction between the 'beingness' as originally created by the Elohim and the genetic constitution organized by Yahweh, comments Benzaccai. Sananda removes the notion of fate or supernatural intervention. It is left to each individual to make the crucial decision of coming to Earth. Anyone who wishes to come back into physical existence does so, but there is the added element of an experiment. The individual is behaving like a scientist who formulates a hypothesis and sets up the perimeters of his experimentation. This is the scenario Sananda just suggested, 'It would be interesting to explore that particular genetic matrix, that particular set up of genes, that particular type of physical form'.

'One thing is certain, we have total freedom at all time, we choose our next life, our next genetic make up and circumstances, says Jeremy. Going back to your experience at the yeshiva Benzaccai, things now look like this: Yahweh 'wished to explore ways of working with power'.

'Power? We were non-existent, we were lumps of nothing!

'You came to experiment with the polar opposite of power, powerlessness. You were systematically dis-empowered, we all were from infancy, this is the root of the Jewish condition as I experienced it, says Clara.

'Those who indoctrinated us, like their god, were also experimenting with power, realises Benzaccai. They were at the controlling end of the power band; we were at the receiving end. Gratifying for them, undignified for us.

'Looking at it this way our religious teachers too came to experiment with power, made in the image and likeness of their god, they adopted his aims and method. We rebelled against the use of such power, notes Clara. 'This is not the way you would choose to explore power' said Sananda. No indeed, the way world servers choose to explore power is in the form of self-mastery, self-knowledge, autonomy, self-empowerment. More to the point whereas the loyal servants of the Yahweh-force seek to disempower us, we the workers of the Hierarchy assist in the empowerment of others.

'That's right, nods Levinson, millions of cosmic workers appointed by the Hierarchy are now in incarnation to lessen the power the god-force has on mankind and the Planet. This particular form of energy has been strangling both man and Earth.

'We came under the influence of diehards dancing a weird power dance, a two-step dance, moans Benzaccai. One step is the need to submit to the power of the deity, to 'nullify' themselves before the demigod. The second is the urge-to-power. Servility and power, capitulation and authority, they blend the two, at ease with their own contradictions.

'They experiment with polarity in earnest, retorts Levinson! They go all the way, no half measure for them! And we lived in silent agony! Our Jewish persona coerced to comply, longing to lie down and die and our divine Self silently prompting us to shirk their injurious influence. While we were agonising they were rejoicing in the power of the idol!

'This bunch of harmless bigots who look different, act different and dress different give rise to amusement, irritation and tolerance, concludes Benzaccai. The time is soon approaching when they will be seen not as a harmless bunch of oddballs but as a group bent on embedding deeper the god-force, as agents working to prolong the idol's will-to-power and his influence through unsuspecting Jews who fall under their spell. They will be subjected to intense scrutiny and their motives investigated. Who are they and why are they returning in Jewish garb? It is our function as world servers to ensure that the god-force is weakened and not strengthened. The idol will eventually be toppled.

'This could be misconstrued, inserts Levinson.

'I know. We are talking about the will-to-power discernible in political, social and religious forms and their influence, control and authority. Now this force is well distributed throughout humanity, it is a global phenomenon, at all levels, political, social and personal. It is the function of the world servers and people with a humanitarian inclination to assist in the lifting of all forms of power imposed on us from outside. Our work is to encourage autonomy, awaken the will to freedom and inflame the realisation of our vast inner resources. For as long as we are puppets on a chain we remain blind to our real nature. But when we shake off external forces we rediscover our boundless inner power. The idol literally and figuratively is doomed, being replaced by the qualities of this new era aptly named the Age of the Soul.

The Cosmic Mind

'If I may review, Master Sanaka, the cosmic Mind divides, multiplies and individualises in human form. There is no difference between us. We are all parts of the same Mind. There is no high or low, no superior or inferior, not even good or bad! In a sense, man was never 'created', he simply 'is'. Man and the cosmic Mind are of the same nature. Man is consciousness made manifest. What a realisation!

'First, good and evil are ultimately an illusion since duality is an illusion; behind the polar opposites is unity. Buddha stated that the Self is unborn, uncreated because it is part of the universal Mind. Man is of cosmic dimension, he is the universal Self. Second, the cosmic Force that vitalises man has lost nothing of its creative power. Moses' assignment was to remind us that cosmic Consciousness is the only reality and that man shares in that power. It follows that he too is boundless, infinite, like his Father he is endowed with the same qualities. One such quality is a limitless power to create by thought.

'Like the Father who creates by thought alone, man is able to create by thought, interrupts Levinson, I am sorry to stop the flow, but I cannot resist! Awesome power exploding in the 20th century. It is the power of thought which gave rise to the ideologies which crushed mankind in our time. Stalin and Hitler used the power of mind to initiate and execute the greatest crimes against humanity. The Tibetan informs us that the 20th century wars were fought on the mental plane'. All eyes are on him and embarrassed, 'I apologise for the intrusion!

The reading resumes, 'And the people at Sinai witness and listen, shaking in awe, recounts Sanaka. They remember the ancestral god and the deities of Egypt. The temptation to turn back to the familiar gods they can identity with is irresistible. The gods are more accessible; they have a presence, a form.

'But they are being told that the primeval Intelligence at the origin of the cosmos is also their own mind, infinite, inalienable, immortal, existing beyond time and space, comments Moses. This is too much to take in.

'This the Master hints at with these enigmatic words, 'Before Abraham I am'.

'This infuriated the rabbis who took it literally.

'Do you glimpse now why, asks Sanaka?

'The worldly-oriented rabbis did not grasp with their literal, chronological mind. Their imagination would not stretch to that other reality - permanent, boundless, formless - behind physical reality. They were unable to go beyond the literal, the chronological, the linear, the temporal.

'Excellent Moses, your grasp of spiritual Law is impressive. It means that each and every human being is part of the primeval Mind. But this Law is not grasped at Sinai. The people decide they want meat, water and a visible god they can dance to. They want to lose themselves in a frenzy of sensual delight. Who wants spiritual Law when the flesh is clamouring its due!

'The Fall is even more ancient, notes Moses, boldly.

'With the Fall man loses sight of his primordial nature, he no longer knows he is the cosmic Mind in individuality. Ignorant of his nature he falls into the tragic mistake of believing that he is finite, limited, sinful and powerless. The metaphor that suits his new view of himself is the Fall. Truly he has fallen from grace in his own evaluation of himself. He now sees with human eyes. Ignorant of the boundless Mind that inhabits him, he only sees his finite human mind. His descent into matter is complete, he now identifies fully with his lower self, he no longer is the Divine in physical form, but just a fearful human form that embarks on a desperate journey of sorrow, pain and grief. As he plunges deeper into the darkness of matter, he also condemns Earth to the same fate. Earth has offered herself to assist man's growth and in so doing has made herself vulnerable to the thoughts, emotions and actions of man. Man builds his own mental and emotional bodies but he also builds the mental and emotional bodies of Earth. Both are locked in a continued downward spiral of pain and karmic reckoning. But cosmic Law is operating in spite of our ignorance. Ignorance does not eradicate the Law.

'How am I to explain that man is the cosmic Mind hid under the mask of the ego? How am I to prove that Earth is the Mother of humanity, that she responds to our activity and that she is in darkness because we are in darkness? How am I to show the operation of cosmic Law, when we only know of human law? How am I to explain that our secret thoughts can have such a negative effect on us and on the Planet? Such an intimate relationship between man and Earth! A huge responsibility for mankind. Where does that leave both man and Earth?

'Many of your more advanced religious thinkers have known this as did the Prophets. This is not entirely new, in spite of much distortion on the part of lesser generations.

'So, Master, people understand what they want to understand. The moment one understands, one becomes involved. It takes courage to understand. I never saw this before.

'To understand is to evolve. Many choose the line of least resistance. One pleads ignorance to get off the hook! Or ignorance is forced upon them to let the despotic god-force reign unhindered; this force is fed by faithful supporters. It is easier to govern the masses by feeding them on beliefs that have no foundation in reality. Recently the god-force was challenged; you heard echoes of the rebellion reverberate throughout Europe at the time of the Revolution. It was an earth-shattering time for kings, aristocracy, priests of all affiliations and all their gods.

'I see now that it was necessary for the rulers to keep this information hidden. To tell the people that they share in the cosmic Mind might unleash anarchy.

'To return to the power of thought, creative thought – this divine quality we share with the Infinite – acts either way for good or ill. The law operates for all; all of us are subject to its effect.

'Any fool with his power of thought can send out low-grade thoughts that harm mankind and Earth!

'Indeed Rabbi Moses, the responsibility is great, it has cosmic dimension! One important point I must emphasise: the Law brings on what man himself creates. The enlightened man aware of his power of thought acts with responsibility. He knows that he is the originator of his action and the effects of his action. Your people are the living proof of the Law in action. Ignorant of their unlimited creative power, they opt for powerlessness. They think 'defeat', 'surrender'.

'Master you said, 'the Law brings on what man himself creates'. Thoughts of 'defeat' and 'surrender' create defeat and surrender. The Source creates by thought; we create our unfortunate destiny over and over with our thoughts! It is not the world that plots our demise, we do it ourselves! We create our destiny with our thoughts and we pass on these thoughts to the next generation which imbibes them and live them. Each generation swallows the thoughts of its ancestors and the problem is compounded. And I am expected to take this terrible insight to them!

'Yes, you Moses, who else? They have waited long enough and the world has waited with them. When they know, the world will know, because humanity is one vast body, what affects one part affects the whole. In ignorance of the Law, they cry out in the wilderness, appealing, invoking, imploring, and they rage against their god who has forsaken them. In each generation they pour out into the world their pain, their fear and their guilt. These heavy emotions are not lost; their creative power is still within them, it has not vanished. Endowed with the power to create by thought, they erect the walls of the ghettos which began to hold them in Egyptian times and which are now familiar land marks, painful reminders of what ignorance precipitates.

'We are a living laboratory. We set it up; it seems, to demonstrate the workings of the Law to the entire world. The world despises us, we pity ourselves and neither knows why!

Father & Son allegory

'Well observed Moses. They utilise the divine power of thought to fence themselves in and condemn generations to inner entrapment and outer captivity. The Law is operating at all time, you are still in bondage. Moses and the Prophets initiated the recalcitrant Hebrews to the reality of the universe. The Essenes, centuries later presented the fact of the Son poetically expressed, 'Do you not believe that I am in the Father and the Father is in me? It is the Father who remains ever in me'. He stops to observe Moses who decidedly remains quiet.

'The Hebrews continue to be reminded, resumes Sanaka, of the immovable, unchangeable nature of the law. The Father is not external to you; you do not need rabbis and priests to reach him. No one will ever explain the Father to you. No one will ever give you permission to communicate with the Father. The Father is your very being that you alone can experience. 'I and my Father are One' reinforces the central theme of Oneness. There is no difference between the cosmic Mind and the human mind, they are the same.

'I foresee insurmountable objections, says Moses: 'mere speculation' they will jeer. With respect Master Sanaka, they will laugh, 'all this nonsense about Father and Son', 'Universal Mind and human mind being one'! I shall be taunted as a dangerous heretic.

'You are used to it, laughs Sanaka! All this is real and verifiable and should be taken literally. Deep in the Heart shines the radiant light of the Son and at the centre is the brilliant spark of the Father. In the Heart of man, Father and Son are indeed one. Moses came to show mankind the Father alive, vibrant, and creative. The Essenes came to complete the picture, revealing the living presence of the Son merging with the radiant presence of the Father in that spiritual centre known as the Heart. Man now is increasingly aware that the Father dwells inside him and that the Son inhabits the same space. He senses the essential oneness. Rabbis, prophets and priests, synagogues and temples all intermediaries are now superfluous, an affront both to the Father and to the Son in man. All that man needs to know now is that 'I and my Father are One'.

'This phrase is too provocative.

The truth provokes! But the rabbis are irritated, they recite from memory every word, sign and letter of the great myth of Creation to which they devote their entire lives, they know it intimately and have dissected it for centuries. They claim that the Father is in the sky; there can be no common ground between Father and man. God is in the sky man is alone down here.

'Yet they miss the point. I know I did, sighs Moses.

'They fail to touch the hidden meaning. Cosmic Law is long forgotten, they are still caught up in the Fall, aware only of their limited human self. They study the texts only to find their finite notions about the world and man confirmed. We read what we want to read! Infuriated they turn to blows against the impudent Essenes! How dare they defy their cramped view of the world?

'Man is mortal and material, sums up Moses. He is born, he lives and multiplies and then he dies. Man's greatest ambition is to live in order to serve his god. All else is heresy.

'The Essenes are undeterred, they are on a mission, they have been sent out to herald the age of the soul. They insist 'I and my Father are One', but to no avail. And they say reassuringly yet firmly 'And the truth shall set you free'.

'O to be free! It has to be not freedom but bondage, laments Moses.

'And they insist, 'Rabbis do you not see that Father and Son dwell inside your chest? Remember the spiritual Law Moses received at Sinai which says that God created man in his image. God is pure Mind, so if man is made in the image of his Creator he too is mind, he possesses the same power. Unsettled by the law long forgotten, the rabbis feel vulnerable, and their authority in doubt. They resort to violence; they throw stones at the blasphemers who insist that the life force pulsates throughout the universe as it does in man! This is real, we are the living proof that God exists. Nature and man are living evidence of this all-pervasive life force. Life, manifest in us reveals the unseen 'It is the Spirit within you that does the work'. The body of itself is nothing; it is the life force within that animates us.

'This is pure heresy, says Moses, they are men of their time.

'And you do know, smiles Sanaka with gentle irony. The rabbis shake their angry heads in obstinate denial. Matter is matter, man is man, god is god, that's that! The world is solid, god and man are separate. One is creator, the other created and no nonsense permitted! When man dies he goes wandering aimlessly into the Underworld. They refuse to grasp the idea of an intelligent life force underlying, underpinning material form. Form dissolves into the one life force. How dare these Essenes insist that spirit and body are the same, that mind and matter are similar, that God and man are one!

The reading is interrupted by Benzaccai, 'If I may be so bold …. Einstein argues the same thing when he states that matter dissolves into molecules, atoms and sub-particles; all is energy or 'field'. Einstein scientifically explains that matter is not solid, ultimately matter is an illusion, it dissolves into energy. The body so real to us is not real at all. 'I and my Father are One', all is conscious energy, all is mind.

'It is time to pause for a walk around Mount Sinai to enjoy the glory of the sunset that no cloud can hide or spoil, suggests Jeremy. This is a place of inspiration as are all mountains.

'Why are mountains associated with inspiration?

'They stir something deep in us; they are a powerful symbol of the towering spirit we aspire to.

They sit for a while at the foot of Sinai quietly absorbed in the contemplation of the sun setting in a glorious orange and pink orb. Breaking the spell Clara suggests that they contact Sananda; there is a burning issue she wishes to discuss with him.

Smiling at her enthusiasm Jeremy consents, 'there is no escaping your inquisitive nature; we may as well call on Sananda'. They settle quietly at the foot of the mountain. His eyes now closed he turns to Clara and smiling invites her to put her question:

Worship of Separateness

'When it is said of Adam and Eve that they eat the fruit this can be inferred to mean that they choose to enter a world of limitations, a state of forgetfulness. They choose to emerge from a state where all things are known and where all things are of God to an experience of separation. Separation is symbolised by the casting out from the Garden of Eden'. (Master Sananda)

Tree of Knowledge of Good & Evil - Master Sananda

'Master Sananda, would you shed light on the meaning of two myths that have perplexed generations, sparked off much speculation, roused much disquiet and inspired great artistic creations: the Tree of Life and the Tree of Knowledge of Good & Evil?

'First of all, these symbols are given to you as archetypes, that is to say, they stir up within each being a deep understanding that is your own understanding. So although I will certainly say a few things about these myths, I am not going to exhaust the possibilities. You also have your own answers within your own understanding. The Tree of Life occurs in many myths and is perhaps a simpler image than its **extension** the Tree of Knowledge. It can be seen, as you already appreciate, as a symbol of yourselves, drawing sustenance from the depth and bearing fruit which you release into the world and which in turn becomes new life. It is simply, I would say, one symbol of the process of life, of which really are all symbols. The myth of the Tree of Knowledge of Good & Evil is more localised. It offers various possibilities of interpretation. As you know, many of your wise men and women have devoted much time to interpreting it and much value has come out of their work, as some new insight can be gained by contemplating it. The myth of the Tree of Knowledge is about the process of leaving the state of Grace that humanity is now engaged in moving towards again, returning to.

'The original state of oneness before separation occurred?

'It is the state where all things are seen as complete in themselves and neither good nor evil, before occurs the descent into the world of Polarity where the knowledge of good and evil is simply the realisation that it is possible to classify the world in this way, to experience the world in this manner. So that when it is said of Adam and Eve that they eat the Fruit this can be inferred to mean that they choose to enter a world of limitations, a state of forgetfulness. They chose to emerge from a state where all things are known and where all things are of God to an experience of separation. Separation is symbolised by the casting out from the Garden of Eden.

'The Fall?

'It is a fall, a form of fall. But I would prefer not to see it as a fall quite so much as a 'jump'. I would say that it was your choice; it was your decision and expressed intention to explore this state of reality, this way of being. And this exploration is drawing to a close, but it will not be seen as having been a waste of time, a detour. In some sense, it will be seen as a detour, for you will return to a state that you had previously known. And so the intervening time, the time when you have been cast out of the Garden, the time when you have been digesting the Fruit, will, in some sense, vanish from you. For part of the experience of eating of the Tree was to move into an experience of time, an experience of mortality, to leave the immortal state which Adam and Eve first knew and to move into the transient state of three scores years and ten. So as you leave all this behind, your perception of time changes and the sense of wasted time go certainly. But the sense of a 'spent' time may also go and you will simply experience the state that you knew before, but with the benefit of the wisdom you have gleaned in the intervening ages. So with that return to the pre-Fall state comes many changes in the way that you perceive the world and of course, you never truly really return to the same place for you have changed on the journey and so the place looks different to you when you come to it again (with a gentle toned down laughter) you appreciate it more, you might say!

'So is it correct to infer that learning can best be achieved here in the world of polarity and conflict rather than in what the Buddhists call the Bardo state, the state between lives? It is possible to learn, they must be learning somewhere?

'Absolutely, all states offer, as far as we know, opportunities for learning. The Earth plane is simply one classroom, if you like! But no, you are quite right, the Bardo and all other states that you know of also offer opportunities for learning. But just as each teacher will teach you a different subject, so each state teaches you something different. But there is a sense now emerging among humanity, of you drawing to the end of what you chose to learn from this particular state – the sense of completion, sense of the lesson coming to an end and you moving on to the next stage'.

The interaction comes to a close and the group remains silent for an instant before resuming their conversation.

'The Tree of Knowledge symbolises the loss of the prior state of Grace, the state of union before separation, before division took place, points out Tara.

'It is something more fundamental, takes up Clara, Sananda is saying that humanity lost that state of Grace but is now returning to it, moving back to it, going home! All is not lost, we simply took a long detour, time was not wasted, we learnt a lot along the way, like the heir in La Fontaine's fable, we may have fallen asleep or got side-tracked, but we are getting to our destination which was also our starting point. Back to the beginning!

'Something else is crucial; he is speaking of time, not duration but time, comments Jeremy. When separation took place, when polarity was registered, the experience of time became a reality. Like polarity, time is an illusion, for behind polarity is unity where time is not. In other words we are returning to a state where neither polarity nor time is experienced, a state beyond time. But polarity and time could only be experienced by the personality. The personality is our best tool to experience and experiment with both, in spite of its inherent flaws.

AMIRIM IN GALILEE

Late evening after a long and tiring drive, they arrive at Amirim. High in the Galilee hills, this peaceful farming community is entirely vegetarian. They were encouraged by

Benzaccai to choose Amirim for the calm beauty of its surrounding. Benzaccai will direct them through the most difficult regions, he will be their guide. A family is expecting them and greet them warmly like old friends. They open their large house; offer an exuberant and warm hospitality and an attractively prepared vegetarian fare. After the meal they sit outside on the veranda, at last they can rest. They feel so at ease with these kind people they want to stay. This place exerts a strange and enchanted influence on them. It all seems so familiar! The next morning after taking leave of their new friends, they resume their journey towards Capernaum. The view from Amirim is startling. They pass through a Nature Reserve, which preserves thousands of species of plants and animals. They rest for a while in the woods, savouring the peace, enjoying the shade beneath the trees and listening to the birds. A well deserved pause before setting off. The hills of Galilee are intensely green. The rocky landscape has been planted with forests and farms produce a wide range of crops. The region enjoys an ideal Mediterranean climate and scenery. And they were under the impression that Israel was a desert! They drive through woods and hills bathed in glorious sunshine. Their guide knows the geography, the history and culture of this region as well as its archaeology. He explains that besides being an anthropologist, he also spends time working on archaeological sites.

'Why anthropology, enquires Jeremy?

'My childhood was a web of deception, I was born in a lie, I grew up in a lie, and I lived a lie. When as a boy I came to Israel I made myself the solemn promise to discover the truth. My parents were illiterate; I had been rounded up with hundreds of other kids from the slums and shoved in to a Hassidic school where we were subjected to much indoctrination.

'This is their mission round the world; they are the Messianic wing, those on whose shoulders the redemption of humanity rests squarely. At least this is their fantasy, inserts Levinson.

'And in my spare time I am also an officer in a reserve unit, adds Benzaccai.

'A complicated existence, definitely not dull, remarks Clara, why archaeology?

'You get used to it, diversity is the spice of life. Why archaeology? Archaeology yields the truth, it exposes the past, it does not compromise. We can no longer rely on the Biblical account; it was interpreted not by historians using rigorous methods, but by a priesthood who had a vested interest in presenting events subjectively shaped by their beliefs. Only a scientific approach can now put the records straight.

'We create the world in which we live. The law-makers of the past, unaware of the rudiments of psychology shaped reality around their own biased views.

'With our thoughts we make the world', quotes Tara.

'Absolutely, in Israel perhaps for the first time in our religious history, it was the Essenes who denounced human subjectivity and our penchant for self-deception, notes Benzaccai.

'You know of the Essenes, exclaims Jeremy?

'Of course, they lived on these shores. This landscape is filled with their august presence. The clerics did not share this impartiality, they witnessed events which did not match up their inherited notions and which baffled them. Unable to read the meaning behind the events, they explained them from their subjective point of view. Naturally, it was flawed and their conclusion outdated. They were out of touch with the times.

'Out of touch then, what about now, exclaims Clara!

'Their rendition cannot be taken seriously by our more mentally-developed generation.

'Yet the past still exerts its fascination and retains its hold on those who come in search of themselves, remarks Jeremy. They call it by different names, the fact remains that they come back. This more rational generation is also in search of the past, the past you denounce.

'We have not yet severed the umbilical cord that keeps us attached to the past. Reason and knowledge tell us that the ancient notion was flawed and imaginary then as it is now, yet we cannot break away, we go on celebrating Passover, the Red Sea passage, the giving of the Law as if they truly happened in the manner the writers wanted us to believe they did, replies Benzaccai with a touch of irritation.

CAPERNUM

They continue their journey to the Sea of Galilee, rich in symbolism and connotations. They arrive at Capernaum, a name that stirs up a wave of emotion and dimly remembered events. The old Capernaum was destroyed, but so steeped in religious history it had to be restored. At the end of the last century the Franciscans acquired the site and began excavation. The reconstructed ruin of the synagogue dominates the town. The friends decide to visit the vestiges of this fine synagogue in black and white marble with Roman-style façade. Then driving out of Capernaum on a winding road, they admire the green and beautiful Galilee, rich in history and steeped in mystery, scene of events of a mystical nature. They prefer to do the rest of the journey on foot. Walking through fields, they climb the Mount of Beatitudes where the basilica set among gardens commands a startling view of the countryside and the lake. They stand in wonder and awe. For centuries, the Sea of Galilee has fuelled the imagination of artists and believers. Now they are standing above it. Are they looking at the Sea of Galilee? Is it a mirage? They remain silent, rapt in thought. Breaking the spell they walk to the chapel where they are greeted by a monk. 'Welcome to our modest abode; I have been expecting you. Do come in, you must be tired; a glass of cool lemonade will refresh you. Which one of you is responsible for the manuscript?

'I am, replies Benzaccai; may I ask how you came to hear about it?

'We have known about it for some time, rumours have dispersed through churches and monasteries, like a sound echoing all over the land that an important scroll was hidden in a monastery and that it contains priceless information for humanity'. And with a sweeping glance at the group, 'you see the time is ripe, it must be now. Everything has converged to the present; you are making this moment. It is a great responsibility you are taking on, but it does not seem to concern you, he adds with an enigmatic smile.

Sensing the ambiguity of the remark, Jeremy replies, 'we do not evade responsibility, we consciously accept our duty to mankind; our very existence is one of service, the recovery of this manuscript is an aspect of it.

The monk looks intently at Jeremy; he muses to himself, 'Is it possible for a group of unbelievers to be entrusted by God with a mission for humanity? This was indeed unsettling. His deep-seated belief in his own mission and chosenness was somewhat shaken.

God made man in his image and likeness

Rabbi Moses is engaged in an intensive programme of study at the monastery under the enlightened guidance of his Master. He writes in his manuscript, 'Master Sanaka, I soon found out, appears to have a special interest in the Old Testament. I put the question to him and he replied with his luminous smile that the study of religion had occupied several of his life times and that this life was no exception. Quite apart from his involvement with the sciences and the arts, he has devoted some academic endeavour to religion. Intrigued, I put the question to him, he replied, 'Religion was for a long time the main source of information about the world. It offered, in coded language references on the origins of the world and the history of long lost humanity. Under the literal form which has captivated the imagination of mankind, is a wealth of knowledge about the true nature of man and his cosmic status which has eluded the most insightful among the seekers. Unable to lift the veil to seek the deeper meaning intended by the Hierarchy, the official scribes simply brushed the surface.

'Were they afraid of what they might find?

'Possibly. There are two divergent strands running through the text. The first is woven around Yahweh, disturbing by his negative outlook on man and the world. He is the sovereign who seeks to dominate. In the god of Genesis the world discovers despotism and inequality; humanity is now divided up into rulers and subjects, a better humanity which seeks to rule and a lesser humanity which accepts and expects to be ruled. The world will explore, through the ages, the theme of despotism, racial advantage, social differences, authority and inequality and the misery arising from all these. In contrast you have the 'God made man in his image and likeness' strand. You have at the outset two divergent views of man and the world. I would like to explore further the theme we examined when we discussed the Cosmic Mind. You may wonder why I wish to return to it, it is central to the Path and you are firmly on it. You have been on this path for several incarnations and this time it must be realised. All is mind as you know, now you must live it, you must experience yourself as mind, as an integral part of the universal Mind. There can be no initiation without this realisation, no liberation from Samsara.

'I have observed the conflicting strands, I have lived that conflict, says Moses!

'Remember that the texts were given by the Hierarchy who, as impartial observers of the world, presented the dominant outlook, the major trend. We all are acquainted with the first verses of Genesis, common heritage of mankind, known by all and yet barely understood. God is the Father who esoterically stands for the All That Is, all pervading, all-knowing.

'But this is precisely what Yahweh is not, he is framed in space and time.

'Precisely Moses. The question neither correctly tackled nor effectively answered is, 'if man is created in the image of God then man is like god, he is endowed with divine qualities, particularly the attributes which form the Trinity, known in all ancient cultures: Will, Intelligence and Love. Shamballa stands for divine Will, the Hierarchy stands for divine Love and Humanity stands for Intelligence. We will narrow down our investigation to the law of mind. Just as the Creator creates by thought alone, so man 'made in his image and likeness' also has the capacity to create by thought.

'We have covered this ground, notes Moses puzzled. The implications of this law are far-reaching. If man inherited his Creator's mind, if he shares the same creative power, then he can create by thought alone anything he wants.

'Yes, the implications are serious, too daunting or too intrepid to contemplate in earlier times. They took fright, if they acknowledged their own power; the lesser god would punish them. You see man was held back by his own power, fearful of his own magnitude!

'We let go of the creative power of our mind, we caved in to the threat of the lesser god and the fear of man!

'But you relinquished something else: responsibility for the nature, quality and content of your thought. Thought can also be destructive; your troubled history illustrates the reality of this Law; it conclusively proves the destructive power of thought. As you aligned with the demigod, you lost sight of the universal Mind, your fundamental mind! Disempowered man settled for a diminished state. Man as a spiritual being shares in the cosmic Mind, but man as mortal being has forgotten his primordial magnitude. And he passes on to the next generation his cramped view of himself. Distressed by his powerlessness he seeks the protection of a 'higher power', a demigod to adore, to mollify, to resent. A transfer of power takes place. Having stripped himself of his innate power, man invests that power onto his demigods. You invested Yahweh with your own divine power, divesting yourself to robe a temporal being. If this is not heresy!

'But this is only the start, continues Sanaka. Now that man is firmly established in his mortal status, he must lay down rules of conduct, moral, social and religious laws that all must obey. He will raise armies to secure them and build courts of law to punish offenders. You recall the aims of the Revolution. It was a partial attempt at reversing this state of affairs. Man today is claiming back some of the power he invested in his rulers and gods, he is also rediscovering the forgotten universal principles the Hierarchy taught on the shores of the Sea of Galilee.

'The Revolutionary movement confounded my teachers back in Vilna; they condemned it, interpreting it as a move away from order and into chaos. Orthodoxy approves of absolute power, it seems.

'That's right, the spiritual principles of freedom, equality and liberty are a threat to those in power, be it in politics or religion. What is the outcome of the loss of the law of mind, I invite your analysis, Moses?

'I can think of two outcomes striking in their nature. Man having lost his primal power needs a light to travel in the dark. So the first outcome is the need for a strong deity to protect us, the other follows from the first, if we need a god we inevitably need rules, precepts and a court of law to keep men abiding.

'Excellent deduction Rabbi Moses, you are a credit to your Talmud teachers. You see, when man forgets his divinity, he is 'fallen' and as finite individual he must be coerced into behaving in a manner acceptable to his society. Any infraction to the code is severely punished either by death or banishment.

'The more coercion the less likely he is to use his freedom of choice and personal responsibility, suggests Moses.

'You spot the paradox, teases Sanaka?

'The more precepts, the lesser his sense of moral responsibility! First, the group takes over responsibility for action and the individual is less likely to measure the impact his thoughts have. Second, having lost the memory of his initial power he is unable to anticipate the long term outcome of his thinking. But what am I saying, he is not permitted to think, the thinking is imposed on him!

'Well done, my son! Man is aware only of his pain, sorrow and tribulation. He does not begin to visualise the thread that extends from his present distress to the cause. The cause is lost in the distant past. And because the cause is unknown to him a third protagonist enters the stage of this human drama, Fate. This force is irrational, incomprehensible. Fate strikes without reason and as man abandons his creative power he needs to justify his situation, rationalise his destiny.

'Where is the cause? It extends so far back in time that it may not even exist.

'But it does, that it the whole point! The cause may stretch back 300,000 years, 4000 years or 200 years, but it remains the cause and for so long as it is not dealt with consciously it will continue to haunt you. The cause lies in the depth of your collective consciousness and you have the urgent duty to excavate your group mind and bring it forth to the light of day. There can be no liberation as long as the truth is ignored. In future, the law of mind will be identified and ancient methods of healing rediscovered. The link between negative thought and sickness will be once again understood, and as thought can cause illness, we are going to restore the power of thought to heal.

'Because the law of evolution works inevitably through repeated incarnations, sums up Moses, it is possible that a disease contracted in one life time may have its cause in former incarnations. This indicates continuity but also something that I find most disturbing, nothing is ever lost, nothing is ever forgotten. We return into incarnation to adjust, atone, align, adapt, correct, polish, and improve.

'Indeed, this is often the case. Masters instruct that disease is mostly of karmic origin, but there is also the collective distress of entire groups. And this distress has been veiled, denied or distorted by the attitudes of the group and the way the group perceives its nature and role. So the picture becomes increasingly complicated, each generation adding on to the distorted view of the generation before.

They sense that Sananda's response is to be startling. They intuitively know more than they realise, for the question touches at the heart of the great

Essenes & Jews – ideological differences – Master Sananda

What about Essenes and Jews? The question is formulated after deep reflection and centres on the split along the divide between soul and personality.

'What features of the Hebrew worldview were unacceptable to the Essenes of 2000 years ago, asks Clara? Was it the claim to divine selection and insistence on separation? Or was it the fact that they bent Moses' instruction to bring it into alignment with their own outlook?

'The Essenes thought to be guardians of a particular aspect of the truth; they were safeguarding a particular truth they saw in danger of being lost. To some extent, they felt that certain sections had a vested interest in extinguishing those strands of the truth, which they sought to safeguard. This was the source of the friction between them. From the Jewish point of view, the Essenes were heretical. So the Essenes also felt trapped, they saw themselves as safeguarding strands of the truth, too. In some respects the two perspectives were incompatible. The origins of this go back a long way.

The Jewish people, continues Sananda, saw themselves as having by right, hegemony, or a role of leadership over the other peoples of Earth. They had a sense of **having been** chosen for this role, by virtue of their genetic inheritance which led to often substantially greater ability than some of the peoples around them, at least in their own perception …. One cannot accept this as an objective truth. They felt they had a leadership role to perform by god-given right. Their perception at that time was that this leadership function should be passed down genetically through time. The Essenes, on the other hand, were in essence totally unconcerned with the role of genetic inheritance. They were much more concerned with spiritual inheritance, that is to say, they sought to pass on wisdom to those who displayed the spiritual characteristics they sought, regardless of what their genetic lineage might be. Since many were Jewish themselves, for those who followed main stream Jewish thought, this was - from the point of view of the religious leadership - a dangerous dilution of the genetic spark which carried those abilities they most sought to preserve through history. Without going back to the historical origins of these two views, you can see how there would be a powerful conflict between those who believed in a handing down of a lineage, a spiritual handing down, a recognition of the soul which inhabits the body, regardless of the genetic origins of the body, and on the other hand, a physical handing down, down the family line which must be kept pure because particular qualities were stored in the genes. Ultimately neither of these view points is incorrect, they both had validity. There were good reasons for each of the two camps to hold the views that they did, but nevertheless, most of those involved were unable to incorporate both views simultaneously, they were too contradictory to be sustained alongside together, hence the conflict.

'Master Sananda, you mention the genetic inheritance and the passing down, through the blood line, of essential characteristics, yet the Hebrews were keen enough to absorb other people's views. Quite apart from integrating ideas and beliefs from outside, they have drawn to themselves people genetically different, strangers who have added their own gene pool. It seems that the genetic argument does not hold.

'It is not proved to be a viable way of achieving the goals they sought. It remained a strand of thought, but only one strand. It turned out to be rather unworkable. In practice to keep a genetic strain pure on this Planet is not feasible, because of the way you all interact, nevertheless it remained at that time and since, one of the core principles that Judaism sought to sustain or extend itself through. It is seen as a route toward a particular goal, to keep the genetic lineage intact.

'In order to keep the lineage pure they must have had deep conviction in their mission. What convinced them so resolutely?

'They retained memories, partly conscious, increasingly not conscious of their origins. Humanity has come from a number of different sources; there have been genetic input into the human race at different times in its history. The Jewish people was the recipient of a particular strand of DNA which contained particular types of information concerning the role to be played by those people who had this aspect of DNA within them. The safeguarding of this DNA strand took on the character of a goal; it offered the possibility of exerting a kind of stewardship over the rest of humanity.

'Was the intention one of political domination encouraged by their singular genetic inheritance?

'The inward intention would be benign. Early in their history, they were distinguished from the rest of humanity with whom they shared the Planet by some characteristics, among which generally superior abilities and intelligence … but not always. This had to do with that particular type of DNA. Hence the desire to maintain the strand of DNA within the family tree.

'Leadership because of genetic advantage. This sounds surprisingly modern!

'This strand appeared as a goal. It offered the possibility of exerting a kind of stewardship over the rest of humanity.

'But why them, why not other human groups?

'Part of the purpose of giving to some people and not to others those specific qualities, was that other groups, not living on the Planet at that time, wished to observe the consequences. They had a plan. Those who set this experiment off, sent and put forth of themselves onto this Planet, the people who became the Jewish people. They sent some of their own people with specific abilities to follow track through time - a long time scale - in the belief that their people would move to the fore, would come to be regarded as superior in term of leadership. So a strong deeply-held inherited wish of those people to play that role. But because of the way things have been operating on this Planet for thousands of years, the picture has become much more complicated. This gives you some of the reasons why they have sustained this goal for such a long period of time.

'It looks like a conspiracy on the part of the galactic civilisation you mention to exercise leadership. Did they have a political or a spiritual goal?

'Neither political nor spiritual. They speak of leadership.

The interview with Sananda comes to an end, leaving the group numb. The same thought is churning in the mind of all. How was all this possible, had they heard right, were they under a spell? Finally Clara erupts, 'leadership, bloodline and survival! It's all to do with the temporal world. All to do with this world, no transcendence! We are fanatical about extending the biological experiment started aeons ago by a galactic civilisation and we do not even know it! Dominion of Earth through genetic enhancement discreetly hid under a moral obligation to lesser humanity. But what we do not know is that we are keeping alive the dream of domination of a stellar civilisation!

HEBRON

Sin & Atonement - a pessimistic view

News arrives the following morning at St Katherine Monastery that Benzaccai has not been seen at the university. His wife rings Jeremy in distress. He has never missed a day at work nor has he gone anywhere without telling her first of his destination and intentions.

'Do you have any idea where he might be, she asks in a trembling voice?' No but they will search for him. As they are leaving, the telephone rings. Jeremy goes back in to answer. He returns minutes later smiling, 'Benzaccai is fine, he is in Hebron with doctor Suleiman who invites us to visit him; he has the next chapters of The Hebrew Gods.

'Is Benzaccai staying at the doctor's at the moment?

'The doctor was brief and deliberately so I felt, I preferred not to question. But my impression is that Benzaccai is not with him at the minute.

They call his wife to put her mind at rest. The group, concerned for the safety of Benzaccai set off to call on Dr Suleiman who knows Benzaccai' s whereabouts and will certainly reassure them.

'How long will it take to get from Sinai to Hebron, asks Clara who suffers from travel sickness?

'We shall make several stops to give you a chance to stretch your legs, promises Jeremy with kind concern.

They stop in a village for the night. The next morning they head for the doctor's house where they are greeted by a mild-mannered, courteous and smartly dressed man who speaks excellent English. 'I can detect a hint of surprise, he observes with a smile, I studied medicine in the United States and after qualifying came back to work for my people. They need all the help they can get. I am not a politician, which I am sure is a blessing, he adds with yet another smile. I am a simple country doctor but also a thinker, a seeker after the truth and a keen student of Sufism.

'I too am a student of Sufism, says Johansson with visible satisfaction, it is a pleasure to meet a fellow traveller on the road to enlightenment.

'I did not know there was an awareness of Sufism in the West, admits the doctor with joyous surprise.

'It is in many ways the foundation platform of Western civilisation, as you know, explains Johansson. In the Middle Ages Sufi scholars and a few distinguished Hebrew scholars spread Greek science and philosophy. It was the first Golden Age of Spain in which Sufism played a crucial role. I am also convinced that the Kabala which appears out of nowhere in 12th century Spain can also be attributed to Sufi scholarship.

'This is a bold statement, smiles graciously Suleiman.

'Bold it may be. The Wisdom in Sufism is being rediscovered as we are forging ahead into the New Age, a time of change for mankind.

'We are among friends, says the doctor visibly relieved. I asked you to come to me in spite of the difficulties involved, because Benzaccai asked me to.

'Where is he, asks Jeremy concerned?

'He is not with me at this moment, he stayed in my house for a night, a long night we spent talking about the manuscript and drinking tea. Concerned for his safety I sent him on to Jerusalem to stay with my brother, also a doctor.

'We must go to him, butts in Tara.

'This may take some planning, replies the doctor. You see, Benzaccai is not a popular figure right now, in Jerusalem for religious reasons, here for political reasons in spite of the fact that he is a staunch liberal and humanitarian, or perhaps because of it. He insisted I call you to give you the next chapter of the manuscript. Before we begin we shall have some tea. His wife brings tea, honey and almond cakes which they all enjoy.

'Are you ready, asks the doctor?

He closes the curtains and locks all doors. 'We can never be too careful'.

He turns the key in the drawer of a carved desk and draws a few handwritten pages. Slowly, with reverence he begins to read the text. Master Sanaka discusses with Moses the Day of Atonement.

'What is the role of the Day of Atonement when we are commanded to fast, pray and repent for negative actions performed during the year, asks Moses?

'To regret negative actions is a personal thing. Genuine regret springs from the evolved individual who sets himself high moral and spiritual standards. When he falters he is overcome with regret for having failed to live up to his principles. This is why an imposed day of penitence is rather futile; the unevolved does not know what he should feel guilty about. He abides by the rules for fear of the group and terror of retribution from the vengeful deity. After the fast he returns home to repeat the same behaviour.

He has not grasped the basic idea of transformation; he must change in a fundamental way. He does not feel the urgent need to review his thinking and actions. He simply had an empty stomach for a day! This is what happened in the Temple of Jerusalem with the priesthood and the money-lenders. Fast they did, pray they did but to no avail, they had no comprehension that change is imperative. Without change there is no evolution. Evolution is the Law of the universe.

'To pray for forgiveness is pointless.

'Not necessarily, says Sanaka, if regret springs from the depth of man, it is not pointless. But I understand what your question implies: no entity outside you can forgive you or punish you. There is no judge, no prosecutor, no defence, and no executioner 'out there' to punish or reward you, no agency to alter the course of your existence. Your life course was traced by you. Cosmic Law states that no being in the cosmos can alter it!

'Any request is pointless, insists Moses.

'Selfish request usually is, but deeply felt request for clarification, for knowledge and progress is not pointless. The Masters search the world for the tiny points of light men are and when they detect genuine endeavour, they respond. Do ask for help at all times, Moses, do not hesitate, the Masters will surely hear you, so long that the assistance you request has to do with your spiritual progress and not personal gain.

'So trying to change our life conditions is futile, concludes Moses.

'Trying to change life conditions is futile if you petition some extra-Planetary entity to do it for you. It must come from you and you alone. Your life conditions are of your own making, they are the outcome of your thoughts and actions over many life times. Our life conditions are our creation, they reflect our nature, expose our emotions, and divulge the thought forms we have entertained over many lives. The day will surely come when skilled individuals will diagnose deep-seated life problems in the same way a physician diagnoses a malady by studying the symptoms. Looking at life problems and their resultant health disorders, they will be able to disentangle the mental and emotional problems that are rooted.

'To change our life conditions through prayer and rituals is pointless.

'Would you expand on this, smiles Sanaka?

'If our life conditions are the outcome of our thoughts over many life times, who can change what we set into motion? In order to change our conditions we have to change our thinking. No god is responsible for the quality of our thoughts, nor can he change our mind for us, we have to do it.

'Excellent grasp, Moses. Changing life circumstances by your own endeavour is the raison d'être of reincarnation. Man returns to Earth in order to change his nature, refine, polish, chisel and smooth out sharp angles. He is like Michelangelo who intuitively glimpsed the form of David, the ideal form, concealed in a block of marble; all he had to do was to chisel it out. Man harbours the perfect image of himself. He has to sculpt it out of the raw block of clay he is at present. He does this over countless lives and without the help of the gods, in spite of his naïve beliefs. This slow and thorny process of change may or may not alter completely the outer circumstances in this life but will change everything for his next incarnation. Change must come from within with the full sanction and intelligent grasp of man. Change is the law of life. Life is perpetual change; life is a stream ever-flowing, ever-moving, ever-changing. When the law of life is ignored trouble ensues.

'What is the mechanism at work?

'When you solidify the life impulse, when you arrest the vital flow of life, when you discontinue its course, when you carve in stone a rule that is obsolete the moment it is engraved because the natural inclination of life is motion, then trouble ensues. Life forges ahead to its ultimate destination like a river flows to the sea. Evolution is written into all things. Have you ever collected sun rays in a wooden box? Does a river flow away from the sea?

'What happens when we try?

'You get the legends you read with devout awe in your story books! These stories were included by the Hierarchy for their emblematic content. Their symbolic meaning is plain for all to see: you get the sad stories of pain, suffering, disillusionment, abandonment, disaster, anger and resentment. Life will not be bottled; life will not be imprisoned in a wooden box, a room, a temple or anywhere else. If you resist change, change will come, but it will come from outside without your consent. It will be imposed by the forces of evolution.

'The day of fast can be dispensed with, concludes Moses?

'Again it depends on the intention. If you hope to gain favours and rewards, you are wasting your time. The undeveloped man who implores his god but remains selfish, grasping, envious and sensuous is wasting his time. He simply grows angry at his god.

If he refuses to improve his nature, then fasting can be dispensed with. It all has to do with progress.

'Then fasting and petitioning are futile whether we change or whether we do not change. In the first case we demand favours from outside without effecting change, in the second case we embark on a programme of change which emancipates us from the need of outside interference.

'Excellent grasp as always, rejoices Sanaka. It all stems from a key misunderstanding; humans have stumbled and fallen over this misunderstanding for ages. The underlying assumption as always is that you are puppets on a string that an outside entity pulls at his leisure. Man, you are told is ignorant, corrupt, lazy and easily led astray. Sinful man must submit to the deity. His reason for living is to 'do & obey', his ambition is to 'walk before the lord', and his life goal is to gratify his god with the 'go & multiply'. All these demonstrate a profoundly negative view of man: man is insignificant, he must be compliant, clean and 'doing'. What a demeaning view of human nature!

'I was urged, with implied threat, never to try to comprehend the ways of god, recalls Moses, 'do not question, do not doubt, this is idolatrous, you must accept, this is your greatest duty, god knows best. You must have complete faith, you must bend in total submission'. Have I heard these phrases often in my life! Ignorance, obedience, surrender, capitulation were hailed as the greatest spiritual qualities a man could aspire to!

'This is the key misunderstanding and one which has cost you several millennia of suffering. You are the perennial pawns of fate, 'prisoners of the Planet'; captives of both the astral and physical planes of existence. Our individual blueprint for earthly existence is drawn by us before birth, no change can occur on the Day of Atonement, no change except in your thinking. Do tell me about that day, asks Sanaka.

'Are you interested, asks Moses surprised?

'Only because if affects you. You need to examine it in order to release it. That which is not understood tends to cling to our emotional self.

'We fast in expiation for the sins committed during the year'. The fasting, the praying, the expiating, the sinning, the threat, the horn blowing, all seem so embarrassingly ineffectual and archaic. He thinks, 'I am a prehistoric man explaining prehistoric practices to a Master of the Wisdom'. He feels sick at the pit of his stomach, he wants to lie down and die. Sanaka observes him closely and respecting his pain looks away at

113

the white peaks. Moses finally collects himself and to conceal his emotion asks, 'Master Sanaka, are the events recounted in the Books to be received with trust, or should they be dismissed pending a time when they can be deciphered by the Masters who gave them?

'I was coming to that. The ancient scribes did record events but events filtered though their imperfect intellect, inherited beliefs, inherent prejudices, attitudes and predetermined views. The original Sumerian texts, foundation of the Old Testament are modified to confirm old beliefs.

'What did truly happen, enquires Moses?

'Darkness hit the Planet, the innocence of the past was no more, the light that humanity knew was veiled. The soul, Eve, plunged into darkness.

'She is cursed to bear children in pain, says Moses.

'As always the problem is one of interpretation. Patriarchy seizes a universal myth and adapts it to suit its end. From that moment on the cosmic myth is confiscated by patriarchy. The truth is hidden deep into the fabric of the texts to be deciphered at a later time by more advanced minds. No sin is committed; no vengeance is inflicted by the deity on man for his wickedness. The blame for the incoming negative forces is shifted on the confused victim, man. Man is not the cause of the disaster; he has not eaten any 'fruit'. The commentators fail to grasp the allegory. Man is blamed for something outside his control. The world is turned upside down. It is not man sinning against the gods as much as the gods sinning against man!

'What did happen?

'Dark conceptual energies spread to envelop the Planet, pervading the energy field of both man and Earth, causing confusion and distortion in the mind of man who has lost the memory of his true identity and origin. He no longer is able to make sense of what is happening in his world. He believes himself to be inadequate and responsible for his decline and impoverished state.

'Modern psychology is born, bursts out Levinson, it does not originate with Freud and James but with the biblical commentators! They offer us the familiar ferment of guilt, fear, self-blame. These malign energies are already present and fused'. Sensing the audacity of his outburst, he apologises.

'You are right, doctors and psychologists have to deal with the long term effects of those waves of low frequencies that hit Earth long ago, smiles Suleiman. Early man was unable to explain them, he had no antidote; he could neither assimilate them nor release them. A plausible explanation had to be given that would appease his disquiet. I picked up a few points, roots of modern psychosomatic medicine. 'Change must come from within with the full approval and intelligent grasp of man. Change is to be fostered. Change is the law of life. Life is perpetual movement; life is a stream of energy ever-flowing, ever-moving, ever-changing. When the law of life is ignored trouble ensues'.

'He also says something which held my attention, notes Clara: 'When you solidify the life impulse, when you crystallise the inherent flow of life, when you attempt to discontinue its course ... trouble ensues'. We see this in our counselling room everyday. Life is frozen; people are arrested in a certain mode of feeling. They modulate the minor keys of pain.

'There is more, quotes Suleiman, 'Man is blamed for the crime of his gods. The world is turned upside down. It is not man sinning against the gods as much as the gods sinning against man. Man has learned to be passive, submissive, sensitive, resigned. He has abdicated his divine nature.

'Sufism is the Timeless Wisdom and it must be as painful to you as it is to us to observe the damage perpetrated by the patriarchal ego, says Johansson.

'I am also a doctor of the soul. I endeavour to return to my patients what they have lost, their innate freedom and responsibility, the sense of their inherent divinity and power.

'Sanaka anticipates modern psychology, continues Levinson, I quote, ''Man inept and corrupt must submit to the deity who knows best. His glory is to 'do & obey', his ambition is to submit and 'walk before the lord', and his achievement is to accomplish countless acts ... A profoundly negative view of man. What a demeaning view of human nature!' Modern psychology is contained in these few sentences.

'The field of abnormal psychology is contained in the interpretations of the opening verses of Genesis, replies the biblical expert Johansson. The suffering of humanity is held in a nutshell. Infinite, deathless, timeless man reduced to 'do & obey', 'go & multiply'! A tragic fall!

'And we wonder why so many are distressed, exclaims Clara!

'Self-blame, sin and shame are at the root of it all, replies Levinson, I guess.

'You guess right, agrees the doctor. This is the reply of Sanaka, I read on: 'In ancient Sumer, the Day of Atonement – Kippuru - was prescribed as an antidote to man's flawed and sinful nature. Later it reappears in Hebrew practice with the same claim. Man is now on the familiar treadmill of appeasement: 'adore, sacrifice and obey'. Man must expiate for imaginary sins he must believe he has committed. He is responding to negative forces over which he has no control'.

'To insist on man's sinful nature and demand that he wallows in fear is to keep him guilty, disposed to defeat. Fear and defeat are interlaced, interrupts Levinson, who as a therapist encounters the effects of fear and guilt in his work. These negative energies are insidious, causing not only emotional disquiet but physical disorders too.

'We will discuss this at length later, says the doctor, emotional causation of disease - psychosomatic medicine - is my field of interest, may I read on:

'Do go on, Moses, smiles Sanaka encouragingly, it will soon be over. Tell me more about the Day of Atonement, the most holy day of all.

'The horn is blown to cast the devil away from the midst of the community. Israel is purified and readmitted within the circle of god. The Book of Life is open and god inscribes our names for another year. We go on living to the extent that we please god and perform the duties he has ordered. The bulk of practices stem from the Talmud not from god, though they pass for divinely given. Neither Moses nor Solomon would recognise them; they are a human creation with the approval of god who manifests in the 'voices' heard.

'Human law endorsed by God, chuckles Sanaka! And they want you to believe it? How can laws that originate in the mortal mind of man be sanctioned by God? You see, man in order to impose his will ascribes it to his god, and the people trust, revere, abide, obey, observe, suffer and die!

'Their god-approved rules are just as biding today, says Moses. I know! I admit with sorrow that I thrashed them out! I still cannot come to terms with it. I wonder if the infamous felons of the world can appease their conscience more readily than I can mine'. Deeply moved he is about to break down but controls himself with effort.

'Man hoists himself to his gods' pinnacle, continues Sanaka observing Moses closely and assessing his response. Man playing at being god, man emulating his gods or is it the gods emulating man? You have played this game so earnestly for so long! The truth is very different, before coming down to Earth, before choosing a suitable body we construct an energy shape, a plan for our lives. We write the script and we sketch out the characteristics we need in order to go through certain experiences. It can be likened to the architect's plan for his next building; material, measurements, textures, colours, all is there. So you see it is impossible for any extra-planetary entity to change the course of your life on the Day of Atonement, because that course was decided by you and by you alone, in association with those who are willing to act out the chosen drama with you.

The Serpent fosters man's freedom

'Master Sanaka, we have reflected on the core issues of Genesis. You have left out one of the main protagonists, Satan. May I ask why?

'You are now ready to grapple with the Serpent, smiles Sanaka his radiant smile. In the opening verses of Genesis we come unstuck as we confront our own confusion. The Serpent explains to Eve that eating the Fruit will not cause her death and that god will not implement his threat to destroy her. He is right, Yahweh surrenders the moment man recognises the wisdom of the Serpent and discards his order. This is god's defeat and man's affirmation.

'What does the Serpent stand for? Why does Satan take this form?

'As you imply, there is no serpent at all! Others will explain this myth differently. Some would say that the Serpent is the embodiment of evil. I would say the reverse; the Serpent is reminding man of his essential autonomy. Yahweh denies man the freedom that he himself enjoys, while the Serpent gives it back without imposed restrictions. The scholars were really perplexed: 'should man be free or should he be dictated to? This is the central question they are confronted with. Their answer is predictable: they do not recognize man's divinity and his innate perfection. Man must be coerced and controlled as he is incapable of making decisions on matters regarding the conduct of his life. Satan adopts the opposite stance; he recognises man's essential ability to take charge of his life. In this allegory the rabbis put across their own views inevitably endorsed by their god. You do know that the Old Testament is built around selfhood, the mounting dynamism and assertiveness of the self?

'Is the experience of the self such a disaster?

'It does not lie outside the Plan, if this is what you imply. It was intended this way and the Hierarchy records the development of the self from its first whisper to its full-blown expression. It is an objective account, an impartial presentation of the development of the self.

'Is the Old Testament just an objective record of the rise of the self?

'Its main justification. Still, as you know several verses describe the creation of the world. You boast a profound knowledge of the origin of the universe. Yet it is only the creation of the Solar System that is given in Genesis. It hints at a former Earth and a prior Solar System. Following this partial creation comes the long and tedious recounting of the generations of man.

'There is more to it.

'Three main themes emerge: the creation of the Solar System, the history of lost humanity and the development of the self cloaked in allegorical form.

'You leave out a key player in the drama, Yahweh perceived as the god of Creation, Yahweh creator of time and matter. The 'go & multiply' is eloquent! The purpose of man's existence is to 'multiply'. This your ancestors believed, to them Yahweh is the god of physicality and man is trapped in the material world. There is no essential freedom, no way out. Not so with the Serpent who convinces Eve of her fundamental autonomy. Eve fears the disapproval of Yahweh. This is crucial since the soul is in physicality, in Samsara; Eve hesitates for fear of antagonising the god of Samsara. That is, she refrains from breaking natural law. She has forgotten that she transcends nature.

'Do the orders emanate from the Hierarchy?

'Never, never! The Hierarchy never instructs. Coercion and control originate with the self, never with the soul. And the Hierarchy operates at soul level. They communicate with man on the mental plane, never on the emotional plane. Fear is of the emotional plane. The Masters never dictate, 'thou shall not' and 'do & obey' do not stem from them. The Masters respect man's autonomy for they are aware of the divine majesty conscious in man.

'They never order, never judge, never decree, yet we have thick volumes of laws that order, judge and decree, mumbles Moses.

'Draw your own conclusion! In the allegory, man dares to rebel against god, and this first act of insurrection is also the first act of freedom. Yahweh stands for absolute power and is revered for it! Eve rebels against arbitrary rule.

'Today the god of nature is medical science not Yahweh, burst out Clara unable to refrain herself. Genetics tell us that we are our genes, that heredity makes us what we are, that disease is an act of nature, that human aberration is encoded in our genetic make up and that there is nothing we can do to change that! Determinism in science, philosophy and psychology has its roots in the Book of Genesis. The cancerous individual is a 'cancer victim'; the heavy smoker who needs a triple bypass is a victim of heart disease! No allowance is made for the man inside the body. What rift, what split, what rupture, what discord in the mind and heart disrupted the life force and unsettled the natural process, replacing order with chaos? It is the body that 'catches' a disease and the individual is a passive recipient, victim of the laws of nature that he does not comprehend and certainly does not control! To try and explain that degenerative diseases and others are the product of our thinking, attitudes and emotions is anathema, this goes against the trend. Natural law governs and is implacable.

'The god of nature is Yahweh, echoes Levinson! This is the message secreted in the opening verses of Genesis. He is worshipped today as never before. He controls our minds, takes cover under social norms, animates social values and vitalises ideologies, theories and doctrines. Graduates swear allegiance not so much to Hippocrates as to Yahweh, unknowingly.

'I am sorry for the outburst, apologises Clara.

'We value your outbursts, laughs Jeremy.

The reading resumes, 'The rabbis do not see it that way, interrupts Moses, for them man has committed the ultimate sin in resisting the absolute rule of god. Man should be subservient to power, obedient to authority. They compiled painstakingly thirty-six volumes of rules that pass for the unalterable, permanent word of god. They took side with Yahweh against man!

'In the Greek myth, Prometheus steals the fire from the gods to give it to man. His concern was for man; his responsibility was mankind, not the gods!

'The humanism, rationalism and idealism of the Greek mind was foreign to us, Greek civilisation was derided as 'darkness', reflects Moses.

'It is this pessimistic view of man that has prevailed, continues Sanaka. Gone is Satan's recognition of man's right to choose. Centuries ago in the land of the 'one people' and the 'one god', the simple, uncultured masses rebelled as had done Eve. They wanted to keep the many manifestations of the divine, the world in all its diversity, the many facets of life. They had always worshipped the gods to whom they turned for consolation in Egypt, in Sumer and now in Canaan.

'Master, you do not appear to esteem monotheism, yet it is held as the greatest achievement.

'By whom, smiles Sanaka? By the people who invented it, naturally! Caligula would praise tyranny just as Pericles would praise democracy. Monotheism is repressive, man has been experimenting with various forms of rule and he will do so until he wakes up to himself.

'I thought of it as our great achievement, a major landmark, says Moses.

'You thought what you were told to think! The simple people of Judea showed a measure of freedom. They were unresponsive to Yahweh, they knew in their simplicity that he was on a level with the gods they trusted. Buddha stated that the gods do exist but that they are no better than we are. The gods, explained Buddha, are like earthlings, they live in illusion, not having realised the true nature of Reality. We are better off, we share in the divine attributes, we have a set of chakras dotted along the spine, spiritual centres in the brain, meridians in which circulates the cosmic life force and the Heart is the gateway to the visible and invisible universes. The chakras draw the cosmic Life Force; they act as intermediaries between the spiritual plane and the physical plane. We have all it takes; we need no external intervention from gods or men. We are complete.

'At the time Buddha was teaching man how to come into the fullness of his own being, the priesthood in Jerusalem was denying man' s innate freedom and demanded that we revere the one god they supported, notes Moses.

'Monotheism was not thought through. Who is this being with human flaws and mood swings? Who is this god who orders the execution of entire groups, who makes wars in which all must be destroyed, men, women, children, cattle even crops! Let's be realistic, one Samsara god is as good as another, this the masses knew!

'May we interrupt the reading for a while; we have to reflect, suggests Jeremy. I feel that we need a refreshing break.

'A glass of lemonade will do wonders, suggests the doctor. Minutes later his wife enters with cool lemonade and almond cakes. She is invited to join in the discussion but she declines gracefully.

'We have come a long way, begins Jeremy. The mind of modern man has made giant strides forward. We are better equipped to receive revelations now the Hierarchy is drawing closer than at any time since the days of Atlantis. Under the inspiration of the

Masters we are rewriting the Old Testament, lifting the veil of symbolism to penetrate the form that has confused generations.

'We have evolved a critical mind, we are endowed with reason and now more than ever before, we are able to grasp the knowledge the Hierarchy refrained from giving out in the past, simply because man was not yet developed, explains the Sufi doctor.

'You did rather well eight centuries ago, remarks Johansson!

'We had the Ancient Wisdom, confirms the doctor, the priceless wisdom of the ages we shared with the mystical East. This enabled us to reach a degree of culture and sophistication unknown since the days of Greek Enlightenment.

'The Masters who guided the faltering steps of our remote ancestors are returning to teach us again, says Levinson. This time they are addressing us as intelligent and responsible adults. Perhaps for the first time since the days of Atlantis they are using the language of science and philosophy to convey their ideas. They gave our perplexed ancestors at Sinai limited instructions intended to encourage them to behave less destructively.

Good & Evil

The reading restarts. 'World mythologies recount stories of a hero who is confronted with almost insurmountable hurdles. The hero must withdraw from the world and live in solitude. In the wilderness - symbolic of the material world - he faces an awesome challenge: the devil'. Rabbi Moses identifies with the hero but needs some clarification.

'Master Sanaka, mythologies narrate similar events; it is as if the heroes in most cultures must experience similar tribulations, why?

'Sound question. Encapsulated in the myths are certain great truths and these are progressively unravelled by man as he progresses on the Path. At one level of meaning, the plight of the hero is the plight of everyman in the course of his evolution, through time. The hero is finally an initiate when he has surmounted all the hurdles placed before him. He is now master over his body, mind and emotions. He has attained mastery over his mortal self. He embodies one of the primary qualities of the soul, power. But the myth is not limited to the hero, the myth applies to all men, for all men travel the same road, must suffer the same hardship and confront the same obstacles. How else would he know himself? How else would he attain self-mastery?

'So the terrible evil that befalls man may not be evil after all.

'Excellent deduction, Moses. We'll come to this point in a moment. First let us explore evil. Evil, the 'devil', is not the dark entity with pointed ears and red eyes, but that hostile force in the world which is intent on keeping man's soul entrapped in physicality, imprisoned in the lower emotions of fear and guilt. The 'devil' is the force that prompts man into thinking that materiality is all there is, that any quest for the higher reality is superstitious nonsense.

'The devil is the force of materialism, enquires Moses?

'What else could it be? The materialism of separateness, fear, guilt, authority and obedience.

'Why materialism at all?

'Because separateness excludes. This is a deviation in the eyes of the soul. The soul is all-inclusive; the nature of the soul is empathy, understanding, tolerance and acceptance. The soul does not know separation, division, authority and obedience.

'If it is not of the soul than it can only be of the self.

'That's right my son. Materialism because it affirms the supremacy of the material nature of man. Physicality is not all there is, man is a cosmic being who transcends matter, space and time.

'But Master, man lives and functions in a material world. He is also bound by customs, traditions, beliefs and prejudices.

'Indeed, matter and beliefs hold him tight. They suggest to him ways of behaving and believing which may be quite alien to his own nature. He feels imprisoned and the temptation is to yield to outside pressure, society is stronger than the individual and the pull of matter irresistible. His group may uplift him when it gives him beliefs which ennoble him and principles that are life-enhancing. But group beliefs often are of a kind that restrain his innate talents, inhibit his potential, suppress self-expression and disable his intelligence. Man is diminished as his soul is muzzled. These beliefs drag him down deeper into the darkness of matter. Controlled through guilt and fear man is reminded of his sinful nature, his weakness, his corruption. He may be forgiven for thinking of himself as a play thing in the hands of fate!

'Is it evil to remind man of his weakness?

'No, so long as you give him a rational method and a spiritual discipline to help him overcome his weakness! If you insist on his weakness and offer him only dogmas and rituals, you have done nothing except push him deeper into darkness. Evil is darkness.

'Instructing and punishing are not interchangeable, Master?

'Absolutely not! Buddha instructed humanity he did not punish. He listed the causes of suffering, elicited the nature of man and explained the purpose of life in incarnation. He proposed a doctrine of liberation built around his insight into human nature. He blended cosmic law with insight into man's nature. He applied his theory to himself. Punishment, guilt, fear and blame have never worked and never will. Man needs to be reminded of his higher nature; he must be awakened to his cosmic dimension.

'Why is man continued to be presented as sinful and primarily bad?

'This is a question you should put to those who endorse the old world view, giggles Sanaka! You approach your god with lavish images of power and exaggerated images of authority. What has escaped your attention is that he never is associated with the power of love. He is the personification of power but power not mitigated by sympathy. Throughout the Old Testament he appears in his role as the judgmental sovereign, the ruthless ruler who demands deference and capitulation and who deals out punishment.

'Is our image of god one tinted by our fear of evil?

'It appears so, he is portrayed as unjust, menacing, unpredictable, power-thirsty, yet he gave early man the capacity to discriminate between right and wrong, he taught primitive man how to behave decently. The existence of evil in the world has troubled many true believers who ask in their anguish, 'if god is a power for good, why does he permit evil to thrive?'

'Each generation asks this question, continues Moses, Moses himself is said to have agonised over the apparent success of evil.

'You must recognise, Moses, my son that all life arises from the All That Is. He is the all-embracing life force, from which diversity ensues.

'God includes evil too? My teachers back home would shout 'blasphemy'.

'That is because they do not think duality through to its logical conclusion. We live in the world of illusion. Ultimately duality is an illusion and so good and evil are an illusion.

'How can a just God tolerate evil, asks Moses, not yet convinced, or perhaps afraid of finding out the truth?

'You have to recognise that the gods that man fashions do not transcend the limits of the human mind. Man is bound by his society and culture as he is bound by physicality. And so man of long ago who lived in a climate of fear, threat, doom and gloom attributed these to his gods. Mentally undeveloped and spiritually unevolved man was unable to conceive of anything else. His god was a reflection of his beliefs about the world. Faced with evil, he projected that evil on to the gods.

'But what is evil, enquires Moses with a feeling of urgency?

'Evil is ignorance of good. As the mind of man progresses through time and improves through countless incarnations he gradually revises his definition of evil. Evil is no longer portrayed as the devil with red eyes and a tail, but is seen by the more discerning mind, as an absence of … a lack of … a deficiency in … The notion of evil for primitive man was different from the notion of evil for modern man. Modern man understands that evil does not fall from the sky, many factors contribute in its formation.

'The definition of evil is becoming more complex, remarks Moses.

"Father forgive them, for they know not what they are doing!' This invocation says it all, the finest definition of evil you will find, <u>not knowing</u>. Evil is not inherent in man. If he knew his true nature, he would never commit evil acts. When man knows, in biblical imagery, that the Shekhina burns bright in the Temple of Jerusalem, in his own Heart centre, when he realises at a deep level of awareness that there is only One Life and that he is that life, then evil will vaporise. 'We are what we think. With our thoughts we make the world.'

'We make evil?

'We perceive evil! 'See yourself in others then whom can you hurt'? What harm can you do?' Man commits evil acts through ignorance. You cannot hold your god responsible for your ignorance.

'Yet a great deal of evil befall man, often from birth, is it ignorance too?

'He returns to Earth life just as he was before he died. The same man with the same beliefs, prejudices, desires, emotions and thought forms.

'Karmic hurdles he encounters force him to rethink in each life?

'Who said that karmic difficulties are evil? The Lords of Karma supervise the progress of mankind. Karmic events may be unpleasant, but sadly all too necessary. Karmic happenings are forcing us to review our lives, re-evaluate the nature of our thoughts, reappraise the quality of our emotions and examine our actions. Karma is our teacher, our ally. There would be no learning if it were not for Karma. Expansion of consciousness is the result of karma. If it were not for Karma human beings would still be eating one another in the dark forests of primeval Earth. So evil has its place in the evolution of humanity. If you can call it evil!

'But evil can also be viewed in terms of the polar opposites, says Moses who feels uneasy with the notion of Karma. I know of 'an eye for an eye' and never felt at ease with this aspect of divine justice.

'What made you so uneasy, teases Sanaka?

'Its brutality.

'That is why it cannot derive from the Source, it can only stem from man.

'Is not polarity itself in a sense evil?

'Right. Evil is the polar opposite of good, and as the universe was built around polarity, there is equilibrium. So any attempt at destroying evil would precipitate the disintegration of the world. Good will not exist alone or the whole fabric of the universe would crumble as Buddha rightly pointed out. Polarity must remain until it is transcended or the world will return to chaos. Evil has its role to play, a major role, it gives us the resistance, the tension we need to grow and evolve. We have to grapple with it in order to prevail over it and in so doing shape our character, learn and evolve.

'So evil is not to be despised or destroyed. Is all evil to be accepted?

'As we just said our perception of evil changes as we evolve. Do give me an instance of this, asks the Master unexpectedly looking deep into Moses' eyes.

'My past is coming to the rescue, smiles Moses. Where I come from disobedience to god or disregard of a ritual is the essence of 'evil'. But someone who has moved up the ladder might consider a personal god, a ritual or a dogma meaningless.

'Well reasoned, Moses. The forces of good and evil befit our level of evolution, they change as we change. As you point out, evil for a man who lives in fear of a Samsara god is different from evil observed by rational man.

The Fall - Dark Energies corrupt Earth - Master Sananda

'Know this O man, the sole root of sin in thee
Is not to know thy own divinity' (James Rhoades)

Clara and Levinson are absorbed in the issue of the genetic origins of their people. They request a question and answer session with Master Sananda which is immediately granted by a teasing Jeremy.

'I longed for this, confesses doctor Suleiman. I know from Benzaccai that you channel a Master, Commander of the cosmic workers. I am too excited to express my gratitude; I have not felt so elated in a long time'. His eyes are shining with tears of joy. They sit down with a thrill of anticipation and after the introductory greetings Clara is invited to put her question:

'Was the manipulation of their gene pool responsible for the Hebrews relinquishing immortality? In ancient Egypt immortality was ever present; life was suffused with the certainty of eternal life. In rejecting eternal life, man resigns himself to being mortal. Is this what the priesthood wanted? Can we speak of materialism? Were the Hebrews materialistic in that sense?

'It has been the general pattern for humanity, that at one stage all of you, regardless of the particular strand you belonged to, all of you experienced lifetimes much longer than you currently tend to. There has been over a long period of time a gradual shortening of the life span down to the point that it is at present. One way of picturesquely describing it is with the myth of the Fall. It has come about through the Fall, through a changed view of your true nature. The adoption of the energy of guilt has a powerful effect on the physical entity and has tended to shorten the life span. You actually have the capacity to renew yourselves indefinitely but as part of your exploration of limitations you have chosen, at the highest level, at soul level, to relinquish this possibility and to believe that it is something that you can no longer do. Consequently you also experience the kind of illnesses that tend to affect much of humanity, such as cancer. All of these conditions are not intrinsically necessary to the human form. The human body has the capacity to simply renew itself for as long as the spiritual being within the vehicle wishes it to happen; a skill that can be re-learnt. So this is not simply something that the Jewish people alone experienced, it is a much wider issue which applies to the whole of humanity. And what you find in the Bible is simply their version of that experience. I think that if you explore the myths and religious writings around the world you find that it is by no means a memory unique to a particular group.

'You just stated that mankind felt shame and guilt. The Book of Genesis recounts the myth of Adam and Eve and the Fall of humanity, there have been so many interpretations of the Fall. What is the true nature of the Fall; surely they did not eat an apple!

'Take it as a symbolic story, as an interpretation. It contains symbolic truth, but it is not to be taken too much as a literal account of what happened. Historically speaking - we are going back thousands and thousands of years -there came a point where the comparatively small number of people living on the Planet at that time became aware of an incoming flow of energy which broadly speaking you might describe as 'dark energy', a slower, heavier vibration which they felt was part of their divine mission to accept, to come to an understanding of and to learn to integrate'. A few more questions are put to the Master before the encounter comes to a close.

The Fall – group discussion

'As I see it, there are two sides to the story of the Fall, remarks Clara. She detects a look of surprise.

'The Fall again, it's ancient history, says Tara not at all amused.

'The Fall is still with us, replies Clara. What makes you think it is past? We are in the Fall and the Old Testament is a potent reminder of this. If I may be so bold, the Book is the Fall, it is a giant metaphor for the Fall of man, the symbolic illustration of 'fallen' man. For as long as man is 'fallen' this Book will be read. The Old Testament was to early humanity what psychological theory is to modern man.

'You are saying, inserts Levinson always in tune with Clara that in allegorical form the entire text narrates the history of the Fall of man and the expansion of the personality?

'I agree, in his completeness, in his pre-Fall state man knew himself to be unlimited. He was functioning as a multidimensional being, existing in several realities, apprehending the world in its wholeness, aware of the reality that underlies the material world, comments the doctor.

'Then came the Fall and forgetfulness, comments Johansson. The Old Testament is the narrative of the descent of boundless man into limitation, ignorance and 'sin'. Sin most horrid: the forgetfulness of his prior fullness. Man did not fall once and for all, having lost the memory of his multidimensionality, he had to be told what to do, rules and regulations had to be put in place.

'The descent of man into physical reality, into the world of limitations, also ushers in a 'new' religion, not the spiritual religion he once knew, but a ritualistic religion that keeps him obedient and fearful, remarks the doctor. The salient feature of the Fall is the rise of the self, aggressive, dynamic and effective.

We follow the expansion of the self as it is projected on to the deity. The judging and unforgiving self finds full expression in the gods man adores.

'And much later when the moral faculty appears, butts in Clara, it too is projected on to the deity and he becomes an ethical god who shows concern for the weak, the widow and the orphan. Remember the haggling between Abraham and his god on the fate of Nineveh.

'Interesting, notes Levinson, one might say that in a sense the Old Testament is a kind of history of evolution which charts the development of human consciousness, the precursor of Darwin's theory of evolution.

'Not a good example, laughs the doctor, Darwin was a biologist. The Old Testament illustrates the evolution of consciousness after the Fall. Or rather the rise of the personality after man has lost his many-sided perception.

'He no longer knows that he holds the universe within, inserts Tara.

'Right, continues the doctor visibly relieved. The revealed text is the allegory of the descent from unlimited consciousness to limited consciousness, from wholeness to separateness, from love to fear. This is truly the Fall. We have been falling ever since, until the 20th century when the curve fell to its lowest point, but is now ascending.

'The waves of light coming to the Planet are assisting the ascending curve, enlarges Jeremy. We are gradually leaving the Fall behind as we are focussing on integration: the soul is drawing near. Time is collapsing and we are aiding in the process. Sananda has shown us how to experiment with time; under his guidance we travelled into the past to meet our former selves and into the future to encounter our future self.

'The movement is going in reverse, repeats the doctor, from limited consciousness to unlimited consciousness, from fear to love as you rightly stated. We are going forward by reverting back to our primeval fullness.

'The Old Testament as testimony of the climb of the ego-self is becoming superfluous. As image of the rise of ritualistic religion to mirror the rise of the self it is also outdated. As formal religion to control the power of the ego, it is also becoming redundant, concludes Levinson.

CHAPTER 2

DESTRUCTION -- THE FATHER & SATAN PLOT THE DOWNFALL OF HUMANITY

'God degenerated to the contradiction of life, instead of being its transfiguration and eternal Yes! In God a declaration of hostility towards life, towards nature ...'
(Nietzsche)

JERUSALEM UNIVERSITY

On their return to Sinai, they receive a telephone call from Benzaccai. He is at his desk at the university where he has resumed his teaching duties that day. Jeremy enquires about his safety, Benzaccai declines to answer. 'Come to Jerusalem to my office for the next chapters. Preferably today I may have to go away soon. Sorry for the urgency, there is no time to waste'. He sounds curiously dramatic.

'Another trip chasing after Benzaccai moans Clara who dreads yet another long journey in the heat of the day.

The trip proves more pleasant than she anticipated. The journey across the Judean Desert is stunning, awe-inspiring. She is so absorbed in the dreamlike quality of the Desert that she forgets her sickness. The wilderness may be a metaphor for the treachery of the physical world but it has an eerie spiritual quality, an awesome power. Hours later they stop at an inn for the night. In the morning they resume their journey. Finally they knock on Benzaccai's door. He greets them with his usual warmth. He looks older, weary, his shoulders slightly arched. This man is being chased by his inner torments!

Sensing their silent questioning, 'My demons have finally caught up with me. The translation of 'The Hebrew Gods' brings elation and torment, illumination and darkness. Elation because it lifts me out of ordinary reality and confirms my own findings, torment because it rekindles awful memories, the enormity of what I experienced as a youngster in the hands of orthodoxy. I am being knocked over relentlessly. Every day I emerge from The Hebrew Gods dazed, exhausted, disorientated. It takes me a while to get back to normal, to find my bearings. Paradoxically as I am thrown back in time I also age with each chapter I translate.

Past and present grapple pitilessly, I am a battlefield. It is as if the whole of the Jewish condition is battling it out in me. This is Armageddon, the final struggle.

'I know exactly how you feel, says Clara holding back tears. I have come to feel that this is a personal war, not a war that will be fought by humanity at large, but by each one of us.

Job & the temporal god of Genesis

Rabbi Moses now turns his attention to the ambiguous and disconcerting legend of Job. The version he is familiar with is no longer tenable, because as with all else, it is flawed. The outpouring of the simple imagination of simpler minds of long ago is unreliable. He has moved away from the old self-deceiving, self-enlarging picture of the world. He realises now that he never received answers that satisfied his inquisitive nature. He had endorsed the outburst of emergent minds whose limited perception could not grasp the scientific and philosophical genius of the enlightened Greeks. Moses was also discovering that Greek knowledge his ancestors had discarded as 'darkness' was founded on the Timeless Wisdom imparted long ago by the Masters.

'Never again will I 'make do'! Never again will I settle for defective versions. Never again will I languish in the devotional sphere of experience when the world is lifting itself to higher planes of consciousnesses. He made this passionate promise to himself and one he was never going to break.

'Master Sanaka, I would like your view on the story of Job, the righteous man who endures severe blows from fate.

'The story of Job is one of the most fascinating, begins Sanaka. As with most myths and allegories there are several ways of approaching it. It is one of the oldest allegories of the human condition. Let us start with one such approach. The legend of Job belongs to the intellectual tradition of India. Its universality indicates that it holds an important message for mankind. If the Old Testament was to disappear, future generations will remember the moving story of Job, more so than any other. It may be a figment of the imagination but one that sheds light on the human situation. Here you have a devout man, an upright man who has devoted his life to learning and serving his god. Suddenly god and Satan devise a wicked plot to trick him. He is tested to the limit of human endurance. He bends under the furious blows of fate but does not break. God is forced to recognise Job's moral superiority. Something strange happens, Job surrenders to the will of his god in what appears as a contrived conclusion, for it is Job who is victorious, Job who triumphs over evil, darkness and death and emerges unscathed, undamaged, whole. This myth more than any other illustrates the plight of the Hebrew and the nature of his relationship with his god and the world.

'Does the story illustrate the triumph of man over his fate, enquires Moses?

'That's the way it appears. There is more to it than that. First, Job stands symbolically for the Hebrew people; you are a virtuous, upright, learned people who submit to the blows of fate. Secondly, fate is blind, god unjust, unethical and arbitrary. Man is moral and noble, his god is not. The roles are reversed; the world has been turned upside down. You see, it is god who needs salvation, not man. The story of Job is the story of man living in Samsara, the world of time and space. For as long as man thinks of himself as powerless and his gods as powerful forces, things will never change and mankind will go on asking the same vital question for ever, 'Why is the righteous man suffering'?

'Is it not a central question, one all men ask sometime in their lives?

'We do not. We never ask this question because there is no one to ask!

'The Buddha, the Masters?

'Each man has to answer this question for himself. He is not to expect an answer from the world; he must find the answer himself if only to justify his existence. Your situation is untenable; the god who forbids you to use your mind is the same god you ask an answer from! Is it not strange to expect a rational response from an irrational god?

'Man pictures his gods according to his own point in evolution. Greek enlightenment was assertive, rational, ethical, and idealistic. The enlightened Greeks relied on reason.

'Indeed Moses, you understand. Pre-rational man has need of gods that he endows with his own emotional nature while rational man relies on his own reason. Man who imagines his gods to be like himself is fashioning gods of clay. He adores the images that spring from his fearful mind. As Buddha said, 'We are what we think. All that we are arises with our thoughts. With our thoughts we make the world'. You must take his words literally. Our gods and demons arise with our thoughts. Our circumstances, our troubled lives, our suffering arise with our thoughts, this is our world and with our thoughts we make our world.

'There is no god to blame, no fate to curse, no malignant forces to charge.

Who are the gods?

'The ideas you are ready to die for and to kill for are the gods. Man having lost his soul power is a fragile leaf blown by external forces. The life force that supports the universe is available to you. How that for a leaf blown by the winds of fate? But you forgot your unlimited cosmic power. Deserting your soul, you deserted your power. As you disempower yourself you empower external forces.

'Man at once powerful and powerless.

'Man is still thinking in terms of god 'out there' and man 'down here'. That is the root cause of his sorrow. There is no god 'out there' sitting on the clouds. The one God dwells in the Heart. In meditation when we move into the inner spaces, into the Heart chamber, we gaze at the flame in the centre of the lotus and inside the flame is the brilliant spark, the radiant 'I AM Presence'. This is where you must look to find him and to find your answer. You recall the Sufi Master who travelled the world in search of God only to find him in his own Heart? So near yet so far!

'So you find the answers to the great life questions within your Heart temple?

'Where else? Can you think of a higher place? When we have a question we do not look up to the sky for answer, we travel within; we ask the cosmic mind inside us. God is not in the sky except in the Bible narrative and there is a good reason for this: Yahweh did come from the sky. The cosmic mind has always inhabited the Heart of man. So near yet so far! Buddha knew himself to be the universe, he was aware of his own all-pervasive presence. Heresy to the law-makers.

'I always try to come to the defence of my people; I am in a way their advocate for they are not present to defend themselves. To them it is pure heresy that a man should declare himself at once God and the universe.

'It is heretical to those who project their god outside and believe the universe to be real and solid. The enlightened minds of India and Tibet know intimately that the cosmos is neither solid nor real in a significant way. Buddha taught men but he also taught the gods. The god you project outside is distinct from you and indeed it is heresy to try to align yourselves with him. Imagine a simple Roman centurion living under Titus or Caligula claiming to be one with his supreme ruler? But the cosmic life force pervades all creation and is as much 'inside' as it is 'outside'.

'We do not know how to know, mumbles Moses.

'And when illumined Beings move down to show you how, you cast them off with furious derision. Power does not confer right, yet power makes your god right! You have worshipped his power since prehistoric times, but what have you learnt from your powerlessness? Power is legitimate in the hands of the gods, why! You have journeyed down the ages with the slogans that echo throughout Christendom: 'the will of God', the 'power of God'! A strange mix, the power of god is plotted against the powerlessness of man; yet man in his insignificance is 'chosen' and erupting with pride! Do you spot the inconsistency, how can man be powerless and so important in the same breath?

'So our very dis-empowerment has taught us the legitimacy of power!

'You became an active force, an agent of power. Dis-empowerment and arbitrary power found together in one people!

'What should we do, protest?

'I think that the story of Job depicts vividly the situation of the Hebrew in the world. Saddled with a powerful, unreliable and amoral god, the Hebrew is alone and forlorn. He is alienated from his soul, from his fellow men, from Earth and from the universe. In part the story of Job is the story of the Hebrew in the world.

'Why, what went wrong?

'He turned his back on cosmic Law. Had he not ignored the law of Karma, his situation would be very different. From passive victim of fate he would be the active agent of his destiny, the creator of his future. Like Buddha he would have arrived at the earth-shattering recognition of his all-encompassing power. So you see the story of Job borrowed from a variety of ancient cultures does reflect the position of the Hebrew in the world.

'So Job is an allegory of Karma, asks Moses disappointed.

'I also told you that the allegory of Job has many facets. You may liken it to a cut diamond which reflects the colours of the rainbow. If Job is man acting out his inexorable karma, it is also the epic story of man triumphant over fate. The story of Job is the story of the mythical hero, the song of the Self. Every affliction that can befall a man strikes Job: he loses wife, home, children, wealth and health; still he maintains an inflexible allegiance to higher values. He will not be beaten by fate. He rides the storm of life with unflinching courage, undaunted spirit.

'Is this the core of Job's story, the human spirit?

'Absolutely, confirms Sanaka. Job symbolises the human spirit, the observer, the onlooker, the objective analyst who examines with detachment, refusing to give in to the tyranny of the self, to the force of the emotions. His friends engage in theological debate, they argue, dispute, censure and blame: they are the embodiment of Yang, the masculine energy. Job, the timeless Self refuses to be drawn into theological debate, judgement or blame. Immersed in tragedy he is able to distance himself from it; he refuses to be dispirited. He listens to his friends, he understands their viewpoint, he knows the games the self plays. The reality his friends stand for – time - is an illusion. He sails the stormy seas with great dignity, triumphant over evil, darkness and death.

'In this light, he is hardly a victim.

'You are right. Job is not a victim; he is master of himself, of his mind and emotions. He is at the helm; the mythological hero who has conquered. He has transcended the self and its drama. His human nature has been purged, his emotions purified. He knows the true God: his own Self.

'Job by refusing to engage in theology does something else, remarks Moses with perspicacity. He has outgrown any dependency to the gods. Liberated from the self, he is also liberated from the gods.

'A brilliant conclusion, Moses. He is also liberated from his group values, attitudes and beliefs. He lives the phrase, 'And the truth shall set you free'.

'Master, it seems that the story of Job has nothing to do with courage and endurance. Nor is it about theology for in his darkest hour his eyes finally open and he perceives the gods as the perpetrators of crime against man. It has to do with the subjugation of the self.

'Indeed, replies Sanaka, remember that the story of Job like all biblical stories is an allegory. The gods symbolise the lower self, the forces within man that keep him dependent, fearful and subdued. The Self stands free and triumphant over the gods.

'In biblical rendition the one god, remarks Moses.

'One god or many. It is still the human self bogged down in Maya. Let us leave it for the moment, time for tea. They return to Sanaka's study and have tea. A meditation follows in which Sanaka invites Moses to reflect on the nature of Job. Feeling refreshed Moses also feels emboldened.

'Job is perhaps of all biblical characters the most enigmatic, why is that?
'Because he is not a biblical character at all, laughs Sanaka, he is an import, foreign to

the biblical mould. Your tradition concentrates on the separation of man from his own Self and from the cosmic Self. If you read the texts with clear vision this is what you find in every myth, every legend. The myth of Job is different. Job is confronted with challenges to break a weaker individual; he bends but does not break. His pious friends live by the rules of the group. Immersed in group beliefs and opinions they do not make sense of Job's predicament, they assume that Job is cursed. They even call him a heretic, a blasphemer! But Job lives and moves on a plane of existence beyond their reach. He knows himself to be 'good'; his goodness is not externally-derived; it does not stem from the rules that keep his community in thrall. His goodness springs from his cosmic nature, he lives as his Self. While his devout friends live by group rules and exist in a world of duality, Job exists in the world of unity. He lives in harmony with the universe. His pious friends have lost their intuitive nature to embrace the artificial, separative and verbose world of theology. Job moves in the world of reality, his friends are frozen in duality. Job has passed the test. As his Self he is immortal, aware of existing beyond time. He is timeless. As his Self he knows no fear, no regret, no anger, and no resentment. He is conscious of his Buddha nature.

'I know now why I found Job so fascinating. He is an outsider.

'He is the man who has shed his lower nature and realised his oneness with the universe, his Buddha nature. You are the sentries of the Fall. You have transmitted the Fall, the limited perception of yourselves. When you wake up to the realisation that you have perpetuated an illusion you will be free.

The Father – Yang, the cosmic Masculine energy

Moses had direct and intimate experience of the problems facing the Hebrew in the world. Abhorred by men, alienated from Earth, fearful of his nature, alone in the universe, the life of the Hebrew has a tragic quality. Possibly the most disturbing aspect of his condition is the encounter with the Father whose actions are enigmatic, whose intentions are ambiguous and whose demands are unreasonable. Echoes of the Revolution had reverberated throughout imperial Europe and had reached Moses in Vilna. Ordinary men and women were rebelling against the absolute power of their kings. Soon after he was excommunicated by the rabbis of Vilna, his friends and colleagues. His life, he felt, had come to an end. Why should intelligent, learned men cast him out of the House of the Lord simply because he wanted to know about the world? The urge to explore, to learn, to know and to expand his mind rose from the depth of his being; he was unable to resist the force of the impulse. In the mystical land of India he was now reviewing the terrible experience and decided to grapple with it. Why was god so merciless, why was man so hurtful? These questions tormented him. He had to approach the Master.

'After listening intently, Sanaka replies, I would say that god has nothing to do with it. And those who cast you off did so with a heavy heart, they felt that they had to. They are the guardians of the law, the sentries of the Father who is the energy of the 1st Ray of Power. The power of the Father is absolute and must never be challenged for fear that the world may return to chaos. You were challenging the established wisdom elaborated over thousands of years. The Father is unconditional, unalterable Power. Long ago in the perception of primitive man, the world was a terrible place and its creator was awe-inspiring. Early man was emerging from the unconsciousness of matter and probing the mystery of self-consciousness. As he was opening his eyes to the world around him, he conjured up the notion of a Creator. That was a giant step in evolution. However, the world was not a dependable place; great cataclysms struck Earth over the ages. It was sensible to assume that the Father of Creation was the cause of these disturbances. Man grew fearful, anxious. The Old Testament is a record of attempts by primitive man to make sense of the world, of his own life and of the originator of both.

'I encountered in my own life what ancient man sensed. Why?

'For this you were born, Moses, remember! You designed your own research mission. You knew that the Jewish condition was the laboratory in which to observe at first hand the workings of the 1st Ray of Power. You came to observe the ways of the Father through his people.

'Why should I incarnate for the sole purpose of studying the workings of the Father, the mechanism of power? For this, Versailles would have been the best place and Louis XVI a living illustration of power in action.

'The rumblings of the Revolution reached you and forced you to question your inherited beliefs. You came into incarnation to observe the Father at work through his agents, but you also came to participate in the experiment. You came to observe and to participate. You know the 1st Ray of Power as it manifests in the Old Testament and through the people who regard the Father as absolute ruler. But the energy of the

Father jars with you. Your soul rides the 2nd ray of Love and your personality the 3rd ray of Intelligence. You could not exist in an exclusively 1st Ray environment.

'Master, this is the Divine Trinity!

'Most advanced humans share in it. However taken to extreme the Rays are a problem. The Father - figuratively the 1st Ray of power - constructs forms that solidify. When forms become rigid they threaten the progress of man.

'The Father is potentially dangerous.

'When the thing created turns to stone like Lot's wife, death follows. Life is fluid, life is change, life is creative, and life is flowing. Power is neither good nor bad; it depends on how it is utilised. When power - the Father - indulges static forms, solidified states, inert circumstances, it is time to 'destroy'. Realised cosmic beings come to 'destroy' encrusted forms and crystallised beliefs.

'The Father is irrelevant?

'The Father was relevant long ago to assist archaic man groping in the dark. Today he is irrelevant. The force of the Father has cast its giant shadow over Earth, choking the Planet and stifling the initiative of man. It has imprisoned soul life, prevented the expansion of consciousness and obstructed the development of mind. The Father keeps man in fear, arrested in the emotional life. You have a strange mix: the Father fixed on the 1st Ray of Power and man fixed on the 6th ray of emotional life. The absolute ruler demands and expects his subjects to stagnate on the plane of emotions.

'Man's progress is incompatible with the idea of the Father?

'The Revolution answered your question. The process of disintegration will continue until finally the idea of the Father dissolves away. Despotic power, injustice, animosity, rule of law, unfreedom, centralisation, separation and division are all 1st Ray characteristics. Humanity has explored this ray at length.

'So this is where I come in, asks Moses with hesitation?

'This is where you come in. The Father must release his hold on man and on the Planet. Your people, as custodians of the Father-ray, are to grasp that this ray taken to excess is a peril for mankind, the Planet and the world.

'It has cosmic implications?

'It has indeed; remember the oneness and unity of the universe.

'What will replace the 1st Ray?

'The 2nd. The Ray of Love which was introduced to a terrified humanity some 2000 years ago. The curtain has fallen on the Father and is rising on the Son, the Ray of Love-wisdom, once again. This is the task you set yourself, your part in the Plan. This brings us to the next chapter of our instruction, destruction. The Father created the world and now he decides to destroy it.

'The Deluge?

'The Deluge. But before we come to it, you recall how the Psalms lament at the severity of god's handling of the world.

'The author of the Psalms laments the injustice of god's rule: the insolent lives in abundance and the just is plagued. Like Moses before him, he asks the question that has tormented mankind.

'In the absence of a doctrine of the soul, this question has no answer, how does evil exist in the world created by a just god?

'The doctrine of the soul, asks Moses?

'Yes, the soul is a fragment of the Source destined to journey through time.

'That God created man, we know, but the purpose of this creation is unclear.

'He did not 'create' man to cast him on this far away Planet. Man is an emanation of cosmic consciousness. Man never was created in the sense you think, the Great Life fragmented itself and embodied itself into all forms.

'But Yahweh did 'create' man, reminds Moses.

'Yes, he did, but the Creator did not! How that for a paradox, he chuckles!

'Why did God insert a fragment of himself in man?

'God came down to school! He wanted to find out if he could prove himself in matter. The soul buried itself in matter millions of years ago and began an endless cycle of incarnations in order to regain knowledge of itself, its origin and its destiny, to become liberated and illumined before returning to the Source. The soul evolves through successive incarnations. The answer hastily offered is that of the Fall. Man was high and noble but fell from grace as he sinned against god.

'The injustice of god is an illusion.

'Man interprets the world from the boundaries of his mind. Man's outlook is limited to his environment and his moment in time. With hindsight what appeared unjust may turn out to be quite different with the passing of time. And so going back to the Psalmist, he was a man of his time; he voiced the mood of his generation. He knew only of the god who is the embodiment of the 1st Ray of Power and like his people he laments the fate of humanity condemned to suffer the random power of an arbitrary god.

Atlantis & the Lords of Form

One early morning after meditation, Master Sanaka looked strangely solemn. He did not greet Rabbi Moses with his customary warmth. He remained quiet, standing tall and regal by the window, observing the snow-capped peaks, majestic unconquerable wilderness that fills man with awe and reverence. Slowly, almost reluctantly he emerged from his reverie and turning towards me with a melancholy expression I had not seen before, he began in a deep voice: 'Moses, my son, in the past the Hierarchy sent out some of their most able and experienced ambassadors to Earth. Your great Prophets were dispatched from Shamballa to lift human beings out of the predicament they had plunged into.

'We no longer have prophets or even rabbis of inspiring presence and regulating moment. Why is that, has the Hierarchy given up on us?

'Certainly not, replies Sanaka with surprising force. They have pledged to guide, inspire and enlighten mankind from the dawn of time and nothing will change that. Their field of action is the mind of men, they work on enlarging human consciousness; they are responsible for the new lines of thought, the new intellectual and scientific movements which help mankind forward; they fight obstacles that stand in the way of human progress, they fight for the freedom of the human spirit against all manner of oppression. They evaluate the spirit of the time, they know how and when to adapt their methods and adjust their procedures.

'We no longer have prophets to inspire and enthuse, what does it say about the spirit of the time?

'Prophets were appropriate to a certain period in history, sent out by the Hierarchy, they emerged into the world of men to guide, teach and lead the way. Then you had rabbis, distinguished individuals who emerged from the ranks of humanity, but their style too is becoming outdated.

'To be replaced by?

'Cosmic workers are artisans who work not with bricks, wood, clay or laws but with light. Their material is light. Their explicit or oblique intention is to shed light, to enlighten. Their task is to lift dense, dark energies to the light. Their mission is to raise the consciousness of humanity. And they are doing this in different ways; they follow the avenues to knowledge, from literature and philosophy to science and the arts. The divine in man is manifesting this way.

'Arts, literature and science are profane, only the study of Torah is permitted.

'Sadly so, this is why the Hierarchy is engaged in an unremitting battle against superstition, bigotry and ignorance. And they are sending intelligent, enquiring, spiritually-oriented individuals who are coming to lift mankind out of its self-erected prison. Their appointed task is to liberate the soul from the prison of religious dogma, fanciful beliefs and uncritical opinions.

'They are born in it and so naturally they stay in the mould, notes Moses.

'Just what they should never do! The key test in life is to break the mould. Why should our action be dictated by men who died thousands of years ago? The self brings back in successive incarnations thought forms, desire and emotions which spill over into the global outlook, but the global outlook in turn feeds personal desire and fantasy. And so the problem is compounded generation after generation. The individual is sucked into the social group which offers him the opinions and beliefs he knows and craves.

'It is a never-ending cycle of returns into the same mould of opinions and beliefs, emotions and thought forms. Is this ever going to end?

'When man learns that each incarnation is an opportunity for growth and change. When he grasps that the forms of the past have to be dissolved, because they constrict and obstruct. The forms of the past are a tomb. Rather than stumble back into the same mould, his task is to break that mould, for his own liberation and the liberation of others.

'Mankind in general or the Hebrew people in particular? Is it ever going to happen?

'To this end you were sent out by the Hierarchy, for this you are being developed, taught and equipped. It is light, my son, light that will renew and regenerate mankind. The damage wreaked by superstition, sentimental devotion and dogmatism is unfathomable. I exhort you, he continues with a slight trembling in the voice, go back and urge men of good will to break down the fog of negativity that is choking Earth. The Planet is plunged into obscurity, literally as well as figuratively. Cosmic beings know of the thick cloud that envelops Earth, a layer of darkness that they find difficult to penetrate. Go back and tell the world to wake up. Do not repeat Atlantis.

'Atlantis? Atlantis is a legend.

'Legends are based on real events. Atlantis was submerged by the rising sea. This event is recounted in the Flood. Atlantis destroyed itself. Noah was rescued from the Flood.

'How can the story of Atlantis be repeated, it is promised that Earth will never be destroyed by water?

'In order to prevent a similar disaster, Shamballa sent out some of its most competent and experienced ambassadors 2000 years ago at the dawn of the Age of Pisces. The world was living on the edge and only the discerning mind of the Hierarchy did appraise accurately the situation.

'What made them decide to send the Essenes?

'The forces of Light and the forces of Darkness must be balanced: we live in the world of polarity and so when the scales tip into the Dark section, this sends a danger signal. Besides, the Hierarchy is monitoring mental activity on Earth at all time. The Atlanteans are coming back to share their knowledge with you and to make amend. Atlantis had a powerful impact on the thinking of ancient Hebrews and now on Western culture.

'We are the product of Atlantis. What rabbi would believe me?

'He would shout 'heresy'! If he has studied the Book of Genesis in depth, he will know that his thinking and devotional feeling originate with the fall of Atlantis. The legend of the Flood occupies central stage in your thinking; it has shaped your entire outlook. The Flood intensified your pessimistic outlook, your separative consciousness and your tendency to feel guilt. The Flood feeds your reliance on authority and your dependency on a supernatural agency. It was after the fall of Atlantis that the idea of the Saviour appeared in Sumer and found its way into the Old Testament. You never forgot how mankind precipitated its own downfall. The dread of a similar event occurring again inspired you to seek a force that would protect you, Yahweh was the obvious choice. What a paradox, you go for refuge to the god of nature to be shielded from the natural course of nature!

'So our beliefs about the world are the outcome of the collapse of Atlantis?

'The energies of Atlantis have not vanished. Negative energies never disappear; they are not dissolved by prayers and fasting. The energies of Atlantis are alive in human consciousness, more so in the memory of the Jewish people, where they crystallised.

Humanity was understandably in a state of shock. It seems that your people have perpetuated that state in their interpretation of events.

'The demise of Atlantis came about by an act of god, says Moses.

'What god, asks Sanaka? Man creates his circumstances at all time. His outer world is a reflection of his inner world. What he projects outside springs from the deep of his own mind. 'Energy follows thought', this is cosmic Law. You are the demonstration of this Law; you are the Law in action. No god judges or punishes man; should there be such a god, he is not worth knowing.

'Why do they not let go of these energies?

'They don't know how, nor would they dare to either. When man has suffered such terrible experiences, he is too fearful to either rebel or resist. You must also remember that the Hebrew people are the guardian of humanity's past. Your people have the incredible courage in the face of adversity to keep these memories alive. They should be admired for their courage and endurance! They endeavour to transform these negative energies by constant and urgent application of precepts. They believe this to be the only way to raise mankind into the Messianic age, the time when men will be redeemed. But if the intention is admirable, the method inhibits its success.

'Are prayers and moral conduct not the method?

'Who are you praying to? Moral conduct, though important is of the personality. Morality is of the Fall, 'When the Tao is lost there is need for morality, legality, knowledge and much pretence'. Healing comes from the light of the soul, from kindness and compassion, from sympathy and understanding, from cooperation and conciliation. Love is the substance the universe is made of, it is the reality underlying all forms. Love heals everything. Yet love is clearly absent from your schedule.

'Why is love absent?

'Because of the Fall. Because of the demise of Atlantis. Prayer, fasting, precepts and practices change nothing; what they do is to aggravate your inflated sense of separateness. They tend to intensify your sense of specialness. It is the self which has the last word.

'So the Day of Atonement is pointless.

'In terms of healing the energies of Atlantis that hold man captive and have shaped your religious belief, it is indeed pointless. But as a way of expressing guilt, sorrow and regret it serves a purpose. Many people like feeling guilty; they find relief in pain and regret.

Since the days of Ancient Greece, physicians have known the role played by guilt, shame and fear in the causation of disease. Healing is invariably self-healing; one must want to heal and not every one does.

'Why healing, why not contrition?

'Do you really believe that rinsing and salting meat, chasing after bread crumbs, praying, fasting, ablutions and other rituals can transform energies? Healing is vital; this was taught by the Essenes. To heal the lingering energies of Atlantis is to let go of fear and guilt and to relinquish the feeling of powerlessness. Fear, guilt, shame stamped in man's psyche are keeping him in captivity. It is only with love and light that we can begin to heal and transform the energy of those memories as they exist within us and in this way the past itself begins to change. 'Love heals everything' say the Masters. The emotions of fear and guilt perpetuate the crisis, they prevent its resolution.

'How did the crisis precipitate in Atlantis?

'The mind of Atlantean humanity was lagging in immaturity and yet Atlantis had a brilliant civilisation with an astounding scientific achievement which it owed to the Hierarchy. Two distinct forces were operating on that continent, expressing the two opposite views of life: the forces of Materiality and the forces of Light were engaged in a relentless struggle.

'Gog and Magog?

'In a sense. The divide was growing wider and the crisis was inevitable. Chaos and devastation engulfed a civilisation that had lost its way into materialism and emotionalism.

'The Hierarchy did intervene, Genesis informs us that god at the last hour saved Noah for he was the only deserving man.

'Yes, the Hierarchy did intervene to rescue Noah and his group. So the Hierarchy stepped in to provide emergency rescue and the story of this daring action is graphically depicted in the allegorical story of Noah's Ark. Ancient texts tell of 'the sons of men led by the Sons of Wisdom'. The central theme of the Old Testament is the rescue of the 'sons of men'. According to your version of events Noah was the only group saved and this inflates your sense of worth and purpose. The truth is that many escaped and travelled in all directions, to the Americas, Egypt and India where they laid the foundation of splendid civilisations. The Hebrews are a part of the salvaged posterity of

143

Atlantean humanity – saved by the Hierarchy, not for their merit, but because it was felt that humanity had to be saved.

'They were undeserving?

'Noah was a man of his time, unable to transcend the point of view of his generation and culture.

'Why were they not allowed to perish? In this way humanity would have started from scratch without any psychic residue from Atlantis.

'The Hierarchy felt that humanity should not perish and so the group known as Noah was saved. The Masters salvaged what could be salvaged of humanity'. He pauses to observe Moses.

'There is a parallel with the events which marked the dawn of the Age of Pisces, resumes Sanaka. A similar conflict was repeated by the descendants of Atlantean humanity and the Sons of Wisdom. The 'sons of men' were holding on to the world view that had precipitated their demise in Atlantis. They chose to focus on materiality, emotional devotion and physical survival. Attachment to the physical survival of the group was paramount while the cosmic nature of man was neglected and ignored. They were restaging the drama of the Flood.

'And the Hierarchy wanted to avoid a repetition of the tragedy?

'That's right! The Forces of Materiality were influencing humanity as they had done in Atlantis. So the Forces of Light came back on a rescue mission before the disaster. The elemental battle between the forces of Form and the forces of the Soul was raging once again. The assistance of the Forces of Light was rejected in a storm of protest. Imperial Rome, seat of power and materiality was also involved. The enduring preoccupation with materiality was showing no sign of subsiding. The epic encounter between the Ambassador of Shamballa and the authorities symbolically illustrate the cosmic struggle between the Forces of Form and the Forces of Light.

'The outcome was inevitable, says Moses with profound sadness.

'Regrettably so, remarks Sanaka with melancholy. The guardians of form – dogmas, rituals, taboos and separateness - dispersed all over the globe. Form had triumphed over being. The guardians of form changed the course of history: Western civilisation is the outcome. The Lord of the World – Sanat Kumara - and the Hierarchy had sent out their ambassadors to accelerate the coming New Age intended to liberate humanity from the burden of religious belief and superstition and heal the lingering energies of Atlantis.

'Dispersed to learn from their mistakes?

'Yes, to learn in exile the illusory nature of form and realise the unreality and impermanence of all things. And this is coming to pass.

CHAPTER 3

ABRAHAM & THE FATHER –- the gods of Sumer accompany Abraham into Exile

JERUSALEM - The church of Mary Magdalene on the Mount of Olives

The next chapter of The Hebrew Gods will be handed in at the Church of Mary Magdalene situated on the Mount of Olives. The friends head for the Wailing Wall to meet a young soldier who is to take them to Father Gabriel who has the translated text. The Church of Mary Magdalene enjoys an elevated position on the Mount. At the designated spot, the friends are approached by a tanned, confident young soldier who walks with an assured gait.

'I am not in the army, begins Nathaniel, I am a student of captain Benzaccai, but I belong to a reserve unit. Captain Benzaccai put me into the picture, he knows of my interest in anthropology which I am currently studying at his faculty'. He hesitates, embarrassed, both bold and shy. I am also studying Existential philosophy, he whispers.

'How do you reconcile philosophy and military training, asks Jeremy?

'War and military service play a central role in all our lives. We have to engage in activities we would prefer not to engage in. But I have the survival of Israel at heart; I accept sacrifices and agree to compromises. I know I can talk freely with you; there is one more thing I intend to explore.

'Which is … asks Jeremy encouragingly?

Now more assertive he speaks faster, 'I am looking at all aspects of healing, all areas of mind training, from Existential therapy to Buddhist meditation practices, including the neglected areas of karma and reincarnation that may shed light on the origins of illness.

'Fascinating, says Tara, the Buddhist. If I can help in any way?

'I accept your offer, now it is time to go'. They climb in his military four-wheel drive vehicle and speed up towards the Church of Mary Magdalene.

'This is no way to travel incognito, remarks Jeremy, we are attracting much attention. But this is quite something! Look over there to your right'! They are at the top of the hill with the whole of Jerusalem stretching down below in all directions, 'this is truly impressive.

To which the soldier replies with visible satisfaction, 'I took this road for the view, you have beautiful scenery down the Mount of Olives. The Mount is shrouded in myth and mystery. Delivering his apocalyptic prediction, the prophet Joel warned that at the end of times, the nations will be judged on the Mount of Olives. This terrible prophecy I hope will never come to pass, unless some cataclysm strikes Earth. This is the terrifying vision Joel imparts, 'The sun shall be turned into darkness and the moon into blood before the great and terrible day of the Lord come. In Mount Zion and in Jerusalem shall be deliverance'.

'The doomsday scenario of astro-physicists who predict that in some distant future Earth will be swallowed up by a 'black hole', notes Jeremy.

'Or destroyed by a passing comet or struck by a meteorite, adds the soldier. The future looks bleak.

'Enough to make you shudder! Too bad for those who do not abide by the will of your god, says Jeremy in jest!

'That is not all, Joel has this powerful message, 'Assemble yourselves and come all ye heathen …. Let the heathen be wakened and come up to the valley of God's judgement for there will I sit to judge all the heathen round about'.

'Are we the heathen Joel discriminates against? This is no prediction from a god moved by love!

'The idea of love was absent in biblical times, replies Nathaniel. We have 'Love your neighbour like yourself' from a Babylonian exile, but the notion of love is absent, generally speaking. It is a recent idea, one we have not as yet fully endorsed.

'The prophet's imagination is bursting alarmingly. Which of the two is going to sit in judgement, Joel or his god, asks Jeremy?

'Who are the 'heathen'? Those who disobey the temporal, secular god or those who submit to him implicitly, snaps Clara?

'Wait until you hear the rest, warns Levinson. This is bland compared to the hallucinatory scene by Zechariah who predicts that at the end of days, 'the Mount of Olives shall cleave in the midst toward the east and toward the west and there shall be a very great valley and half the mountain shall remove towards the north and half of it towards the south'.

'I hope the Mount does no decide to cleave right now, laughs Jeremy, trying humour to dispel the tension he senses in Levinson.

'I spent my youth reciting this apocalyptic delirium, retorts Levinson. What a stuff to fill young minds with! And all for what? In my opinion, neither Zechariah nor Joel were inspired prophets, they rose from the ranks of the people and so were not sent out by Shamballa, they were, I feel, no more than alert social observers who knew what made the people tick!

'I find this picture of doom interesting, says Tara. A cataclysmic event is going to occur; a violent tremor will reshape the landscape. Such disasters have been predicted for centuries by all nations. The ancients knew that the Planet is a living and turbulent organism, they witnessed massive land masses shift before, and they also knew that in the end, the coming of Buddha would be heralded by terrible events. To avert the ultimate catastrophe Shamballa sent out a call which resounded throughout the universe and to which millions of cosmic workers responded. We came down to avert the final destruction.

'To avert the final showdown between the Forces of Form and the Forces of Light, says Jeremy.

'How is this possible, enquires Nathaniel?

'Your prophets speak of Judgment Day, of final retribution, of ultimate destruction, which the Planetary Logos wanted to avert. He sent out a trumpet call to which cosmic Beings responded, explains Johansson.

'How do you do it, asks Nathaniel excitedly?

'We don't engage in prayers and fasting, we don't sit on the floor mourning in ashes, we don't atone for imaginary sins nor do we wallow in self-reproach. And we most certainly do not swear allegiance to the god of fear, this is the way we don't do it, replies Clara!

'We do it through transmutation, our task is to absorb and transform the negative energies that were choking the Planet and threatening to precipitate the very cataclysms Joel and Zechariah describe, explains Jeremy.

'You do it by absorbing negative energies and changing them?

'That's it! Energy is indestructible, fighting evil is pointless, it only serves to reinforce it. According to cosmic Law we give life to what we focus on. If we fight evil we strengthen it. The only way is to absorb it and convert it into something harmless.

'It is a risky job, notes Nathaniel.

'Very risky! We ran the risk of getting swamped into the quagmire. Our work attracts some unwelcome attention from entities on and off the Planet.

'What the Buddhists call 'conceptual evil', says Tara. When a civilisation reaches a certain degree of enlightenment hostile forces step in, this is what happened in Atlantis and other advanced civilisations before Atlantis.

They continue their journey down the Mount of Olives rich in symbolic significance. Each church they pass has some biblical reference. On this side, a mosque converted from a church, further down the hillside, the Paternoster church, a Carmelite sanctuary. The young soldier explains, 'this road leads down to the Tombs of the Prophets and over you can see the domes of the church of Mary Magdalene.

'It's a Russian church, exclaims Tara. What a lovely church, so colourful and of such complex architecture, so much detail. It's like being in Leningrad.

'At the bottom of the hill you can see the Garden of Gethsemane and its olive trees with all the many mystical associations!

At the church of Mary Magdalene, they walk in an ornate interior beautifully lit with numerous candles which give a radiant white light. The light and the tranquillity have a calming influence on them, even on Levinson who was withdrawn and visibly tense. In the church, a priest simply dressed in a black robe, in stark contrast to the elaborate and luminous Byzantine church, walks down to greet them.

'Welcome, smiles Father Gabriel with arms wide open to embrace them. It is a joy to greet you. I have often been used as a mediator to resolve situations involving religious politics and negotiate to bring a solution to conflicts between opposing factions'. Detecting enquiring looks, he explains, 'you will be surprised how much acrimony simmers under the surface between groups of opposing views, who refuse to learn to live amicably side by side.

'The legacy of both monotheism and patriarchy, remarks Levinson with barely repressed exasperation. Both are inimical to peaceful coexistence. Both are a recipe for intolerance. Both foster hostility and division'. Father Gabriel remains silent in surprise; he did not expect such an outburst.

'You are a diplomat, says Jeremy always appeasing.

'Diplomacy is an important part of church work, replies Father Gabriel. So you understand why I was picked to give you this revelation. I have to say that I am delighted and honoured to have been asked. Let's us proceed.

'Can we take away the translation?

'Regrettably I have to refuse; it will always be associated with this church, so that anyone can access it. It belongs with us, it is clear that god wanted it this way'. They sit in a circle and the priest starts to read by the brilliant light of the candles. 'I glanced over the pages, they all speak about Abraham. It is a long and fascinating dialogue, very intense on the part of Moses who seems to be pouring out his very soul, adds the insightful priest.

Father Gabriel reads from The Hebrews Gods: Abraham

'Abraham, the Sumerian as he migrates out of Sumer takes with him the beliefs and practices of his people. The culture of Sumer is enshrined.

'He left Sumer to preserve its culture? The father of the Hebrew people?

'A culture as brilliant as that of Sumer had to be preserved, replies Sanaka. A similar thing happened to that other great culture, Egypt which Moses took with him. Ancient Sumerian and Egyptian cultures are alive today through the Old Testament and the religious enthusiasm of your ancestors in preserving them.

'They did not know that. Both were pagan abomination to them!

'Abraham the father of the Hebrews is a religious and political figure in Sumer. The biblical text hints at his identity and conviction. Ardent Moon worshipper, he moves out of Sumer in protest at the inauguration of the new solar religion. Genesis tells us that he originates in Ur, the intellectual city of Moon-worship. Why should Abraham embrace Moon worship and reject Sun worship?

'I am baffled, admits Moses. This is new to me! The father of the Hebrew people entrusted with a historical purpose on Earth worshipping the Moon!

'And you were a learned and revered Hebrew scholar, chuckles Sanaka.

Embarrassed Moses attempts to come up with a plausible explanation over an issue never raised. The father of Israel could never be a Moon-worshipper! 'What troubles us we remove, what does not match the preconceived idea is eliminated. A tentative answer may be the 'bride of god' metaphor. The Hebrew people is depicted as the 'bride of god', a feminine entity. It may seem natural that the father of the 'bride' should worship the Goddess. Worship of the Sun, a masculine force would be inappropriate. Our lunar calendar may well hint at this. This is pure conjecture, confesses Moses mystified.

'Good try! The Goddess is frequently driven out with thunderous protest. Derided and reviled she hides under the surface of your stringent monotheistic history. Moon-worship implies reverence to a single god, solar worship in contrast approves of a plurality of gods. So we are introduced to the father of the Hebrew tribes, the originator of Western civilisation, the custodian of the Nefilim civilisation! The text sketches an ambiguous portrait of Abraham, dotted with clues which help us infer much about his past. He was a leader of men in battle and a political figure in Sumer who worshipped the Moon-goddess. It is interesting to note that on the Sumerian clay tablets Yahweh is depicted with a moon crescent over his head. As Abraham comes on to the stage of history, Moon worship is being threatened by Sun worship which in the end does spread all over the world. The Sun, the masculine principle, is now adored. Mankind is leaving behind the cult of the goddess and is entering the phase of patriarchy.

'Is it not strange that the custodians of patriarchy should unwittingly worship the Moon Goddess when it would be more coherent to worship the Sun God?

'Coherence and consistency have nothing to do with faith. Faith stems from the emotional nature of man, not from reason. Faith predates reason; it is deeply rooted in man's unconscious nature. Going back to Abraham, he rejects the new solar cult and joins forces with warring groups. At the head of a small army he marches on Canaan where he defeats Nimrod and invades the country. Genesis presents him as a leader in battle, both literally and figuratively, he fights on the battle field just as he fights the birth of new ideas. He is the man of the old world order who resists the new world order. The land of Canaan, contrary to the embellished Biblical account is not miraculously given but fought over on the battlefield.

'Yet Abraham is the bringer of the New Age.

'Indeed! In order to impose Moon-worship, Abraham reinvents the role and nature of Yahweh, one of the Babylonian gods. In Sumer Moon-worship was associated with Yahweh. Abraham formulates his personal vision of Yahweh who he adopts in preference to all other Sumerian gods.

'So in what way is Abraham the bringer of a new age, insists Moses?

'Your insistence does you credit, smiles Sanaka. The distant god of Sumer adopted by Abraham becomes a personal god. Abraham, the monotheist sets in motion a new religious style. Interested in the progress of mankind Yahweh involves himself in human affairs. The god of Abraham becomes a personalised deity that man can relate to. Whereas the god of Noah and Job was vindictive and unprincipled, the god of Abraham has progressed to meet the mood of the times. Endowed with moral qualities he has outgrown his cruel nature and is now fashioning a coherent plan for the future of humanity. Yahweh, this eminently 1st Ray ruler will survey the workings of the Ray of Power. The Planet and mankind will be his living laboratory.

'It makes sense that emphasis is now on purity, moral perfection and separateness: 'Walk before me and be thou perfect' is the command to Abraham.

'So it is, pursues Sanaka. A personal relationship is forged between man and his god. Man lifting himself to his god and god engaging man to 'walk' with him. A new age is dawning as man and god strike a partnership.

'What of the Plan for humanity that rests with the Hierarchy?

'The new age introduced by Abraham is a plan for the Planet distinct from the Plan which resides in Shamballa.

'I was taught that Abraham's plan for the world was the only true plan, the ultimate plan conceived by the unfathomable mind of god.

'You would, of course! Quite apart from the plan, it is a giant stride in human consciousness, a significant shift from passive subject to active agent. Abraham sees himself as collaborator of god. Man is no longer a puppet on a chain, he is an active force. Great stride forward wouldn't you say?

'Man becomes aware of himself as a creative force, as an active being. Though he still has to 'do & obey'! But what of the plan?

'I am coming to this. Abraham is a man of his time, the god who has 'chosen' him, who influences him and for whom he conquers Canaan is 'El Olam', the 'God of the World'

'We praise, we evoke, we esteem, we revere, we acclaim, we pray daily to him. Every morsel of food we eat is blessed with the phrase 'Melekh ah Olam', 'King of the World'. What is so significant about this?

'Smiling at Moses' s outburst, Sanaka replies, 'Olam' is Samsara, the world of time, space and matter, the tangible, finite, created world. The god of Abraham remains firmly anchored in Samsara, rooted in the world of polarity. In arcane tradition, polarity is symbolised by Moon and Sun. Esoteric doctrine explains that the Creator in order to explore himself and the world decided that polarity was the method best suited for this experiment. In the opening chapters of Genesis, polarity is an established fact and runs through the whole of Genesis.

'So Yahweh and Abraham are functioning within the boundaries of polarity, they abide by the primeval intention.

'This is a good way of putting it! Let us explore further the nature and objectives of Abraham. He moves out of Sumer in a mood of protest against modern times. Tradition presents him as an innovative figure who rescues mankind from the decadence of idol worship; he stands as the towering bringer of the worship of 'one god'.

'This is the perception we have of him, but it is only a partial representation.

'Abraham it seems turns his back on modernity. He reacts against novel ideas and the new awareness of his time; he opts for the conservative line.

'What is the new awareness of the time? Is it the sense that the feminine principle has been overplayed and that it is the turn of the masculine principle to be explored?

'I would accept this. His reform is directed against the dominant idea of the time. His monotheism thought to be a giant leap forward for humanity is a protest against progressive ideas. The theme of the Moon echoes through Genesis woven into the fabric of the narrative and around the lives of the Patriarchs and their wives. Esoteric doctrine calls the moon the 'wanderer'. Abraham too is a 'wanderer'; he wanders from East to West like the moon in its trajectory around the Earth. The theme of the polar opposites, Moon and Sun is found everywhere.

'Abraham and Lot, Jacob and Esau, the text abounds in such imagery, says Moses. I see the text in a new light, in terms of the primary forces of masculine and feminine, Sun and Moon, of primeval polarity.

'The story of Esau and Jacob is a dramatisation of the cosmic reality of polarity. The Sun-Moon imagery is also found in carvings and paintings of Buddha. But for the 'Awakened One' there is no polarity, only primordial unity restored. Buddha is always depicted with Sun and Moon implying that he has blended polar opposites and effected union between matter and spirit, light and dark, Moon and Sun, masculine and feminine principles.

'All suffering stems from duality.

'Buddha made it clear that the root of suffering lies in duality. He explained that duality has floundered humanity and will continue to do so until man wakes up to reality.

'Neither Abraham nor his god transcend polarity, they are encamped within it.

'The theme of polarity is dramatised throughout. Duality is everywhere to be found in the Old Testament, storehouse of the eternal Manichean struggle between light and dark. The image of the twins fighting in Rebecca's womb hints at polarity. Man is the battleground in which all opposites are waging a relentless war.

'Polarity is the dominant theme of the Old Testament and we are its carters.

'Polarity is the fact of Creation, but your handling of polarity is altogether unique. You see polarity everywhere, you magnify it, you embellish it, and you exaggerate it. You divide and subdivide to justify your sense of separateness and chosenness. These two themes which run throughout your tradition are instances of polarity gone astray.

'Endorsing duality we have endorsed the source of human suffering. We have approved the fount of pain, the origin of wars and all human misery. We made it an asset, a god-given privilege. And the people I knew, my Hassidic teachers were commanded by their spiritual leader to spread the word to the four corners of the globe!

'Light, my son!

'So the future for humanity and the meaning behind the theme of the Messiah is the dissolution of polarity.

'Absolutely. Awareness of duality is the root cause of human suffering. The Law of Grace will bring an end to it and restore the perception of wholeness.

The reality that lies behind the illusion of duality is undivided Oneness as Buddha declared. Your people are imbued with the idea of duality and separation and so trudge down the perilous path of illusion.

'A paradox, notes Moses, we are ardent defenders of the idea of the 'one god' and fervent defenders of polarity, the very negation of the One! God says 'I am the god of Abraham, the god of Isaac and the god of Jacob'. In the light of what you just explained what does this daily prayer mean?

'At a deeper level of meaning, Abraham symbolises the spirit in manifestation, the Father. Isaac hints at Isis the Goddess who was the 'breath of life', the soul. As for Jacob, he stands for the body just as Adam did. And so emerges the foundation platform of Creation: body, mind and spirit blending into One.

'If Abraham, Isaac and Jacob represent humanity, the Trinity embodied in man, then all is One, there is no separation, no division, no fragmentation. Differentiation is only appearance.

'That's right. All separation is illusory; Genesis tells you that, yet your learned rabbis have insisted on the illusion of separation and on affirming duality.

'If all is One the Father is at the same time the Son. And time is an illusion.

'Precisely. Well done, my son! You can now understand the words of the Master, 'I am before Abraham' which so incensed the Rabbis. Anchored in temporality, in Samsara, they did not know that time is an illusion.

'Jacob after his struggle with the angel – or Yahweh - is called Israel, does he become all three at once?

'If you forget for a moment the literal meaning, then yes, Jacob becomes all three. His struggle with the angel or Yahweh has opened his eyes. He is now aware of who he truly is: body, mind and spirit. He awakens to reality, he contains all, he is all! Furthermore, the three syllables IS-RA-EL reveals as it conceals the essential nature of Jacob. IS symbolises the soul in man: Isis as you know was the 'breath of life'. RA is the Sun god and alludes to the physical body. EL is the spirit in man. Once again we stumble on the primal trinity of body, mind and spirit!

'The Goddess Isis and the Sun god are hiding in the pages of the Old Testament, mumbles Moses. I am mystified.

'What do you think your ancestors were doing in the luminous land of Egypt, if not harvest some of its spiritual treasures? They took perhaps more than they could grasp! Moses, Initiate of the Egyptian Mysteries, did not leave behind Isis, El and Ra; he brought them out and gave them to the Children of IS-RA-El. You see, you are an integral part of humanity. Your name says so!

'One of the fundamental tenets of Hassidic doctrine is that only the Jew is endowed with soul and spirit.

'And what of the rest of humanity, I wonder? What became of the One humanity in the mind of the messianic people? What happened to the promise of a messianic deliverance for the world? When did the split occur? When did confusion set in? Is it possible to be so forgetful when the text reminds you at all times?

'There is no One humanity, states Moses with profound melancholy.

'O yes, replies Sanaka with unusual animation, there is One humanity and you are it! Did the Baal Shem Tov sense the hidden meaning in the name he gave himself, Israel? Israel represents humanity and stands for unity, for oneness. So why do they clutch at a notion they know to be untrue? Is it a plea to abandon the command 'Love your neighbour like yourself'?

Benzaccai enters the Synagogue - Quarrel with the rabbis

Benzaccai arises one morning with the tormented enthusiasm of an evangelist, the anguished fervour of a missionary. He dresses in his best clothes, folds his frayed prayer shawl and heads for the synagogue, his mind feverishly churning over the issues that have kept him awake these last few nights. He intends to address the congregation and awaken them to a new way of looking at their condition. He enters the synagogue in a state of inner turmoil, walks resolutely to the first row of chairs and sits down. The older rabbi, surprised to see this well-known unbeliever greets him in a guarded but polite manner. Benzaccai replies with courtesy, but the gracious manners soon melt away to give way to a universal feeling of shared distrust. A tangible feeling of disquiet spreads rapidly. Now is the moment he had been anticipating with gloomy certainty.

'I am not a religious man, begins Benzaccai, we are reading today the Verses we read 2000 years ago, in exactly the same manner, head down in humble reverence, moved to tears, head covered in deferential acceptance. Some of you show great concentration and adoration, yet beneath the reverence and humility ferment much pride and prejudice. Deep in our genetic memory strong emotions are stirred up, not love and reverence but anger and frustration. I know, I have monitored them all my life, I hold them inside me, we all contain them in our being. They are deeply encoded in our genetic material. We are born with them and we pass them on.

The rabbis listen in disbelief. They sensed trouble the moment the man entered the synagogue but were not expecting such an outburst. They remain silent for fear of upsetting the faithful and not entirely sure what to do. They expect respect and obedience and never deal with unbelievers. The unbelievers are 'out there', out of sight, out of mind. They are not worth bothering about, they will not be saved. The synagogue belongs to the devout, those who revere god, those who profess devotion.

Playing on the element of surprise, Benzaccai proceeds, 'yet I glimpse not the slightest expression of doubt or enquiry. Things are as they always were, yet the world has changed beyond recognition. We are sending men on the moon, space satellites are probing the universe, we can establish how the world came into being, we know the secret of life at atomic level, we even know how to manipulate the genes that make up

156

our body, and we understand the function and nature of DNA. 'We are beginning to suspect that the universe is more a great thought than a great machine', said the physicist James Jeans.

The rabbi, visibly annoyed interrupts, 'This is not the university, in this holy house we study the word of God, not the product of foreign wisdom. All that comes from the world is profane and contaminated. Only the word of God is worthy of study. We know who created us and why.

Benzaccai, well rehearsed, replies with equal certainty and vigour:

'You do not. Torah is not the final word of God, it was not written at Sinai, but after the exile of Babylonia 800 years later and the scribes who etched it did so not under divine inspiration, not to shed light but to shroud the original text in mystery. The original texts were so doctored as to become impenetrable.

'Are you a heathen? Do you believe in god, asks a rabbi?

Without losing his poise Benzaccai questions back, 'do you?'

The rabbi is never questioned. The question is provocative, 'Is it not obvious, are you sightless, even a heathen like you surely can see that!

'What is so special about 'belief' and demonstration of piety, protests Benzaccai? Belief is an emotion and emotions are unstable. Knowledge is of the mind and is more stable, more enduring. Emotions bring suffering, knowledge attracts more knowledge.

'We have believed for thousands of years, insists the rabbi exasperated.

'That is our misfortune and the root of our suffering. Belief was appropriate to the past when man had basic emotions and nothing else. Since then mankind has evolved a mind and even a 'new brain', the cortex. To believe is not only archaic it is negative. We are bolted in emotional devotion, keeping humanity locked with us. In order to palliate to your archaic god you are preventing the emancipation of the Jew and the much promised unification.

The angry rabbi is now vulnerable and Benzaccai emboldened bombards him, 'The more obvious a thing is, the less credible, you protest too loudly.

The angry rabbi does not let go and recklessly shouts, 'I am asking you again, do not try my patience, do you believe in god?

'Which one, asks Benzaccai tantalisingly?

'Which one, shouts the rabbi, don't you fear for your soul? Get this madman out of my sight! This 'rachah' is offensive to our virtuous eyes.

157

'Rabbi, which god or gods, repeats Levinson enjoying the dual of words?

'Please answer the man, says hesitantly a rabbi who had remained quiet, a sad and gentle looking man with a noble expression.

Benzaccai looking at the angry rabbi, 'I am simply asking you to answer your own question. You ask me if I believe in god and I am returning the question, I see no offence in this.

'You see no offence, do you?

'You question me with scorn; you throw at me the question that has occupied my thoughts all my life. I delved diligently in the studies you advocate, to no avail. Dissatisfied but determined to discover the truth, I turned to the wisdom of the world you so despise, in the hope of finding the answer to the most fundamental question a man has to address in his life.

'The truth is in this book, nowhere else, the truth that God himself gave to Moses. There is only one truth and we have it, replies the angry rabbi waving the Book in wrath. You want to know if I believe in the one god, fear for your soul, heretic, well I am telling you, I believe in the one god!

'Which one, insists Benzaccai brazenly.

'There is only one, stubborn unbeliever, 'rachah', you will roast in hell!

'This has not always been the case. Not long ago, we worshipped many gods, in the land promised to Moses. Our rowdy ancestors danced a wild dance around the Golden Calf, shamelessly, in the holy presence of Moses. When the Temple was destroyed and as the people was about to be scattered to the four corners of the world, the rabbis seemingly unsympathetic to the fate of their people sighed a sigh of relief, 'at last the genius of idolatry is going to be stamped out'. They hoped that great suffering would pluck out the people's penchant for idolatry.

'The rabbis knew and this came to pass, replies the Rabbi with satisfaction.

'They must be rejoicing in the netherworld, for they were proved right. We no longer worship many idols, we worship only one. The many gods that gave us consolation and succour were replaced by the one god who gives neither consolation nor succour. The one god, who has disabled us with decrees and taboos, disempowered us with his practices and precepts, the same god who plotted the annihilation of mankind in the days of Noah. The god of destruction and death', concludes Benzaccai with the passion of a preacher.

'How dare you come here and insult god in his very house!

'I am not insulting God. I am questioning your intelligence or the lack of it, I am stirring the knife in the wound inflicted thousands of years ago that you refuse to heal.

'You are an impostor, an ignorant, you insult god and you insult us.

'How could I insult a god who does not exist? In your heart of heart you know this. Listen to the still voice of the soul that you smother. Hark to the silent voice of the inner God that you have silenced. In a concentrations camp of Poland, a few sincere, god-fearing men made religious history when they came together in an unusual assembly, a human tribunal to try god. They fasted, prayed, wept and brought god to justice: they found god guilty of crimes against his Children. But they did not go far enough, they did find god guilty of crimes against the Jews but what of mankind?

'What of mankind indeed, replies the rabbi furiously, what have they done for us, they have killed us in every generation and they enjoy it.

'That is the point! They have been killing us for thousands of years and we still do not understand why! We refuse to find out why! Is it because the source of our predicament springs from us and not from them? The reason is buried deep in our collective unconscious, but our heads are buried in the sands of ignorance.

'I have heard as much as I can take from a renegade, get out of here before I put a curse on you and cut you off from god.

'You have neither the right nor the power to cut me off, I am a fragment of the Creator, he incarnates in me as he does in all life.

'Out of here, blasphemer. Do not anger god. I am ordering you out. The rabbi unable to control himself shouts, 'you heretic, out of the house of god. May god forgive your sinful soul, if it is not already lost.

'There is no such thing as sin, replies Benzaccai endeavouring to remain poised. It was unknown in the ancient world, we invented it. Nothing to be proud of! As for my soul, how can I lose that which is indestructible, boundless and timeless? Your god gets angry, the Divine does not. Your god judges, the Divine does not. Your god forgives when the mood takes him, the Divine does not forgive because he neither judges nor condemns. The universal Life force that holds all the universes together is not in the least concerned with your irrelevant squabble. He is Life in all its diverse manifestations, but you would not know, because you have not as yet grasped the reality of life. The entire universe is a giant thought, a sea of energy, pulsating with life. The nature of Reality is consciousness and your god is to the Divine what an atom is in size and importance to the universe.

'Out of the house of god, commands the rabbi with fiery eyes, livid with righteous anger.

'How can I get out and where would I go?

'You should have thought of that before I placed a curse on you.

'You don't understand. There isn't an atom in this vast universe that is empty of His Presence. Where could I go? Wherever I go I am sure to be contained within Him. Wherever I go he is contained within me! We are inseparable; I cannot escape him any more than he can escape me!

'Sacrilege, blasphemy! Out of this sacred place!

'At Sinai, our ancestors caged god in a wooden box. To this day you narrate with pride the story of your incarcerated god, how he came to be locked in that box and you teach it to your children like other parents narrate the story of Aladdin and the genie in the oil lamp. Your thinking has not changed, continues Benzaccai emboldened by the lack of self control of his opponent. You accept as true that god can be locked in a box, like a doll in a doll's house! God is to you an object that occupies a space and exists in time. You see your god as you see yourself: a three-dimensional being, one who lives in a physical world bound by space and time.

'Are you immaterial, you look solid to me, jeers the rabbi.

'I am no more solid than you are. The true nature of the world is not matter but energy; it is not solid and inert but empty and pulsating. The world is alive. That's what the Essenes challenged you with long ago, they too said that the world is not solid, that the world is thought made manifest.

'And we dealt with them as we should deal with you!

'You claim that you study only the word of god, and this you do. But the old books tell you nothing about your true nature, the purpose of life on Earth, the nature of your soul, the nature of the world and the nature of God himself. What you learn concerns this world and this world alone, yet you condemn modern science!

'You are damning yourself!

'They told you who you truly are; they told you that you are deathless, boundless beings. You rejected your own divinity because you had devoted centuries to erecting laws, rules, taboos, precepts and practices in a towering structure, a Tower of Babel in celebration of physicality. 'When the Tao is lost there is much need for legality, morality and knowledge', says the wise East. As man lost the memory of the Divine, he became neglectful of his own essential nature. Separated from his soul man had to make up for his loss. The Talmud was manufactured, faithful record compiled over centuries of your entrenched belief about man and the world. And this belief is effectively materialistic; it revolves around bloodline and survival. The Essenes were bold enough to teach you the true nature of man and the true nature of the cosmos. They explained in allegories and fables that the diverse forms are an optical illusion generated by the mind. Those who can truly see know that the world is not solid, that it is thought 'solidified', light 'congealed'. Our brain interprets light as form.

'What are you rambling on, you make no sense at all, says the quiet rabbi.

'How can god be trapped in a box when the many interlocking universes cannot contain the cosmic Mind?

Looking around at the silent rabbis for support, the loud rabbi explodes, 'do you understand a word this blasphemer is muttering?

'They will one day, replies Benzaccai. We all are advancing on the Path, the march is irreversible, for humanity and for the whole of Creation, but not all of us are on the same point. We all emanate from this limitless Being and as such we too are limitless.

'This is an outrage!

'This shocks you! You want to go on believing that we are leaves blown by the wind of fate and dispersed by the whims of your god!

'You come down from the apes then, roars the rabbi?

''And there was light'. We are emanations of that primordial light. It is the Presence pulsing and radiating in your chest. God is 'out there' and 'inside here', we are One with the light, we are the light. 'I and my Father are One'. What infuriates you the most the fact of God living inside your chest or the fact that the real God is Love? That's it! Love is anathema, your god is fear?

'Yes, god is fear! God created all, contains all, owns all, yet the only thing he demands from us is fear, he wants us to fear him! This is the only thing he does not own, the only thing we can give him, replies the rabbi proud of his piety, unaware that he is quoting an aberration.

'Patriarchy, monotheism and leadership because of moral superiority! It is all there in a nutshell, the unchanging predicament of the 'chosen people' and through them, the enduring predicament of mankind. Weary, Benzaccai combs the group of rabbis and notices a young man among them who listens intently with an earnest expression. Drawing a coloured ball, he addresses him, 'look at this multicoloured translucent ball, what do you see?

The young rabbi hesitantly replies, a multicoloured ball.

'Is this a Jew, asks Benzaccai insistently?

'Of course not, if this is a joke, it is in poor taste, replies the young man.

'Is this a woman?

'No, replies the young man. What are you getting at?

'If I placed you under hypnosis, I could make you believe it. There is an irrational part of the mind, the 'unconscious' which believes with no trouble. This may be a sick joke to you but one we have lived with for millennia. The human soul looks like this, he continues, wanting no interruption. A sphere of light, pulsing, pounding with life and knowing only love, freedom and compassion. This sphere of light knows no separation, no gender, no race, no dogma, no colour, no ethnic difference, not nationality.

'What are you getting at, repeats the young rabbi?

'The priesthood long ago conspired to place us under a state of hypnosis and made us collectively believe that this beautiful sphere of light was an object. Since those dark days each male Jew must blurt out his gratitude at not being a woman.

'And what if it is a woman, boldly asks the young man?

'Well, if it is a woman? An object of lust and stupidity.

'And what if it is a Gentile?

'Ah! Well now, if it is a Gentile, a lesser being, unclean, untouchable.

'What if it is a Jew?

'Now, let me think, mutters Benzaccai feigning to mull over the question. Well if it is a Jew, he can only be the purpose of Creation! 'There is neither Gentile nor Jew' said the Essenes. The human ego is trapped in identity and gender, make- believe situations and role-play. It is a delusion, a mirage. Have you ever been to the theatre?

'No, of course not, I don't go to the theatre, he replies with animated conceit.

'As a deprived child attending religious school for the destitute, Benzaccai had to endure the smugness of the devout missionaries who would mouth with sensuous piety, swollen with conceit, 'we don't eat this, we don't wear this, we don't drink that', 'we don't touch that'. They were too holy to dirty their hands with life, so they kept apart.

Endowed with a large ego they believed that the Creator had selected them to be 'special' and to show off the crust of their piety. Their spirituality expressed itself in the outer coverings.

'Time for prayer, commands an older rabbi, you have listened to this impious talk for too long, do you want to corrupt your mind, are you trying to offend god, heaven forbid, he insists in devout distress! They move out; Benzaccai breathes a sigh of relief, but he knows that their exit is not the end. However he presses on now that he has the attention of the young rabbi, 'An actor called Orson Welles played Macbeth; he played the character but never believed himself to be Macbeth; he was just pretending to be Macbeth. As an actor he was 'cheating' his audience. That's alright, his audience wanted to be cheated and delighted in it. He was pretending with our tacit acceptance.

'What are you saying, asks the young man increasingly concerned? 'We have been playing roles for ever. The ego seeks to reincarnate, it has to. It is driven by both the law of evolution and the law of opportunity. Many human beings choose to reincarnate as Jews. They come back on the stage of life believing to be Jews and wanting the world to believe it too. In other words, they play at being Jews, they pretend! All human beings who come back into incarnation pretend, they return in a make-believe world. That's what we did you and I! We have put on the cloak of flesh and convinced ourselves that we truly are Jews. Yet, the soul mocks the self-deception of the ego. The soul knows; it was its decision to dress in this garment in order to do things in a different way and learn things from a different angle.

'This is heresy, mutters the young rabbi distressed!

'But the soul is not hoodwinked by role-play. The soul takes what it needs from the experiment and discards the rest. The ego believes the whole charade to be true, the whole mirage to be solid. Like children playing cowboys and Indians, they get so engrossed in the game that it is real to them. The soul goes along with the game in order to explore, experiment, observe, analyse, consider and conclude.

'The soul is a scientist, exclaims the young man perplexed?

'You hit the nail on the head! The self is lured into the experiment and can't see the wood for the trees. The soul incarnates into the Jewish frame in order to learn and grow. But why the pretence? To finally explode the illusion and break the mould! Plato said that 'the body is a tomb'. Other mystic thinkers have used the same image of the tomb and death. Whoever identifies with the mortal self is 'spiritually dead'. Our religious doctrine built around man in physicality perpetuates our materialistic view of life.

'Materialistic view of life, we, the most religious people on Earth, exclaims the young rabbi genuinely offended.

'Again you hit the nail on the head! Our predicament stems from a mix-up. We take religion and spirituality to be identical. Often religion excludes the spiritual. Religion is of the personality, the soul has no religion. The soul is love, freedom, compassion, understanding, conciliation, consent, tolerance, beauty, unity, joy and light. These are conspicuously absent from our doctrine. Our tradition which revolves around survival keeps us in the 'tomb'.

'The Jew lives in the real world, not in the heavens.

'Indeed, but the Jew is also a being of light who does not belong on Earth. He is the Infinite in incarnation like all human beings. And the Talmud – that Tower of Babel - should at least hint at his true origins, the heavens!

'Why am I listening to you, moans the troubled young man? Yet I must, I am going to incur the wrath of the rabbis, worst still the wrath of god, but I must go on. When I was a child, I would lie awake at night waiting for my father to return from the house of study, my heart pounding in anticipation, I knew that he had a secret for me, something wonderful to tell me. It never materialised. Later I would walk in the study room or the synagogue yearning to hear the magical words I so longed to hear as a child, dreading and longing. It never materialised. I dismissed the whole thing as childish and futile.

'Until now, smiles Benzaccai sympathetically.

'Until now, sighs the young rabbi. Dreading because I knew that the words I hungered for would change my life for ever. Fate has brought you, let's withdraw to the back room, I must hear more, don't let me down he adds with a touch of desperation. They withdraw to the quiet study room.

'Thought creates, continues Benzaccai, 'As you think in your heart so you are'. Not only do you create yourself with your thoughts, you create the world around you. Do you guess the far-reaching implications? Thoughts manifest in the material world. Look around you, everything you see is a manifestation of a thought. Emotions are powerful agents; the strongest emotion is fear. Fear influences action. Thought forms of distrust, apprehension, anxiety and devastation are of the densest, they are so potent that they precipitate swiftly in our reality. They take shape.

'We are the most religious people on Earth, what has this got to do with us?

'We speak fear, we think fear, and we live fear. Our unconscious mind dreams fear, we pray fear, we carry the genes of the god of fear. And fear is the densest, most destructive emotion and one that keeps us solidly implanted into physical reality, separated from the Source, separated from the soul. Do you understand what I am talking about?

'Thoughts make us what we are; thoughts make our world. Thoughts produced by fear have shaped our history. Is this what you are saying?

'You have the knack of hitting the nail on the head each time! If this is what you have been longing to hear since childhood, then you are in for trouble, smiles Benzaccai with sympathy.

'There is no going back, sighs the young man in tears.

The synagogue was filling with people. It was time for prayer and this was an opportunity to make a stand. He returned to the main room and decidedly stood on the pulpit facing the congregation. Luck was on his side. The men who on entering the temple looked preoccupied, inattentive or even agitated were now silent, their attention fixed on that impious man who was not wearing a hat. His quarrel with the rabbis became a sermon. Turning to the congregation and with a deep emotion which soon was shared by all, Benzaccai paused, undaunted by the excitable rabbis draped in their prayer shawls. He was determined to say his piece, uninterrupted. His tone changed, the timbre of voice and demeanour resolute.

'I take this noble Torah as my witness. When you build temples of bricks and stones, you hark back to the formative years of humanity. There is only one temple, the Heart of man. You focus on the outer form in all things, in man, in nature. The dark energies of materialism descended on Atlantis and mankind felt powerless to resist its pull. Both disappeared into the waves, the story of Noah recounts that terrible event. Form should be balanced with its opposite, spirit. When you invest so much attention on the form, you neglect the Idea concealed in the form. Every form contains its own meaning, its unique quality. You read Torah every day, the form gratifies you, you no longer wonder if there is an Idea hidden. Science is discovering ideas concealed in all forms, you have been given the great Book of Creation and you play with the stories!

'The only Temple God is interested in is your Heart. The universe does not contain him, yet your heart does, if you care to look. You knew all this long, long ago, but you forgot and you began to build temples of stones and bricks, and the more you forgot, you more you indulged in legality, procedure, debate and conjecture. The Temple of Jerusalem was intended as a reminder. It stood as a metaphor for man himself. The Temple of Jerusalem is the heart of man, the Shekhina dwells within. Unlike the Temple of stone which is transient, the Temple in man is indestructible. We fast and mourn inconsolably the destruction of the Temple, unaware of the Temple within which can never be destroyed. With a poignant irony it is the Temple of stone which is the object of our desire, the focus of our lamentations. As we mourn we ignore the real Temple within, invincible, imperishable, unassailable. Our tragedy stems from our fascination with the transient, the ephemeral, that which has no substance, no reality. We look outside searching for what is inside! It took man millions of years to emerge from unconsciousness into consciousness. He is now poised to rise from self-consciousness to God-consciousness. He is ready to accept that he is God incarnate walking the Earth. For this shift to take place man must be willing to break free from the past. He must 'be born again'.

'If the Temple is in the heart of man, then it is in the heart of all men, says the young man sitting on the front row.

'You hit the nail on the head again! How can you disdain another when the light that shines in your chest also shines in his? How can you revile the other who shelters the Shekhina? And so when you exalt your god but despise the other, you are living a lie, you accept as true an illusion.

'To glorify God is to glorify the other and if you cannot do this then your life is a charade, utters the young rabbi.

'You have done it again, exclaims Benzaccai! Each time you utter 'thank god for not making me a woman, for not making me a Gentile, my god is the only god, he created the world for me, I am the purpose of his creation', you live a lie, you live a sham. Your pride is founded on a delusion. You recall the Psalmist, 'Vanity of vanity, all is vanity'. You confess your ignorance of the nature of the world. God created man in his image, on this you should meditate every day of your lives. To exalt the true God is to exalt the other and not just man but all life forms, the most humble, a pig, a wild flower, a worm deserve respect for the life that animates them

'I never thought of it that way, the life of God in all things!

'You barely admit the life of God in human beings! There is no escaping this truth; you love God to the degree that you love the other. You love God only to the degree that you sense his living presence in all forms of life. Think of the sun; the rays radiating from the sun are neither separate nor different from the sun; there is one sun and one light. There is one Life and humanity is arriving at this realisation, enabled by the findings of science. It is a tragic fact that the Revelation given to enlighten us has kept man in darkness and ignorance. Ignorance is the source of all suffering.

'But I know who I am, says the young rabbi in pain.

'Who are you?

'I know perfectly well who I am, I am a Jew, do not taunt me!

'This is what you think you are! You were indoctrinated into thinking this way. Had you been adopted at birth by a Gentile family, would you know that you are a Jew? No, you would be a Gentile; you would be indoctrinated into Gentile beliefs. No child is born with a doctrine pinned on him, each newborn is a blank slate and we write on it what we like; such is the misfortune of mankind. This is what your separated self, alienated self thinks you are! The ego seeks its own survival, the ego seeks separation, the ego negates union, the ego abhors unity. When you broadcast, 'I am a Jew, I am a man, I bless god for not making me a woman or a Gentile', you are in fact refuting the soul in you and in all beings. You are obstructing unification with the soul and with the Source of your being. You do not know who you are!

The incensed rabbis cannot tolerate this madness any longer, they are about to blurt out when an old man sitting on the front row intervenes, 'Let this mad man speak, I want to hear him out, we all do.

'When you see the other person as a lesser being this gives you the right to hurt him and even destroy him. You perceive an illusion. When you collect in the house of prayers and you shut the other person out - be it a woman or a stranger – you broadcast a message that reverberates throughout the world, you are saying ' God dwells with me but not with the other, I am special, he is not, I am chosen, he is not, he is lesser than me'. You are denying his divinity by asserting yours too brashly! You broadcast that humanity is broken up, that the world is dislocated and that you are disconnected. You shout that you have forgotten the Oneness before Creation, before duality appeared, before the Fall. Why build temples of stone when God himself built temples in the heart of each human being? He does not want bricks and mortar, he wants the human heart, it is his natural home, the space he has always occupied. And when you realise this, the scales will fall of your eyes 'And the truth shall set you free'. You will save the world because every human being is his own saviour and the saviour of humanity. We promote the physical ego and as ' the body is a tomb' it is 'death' we promote. Ritual performance reinforces our solidity, our endurance in physical form. The law was thought to be a curse, *'All who depend upon works of the law are under a curse'*. The same text denounces *'the law that kills'*.

'Another blasphemer, screams a rabbi!

'The ego hungers for enlargement, the ego thirsts to be 'special', 'unique' and 'chosen'. Every word you utter exacerbates your predicament because every word inflates, distends and swells the ego. The ego is false, it is manufactured, it is conditioned. The more you pump it up the more fragile, the more threatened, the more vulnerable it is. Our sad history is the dramatic evidence of this. Our law is a monument to the human ego. 'As long as man has any regard for his corpse-like body, he is impure and suffers from his enemies as well as from birth, disease and death', said a Hindu Sage. Doesn't this encapsulate our condition perfectly? The body is all. Our law is built around this corpse-like body to keep it disease-free and to instruct us not to bump each other off. Survival is the key; yet it brings only suffering because we worship on the altar of this corpse-like body. Our law keeps man chained to his fake identity – the ego – and denies him access to his real Self, his true identity. This is 'death' not life!

Benzaccai decides to take his leave with these last words carefully chosen to produce the most impact, aware of the impression he has made. The congregation is under a spell and he wants to exit before it is too late. At this very moment two angry old rabbis enter the synagogue, they overhear the last few words and are seething with rage. He observes a look of horror and deep resentment on the faces of all present. Feeling drained of energy, 'I am not talking your language', he concludes in a whisper. The men rise to their feet, a surge of anger swells like a shock wave sweeping outward from a point. They grab him and hurl him out. The older rabbi orders that Benzaccai should be dropped in the occupied Territories. Blindfolded, he is driven in a truck to a distant location; the journey seems endless, he feels sick at heart and ill at the pit of his stomach.

Disappointed by his performance, Benzaccai is a changed man. A short while ago, he had entered the synagogue with the enthusiasm of a man with a mission. He was reflecting bitterly as the truck was rattling down the roads and tossing him awkwardly. To change our history is to change our thinking. Change begins in the realm of thought, change originates in the mind. The rabbis want the old pattern of doing, thinking and feeling to persist; they want to perpetuate the 'drama of pain'.

Dumped in a crowded street of Hebron, he tries to lift himself off the ground. Surrounded by an agitated crowd, in his best Arabic he explains that he got into this mess because he tried to make the rabbis understand that we all are from the One God and no one can exist outside of the whole. They calm down and on the order of their leader armed with a machine gun, they whisk him away and hurl him in a dark room. The Sufi doctor hears the news of his ordeal and captivity and goes to the rescue. A sensitive and thoughtful man, the doctor feels sympathy for this strange man with a message. For the second time doctor Suleiman is going to help Benzaccai. Destiny has knocked on his door once again. The Sufi knows that any event is a learning opportunity. Suleiman is aware of the spiritual meaning behind events, he senses that the universe is beckoning him to utilise this event. The time is soon approaching when major changes are to take place. He intuits that the manuscript that has so infuriated the rabbis in Jerusalem may well speak of such changes. He is like the inspired and perceptive Magi of long ago who had travelled from far-away lands to usher in the New Age, the new spirit of the time.

The friends were feeling apprehensive. Furtively glancing at their watches they were silent. Benzaccai had not returned. A feeling of doom descended on them. Jeremy broke the heavy silence, 'something is wrong, Benzaccai is two hours late, we must phone his office'. He had not been in the office all day. Puzzled, Levinson suggests they contact his family. Their search is fruitless. Finally, he remembers that Benzaccai had casually mentioned his intention to visit the rabbi to discuss a personal matter. They call at his house, but the rabbi was still at the synagogue debating vehemently the unusual and disturbing events of the morning. They hurry to the synagogue to ask the rabbi if he knows where to find Benzaccai. He shouts that as far as the law is concerned, Benzaccai is a heretic, 'he no longer is a Jew, he has been struck off from the Book of Life and pronounced officially 'dead'! That was that. The group, stunned by the violence of his denunciation, are silenced in awe and disbelief. What has he done to deserve such a curse? The rabbi has no time for them; they are a bunch of unbelievers. 'Liberalism is the evil of the time and the scourge of this country', he shouts'. He has

169

been campaigning for a return to the autocratic rule of the ancient god. He felt with deep conviction that religious repression was the only solution to the problems of his people!

The friends weary and worried left. They had been brooding over Sanaka's portrayal of Abraham and wished to explore this enigmatic biblical character further. The revolutionary nature of Abraham had always fascinated Levinson and Clara. Could Abraham be justifiably regarded as an epoch-making figure, an innovative spiritual and social reformer or was he an astute political individual who wanted to exploit his social position in Sumerian society? Or was he a retrograde theorist who wanted to hold on to the obsolete ideas of the past? They decided it was time to put these questions to Master Sananda.

Abraham by Master Sananda

'Master Sananda, begins Clara, would you shed some light on a few enigmatic but significant biblical figures. If I may, I would like to start with the first major protagonist of the Old Testament, Abraham. At the time Abraham takes command of the group which becomes the Hebrews, several encounters take place between him and his god. The dialogues are disconcerting in their ambiguity, some are friendly, as if between equals. In other dialogues god imposes his supremacy and asks Abraham to walk a certain path: 'You shall walk before me!' Who was the god Abraham was talking to?

'In part, answers Sananda, Abraham was talking to the God within. He had a sense of his own divinity. He recognised that there was a spark of that divinity within him that he could connect with, in the same way that you might feel able on occasion to connect with your own I AM Presence. That was one aspect of it. Abraham, as you might appreciate, had his own specific origins in relation with this Planet, that is to say, he was the representative of a group who had come to Earth with a specific purpose. Therefore, when he spoke to his god, he was, to some extent, tracking back along the energy line of the purpose that he and his community were acquainted with. In practice, this means that he was channelling the collective wisdom of a group of beings who were genetically responsible for an important part of his own racial origins in terms of his human form. That is to say, he was connecting with a group who played a major role in transmitting information at the genetic level into the human form that was his and his forbears and descendants.

'May I ask which group?

'The group from which he originated had their own collective wisdom which by that time was highly evolved and which in turn came from the Source of All. Their collective wisdom was tailored by their experience which emphasised particular aspects of the Divine and underplayed or played-less upon other aspects of the Source, so that they were acting as a relay station for those of their members who had chosen to incarnate on Earth and Abraham was one of them. He was a leader among those who chose to incarnate and became their leader on this Planet.

'He was a leader among his galactic group and when they decided to incarnate on this Planet, he became their leader on Earth too, sums up Clara.

'For him, continues Sananda, to expand his understanding of who he was, he would experience the inner space. It was like having a temple of peace, a temple of stillness within him which in trance-like states enabled him to connect with the group of beings he had been part of before he incarnated on Earth. They, in turn, were doing their best to relay information and energy from the Source of All.

'In meditative states he would move into the inner spaces to connect with the people he had left behind on his galaxy of origin, again sums up Clara.

'There is a third strand to the nature of Abraham's inner experience. The being you traditionally know by the name of Yahweh was also playing a part in this particular drama. You can think of this being, in a way, as something of an 'interloper' - not using the term in a critical sense. He was a being of great power and energy who also experienced himself as divine and who was using the flow of energy that Abraham connected to, the Source of All, to flow through particular messages. Messages of importance from the perspective of the group of non-physical beings whom Yahweh represented in their plan for the generation of a particular type of civilisation here on Earth. To return to Abraham's experience, the whole thing would have been like a single rope of communication, comparatively speaking undifferentiated. What I have done is just to unravel that rope slightly to suggest that this single rope was made up of different strands.

'If I may go back to the second strand Abraham was linking up with a galactic group he was associated with. Was it his soul group or a civilisation that had flourished on Earth long ago?

'You can think of it as a soul group, in many ways it was his soul group. We are talking about a group of people who incarnated together on this Planet but who had not chosen, by and large, to live on Earth at any time. They had sent forth representatives among whom Abraham to experience life on Earth. Just to explore what it was like, in order to help them develop their own civilisation. This group lived and still live on a separate galaxy to your own galaxy, so there is some distance in astronomical terms from your Earth, in physical terms.

'They had an interest in what was occurring on this Planet?

'Absolutely, that's right!

'For what purpose?

'They had a particular interest in developing ways of transforming energy. The type of energy they were interested in transforming – they foresaw correctly – was likely to develop on Earth. Broadly speaking, we can call this the energy of polarity. They were interested in discovering how you transform those polarised energies into unified energy. They invested much effort and the intention directed by their whole society focused toward understanding the nature of these energies. Earth was by no means the only Planet they chose to explore, but it was one which, they felt, would be a very fruitful place for them in which to explore these concepts.

'The Old Testament is the repository of polarity which has caused much misery, because it implies division. Was it a natural choice to use Abraham as the father of a human family which would be repository of these polarities?

'Abraham was not the first but certainly one of the earliest members of this particular wave of exploration and indeed it felt for all involved a very natural progression in the work they were engaged in. Abraham himself had some awareness - although you appreciate that the density of the Earth plane made it difficult for him to retain full awareness. He had to some degree an awareness of that wider mission beyond his individual human life. This is one of the things he expressed or did his best to express in the way he guided his people.

'Was he connected with the Hebrew group he guided, asks Clara?

'O, yes, yes

'Were they the same people who came from his distant galaxy of origin?

'Not all, but a fair proportion had genetic input from that particular galactic civilisation. Something of a genetic broth if you like, a mixture of different sources, because a number of different groups were interested in having input into that particular racial grouping.

'Quite apart from Yahweh and his group?

'That's right, absolutely! As history often is, quite a complex picture.

'If I understand, other galactic civilisations were interested in having some genetic input into the early Hebrews?

'Yes.

'It certainly is a complex picture. Were all these different galactic civilisations concerned with exploring polarity?

'Broadly speaking, yes. You could say that everyone who comes to the Earth plane is interested in exploring polarity. Polarity is such a large feature of this particular level and area of existence. It would be more specific and more accurate to say that they had interests other than the study of the management of polarity. One of the shared interests of all the civilisations which had energy input into this particular group – the early Hebrews – was a belief that somehow it is possible to take energy and split it so that it becomes polarised. Then to bring back, to combine uniquely or unify that energy in a new way so that it has transformed into something very significantly higher and more evolved than the energy that was originally split into polarised forms in the first place. That was the kind of shared methodology.

'Is this the reason why the Old Testament seems to embody polarity and takes it to its ultimate expression?

'That's right, in some respect. You tend to find in the Old Testament the manifestation of polarity and coupled with it that constant striving for oneness, for unity. So the two are coexisting as you might expect. So yes, a marked experience of polarity in all kinds of way, through the stories of that people as they are recounted in the Bible, but also always a search for oneness: oneness of the people, oneness of the land and oneness with the Divine Source.

'After reading that Abraham was the Ascended Master Morya, I came to the conclusion that the god he was talking to was not Yahweh. Was he Morya?

173

'Yes there is a lot a truth in this. Perhaps not an exact translation but it would be fair enough to say that the being who was Abraham then evolved to become El Morya.

'I assume that Abraham given his eminent origin would have made contact not with Yahweh, but with the Planetary Logos, focussing his energy on the vision of the divine Plan that the Hierarchy is holding for humanity.

'You must remember also that Masters too are on a path of learning. I understand the line of your reasoning, but it is not necessarily the case.

'May I ask what is not necessarily the case?

'It is not necessarily the case that Abraham would not be connecting with Yahweh because he would consider it to be more appropriate to connect with Sanat Kumara. For, you know, all of us have a great variety of experiences and part of the purpose of having many different incarnations, is to elude, to avert connecting with one particular source of divine energy, but to find it in many different ways.

'To what extent was Sanat Kumara, in his function as Lord of the World, associated with the Old Testament? Did he play a leading role in the dramatic events of the Old Testament?

'It would be more accurate to say that Sanat Kumara, as you experience him now is operating outside of time, in the sense that his energy can be present in any situation, at any time and in any place that he chooses. The past is less fixed than it appears.

'I understand that Sanat Kumara exists outside Creation, outside polarity, beyond this reality whereas Yahweh like us is subject to the limitations of time and space.

'Yes. This part also can be transformed. At the moment the human race is undergoing an important change. It is going through a phase of releasing in a fairly short time images, forms and systems of the past in order to transform them, to replace them with images, concepts and forms that contain more of Sanat Kumara' s energy than those you have experienced as being real.

'The forms and systems we experienced as real were only one way of looking at the world?

'You could say, continues Sananda, that Sanat Kumara' s energy is entering more into that experience of the past than it has so far. The past is not sealed off from the present. You can look upon your own life purpose as being part of that work. You yourself are seeking and indeed are creating doorways through which the energy of Sanat Kumara can enter into particular areas of human consciousness. You have a specific interest in aspects of the Old Testament, in the Semitic people. So where you direct your attention and focus your intention with the underlying wish that more light move in those areas, then to that extent Sanat Kumara's energy is able to move back into the past and transform even the past. This is one way of answering your question. For, as you understand that particular past we call the Old Testament, as you understand it in the manner it was given to you, there is not much of Sanat Kumara's energy present. But at the moment, a kind of dissolving is occurring of the boundaries between different racial experiences of the past. This means that energy from different cultural experiences, different spiritual strands are flowing into one another to create a greater experience of harmony and Oneness in the world as you are creating it now. So that for instance, to give you a small example of how this works, if you go back 150 years you will find there were no Buddhist in this country and virtually no one had heard of Buddhism. Today in Britain you will find a lot of people who call themselves Buddhists. This is one way; a particular kind of experience of being on the Earth plane is being introduced in another country. A country which has had the experience that you might broadly call the Christian-as-of-Pagan experience, if you look at it in religious terms. There is a constant inter-pollination of experiences which does not just happen in the present it reaches back into the past.

'We just read that Abraham journeyed out of Sumer in order to secure Moon-worship which was being threatened by Sun-worship. Now, was Abraham determined to save Moon-worship with Yahweh at its head? Did he conceive of the resolution of polarity at the time or is it an entirely different idea altogether?

'For part of him, the consciousness of being engaged in the resolution of polarity was always present as this focus formed part of his known agenda. It was not always easy for him to keep this aim at the forefront of his consciousness, he was having a human experience and sometimes dilemmas and conflicts would arise in his life that made it difficult for him to retain this guiding light before him. There is some truth in this theory, not a sizeable amount of truth, as it is an attempt to oversimplify things, to tie things up neatly.

'Moon-worship was not paramount for Abraham but the resolution of polarity or the management of polarity was?

'It would be true to say that for Abraham both Sun and Moon were important not simply as heavenly bodies influencing this Planet and life on Earth, but as pathways to

175

establish the kinds of connections I spoke of earlier. For Abraham, the Moon was an effective gateway back to his own galactic people, so it was important for him to retain its status. Furthermore, he recognised and understood the particular qualities of lunar energy that affected the Planet, influenced his people and mattered to the work he was doing. But he did not feel unduly threatened by the rise of Sun-worship, nor was there some kind of battle raging to suppress Moon-worship. His understanding of cosmic events and their effect on the Planet was more sophisticated than this. Now we are going to bring this talk to a close'.

'This calls for clarification, suggests Clara, Sananda was speaking of the work we came to Earth to do. We are working toward unification through the dissolution of outworn systems, forms, beliefs and ideas. But I did not realise that I was bringing the energy of Sanat Kumara back into the Old Testament. This gives me quite a thrill!

'The energy of the past we experienced as real is being transformed to come into alignment with the energy of Sanat Kumara, the Planetary Logos, notes Jeremy now alert.

'Something Sananda said puzzles me, admits Clara. I quote, 'part of the purpose of having many different incarnations, is to elude, to avert connecting with one particular source of divine energy, but to find it in many different ways'. Jeremy?

'I was hoping you wouldn't ask, smiles Jeremy. I think he means that the primordial energy we call God differentiated into the seven cosmic Rays or qualities of light which make up the universe. These contain the full range of experiences, the full scope of qualities and the full extent of ideas. So the gods are aspects of the Divine, they have qualities of the Divine, even if they are inflated or warped.

'I see, exclaims Clara! It means that Yahweh as embodiment of the will-to-power manifests a divine quality, the 1st Ray of Power. In this case we all do.

'Yahweh embodies an inflated 1st Ray. With him the distorted will-to-power descends into the lower octave of polarity, remarks Levinson. The Father in Jewish consciousness is a negative force.

'Excessive, inflated, distorted but why negative, asks Clara?

'Negative because polarity is no longer held in balance, but sloping dangerously into the lower spectrum, replies Levinson. Power alone can be ruthless; it must be balanced with justice and compassion. We have been stuck in this warped Ray of Power and some loud voices want to keep us in its thrall. In some parts of the world it is getting louder. A point that strikes me, 'it is not necessarily the case that Abraham would not be connecting with Yahweh because he would consider it to be more appropriate to connect with Sanat Kumara'. That's the whole point, he had to do it this way, he came to Earth to explore polarity. He wouldn't get polarity from Sanat Kumara who exists outside of it!

'Another major point, notices Jeremy, we all reincarnate over and again 'to avert connecting with one particular source of Divine energy but to find it in many different ways'. Unity is the outcome of having explored the many sources of divine energy. Divine energy is made up of myriads of strands and we need to explore all those strands before blending them into unity.

'There is no single god above all others, except in the mind of the bigots, concludes Levinson. There is a myriad of 'gods' or ideas that we must explore through countless incarnations. All god-ideas emanate from the Source and we must discover each one. 'My god is the only god' slogan is a sham. The Source is an infinite potentiality of ideas. This infinity of ideas we project as 'gods', these are our religious packages, ideologies, theories, systems and doctrines.

'But all these god-ideas are bits of the real thing; all these god-ideas make up the Whole. They all contain traces of the truth, notes Jeremy.

'Yahweh embodies the destructive aspect of Power, reflects Clara. Ponder over the history of humanity over the last few millennia for evidence. It is interesting to note that Sanat Kumara too embodies Power, the creative power of the Divine.

'But the negative side of polarity is not inactivated yet; it is alive and kicking a fuss intent on thwarting our efforts, concludes Jeremy. They are regrouping and gathering strength, grasping at the ancient bankrupt ideas, obsolete beliefs and archaic thought forms that have kept mankind arrested in illusion. The purpose of reincarnation is to bring us into contact with new and varied experiences not to keep us stuck in the bankrupt ones. The purpose of reincarnation is to become more alive, not to freeze into stagnation.

''What is stiff and unbending is disciple of death' says the Tao. The disciples of death want us to be more 'dead', inserts Clara.

They are concerned for the safety and wellbeing of Benzaccai. The next morning brings no news from him. As they feel the need to calm down and be collected they decide to go into the church. A military vehicle stops at the gates, a young soldier alights. A monk slowly appears and invites the soldier in. The young man is led to the church where the friends are absorbed in meditation. With reverence he waits at the door. The meditation over, he enters the church and hands over a letter to Jeremy. The brief missive reads: 'I am staying with doctor Suleiman who you already met. He has the next chapters of The Hebrew Gods. Do come as soon as possible, Solomon the young soldier will escort you to Hebron. There is some turmoil at the moment; a few military vehicles appeared in the street this morning. I may have to leave soon. Love and light. Signed Benzaccai.

'Let's go, exclaims Jeremy. There is no time to waste. We shall travel in our car under the protection of the soldiers. I wonder if passing through the streets of Hebron in a military vehicle is a good idea.

'Let's go, says Clara, we are like the perennial wandering Jews relentlessly moving on, laying anchor nowhere.

'Our wandering has meaning and orientation, corrects Jeremy. We have a manuscript to bring to the attention of the world. We are not meandering aimlessly cursed by a blind fate we do not understand. We know exactly what we are doing.

'But not where we are heading for, laughs Clara trying to dispel the tension and cheer all who look rather tired. Hours later, weary in mind and body they are greeted by the doctor who looks somewhat tense.

'The situation is deteriorating in the streets of Hebron, says Suleiman. I sent Benzaccai away to my brother who lives in Jericho. I had to see a few people this morning. Women are frightened for their children; men are determined to fight to the last. I am worried especially for the children who have never known peace. Do come in my study we shall read the next chapters they seem to be more urgent than I first thought.

'The qualities of light the text is permeated with will have a positive effect on all. Light is a powerful weapon against fear and hatred, notes Jeremy.

'Absolutely, love is a powerful weapon against fear and hatred, echoes the doctor. Let us transmute darkness into light. We all need it; the people of Hebron need it and deserve it. Guess what, the text is about Abraham'! The reading begins:

Abraham offers Israel to the idea of the unchanging Father

'Like Agamemnon in the parallel Greek myth, the deity demands of Abraham that he immolates his only child, begins Sanaka. To obtain the favours of the god of war,

Agamemnon must sacrifice Iphigenia. Similarly in order to appease the Father - the 1st Ray of Power - Abraham must immolate Jacob. Such immolation is a violation of the natural order and a denial of basic moral principles. We know that Abraham was the ambassador of the Sumerian civilisation that had long abolished human sacrifice. Even in the wild, animals do not kill their offspring, as this would put an end to the survival of their own species. So what does this bizarre, unnatural, ill-timed story is telling us?

'This is the ultimate sacrifice and one Abraham is willing to make for an ideal.

'An ideal greater than man himself? Is it an ideal to put an end to one's bloodline when the safeguard of the bloodline is the reason for living of the Hebrews? First, we know that it is a test of faith because at the moment Abraham and Agamemnon are about to sacrifice their child, a goat is substituted to prevent slaying. Abraham is willing to kill his son in order to appease his god, a god who has made his intentions known. But it makes no sense at all, since the continuation of the bloodline is so crucial to Yahweh's aims for the Planet. But humanity is evolving a moral conscience and rejects this kind of pagan behaviour. Modern man Abraham inaugurating a new intellectual era allows reason to prevail over the capricious rule of his god.

'Modern man Abraham tolerates this capricious rule it seems, says Moses.

'Second, Abraham is inaugurating a new age of human consciousness. He is aware of the immorality of his gods and he is also aware of his own inner power. It is an age when man begins to view the world from an ethical angle. And so Abraham breaks with pagan tradition. The ancient tribal deity has to acknowledge Abraham's superior moral nature.

'Abraham stands for a new phase in human evolution, notes Moses.

'But there is more to it than this. A soul incarnates in Jewish form to play the role appropriate at that point in its evolution. The soul is only interested in the learning gain it will get from that incarnation. Initiates have a loathing of the physical world - the world of illusion, Maya. Plato describes 'the body as a tomb'. This disdain for physicality has resounded down the ages.

'Why, the soul cannot function without the body, inserts Moses?

'You made a formal pledge to the body, you made a solemn contract with the material self and you have never vacillated since! The body is that part of the mortal self you identify with. Is this not what the dispute was all about between Rabbis and Essenes?

179

The Rabbis were given a chance to glimpse at another reality, to no avail! When we identify with the body – 'my body is me' - we confess to being 'spiritually dead'. 'The foundation of our tradition is 'I am a Jew because I have Jewish blood'.

So, returning to the narrative, two previously veiled messages now come into view:

First, symbolically Abraham straddles two epochs, two outlooks. He refuses to give in to the idolatrous impulse which is no other than ritual murder. He initiates a new age for humanity. His descendants will not regard the slaughter of a first born on the altar of the deity as virtuous. They are experiencing a growing sense of morality with the dawn of intelligent thought. Second, biblical man sacrifices his son to the unconscious force that imposes its will on conscious man. This may be the subtle message the Spiritual Hierarchy hid in this mystifying story. Yahweh was known in Sumer as 'God of the Sea'. Abraham exerts control over the impulses that rise to the surface from the deep.

'Sacrifice comes from the deep of the unknown mind?

'It locks itself there! Many ancient societies have offered human sacrifices to make the sun rise, to win wars and to appease the gods. The sacrificial urge springs from the most primitive part of the mind.

'Is it a form of insanity?

'It is today. Thirdly, apart from the mind factor, there is a cosmic factor to the story. To the Hebrews, Yahweh exists outside man and outside Creation, remote from both. In biblical times mankind witnessed terrifying cataclysmic events. In the imagination of ancient man the idea of a separate god and an arbitrary universe fuse. In the absence of known physical laws, the deity controls man and Nature.

'So Isaac is sacrificed to the unconscious forces in man and in the universe?

'Symbolically Isaac was sacrificed. Isaac is sacrificed in every generation. Each one dies on the sacrificial altar of illusion, slain by the mortal self. We sacrifice every generation on the altar of putrefying thought forms, decaying notions, decomposing beliefs that sprang from ancient man not yet endowed with a mind. You have been caught up in inherited habits of thoughts, in habituated emotional reactions that you never questioned, because fear was clutching at your heart. Fear, the densest emotion known to man and one which harks back to his pre-human past.

'A heavy emotion governs our lives?

'Humanity is climbing the ladder of evolution slowly. This brings us to yet another Greek myth which illustrates the plight of Abraham's progeny, the myth of Sisyphus. Cursed by the gods, Sisyphus is condemned to repeat the same action for ever: he has to carry a rock up a mountain from which it will roll down. Battered, exhausted, defeated, he goes on for ever. You insist on passing the affliction on to the next generation. It is the turn of your children to perpetuate this terrible predicament. The myth of Sisyphus illustrates the plight of IS-RA-EL and through you the plight of humanity.

'We yield to the whims of the gods that rise from the deep caverns of the mind. Man is born in ignorance of his true nature and he perpetuates the myth of his frailty and limitations.

'Excellent Moses, my son. Believing himself victim of the Fall, man elevates fear and separation. Believing himself to be guilty, he promotes guilt. 'Man is born in sin', the sin of ignorance: 'Whatsoever ye believe ye have received, ye shall have'. Not a curse, but cosmic Law that the Master is citing. What we believe comes to pass. We are makers of our situation, makers of our world. At yet a deeper level of meaning, Isaac is Isis, the Goddess who breathes the 'breath of life', the soul. So Abraham is willing to sacrifice to an irrational god the soul of humanity! The soul is symbolically immolated to the irrational nature of man.

'Man who was created divine is truly fallen. The split between the self and the soul has impoverished him so much that he sees himself as a victim.

'Absolutely, Moses. At yet another level of meaning Abraham knows this and the false immolation of Isaac proves it. It is as if he was saying, 'I am acting out the original drama between self and soul. I am a man of the Fall; I am playing out the drama of the Fall, the break, the separation. But I am not dupe, I can recover lost unity; every man can achieve union within himself'.

'So he does not sacrifice Isaac at all!

'He slays the personality, the mythological monster that keeps man split from himself and from the Source. He sees through the illusion.

CHAPTER 4

MOSES & THE FATHER –– the gods of Egypt escort IsRaEl out of Exile

'Each man is his own absolute law-giver, the dispenser of glory or doom to himself; the decree-er of his life, his reward, his punishment'. (Dr Douglas Baker)

HEBRON

Moses the law-giver

One morning after meditation, Sanaka informs Moses that the subject of investigation for the day is to be Moses the Master.

'I have been waiting for this for a long time Master, confesses Moses.

'I know your empathy for Moses; you are of the same cosmic Ray line and the same spiritual lineage. But you already know what I am going to say because it is carved in your mind. It is just a question of retrieving this information.

'The same lineage?

'You belong to the same spiritual family of Light. Those who come to humanity to initiate new religious movements or new development in civilisation are usually sent by the Hierarchy. They are beings of spiritual eminence, as was Moses, which is why he was born in a spiritual land, in the imperial family of Egypt who gave him an arcane, scientific and spiritual education that his cosmic status as a Master of Shamballa demanded. He appeared on the world stage to 'release from crisis the sons of men'.

'Moses born of the Pharaoh?

'To have been born in the Hebrew colony would have narrowed his field of action and confined his spiritual goal to a specific group and became their voice. Besides, it matters little whether he was born an Egyptian or a Hebrew, he was an emissary of Shamballa who came to carry out a mission, and this is all that matters. The issue of blood is negligible.

'He did lead that specific group and no other though, notes Moses.

'Indeed, but through that group it was humanity he was directing. The Hebrews saw themselves as a moral and spiritual force responsible for the direction of mankind. They remembered the role of leadership Abraham was called to play by their 'creator' god.

'So Moses was pandering to the desire of that group?

'No, Moses was in constant contact with the Hierarchy and was able to plan ahead. Their deep-seated belief in 'chosenness' and moral mission would take care of the information through time. Sensing the nature of the life force that drives the group he was able to plan to prevent stiffening and stagnation. He could arouse the qualities slumbering under the tribulations of exile and the force of tradition. But tribulations and tradition are double-edge swords, while keeping the memory alive they may also obstruct the development of higher qualities.

'But what does the soul want? We have been mulling over this question for some time, asks Moses puzzled?

'The soul is never inert, never slumbering, the soul is thriving to break free from the forces that oppose its growth and conspire to keep it suppressed. The soul rejects the limits imposed by the self, society and religion. It shrugs off the bondage imposed by man upon himself.

'Yet the soul incarnates into the Hebrew condition to experience the very conditions it rejects. Shall I ever understand, laments Moses?

'You will and on your own. Moses saw that the hardening of ancient belief was crippling the soul; he came to set the soul free. Moses originated from Shamballa, the 'centre where the Will of God is known' and as a Master of the Hierarchy from the 'centre where the Love of God has full sway'. He was highly qualified for the task. The sad irony is that the Divine was beating in their chest and they did not know! They had pledged allegiance to the most numbing, the most disabling, and the most disempowering deity in the pantheon of gods. As a result the soul life in man was suppressed.

'Yet the soul incarnates in the Hebrew condition repeats Moses much troubled

'The soul incarnates in any condition it chooses to learn and assimilate that which is of value. It extracts the germ- wisdom and discards the rest.

'A learning experience, nothing to cling to or go haywire over!

'The soul has the task of breaking the mould that has kept it in thrall!

'Breaking the mould, outrage to my people!

'Few individuals are able to break the mould. To break the mould of core beliefs, attitudes, dogmas, emotional response and thought patterns is perhaps the major trial in any incarnation. The dilemma for the Hierarchy is to decide how much information to impart at any period in time. This instruction must match the nature of the people and their point in evolution. Truth is never revealed in its totality. It is given in fragments over periods of time.

'Truth was delivered in its totality at Sinai, we insist.

'Would a rational person accept as true that the 1st Ray of Power – one attribute and only one - explains the totality of the Divine? It is the same as saying that the head is the totality of man; the head is a part of man! Early humans imagined the Infinite as a cripple. Stubborn belief in a 'cripple' Creator and a cripple human being has kept you 'prisoners of the Planet'.

'Why 'prisoners of the Planet'?

'The reason behind repeated incarnations is to learn to move from the unreal to the real, from illusion to truth, from darkness to light. As long as man is unable to raise his consciousness to the Real he will have to come back time and again until he is able to peer beyond the illusion of polarity, the illusion of separateness and 'chosenness.

'But truth is not static, it changes you said so!

'Right! Truth is evolving like the universe, like man and like the Creator himself. Truth is dispensed in stages to match the ability of the people who receive it. It would be inappropriate to tell a group almost entirely destroyed by apocalyptic events that God is a God of love! It would be equally inappropriate to tell them that God is alive in their chests for they only knew of the Father, a stern and distant figure, judging and punishing.

'Why would it be inappropriate to tell them about the principle of Love?

'The great majority of the Hebrew people had been destroyed in the apocalyptic events, so love and brotherhood seemed unreal. People want help, direct and effective help; they need a guiding light.

'So it was all for later, suspended, postponed for a later time?

'When the mind develops. It would be pointless to encourage them to 'Hold fast to the truth as a lamp. Be ye islands of refuge unto yourselves'. They desperately needed a strong guiding hand rather than an exhortation to freedom. Spiritual sensitivity was embryonic. To receive the truth three conditions must be met: moral discipline, the will-to-progress and a sense of social responsibility. These qualities are very modern.

'Let us take a pause, interrupts Tara, to let the Tibetan sum up the difficulties encountered by the Hierarchy'. In spite of the slightly surprised if not disapproving look of her friends, she quotes: 'The problem of the Hierarchy has been how much exact truth humanity can comprehend…They have to decide which aspect of universal truth will enable man to emerge out of his difficulties and move forward on the Path…'

'Your incursion is timely, chuckles Johansson. Moses had to tread gently; the archetypal image of the Father was the most potent, the most realistic and the most appropriate. The vengeful Father was manifesting through the terrible events. In a random world struck by an apocalyptic devastation, the image of the Father is best adapted to the emergent consciousness of the time. Well done Tara, you may interrupt anytime!

The reading resumes: 'And so it seemed appropriate to confirm their experience of a powerful Father, creator of all things, says Sanaka. Yet in spite of the calamities he had piled up on them he was still the Father who demanded that they lead an honourable life. That was quite sufficient for the time, the place and the people, the rest would come later; safety measures were put in place to that effect.

'In spite of these safety measures, we have maintained that the whole Truth had been revealed and that nothing new can ever happen.

'Nothing? And what of the messianic dream? What of the messianic age of reconciliation and harmony, Moses you have not forgotten?

'We have lived in expectation of a Messiah who would drop in on us, a kind of benevolent cosmic catastrophe! Not the Messiah in our chest! That is at the root of our perennial problem.

'Excellent! 'Be ye islands of refuge unto yourselves'.

'How pessimistic, man is alone in the universe with only himself to rely on.

'In a sense you are right Moses. Man is alone responsible for his own liberation. Truth dwells in the inner man and it is there that he must turn for refuge. You insist that the segment of truth you got at Sinai was the whole truth. This misreading is at the root of your perennial suffering.

'Truth dwells within man yet truth is never static, it changes.

'Well done, Moses. Truth is universal, ever-changing, ever-evolving, but the way to access this moving, changing truth is through the Heart, doorway to the universe and to other dimensions. But there is another crucial point, what is it Moses?

'Truth is not of God alone; not of man alone. Truth is the result of a grand cosmic undertaking; the convergence of many strands and many forces.

'Well summed up! Truth is of the soul, not of the ego. To sense the truth one needs a balanced personality enthused by the soul. Unevolved man clings to the materialism of separateness, fear, guilt, authority and attachment. The unevolved ego is 'split' from the soul'.

'The split between personality and soul seems to govern our world?

'There is a strong affinity with form, all that is approved - tradition, thought forms, precepts, bloodline. This mix-up about form delays contact with soul life. Devoted to physical lineage you have forgotten your divine lineage. When you label the body as the totality of who you are, you neglect the reality of the soul. When you identify the soul, the actor who plays all the roles you have incarnated into from time immemorial, 'The truth shall set you free'.

Moses' mission by Master Sananda

Rabbi Moses' abiding interest in Moses stems from an energy linkage, a spiritual lineage. The group spurred on by Rabbi Moses' inquisitive nature set out to do some researching of their own. Jeremy accepts to channel Sananda. Clara finding it difficult to contain her enthusiasm asks Sananda:

'I once raised the issue of Moses' origins with my teacher who confirmed that Moses was an Egyptian. Would you tell me more about his identity?

'I would say that it was part of his purpose that his parentage should remain mysterious. It gave him the ability to represent divine energy, to act as a leader more easily for, in anonymity, he could step forward without too specific a background to give bias to his leadership. As a being, you are looking at someone who, as you might imagine, is quite evolved, who came in very specifically to perform a task in that lifetime. It was his wish to bring to a speedy close, a speedy achievement the historical goal of the Jewish people. He wished to lead them into a state which would become recognised by them as being, in essence, a spiritual state rather than primarily a physical or material state, and he hoped that in so doing, they would be able to move up to the next plane of their existence. Not exactly in your modern term to 'ascend' but something like that, to achieve a kind of spiritual transformation, to become an enlightened society. That was his sole aim for that life time. As it is, although he made strides in that direction, he was not able to achieve it. And I would suggest that his goal is beginning to come up over the horizon now.

'For mankind at large?

'For mankind at large also for the Jewish people.

Clara was musing over Sananda's reply to the questions she had pondered over for so long. She intended to return to the subject at the most opportune time, for his answer had triggered more probing questions still. The occasion arose the next morning after breakfast when Jeremy was sitting quietly by the lake in a rare moment of solitude, which he graciously accepted to break. Her request was not intrusive he said reassuringly. In the transparent light and renewed freshness, all was still and vibrant at the same time.

'Master Sananda, I would like to return to a subject which preoccupies me. I wish to tie up a few loose ends if I may.

'Welcome again, yes sure ask your question.

'It is a very lengthy question. Moses, both as an Initiate of the Mystery Schools of Egypt and as a Master of the Hierarchy must have known of the existence and reality of the Goddess. Why did he promote the worship of the one god, artificial in principle and in reality? Why did he allow theism to gain prominence? Is it because the denigration of women, the war against the Goddess, monotheism and patriarchy, all these features make up the unique character of the Hebrews? Could it be regarded as the portion of the cosmic Plan they had to implement as their own crowning achievement?

'As with all answers there are several aspects to consider. Let me suggest this: Moses thought to create unity among a specific group of people. He perceived that one way of achieving his goal was to focus on what lay beyond the individual god that the people were devoted to, to show them the One that lay behind. This desire, in its highest aspect, at soul level, motivated him. He wished the people in his charge to know that there is Oneness, the Source of All. Part of this desire would be to help a splintered group of people who were falling out among themselves to find that concept healing of division, and in so doing impart a feeling of unity. This was important for their long journey ahead across the Desert and through history.

'What of the Plan?

'The qualities you refer to are not unique to that group. The experience of patriarchy and monotheism, the rejection of the Goddess and the suppression of women were a reflection of what was happening and which was becoming widespread in the world.

Broadly speaking, the movement toward patriarchy was advancing. You live in a world of polarity and all these features were part of the experience of polarity. Indeed, in the pre-historical, mythological world, female energy was dominant, whereas male energy was marginalized. In terms of gender, humanity chose to live through the experience of a society where female energy was predominant. However, for centuries and until now, in your world male energy has been dominant, and part of what modern society is experiencing now is an attempt to correct, to rectify this situation. Today, humanity is seeking to find a balance, a oneness beyond polarity where it rescinds either subjection or dominance of one gender by another, until the male discovers in the female much value, until the female discovers much to appreciate in the male. There is a dawning recognition that each gender has much to offer the other. A contented society is one which is in a state of equilibrium. This will be achieved in a society where all will be valued equally. Now, in Moses' time, one salient feature was that men by suppressing women were in reality seeking to suppress their own female aspect, the feminine part of their nature. And women also were seeking to suppress the male aspect of their own nature, suppressing their maleness.

'I thought that it was the woman's femininity that was being suppressed.

'Women were being suppressed in all aspects, they were suppressed as beings. This element, this development is not necessarily a consequence of monotheism. It happened among a group that was experiencing monotheism and seeing that one god as a male while simultaneously exploring patriarchy and using the male god to justify and bolster up monotheism and patriarchy. For Moses, this was a gender-free experiment; his higher purpose was not running alongside issues of gender. Nevertheless, he was a man of his generation, subject to the currents of his time. He was not able to bring forth the full implications of the main themes he was presented with, the main currents he was engaged in, because as well as being a great man; he was a man of his time. So part of his higher being, his higher Self had the real experience of unity, of Oneness which is monotheism. At the same time he was riding the current of his time which was the exploring of the male energy. And so, it was automatic for him to refer to this one God as 'he' rather than 'she'. When he strived to evoke the dominant life current, when he tried to speak of energy, the image of the Father was the natural image that would come to him.

'This is surprising, he was an ambassador of the Spiritual Hierarchy, an Ascended Master, was he not in contact with you?

'These were not easy times for humanity, surrounding energies were dense at that time and so you could think of him in a role of translator who was first of all experiencing a clear and strong connection - but not always. As a translator, he had to translate into a language that could be recognised, communicate into a form that those he had charge of would understand. Like all of you living in the world of polarity, he did the best that he could under the given circumstances. The survival of his people was his primary responsibility; to help them cope through time was very important to him. Part of the way in which he sought to reach this goal was, as well as being a spiritual leader, to become also a political leader and do what political leaders do: make deals, negotiate and make alliances. Was he not to speak the language of patriarchy he would not have fulfilled his political mission; he felt that adopting patriarchy was essential. To speak another language would jeopardise his mission. This would disintegrate the group which was his primary charge. At the human level, looking at it in psychological terms, his own relationship with that one god felt like a relationship with a firm father. He grew up as an orphan, although he was adopted and much loved by the Pharaoh, he knew himself as an orphan. And so the notion of the Father, at a personal level made psychological sense, the one god becoming the father he never knew.

'He pretended to be human in spite of his association with the Hierarchy?

'He did not pretend to be human, he was! He existed at different levels, like all of you. The human aspect of him was a gifted, extremely gifted human being. He was fully human! Throughout his life, from an early age, he had a conscious connection with the Source of All, this made him more than human, but the human part was there too. As I mentioned earlier, the survival of his people he felt was his primary responsibility, he cared profoundly, very deeply. He felt that this was the task he had been given. Everything else came secondary to him.

'Why feel so strongly about that people, he was not one of them?

'He understood that there were deeper purposes. He consciously was fulfilling a contract going a long way back and this was not just escorting and leading a group of people across the Desert. He had a deep understanding of the evolution of the Plan. He knew a lot of what humanity is just beginning to discover or uncover at present. He remembered that he had known other states of being, he had memories of having existed on other stars, he knew that his people also came from the stars. So he was aware that he and his people did not originate on Earth, but had travelled to this Planet from other world systems. But nevertheless, the purpose he envisioned for his people across historical time remained intuitive; how the Plan was to unfold was not known. He had to trust the instructions of his Father.

'Who is the Father?

'This is a complex question. He was receiving instructions from a number of sources. He did connect with the Source of All, he was connecting to the Source through other beings, and particularly through a being he would have recognised as the founding god of his race, known as Yahweh; the name is a label attached to several energy forms. He also received instructions from his soul, his inner guidance. He sought to hear as clearly as possible his own God-self.

'Shamballa seems to have invested much in the Hebrew group, why is that?

'Many groups have come from other star systems and so in many ways the Jewish people are not unique. But they do have some special qualities they manifest as a group consciousness, a particular way of experiencing the world that outwardly expresses itself with the unmistakable characteristics you associate with the Jewish people. You are familiar with these qualities, you have them yourself: intelligence, artistic talent, versatility, motivation. And so they made the conscious decision as a group, at soul level, to explore the world in particular ways, not altogether unique to them, but in ways which are more marked in the Jewish people and which has secured them both prominence in the world and also which has brought them great difficulty. You see, in the world of polarity, groups which love their uniqueness tend to be marked out by themselves and by others. I must emphasise that the vision they have of themselves is not unique - certain Aborigines too come from other star systems, little known to the West they are working in individual ways but they are more shut away. Now is the time where all of you, the human race, are learning to pool the individual visions of all the various groups and are looking to use the 'us' motto, to create Oneness out of diversity, out of the many.

'But the Jewish people seem reluctant to go along with this unification, although things are changing, at least since the war. Are they inhibiting unification?

'They see themselves holding some of the keys that can liberate humanity that others have forgotten.

'What keys do they hold?

'This is to be grasped in an abstract way. It is a form of energy that comes into the Heart centre, opens the Heart, encourages liberation and stimulates the process of ascension. Some have this feeling unconsciously, for it is difficult to hold that awareness. But the real challenge the Jewish people has met is the challenge of attachment. They safeguarded the consciousness of their special role and they have become attached to it and its outcome. The lesson to be learned is the experience of becoming detached. They have to learn to practice non-attachment to the past. They are at present working through the major drama of releasing attachment'.

The meeting ends. The friends remain silent for a short while reflecting on the significance of what Sananda has divulged.

'What is the nature of the 'keys' Sananda is referring to, I wonder, asks Clara always inquisitive? I quote, 'it is a form of energy that comes into the Heart centre, opens the Heart, encourages liberation and stimulates the process of ascension'. I looked for these 'keys' when I was living under the oppressive shadow of the Yahweh energy and never found anything, and not through lack of trying either!

'I never found it either, echoes Levinson, and not through lack of trying either, the more I searched the more disillusioned I became.

'I felt betrayed, says Clara. I was being palmed off with the abhorrent 'do & obey'.

'You were searching for the truth; they were not, smiles Jeremy.

'I may have a tentative answer, suggests Johansson, the biblical scholar. You recall the myth of Osiris, the Egyptian god dismembered by Set who scattered his limbs over the Nile. It was the task of his wife, the Goddess Isis to gather his limbs.

'The myth has its echo in Exodus when on leaving Egypt, Moses goes to the Nile to raise the body of Joseph, notes Clara. What do you think Moses was doing? Was he 'gathering the limbs' of Osiris?

'Joseph was not Osiris, but may be the Hierarchy when hinting at the 'gathering of the limbs' were alluding to the gathering of the fragments which were 'torn off' from the Logos - the souls, expands Johansson. Sananda just said that Moses was attempting to create an enlightened people that would move beyond polarity. He failed, but the process was repeated 2000 years ago when the Essenes tried to lead this recalcitrant people towards liberation through the recognition of the feminine principle in them: the soul. They too failed. Patriarchy and monotheism triumphed in a torrid and well orchestrated rejection of the feminine energy.

'Returning to Osiris, what is the link with what Sananda just said, asks Clara?

'Alright, let' s go back to Plutarch' s description of the death of Osiris, 'Set scatters and destroys the sacred Logos which the Goddess Isis collects and puts together and delivers to those undergoing Initiation'. Do you see the implications for us today, invites Johansson?

'Plutarch seems to be describing what is happening now, muses Jeremy. First, the Logos split himself into fragments which he inserted into sentient beings. Back to the first verses of Creation: primeval unity was 'destroyed' when the Logos - Osiris - split himself into fragments, allegorically the 'scattering of the limbs'.

'Right, continues Johansson, but there is more. The Goddess Isis is gathering the limbs of Osiris and this is happening now. Sananda is taking us into Initiation to do precisely that. He is taking us into inner journeys to the Heart centre, the gateway to the inner dimensions where we met the Goddess herself and where we are connecting with the soul. 'The gathering of the limbs' is now and we are directly involved in it.

Moses & the self

'Moses is the bringer of the New Age like Abraham before him, begins Master Sanaka. Moses is the liberator, the long awaited for Redeemer, but the liberation intended by the Hierarchy is more figurative than literal. Egypt was not the oppressive land of darkness depicted in the Bible. Egypt was a spiritual planetary centre where the antediluvian knowledge of Atlantis was recorded in colossal stone structures. Egypt was the spiritual realm of Hermes and the great Temples of Initiation. The Hebrews understood the liberation as a flight to a concrete land of 'milk and honey'; the original intention of the Hierarchy was lost. The outline became blurred as Moses was being diverted from the hierarchical course - and his self-chosen path - to follow the itinerary set by Yahweh whose agenda was not aligned with the Divine Plan. Like a general on the battlefield who has to evaluate the situation at regular intervals to revise his strategy, Moses has to defer his dream, subdue his vision to submit to the reality of the moment. He must pay tribute to the god of the day. Unwittingly like Abraham before him, he becomes the steward of the god of selfhood. The ruthless advance of the self does not brook any interference.

'That was his appointed mission, yet he failed. As an infant he is rescued by the Egyptian princess. What is the hidden meaning?

'The Goddess Isis saves him from certain death as he drifts on the Nile in his basket, just as she had rescued King Sargon. The parallel with Sargon is not unintentional. Sargon was the Babylonian redeemer 1000 years before Moses, and Moses was seen as following in the footsteps of the Sumerian liberator. We must not forget the Sumerian origins of the Hebrews and their leader and father, Abraham. In the bible story, in order to keep within the artificial bounds of monotheism, the goddess Isis is replaced by the princess.

'The Egyptian goddess Isis saves Moses?

'Isis is temporarily exiled, Isis vanishes but is not destroyed, she lives on in the consciousness of humanity. She reappears in Christendom and later in the Hassidic community. The Goddess lives on in the heart of humanity.

The Plagues of Egypt – a Narcissistic interpretation?

'One early morning we were walking through a wood. Spring had arrived early that year: flowers were gracing the lake and their bright and varied colours were a joy to behold. 'Such beauty, I remarked moved to tears, as I looked to the snow-covered peaks in the distance.

'Let's sit by the lake for a moment. Suppose that a meteorite came hurtling down from space, hit this land and destroy the landscape and the people, how would you feel, asks Sanaka observing me from the corner of his eyes, watchful to my every move and expression.

'I would be most upset.

'Why, he asks relentlessly?

'I really don't know what you are probing for, Master.

'Would you rejoice?

'Certainly not, retorts Moses.

'And yet you sit at the table on the Passover night to praise your god for the wonderful miracles he wrought! The Ten Plagues were attributed to the god of wrath who in the legend precipitated these terrible calamities on the bewildered and defenceless people of Egypt in retribution for their sins! Sin was unknown in Egyptian consciousness. The sensible Egyptians did not 'sin', they made 'mistakes' which could be redressed through learning and progress. A mistake affects the person who makes it not the deity. But enough of it, I am digressing.

'What about the plagues, enquires Moses hesitantly, regretting asking?

'One day, continues Sanaka, scientists will explain in an intelligent and intelligible manner what truly happened. They will discover that for a disaster to be unleashed all it takes is a small rise in temperature and a chain reaction follows: microbes, insects, tadpoles, flies, locusts all begin to multiply randomly to provoke the kind of infestation your Bible story recounts with characteristic candidness. You interpreted events through your preconceived ideas. Greek mythology offers and illustration of this flaw in the myth of Narcissus. Narcissus was a handsome young man whose attention was turned inward. Sitting by a pond, he saw his own image reflected in the water and fell in love with it. For Narcissus, the world existed as a mirror to reflect his own image. Like Narcissus you fell in love with your image. You wandered through the Desert - the Desert symbolises the emptiness, illusion and unreality of the self - aimlessly through raging fires, earthquakes, tidal waves, volcanic eruptions and darkness cast by the clouds of dust. You witnessed cataclysmic events, yet the women danced for Yahweh in gratitude! Humanity was being annihilated and you danced! The world was being shattered before your very eyes but you only saw your image and you fell in love with your idea of yourselves.

'I get your point, says Moses, unwilling to prolong this painful encounter.

'I am distressing you, remarks Sanaka, this was never my intention.

'If only you knew! I lie awake at night unable to sleep. Not a day, not an instant goes by that I do not mourn my loss. I have no word to describe the feeling of loss, nor can I find words to express the pain.

'I know. You are moving toward the realisation of the present. Time for you is changing as you perceive yourself existing in many realities at the same time. The personality exists in time, the Self moves beyond time. You exist beyond time, Moses, you live in eternity now. Besides, what you are experiencing extends beyond your personal life. You set yourself up as a laboratory to live the Hebrew condition in order to explore it, understand it, love it and transmute it for your people, for humanity and for the Planet. You should celebrate and rejoice, not grieve. If you are not too distressed I would like to continue, for you are going to take back all this with you, back to Vilna.

'Is my time with you coming to an end, asks Moses visibly distressed?

'Not yet, you will be going away but I shall always be with you.

The Old Testament: celebration of Samsara - Song of all Mythologies

'One morning after the meditation, Master Sanaka asked me to join him for a walk in the monastery court. The air was luminous and pure. He looked at me while I was breathing in the pure air and smiled gently.

'Rabbi Moses ...' I interrupt him to remind him that I had been stripped of his title and name.

'Naming was important in the Ancient East, to name was to give life, replies Sanaka. To rob someone of his name is a symbolic way of robbing him of his life. Your name is Moses, not an accidental choice, it was most certainly chosen by you long before this life. Like Moses with whom you share a certain quality of being, with whom you also resonate, your karmic task is to be of service, to lead your people back to the light. You chose service to attain enlightenment.

'I am mourning, replies Moses repressing tears.

'Begin to see yourself through the eyes of the soul. Identity is of the self, not of the soul, the soul simply 'is'. It is never defined in any other way. In the past you focused on your personality. When you see your life through the eyes of your soul, you will no longer be troubled by the past. Your soul exists beyond space and time, beyond Creation, beyond Samsara. That was the core of Moses' teachings, too advanced for the literal, prosaic mind of the time. They knew physical certainty and the solid world around them. The ancient texts are a literary masterpiece in celebration of the visible, tangible world. Mythology of all mythologies it encompasses the beliefs held by the Ancient World. In the world of sacred texts it must rank among the most passionate declaration, not of the right of men, not of the sacredness of life, but of the power of the physical world! Your deity is personalised. The stars are personalised: the twelve sons of Jacob, the twelve tribes of Israel symbolically stand for the twelve constellations. Your revered heroes are given god-like status. Under the thin veil of historical fact you can identify the gods of Egypt and Babylon. Think of Abraham his name conceals the Babylonian god Tammuz. Abraham-Tammuz has a sister-wife Sarah, the goddess Ishtar. But Tammuz and Ishtar are also Osiris and Isis. The gods of Egypt are the gods of Sumer and the gods of IsRaEl.

'Master Sanaka, is it my goal in this life to inform my fellow men that they have worshipped and died for Tammuz, Osiris, Isis, Asherah, El, Aton, Baal and other gods while declaring undying allegiance to Yahweh?

'Yahweh was the god of the priesthood. He was the official god, the national deity. The religion of the people of Israel was pagan. Neither the people nor the kings were ever deceived, they knew!

'You are asking me to shake them to their foundation. With respect, Master, do you realise what this is going to do to them, the awesome realisation that they worshipped foreign gods all along and that the one god they thought had created the world is no god at all! I cannot do this!

'Because you fear their wrath or because you wish to keep them slumbering, questions Sanaka whose insight unsettles Moses? There will be an outpouring of anger, like a river that breaks its banks after heavy rain and floods the land. But behind the rage is anger at themselves for having lived in ignorance, anger at having been deceived. It is hard to wake up from a long sleep, even if this sleep was filled with nightmares, because reality is fluid, uncertain, and impermanent. They endure the nightmares as long as they have a glimmer of certainty. However, the certainties of the past have been washed away and they are bereft.

'You want me to do this to them? Have they not suffered enough? Why take their glimmer of certainty away. There is such a thing as a saving lie!

'There is no such thing as a saving lie! Only the truth saves even if it hurts. They have the right to wake from their nightmare, 'And the truth shall set you free'. Without truth there is no spiritual freedom and ultimately no enlightenment. Do you have the right to refuse it to them? You have to inflame a new vigour, stir in them the desire to take charge of their destiny. You will articulate the long lost dream of a condition ruled by reason, justice, liberty and spiritual wisdom for all. The Enlightened State that Moses set out to establish. I know what you are thinking, 'why me'?

'Indeed Master, why me?

'If not you who? One of your Rabbis when facing a national crisis said something like, 'if not me who and if not now when'? You may feel irrelevant, brittle, unworthy as your people often feel in their heart under the brash exterior and abrasive sense of group aloofness. But this is an illusion; all of you are beings of light. Your souls are powerful and boundless. When you escape the prison of the god-idea you will soar to great height.

Moses & the Hierarchy - Master Sananda

Moses' Egyptian origin was suggested by Freud and is being confirmed by a recent academic study. Why an Egyptian? Who else could lead an unruly mob out of Egypt at a time of great natural cataclysms? It had to be someone with strong social, political status and connections. Who else had such profound knowledge of the Ancient Wisdom? Who else had the spiritual stature and the intellectual achievement? Clara was musing on Moses and his origins as she had done so often. She finally approaches Jeremy. 'I know, don't say it, laughs Jeremy, you want to speak with Sananda!

'Is it possible, I want to clarify a few points raised by what we have just heard. It is never ending, one question leads to another.

'The others are planning a walk; you may stay behind and put your questions unless you prefer a walk.

'I'll put the questions!

The encounter with Sananda begins: 'Master Sananda, when Moses was at Sinai, we are told that he received a Revelation. Did he receive it from the various channels that link up to the Source?

'Yes.

'The Brotherhood of Light. Were these Beings from Shamballa?

'That would be a reasonable description I would not quarrel with it. It becomes difficult to be precise in those terms simply because we experience ourselves – and here I speak of myself as a member of that same Brotherhood – as being very much connected in a way that is not quite part of your human experience.

'A collective consciousness or group consciousness made up of very distinct individualities?

'Yes. It's as if you felt yourself to be as much Polynesian, as much Russian as much Greek as much Paraguayan as you are British. Suppose I said 'are you Russian?' If you felt that connection you would say 'well, yes, I guess I am Russian' (he says this with a light laughter). So it is something of that order, when you say 'were these Beings from Shamballa?' I would say 'yes' for indeed there was a connection. But it would not quite be a primary connection. To return to your question, the passageway of this particular

Form of Light which became the message Moses received was through the Elohim and they used angelic helpers. So you have an angelic presence, also and beyond that there were many, many interested Beings, including Beings who had no real connection. They wished simply to hold a space rather then to actually give the message. In other words, they wished to assist in the process.

Essence of Moses' teaching – Master Sananda

'Master Sananda, what was the essence, the nucleus of Moses' teaching? Was it the energy of Sanat Kumara he embodied or was it that same mainstay energy that you referred to, that core energy around which our physical reality is formed?

'You could think of Moses as having been very strongly aligned with that core energy, almost as if a manifestation of that energy; though actually human energy and the electromagnetic field are not the same kind of energy. It is not that Moses was a manifestation of that energy, but he was aligned with it, he was, to some extent fulfilling the purpose of that Energy Form willingly in order to work within a shorter time scale.

'Was he using Earth energy as a building block and short cut to achieve his ultimate goal?

'His purpose was to set up more localised structures of thought and beliefs - and the practical laws of course – that would assist his people especially, to understand more clearly their role not just on this Planet, but their role in universal terms. One such purpose was to inspire a greater vision, so that they may see more, so that they may remember more of their own true nature. So in a way you can view the epic journey he undertook, the odyssey he embarked upon as being real and concrete in space and time. But it also has to be perceived as being symbolic. It was intended to show his people (this is something of a truism) that this life is a journey and that the important thing is for people to realise that there is a purpose in that journey; life is not a matter of surviving, getting up and going to sleep and surviving again the next day. He wanted to demonstrate that there was something to follow, that there was a connection to be made.

'Master, the Nefilim left a profound imprint on Hebrew consciousness: their negative view of the world. Emulating their 'makers' they adopted a self-centred style: they focussed on the personality. This preoccupation with the self led to a contraction, a turning inward. Was it not the very opposite to Moses' intention? He wanted to dissolve that contracting, that turning inward and encourage an openness, a turning outward, and expansion.

'I would accept this. This is a fairly accurate presentation of his intention.

'Was that 'connection' to be made with the divine, with the inner Self or like Abraham with a specific galactic group?

'Moses was working in a rather different way; he did not have the connection that Abraham had. He was seeking really, a more universal connection.

'With the Source of All?

'Yes, that's right. In his own view he was not terribly successful in achieving this, but it absolutely was his intention. He had that sense of God being everywhere and longed to communicate his conviction and intuitive feeling.

'I might be going on a tangent, yet my next question does concern Moses even if in an oblique way. A book I just read speaks of an advanced civilisation of long ago which ascended to a higher dimension of being and migrated out of this Planet. They left behind a daughter civilisation which chose to stay on Earth. However there was a serious flaw in their biological and psychological make-up, they became a fearful and timid people, and to deal with their fear, they adopted, as a coping mechanism, a fearless, virile, powerful god which later re-appeared as Yahweh. Is this the people of Lumenia? Are they genetically and culturally linked with Abraham, do they originate from the same galaxy?

'No. There is no direct connection at all. They are of different lineage altogether. There are connections in genetic terms in as much as all of you who have chosen, at one time or other, to live on this Planet are broadly of the same family. There is a very loose sense of there being a connection, but not in the way you suggest, no.

'They are of the same cosmic family?

'That's right. Broadly speaking, all are of the same cosmic family. Some from this galaxy, some from other galaxies.

'Are their genetic ancestors from the star system of Lyra?

'That's right. This picture is correct of being a space from which a particular family develops and then spreads out across this galaxy, but there are also additional complexities. Again very much in the way in which the human race has spread across this Planet. Imagine this movement of population expanded up to galactic and intergalactic scale! You will find general patterns that you will trace easily and all sorts of anomalies creeping in as well.

'They are all physical beings living on physical planets or not necessarily?

'Not necessarily. In the course of the general history of the human race, you have become more physical as time has gone on. There was a time when you did not experience yourselves as being physical in the way you do now. But you chose to explore physicality in greater detail, so you have become more closely identified with physical form than was originally the case.

'After this digression may I return to Moses?

'Yes, certainly.

'One more detour! I apologise.

'That's alright

'Those who incarnate in Jewish form come back to either develop certain qualities or to resolve the experience of pain from the past. You spoke of a 're-stimulation of pain'. They also need to realise that in the eyes of the Source all are equal. Do they realise that they are in Samsara, stumbling from incarnation to incarnation?

'It is impossible to generalise. It varies from person to person.

'You also said that Moses came to perform the task of bringing to a speedy close the historical goal of the Hebrews. What exactly did you mean?

'You might think of it as Moses' soul purpose. What tends to happen in incarnation is that it is not easy to fulfil absolutely a soul purpose. Moses' soul purpose in coming to Earth was to manifest a new kind of energy which he wished to inflow, to transmit to the Hebrews, so that through transmission of this energy, through his beingness, he would assist them to dissolve certain patterns of behaviour or habits of existence which could be seen as a form of entrapment. That is to say, there was at that time among the Hebrew people the sense of being in some way 'chosen'. But they were unable to interpret it in a way that was liberating for them …. the meaning of being 'chosen'. They were unable to experience it other than by being 'separate'.

'To feel 'chosen' does not imply to be 'separate'.

'It was Moses' soul intention to come in and transform the experience of being 'chosen' into the experience of being 'leaders' whose purpose was to steer and focus love to all of humanity. That was his wish at soul level. He was not fully able to accomplish this. To some extent he was successful; he made some progress on that path; it was his aspiration to create an opening in the energy field. Visualising energy in the abstract, you will perceive that the energy of the experience of being 'chosen' had turned in on itself into a form of protection. His objective was to let his own particular qualities of energy flow in to facilitate that 'closing in' to turn into an 'opening out' and a radiating outwards. The sense of being 'chosen' would remain but the purpose of being chosen would change in the way that it expressed itself. This was his intention. You may want to ask more about this.

'So that their sense of 'chosenness' would not crystallise into inertia? You also said that he aimed to create a spiritual State, an ideal or enlightened society. It is very difficult to visualise what Moses might have been. He is so remote in time and culture. Was he in some way a Plato before his time? Was he attempting to create the ideal 'Republic', the humanity visualised by Abraham Lincoln, a new social utopia as envisioned by Rousseau?

'Some elements of those people you mention. Let's see if we can find you a close contemporary model. Perhaps you might choose Nelson Mandela as being more of a model. Now, don't put too much weight on this, but the similarities might be along this line: the ability to hold a vision over a long period of time is a characteristic both these beings share in common. The ability to accept privation and difficulty and yet still hold the vision, both these two beings share. Something else, both hold in common the ability to inspire others to become the politicians rather than becoming politicians themselves. I don't want to push this too far. Certain suggestions you made pointing to Moses playing a role of statesman or politician in the modern sense ... I think that would not be quite the case.

'A philosopher, a thinker?

'Yes and more than that, a spiritual leader whose leadership came out of his experience of Divine Energy and so a little bit more like your Abraham Lincoln, to give you something of an idea. Let's see if we can describe this in a different way, a different track. He was a being, at least at soul level, who was to be the pillar of flame that others were to be guided by. In other words, he hoped to bring out the best in people, so that they themselves would create that ideal State. It would not be so much that he would say 'Do this, do that'!

'Inspire them?

'Exactly, the perfect word.

SINAI

The friends are travelling back to their initial destination, Mount Sinai, where their journey began and from which they embarked on unforeseen travels and discoveries. They are accompanied by a student of the history of Ancient Sumer they met and to whom they graciously offered a lift.

'Did you know, begins Jonathan who is visibly in his element, that the Sinai Peninsula was known in ancient Sumer as the 'Land of the Missiles'? Modern researchers argue that after the Flood - which, as you know ended the last Ice Age, some 12,000 years ago - the Nefilim who had abandoned humanity to perish in the Deluge, returned to Earth.

'To salvage the remnant of mankind, enquires Clara with a touch of sarcasm?

'Humanity had already been salvaged; it was not compassion or remorse that brought them back, replies Jonathan repressing a slight displeasure.

'The Land of Missiles, were they at war with other powers, enquires Jeremy?

'It is suggested that the Sinai Desert was a launching space station, where they landed their space ships before deploying them. The modern equivalent would be Cape Canaveral. The Hebrews call Sinai the 'Mountain of the Elohim' in the misidentified notion that Yahweh and the Elohim are one and the same.

'It may not be mistaken. At Sinai, it was in part the Elohim who imparted the specific document we call the Old Testament.

Levinson and Johansson pay scant attention to the brash American student who seems more interested in settling scores.

'And Mount Sinai was completely engulfed by smoke for Yahweh had descended upon it in a fire. And the sound of the Shofar continued to wax louder...' quotes Levinson, moved by this extraordinary experience. Unable to explain the conflicting emotions battling within him.

'I always thought of it as the horn blown on the Day of Atonement to ward off the Devil, inserts Clara.

'It is, but in this instance, it was the device used by the Nefilim to amplify the voice of Yahweh, so that it could be heard by the multitude amassed at the foot of the mountain, answers Jonathan proudly asserting his knowledge.

'A loudspeaker?

'Yes, but to the gathered people who had never had any encounter with technology, it must have been a terrifying experience, says Johansson.

'And it was, replies Jonathan with brash confidence, they begged Moses to intercept the verbal command from Yahweh 'lest we should die' they implored terror-stricken! An event intended to strike terror in the heart of the multitude and make an indelible imprint in their psyche. Yahweh is, among other things, a great stage director. He orchestrated the descent upon Sinai in his dazzling and thundering space ship to terrify the masses into obedience and so ensure his continued, undisputed sovereignty over the Planet.

'That's right! With this amazing display of technology, he was certain of the capitulation of the masses, says Levinson. All he had to do is let the engine roar higher, the cloud of dust and smoke thicken further and he has the undivided, terrified, captive attention of the people. They are his!

'They have been his ever since, continues Clara, they are in the words of Yahweh himself, his own property, 'a treasured possession to me you shall be, for the whole Earth is mine'.

'You shall be my kingdom of priests and a holy nation', echoes Jonathan.

'Daunting inferences, remarks Clara. First, 'I am your one and only god and you will serve me unconditionally. Second, as a 'holy nation' you must stand 'separate'. Third, a 'kingdom of priests' to orchestrate things.

'All the roaring, the dust cloud, the mountain quaking, the tumult and the amplified voice thundering orders convinced the multitude that they were dealing with a mighty god and that it was in their best interest to become a 'kingdom of priests and a holy nation'. They had no choice; the basic law of survival demanded it, analyses Levinson. And so they embarked on a religious odyssey of capitulation and compliance tainted with resentment, frustration and fear which has lasted to this day.

'The 'service' to Yahweh today, continues Clara with bitter memory, is no more enlightened than it was in that long gone age when gods mingled with mortals, when they lusted after the daughters of men and when they demanded to be worshipped by mortals, as they walked among men.

The Renaissance Movement

On the grounds of St Katherine Monastery, at the foot of the forbidding Mount Sinai, the group are about to meet, in this majestic and desolate wilderness, the founding 'fathers' of the Renaissance Movement, who had outlined their main ideas and aspirations and who now wished to discuss their 'manifesto'. It was felt that in such a secluded area, away from the bustle and noise of daily life, they would have greater freedom to discuss serious issues. The choice of location was deliberate; they seek inspiration as well as tranquillity. They had arranged to meet in the cool shadow of the Monastery, where all is calm, peace and tranquillity.

They finally arrive in an old American car that emits a cloud of smoke and squeaks indiscriminately and which could be heard from a distance, disturbing the immense and proud silence of this grand and terrible Desert. The presentations get under way as they alight from their dusty car which has seen better times.

A tall man with greying temples, blue eyes and a short beard introduces his colleague, Sarah Gihon, a young-looking woman casually but smartly dressed, who radiates an air of gentleness and warmth. The man explains that after completing their doctoral thesis in American universities, they had stumbled upon the new spiritual movement vibrant over there. They also took part in advanced meditations workshops planned and organised by the Masters. As they rightly concede, the United States is the melting pot for new ideas. Before returning to Israel, they had met Jeremy who was running a workshop on Star Consciousness, a course which galvanised them into action and which became the inspiration and foundation platform for the launch of their Renaissance Movement.

After this preamble, they sit down and rest a while from their journey. They share around grapes, water melon and quartered oranges they have brought. A monk brings cool lemonade. After the pleasant remarks on the food, the drink and the awe-inspiring surroundings, questions are fired.

You have a doctorate in which science, enquires Jeremy?

'We work in the field of social sciences, I specialise in philosophy and anthropology, Sarah in psychotherapy and holistic health. Applied science might have limited us. These disciplines do not lock us in; we retain an open-mind and an insatiable inquisitiveness. Coming together we began to exchange ideas. Though it was the study of religion that brought us to the United States, we sought to expand our field of enquiry and before long we abandoned the uninspiring area of theology for that of spiritual philosophy, while continuing with our respective field of research. Fortunate to meet spiritual teachers who were also academics, we were launched so to speak, nothing could arrest our trajectory.

'Are you still being propelled, asks Clara with slight irony.

'Yes, we are still on our ascending curve, and we do not intend to begin a descending climb. My name is Macchabee.

'Judah Macchabee I presume, asks Clara?

'Maimon, my father, a freedom fighter named me after his hero, and so I have to live up to the name! Like Macchabee I am a resistance fighter.

'Fighting what and who, asks an inquisitive Tara?

'I am engaged in a spiritual conflict, clarifies Maimon. I have declared war on the hereditary state of inertia and static beliefs, against all that imprisons us: attachment to dogmas, denial of man's creativity, and denigration of man's ability for decision-making and his freedom of thought. It all springs from fear.

'"I have a dream ..." quotes Jeremy in jest.

'I have a war, replies Maimon calmly, I disagree with our relationship to humanity and to the world. When we finally allow our higher nature to manifest, an inherent, fundamental order reveals itself. As victims of the whims of fate, we wander the Planet, rootless, hapless in a world in which we have no place. Alienated from our being we are also alienated from the world. When we finally wake up, the world is transformed; we find our rightful place that had been denied us.

'Quite a programme, remarks Levinson, the more enlightened may understand your passion, but what of the minority who worships the past?

'It is too late for the past! We are living through a unique period in human history. We are being presented with a choice we rejected centuries ago. The choice is simple, either freedom from the bondage of religious law or continued entrapment.

'26,000 years before the Planet enters the next Aquarian Age, replies Tara quickly. Going back a bit, you are echoing the thought of Buddha. To Buddha the world is a vast field of consciousness which responds to our presence. A vast expanse of mind to which our human mind belongs.

'The cosmic nature of mind! A far cry from what we believe. We see the world the way our ancestors saw it, says Sarah, the way we are conditioned to see it. We project on to it the inherited cargo of bygone beliefs, perceptions, fears, prejudices, which weigh us down through life. In other words, we project our subjectivity onto the world, we do not see the world as it is, we see the world as we are.

'As your distant ancestors saw it, inserts Jeremy.

'So, common sense dictates, continues Maimon, that if we don't like the world as it is, we simply have to change the way we see it. From time immemorial we have been playing the same tune, like a broken record which plays the same bars over and over until we stop it.

'We act; we make decisions all the time while believing ourselves determined by fate. We act along the line of the worn-out patterns, and as we engage in daily activity we leave our imprint unaware of the impact we have on the world around us. In other words we act unconsciously, says Sarah.

'Right, continues Maimon, to recognise this opportunity is to face a crucial choice. If we choose the way of freedom we will enter the Promised Land.

'You are in it right now, laughs Clara.

'If we misread the signs and go on as before, we will simply perpetuate the errors of the past and live in a regressive state in which the defunct past continues to condition our lives, explains Maimon ignoring Clara' s mocking

'And the lives of those around you, remarks Jeremy.

'Why a spiritual movement, enquires Levinson?

'Ritualism blighted my early life, answers Maimon. Spirituality is the ancestral dream as yet unfulfilled. If we remain focussed on the materialism of tradition then it will remain an unattainable dream. The vision of a state at peace with itself and the world, a mirage!

'The way is not in the sky. The way is in the Heart', quotes Tara.

'We briefly encountered spirituality on rare occasions, with Moses, with the Essenes, with Spinoza and with the Enlightenment Movement which briefly blossomed in the 18th century. And they all vanished, just a memory, a mirage, remarks Sarah.

'For as long as our religious tradition is grounded in physicality, spirituality will continue to elude us, insists Maimon. We produce many atheists and many pietistic individuals. The label differs, the kernel is the same, and both are rooted in physical reality. The pietistic ones adore a materialistic god; the others prefer the laws of Nature.

'As long as man has any regard for his corpse-like body, he is impure and suffers from his enemies as well as from birth, disease and death', quotes Tara.

'Our pietistic men bless their god daily for giving them the body of a man and not that of a woman, think of it, mocks Clara!

'A corpse-like body is a corpse-like body; it is impure and attracts enemies, disease and death. That's what happens when we worship the body. But the body is all we know, echoes Levinson!

'Both theists and atheists focus on the material world and hate each other's guts, picks up Sarah. I am aiming at the restoration of Goddess culture and the recognition of the power of woman. When I was in New York I joined a women's movement dedicated to the resurgence of the Goddess.

'Tara, I presume, asks Tara?

'By any other name, the Goddess is and will be, smiles Sarah.

'We have never been closer to fulfilling the dream, continues Maimon. My dream is the demise of religious Judaism and the emergence of an enlightened State.

'That was Moses' aim too, in part. A political goal, asks Clara?

'Both political and spiritual, I don't think we can split the two, not any longer. The Declaration of Human Rights is a political as well as a spiritual statement about the inalienable rights of man.

'I agree, approves Jeremy. Love is within the reach of mankind. Not sentimental love but the compelling force that encourages change and promotes expansion. Love as a conscious evolutionary force.

'The inalienable rights of man, resumes Maimon, freedom of expression, access to education, the right to work for all without fear of reprisal, freedom 'to do and to be'. It is the impulse to fulfil our potential, social justice, humanitarian aspirations, concern for the dignity of man, the right to freedom and regard for human relations.

'This is the principle of love we discarded 2000 years ago and which we endorse today, inserts Clara. It is the love-energy which will release us from the bondage of the religion of fear and the god of fear.

'If we fail to arrive at this realisation, we would have learnt nothing from our painful history. It has to do with fear. Fear is the great aberration, the great distortion, adds Sarah. I observe its devastating effects in my patients.

'Hermes, Krishna, Buddha and the Essenes came to eradicate fear and replace it by love, says Tara.

Sarah pursues with a note of resentment, 'not for us, we excluded ourselves, preferring to grab at fear, and we have never let go of it. Our history hinges around fear, it is replete with events, stories and fables built around the energy of fear. Our law and religious beliefs depend and hang on fear. Fear is our driving force and our downfall. Instead of denouncing fear we have erected it into a guiding principle. Our god is the god of fear; we instil fear in the heart of our children. We perceive god in his most destructive aspect.

'The religion of fear has given rise to the politics of fear, says Maimon.

'Pictured as the Father, the originator of time matter and space; the static universe.

'The 'destructive' Shamballa force was released into the world in the 20th century and detonated with the apocalyptic violence we know. Destruction brings about new creation, reflects Jeremy. The Masters are coming closer to help us transmute fear into love. They are focussing on our Heart centre which is gradually opening, and love, excluded from our awareness for too long, is entering into human consciousness. It has taken many centuries, but the catastrophes of the 20th century have been instrumental in bringing about this change.

'Like you Sarah, my aim is the reinstatement of the Goddess. The return of the Goddess heralds the opening of the Heart centre, the birth of love. Fear is the weapon of patriarchy, love is with the Goddess. The feminine principle is entering our consciousness once again, says Tara.

'This is something we cannot as yet fully grasp, continues Sarah, our attachment to physical form is such that we forget the living essence within the form. Form and fear pervade our existence and blight our lives; they are the great challenge we have to confront. We have to realise that the feminine principle - the soul - must assert its dominance.

'Death is followed by resurrection, notes Jeremy.

'That's right, like spring follows winter. The long winter of fear which tradition has nurtured and perpetuated is coming to a natural end, agrees Sarah.

'This is one of the great contributions of the Essenes. As the nature of the soul is love, they proved the existence of the soul through unconditional love, remarks Jeremy.

'And showed that there is no death. With Berechit enters time and with time enters death, mutters Clara. Death is linked with time and time is an illusion that swept in with Creation.

'This is a paradox when we recall the manner of their death. They demonstrated that death is an illusion. They imparted the secret of immortality which is love. Love confers immortality and eventually releases us from the bondage of physical life.

'To prove the illusory nature of death to a people steeped in the material world was daunting comments Levinson. Bronze Age humanity could not grasp such abstract an idea. The human mind was forming and it took 2000 years for it to evolve to the point it has reached today. We are beginning to grapple with the world of meaning which lies behind the form.

'Why did it take so long, asks Tara?

'Because man tends to be beguiled by form - physical, social and mental, says Maimon. The great heresy was to believe that the information given at Sinai was the be-all and end-all. It was intended to be only temporary. Form, social or intellectual serves a purpose and is retained for as long as it is useful. When it calcifies, it is 'dead' and must be discarded. We were taught in legends, fables, allegories and commands. These symbolic and visual instructions were adapted to the mental ability of the time.

'The simple teachings we received at Sinai we dare not discard for fear of retaliation. Expansion of consciousness has been a slow process partly because of the resistance of the rabbis who abhor questioning. To pacify their deity they block progress.

'In earlier times, forms endured for considerable periods, but as evolution gains momentum, existing forms expire faster and are being replaced by new forms. This process of rapid birth of form and death of form is gathering speed. As we evolve, old forms become obsolete, explains Jeremy.

'The form we received at Sinai served its purpose, it helped a group develop a social and moral conscience, says Maimon. But it got to tight, strangling us, obstructing our progress. It became a liability, a peril to our very survival. Miraculously, exile came to our rescue. In our endless peregrinations, we were exposed to advanced forms of thinking. And the devout wail and mourn exile! Exile is our ally, the driving force of progress and emancipation. That which resists change inevitably dies.

'Did you see the representation of Hell by Botticelli, notes Jeremy, the artist. Lucifer is entombed from the waist down in ice; he is rendered immobile, inert, frozen. Hell is immobility, inertia, stagnancy.

'This hell, we have endured for too long, says Clara, whose experience of it is vivid; after all these years it still haunts her.

Jeremy enquires: 'When we met on the Star Consciousness workshop some time ago, we hardly had time to exchange meaningful information. You are laying the foundations of a new movement, give us the gist of it, formulate your agenda. From social sciences to spiritual philosophy, this is quite a leap! How did you make that leap?

'It was not a leap but a progressive and considered development.

Our agenda is clear and relatively simple in contents and scope while possibly considerably more difficult in implementation, replies Maimon. First, we propose to depose the gods of the Old Testament who hang around like insensitive and tactless guests who do not know when to leave. The gods who established civilisation must be persuaded to leave or be driven out.

'You know all about the origins of the gods, asks Clara?

'We devoured avidly recent research on ancient Sumer; we read among others Kramer, Patai and Sitchin.

'As Sananda explained, proceeds Jeremy, the energy of Sanat Kumara is entering more into humanity's consciousness. The new forms, ideas and images are displacing the old ones registered in human consciousness and recorded in the Old Testament. We can regard this document as a database for events of the distant past and a filing system for archaic ideas about the world and man.

Everything that is wrong with humanity and the Planet stems from those antiquated ideas, forms and images, says Clara whose bitter experience of this dismal reality is all too vivid.

'With the demise of the tribal god the demise of his first command, the odious 'go and multiply'. In its place we will carve, 'Love and revere the child that you bring into this world, for he is the Logos incarnate, do not multiply inordinately and randomly, create the child consciously', enounces Maimon.

'You will need a large stone tablet, laughs Clara!

'So far we have the war against religious inertia, sums up Jeremy whose logical mind needs order, the return of the Goddess, the creation of a spiritual state and the overthrow of that first command 'go & multiply'.

'The 'go & multiply' not only demeans humanity it has led to the population explosion we have today and which no country seems able to contain, says Clara who does not hide her repugnance for this and other demeaning commands. Some laws set men free. This one is definitely of the kind that enslaves human beings.

'Next, continues Maimon, the phasing out of the offensive 'do & obey'. When the despotic god is finally toppled, no man will ever 'do & obey'. Equally no man will ever force another to 'do & obey'. Man-child in Genesis was forced to serve his master unconditionally. Our tradition presents man as a mindless servant and takes great pride in it. Modern man is no longer a docile or recalcitrant serf, he is his own master, and some find this shift in awareness almost impossible to attempt. Religious perception today is no different from what it was in the Stone Age. In its place we shall inscribe: 'Be & know'. Humanity's consciousness has been dominated by the 'do & obey' and Western culture echoing Hebrew tradition has glorified action and promotes 'doing' above 'being'. 'Being' is for the contemplative Eastern mystics while 'doing' is for the modern, technological, scientific West.

'The Masters aim at developing both in us. They seek to blend the contemplative with the dynamic, the meditative with the creative. To achieve equilibrium East and West must unify. In cosmic terms it is the merging of mind and heart, action and contemplation, explains Jeremy. Unity comes not in exclusion but in the fusion of opposites. The civilisation in the making which the cosmic workers are manifesting is such a fusion. We are aiming at unification; we seek to bring about the state of Grace.

'The state of Grace, fusion of opposites, end of polarity, oneness restored, whispers Tara.

'I fully agree, I have been saying this all along, salvation in our society is with 'doing', insufficient attention is paid to 'being', says Levinson...

'The scales tilt heavily toward 'doing' continues Jeremy. The more we do the more we are perceived as successful and valued by society. 'Being is the most valuable contribution you can make to the world' told us Sananda, and emphasis on 'being' is going to reverse the trend that was set in motion in the Book of Genesis.

'Distress can often be laid at the door of this biblical command, says Sarah who encounters much despondency brought about by a feeling of inadequacy and failure. Not every one is willing to justify his existence by incontinent action. People tend to compare themselves unfavourably to others who they see as more successful. Too often they reach their mature years only to break down in sorrow for not having achieved enough, for not 'doing' enough, when they should feel sorrow for not 'being' enough. We need a revolution in thinking!

'I drink to the revolution, chuckles Clara raising an imaginary glass!

'Separative attitude, karmic baggage from the past, fear, shame, all split us from ourselves and from the world, comments Jeremy. Sanat Kumara teaches that we are entering the time of Grace. Grace is the opposite of separation. Grace is the knowing of your oneness with the All.

'What is the working of Grace, asks Sarah eagerly?

'Grace brings you into the present, teaches Sanat Kumara, replies Jeremy. 'You are free to gather up the past and the future and roll them into the present. Forgive all, especially yourself; for all you witness outside of yourself is a reflection of what lies within'.

'That's it, exclaims Sarah. Past and future torment people, they lament the past and dread the future, they fail to be here in the present. Grace is the point of balance, the point of harmony, the point of healing.

'The point of balance where past and future blend into the present is the point of equilibrium: the end of tension, the end of fear and separation. All is realised: union, harmony, balance, in other words healing, echoes Levinson.

'Our inherited nature predisposes us to splitting, separating, dividing, continues Sarah. It predisposes us to tension and distress. In other words, our inherited nature and our tradition predispose us to illness. We are the people of the past. We are the people trapped in 'time'. Because of this entrapment we promote separation. We are split from ourselves and the world. We need to heal, we need Grace.

'Grace is the knowing of your Oneness with the All', quotes Jeremy.

At this point, Maimon inserts, 'I would like to quote a phrase by Oscar Wilde that made a lasting impression on me, 'In the opinion of society, contemplation is the gravest sin … In the opinion of the highest culture, it is the proper occupation of man'. We are beginning to sense the reality of the inner man, and we are progressing toward a concern with 'being'. Our reverence for 'doing' at the expense of 'being' is becoming an embarrassment and will demand a revolution in thinking. 'We aim to erode to its final dissolution the twin evils of 'do & obey' and 'go & multiply', not forgetting the third evil 'obey your parents'. And when these malignancies are cut out, those who wish to embody in the Jewish garb may do so more safely. But even if they prefer to incarnate into this genetic mode, they will begin their Earth adventure on a higher octave, a higher vibrational note. Once the deity is no longer absolute master, 'fashioner', father and jailer, we shall abstain from the 'do & obey'. We, humanity can now make a full declaration of independence.

'Mankind is entitled to demand the freedom that is its birthright and which was taken away from us, agrees Levinson.

'Change is unfolding at an unprecedented velocity. Our teacher in India warned us that this acceleration eludes even the most critical eye, expands Maimon, slowly as if testing the waters before venturing too far. This is no time for complacency and there is work to do, even if the outcome is blurred in the distant mist. We are reformulating the fundamental tenets of the Old Testament. We formerly declare them obsolete, an obstruction to our progress and the progress of humanity. This bygone theology has locked us up and detained us in an archaic past. We are turning our back on the past to look right into the present and unravel the trends.

'How do you propose to tackle these issues, enquires Levinson with acute interest, I have been writing about changes taking place globally and working on an analysis of our inheritance. I strongly agree with you, change is upon us in ways which are still not yet clear, but the ancestral world view is undergoing a profound shake up, we can hear the underground groaning.

'Indeed, I am glad that we meet on this point, continues Maimon with a visible expression of relief. We are dealing a fatal blow to the most odious injunctions that struck primitive man, the 'do & obey' and the 'go & multiply'.

'The 'do & obey', picks up Sarah is a relic from a bygone age to which we cling with disgraceful servility. Have you read 'The Island of Dr Moreau' by HG Wells? It was an eye opener for me, the character Dr Moreau is a benevolent geneticist who has humanised wild animals by inserting in them human genes. In deference for their 'father' they 'do & obey' without question. But eventually the docile creatures rebel and kill their 'father'.

Later, after a stroll at the foot of the mountain, they sit down in the golden light of the setting sun. 'At the foot of this majestic mountain saturated with symbolism, we are trying to grasp something of what Moses experienced, remarks Jeremy. Each man has to 'go up the mountain', scale the peak in the course of his long climb to the light.

'Symbolism, asks Tara?

'Figuratively the mountain stands for higher states of consciousness, explains Jeremy. This is why Initiates 'go up the mountain'. They leave behind ordinary awareness to partake to the Mysteries. In that altered state of consciousness can be found spiritual reality. They abandon the mundane, the pedestrian to rise into the higher realm of Mind, and from this altitude they look down on the sorrowful world of men and they 'know'. The full panorama of life unfolds before them and the meaning of life is revealed. Our limited mentality, our narrow picture, our trivial squabbles, our prosaic concerns dissolve into nothing. When the Initiates symbolically descend from the mountain they find the world as it truly is, clouded in darkness, shrouded in illusion. They veil their faces because those gathered at the foot of the mountain cannot endure their light. We are not there yet!

'The high priests of Jerusalem distanced themselves from the impure masses to protect their purity, chuckles Clara.

'They protected not only their idea of purity they also protected their lavish lifestyle. The Essenes were appalled by the social injustice and corruption of the day. They denounced the extravagant lifestyles of the high Priests who built for themselves elegant Roman villas with private baths, discloses Levinson. The corruption of the money lenders who organised a banking system in the Temple is something we prefer to forget. Yet the high Priests built a bridge linking their villas to the Temple to avoid contact with the 'impure' masses! They would not compromise their purity!

'While the lame, the sick, the disabled, the lepers, the insane were banished and sent to die in the wilderness where they lived in caves like animals, discarded as sub-standards and abandoned to die in the desert! The decadence and corruption of the time is hard for us to even imagine. The establishment was corrupt, yet the Essenes did challenge the priesthood and the learned Rabbis with resilience and determination. They rejected the prevailing view among the priesthood that the sick were imperfect, unclean, impure and unworthy. The Essenes began a healing programme to return the sick to society. As a therapist this is particularly relevant to me, says Sarah.

'They were witnessing eugenics in action, long before our 20th century when those considered inferior or imperfect were forcibly sterilised in the United States and in Sweden, inserts Levinson. But it was in Germany that eugenics took its most diabolical form. We invented eugenics long ago.

'The idea was to phase out defective genes and encourage the perpetuation of healthy genes, says Sarah. The discarding of the sick was their own version of natural selection centuries before Darwin shocked Victorian Britain.

'Natural?

'Let's call it contrived 'natural selection'.

'Father forgive them for they know not what they are doing', quotes Jeremy.

'Amen! They certainly knew not what they were doing: they shrugged off in contempt cosmic Law. They knew not that each human being is the receptacle of the Presence. They knew not that the Shekhina dwells in the inner Temple of the sick, the lame, the lepers and the insane. This was true of the arrogant priests as it was true of the 'substandard' sick they despised, says Levinson.

'Let's put things into perspective, continues Maimon, it is an aberration with its own logic. The presence of the sick and disabled is intolerable among a social group which sees itself as biologically perfect. The pure race Yahweh genetically engineered could not sanction imperfections. Disease and flaws clashed with claims of purity, selection and racial advantage. To the priests it was a violation of the 'divine' order. The genetically modified people had to discard those who did not meet Yahweh's specifications. The myth of the pure race had to be maintained at any cost.

'Our infatuation with genetic purity has screened us from cosmic Law, repeats Levinson. The priests condoned corruption because they functioned as their egos, ignorant of a higher reality. They saw the flaws in the sick but did not see their own flaws. The 'money lenders' episode is a reminder of human frailty; it symbolically stands for the arrogance of the ego. The symbolic gesture against the money lenders is a reaction to corruption and selfishness. This gesture was anchoring the fundamental principles which 2000 years later became enshrined in the Declaration of Human Rights: social justice, equality, liberty, respect for human rights, and the recognition of human dignity.

'Had the high Priests shaken off their complacency and adopted one single cosmic law, just one, they would have spared the Jewish people's unimaginable suffering, remarks Jeremy in thoughtful mood.

'As the 'do & obey' is dissolving, we insert 'being & freedom'. The Old Testament is coming of age!

'Why not 'be and assert your freedom', suggests Jeremy.

'That would be a command. We do not command, we do not coerce.

'Would you outline the tenets of your vision for a new version of the Old Testament, I have a special interest in the subject, asks Levinson?

'I share your stated desire to undermine the old system and present it in a form that is acceptable to 20th century minds, echoes Clara.

'The religion we envision will be founded on two related ideas and the methods by which these ideas can become reality, begins Sarah.

'A religion, exclaims Clara alarmed!

'Not in the narrow sense of 'do & obey', not the religion of the masculine ego, picks up Maimon. The new religion focuses on man in relation to his own Self and to the cosmic Self.

'Your new 'religion' unchained from dogmas, untied from the externalities of rituals, unbound from theology does not mention the central principle underlying all creation, reflects Levinson.

'It certainly does, to establish a relationship with the Source and with the Soul is the ultimate.

'What about 'love thy neighbour', probes Levinson? Had our ancestors understood the relevance of this principle, all the other tenets would have vanished into smoke. This is beginning to happen now. If you love the other, you know the divine in man and in all creation. You have attained the goal of creation; you have verified the purpose of evolution. The rest flows from this realisation, so avoiding many centuries of painful exile.

'Yet, some are fashioned on the Stone Age model, but their numbers are dwindling and will go on dwindling, for no other reason than the world is changing all around them and they are being influenced by those changes, in part unconsciously, adds Maimon.

'Judging by newspapers articles and television reports, they are making up the numbers by their loudness, inserts Clara.

'The liberation of man from his religious prison and his entrapment in the ego is the object of our master plan, continues Maimon for whom this is visibly a painful reality. We are addressing the constricted view man has of himself as finite entity doomed to die. Many will rebel at our endeavour to subdue both the ego and the tribal consciousness that has crystallised around it

'Many are buried in the sand of dogma and superstition, too timid to accept the magnitude of their true identity, notes Clara. Man will know himself in his nature as he truly is. For the pious individual who has adored his projected self 'out there' in the cosmos, it is an unsettling probability.

'This leap is unsettling, notes Jeremy, in a pacifying tone. The swing from being a child to being self-governing is daunting. Man-child is petrified and who would not be? One instant you are a helpless child and the next you are master of your destiny?

'For them, to be spiritual is to exclude the world and suffocate in their own confined space, caught up in a time warp, notes Clara who recalls too well. To be spiritual for them is to contract, to shrivel.

'To be spiritual for us, says Jeremy, is to expand to the four corners of the globe, indeed to the four corners of the cosmos. To be spiritual is to accept, to assimilate, to comprehend, to integrate, and to feel part of the universe.

'To be spiritual is to include, agrees Maimon. Everything which pushes away our boundaries is worthy of investigation. Science, humanities, arts, philosophy are spiritual because they cultivate expansion of mind as they push further away the frontiers of the potential. Denying the whole range of educational opportunities is to condemn children to ignorance, fanaticism, intolerance and deficiency. That is not all! The resultant resentment and anger will send out shock waves into the world, striking man and Earth equally. All facets of experience, all aspects of knowledge unlock the nature of meaning. Exploring all things is what makes us spiritual.

'It is encouraging to hear this new definition of religion, I like it, says Jeremy!

'Resentment and anger are spilling over, echoes Sarah. They are palpable even if disguised under the cloak of piety. Our social life bears witness.

'In our new religion, continues Maimon, all children will receive a broadly based education and parents who restrict their children to ancient fables and allegories will come under scrutiny. Our declining religion authorised certain views and beliefs but denied others just as valid.

'Such as, enquired Jeremy?

'Intuitive knowing was profane, genuine religious experience heresy. We were not allowed to know, feel or experience anything outside the authorised instruction; the 'do & obey' was absolute, says Sarah. The mind was the possession of the religious establishment who decided what to feed it with. Women were denied elementary education and given inferior status, forced to cover their heads as a sign of inferiority, obedience and humility, or was it humiliation? At all levels of human expression, it was a dictatorship.

'In tyrannical regimes the real enemy is invisible, it is man himself, says the radical Maimon, truly a freedom fighter. Through propaganda he is denied information on his true nature. Information is either distorted or suppressed. Where it is distorted man is perceived as essentially flawed to be broken down and rebuilt for the benefit of the party, the regime, the Father land, or the one god. Where it is suppressed, the talents, aspirations and potentialities must be stifled.

'So much for dictatorship among our people, retorts Levinson! What of other people? We decided that religious sensitivity was our right so we denied it to others. As lesser beings they were incapable of it. Religious feeling is inherently human but we denied it to others. We failed to realise that all men are made of the same cosmic essence and so we invented a biological and mental superiority no more founded on scientific evidence than the racism of Hitler was.

'Religious feeling is fine but redundant, what about religious 'knowing', argues Jeremy?

'Right, continues Maimon, we are clinging to the antediluvian era. As we drop the baggage of prejudices, archaic thought pattern, images and beliefs: all conditioned responses learned in childhood, something wonderful will happen.

'Tell us what, exclaims Clara!

'We shall make out our own divinity and recognise the divinity in all men, clarifies Maimon. We will have completed a six million-year trek across time! The first verses of Genesis we shall read as the Initiates read it, 'And the Word said: Let Maya flourish and let deception rule'. Governed by deception we embraced Maya without inhibition and choking in its embrace we have endured much pain and inflicted much suffering on the Planet. This was the focal point of our training in India.

'Group consciousness is the goal of this age, yet it has been our downfall. Inwardly oriented, oppressive and claustrophobic, our group consciousness was attended by fear, narcissism and condescension, reflects Levinson. The new awareness of Aquarius externally-oriented is liberating and encompassing. From contraction to expansion, from self-consciousness to world consciousness.

'Control by Maya implies not only duality but suffering, expands Maimon. Maya, the world of illusion reads out suffering. Where Maya rules, the soul slumbers. Where Maya governs conflict thrives. Instead of fostering spiritual life, we thwart it. Self-conscious man frustrates spiritual life; he fails to be the conscious servant of humanity.

'Quite a paradox, the more robust the religious reaction, the less self-knowledge. Man loses himself as he worships his gods; he loses sense of the cosmic dimension of his nature, sums up Jeremy

The End of the Jewish condition - Determinism is no longer

'Should the Jewish condition come to an end or does it serve such a valuable purpose that it must endure? I have grappled with this concern for a long time, asks Maimon?

'We all have, smiles Sarah, we have done more than grapple, we have agonised over it.

'The answer must be 'yes' to both. You are raising the vexed questions of determinism and freedom, replies Clara.

'That is not quite what I meant, replies Maimon. I was asking if the Jewish condition still serves a purpose or if it is redundant.

'There is more to it than purpose or lack of it. It spills out into the realm of determinism and freedom. The answer is 'yes' to both, insists Clara.

'Can you explain this ambivalence, asks Maimon wonderingly?

'The answer is ambivalent, picks up Levinson. If the conditions are ripe for its germination, the Jewish condition will arise. The presence of desire, prejudices, temperament and attitudes are predispositions that make the Jewish embodiment necessary. The answer to your first question is 'yes' it serves a useful purpose; human beings need it for learning and growth.

'The desire to develop and grow in moral and spiritual stature is also a fertile ground, inserts Tara. You all incarnated in the Jewish condition to grow into wonderful spiritual beings, don't forget.

'The spectre of determinism rears its head, says Jeremy who has pondered over the issue and seeks to clarify his own thought. Yet this situation - desire, attitudes, prejudices, challenging relationships, emotional distress, and negative thought forms - is not the work of some malign deity who seeks revenge on man by throwing him into the quagmire of Maya. It is the work of man himself. No external pressure is applied. His destiny is the outcome of his own actions. Man is in charge of his Karmic destiny at all times, since the beginning of times, in fact. The inexorable law of Evolution is at work.

'You are saying that man oscillates between change and stagnation, movement and inertia, longing for progress and dread of progress, yearning for freedom and fear of freedom, sums up Maimon.

'Exactly, replies Jeremy. You have just enounced polarity with its positive and negative signs. Man, down the ages, like a pendulum has oscillated from longing for freedom to fear of freedom, from change to stagnation.

'As for us - and we have tradition as a back up - we are arrested on the negative side, says Maimon. I made my position clear; my aim is the demise of religious ritualism and the birth of an enlightened State. For us it is the fear of freedom that is the core issue, we opted for stagnation, inertia, apathy, obedience to authority. In other words we believe ourselves to be determined. We believe in a vengeful Father rather than in our autonomy.

'The answer to your question must be that the Jewish condition is both unavoidable and preventable. It serves a purpose for as long as man avoids facing up to the truth of his being. It will evaporate the moment man - the human race - knows his infinite potential, concludes Clara.

'Is there anything valuable about the Jewish condition, asks Sarah perplexed?

'Its disappearance, retorts Clara! As long as man remains in infancy the condition will endure. It will disappear when man – humanity - finally decides to take charge of his life.

'It does serve a purpose, smiles Jeremy.

'Yes like a pushchair serves the purpose of pushing an infant. No one expects to see a grown up man sitting in a pushchair!

'Santayana declared that those who forget history are condemned to repeat it, notes Maimon. If we refuse to make sense of the painful events that blight our past, history will be repeated. As long as we keep our heads buried in the sand, we will replicate the past. I for one do not want to see a repeat performance of the events that nearly brought to a close life on Earth in the 20th century. The civilisation of Yahweh died a terrible death in Europe before finally exploding at Hiroshima. This must never happen again!

'It was the energy of Will released by Shamballa in its full potency which detonated, says Jeremy.

'I want to send out a trumpet call to all people of good will, inviting them … no, urging them to erect an insurmountable planetary wall. The civilisation of Yahweh must not be exported and dumped onto another planet. It must be confined to Earth and fade away, says Levinson with passion. The dissolution of the Yahweh culture will facilitate a shift in awareness from narrow perception to an unlimited sense of freedom.

'The civilisation of Yahweh was not all bad, suggests Jeremy the artist.

'True, agrees Johansson. Without it we would not have walked on the moon, built supersonic jets, computer systems of bewildering complexity, harnessed electricity and discovered DNA. By the way, some of the most distinguished scientists are Jewish, not a coincidence! Furthermore it is the civilisation of Yahweh which gave us the cathedrals, Galileo, Newton, Beethoven, and Michelangelo, astrophysics, psychoanalysis, genetics, literature, philosophy, microsurgery and biotechnology. At no time in the history of humanity was so much achieved in so short a time. This stupendous civilisation built around the masculine ego has achieved much.

'Yet it is the negativity of this civilisation which often eclipses its great achievement, notes Jeremy. After all, the masses never heard of Newton, Beethoven and Michelangelo. Their priests, monks and rabbis would have forbidden it with lavish threat.

'Humanity endured it for thousands of years, says Clara petulantly, it will not be inflicted upon another galactic race which does not deserve to be so chastised or so cursed. We have no right to do this to any one else, anywhere else.

'How can we prevent it?

'We will expose any resistance, continues Clara with passion, enlist all men of good will. I lived through the horror of it and I plan to spare others the same fate whoever they are wherever they may be. We must never allow the old system to be restaged somewhere else. We shall erect a fortification of energy, a ring of radiation, a giant thought-form of light round the globe to prevent a last charge from the old order, the old energy. We will spare other cosmic beings from having to appear on the stage of the most repressive, regressive, dispiriting and disheartening system. I was immersed in it for a large segment of my life, I know the agony! What we do now will have far-reaching consequences.

The End of the Jewish condition - Belief is archaic

The following day a car arrives with two of Benzaccai's students. The young people have a probing curiosity in Holism and the new psychologies. Almost by accident they discovered that they are not alone in this. David is studying the psychology of Jung and

Rebecca is writing an essay on the 'role of emotions in the causation of disease'. After the initial greetings, they rest for a while outside the monastery, in awe of Sinai. They are invited to share a wholesome lunch prepared by the monks.

'Man needs to worship the gods of his society, says Rebecca who shows a serious interest in the religious. Where a society retains its ancestral gods, all is acceptance. But where there is a clash between ancestral gods and societal beliefs there is conflict, questions are asked but not answered.

'The age of belief is coming to an end, says Levinson reassuringly. The ruling force relied on worship; it had to for it was not of the Light. When the ruling force is laid bare, man will no longer need to worship; he will rediscover his innate power.

'He will know who he is; he will know that he is on Earth of his own free will. Man reincarnates over ages and he does so consciously and deliberately. When the controlling force dissolves, man will be in control, reinforces Jeremy

'I made the decision to come into incarnation, without any input from any outside agency, of my own free will, says David excitedly! And not for some vague collective goal, but for me – to improve my character, mend relationships, refine my nature, develop faculties, fulfil my potential and explore the world. I am a free agent; I planned the whole scenario and put everything in place – people, backdrop, props, and events. Scriptwriter and actor!

'I am no victim of circumstances! I am the instrument of my own evolution, says Rebecca spiritedly. The implications for therapy are huge. When people know that they came to Earth of their own decision, the world will change.

'That's right, continues David avidly, the whole picture has changed for ever. I am no longer designated for some imaginary group purpose. I made the decision to visit Earth with a goal of my own, not a collective goal nobody knows anything about or cares about.

'That's right, says Rebecca, for so long as a capricious god planted me on Earth, there was no meaning and no recourse action.

'Now the ball is in your court, smiles Maimon.

'Exactly, continues David confidently, the ball is in my court, I am in charge of the whole process. I am master of my destiny, author of the way in which I shape my belief about the world. What I am here for? I cannot evade this central question. God did not dump me here, so why did I come back?

'The decision was yours, so the reason behind it is yours too, says Maimon.

'So not only I am on Earth as my decision, I also know the reason, I am in charge of the whole process, exclaims David!

"Everything has changed, contributes Jeremy who is visibly enjoying this input. What one of us changes is changed for all. What has been achieved cannot be undone. Who moves forward in his own progress, moves the whole of humanity with him. He has set new records; just like the Olympics games; the runner or swimmer who wins a medal has set the standards for all who will come after him. Nothing moves backward, only forward. The discovery you made today belongs to all, you have broadcast it to the world, you are setting new standards for all.

The Ten Commandments – an overview

Rabbi Moses continues to narrate his epic quest for the Self. He notes, 'I used to think that the Ten Commandments were a major advance and that we had given the world an essential tool for correct living. In the light of my experiences in India, I have had to reconsider all that I held true. Many of those who reside in this monastery are advanced beings; they form the fabric of a new and more evolved human race well ahead of the rest of humanity. They incarnate not to make amends, not to heal psychic wounds, not to gratify desire, not even to climb the evolutionary ladder, many are already liberated. They incarnate to be of service to humanity. Deliberating on this issue I approached Master Sanaka who is apt at discerning my secret thoughts almost before I am able to formulate them to myself.

'You are reflecting on the Ten Commandments, are you not, he enquires with that characteristic twinkle in his eyes in which mingles a touch of irony, kindness and challenge.

'You know?

'You wonder how I do it, he replies with the same sparkling smile. It is simple; I follow the logic of your reflection and anticipate your next enquiry'. He remains silent for a minute looking intently into my eyes as if penetrating into the deeper regions of my mind. 'The science of mind, he begins very slowly choosing his words, the sum of esoteric knowledge and mental discipline was given long ago by Patanjali to achieve spiritual freedom.

Somewhat confounded I hesitatingly say, 'the Ten Commandments and the Revelation intended the same, did they not?

Smiling again, Sanaka replies 'the Ten Commandments were a giant stride forward for humanity. A few thousands years ago enlightened cosmic Beings came to Earth to instruct and inspire mankind, Hermes, Moses, Buddha, Krishna, Lao Tzu. The Ten rules were intended to turn a wandering tribe into a civilised sedentary society. Note that Buddha did not formulate rules for daily living. His concern was liberation from the illusion of Maya, the world of time, space and matter. Your commandments do not serve that purpose. They instruct you to lead decent lives but do not aim at lifting the veil of Maya.

'Buddha did not give rules for living?

'Rules for living are vital to people absorbed in physicality to show them how to perform basic activities and to teach them basic conduct. Buddha was addressing advanced individuals searching for spiritual liberation.

'Rules for living are other than spiritual liberation?

'Spiritual liberation is the ultimate goal. But those absorbed in physicality have to proceed gradually, from the material to the non-material, from darkness to light, from the unreal to the real, from matter to mind.

'The rules which set us apart from the rest of humanity, we regard as a sign of our chosenness and moral authority.

'Indeed, but too often they are taken as an end in themselves rather than as a means of refinement, improvement and progress. And instead of taking you gently to the time of liberation they arrest you in Maya. You descend deeper into the illusion.

'We descend into the illusion because we get attached to physicality and perceive our body as who we are?

'That's right. You come to the dense atmosphere of Earth and the illusion of the Fall and you need a body of flesh to move about. The body is only a garment yet you devote your lives to this mantle, your religious practices demand it and revolve around it. And so instead of moving toward spiritual liberation you stand still adoring your body and neglecting soul needs.

'Our body is who we are. The 'do & obey', the 'go & multiply' remind us at all time of our physical identity.

'And wisdom teaches that the perishable body attracts foes, disease and death. It keeps you in the illusion. Sanaka smiles with a hint of irony and melancholy. He seems to be waiting.

'So it is to no avail, it has kept us in ignorance, attachment and illusion.

'All the great avatars and Prophets who came to advance mankind knew that evolution is a slow process. But to return to what I was saying earlier, one precept stands out, I AM. The others instruct you to interact in a sensitive manner and behave in a sensible manner. These rules perceive man as a physical and social being.

'Are we not commanded to love god with our heart, mind and whole being?

'Indeed, but the god you are commanded to love is the god of Samsara who, like you is trapped in the world of illusion.

'We send out to the world our allegiance to the one god, the 'Adonai'!

'It may be that the I AM and the Adonai are not the same, or are they? Some tangle set in over time as you fused the I AM, the Elohim, Adonai, the King of the World and others. You refer to these Manifestations interchangeably; you worship them as if they were the same entity. The King of the World is Sanat Kumara, a cosmic Being who exists outside time and space, unlike your Samsara god.

'Which is the correct one? I am confused.

'It is not for me to say. Your people will have to make an informed decision in the light of spiritual Law and not under the spell of caprice and fantasy. This much I can say: the I AM command is an enigma, it hints at something of a different order, something other than your mundane existence, it does not hint at earthly man.

'Is the I AM implied in the teachings of Buddha?

'Buddha did not define man as a physical entity, he was fully aware of his own cosmic nature; he knew his mind to be the universal Mind. Later the Essenes reiterated the cosmic nature of man with the much vilified, 'I & my Father are One'. They spoke of the soul, the enduring, deathless core of man.

'Why us, why select us, why entrust us with a treatise on the history of the Planet? India is the land of spirituality and wisdom. Why not give it to India?

'The Hebrews had another mission, willing to safeguard the historical records of this Planet. Their intellectual ability predisposed them to understanding physical reality, to exploring the energies of Duality. They were also inclined to identify with the self. They made the apparent, the visible their area of interest, interpreting and controlling as best they could this world. Much later their outlook was integrated into one of the most brilliant civilisations of all times. They had planted the seeds of science.

'I find your explanation illuminating as always, but Master may we proceed with the commandments? They have preoccupied me all my life, inspiring and exasperating me at the same time.

'Why inspired and why exasperated, asks Sanaka with humour?

'Inspired because they were of such moral elevation, such spiritual altitude. Exasperated because I sensed none of this.

'They were thought to be moral, they passed for spiritual. In a very real sense they were, to Lemurian man they were all these things. Well, let us look at the rules which trigger your disquiet. They imply something new and important: responsibility for one's actions. With the 'do not steal' and 'do not kill', man encounters responsibility, moral decision. He is invited to reflect rather than act on impulse. He is confronted with his own conscience. But again we are dealing with the ordinary, the mundane, and the social. I do not denigrate, I state.

'Self-rule is introduced; man is no longer driven by instinct. He is presented with moral choice, says Moses. Am I trying to reassure myself?

'No, you are not. No hint at the soul journeying through time, though. The nature of the soul is freedom. Not social or legal freedom, but freedom from the boundaries you erected, sign posts hurled outward that mark out your space on this Planet. The most religious people yet the least self-governing, the least self-determining, bound by your own perception of the world. Shackled to the wheel of rebirth with the rest of humanity you leap into one life and then another in a never ending cycle. You are figuratively the Sisyphus of the Greek myth, the ill-fated mythological character cursed by the gods.

'I have often felt like Sisyphus, sighs Moses. I was on a punishing climb leading nowhere, endlessly repeated and from which I could not escape.

'This myth illustrates so aptly your condition. You were given a freedom of a sort, just to find your way on solid Earth. No map, no compass to guide you away, to set you free from the perpetual ascent and perpetual descent, the never ending cycle of pain. But you are a mirror which reflects humanity's suffering, confusion and sense of loss, its feeling of desertion and aloneness.

At group consciousness, humanity long ago agreed to give up primeval unity. Duality entered the world stage. To embark on this cosmic journey you had to cut off the cord, symbolically, since then you have been separated. Your people have been afflicted more by this separation. You have suffered more, you erred more, you roamed and meandered in search of an ever eluding unity. And so you built vast structures of opinions, suppositions and interpretations, hoping beyond hope that this would do the trick. Alas, the more you built your towers of words, the more alone and forlorn you felt and the further away the point of contact and reunification.

'Sadness runs deep like an underground stream, notes Moses. Like Sisyphus we persist in climbing the mountain and like Sisyphus we must slide down in a perpetual cycle. We failed to grasp that this cycle must be broken at some point. It became the norm; we erected it into a grand religious purpose!

'And such ability for self-deception!

'To bring to an end erring and meandering we needed more purification, more remorse, more self-immolation, says Moses. We had more things to do in the hope of restoring our lost memory.

'The more you 'do' the more you harden the shell. What is crucial is to break the shell to go into the nature of things, into the core, the life, the Idea. Rules did not do the trick! You were deceived away from the centre, from the life at the core, remarks Sanaka. Union is not achieved by the salting and rinsing of meat, the washing of hands, the shaving of the head for women and immersion in the ritual bath more times than prescribed. Your rabbis gave you more things to 'do' instead of counselling you to quit doing things! 'Doing' is salvation they thought, to no avail. When you finally grasp that 'being' is everything, union will draw closer. When union was lost, also lost was the memory of who your truly are - beautiful beings of light – who harbour the divine presence, the I AM that Moses carved in the stone lest you forget.

It was time for their walk in the inner courtyard before the tea. A chilling wind was blowing, the sun was setting and there was a feel of snow to fall. Moses shivered. Was it the penetrating cold or melancholy rising in him? They walked silently for a while and then Sanaka broke the tranquillity of the moment. He continued his train of thought, picking it up where he had left off:

'... to forget your divine essence, to come down and be caught up in human form, oblivious of your origins. Once marooned on Earth shores your collective invocation ascended into the spheres of Light where it unleashed a response from Shamballa. After Moses the I AM lost its magnetic pull as the people reverted back to the old ways, the ways of ancient worship. Emphasis shifted from God within to the god without. 'Love your god with all your heart', you became monotheistic: you forgot your own divinity. Your feet turned to stone like your laws. Your essential freedom taken over by legality.

'I never saw it as a great loss, it was always perceived as a great gain.

'The force of legality is keeping you where you are in terms of evolution. 'Walk before me, thou shall be holy before me' encapsulates this divergent course of evolution. To us obedience and separation are obstacle to progress and liberation. To you obedience and separation are the ultimate sign of spirituality. How can you lead humanity when you distance yourselves from your fellow men? You erect barriers that prevent your escape from the external prison of Maya and the internal prison of illusion. What takes shape outside is the projection of what is inside; physical events are the manifestations of mental events. What you see outside is a reflection of what is inside, the material walls of the ghettos are the walls of your tormented minds. Thoughts create, this is cosmic Law.

'No blame to apportion, the outside world is a solidification of our mental world for all to see! There can be no denial, no pretext.

'You create your world, you fashion your experience. You deserted the inner world that once was the natural environment of man, like water is to fish. You deserted soul power for rules that engorge you with nervous pride and forlorn self-righteousness. But your inner torment erupts, like lava. Reeling in self-absorption you forgot the enormity of your loss, the scale of the betrayal. The ruling-force you revere is your own creation, your idea of what a god is. He gave you this world, but at a price.

'Is it not what Lucifer does to Dr Faustus, asks Moses? In my Haskala period I was bold enough to read forbidden books.

'There are many more forbidden books you should have read, chuckles Sanaka! In the world mythologies Lucifer, grieving his loss, lusts after the light. The key is that he does not tempt man to sin against God! He retaliates by persuading man that he is just a body. His vengeance? He keeps man grounded in physicality. Man believing himself to be matter forgets his primordial nature which is Light. Lucifer wins the day!

'Man does not have to sin at all! To believe that he is his body is quite enough, he has hooked himself on the wheel of illusion for how long?

'Time is an illusion so it does not matter how long it takes. The Serpent urges Eve to think again. The Serpent – Wisdom - alerts you to the reality of the danger lurking as you are about to capitulate to the will of a Samsara god. The demigod gave you the physical world with the promise of a distant reward: the leadership of the world. But at a price, you exchanged the cosmic Plan for the earthly plan that revolves around the future of a stellar civilisation. You got rooted in the world of form and multiplicity.

'The Myth is disturbing, mutters Moses.

'You are right; of all the myths this must be the thorniest, the most paradoxical. On the one hand Eve, the mind ....

'The mind, the soul, butts in Moses puzzled.

'Buddhism accepts only the existence of the mind. All is mind, the universe is mind. Buddha is the embodiment of the universal Mind. Eve 'sins' against primal unity as she enters the world of confusion, duality and matter.

'Eve does not sin. Eve is becoming conscious. Se has left the herd and is developing individual thought.

'Excellent Rabbi Moses. She begins to manifest individual thought. Is it not strange that your experts regard that momentous event as a 'sin'! You must place the myth in its prehistoric context. The dual world emerges from the fogs and man starts to discriminate between things. He starts to give qualities to things. The myth recounts the birth of the human faculty that discriminates between good and evil. You locked yourselves into it for all times, unwilling to grasp that nothing is ever static, everything is change. The cosmic Life Force is constant movement and change, but you depict this ever-moving, ever-changing life stream as a static, unchanging, frozen Father!

'The 'sin' of Eve is not a sin, repeats Moses.

'Entering duality she enters the world of thought. Yes she 'sins' by thought, but in the end it is thought that will redeem her. The Hierarchy has been pressing ahead with the development of the intellect, the expansion of the mind. This is the next fantastic journey in evolution. You see, good and evil in the end converge to the same point, the point of realisation, the point of integration, of synthesis. Nothing is good or bad, duality is an illusion.

'But it is a valuable learning tool, without it there would be no culture, no progress, realises Moses.

'Absolutely! But we need to look beyond good and evil. The 7th Ray of Integration will herald Paradise regained. This ray will herald the reappearance of the Hierarchy and the emergence of Buddha Maitreya, your long awaited-for Messiah.

'Paradise regained! Not by pious deeds, not by devout petitioning, but with the rise of rational thought. The mind is the gateway to the soul. It is already happening before your eyes, the Haskala movement was a vibrant expression of this reality. Nothing can indefinitely restrain soul life. The life impulse forces its way through obstacles put up by man, eventually exploding the form that prevents its normal flow. Forms have a limited duration, the Hierarchy release ideas into the world for man to learn from. When the form solidifies and no longer serves a purpose it must disperse. At the moment an idea becomes obsolete, the Masters release another idea better suited for the time and the point of evolution reached. History is a catalogue of such 'divine' interventions, cultures and civilisations have come, flourished and vanished, intellectual and artistic movements rise and dissipate. Why do you refuse to learn from the millions of years past in which races and civilisations have come and gone?

Worship of Form

'Always the building of the form, always its utilisation for as long as possible. Always the destruction of the form when it hinders and cramps the expanding light'.
(Master DK)

Form & the destruction of form

Levinson draws a paper out his pocket and reads the words of the Tibetan:

'The Masters utilise the form. They seek to work through it, imprisoning the life for just as long as the purpose is served and the race instructed through that form. Then the time comes that the form no longer serves the purpose intended, when the structure atrophies, crystallises and becomes easily destructible'.

' I had to quote this text, explains Levinson looking at David, you said that after the war a small group formed and scattered around the globe firmly intent on resurrecting the 'defunct beliefs'. They are more dogmatic than at any other time in our entire history. Let's face it, religious fervour was more than lukewarm in ancient times, we know from biblical texts that the priesthood had to do a lot of coercing to bend the masses to the will of Yahweh. What is this post-war group? What is its agenda? I think the quotation answers your question. The Hierarchy build form ….

'Sorry to interrupt, moves in David, what do you mean by form?

'Right! A thing exists in form; form is the crystallisation of an idea. Think of the Baroque period with Bach for example; musical form then was very different to what it is today with Shostakovich or Stravinsky. What goes for the arts also goes for ideas. Form appears in every area of human activity: in economics, politics, literature, philosophy and so on. If I may resume, smiles Levinson … so the Hierarchy utilise form for as long as possible, before encouraging its destruction when it restricts the developing mind. This they attempted 2000 years ago when they sent out their ambassadors. The Father who stands for the static universe is unchanging. He restricts the development of mankind. The law-enforcers reject this. The agenda of the Hierarchy is liberation from the fetters of belief.

'In contrast the agenda of that dogmatic group is to keep us locked in those same fetters, inserts David.

'I would say the agenda of this dogmatic group is to prevent the emancipation of humanity. Unconsciously their agenda is to spin out the illusion. The Hierarchy help us dissolve Maya and achieve the state of Grace where polarity is transcended.

'This sheds a new light on the hidden agenda of a group we never could understand, ponders Maimon.

'So if the dissolution of illusion is the aim of the Hierarchy, then of necessity, the dissolution of the Old Testament in its present form is a precondition, says Clara with the elation that clarification brings, because it stands, as I experienced it, as the embodiment of illusion.

'Tell us more about the Hierarchy.

'This will take time. At the dawn of the Age of Pisces, they denounced the god-force who needed 'to be placated by death', a god who demands 'blood sacrifice instead of loving service'. This elemental deity was dealt a severe blow 2000 years ago when the Essenes made the first rupture in the dam of tradition.

'It was only a break not a dissolution, clarifies Sarah.

'Buddha Maitreya, as he is known in the East, is directing his effort towards transforming this situation. Under his banner and inspiration millions of cosmic beings have come to Earth to raise the consciousness of humanity in anticipation of His return and are clearing the way for His emergence.

'Not a thought that will amuse the rabbis, remarks David!

'When we held tight to the old Earth beliefs the end was not in sight. Now that the old world is disintegrating, that the old energy is being transmuted, the goal is coming into focus, explains Clara. Some hold even tighter to old Earth energy and they call for the Messiah promised to primitive humanity: a mass exterminator who will come in to wipe out humanity and ravage the Planet.

'Maitreya, the manifestation of cosmic Love, is to embark on a global genocide to salvage a few devout! Dhjwahl Khul discloses that Maitreya, when he appears on the human stage, will eradicate religious Judaism as one of His first priorities!

'Would you clarify, asks Rebecca?

'Well, one edict contains all the others and repudiates them at the same time: 'Love thy neighbour like thyself'. What is so revolutionary about it is the affirmation of the oneness of all humanity, it is hinting at something new 'I and my neighbour are equal, we are of the same essence, we are rays of the same Sun, all else is an illusion'.

'There is no separation, no high and low, exclaims Rebecca.

'That's right. Some startling realisations, 'if I am you, how can I hurt you, how can I steal from you, how can I kill you'? 'If I am you, hurting you would be hurting me'. When one part of the body hurts the whole body hurts, when one individual is in pain, the whole of humanity is in pain. This is when one edict intuitively grasped renders the others obsolete. Note that it is a 'positive' one. It appeals to the reason and intuition of evolved man, not to the man-child of long ago.

'The affirmation of the one humanity changes our entire outlook on the world, continues Jeremy. Because cosmic consciousness is the prior energy that created all and pervades all, we can take our debate a stage further. The Master said 'I & my Father are One', Clara just said 'I and my neighbour are one' so if 'I and my neighbour are one' we get a combined definition 'I and my Father and my neighbour are One', and stretching this to the limit 'I am the Father, I am humanity, I am the lion in the wild, the blade of grass in the field, the leaf on the tree, the worm in the soil. I am in all and all is in me'.

'Only the great mystics have attained such illumination, **notes Tara.**

'Yes, but it is within reach, replies Clara. Monotheism we esteem as a brilliant achievement is beginning to look more like an embarrassment than a gratification. The more perceptive see it as a liability.

'That is why we came to Earth when we did, in the war years, reminds Jeremy, at a time of major transformation in consciousness : from theology to humanism, from dogma to humanitarian concern, from the implacable rule of law to social conscience that embrace humanity rather than shuts it out.

'Theology is our great invention, adds Clara with sad irony, it was going to make sense of the world. All it did was to keep the masses dormant and suffering. When the soul is lost, mankind needs gods to fill the void.

'That's only too true, agrees Levinson, we were appointed to undermine the calcified thinking, dissolve the fossilised beliefs, refute the theology, redeem our bloodline while being choked by the prevailing thought forms of the group!

'In my case, probably more choked than most, continues Clara I am not recovered yet.

'What is the core of your assignment, enquires Maimon?

'The reiteration of the message our ancestors discarded. Now the message is being presented in a new form.

'What will it be, insists Maimon?

'The Messiah whose appearance is imminent, the Tibetan tells us, Lord Maitreya plans, as He prepares for His emergence, the gradual eradication of the fundamental tenets of theological Judaism.

'The rabbis won't be amused, notes David.

'The same tenets that precipitated the split from the rest of mankind, the split from the Self and from the world, says Levinson. 'The gradual dissolution – if in any way possible - of the orthodox Jewish faith, with its obsolete teaching, its separative emphasis, its hatred of the Gentiles …'

'Why the cautionary 'if in any way possible', asks Clara?

'Because the Messiah will not impose, he will suggest and inspire, but never command. The doctrinaires command, the Masters do not. The Masters respect our autonomy, the doctrinaires do not. The distinctive feature of the genuine spiritual master: he never dictates, he never says 'do and obey'. And whoever comes to you and proclaims 'I am sent by god, I tell you what to do', run, run for your life! The 'do & obey' is the

233

signature of the religious despot, the devout dictator who must control the mind of others.

'He has no positive statement to make about us, remarks David.

'Yes, the Tibetan has these uplifting words for the liberal, secular Jews, 'I do not fail to recognise those Jews throughout the world ... who are not orthodox in their thinking; they belong to the aristocracy of spiritual belief to which the Hierarchy itself belongs'. You see you belong to the aristocracy of humanity and you are aligned with the Hierarchy, what more do you want?

'Quite a tribute! We are this aristocracy! Our people have been held captive by fear', muses Sarah who has made a study of it, 'fear has been the conditioning influence in our history. Fear is the driving force, the malign force which dictates our responses, motivates our actions and governs our emotions. It is both the driving force and the inhibiting force. Fear sends out negatively charged waves which attract the same. Fear is one of the most potent, most injurious emotions. As a therapist I deal with the harmful effects of fear. Religion and family conspire to instil fear. Fear is the weapon of religious tyranny. Our religious system relies on fear for its persistence.

'It magnetically draws a negative response from the astral realm of existence, the realm of lower entities which feed on our lower emotions, adds Tara. Fear emits negatively charged waves which reach their targets to play mayhem with the world.

'Apart from the harmful effect of fear on us, inserts Jeremy, the frequency of fear as it permeates the Earth field, affects all that lives on it. The fear we release is deeply injurious to the Planet, as it adds density to the already dense energy field of Earth.

'As the Tibetan explains the time comes that the form no longer serves the purpose intended, when the structure atrophies, crystallises and becomes easily destructible. I assume that you seek to abolish the existing Ten Commandments and replace them by ethical precepts that will befit the time in which we live, enquires Levinson

'That's right, replies David. As negative commands, they are vestiges of the ancient past and as such have no place in a liberal, secular, intelligent society that is progressing in quantum leaps.

'I for one will not bemoan their disappearance, says Levinson, they have caused me enough grief, and I am still grieving, three decades on.

'I am still grieving three decades on, echoes Clara.

234

Tara had been staring at the setting sun, enthralled by the charm of the moment. She suddenly mumbles 'Who?

'Not who, what! The Ten Commandments were given with the best interest of mankind in mind. As with all else, confusion took root over time.

'They are considerably older; they antedate Moses by thousands of years.

'What do you mean, what confusion, asks Tara not quite with it?

'The whole document was given for safekeeping and with built-in safety valves, built-in obsolescence at it were, explains Maimon.

'It passed its sell-by date, jokes Tara.

'Quite something, chuckles Jeremy! If I am not mistaken your Earth assignment was to destabilize that faith, to undermine that belief.

'They are outworn, inserts Rebecca who is listening while ingesting the beauty of the scenery. They must be adapted to our time. It is our responsibility to attempt it, and so give others non-verbal authorisation to continue; make it easier for them to complete the task.

'Always the building of the form, always its utilisation, always the destruction of the form when it hinders and cramps the expanding light, repeats Levinson.

'I don't think that we came on this assignment to 'attempt' but to execute in more ways than one, replies Clara, stimulate a shift in perception, remove the stumbling blocks and undermine the system. We came with the specific mandate to infiltrate outworn forms, learn them, absorb then and explode them or transform them. As I have not the slightest intention of revisiting Earth to implement belatedly our programme of transformation, it must be done now and without delay 'always the destruction of the form when it hinders and cramps the expanding light'. I am on a 'destructive' mission!

"It took me a long time for find out who I am, continues Levinson, to recover the memory of what I came to Earth for. I feel a compelling need, a pressing tension to transmute the controlling energy and all that it stands for: the tyranny of the patriarchal ego, power struggle between man and woman, separation and discord in mankind, egotism and intolerance, an unverified sense of mission and a civilisation that is born of all these.

'In my counselling work, informs Sarah, I meet numerous women who have suffered terrible injustice in the hands of their fathers, husbands, sons, lovers. They tolerate the

235

intolerable, they submit to the unacceptable, in spite of the giant strides women have made since the war.

'Religious women have made no progress; they reel in their lesser status.

'We have to realise, says Sarah that matriarchy was the dominant social mode. I aim at the resurgence of women's spiritual awareness and the re-emergence of the goddess. Thousands of years of patriarchal domination erected the basic structures on which our civilisation is built.

'What is the way forward, asks David?

'To declare the gods redundant, replies Clara decidedly, as we overthrow them we reinstate the Lord of the World, Sanat Kumara.

'A new God in place of the old god, mumbles Rebecca!

'Too much trespassing for too long! This beautiful Earth has been their play ground and experimental laboratory, retorts Maimon. The old gods violated the laws of the universe but were tolerated because Earth is a free-will zone. They must be reminded they are neither required nor tolerated any longer. They must leave with an ultimatum

'How do you propose to do this? If they were powerful enough to conquer the Earth how can we succeed, asks David?

'Millions of world servers are working with the Masters, waves of light are being transmitted from other sectors of the cosmos, informs Jeremy.

'I propose a full re-examination of the Old Testament, intervenes Maimon. We have to rewrite this document which has been for too long regarded as untouchable. Its symbolic meaning has eluded us. It is to us to shed light on the psychodrama being played out in our synagogues. The original meaning has been warped. It is a data bank of the origins of Earth, lost civilisations, the birth of modern man and modern civilisations, information concerning galactic raiders, data relating to movement of Moon, Earth and constellations. All this information has been deified. We bow to it, mutilate new born infants to it, offer blood sacrifices to it.

'No more Old Testament even in a new presentation box, exclaims Clara, my soul purpose was to undermine this one and I am doing just that, 'always the destruction of the form when it hinders and cramps ...' The reason for our being on Earth is 'the destruction of the form'. For me there will be no next field trip to Earth. I will not come back to mend the unpredicted damage this revised version will unleash. However

I don't refute its reinterpretation in the light of recent scientific research and newly released information from the Masters who long ago gave it in its pristine state.

'I wish to see the Goddess reinstated, whispers Rebecca, because women need to wake up to their own potential. This is the new form for today.

'I have no wish for the cult of the Goddess to be revived, replies Clara with conviction. We cannot regress to a lost age of evolution. We left the enveloping arms of the Mother long ago to freeze up under the menacing glance of the Father. A turn up on the spiral of evolution? Possibly, but we have in the last couple of centuries relinquished the need for the Father too. Humanity is advancing, except those of Neolithic mentality who still cling to the Father. You want to replace the Father by the Mother, what are you hoping to achieve? It is a way of eluding the real issue. Don't count on my support. 'Always the destruction of the form when it hinders and cramps the expanding light', our assignment in this life.

'I work with women and they express their desire for a loving, intuitive, supportive feminine presence, says Sarah with conviction.

'I agree, the women I work with yearn for a more gentle, caring and nurturing presence, for softer times, echoes Tara.

'We are leaving in the morning, says David. For some curious reason we feel at home here, we don't want to leave, so we will not say goodbye, you understand.

It is getting late; the guests are spending the night at St Katherine Monastery on the invitation of the monks. They are invited to share the evening meal. The food is wholesome: freshly baked bread, soup, baked potatoes, figs and grapes. They feel the majesty, the simplicity and the serenity this place is imbued with. The soft gold light in the refectory gives the food a unique transparent glow. After breakfast, they go for a stroll at the foot of Mount Sinai bathed in the morning light. A car in the distance breaks the silence. They exchange enquiring glances. A feeling of unease is registered. A young soldier alights from a military vehicle and smiling warmly: 'Are you Jeremy I bring a text from Benzaccai, the most recently translated. He insisted that I should bring it without delay'. Then with a slight hesitation … 'may I listen to it, I am one of his student … in spite of my uniform? He is invited to stay. They settle at the foot of the mountain to listen to the new text.

'Would you like to read the text, offers Jeremy?

'I would love to, replies the soldier, visibly moved.

The Four Deceptions

'As I see it, four biblical decrees have held you back in your slow march through time, begins Master Sanaka. By a strange quirk of human nature they have led you in the direction opposite to the one you thought you were going! While the rest of humanity is treading the Path of Return you move away from it. Let us mull over the Four Deceptions: 'go & multiply', 'do & obey', 'respect your father and mother' and 'love your god with all your heart …' If you scrutinise these precepts you discern a common thread running through them.

'Unconditional orders, they brook no disobedience and imply a real threat.

'Exactly. A controlling force is imposing its will, as you indicate this force demands obedience. No criticism or deliberation. It is not a dialogue but an instruction from ruler to servant. Serfdom enters the human energy field. Serfdom becomes the new reality. First 'grow & multiply: to bring souls in incarnation is to give them a chance to balance their karma and so help them evolve, but it is also short sighted. Quantity is no substitute for quality. These impatient, impetuous souls coming down - or precipitating down - in often poor and congested homes rob others of personal space, vital peace and freedom of movement. The more sensitive in desperation turn inward, in search of inner protection. The more assertive turn outward to vent their anger and frustration often in a strident and destructive way. Precious moments of silence are unknown, indeed frowned upon, you have to live in a perpetual whirlpool of agitation, in a constant whirlwind that saps and depletes your strength. The need of the group displaces and overturns the need of the individual. The individual is swamped.

'Just as damaging is the 'do & obey', continues Sanaka, which prohibits intellectual probing and moral appreciation. The controlling force 'out there' knows all; you are credited neither with reason nor comprehension. The slave does not and must not understand his master. He must obey that is his only right and obligation, his only reason for living. The third order contains the first two parcelled up together in a potentially lethal mix. It repeats the 'do & obey', this time not to the deity but to his representatives on Earth, the parents. Parents are the guardians of tradition, customs, prejudices and superstition. Your parents, aligned with the god-force are originators of your body, but your mind belongs to you and you alone and this is never hinted at in your texts. You know why?

'There is no mind worth considering, ventures Moses.

'Not quite, remember the allegory of Eve and her fateful curiosity. As you know, Eve is the embryonic mind trying to rise out of the darkness of unconscious life. But to the rabbis she is the great 'sinner', she has committed the ultimate crime, she has dared to question, dared to doubt. The allegory of Eve hints at post-Flood humanity, it elusively hints at the role the mind is going to play in the new humanity but it also tells us that your people are not going to like it a bit!

'So for us the mind is the 'sinner', it must be restrained. What is left?

'Emotional devotion, replies Sanaka.

'I remember well, butts in Clara, the agents of the controlling force insist that the Jew's highest purpose is to nullify himself before the altar of the deity, to believe unreservedly, absolutely. To promote sentimental devotion and the capitulation of mind they scour the world in search of desperate Jewish souls to 'save'! Sorry for this intrusion.

'A valuable one, says Jeremy.

'The allegory of Eve, the mind dawning after the Flood, is foreign to that particular group comments Maimon. They derive a sense of self-righteousness from religious sentimentality and reject insinuation of mind. The mind is what would estrange them from their god. Do intrude Clara!

The reading resumes after this brief interlude. 'Finally we come to 'Love your god....' This is a difficult one, because it looks so benign, who would quarrel with it? A shiver of smugness runs through you: just below the surface lurks theism with its rush of pride. And this sets you apart and gives you an aura of elevated spirituality. How many dare to mull over the oddness of the whole thing and ask this heretical question 'what god are we talking about, could there be two gods in the Book of Genesis and in the Ten Commandments?' Startling thought, yet the answer must be an emphatic 'yes'. Existing beyond time and space are the Elohim, the 'Creator Gods' and existing within time and space is the god of the flesh whose prowess you celebrate in serfdom.

The I AM

'I AM the one who is' stands alone as the first precept but it also stands out by its very nature and meaning. The I AM attaches man to the Source ...

'... Attaches, inserts Moses?

'Literally 'attaches'. A thread of light stretches from the I AM spark at the centre of the Heart right up to the Source. You may prefer 'continuation' or 'extension'. The enlightened Greeks knew that each ray emitted by the Central Sun enters a human body. And man feels alone?

'They will brand me a heretic!

'What they call you is no concern of yours. Your role is to radiate light and light disperses darkness. Light will dissipate defiant resistance to progress, unevolved attachment to the past and uninspired devotion. Light will rouse them out of the long sleep; excite an urge for expansion and a longing for liberation. Two simultaneous moves, inwardness and expansiveness.

'Love and light will be my only tools?

'Can you think of any other more potent or more enduring? They are the primary substance the universe is made of! Let's return to the I AM, not a command but evidence. It contains the whole essence of the revelation, which may explain why it has eluded infiltration. The I AM, cosmic in its magnitude has dodged probing. In its infinity it extends way beyond the universes. In its minuteness it nestles in the Heart of man.

'The I AM encompasses all the universes. It is also the atom in the Heart. I understand "Understand' is not enough, you must 'experience' and you will. Your integrated personality is coming into alignment with your soul. You will see the spark, in other words you will see the Divine snuggling inside your chest. Who said that we need temples of stones, when you can see, talk and hear the Divine directly without a negotiator?

'What is the significance of the I AM?

'It answers in two enigmatic words the crucial questions man has grappled with since the dawn of thought. To this end I refer you back to the allegory of Adam and Eve. Eve, symbol of our mind nature, finds herself plunged in the world of polarity and attempts to make sense of it all. Polar opposites, good and evil trigger tormenting questions. Eve must grapple with questions and find answers. This is the beginning of knowledge acquired painfully through physical reality, in the throes of polarity.

'How does the I AM answer all questions?

'I view the I AM as the answer to the twin question of the nature of man and the nature of God and the relationship between the two. Others will see it differently. The God within is the God without. Or, God exists in transcendence - the universe – and in immanence - man. So looking for God outside of you is pointless, no building of stone can ever house the I AM presence because it is inside us, it animates all, it permeates all, it is in everything, it is everything. More to the point, the All incarnate in man is accessible and a dialogue can begin.

Two gods in the Ten Commandments?

'A similar thought flashed through my mind, butts in Clara, I am invited to intrude, am I not? As I was listening, the I AM lit up much like a crystal when exposed to light. I sensed that the I AM that shines down through the universe was carved in the Tablets as a tribute to Moses. Moses, the Egyptian adept of the universal Mysteries, knew the I AM in the universe and in man. But it seems out of place on the Tablets for it clashes with the second commandment 'Thou shall have no other gods before my face'.

'I don't quite follow mumbles Levinson, normally on the same wavelength.

'I'll try again. It seems odd that the I AM should concern himself with other gods, don't you think? Why should he disapprove of man's evolution in stages? Man needs to explore the many facets of the world. To explore the world he must ignore the unity in all things. He must see things separate and different. In other words, he must immerse in polarity and play the game!

'To use the religious imagery it is to 'adore many gods', echoes Jeremy. That is what the All wanted when he incarnated in the universe. That is why polarity came about to throw in complexity and even confusion, so that questions would be asked. To 'adore other gods' is essential, it is the purpose of Creation.

'To adore many gods suggests that man does not see the whole picture, inserts Maimon. The idea of the one god is an attempt at reconstructing the whole picture. It is to gather the pieces of the jigsaw into a meaningful image.

'To see the whole picture is the goal, the finishing line, notes Tara.

'But to adore one god, eliminating all others, is pointless, because you replace the whole picture by a broken piece of it, explains Johansson! After all the 'many gods' is well within the framework of the Plan of evolution. In other words the exploration of the infinite diversity was within the divine Mind.

'It makes sense, admits Maimon, Moses knew that the march of evolution was going to be perilous, long and arduous. Why ban the many gods when Earth is the school man visits and revisits to learn about the bewildering diversity before he rediscovers unity? We do not grumble when our infants come home from playschool with clumsy, naïve, primitive little drawings. We know that it is part of growing up and we love them for it.

'What are you suggesting, asks Levinson still unclear?

'I suggest that the I AM encoded Moses' idea of the Logos, replies Clara. For Moses the I AM was the Logos, but this was rejected by later generations unable to fathom out his intention.

'Are you suggesting that there is competition between the two?

'Not at all, only a substitution at a much later period, clarifies Maimon who is engaged in a war against the static religious mould that has kept his people in a prolonged state of inertia. Brilliant insight Clara, truly inspirational. Why did I wait so long to see it? I would say that the first Commandment dates back to Moses and the events at Sinai. The second is more ambiguous and is of a much later period, the Babylonian exile where they encounter the Sumerian god Ea, Yahweh in Genesis. The god of the Hebrews before and after the Babylonian exile is a possessive, aggressive, wrathful, vengeful and materialistic deity. He hates strangers and demands their eradication. Power is centralised in his hands, he is imbued with an inflated sense of self.

'When we lost the Tao - the Way - we traded our innate harmony with the world for an ego-oriented quasi-religion. The personality of our deity illustrates our grave loss, our serious disorientation, notes Clara.

'Yet he gave the splendid civilisation of Sumer, some 7000 years ago, which inspired the Greeks enlightenment period, remarks Jeremy calmly.

'He certainly did, Greek scientific achievement and the Hebrew religious system originate in Sumer. Through Judaism it is the foundation stone of Western civilisation, explains Maimon.

'We are not archaeologists but we spent many fascinating hours with a specialist of ancient civilisations who wrote a thesis on Ancient Sumer, a university colleague, explains Maimon. The time is coming when his research findings will be taught throughout the land. Our religious and legal system originates in ancient Sumer and we believe them to be divinely inspired! Sumer is the cradle of modern civilisation.

'If your insight is accurate, then the Ten Commandments are stating that two gods are facing each other, challenging each other, begging for man's attention, notes Tara whose loathing of formal religion is no secret.

'It is clear that the first two precepts are hinting at the existence of two gods, interleaves Johansson. I arrived at this conclusion when I was researching my thesis. The I AM permeates the universe and incarnates in man: impersonal in the cosmos, it is individualised in man. The I Am in transcendence and in immanence. The second god as I see it is a metaphor for the age of the Ram, it symbolises the rise to power of the ego in its forceful affirmation.

'Powerful, assertive, forceful, it is this second 'god' that has ruled the world, with documented power and undisputed right, brilliant insight, exclaims Maimon! It has precipitated an avalanche of tragedies upon us. We have stumbled down the ages, fumbling on the bleak road to nowhere. The select few who heard voices imposed themselves as mediators between their idea of god and their idea of man. The projection of their collective ego is still haunting mankind.

'It is certainly still haunting us, sighs Sarah whose dislike for patriarchal religion is no secret.

'Fear still claws, mumbles Clara.

'Why fear, love rather, suggests Jeremy!

'The idea of love is recent, explains Johansson; rejected 2000 years ago, it reappears in the principles of the Revolution and more recently in the United Nations Declaration of Human Rights. Love is the most advanced, the most evolved, the most inspired realisation and one which earlier humanity could not attain. The onslaught of the self in the age of the Ram annuls the possible insertion of love. The disconnected, separative, estranged self stands in opposition to love which is of the Self and which manifests in inclusiveness, bonding and wholeness. What was 'revealed' at Sinai was the true nature of humanity at that point in its evolution.

'To sum up, the I AM, impersonal in the cosmos, individualised in humanity, exists beyond time and space, concludes Jeremy. The second is located in space and time and appeals to a specific group. The I AM informs of the divine nature of all men and their fundamental unity, while the second 'thou' spells out differentiation, isolation and separateness. 'Thou' clearly indicates an outside authority dictating, demanding, and imposing. The first hints at the higher Self in all men, the second at the human self, the ego ...

'... source of attachment, aversion and confusion, interrupts Tara, the three mental poisons identified by Buddha.

'Not to us, we have carved the ego-nature in stone to ensure its permanence, exclaims the young soldier who had listened intently. This is our idea of immortality! So much is making sense now. For the first time I grasp the implications of the I AM. This is a life-transforming experience for me.

'The I AM got buried under the avalanche of precepts, practices and prohibitions, inserts Maimon. It got stranded in polarity, the world of time, space and matter. Man forlorn and estranged is grounded; the I AM takes refuge in the Heart where it was ignored until now.

'It is all so clear, exclaims the young soldier, I feel like dancing, screaming, weeping, I don't know which.

'Do all three, laughs Jeremy. Let's dance together.

'I have seen so much distress among the devout group to which I once belonged'. Noticing a look of interest he quickly adds, 'this is a story I don't want to go into. Some, when faced with a crisis just fell apart. It is as if they had not inner resources, nothing to fall back onto, no inner solidity.

'They had burnt up all their resources in the 'do & obey' and the 'go & multiply', says Clara. A ritualised life is often superficial; it peels off fast. Automatic execution of rituals is often a way of hiding one's shallowness. Too often it is a place to hide.

'I see that now, continues the young soldier, when my head teacher was removed from his position he broke down, he was ill for months, he caved in; he had no foundation on which to rest in time of crisis. He had spent his life in rituals, prayers, study and yet when the crunch came he collapsed.

'Our tradition commands us to keep separate in faked or genuine purity, explains Levinson. But most alarmingly its role is to disempower, to render us vulnerable.

'Buddha restores balance; he empowers mankind, inserts Tara. He reminds forgetful man of his primeval, invulnerable nature.

'In other words it expects of us everything that the Hierarchy fights against, everything that insults human dignity and the divine Presence within each one of us, completes Clara.

'I see now, adds the young soldier, we have spent ages doing just that!

'Because it offers no method of self-knowledge and self-mastery, when crisis comes, downfall comes, concludes Clara who knows only too well the devastation unleashed on the unwary, she lived it.

'Thou shall love your god with all your heart …' a positive command. The question is 'why love god' when you are God, observes Jeremy always logical. The order to love is strange; is it a hint that you should love yourself wisely, because without self-love there can be no love of the other? Sananda insists on this. So love yourself in order to love your god, but you are god?

'I would reply, 'do not love your god' for you are deceiving yourself, there is no god. You love your ego and the ego is the source of all illusion and the cause of your endless rebirths and deaths, says Tara. It keeps you entrapped in the world of illusion, Maya. The Buddhist always surfaces in Tara, sometimes provoking a slight annoyance combined with interest for she brings to light a new angle.

The residual Commandments

'Thou shall not kill'. A negative order, begins Johansson. A society must formulate rules in order to maintain law and order, rules that all acknowledge and will internalise. So in the age of the Ram a crucial command. But viewed from soul perspective, it is rather meaningless: no one can ever be killed, life is indestructible, the true being of man is deathless, it exists beyond space and time. From the angle of the soul no one can ever be killed.

'Thou shall not take your neighbour's wife'. How about that, exclaims Sarah! The epitome of patriarchal authority! It harks back to archaic times when men owned their wives and cattle! The wife of your neighbour is an individualised aspect of the Divine. She cannot be stolen because she does not belong to anyone. In the present climate of awareness a woman knows that she is accountable for her actions. No wife can be taken from her husband because no woman is owned; no human being belongs to any other human being. Each woman is her own master even if she does not know her own divinity. Her pre-natal decision was to be a woman and the decision was hers and hers alone. She is accountable only to herself. A woman is her own person in social and psychological terms but also in cosmic and spiritual terms too.

Shabbat – Day of rest?

'It is interesting, notes Jeremy that God had to 'rest' on the 7th day! What is the chronicler really saying: is God so human he tires of work? Just as baffling, God created the world once and for all, impossible, nothing is static in the universe, stars are birthed and stars die as we do.

'Rest' should be read 'withdraw', or 'to appear to withdraw' behind the veil of Maya, suggests Johansson. We know that the Shabbat day is Saturn' s day and as such signifies a day of contemplation, a day reserved for the spirit in us. Saturn is an exacting ruler who demands the highest standards of spiritual achievement.

'So this explains why the Master went into the Temple to heal the sick, on the Shabbat day, says Jeremy with a 'eureka' inflection.

'He entered the Temple on the Shabbat day, explains Johansson, to rouse souls slumbering in the materialism of fear, authority and ritualistic routine, to awaken them to the inner whispers of the soul. To heal is to free the soul from the entrapment of the ego.

'Ingenious insight into the healing on the most sacred day, which shocked so many, remarks Sarah and a new slant on healing. In this light 'rest' is almost irrelevant. The transgression was no transgression at all.

'I was conditioned to believe early in life that the Shabbat sets us apart, a sign of our spiritual loftiness, says Levinson.

'Genesis narrates that God created the world in 6 days and on the 7th he withdrew in order to provide man with an opportunity to prove himself in a universe empty of its Creator in which Duality had full sway and where the likelihood of error and misinterpretation were great, suggests Jeremy.

'The risk of failing to recall his origins, of forgetting his true nature was a menacing probability, interleaves Sarah. To be tested man is placed in an 'empty' cosmos, a bewildering world of polarity where good and evil will throw him into the deep end. Therapists observe the effect of this all the time.

'Le silence de ces espaces infinis m'effraie', quotes Clara. Pascal describes the fear and isolation man feels as he confronts an empty universe.

'And right he is too, replies Maimon who values the insert. Ancient man is caught up in the tangled web of polarity. He has to make sense of the world and his place in it. How is he going to relate to the world? The 'do & obey' comes to the rescue early in his evolution. He has now a map to guide him through the dense forest of the dualities he encounters. But this assistance comes at a price as he comes to rely on it. He sacrifices his autonomy, his initiative, his curiosity, his intuitive ability. Furthermore, should any one try to do things differently, they will be chastised, persecuted or even killed!

'The picture has now dramatically changed, notes Sarah. Man placed on the Planet to measure the expanse of his power is now a frail and flawed creature who must conform to a set of rules. The splendid embodiment of the Creator is now a shadow of his former self. In the intervening period patriarchy and monotheism have stepped in to cut man down to size. Diminished and bemused man worships the nature god who is responsible for his fall from grace. Miniaturised man breaks down and weeps on the therapist's couch, he yearns to reconnect with his lost Self.

'From a timeless and boundless being man has been demoted to a physical creature who defines himself with external labels, 'I am a man, I am a Jew, I am a son, I am of this or that family or country'. Demoted and devalued man now owes allegiance to a Samsara god, a finite god, a temporal god. No wonder the Master entered the Temple to remind them of their forgotten divinity, says Clara!

'The message is that man must not be left to his own device, he is unable to act or be trusted with the direction of his life, says the soldier who seems to have a deep-seated resentment. Sorry to interrupt.

'Interruptions enrich the debate, resumes Levinson. Science is part of our life and is transforming our perception of the world; we cannot revert back to a pre-scientific mode of thinking to broadcast that god created the world in 6 days. Faith is bankrupt.

'First, the universe was never 'created', it was contained in the initial atom that exploded releasing vast amount of energy at the moment of the Big Bang – and it evolved over billions of years, explains Maimon.

Second, barges in Johansson, Eastern mystics give us some insight into their sensitive knowing of the universe, which they intuitively grasp. Buddha was the first to enounce an atomic theory long before Einstein. Einstein expounded Quantum theory in which he argues that matter appears solid but that under scrutiny it dissolves into energy.

'Buddha said, 'emptiness is form, form is emptiness'. The nature of the universe is 'emptiness', energy, says Tara.

'Rabbinical authorities, whose views were unquestioned for centuries, have nothing more to say, concludes Maimon. They are bankrupt. The physical universe which they describe as solid and inert is neither solid nor inert, it is movement and pulsation. The physicist James Jeans suggests that the cosmos is 'more a giant thought than a giant machine'. There you have it! The cosmos may be as real as it is unreal, as material as it is mind!

'And so Maya the world of forms, objects and events is also Nirvana the world of ultimate reality, notes Tara. The tangible is also the intangible. So we arrive at a new idea of the universe which blends the vision of the East with the scientific findings of the West ... it is a mind, alive, dynamic, conscious, intelligent.

'This raises some pertinent questions, proposes Clara, 'why do some people in the scientific professions leave behind their critical mind on Friday night?' When they go home they disconnect from their modern self to connect to an archaic self. They chant praise to the god who created the world in 6 days and rested on the 7th! Why do they switch off their critical faculty, how do they deactivate their questioning intellect? Do they forget every Friday that the universe is energy in movement? And how can Yahweh who walked the Earth alongside man be that 'giant thought'? And how do they, as they wake up on Monday, decide that it is time to drop their archaic self and change into their modern self?

'The expansion of the universe mirrors the expansion of consciousness in man, suggests Tara.

'At another level of meaning, contributes Jeremy who brings the debate back on the spiritual tract, all that exists in the world manifests under a certain frequency of light and adopts the qualities of that light or Ray. When white light passes through a prism it is broken up into the 7 primary colours. The white light unbroken before Creation was 'broken' into the 7 Rays. Each Ray has its own unique qualities, but together they fuse back into the complete white light. The return to the 'white light' or integration lies behind the process of evolution. The universe came into existence when separation into the primary colours occurred. Separation gave us the huge diversity of forms.

'What are you getting at, asks Tara?

'If the universe was formed by a process of division, explains Jeremy obligingly, it follows that the world was not fashioned in seven days, but in the seven rays of the spectrum. And so I am tempted to replace the verse 'and God created the world in 6 days and rested on the 7th' with 'and God created the world in six Rays'. The 7th Ray coming into play at present is the ray of integration, of synthesis. We are recreating the primeval 'white' light.

'Right, the age of Grace is now, says Clara. Grace is the still point, no past, no present, no division, no separation, the point of Oneness restored.

'Let's go back to the Shabbat', suggests the soldier. They are not quite sure whether he is sympathetic or critical of religion. 'For a society learning the basics principles of good conduct, the Shabbat is an affirmation of the dignity of the individual. The Shabbat gives ordinary existence a dignified character.

'We have not exhausted all the facets of Shabbat; perhaps the most significant is the goddess aspect, contributes Sarah. Shabbat, the divine Bride visits Israel; she brings consolation to communities. In spite of their suffering they receive with deference the Goddess on Friday night! The 7th day takes on a new significance as the Bride when the feminine principle enters the humble home. A subtle reminder that the Goddess dwells deep in our psyche. 'Revere and observe the Shabbat' may now read 'Receive and revere the Goddess'.

'We are entering the age of the Goddess, the age of the soul, notes Tara.

'So much for the most vocal monotheistic people on Earth, remarks the solider.

'The adoration of Shabbat may allude to the worship of time, notes Johansson who finds the digression too long. It hints at the inescapable reality of Samsara, the temporal world. Whichever way we approach it, we invariably come back to polarity.

'And we invariably come back to the world of illusion, echoes Tara

'A rabbi recently declared, 'if you don't stop the normal lifestyle of the week, how can you make the transfer into spirituality', quotes Levinson.

'Unconsciously the rabbi is confessing that life to him is profane. We engage in profane activities in the week, our lives are profane, all human activity is profane, all human creativity is profane. How undignified!

'Duality within duality, there is no end to the splitting up, inserts Clara.

'Duality within duality! We never can resist the temptation to split the world, echoes Levinson, proof that we are still gasping for breath in the deep waters of the Fall! With the Shabbat the world is split between two conflicting natures of time, the sacred and the profane. Time, space and matter come into existence at Creation; this is central to our thinking. Our doctrine is the first materialistic ideology. We may be the first people on Earth ever to perceive the world as a giant mechanism in which mind, spirit and the latent powers of man are absent.

'There is no sacred or profane time, all in the universe is sacred, all is divine, even matter, notes Jeremy. We agree that the 7th day symbolises many things, other than what tradition ascribes to it. Viewed from a scientific perspective the world was never created, viewed from an esoteric perspective the world is an emanation of the cosmic Mind, a 'solidified' thought. There is no 'transfer into spirituality' to be made, time is spiritual, life is spiritual, human activity is spiritual as is human creativity. The cosmic Mind in each of us and in matter makes everything 'sacred'.

'Love thy neighbour'

'Much cited, much extolled yet much misconstrued is 'Love thy neighbour'. It conjures up the image of a society in which equality and justice prevail, comments Johansson. It gives us an insight into the mind of those who formulated it, a glimpse into their vision of a more caring society. Regard for social justice discourages selfishness and prevents conflict. Social concern when implemented is the path to enlightenment.

'How?

'Selfishness is the root of all evil as Buddha observed, replies Tara. Attachment, hostility and confusion stem from it. It gives rise to separation, conflict and wars. It is selfishness which keeps humans 'prisoners of the Planet'. Selfishness is the root of suffering.

'Yet we celebrate separateness, notes Sarah. We foster division when we should be fostering unity, conciliation and cooperation because this is the way to liberation from the snare of the self and the entrapment of Samsara.

'The cynics might say 'love thy neighbour' makes social sense for a people which defines itself around group life, inserts Clara.

'What is 'love thy neighbour' for us, asks Maimon? Do we have to love humanity? How can one 'love' an impure, lesser creature? To love others is to see them as equal. It is to identify them as fragments of the Source.

'Love thy neighbour' banish the illusion of separateness, quash the illusion of polarity, inserts Jeremy. Love unites and unifies all into the primal Oneness.

'All humans are rays emanating from the Central Sun, confirms Maimon. All of us are photons of the same light source. We all are equal because we all form the light. 'Love thy neighbour' should extend out to embrace all photons. Can one photon shout 'I am chosen' and by whom? If I say, 'I am chosen' I show contempt for the Light source. I confess 'I am blind to the presence of the light in all beings. I can't see the wood for the trees because I can't make sense of anything'!

'Right, picks up Johansson, man loves the 'other' when he identifies with the 'other'. Man loves the other when he sees himself in the other. A society in which 'love thy neighbour' is enshrined is like the enlightened Athens of Pericles and Plato. A State which respects the dignity and defends the freedom of the other is truly an enlightened state. This is the society we are creating in the face of hostility from the forces of retrogression.

'See yourself in others. Then whom can you hurt? What harm can you do', quotes Tara.

'Love thy neighbour' is restricted to the other Jew, filters Clara. Buddha was not born in Jerusalem, neither were Pericles or Plato. 'Love thy neighbour' rather than embrace, excludes, separates. Not quite the sign of an enlightened society!

'Honour your parents '.... Experience teaches us the fallacy of this command, pursues Levinson. Parents are transmitters of the past, custodians of the archaic tradition which has driven us from disaster to disaster. Parents are guardians of all that has calcified, ossified, solidified, fossilised, all that is dead. In other words parents are the 'disciples of death'. Many of us who originate in other dimensions are born in the most dysfunctional, the most unbalanced families. Who expects us to honour disturbed parents, unstable progenitors who have brought the human crisis to a head in the same way that a boil finally bursts to release its morbid matter?

'I fully endorse this, says Maimon. I am at war with religious constraints; I have sworn eternal hostility to the formalism that keeps the mind of man in shackles. I urge them to repeal the old rule for the new one which goes something like this: 'Honour your children'. I say, 'Parents be humble, your children are unknown to you; they plunged into your mayhem for reasons of their own. Some of them chose this assignment to put order into your chaos and release you from your self-erected prison.

'Respect and love your children, they came into your wretched lives to 'save' you, to salvage what little there is to salvage of your ancestral testament of words, of your desolate inheritance, of your flawed blood line. The only ones who can salvage you', takes up Clara as she recalls her neglected childhood.

'The tribal god relies on the old generation to perpetuate the past. Our emphasis is on the young generation, creators of the new reality.

'In esoteric terms, I declare the Father superfluous and I am crowning the Son, says Jeremy amused.

'Child dishonour is inscribed into our archaic constitution, continues Sarah not amused. Child disgrace is enacted in the 'go & multiply'. Procreation is imposed even in hostile environments – overcrowding, poverty, malnutrition, squalor, often verbal abuse and physical violence. The poorest of the poor multiply inordinately in superstitious fear. Child indignity, woven into the fabric of tradition has been advocated. As a human being, as a therapist I abhor it.

'They made it a virtue, goes on Levinson. 'Grow and multiply' reverberates down the ages. Under Talmudic law, couples are commanded to resume sexual activity at the moment of ovulation when the woman is most likely to conceive. Marriage was instituted for one goal, to multiply, in order to satisfy the needs of the god of the flesh.

'I have sworn eternal hostility to a system which violates human dignity, adds Sarah. Child disgrace may be written in the law; I set myself the task to un-write it.

'Thou shall not steal the ox and the ass and the donkey ...' who cares about the ass and the donkey, or about the country residence or the Rolls Royce, says Jeremy who sees the amusing touch in all things? To a simple society this precept was certainly of importance, they were making their first steps into civilised life. Respect for the property of others was a stride in the direction of peaceful coexistence.

'It was hailed as the pinnacle of moral advance or was it? 'Thou shall not steal' alludes to things, objects, possessions. It shouts, 'hands off my stuff', 'don't you dare touch my belongings; they are mine, mine, mine'; back to the grasping ego: material man clinging to his material stuff! With the 'Thou shall not', what we strike is not the high moral chord but the strident lower chakras that ground us in physicality. The 'Thou shall not' addresses unevolved, undeveloped, unregenerate man arrested in the reptilian and mammalian brains; primitive man in whom the cortex is not yet fully activated.

'How would it read to modern man not to Lemurian man, asks Clara?

'The command ... repellent word ... the remainder, replies Maimon would read something like this in the old formula:

'Thou shall not steal the peace of mind of the other.

'Thou shall not deprive him of his right to think as an individual.

'Thou shall not rob him of his personal responsibility.

'Thou shall not take away his freedom of choice.

'Encourage self-reliance.

'Respect his intelligence and his ability to make informed choices.

'Pay homage to his mind'. This is what I would like to see engraved on the Tablets of the 'new' Ten Commandments. I abolish the crude, negative injunction 'thou shall not' and I replace it with the noble pledge visible on the dome of the Capitol, *I have sworn upon the honour of god, eternal hostility against any form of tyranny over the mind of man'*. Be it the tyranny of the demiurge and his earthly civilisation or the tyranny of any political system which seeks to repress man, unsettle his mind, thwart his aspirations, cripple his creativity and deny him the right to be all that he can be.

'Hurrah, claps Jeremy, is your middle name Moses by any chance!

'I am a rebel. Sinai man personified the tyranny of the self, replies Maimon. Modern man personifies the emergence of reason.

'I have one more idea, inserts Clara. 'Do not treat modern man as you did his ancestors'. Long ago our ancestors, under cover of darkness, ran riot in the streets of a deserted and desolate Egypt that had just been stricken by a terrible catastrophe, and fled with the ox, the ass and the donkey! They plundered the land that had sheltered them for centuries!

'But the looting was god's order, replies Sarah mockingly, so it was right! Such wrongdoing is fine; this is what we have been conditioned to believe.

'Does stealing on god's orders redeem stealing, retorts Maimon? Not for me it does not! No god would get away with it! Stealing from an enemy is still stealing. Sinai man lived before the days of Jeremiah and Ezekiel, before the dawn of moral conscience. Now their religious descendants tutored at the schools of European life scorn such crude forms of theft. They reinterpret the commandments as they do all else.

'I heard that the Talmud says everything and its opposite, inserts Sarah.

'The descendants of Sinai man are more subtle, they lived in Europe for centuries, and they had incarnations in Christendom as monks and nuns. They go for the delicate morsels: the mind. They pillage the soul and despoil the mind, leaving a trail of desolation behind them. Do you recall who long ago stole the soul of man?

Honour your father - Levinson & Johansson

Levinson has a natural ally in Johansson. They share a similar early life experience. One the son of a rabbi, the other the son of a Danish parson, they both grew up in a rigid biblical and patriarchal system. The god had a different name, the rest was the same.

'The changes affecting the Planet at present are the most significant since amphibians climbed on to the shores of lakes and seas and settled on dry land, begins Johansson. The thrill is that we are playing a part in this transformation. The Masters have disclosed that aspects of DNA that lay dormant for eons are about to be activated. The light now being transmitted is altering our genetic make up; we are becoming lighter, less solid. The Planet is gaining from this upsurge in light energy. As we receive more light in our cells and in our energy fields, we attract more light and the whole of humanity is lifted, including our parents and their parents.

'It works on the principle that all life is one.

'Yes, and on the principle that light attracts light! The laws of the universe are just as precise as the laws of physics. There is no point in petitioning the gods to destroy the darkness we engineered. Only light dispels darkness.

Something else of great significance is emerging: now that we are aware of our true identity: it seems futile to honour our parents or any authority that claims to be the receptacle of the whole truth. As man evolves, truth evolves, nothing is stagnant, nothing is solidified. If truth given at Sinai was for all times, truth would have fossilised; fossils are long dead. All is life in the universe. There is no death. Besides, reincarnation forces us to re-examine our family roles. I know that my father was, long ago, a Roman centurion who enjoyed finishing off the victims dying on the crosses. Now he is a stern religious figure who hands out absolute truth, a moral authority.

'Which is the dynamic energy the centurion or the parson?

'The parson. Under the humility the boiling lava of guilt and confusion.

'And I know that my father was once, long ago, a crusader who looted and cursed his way to the Holy Land.

'And which of the two is the driving force, the crusader of the rabbi?

'In disposition, attitude and conviction a pious man, but underneath a man tortured by doubt and self-loathing.

'And we are cosmic workers working for the Spiritual Hierarchy! What do we have in common with our fathers? In the light of the doctrine of reincarnation, relationships are changed for ever.

'Our parents are brokers between god and us, guardians of god's law. For Freud, parents are the guardians of the moral and social laws which they instil in us, to make us conform to the social code of behaviour. These laws form the content of the superego.

'The law of reincarnation cancels all. 'Honour your father and mother' is untenable. Respect, yes, honour, no! Honour your father for having been a cruel centurion, a merciless crusader, Attila the Hun? Honour your mother for having played a part in the Inquisition, for burning witches, for offering human sacrifices to Moloch?

'Don't get carried away, you chose your father in the clear light of knowing. You had something to learn from him in your present life. So, why not honour him, he is serving you!

'No way! I learned all I could learn from him and left him and all that he champions a long way behind, in fact thousands of light years behind.

You, as a cosmic worker had something else to do: take on his negativity and transform it.

'And pile up on me those negative forces?

'To transmute them into light.

'My father is a member of the human race; the emphasis is on 'human'. A human being who at a certain point on the ladder of evolution found in the Jewish role-play something that captured his imagination.

'It resonated with his nature. He felt at home in this particular mental landscape, this specific energy frequency, this distinct group consciousness.

'People in this more discerning age will honour their children. A complete turn around! 'Honour your parents' was a central cog in the old religious mechanism, crucial to a society anchored in the masculine ego. Now that the energy of Sanat Kumara is emerging after a protracted effacement, planetary civilisation established on the will-to-power will subside and fade away.

The two interrupt their conversation for the moment. The discussion has caused them a distress they are trying to conceal. They concentrate on taking in the unspoilt scenery around them, unwilling to be distracted from their reverie, feeling that they need to focus attention on something other than their current problems. Later feeling calmer they are able to resume their conversation.

'The subject is serious and painful, admits Levinson, breaking the long silence. I have been grappling with this issue for a long time and with each insight I feel a flutter as if I had finally resolved it for good. But the resolution eludes me, I find myself churning it around my mind once again, with more intensity and tension than before.

'Same with me, replies Johansson. I despair at ever coming to an understanding that will appease me. I also feel that for as long as we insist on trying to resolve it with our intellect, the answer will elude us. Look at it this way, thoughts are just thoughts, they come and vanish, they are nothing more than fleeting waves, electrical impulses between neurones. The truth lies within and is only accessible through inner exploration rather than through reasoning. We need to let go of the need to rationalise.

'Not the truth, aspects of the truth, there is no absolute truth. Individual truth. Look within for your unique truth. To give intuition full sway in the matter is difficult for us yet so natural to the artist, the child, the prophet.

'Attachment to our parents and their god has been a factor in keeping humanity in a trance-like state, broods Levinson. We have been attached to 'dream-like forms': parents, beliefs and gods are 'like dreams', they have no inherent existence. All this 'unreality' has blighted the seeds of freedom and responsibility. It has disempowered us. Attachment offers no window on another reality. We are marooned.

'We fail to realise that attachment to others is inevitably attachment to their physical self. Attachment to our parents and their god is attachment to their ego and their god's ego.

'You hit the nail on the head! We form attachment to the part that is changeable, transient; the part that dies. The perishable self is taken in isolation and fussed over as the real being when it is truly 'empty' of existence. The real being is deathless, unborn, formless, and autonomous. Why mourn the ephemeral part, the role we play on the Earth stage?

'Confusion has had full sway. We are attached to the peripheral, the form, the part that appears solid but is only the result of external forces, conditions and circumstances, 'empty' of genuine existence, as you said. So much for physical form, what about cultural forms? Our beliefs and attitudes come from our social group; they are not ours at all! They are 'empty'; nothing is reliable or permanent. Yet we die for them! 'Think that all phenomena are like dreams'. Conditions and forces we ascribe to our gods are denounced by Geshe Chekhawa as being 'like dreams', they have no reality, they vanish when we wake up.

'Except that we do not wake up, we refuse to wake up! 'As long as man has any regard for his corpse-like body, he is impure and suffers from his enemies as well as from birth, disease and death'. This encapsulates our condition. We invariably revere that which is impermanent, fenced in time and space. Our gods are temporal gods; they are fenced in with us.

'Think that all phenomena are like dreams', we live in virtual reality. Objects we come across in our waking state are like those we see in dreams, virtual reality! We are bombarded by images. To Buddha the world is virtual reality.

'Like the table we see as a table because we have a mental image of what a table is. The artist would gaze into the mystery of the wood, the carpenter would appreciate the grain, varnish and finish, the physicist would see a myriad of whirling atoms and the mystic would see a whirl of cosmic energy. They all look at the same object but see it in a different light. Each mind interpreting reality in its own unique way.

'We can say that the table is an appearance because we do not see things as they are. The true nature of things is energy. Matter observed closely dissolves into energy.

'The dream-like nature of all things and situations has prompted Shantideva to ask, 'Why should a wise person develop attachment for dream-like forms?' When we develop attachment to things we are held captive by the desire to retain the objects forgetting that all things are impermanent. They only appear solid because our mind makes sense of the world in this way, they are in fact dream-like, we grasp at an appearance, a dream, a shadow. Like the sub-particles in Quantum physics, they appear, whirl for a while, then disappear.

'This bothers me. Buddha dismisses the need for gods; he urges man to seek alone his liberation. In contrast our tradition appeals to the 'Children'. Stretching way back to pre-rational times, it demands absolute reliance on the god who usurped power from all other gods. We have no time for defeated gods, we serve the god who affirms his will-to-power even if this affirmation is the negation of life as Nietzsche observed. This triumphant god will rustle up our liberation. No point in trying to redeem ourselves!

'Going back to 'Honour your father'. Your father is the earthly representative of his god. 'Honour your father' is indefensible, your father, like my father, was the recipient of his god's intentions and his god's 'will-to-power'. The planetary civilisation built around the masculine ego and the will-to-power will vanish in time. So 'Honour your children' for they will usher in better times, more just times. 'Honour all life' for all life is One. The Ten Commandments were adapted to a pre-rational age ... In the wild animals put markers to protect their territories; we have a religion to do it for us. Materialism is endorsed with assets safeguarded by religion and law. Capitalism is born.

The 'new' Ten Commandments

'Your children are not your children.
They are the sons and daughters of Life's longing for itself.
You may give them your love but not your thoughts ...
You may strive to be like them, but seek not to make them like you.'
(Kahlil Gibran)

The evening is bathed in the gold light of the setting sun.
'Long ago a vast crowd gathered in fearful expectation at the foot of this imposing mountain, says Sarah in a dreamy mood.
'And they heard Earth shriek, they saw clouds of volcanic ash rise that had been released by the eruption of far away volcanoes, the Santorini and the Krakatoa. The clouds of smoke plunged Earth into a nuclear winter, continues Maimon. This is the modern version of a natural event of such destructive power that Earth was darkened for years.
'A passing comet came too close to the Planet and threw Earth axis off balance, is another modern interpretation, expands Levinson. Earth was quaking and howling. The end of the world!
'An edible substance poured from the sky; the Children of Israel gathered it and called it 'Manna from Heaven' and ate with gratitude, reminds Clara.
'Something else fell from the sky too, adds Maimon. To appease their terrible god, the sons of Aaron in a gesture of devout terror, took some of the oil that poured from the sky and lit it as an offering. They were burnt alive. They had ignited liquid petroleum. To this day we read this text in religious awe, marvelling at the greatness of god! The account of these events we read year after year, with the same credulity.
'A 'miracle' that the Planet is hit and humanity destroyed, wonders Jeremy?

'Every calamity is explained away as a 'miracle', explains Clara. I used to wonder how many miracles the vengeful god could conjure up. Did he not stop to 'rest' on the 7th day after his arduous work of Creation! Evidently not, he was at it long after, this time busy in destruction! Cosmic cataclysms were as many miracles in the animated imagination of that time.

'He may have needed to 'rest' on the 7th day of Creation, but not at Sinai where he went on performing an endless string of 'miracles' with unrelenting consistency, echoes Levinson.

'We are going to repeat the events, this time without the crowd, without the manna and the petroleum discharged by the tail of the comet, says Maimon.

'Blasphemy, retorts Tara in jest.

'Faith or the simulation of faith is often a way of neglecting our obligation to think and to act, notes Clara. We use faith to absolve us from exercising our divine right. What they refused to do they shrugged off for later generations to grapple with. For us today.

'This is precisely the reason that brought us to Earth, retorts Levinson, to do the job they declined to do all those centuries ago. We signed an agreement with the Hierarchy. One task is the release of the archaic thought-forms that still condition the Hebrew psyche. The other task is to assist the disintegration of the old world order which is hampering the liberation of mankind. We are on the Planet to dispel the 'great illusion', the vast web of all thought forms emitted by humanity which enshrouds Earth. Our people are master weavers of thought forms, master spinners of illusion.

'After this fine introduction, let us begin. Which of you is going to give the Ten Commandments to the world, enquires Jeremy laughing. What about you Levinson, your name is Moses, most pertinent and auspicious for the task.

'This feels awesome and the responsibility daunting. Do I have the right to do this, questions Levinson with uncharacteristic unease?

'I know how you feel, says Clara reassuringly. I have felt like this all my life. You have to shake off the reticence, the fear that clogs every cell of your body, the feeling of powerlessness, nurtured by tradition and reinforced by upbringing and which is choking us. 'What's the point', echoes with a sinister ring in the background.

'I agree, continues Jeremy. You heard Sananda say that vast numbers of world servers have taken up their assignment on Earth to heal, to enlighten, to herald the brave new world. Sananda with Sanat Kumara remind us that we came 'to create a new world'.

They know that we are hampered by self-doubt and hindered by the conditioning that has kept human beings 'prisoners of the Planet'. At the foot of this noble mountain, long ago, the Masters of Shamballa entrusted Moses with the 'document' we call the Old Testament.

'This does not make me feel better, moans Levinson.

'It should, continues Jeremy unperturbed. Don't you see that this is precisely what the Masters expect of us, to restore balance, to heal the past, to transform the past? This is our task, not a figment of our fanciful imagination.

'I agree with Jeremy, says Clara. Some are scouring the Planet in search of immature souls to indoctrinate. As they rake the embers of separateness and powerlessness, they fan the old materialism. As they move around the globe they ignite the fear that lay dormant in the human energy field, re-activate guilt and rekindle helplessness in those who long to shed the crippling ancestral negativity, those who yearn to be free. They are soon wrapped in the dark cloak of the god of fear.

'They are hindering those able to let go of the stagnant thought-forms that have suffused the human psyche and were believed to be 'real'. It has been the role of the 'world servers' in recent times to deflate, to stab at the 'great illusion'. Those of us who seek 'being' in preference to 'doing' are being criminalized! The forces of Form never rest; they are engaged in a total war with the forces of Being, says Levinson.

'All this gloom and doom! In this beautiful country, liberation is imminent, proclaims Johansson in his optimistic mood. Finally, it looks like Moses' spiritual vision is coming to pass and the spiritual values he taught are within grasp. If the Hierarchy appointed us and support our effort, you can be certain that Moses, affiliate of the Hierarchy, does too. Enough to send shivers up the spine of the Pharisees but they too can wake up from their nightmare, nothing is preventing them except their own fear. So Levinson, no more self-doubt, read us the new commandments, your people have waited long enough.

Before I read the 'new Ten Commandments, I have a confession to make: the reading of the 'old' ones used to fill me with disquiet and unease. A force in me was resisting, whispering that it was archaic, undeveloped, uninspired, unsuited to our time. I recoiled each year when the time of reading them at the synagogue came round.

'The spiritual principle the Hierarchy entrusted to Moses originated in the abstract world of Idea, but as it hit Earth it began to weaken, remarks Jeremy, slowing down to human frequency. The finer vibrations initiated on the plane of mind deteriorate as they traverse the plane of emotions. And so a noble movement born in the highest realm of mind plunges in the dark waters of the emotional plane and begins its struggle for survival. Untutored minds unable to penetrate the meaning behind the form fall into religious devotion.

'Moses' dream of spiritual liberation deteriorates into devotional serfdom and ritualism, notes Sarah.

'Not all surrendered! Noble ideas they rejected, they wanted concrete results, corrects Johansson. The intention of both Moses and the Hierarchy to lift the masses to the plane of mind failed. The masses long for emotions, they yearn to venerate, idolise, adore, 'do and obey'. They want to be told what to do, they want others to take responsibility, they want someone else to blame. Or they neither do nor obey, they riot instead! The intention of the Guardians of humanity was to subdue the raw emotional response of the Children, tame their unruly nature, polish rough angles and lift them from the lower triangle.

'What triangle, asks Tara, the triangle of the 6-pointed star?

'Something like that, replies Johansson. The lower triangle is concerned with reproduction and survival, with physical man. The higher triangle is concerned with the higher faculties, with spiritual man. The purpose was to encourage the climb from the lower to the higher triangle. The aim was to subdue the self, discipline the mind, tame the tyranny of desire.

'Only now I grasp the nature of the malaise I felt then, resumes Levinson. Our precepts are grounded in space and time.

'They aim not at soul-man but at natural man, clarifies Clara.

'That's right, confirms Maimon, natural man. The Ten Commandments we flaunt are natural laws. We are not unique, the animal world has similar basic rules within species and they live by them. We refer to them as 'instinctive' impulses. Sadly for man natural laws ceased to be instinctive. Once forgotten, they had to be reiterated.

'They are an edited version of the ethical principles given by the great kings of Ancient Sumer, explains Johansson, specialist in the field. The Hebrews adopted them, in the course exiles, rescuing the thought-forms. It is after repeated 'field trips' that they were able to piece together their version of the moral commands the Sumerians had been living by, some three thousands years before Moses.

261

'The Sumerians ascribed their brilliant civilisation to the gods that came down from the stars, the Nefilim! So the Ten Commandments may well be the reformulation of the rules the Nefilim had given the people of Sumer long before. In his treatise 'Civilisation begins at Sumer' Kramer writes that the Sumerian civilisation was given by the Nefilim, explains Clara. If so how can we account for the egotism of the Nefilim? I am beginning to feel rather confused. At Sinai a despotic god threatened to crush us under the mountain, yet research findings show the same god entrusting a magnificent civilisation to the people of Sumer, a civilisation founded on science, literature, law, medicine, architecture, astronomy, arts and crafts. It is difficult to reconcile the two.

'I agree, says Levinson always attuned to Clara's thinking. It does not make sense; the Sumerians received a marvellous civilisation that inspired Greece before finally being passed down to us. We got the god of fear! It does not seem fair!

'That's because you forgot the cosmic law 'like attracts like'. We attract the god of fear because we are motivated by fear. It's a question of wavelength!

'It just goes to show that we get what we can grasp nothing more, notes Clara. We needed firm handling to secure the Nefilim presence on the Planet and ensure the perpetuation of their genetic coding. We fulfilled our part of the deal and the brilliant civilisation passed us by.

'It is all around us!

'Right, continues Levinson, I understand now why the first three commandments concern the deity. He took the lion share. He wanted to establish monotheism among a social group tormented by idolatry. He declared himself the Elohim, the 'Creator Gods'. Three times he assumes the identity of the Elohim: 'I am Yahweh thy Elohim who hath brought thee out of the land of Egypt out of the house of bondage'. Then, 'Thou shall have no other Elohim beside me' and finally, 'Thou shall not utter the name of Yahweh thy Elohim in vain'.

'The stage is set for confusion to take roots, confirms Maimon. Do you know that the name Yahweh is unpronounceable? Any one bold enough to utter the sacred name was flogged! Today, those who are more Yawist than Yahweh himself, the Hassidim, do not even use the letters of his name, they leave a blank space, so as not to fall into blasphemy!

'They tour the world, says Clara. Heaven help humanity!

262

'The second and third tell about the deity's will-to-power, insists Maimon whose hostility to the old religious system is asserting itself. He takes on the identity of the Elohim who were commissioned by the Logos. He does so from the top of Mount Sinai amid thunder, lightning, Earth tremor and clouds of smoke. Yahweh had a great sense of the theatrical and knew how to stage an impressive epic drama, the memory of it still haunts our psyche 3000 years on. And so we adore a self-appointed god who is also an Earthly king and despot! Possibly the first dictator who ever ruled the Planet. Our 20th century is well acquainted with dictatorship among men. Dictatorship among gods then was new; the gods had ruled side by side in relative peace. The events at Sinai mark a watershed in religious history; for the first time, a god asserts his supremacy over gods and men alike.

'Fascinating, concludes Jeremy, now to the Ten Commandments, Levinson.

'Back on course, chuckles Levinson, I tend to get side-tracked especially when I am helped by friends. Seriously now, the Ten Commandments are basic rules of conduct between mortals. In the intervening ages we have evolved a mind. We exist in three dimensions simultaneously: physical, emotional and mental, as a result the 'old' ten are largely obsolete. Here are the 'new' Ten Commandments for multi-dimensional man:

1   Know that God dwells within you, living and knowing in you. A thread of light extends from the I AM spark in the Heart to Infinity in an unbroken line. Separation from the Source is an illusion.

2   Remember that you are a Soul; your essence is Light and your nature Love. As your soul you express love, empathy, creativity, autonomy, equality, brotherhood, liberty, unity, inclusiveness, integration and harmony. Separation is the illusion of the solitary, fragmented self. In your essence you stand for the 'True, the Good and the Beautiful, nothing less is worthy of you.

3   Let go of attachment to the Father. First there was the Mother, then the Father, now there is Man in the fullness of his power. Greet him with the regard that his greatness demands.

4   Let go of attachment, hatred and ignorance, the three poisons that have blighted mankind. They keep you 'prisoners of the Planet'.

5   Revere your children, for they do not belong to you. They chose you for reasons you do not yet know. Love them, do not use them, exploit or

manipulate them. They bring with them the promise of liberation and new life. In addition, do not engage in unthinking procreation.

6 Love yourself so that you may love the 'other'. You are one another so when you hurt the other, you hurt yourself. To love is to accept, to understand, to respect, to embrace, to encompass, never to judge.

7 Forgive others. When you know that you chose the events in your life and the people who precipitated these events, then you will know that there is in reality nothing to forgive.

8 Know that you are not the plaything of Fate. Let go of determinism, pessimism and materialism. No cosmic entity hurled you onto the Earth plane. You designed your life and you have been doing so from time immemorial. You create your belief about the world, even when it is imposed by your social group. You create your reality and when you know this, you will be free.

9 When you see multiplicity you do not see the One Life.
When you promote separateness you deny the One Life.

10 Recognise that 'form' is an illusion, it is energy in motion. Form is 'empty', it is crystallised thought. Religious form endorses Samsara, the phenomenal world. When we focus on form we empower the Forces of Form, the forces of materialism.

'Quite a programme, exclaims Jeremy. I wonder what the diehards will make of this. They are going to throw their arms in the air in horror.

'Inevitably, comments Clara, they always do. Had Galileo yielded to their demands, we would still believe that the sun turns around flat Earth.

'He lived to disprove flat Earth and died for his temerity, reminds Jeremy.

'So he did, guess what? Earth is still revolving round the sun! Neither Darwin nor Freud were intimidated, delayed perhaps, but not silenced by the doctrinaires of their generation. They boldly enounced their theories. One facet of our assignment is to enounce the theory of Conscious Evolution; we are reminding people that they tread the Path leading back to the primordial unity. We are stating a fact not a fantasy. They will arrive at it in their own time. It may take them several incarnations, several centuries.

'Or it may not, points out Jeremy. They may make the needed shift in consciousness much earlier. Let's wait and see.

The present religious crisis: the spirit is awakening & resisting outside interference

'The post-war period unleashed significant changes, begins Maimon. The forces at work were the cosmic laws that had been ignored. Cosmic laws express the intention of the cosmic Mind.

'Fate, snaps Tara!

'Definitely not! Evolution is not fate, besides we are part of the cosmic Mind, inevitably we participated in the global intent.

'Not what they want to believe! Malign humanity was at it again, retorts Clara.

'That as well. The apocalyptic events were, strangely enough, evidence that universal laws were at work.

'An era is ending, picks up Jeremy. We are beholding with alarm or elation – depending on our view point – the breakdown of values and systems. We are witnessing the failure of archaic religious form, institutions and dogmas. A cocktail of all kinds of things causing much confusion. This melting pot is dissolving all and out of the mix something new and robust is emerging. Moral qualities are being forged to shape the world in the making. These qualities are being forced to the surface by the legions of unseen and unknown cosmic workers who will not tolerate the distortions of the past. They reject the ignorance that passes for profundity, the self-deception that hides behind dogmatism and crawl under the fossilised rules. The fear of being found out makes the weak retaliate. Organised religion all over the globe is shaky. The ground is trembling under its feet.

'They hide their insecurity under a mask of aggressive pietism, interrupts Levinson. Jeremy looks at him with relief; he does not seek centre stage.

Sensing this Levinson continues: 'As I see it, our predicament stems from not having the spiritual system of thought that India has known. Devoid of a coherent doctrine of mind we have given our priesthood the right to do the thinking for us. We declined the search for the meaning of life. Each generation has consistently passed the responsibility on to the next generation. As no messiah was appearing on the horizon and no reliable leader was emerging, shrugging off the obligation was the way of least resistance. Feebleness, vacillation, confusion and indifference have a strange way of passing for profound piety. Our deepest belief is that god is best left alone. But we must pretend!

'In case he hears us, laughs Clara.

'We cannot begin to unravel our predicament, or decode its origin, pursues Maimon. There isn't in our gargantuan religious narrative a hint as to how to dissipate the fog that hides its solution. And so we think in secret, 'the next generation will know what to do, let them grapple with it'! The multitude wants to get on with their mundane lives. Those of us engaged in change have hurdles placed on our path while torrents of pious blame threaten to sweep us into oblivion. Such was the fate of the Essenes, the saviours promised since prehistoric times. Who wants to be saved? It is one thing to weep, fast and petition routinely and quite another to read the signs! In the 18th century the two feuding religious factions, the 'rationalists' of the Gaon of Vilna and the belligerent Hassidim united to fight a common enemy, enlightenment!

'We are reaping a blighted harvest. 'As you sow, so you shall reap'. Vast time distances often separate sowing and reaping. Blighted seeds we planted millennia ago are being harvested now, bemoans Clara. Accounts accumulated over time must be settled. In Ancient Egypt, the god of Karma placed the heart of the dead onto the scales to be weighed as it started its journey into the Underworld. The law of Karma operates for all of us. The religious forms we built have solidified, calcifying our emotions and ossifying our mental life. They are being weighed by the invisible hands that restore balance when balance is upset, order when order is disturbed and reason when reason is garrotted.

'Indeed, the end of the world is nigh, continues Levinson! But not the way the doom-makers roar. The world as we know it is dying a death that no sensible person will mourn. Long ago, the illustrious patrons of the Great Illusion in declaring war to the soul unwittingly ignited the spark of rebellion. Their crystallised rules and ossified beliefs the masses rejected. In its simplicity the people found elsewhere the solace they were denied at home and they adored other gods. But it all came tumbling down in this most appalling of exiles. By a cruel irony of fate, we hold the torch of loyalty to a god that our ancestors disregarded and we have fanned that flame in the midst of dreadful persecution. The ancestors in their crude simplicity knew what was best for them; in our sophistication we do not, we serve the god their discarded!

'I accuse! I accuse the rabbis of crimes against our people, snaps Clara.

'The Jewish people? We know that there is no such thing, only souls choosing the Jewish embodiment for reasons of their own, clarifies Jeremy.

'Good point, replies Levinson. Indeed, the Jewish people attract the souls that select a new stage on which to perform their next act. They choose to inhabit a Jewish body that will offer them the range of opportunities they need. The Jew as a distinct entity does not exist. Those who enter the Jewish condition knowingly enter a collective pool of consciousness. They adopt traits, attitudes and beliefs common to all. They share in a collective experiment from which they cannot entirely extricate themselves. Immersed in this shared experience, they are committed to it until they decide to change the wavelength, to change the quality of the energy.

'The future of humanity seems to be in our hands, admits Maimon somewhat reluctantly. Ancient thought forms of biblical origin have shaped civilisation and still permeate the Western world. Western humanity is the most influential on the globe. So it stands to reason that we have an obligation to change.

'Absolutely, exclaims Clara with an intensity she does not try to conceal. Until now we have relied on the world to initiate change and we simply have adopted ideas and methods. Now, we have to take the initiative. We must collectively denounce our fossilised precepts and archaic outlook.

'I agree, says Sarah, we have a responsibility to humanity, I do not distinguish between groups, I do not discriminate. I have no allegiance to any particular group. However, at the risk of contradicting myself, for as long as I remain in a Jewish body, I feel a strong sense of responsibility to awaken the group I chose to be born into. I cannot disentangle my feelings.

'I find myself confronted with the same dilemma, says Clara. A battle is raging between my objective stance as a cosmic server working for humanity and the tormenting feeling that I must work for this singular group.

'Change is inevitable; change is the hallmark of life. 'Life is change', quotes Jeremy. But it seems to me as an outsider that the Jewish people do hold the key to transformation.

'Our tradition runs counter to everything Krishna, Buddha and the Hierarchy have taught down the ages, says Maimon. Buddha denounced belief in religious authority, yet this is what we have held on to relentlessly, even in the face of tragedy.

'Don't I know, exclaims Clara! I remember a time when I was being chastised for wanting to know, to understand. I was frowned upon as a doubting Thomas. Belief was the ultimate, understanding a sign of spiritual inadequacy. They perched on the highest branch of spiritual awareness, a loftier 'madrega'. There was a broad if silent consensus that I was not as elevated, as spiritually exalted as they were! In a strange way they liked having me around, it gave them a yardstick against which to measure their own spiritual altitude.

'Belief belongs to the astral plane of emotions; as 6th Ray individuals they value all things that can be measured in terms of emotions, in terms of the astral, the 'real' world, comments Levinson.

'Buddha denounced belief because belief is of the lower self. Teachings are to be accepted only if they are confirmed by reason, explains Tara, 'For this, I taught you not to believe merely because you have heard, but when you believe of your consciousness, then to act accordingly and abundantly'.

'This is not surprising, smiles Jeremy, Buddha embodies the third attribute Intelligence. He brought enlightenment to the world. He ushered in the age of reason.

'We never had a Buddha, sighs Clara.

'How could we, replies Levinson? We are advocates of the 'great illusion', marketers of the lower self, broadcasters of duality, serfs to a Samsara god, a temporal god. We are the people of form. We function on the astral-emotional plane. Buddha operates in the world of the higher mind and of pure reason.

'Going back to the issue of incarnation, inserts Sarah, I would like to point out that the souls of humanity that slide into the Jewish form may have 'fallen' into it. It is not so much a decision, more a matter of affinity. They resonate with this frequency band. They tuned into a state of being they already knew and wanted to sample again. Freedom was absent. One does not descend into our condition in search of freedom. The only freedom we recognise is the 'do & obey'. Free expression has not as yet been identified, not yet risen on our mental horizon.

'For those souls that never realised freedom, it is a natural choice to fall into a condition which offers the old familiar patterns of unjust fate and random destiny, adds Clara. Randomness, hopelessness and powerlessness can be attractive to many, if they never knew anything else.

268

'Not to forget the play of evolutionary force and karmic necessity, reminds Jeremy. These forces play a crucial role in the choices of the whole of humanity. The potent Shamballa energy was released in the 20th century. Destruction comes before reconstruction. Old forms and beliefs were destroyed to make room for the new. Hence the profound malaise experienced today in the world.

'The present religious crisis is no crisis at all, exclaims Maimon.

'What do you mean, I know your liking for paradox, notes Sarah.

'I am saying that the religion of man is dying, we are about to switch off its life support machine. There has been resistance and reluctance to analyse the cataclysmic events of the 20th century as analysis demands objectivity and rational probing. Instead we perpetuate the defunct past, powerless to figure out that the old world had to come to an end for the new world to be born of the ashes of the old. And so, I for one welcome the religious crisis worldwide. Besides, humanity is developing a new sensitivity. Intelligence, critical evaluation and greater sensitivity combine to shape a new human race. And you know what?

'Don't tell me! The old world is fighting the birth of the new world, snaps Sarah. The old religious materialism is preventing the birth of the spirit and the emerging spirit is resisting outer interference. Armageddon is visiting us. I witness this elemental battle in my practice, my patients admit to their distress and confusion but cannot figure it out.

'Now for the bad news: the 'chosen' minority is frozen into the old reality that humanity is gradually leaving behind. Floating against the tide, they are drifting away from the reality that is unfolding before their very eyes.

'This is why you embrace the present religious crisis with such enthusiasm, smiles Jeremy?

'Absolutely, nothing is more encouraging or more promising. All is well. The soul of humanity has been in thraldom, but the signs are that it is emerging from the entombment of the religious morass. The spirit is alive. Like a brook that vanishes into the sand to reappear later, we are emerging after having vanished into the sands of ignorance; this time we are determined to run towards the main stream and flow with the rest of humanity towards life.

'Thou shall not'

'The command 'Thou shall not' does not spring from Shamballa, begins Jeremy. The Masters do not command, they advise, inform, inspire, clarify, but do not dictate. They suggest ways of broadening our field of experience, ways of expanding our consciousness, but they do so with great sensitivity and with utmost respect for our freedom. They know in their profound wisdom that man has to grow and evolve and he can only do so in freedom. The Masters never interfere with human freedom. Had the Masters shown a vision in advance of the thinking of the time, they would have violated cosmic Law.

Maimon now in his element is going to speak almost without interruption, he has written a paper entitled "Religious Transformation and the Rise of the Enlightened State' and they all want to hear him out.

'Thou shall not' is the cry of the self, begins Maimon. A cry that betrays the haughtiness of the mounting ego. The ego is asserting itself as it denies the divine that dwells in man. It implies something like this: 'you have no right, you know nothing, you are not to be trusted, you are incapable of responsible decisions, so 'do & obey', I know better. I am the authority. Only I can penetrate the impenetrable mind of god. I alone understand god.'

More than that, it is the first step towards a totalitarian ideology that allows one man to blow the ram's horn to announce his absolute control in religious matters. As he appoints himself mediator he blocks the direct road to the divine, he dams the Path. In the ancient world, the disciples withdrew in the solitude of Temples and Pyramids to be initiated into the Mysteries and taught how to silence the ego. The 'death' of the self was a necessity for entering the Kingdom. The disciple's life effort was to establish a direct link with the Source within. Our law-makers' life effort was to deflect man from linking with the Source. Capitulation *of* the self was not their aim. Their aim was capitulation *to* the self!

'Thou shall not' tells us much on the nature of ancient man who, deafened by the clamour of his own rising ego seeks to smother the divine whisper in his fellow man and substitute his own will, human, mortal, fallible. 'Thou shall not' is the trumpet call of man's torrid ego. It is only fitting that 'thou shall not' be attributed to the tribal god, expression of the self as it manifests in all its intensity and unpredictability; a turning point in the evolution of humanity.

Jeremy having listened intently interrupts, 'What does your movement stand for Maimon? I can see that you are shaking the bedrock of the old order; you are bringing down the walls of Jericho. Assuming that you succeed in disrupting and disturbing the old energies, supposing that you finally overthrow the old order what do you want in its place?

'As you rightly point out, we are shaking the old tradition to its very foundation, but I for one do not intend to raise it to the ground. We are anarchists only in the sense that we want to transform or revitalise the old system, we wish to wake people up from the long slumber of the soul and present them with new choices. But above all we want to remind them of their inalienable, unalterable freedom. My objective, as you know is the demise of the crystallised system that has held us in thrall.

'We intend to reform the old system, not destroy it, pursues Sarah. To bring it into alignment with the original intention of Moses. This must be done in collaboration with all the intelligent, responsible men and women of the world who wish to contribute their talent, knowledge and humanity. We are approaching scientists, philosophers, environmentalists, artists and social scientists. We are drawing people from all over the world interested in launching something new for the Planet, and we want it to start right here, says Maimon with passion embracing the landscape with a sweeping gesture. The old system is obsolete and an embarrassment to a modern, educated, liberal and secular people.

'We intend to regenerate the system we inherited, and to this end we are enlisting all individuals of humanitarian disposition, we are reshaping it, transforming it. It will be reinterpreted as a serious historical record. We are brushing away the cobwebs of tradition woven with the threads of self-deception. What ought to have been an informative manual became a collection of tales exuding fearful piety and oozing devout fantasy.

'When we were in the United States, continues Sarah, we encountered authors we did not know existed and they helped us shape our thinking. They are the new thinkers for today, the Jewish minds who will replace in our school curriculum the dogmatic pundits of the past. To Rachi, Rambam, the Maharal and others, we are going to substitute Velikovsky, Kramer, Sitchin, Jeremias and Patai. They are the men for today; they started their academic careers with religious texts before breaking the frozen surface.

'So, to divulge further the intention behind our movement, we are attracting Jewish thinkers and they will be an integral part of all syllabuses. We want the Old Testament to become a rigorous discipline as it originally was in the mind of those who gave it.

'Never forgetting, inserts Clara that it is a limited body of knowledge! It was suited to a certain place, a certain time and a certain group. The central theme, the pinnacle of this document is the Father, archetypal image that has mystified man from time immemorial. The theme of the Father occupies centre stage and harks back to Lemurian times. On that lost continent, a few millions years ago primitive humans became aware of selfhood. The Hierarchy registering the dawn of human consciousness presented early man with the concept of the Father and rudimentary principles of living. It was tailored to meet the restricted potentialities of prehistoric man.

'And the Father was presented once again at Sinai, enquires Jeremy with disbelief, a few millions years later?

'We relish this fact, smiles Clara with sadness. We parade this pubescent feature with pride. I remember the way they mouthed with sensuous delight, 'God gave humanity 7 commandments of basic living, but he gave us 613 Mitzvoth! Numbers always, quantity is all!

'Two sets of laws for two distinct humanities, notes Jeremy! One law for the 'morally deficient', the other for the 'morally advanced'! The exalted ones got the Ten Commandments!

'Three more, replies Clara, just three more plus the heap of tales, allegories and symbols: images, images and more images and we have a 'thou shall not worship graven images'! We glorify images; to protect images we have suffered every kind of insult, humiliation, persecution and death. This bothers me greatly! Pointless suffering causes me great disquiet. Suffering is not a sign of 'chosenness'; it is a sign of ignorance.

'I agree, says Maimon. We intend to recover that which was buried under the rubble of laboured piety. Our 'manifesto' integrates the findings of science, arts, philosophy, and the Buddhist method of spiritual liberation, psychology, sociology, astronomy and archaeology. No branch of human knowledge will be left out. The dogmatic stance we shall expose as positively irreligious.

'Forgotten is the fact that the Old Testament is the storehouse of the accumulated wisdom and knowledge of ancient Sumer, Egypt, Mesopotamia, Canaan and Chaldea, adds Levinson. Ignorance is a rebellion against the Creator who incarnates in man to learn. The Masters are the most erudite.

'The Masters are masters of knowledge just as they are masters of the universe, expands Jeremy. It is in part their quest for knowledge that made them so. They know that the cosmic Mind incarnates in order to gain experiential knowledge. This universe is a learning zone, and so to deny an individual access to empirical knowledge is an affront to the cosmic Mind and an affront to humanity who is that Mind made flesh.

'Sananda quotes Shakespeare and he told me that he read 'Madame Bovary' in French, adds Clara still amazed. Their scientific knowledge is awesome. Their mission on Earth is to understand the divine Will and implement the Divine Plan. Compared to them we are human embryos, yet they take knowledge in all fields of human enterprise very seriously.

'We want to model ourselves on them, continues Sarah. Our movement will emulate theirs, characterised by open-mindedness, in which all who can contribute are included, and which will take in all branches of knowledge.

'A synthesis, asks Jeremy?

'A perfect synthesis, concludes Maimon. Integration of all fields of knowledge and the birth of the well-rounded man that was the ancient Greek ideal. Paltry bigotry, fearful exclusiveness, narrow-minded specialisation, ignorance masquerading as religious wisdom, all this must go. No one will be fooled. If they intend to retain their aura of mystery they will have to devise a more persuasive artfulness.

'Something bothers me, mutters Sarah, I am a Jungian therapist you see!

'Go ahead, we are therapists too, laughs Clara.

'Alright, the archetypal image of the Father has haunted the dreams of mankind, fills ancient mythologies and is encoded in our genes. It is an integral part of who we are the images of childhood we cannot shake off.

'You want to replace it with the image of the Son, asks Jeremy?

'No, the idea of the Son is not liberating, it will arrest us in the same state of dependency, helplessness and angry resentment that we have known since prehistoric times. The powerless Son living in the shadow of the terrible Father!

'With the metaphor of the Son, Sananda infers not the broken and defeated Son the world knows, but the flowing life force, a new life impulse, a new wisdom, clarifies Jeremy.

273

'The Renaissance Movement marks the coming of age of mankind, expands Maimon. Think of it as a method to exorcise the Father.

'That's right, adds Sarah. We falter in cultivated guilt. To the inner child in us that resists change we urge 'grow up, liberate yourself, it is time to 'die' to the past and time to be 'born again'. Human life is made up of several phases of development, a series of deaths and rebirths. Why do we find it so difficult to abandon an early phase of growth and be 'reborn' into a new, more creative, more effective, more satisfying one? The old world must 'die' for the new world to be born, one that reflects the more evolved, more inspired and 'redeemed' individuals we are now. The metaphor of the Son is apt.

'In place of the 'Thou shall not' we offer 'Thou are empowered to BE'.

'And the truth shall set you free', inserts Jeremy!

They have supper together in the cool shadow of the monastery refectory. The meal comprises freshly baked bread, boiled potatoes, a rice dish, grapes and figs. The monks eat in silence and the group respecting their contemplation eat quietly, reflecting on the fascinating exchange that had just taken place. It is time to depart and the silence is tinged with melancholy. After dinner they warmly thank their hosts. They go for a last walk together at the foot of the mysterious Sinai now lit by the descending rays of the sun in a blaze of orange light. The sadness is palpable but soon dissipated when they all agree to meet again in England shortly after.

Tara's assignment to heal the Jewish people

The next day before setting off Tara reminds Jeremy of a pre-arranged meeting with the Master. To make amends he immediately grants Tara a session. They had their morning meditation at the foot of Sinai and as the others went for a pensive walk, Tara and Jeremy stayed behind in the shadow of the daunting mountain. The Master speaks before she has time to formulate any of the pressing questions that have occupied her:

'The central theme of your life is healing, begins the Master, your chosen path is that of a healer. There are different kinds of healing, healing is not to be narrowly defined, there are many ways in which healing can be brought to people and to the Planet. And so there is no type-casting in some specific role, not for you. Let's look at it this way, in a rather abstract way: the Planet is going through a time of transition. You can see that in the outer world, society is changing quite rapidly at this time, technology is changing, you witness a rapidly growing population. That in itself is a reflection of deep inner changes that are happening, and these changes are acted out in people's lives. You can expect to see great changes in your own life as you move on. Now part of that process of change is a process of healing. In order for the new to come forth, to come into the world, there are aspects of the old world to be healed, to be resolved. And the process of change is catalysed, expedited and in some way created by frequencies of light coming to your Planet; new kinds of light coming from your universe to this Planet that bring transformation. You might think of it as some kind of light that brings 'enlightenment' at the individual level. But there is also a process of 'enlightenment' for Earth as more light is coming into the life of your entire Planet. In effect your Planet as a Being is preparing to move up to the next stage of her evolution and all of you are participating in this process. The human race in one way or another is involved in it.

'Some, like you come in with a game plan, a life plan very much geared to helping that process in a direct and conscious way, continues the Master. Now, one of the ways in which this new light comes to the Planet is within people. All of you fundamentally are beings of light who put on a human body. But in addition, there are beings often called Lightworkers - and you are one of these - who have chosen to embody particular qualities of light which they see as being useful to the Planet at one time or another. Sometimes these qualities of light are quite specialised and you have your own specialism. The qualities of light your bring through yourself you partly embody. But you also partly act as a kind of channel for these specific properties of light; you have the capacity to be like a transistor. You allow particular forms of current, particular forms of light to come through you because of the way you have created yourself as a human being here on the Planet. So you have the capacity to bring particular qualities of light through your own beingness. It becomes part of you, you bring it through but it is also part of you as well. In other words you vibrate to particular frequencies or particular resonance of light. You hold these patterns of light within your being and you radiate them to the world.

'Those properties of light are healing. What I mean is this: it is a bit like sun light. Sunlight can heal a wound, a cut. A cut is helped to heal more quickly in sunlight. The light you radiate out helps to resolve inner pain, not physical pain, but rather spiritual pain, mental pain or emotional pain. Pain that is held in the physical body but is not primarily of physical origin. It can be the pain of a painful memory, exactly the kind of thing you are learning to work with at the moment. So, you are developing at the conscious level skills to harness that energy field, to make it more effective, to find ways of applying it in the physical world.

'You have a particular interest, at soul level, in healing the pain which this part of the world, Europe in the broad sense, has experienced over the last 100 years. There has been a tremendous amount of pain generated by the upheaval that Europe has been through ... tremendous upheaval this century! What has happened is that in the course of this century many people died in Europe, but many of those deaths were unhappy deaths, painful deaths, deaths in war and so on. What often happens to people who die in this kind of situations, they leave their physical body with a lot of unresolved issues, a lot of pain held in the psychic body, the astral body. When they leave this life, they go on to what is called the 'astral plane' which is like a mirror image of this world ... it's not that different really! In the astral plane, people live their lives in a manner similar to what they did while on Earth. Often people who live on the astral plane continue to experience the pain they knew in their earthly existence, the difficulties, and the traumas they went through. Unable to analyse them and release them, the only way to resolve them is by coming back into incarnation and so they think: 'OK, I am going to go back down to Earth and I am going to sort this out!'

'But as you know, when you come back in physical form it is quite difficult to remember what you knew before you took on a body. This is characteristic of the energy of the Earth plane: it moves more slowly, it is denser. You, as a being of light, can zip round the universe in a moment. But you in physical form, you can't do that! Similarly, as a being of light you can access any knowledge you need in the moment that you need it. Easy, very easy! Down here it is not like that, you can't always get hold of what you want to know in the moment that you want to know it. And so you cannot always resolve issues you felt were going to be resolved before you came back, quite as easily as you thought at the time. As a result, there are lots of people now round the world - because those who experienced the traumas of this century in the European area don't necessarily choose to reincarnate in that same region of the globe. Many do, but there will be others scattered all over the world. Those individuals are of all different ages, some people reincarnate very quickly, some leave it for quite a long time. So all different ages, walking around, living their lives, carrying burdens of pain.

'A lot of this pain is collective pain, because so many of the experiences of 20th century Europe were shared by many. Not just an individual pain or individual experience but a shared experience. Whether they themselves were the victims or the people who created the victims does not really make a lot of difference. The pain will be the same. It's the pain of suffering, wanting to understand the suffering and wanting to resolve it, wanting to heal it, in other words.

'Now, the properties of light that you carry within you have the capacity to really assist that particular area of feeling. You will find - should you choose to do so - that you have the faculty not only to heal the deep issues people bring to you, but also to understand, initially intuitively, but later consciously the deeper traumas that lie hidden in past lives but are still held in the energy field. You can help them deal with this present life issues by exploring their lives and looking back at their childhood. But hidden beneath the surface, there will be pain from a previous lifetime which is underpinning the experiences of this lifetime. The experiences of this life time are really after-echoes of that earlier experience.

'You have the ability simply by being you, to help them get in touch with that deeper pain, not necessarily in a literal sense, not in the sense of taking them back to a former life by means of past life regression. Though past life regression, healing the memory is one way forward you might wish to explore. So it is not so much the reliving, the rekindling of the painful memory, and more working at energy level. You have the capacity to help people move out of the past and into the present, come out of the pain of the past and to be here and now. This is actually one of the big secrets of healing, the way healing is done, for so much of the pain people experience - whatever the pain, be it emotional or physical - is actually about the past, because part of them is still stuck in the past. If you can bring people fully into the present - and you have the aptitude to do that - what you are effectively doing is to help them let go of all their past pain. It's a bit like taking a pair of scissors and … snip, snip, snip all the ties that take them back into the past and saying to them, 'Wake up, you are here in the present, look, look the sun is shining, you are alright, everything is alright!' It's a kind of awakening and this is something you can do. You look at people and in the look you give them there is the love of compassion, understanding and reassurance. There is also another quality within, like a very brilliant light, a spark of light you pass on to people which is like the imaginary scissors that go snip, snip, snip… and that light says something like, 'Come on, be here now!' It brings people into the present.

'The people who come to you have some pain in this life or they would not come to you. You have the ability to reach beyond this life and help people heal the pain they carried forward into this life. It is surprisingly seldom the case that the pain people experience in this life is only about this life ... almost always some continuum from previous experience, previous incarnation. You can heal them just by working on the pain of this lifetime; sometimes this will be adequate to blow the circuit on the old stuff, but not always. Part of the way in which you will blow the circuit on the old stuff is through the energy work that you do with people. You are helping a client deal with an issue of now, but all the while there is something else going on, another part of you, let's say your soul and the soul of your client are interacting. Because these persons have come into your life at the human level, they have given you permission to interact at soul level and at soul level you are doing lots of healing as well, you always do ... this form of healing is going on at soul level. So other layers, other levels of that person beyond the issue you are dealing with, are also getting healed.

"What about previous lives, enquires Tara somewhat bemused by the vast amount of information imparted so liberally by the Master?

'I can tell you what you have done in-between lives rather in previous lives. A lot of work goes on between lives. You have had a life time as a Rabbi, you studied rabbinical law thoroughly and carefully, you were a wise man and a respected man, he adds with a crystalline laughter. But you also experienced life in other star systems, and this represents quite an important part of your beingness and your purpose. Though you have had lives on Earth, you are in some respect a visitor compared to many of the people around you. You have a foot in other camps, so to speak, in other places, in other worlds ... and so one of the things you are doing in the larger arena ... looking at a kind of universal scale of things ... is to study the operation of spiritual Law in different contexts. For a part of you - the soul being - coming to Earth is just one small part of your study, one small part of your exploration. You could think of yourself as working under the direction of an angelic group to study the way in which the Spiritual Law that the angels bring into the physical world, actually works in practice. So you have chosen to incarnate in all kinds of different settings to look at the way Spiritual Law works in practice in a large variety of contexts. In particular, you work in connection with the star Arcturus. The Beings of Arcturus are highly evolved beings in this particular part of the universe, in this part of the galaxy, so in universal terms we are talking about a local connection. You have much of their energy, you work under their direction and you studied with them too. You also work with Beings from the star Sirius as they are particularly interested in helping the evolution of this Planet and humanity over the next few millennia. You study with them and you report back to them, you learn from them the spiritual teaching you have chosen to embody. You learned in the first instance from them, they taught you. So you have all kinds of connections, you are a multifaceted, multi-dimensional being, now everybody is, its not that you are exceptional in that, though you have your own exceptional qualities.

'You mentioned my own specialism.

'Yes, your specialism. You have a particular interest as a being - this may be also true of you as a person - as a being, I emphasise this because you don't have to be interested in this subject as a person, it does not matter at all; it's of the being I am talking about. You have a particular interest, as a being, in the experience of the Jewish people in Europe and the traumas they went through in the last 100 years. It's is the kind of pain they experienced that you have chosen to specialise in. So again to make this very clear, I am not saying that you are going to be counselling Jewish people, not at all, because many who were Jewish in a previous lifetime are not Jewish in this lifetime. It is not as it appears on the surface. Your interest lies in a particular kind of experience that was typified by the events that affected the Jewish people this century in Europe. Talking about energy frequencies, you are dealing with a specific type of tangle of frequencies that your wish to disentangle, a complex situation typified by that experience, there is an intense feeling of betrayal. This experience can be found in other social and political contexts as well, other places are experiencing similar events. That is the quality of pain, if you like, that you have chosen to work with and disentangle.

'I have felt betrayal, I fear betrayal, confesses Tara.

'This is one of the key areas you have come to heal - earlier I used the term 'betrayal' to describe the pain you have come to heal. It is natural also, that you should experience betrayal as an issue in your life, as a fear; but remember that a lot of that emotional sensitivity is not yours, but the feeling of those you came to help. Remember that you create your reality, you create the reality of the relationships that you have and of course on a one to one basis it is a co-creation, you are both creating it. Look at your own relationship with yourself; look at areas where you may have fears about your own faithfulness to yourself. So look at all the emotions that other people present to you as in some way mirroring your relationship within yourself.

'Should they accept the energy you transmit, they will sense it and receive help. If they are open to that vibration of 'not-lonely', of connectedness, of oneness - what it fundamentally is. Oneness is the opposite of loneliness, where you experience oneness with the universe; it becomes impossible for you to be lonely. It's simply impossible! So that energy ... a very powerful energy ... when you radiate that energy, anyone who is open to receive it, takes it on. Because it is a vibration it changes the vibration of loneliness, it begins to transform it. You are transmitting the energy of oneness to that person and if they are open to receive it, it is going to do its magical work.

Tara is thrilled unwilling to halt the flow. The rest of the conversation deals with more personal aspects of her life. She finally emerges from the encounter and sits quietly for a while to collect her thoughts, to assimilate. She rejoins the others but remains quiet in spite of the general good humour and chatter around her, even the harsh beauty of the scenery seems to leave her untouched.

Jeremy sensing her disquiet asks, 'You are still under the effect of what Sananda told you. It may take a while to recover and absorb what he said.

'You are right; I cannot rouse from the spell.

'Would you like to share, it might help you, suggests Clara.

'Yes, I need to talk about it. I have just learned that I came into this life to heal the Jews who died in Europe. Further more, I was a distinguished Rabbi in a previous life. As if all this was not enough, I am a visitor to Earth sent from Sirius and Arcturus to help heal humanity. I am an alien!

'You a Rabbi, you are too pretty, exclaims Levinson, what name?

'Perhaps you were Rabbi Moses, suggests Jeremy with a touch of humour, and you came back to bring the manuscript to the world to heal.

Tara does not share in the mirth that Jeremy's wit provokes. 'I think I came back to make amends. As a Rabbi I was keeper of the old world, the old beliefs. I was one of those who kept mankind stuck in the past. I probably failed to serve mankind adequately. For this I am truly sorry.

'Why 'failed' and why be sorry, asks Jeremy?

'Through that Rabbi incarnation I carry a collective guilt. I'll illustrate what I mean; one of my patients is an artistic and intelligent young woman who suffers from psychotic

280

episodes. She is in and out of mental hospitals and takes cannabis regularly to drown her pain. Under hypnosis she relived a previous incarnation as a Jewish woman who was burnt in the York massacre centuries ago. She had been betrayed by her best friend. Her feeling of betrayal is palpable. She is stuck in that distant past as Sananda explained.

'I came across a strange case, contributes Johansson. When my mother was ill, she insisted on going to Lourdes, the place of 'miracle' cures. In Lourdes we came across a group of carers who affirmed with great conviction that the sick are 'special people'. One devout woman said: 'These people are truly special, they are god-chosen'.

'Well meaning, says Clara, but singularly misguided. There is no record of Buddha telling the sick that they are 'god-chosen'. First, no human being is ever 'god-chosen'. Second, illness is a state of dis-ease in which inner harmony is ruptured, equilibrium disrupted. Body, emotions, mind and soul are at odd with each other. That a person whose inner stability is dislocated claims to be 'god-chosen' is baffling.

'All the more baffling that such an attitude deters any attempt at authentic healing, continues Jeremy. Healing as Sananda said has to do with change, inner change, inner transformation. Healing is invariably of the inner person, it is healing of the long-buried emotional pain that obstructs the natural flow of the life force.

'This is our perennial, unrelenting problem, says Levinson. Our law-shapers of long ago initiated the 'god-chosen' myth, this fictitious notion that a group can be selected for a unique purpose. This myth thwarts reform.

'This is what I think you came to heal Tara, notes Jeremy thoughtfully. I think that the Jewish people and humanity through them yearn to be healed from the myths of the past. They long to cut off the umbilical cord that fasten them to that past, break up emotional links, split attachment to old convictions, and dissolve ageless fears. Healing is to be on a global scale. It is humanity that craves healing, arrested in the past traumas of sinking continents, nuclear winters, tidal waves and volcanic eruptions on a planetary scale. All these are lodged in our collective psyche and must be extracted, brought to the surface and healed.

'That's right! The old scriptures rehash that terrible past, stir the knife in the wound and inflict added grief, inserts Clara. It does not attempt to heal, it keeps the wound weeping. It is as if the pundits of the past made it their mission to keep the wound festering.

'They were the winners, exclaims Levinson! As the old wounds festered, imagination was erecting edifices of fear and guilt. The pundits were hammering in the 'do & obey', 'an eye for an eye', 'thou shall not', keeping humanity uninspired, unreflecting, suffused with anger.

'The incoming cosmic energies reaching Earth at the moment are changing all this, notes Johansson with barely concealed anguish. Humanity was forced to creep on the face of the Earth. Earth-man lived in ignorance of his true nature. Human law barred his rise to the mind, convicting him to stagnate in the emotional phase of evolution, easier to manipulate. Healing comes from awakening to our true nature. Ignorance is at the root of most mental distress. Healing is taking place; a giant evolutionary shift is under way as self-conscious man is lifting himself to the plane of mind and to the soul.

'And troubled humanity continues to revisit Earth in the Jewish attire to seek healing and move on, reasons Clara. To heal is to change, but the old views are hostile to change, resistant to healing. We have a dilemma here!

CHAPTER 5

SOLOMON & THE GODDESS – THE 'SACRED FEMININE' ENTERS THE TEMPLE

Yin – Cosmic Feminine energy

'To know Yang and to be true to Yin is to echo the universe. To echo the universe is to merge with the Tao, ever returning to the Infinite'. (Lao Tzu)

JERUSALEM

One morning a young soldier arrives in a military jeep. He leaps out the car, holding an envelope, young, agile, handsome. 'Are you Jeremy, he asks as he walks to Jeremy with a large smile'. Jeremy replies with a weary smile, 'a letter from Benzaccai means a new chapter from The Hebrew Gods" but also a new journey to an unknown destination, a new chase leading nowhere!

'Kafka's Castle, the elusive castle weary travellers never reach, says Clara.

The soldier replies with a look of surprise, 'from Benzaccai's wife!' She invites them to meet her at a secluded spot, the Church of Mary Magdalene in Jerusalem. 'Now, asks Jeremy nervously', he is weary of tearing around in search of Benzaccai? 'Tomorrow, replies the soldier hesitantly. If you decide to go I will stay the night. I have a sleeping bag, I will sleep at the foot of the mountain in the hope of inspiration, the spirit may come down on me in my sleep! I will drive you to Jerusalem tomorrow morning. The journey will not seem so long or so tedious in the relative coolness of the morning'. 'A thoughtful young man and handsome too', thinks Clara.

'We cannot turn down this invitation. We are very tired, but we came for this manuscript and we must get it in its completeness, says Jeremy wearily.

Early the following morning, they set off. In the early morning light the Desert is truly magnificent, lifeless it seems to conceal a mysterious force intimidating yet entrancing. 'Is this journey ever to end, moans Clara'. In the evening they reach their destination. The Church of Mary Magdalene is so quiet as to appear deserted. Built in an elaborate Russian style, its colour façade is a striking feature, a unique marker.

'There is nobody here, mumbles Tara. I am exhausted

'She is waiting for you inside, says the soldier. On hearing the car, a tall and attractive woman steps out of the church, she rushes to greet them with a warm smile. 'So good to meet you at last, I heard so much about you, my husband chose me as his envoy to pass on the next chapter from Rabbi Moses' book, not surprisingly it is entitled 'The Goddess'. By the way my name is Ruth.

'Ruth, says Clara feeling more alert, like my guide.

'I was named after her, replies Ruth enigmatically, tuning in to that wavelength. Encouraged by the attention and interest the group shows in her, she discloses that she is writing her thesis on the changing image and worship of the Goddess down the ages.

'The Goddess was worshipped by that brilliant civilisation called Atlantis, says Tara, do you take this into account?

'I do and my research is extending beyond the radius I envisioned at the outset. It is evolving with me! My thesis and I are growing together. I would like to read the chapter I am working on at the moment, if I may. An animated 'Yes' heartens her.

'This is odd, I came to give you the next chapter of 'The Hebrew Gods' and I start by reading my own paper, she laughs, I am inviting your comments and I shall take them on board. The chapter is entitled 'The Politics of Monotheism'. "To make sense of the present, we must unearth the roots which run deep in the past and in the human psyche. The politics of monotheism have far-reaching implications. To establish the 'one god' was an impressive leap or so it was believed. The idea of the 'one god' suggests concord, greater understanding and equality, a more tolerant and open-minded outlook. It hints at a return to the original unity lost with the Fall. However this unity is deceptive, its aim is not to include but to exclude. Women are excluded along with the rest of humanity. What we have is the masculine ego in control! The god of masculinity is indeed robust! What about the feminine principle, what about the balance of opposites?

'What about 'Yin' and 'Yang', the masculine and feminine polarity, the two pillars of Creation, echoes Tara? Lao Tzu reminds us that the nature of the universe is not Yang as our Judeo-Christian culture holds, but Yin. 'To know Yang and to be true to Yin is to echo the universe. To echo the universe is to merge with the Tao, ever returning to the Infinite'. He invites us to be true to the feminine, since the feminine echoes the universe and leads back to the Infinite.

'It is the negation of symmetry and stability, the denial of equality and impartiality. It is in truth a dictatorship with far ranging ramifications, affecting all aspects of life down the ages. Apart from anchoring a perilous imbalance, monotheism advocates the rejection of multiplicity. The 'one' cannot tolerate the many. There is an erasing of alternative views, a negation of the diversity of beliefs. Individual freedom has vanished. Unity comes at a price, the loss is immeasurable.

'Unity is by definition inclusive. Monotheism is a unity of a sort; it has more to do with exclusion than with unity, reinforces Clara.

'It reminds me of the unity of the old Soviet Union, imposed from the leadership, from the top down, when it should have been encouraged to grow naturally, organically within the masses, comments Johansson. Monotheism imposes itself on an undeveloped people, forced from the top down.

'The style fostered by the Hierarchy is different, expands Jeremy. The Masters encourage humanity to grow, learn and develop so that progress comes from within; it rises from the centre of humanity. The general direction is upward, the responsibility must remain with humanity; humanity is the initiative force, the directing agency. The Masters, our parents and teachers, remain discreetly behind the veil to encourage us to grow naturally, free from outer interference.

'The wisdom of women, their mysterious relationship with Gaia, their innate knowing of natural laws, of herbal medicine, of giving life and nurturing life, of unreserved love, acceptance and tolerance inspire fear in men. All this has been demoted and trivialised. They knew how to relieve pain, assist new life on the Planet, comfort, heal, and sense the invisible world. They also had meaningful prophetic dreams which they could clarify for the benefit of the group. They were high priestesses with a knowledge and wisdom men often feared and revered. In the mysterious and mythical underground kingdom of Agharti, the Atlantean people who survived the Flood and salvaged part of their scientific and spiritual civilisation recognise the power and dignity of women who still occupy significant positions in their society.

'You know of Agharti? Women resonated to the frequency of love, says Tara.

'As I said my thesis and I are growing together! Women understood the mysteries of the Earth and Moon cycles which mirrored their own natural cycle. They did not have to believe, they knew! Belief, the kind of belief imposed by man, hinges around the ancient polarity of good and evil; belief is structured around a divided, fragmented, estranged world. Women have an intuitive knowing which bypasses duality and goes straight to the meaning. They have a global perception, a holistic grasp. They do not break down or dissect as men's belief does. Formal religion is structured by men and controlled by men, designed along a rigorous pattern; no concession is made for intuitive knowing and spiritual perception. Immediate holistic perception of the whole is foreign to structured belief since the pattern is strict and no one is allowed to swerve from it, the slightest variation from the norm is deviant.

'They manipulate through fear. Religious belief hinges around fear, the polarity of love and fear.

'Tara you just said something interesting, interjects Jeremy, belief hinges around the polarity of love and fear. Do comment.

'Glad to be of help, she laughs. Traditional belief hinges around fear, fear of sin, fear of god, fear of hell. It also hinges around love, love of god, love of good. Formal religion plays the love-fear duet, manipulating mankind with both, nurturing both, perpetuating both. However fear always wins.

'Interesting, mutters Jeremy. So belief and polarity became indivisible the moment primitive man became aware of himself as separate from the herd. So belief and the sense of selfhood are connected!

'Belief and duality, belief and selfhood are interwoven. 'I am me, you are you', individuality but also duality. Belief needs duality, belief stems from duality, insists Levinson. For belief to endure you must have division, separation, diversity, in one word duality. Unity renders belief inactive, inoperative. Monotheism for its claim to unity fosters fragmentation, separation, disconnection and differentiation.

'It was naïve to believe that unity can be imposed from outside, continues Ruth delighted with the response. Unity is an ideal, a long-term goal. But imposed by law, unity is a dictatorship; it rules out genuine religious experience, disqualifies intellectual expression and bars creativity, because these lie outside the boundaries of legislation.

'The fog is lifting and unity is becoming more defined on the horizon, now that we are entering the age of the Goddess, reassures Tara.

'Absolutely, continues Ruth visibly pleased. Woman had developed the sensitive, intuitive, mystical aspect of her nature. Monotheism declared redundant these finer faculties which open the gates to the vast unknown, the uncharted unseen worlds. The subjective realms lay outside the control of the priesthood. Women were declared incompetent, treacherous and corrupt. Women perceived the world from a holistic perspective, a global perspective. Patriarchy decided that the Texts would be read not with reason and intuition combined but only with the practical, linear brain. Monotheism is forcefully Yang; it is left brain thinking, a masculine quality. The age of the 'pilpul' was upon humanity. The 'pilpul' is the hair-splitting method of studying the Talmud, which makes the student feel very clever as he engages in mental athletics.

'The planetary civilisation reflects the changes which took place some 5000 years ago when the Goddess lost her ascendancy and women lost their power and influence, reflects Tara. They had ruled society for a very long time, now they were overthrown. It was an entire mode of thinking, feeling and knowing that was lost to humanity.

'Left brain thinking is a male attribute, echoes Jeremy, while right brain thinking is holistic in nature: it is inclusive. Feminine qualities – intuition, sensitivity, empathy, inclusiveness - are also soul qualities. The age we are entering is rediscovering and claiming back soul qualities.

'True, left-brain thinking is mostly a male prerogative, agrees Ruth, women tend to be more right-brain. But this is changing as women are rapidly developing left-brain activity through education. They are about to recover their global, holistic perception. However left-brain thinking dominates religious learning which may partly explain why Jewish women were banned from biblical study. They were declared stupid and incompetent, not surprisingly they were more right-brain developed. Left-brain activity, linear, hair-splitting, methodical is essentially a masculine quality. The totality of perception is a sign of incompetence to our rabbis! Wholeness is stupidity!

'The god-force pervades every aspect of life; it shows in the separation and discord between man and woman, between man and man and between man and Gaia, contributes Levinson. The god-force is detectable in every institution, every field of human endeavour: politics, medicine, economics, education and science throughout the Western world.

'I am taking note, beams Ruth who is jotting down fast. Our god symbolically stands for the masculine side of polarity, for left-brain activity, for contrast and separation, 'thou shall be holy before me' says it all, in a nutshell.

'Why duality, enquires Jeremy, is it because left-brain activity displaces right-brain activity?

'Absolutely, when emphasis is on the meticulous application of the law, on precepts and practices - on the externalities of life - vital energy is squandered on external activity, fearful precision to detail and terror of faltering in the execution of the tiniest points. As a result the feminine side of the brain, the sensitive, spiritual, intuitive, creative aspect of our nature is neglected. Not only is it neglected it becomes redundant, worse still it is refuted as deviant! Figuratively as well as historically we live in the post-Flood era in which humanity functions in a divided world. Our civilisation is being played out on the post-Flood stage: the Father, who stands for both the cosmic masculine energy and the unchanging universe, polarity, fear, a moral and legal code and a strong emotional attachment to all!

'The god-force, inserts Clara, stands for that force in the universe which is unchanging, immovable, judgemental and unforgiving. Fate negates inherent freedom, disregards the law of evolution, and dismisses human creativity.

'Exceptional women were sullied and derided, think of Mary Magdalene this church is dedicated to, exceptional she certainly was, but patriarchy disparaged and denigrated her. A woman in her fullness is an aberration to patriarchy. Decisions affecting our lives were made by custom, common sense and experience along lines handed down, women had knowledge of healing and natural ways of living. Today we hand over to the 'experts' the responsibility to educate us, govern us, heal us, bring our children into the world, operate on us and even remove our organs! Patriarchal rule in all aspects of life has made us powerless. We are not involved in shaping the form and content of education, we are no longer held responsible for our health and we allow those we put in power to make decisions that affect our lives, the Planet and the future of humanity. In the past it was the Goddess, it was women who made vital decisions. The divine Mother and the human mother together made the vital decisions affecting their children.

'In a patriarchal system, education is of necessity practical, mundane and realistic, inserts Tara; it is becoming increasingly technical, utilitarian and pragmatic to serve society. But what of the individual? The needs of the group override the needs of the individual. When a person is utilised to serve the group trouble ensues, there is anger, and there is illness.

'The Goddess valued all her children; they were equal in her eyes. In contrast, patriarchy, spellbound in division, criticism and opinion, grades everything into superior and inferior. Equal opportunity is unknown. In the recent past the monotheistic Western nations sent armies to foreign continents to impose their own ideas, values and beliefs. Their culture was in the Yawist mode, one god, one permissible view of the world, all others denigrated and banned.

As no one interrupts, Ruth goes on. 'Monotheism and patriarchy are interwoven, interdependent. It is tempting to think that patriarchy has it all, but our history brushes a less glamorous picture. Monotheism has forced us to abdicate freedom and responsibility to shift both outside onto a ruthless autocrat. Autocrats, as the 20th century has brutally demonstrated, feed on our deep-seated fear and guilt as they ambush us, to watch us falter and fall. With guilt comes confession. We confess our sins, real or imaginary. With guilt and confession comes retribution. We must pacify the god of retribution and in so doing reinforce his subjective existence, and at the same time deepen our fear and guilt. A merry-go-round!

'Fear and guilt lurk behind much illness, notes Clara. We manufacture disease.

'These are the scrambled energies and entangled forces we came into incarnation to unscramble, reminds Levinson. Not only do our people demand it, the rest of humanity is requesting it too. Dispirited by the selfsame pointless 'doing', humanity is active in unscrambling its own tangled energies.

JERUSALEM

Visit to Jerusalem - Levinson & Clara

Jeremy suggests they all take the day off, 'we need a much deserved break; we have been tearing up and down the country in jeeps and cars, darting in all directions hunting for Benzaccai. I am going to visit the Christian sites that inhabited my childhood imagination. I left all this behind long ago, but now in this mysterious and magical land I am going on a pilgrimage, not only to revisit my youth but to rediscover the past.

'For you the Christian sites, for us the Hebrew sites, declares Clara.

Clara and Levinson decide to stroll through the city to visit the Wailing Wall and Meah Shearim among other sites. Jerusalem beckons the most unsentimental amongst us; such is the power of this ancient place. Jerusalem a beautiful, elegant, yellow stone city is dazzling in the sun.

'The return to the Promised Land must be the result of a web of influences intersecting at that precise point, mumbles Levinson.

'Without doubt. The destruction, the resurrection, the journey back to the Promised Land. Events past generations would not have believed possible.

289

'What of the Day of Atonement, what of the Day of the Temple?

'They beseeched but in their heart probably never quite believed it possible. This is one of our enduring traits, we doubt that which we most forcefully claim to believe in. Not surprisingly, our history has been a tissue of setbacks, betrayals, injustices and oppressions. Master Sananda made an amazing revelation. I asked him, somewhat boldly, why the Hierarchy had not intervened to save Jewish lives during WW2. 'How do you know that we did not help?' was his reply. He said something striking, that many of those who died in such ghastly circumstances had chosen to do so.

'What are you saying, exclaims Levinson!

'Master Sananda disclosed that cosmic beings from the Brotherhood of Light incarnated to give consolation and healing to the Jews and die with them. We know from Sananda that their intention was also to bring to a close the old world order and usher in a new world order, an age of cooperation, conciliation, freedom, tolerance, improved human relations, social justice and equality. The democratic vision of the Essenes.

'The liberal and democratic social order we now enjoy?

'That's right. Think of the sustained efforts of humanists, humanitarians and liberal politicians who lay the foundations of a more sane and rational world with the United Nations, the recovery and unification of Europe. Democratic forms of government and liberal ideals were adopted in Europe after WW2.

'The new Pharisees are not going to accept this.

'They are what I would call the 'Christian wing' of the Jewish people. They became the 'Protestant wing' when they traded Talmudic rule in favour of a lesser avatar who sprang from their ranks. They swore allegiance to the charismatic Baal Shem Tov, an enigmatic figure driven by a form of ardent paganism and a frenzied Christian mode of worship.

'Christian wing? They have a sizzling dislike for everything Christian. You can't be serious!

'They are the 'Christian wing'. They imbibed the Christian idea of the goddess and the god of love - a god of love, can you believe that? From the Puritans they borrowed the idea of religious experience through prayer, respect for hard work and self-denial to attain 'union'. The theme of 'union' became central to their religious life. All this was alien to traditional Judaism, normally associated with enjoyment of living. Christianity has had a profound influence on their feeling and thinking, though they deny it. Just as potent is the influence active in their psyche: they inevitably had several incarnations in a Christian garb.

'This renders their disdain of the Gentiles pointless and farcical. If they are the Christians of yesterday, then why overplay the present role, why despise what they once were? By the same token, why overstate their love for the Jew when in all probability they persecuted Jews in their former Christian personas?

'Ignorance! Long ago we chose to ignore the existence of the soul and its permanent reality. In ignoring the soul we also dismissed the cosmic law of Karma - the law of conscious evolution - and Reincarnation inseparable from Karma; laws which the universe abide by.

'Except us!

'Except us! We fell on the brink and are following our own line of evolution.

'Evolution or retrogression?

'Evolution backward! If there is no soul, there is no karma and no reincarnation. We have stumbled down the ages in the fog of ignorance, unaware of who we are, where we come from or where we are going. To fill the void, we invented fanciful legends. The Puritans among us are myth-makers, skilled at fabricating and magnifying the greatness of the Jew. The nagging question, 'do they truly believe their own propaganda, their own myths or do they need reassurance to cover up their nagging doubt and uncertainty?' Where did this passionate love for the Jew originate? Surely not in their past Pagan and Christian incarnations!

'Pharisees, Pagans or Protestants they are not going to accept any of what Rabbi Moses has written.

'Our history is one of denial.

On the Stormy Quest for the Self

The son of a Danish parson, Johansson spent his early life in a village close to the church. An only child, his fertile imagination was stimulated by the beauty of nature. He sensed at an early age a discord between his parents. His mother originated in the town, she had married without love. Lonely and bored, she felt neglected by her husband who feared intimacy and shunned affection. She had stayed in a loveless marriage for her son who became her only source of comfort. He felt the burden of her love. He was close to her in looks, character and affection, but distant from his father whom he feared. He had to sit in church on Sundays, while his stern father would address the faithful. Gifted as an orator, he kept his audience entranced, as Hell opened up before them in all its terror, darkness and permanence. The sensitive boy shuddered in awe; he secretly detested the god of his father. He had transferred onto the terrible Father the fear he felt for his own father. God was thunderous, implacable, and cruel; he damned the most innocent affections and pleasures. He came to associate his father with god, they were so similar. Which of the two did he fear most, dislike most and distrust most? As an undergraduate he read Religious Studies on the dictate of his father. But he soon got bored with the relentless restating of the tales, fables and parables of his childhood. He longed to read the Scriptures in a rational new presentation. He knew intuitively that the authorised account was only a covering film, a surface layer intended to hide rather than reveal. The rest was pious moonshine to appease the simple minds. He spent his spare time in the library, devouring the books forbidden in his youth. He read Eckhart, Dante, Schopenhauer, and Spinoza. The god of Spinoza was his lost dream of a sensitive, loving, intelligent and rational god. He felt that formal religion lacked intelligence and reason. He abandoned the course chosen by his father and switched to philosophy and psychology. He was at last free from his father and free from the Father. A passionate love affair began with the 'new' psychologies, he was unstoppable. After graduation he headed for the USA. His life course was now clear; he was unswerving in his resolve. He discovered that his own psychic abilities latent for so long were emerging. They included the ability to heal with the power of thought and by utilising the universal energy in which we bathe. This is what Johansson is recounting to Tara. He feels drained, he sits down. Concerned Tara observes him. Finally breaking the silence, she tentatively asks:

'When did you discover your healing ability?

'As a child I sensed this ability. I often came back from school to find my mother sitting in the dark with one of her attacks of migraine. I was too young to understand the link between anger and migraine. I was also too young to realise that people often use ill-health to get the attention they crave. Yet I felt that my father was responsible for her attacks. She would ask me to put my hands on her head and would feel immediate relief.

'The story of the loving little boy looking after his sick mamma and becoming a doctor or healer in later life.

'After I qualified, I returned to Denmark, brimming with all the rich knowledge I was bringing home. I sketched a master plan; I was going to open a practice in Holistic Counselling. I would develop my own counselling methodology drawing from a variety of approaches. It was to be the sum total of all known methods but with a definite emphasis on the spiritual and the philosophical. Buddhism offers an effective tool for achieving self-understanding and self-mastery, what people suffering from emotional distress lack. My father shouted that if I was not yet mad, I certainly was depraved. I left.

'As a child, like you I nursed my mother. She too was afflicted with periodical attacks of migraine. She dominated and controlled the entire family. She was the embodiment of Fate. Hapless, tied to her by our powerlessness, we were held together by the magnetic energy of hatred. The binding agent was hatred. She was the epitome of self-sacrifice and self-denial. I became a healer in spite of myself. Love heals or so we are told, concludes Tara with a sad, incomplete laughter.

'Did it heal you?

'No, it did not heal me. It has eluded me.

After a pause she clarifies 'I understand more, Sananda has shed light into obscure areas of my life. The shadows are dissipating slowly to reveal more of who I am. He explained as he did to you, that I came to Earth as a light worker 'to bring more light to the Earth plane' his exact words. Yet, I have always had to face hostility, hatred and scorn from my family. The hatred my father directed at me was palpable.

'What do you expect, you are an Essene! There is a long tradition of hostility, and scorn directed towards the Essenes.

'In a private meeting, the Master told me that I had taken physical form to bring more light, yet I have had to endure much revilement and sarcasm. The narrow-minded, literal and self-righteous milieu I grew up into looked down on me; I was an outsider. On my return from the United States, they chose to ignore me; to their provincial minds I had become Satan incarnate. Yet, I had embarked on a spiritual journey as much for them as for me. I was born among them to open their heart and mind, to show them that there is another way, liberation from their depressing and trifling rustic existence is possible.

'This is the most difficult part. You know that you came into the world to perform a task. You are on an assignment and your aspirations and actions are all oriented to that end. You remain truthful to your mysterious 'mission'. Your mandate is to help mankind help itself. Do people recognise this? No, they wave the hand of wrath, 'You are on your way to damnation', they foretell with a perverse thrill.

'Think of Spinoza, he remains my inspiration'. He is interrupted by a joyous laughter, 'Spinoza, who dares to mention Spinoza in this holy site'? It is Levinson. Clara and Levinson in their wanderings through the city finally arrive at the Wall and bump into the other two. 'Great timing, laughs Levinson, don't you know you renegade that the name Spinoza is not to be uttered in these holy quarters? He was banished by the puritans and no one, as yet, has lifted the curse.

'Are you making fun of me, asks Johansson?

'Certainly not, I am sorry but it is so funny hearing the name Spinoza in this most 'holy 'of places. By 'holy' I mean unquestioning, conformist, stuck, puritanical, joyless, and stale.

'I respect holiness though I never encountered it, replies Johansson!

'So do I, laughs Levinson. What I did encounter was fixation and self-enlargement. Our talent for self-hoodwinking is matchless, we accept anything so long as it confirms the deeply-held belief that we are 'chosen' for a grand messianic mission, for the purpose of saving humanity, no less. It's in our genes. In our long and tragic history we have not learned how to save a child let alone humanity!

Johansson now seeing the funny side goes along with the ebullient mood, reassured, 'gentle, rational and spiritual, Spinoza was one of the first European philosophers, who, because he envisaged a god of love was branded an apostate and excommunicated by his community.

'Who wants a god of love when we have 'the god of fear', retorts Clara. He was described as 'the Messiah the Jews never had'. We have a long tradition of discarding those who can liberate us from our prison of fear.

'Who wants a Saviour? Its ironic, continues Levinson no longer amused, to note that the puritans who felt empowered to kill symbolically a man and precipitate his damnation are probably wondering what all the fuss is about!

'I must interrupt you, exclaims Clara, I don't agree, the killing is not symbolic, to them it is very real, they eradicate the soul of the person who questions their myths. They did it to me; they also did it to you. Malign it is, infantile it most certainly is because they can no more command a man' s soul than they can a drifting cloud in the sky, nevertheless the intention is strident.

'Where are they now those who damned Spinoza? At death, the trifling details of earthly life vanish like a mirage. Earthly life is a mirage, a mirage they take for real! If they are back in earthly incarnation they are almost certainly born in a different race, colour, creed, social group anywhere on the Planet, who are they damning now?

As no reply comes, Levinson turns round. The other two have been swept away by the crowd, captured in the flowing stream of people. 'They are being carried away by the crowd, we'll see them again this evening, hope they find their way back!

'To 'sin' is to show ignorance of universal Law, picks up Levinson! In other words to 'sin' is to disturb the natural order and equilibrium in the world. Where we upset balance in the universe, balance must be restored, Karmic correction or adjustment is required. This is the gift of Karma in spite of our moaning and wailing, we need it to move on and evolve.

'White Eagle says that karma is 'unlearned lessons'. So exile should be seen as a cosmic gift to learn the lessons we did not learn in former times.

Clara and Levinson have reached the Wailing Wall, the most sacred site in the land. A shrine many visit to pour their hearts in ardent prayers for the restoration of the Temple.

'The restoration of the Temple is to coincide with the return of the Messiah, Lord Maitreya, says Levinson.

'Implicit is a return to primordial unity. But not for us!

'To us the return of the Messiah means more separation. The Messiah will give his seal of approval to separateness or so we believe.

'Then it means that we learnt nothing form our long and painful history!

For a while they observe in silence the men in prayers, austere and sombre, solemn in their long black coats and hats, not bothered by the heat. Clara oscillates between sadness and sympathy at this show of reverence to the past, long declared obsolete by the Masters. She muses a while longer, feeling a growing sensation of discomfort in the centre of her being, a vague anxiety.

Breaking the silence, Levinson makes this strange remark, 'Imagine a minor actress playing Desdemona's nurse who imagines herself the central character of the play and figures out that all the other characters count for less. The play was written for her and her alone; she occupies centre stage, Shakespeare wove the entire plot around her; the others simply fill in the gap, their presence cannot be explained nor justified.

'What point are you trying to make?

'Well, he continues unperturbed by Clara's cutting remark, this man wailing and swaying is doing just that. He believes that he shores up the entire human drama, that he carries the entire world on his shoulders like Atlas.

'To each his fantasy, replies Clara visibly not in the mood to take the debate further. The spectacle of puritanical men praying before the Wall is reawakening painful memories she had shirked for years. She feels vulnerable, unprotected, a wave of panic sweeps over her, she wants to flee. She takes a few deep breaths to calm herself.

She walks slowly to the Wailing Wall where a Hassid at prayers is swaying rhythmically from side to side. Clad in a long black coat and wearing a large-brimmed fur hat, he is in deep concentration.

'Don't' move any further, women are not permitted to invade the space of men. You are trespassing, intervenes Levinson feeling a mounting sense of unease.

'You know what, exclaims Clara, many light years separate this man at prayer from us. He is a relic from the past, primeval man time forgot.

'What I find disquieting is that this man is offering his prayers to a wall that was never part of the Temple of Solomon. This wall was built nearly 1000 years after Solomon; centuries after the Temple had been destroyed. What is he offering his prayers to?

'Devotion feeds on itself; it requires no logic, no grounds. The devout I knew had a horror of reason, they advocated impulsive devotion as unrivalled sign of their towering spirituality. As I observe this relic from the past, I make out the axis around which our tradition revolves: the masculine ego. The ego which clings to segmentation, disorientation and dislocation as it moves away from the centre. As mankind advances under the force of evolution, this man at prayer stands still, rooted, unable to tell the real from the unreal, the core from the shell, the life from the form.

'He is engrossed in the world of form which by its very nature is unreal. I shed all this long ago and if there is regret it is at not having dropped this dead weight long before. I lament my past misguided loyalty. In my dark moments, it all comes back to haunt me. Let's move away, this scene hurls me back to a bleak period of my life, my own prehistoric times!

They leave this place in haste. Clara looks distressed. Levinson guides her to a quiet spot away from the Wall and its disagreeable associations. She sits down and sips some water. Feeling refreshed she suggests they continue their visit. 'You need some rest, he insists'. 'I feel better, besides this may be our last chance to visit the sites.

'Appearances can be deceiving, says Clara calmer. The path of evolution is not linear; it takes various twists and turns. This man at prayer may be evolved but in this life, he may have taken a lesser form of expression to be of service, to make Karmic adjustments.

'He is to be admired really.

'Every human being is to be admired. If over aeons religion was his forte, he probably served each and every god known, except for this one god, because it is now or never, this age is coming to a close. It is unlikely that humanity will ever relapse to the worship of the Father.

'I have read of developed souls who, across time, have travelled the evolutionary path but not necessarily in the linear mode. Pilgrim on the spiritual path he may have sampled all forms of religious expressions, tested all creeds, tried out all skin colours, adored countless imaginary gods.

'In fairness to our ancestors, it is not that simple, devotion uses the imagination for a reason. The only way they knew of explaining physical reality and this should not be derided. Without their effort at making sense of their world, the world would not be what it is.

'You are right, things are complex. The man at prayer is standing at the point where time, ideas and place collide. Arrested in a fantasised past, faltering in the present, clinging to notions long redundant. He is rocking and rolling before a wall which never was part of the Temple Solomon built for the national god, but which housed … the Goddess! Solomon denied allegiance to the god he built the Temple for. Confused? He has every right to be.

No woman in sight. Women are banished to another area away from the righteous eyes of men at prayer. Women are unholy objects of distraction, inanity, triviality and defilement.

'What a strange world, says Clara. Men reel in prayer before the ruins of the Temple to the Goddess, yet women are forbidden to stand there! The Temple housed a Goddess – sacrilege, profanity! The Temple was a site of idolatry yet men pray to it!

'This is the problem with polarity and we are the keepers of polarity. The world is supported by the two pillars of the masculine and feminine principles. When one falls, the other of necessity should fall too. Not so with patriarchy and monotheism! For thousands of years we have promoted, legislated and perpetuated one aspect of polarity, diminishing the other.

'That's right! How to explain exile, if not in the light of polarity tempered with?

'There are many ways of explaining exile; disregard of polarity is one of them.

'It is more fundamental. Patriarchy in downgrading feminine energy - the soul/Eve - upset equilibrium in the world. Balance was disrupted, order was disturbed. Both must be restored under the laws of Karma and evolution.

'Again, how else can we explain the many exiles? Do we learn anything?

'The world does. Enlightenment comes from elsewhere.

'This Wall is a relic of a past in which the god of creation was revered by created man. 'Creator' and 'created' meet at this point. Man in form adoring the creator of form. But what of the formless, uncreated, timeless, unborn?

'It sneaked unnoticed into the heart of the Temple where Solomon glorified the Goddess Asherah. Solomon saw the rupture of the cosmic order and in reclaiming the feminine principle he tried to restore balance.

'The historian Josephus said of the Temple which stood on this spot that it was 'believed to have god as its inhabitant'. But did it? And who believed it? The healthy scepticism of Josephus is to be emulated.

They continue their leisurely promenade through the lively streets of Jerusalem, in direction of Meah Shearim, the medieval city where time stands still. It resembles the medieval streets of the disappearing Jewish world. Cut off from the world it refuses to look beyond its imprisoning walls. The view literally and figuratively is restricted, cramped, and oppressive. Meah Shearim is a strange world in which men dress in long black coats, wear large-brimmed fur hat in the scorching heat and where women shave their heads. They flaunt a mode of dress that connects them to their ancestors of Russia and Poland.

Nothing changes, nothing moves on. The vital impulse has lost its dynamic flow in this back water where life seems suspended. Sunlight hardly penetrates the narrow streets and as sunlight is life, it seems that they are turning their back on the source of life itself. This is the Forbidden City. The men walk with their fringe garments showing, the children look frail and pale, little girls have their arms covered. The women are dressed modestly in old-fashioned dresses, their shaved heads concealed under a wig or scarf. There is no concern for fashion, looks or elegance, why bother with the present when the past will do! The streets are closed off with barriers and signs which read, 'Entrance for women immodestly dressed, tourists and groups, STRICTLY FORBIDDEN'

'This place makes me shudder, says Clara, I brought a light cardigan in anticipation, will they throw me out?

'I want to go in. I must visit this relic from a lost age, is the provocative reply.

'I suggest you don't, warns a soldier guarding the area. These people have a reputation for reacting to any threat to their privacy.

'Why do they respond aggressively?

'It goes back a long way, replies the soldier. Long ago in Europe they were always keen to get into a fight with the followers of the Gaon de Vilna. Over there you can walk, he adds pointing in the opposite direction.

'Thank you for this insight, says Clara to the soldier. Two Judaism appeared two centuries ago, at each other's throat. The one god, two people! What happened to the lost dream of unity?

They venture into the narrow streets with overhanging balconies that look oriental. 'It's like walking in the 'mellahs' of Marrakech or Meknes, remarks Clara. These children are pale, sad, lifeless, do they ever see the sun? In one of the sunniest places on Earth, they should be healthy and active.

'This is what happens when religion governs all aspects of life. These people suffered terribly. Many originate in Poland, a Christian country. And so you have two conflicting patriarchal, monotheistic traditions, both bearing down on them, conflicting yet oddly similar, the Christian being the most dogmatic, unbending, puritanical of the two. And you get this, Levinson adds with a nod and a sweeping gesture.

Levinson & his father

'My relationship with my father was in the Freudian mode. We never got on; he seemed to hold a mulish grudge against me. A deeply religious man, he expressed neither love nor joy, his religious instinct was essentially gloomy. Everything I said, did or studied met with disapproval, he saw me as a foe in spite of my efforts. Before going to university I took a year out to earn some money and gain some experience of business.

On review I think I cut short learning to appease him. I decided to work in his business, again to win his approval and evade his sarcasm. I soon noticed a few irregularities in the accounts; I immediately informed him, thinking that I was doing him a favour. To my surprise I was met with the usual derisive remarks; he wanted me out of the way convinced that I was a trouble maker.

'Well, so much for a godly man, remarks Johansson!

'God and Mammon made peace to torment me, continues Levinson. In counselling therapy, my therapist pointed out that my father may have been either jealous or embarrassed by me. He was slack in his business deals and I had discovered by chance that the upright, righteous man who inspired awe to all in the family and at the synagogue was not what he appeared to be, and I had found him out. The animosity between us grew in intensity, until I was forced to leave. After his death, I saw him in a vivid dream, he asked forgiveness. I was both moved and surprised. I went to a renowned medium to investigate further. My father, he told me, had to redress for heavy karma accrued in previous lives. As a Roman centurion he would take pleasure in finishing off those who were dying on the crosses. Later as a medieval knight he sold himself to the highest bidding rulers in need of soldiers of fortune willing to take part in the long Crusades against the Infidels. The burden of his past actions was so great that he intentionally chose the 20th century to reincarnate, possibly the most harrowing century. Born in Poland, he was captured by the Russians, incarcerated for several years in a Soviet labour camp, before reaching Europe where he joined the Resistance movement against Hitler. He was making amends by fighting the greatest evil of the century, the greatest evil of all times. He had been overwhelmed all his life by feelings of intense guilt and self-loathing he never understood and which he tried to overcome by immersing himself in strict religious life.

'He was asking for forgiveness and it is fitting that it should be to a light worker, a worker of the Hierarchy. He was resolving his past.

Johansson & his father

The two men were walking silently, subdued by the beauty of the sunset absorbed in their thoughts. A feeling of timelessness, of unchanging perfection came over them.

'Is this a religious feeling, muses Levinson?

'Yes. Cosmic energy is everywhere and everything, life ever-flowing, ever-changing, ever-moving. My father believed that god lives in books; he died a desperate man.

'He was a country vicar, but was he a man who seeks god in all life?

'I admired and feared my father, replies Johansson who delays his answer. With a mass of blond hair, a short blond beard, tall and well built, he was truly impressive. A country parson he lacked the sophistication of town rectors and resorted to a sentimental religiosity well suited to the country folks who came to him for solace. He was in my childish imagination like the saints who ornate church windows, stylised, idealised, remarkable and at the same time not human in the usual sense. At university I enrolled on a theology course to satisfy him and emulate him. I engaged with him in vehement discussions, which soon turned into power struggle, as he had to win the argument. Increasingly irritable he withdrew further into his study and into his church. I interpreted his behaviour as disapproving of my evident lack of faith. He no longer encouraged discussion, but when questioned he would burst out in a pious rage. Intelligent discourse was impossible. He became ill and spent days alone in his study neglecting his duties. I would creep into his room in the hope of provoking him to a conversation that would help clear things in my mind. My sincere questions were met with strict theological answers, cold formulations devoid of life and feeling. Later I realised that he was not angry at me but at himself for he had never dared to admit to his dwindling faith. He reproached himself his fundamental doubts. He had all his life believed or tried to believe in a god he did not know, had no intimate feeling for. He died a broken man, convinced that he had been forsaken.

'My father, in all his weakness was like yours, a theologian; he lived by doctrine and dogmas. He never questioned, imbued since childhood with the notion that intelligent questioning was an act of rebellion against god and that the intellect is sinful. Forbidden to think he absorbed himself in repetitive religious practice and tedious study, regurgitating what men of past generations had pre-digested for him. He believed in a god who lives in books, a god who demands, controls, judges and bullies man into submission.

'The god of fear of my father, replies Johansson.

'The god of fear! His god demanded fear. The core obligation of any Jew is to fear god. He never thought of god as a living being that man can approach in a meaningful interaction. A direct experience of god he never had and thought not only impossible, but positively heretical. He was convinced that the Hassidim who claim mystical visions were deluded. Towards the end of his life he became ill and doctors were called to ease his suffering. One of them confided to my mother,' I cannot cure him, his illness is not of the body but of the soul'. He would send the doctors away with angry words, 'my body is dying, let it die, it is my soul that is sick. It is always the soul that is sick and if you don't know this, you should not be a doctor. The body of itself is nothing, the soul is everything. I know now and it's too late!'

The day before his death, he asked for me. He was too weak to open his eyes. 'Don't' mourn, I am free now, I no longer have to pretend. I learned nothing from any one or from any book.

'You are a learned man, I said to appease him.

'Nonsense, I learned nothing. I knew more when I was a child, because I sensed things, my inner senses were alive, but they took that away, they take everything away. For what? ... The religion of the body. It gives no answer to the big questions of life. What they filled my head with is sterile. To them man does not count, they don't serve humanity'. And with a painful, mocking laughter, he went on, 'there is no God, because when they take the soul away, they take everything away. Listen, listen ... There is only one truth and you are that truth'. He sobbed in despair, 'I lived a pointless life and I die a renegade'. He remained silent, lifeless, suddenly he grabbed my hand and in a last exhausting stab .... 'I am free, free at last, but you understand that. I cursed you for knowing what I did not know, what I was afraid to know. Never forget, promise me! Promise me!' 'I promise, I replied'.

Exhausted he kept quiet for a moment, I dared not question, certain that he was gone. But he had more to say before shedding the mortal coil, 'man is his own saviour, don't believe those who tell you otherwise.... they are afraid of the truth ... they want to keep you in the dark with them'. He fell back in exhaustion whispering something I could not hear. Regaining some strength he said with visible effort, 'you are everything and they want you to believe that you are nothing'. He grabbed my hand, 'you are that truth'; promise me never to forget.... I was deceived'. His head fell back onto the pillow. After a long pause he grabbed my arm and whispered, 'I deceived myself .... no man is deceived ... man deceives himself'. He was getting more agitated and distraught, 'I lived my life in a shroud... It is the livings who need to be resurrected not the dead. But I am free to be alive now. Odd isn't it? Know this, there is no god.... I struggled all my life with this … my lack of faith. Nothing can touch me now, I am free at last. There is no god, there is only man and he has forsaken himself. Be who you are, the rest is the delusion of the insane'. He lapsed into a coma.

Levinson & Johansson

'I am not a Jew, neither am I a Christian for that matter, mumbles Johansson, I dropped religious form. I shed all that binds with the past, all that relates, all that imprisons.

'The enthusiasts tend to be satisfied with the form. Try to mention anything else, it is blasphemy, I know well!

'Unquestioning response will come under increasing scrutiny in years to come. Evolved humanity will have the keepers of religious form under scrutiny.

'I share your optimism, keepers of religious form watch out, broods Levinson! Human beings will examine your every move, listen to your every word and poke about your motives. They will examine the evidence and arrive at a sound inference. The realisation dawns that the Jewish condition is ultimately an illusion mankind has kept going; a useful illusion the world needed. It is rather like a stage performance of Oedipus, we know it is an illusion but what an illusion! The Greeks used to send their servants to the theatre. Thinking individuals are poised to figure out that the Jewish condition is of their own making, they are perpetuating it. There will be no anger, no hostility, no judgment. They will realise that individuals borrow the Jewish garment for one life time.

'Driven by the desire to revisit Earth?

'Yes, but it goes further than that … in order to do one of two things, explains Levinson. One is to become psychologists, doctors, musicians, scientists and humanitarians. They make the conscious decision to return to Earth with a view to engaging in activities that enhance and empower mankind.

'And the other, asks Johansson tantalisingly?

'Or to become the keepers of 'the law that killeth'. Inertia, stagnation, stupor!

'Quite, many clutch at belief not to assist people but to freeze them in their tract, interrupt the natural flow of life and hinder progress.

'Quite right, the disturbing thing is that they are doing 'god's work', whatever that is! Yet, all the while they frustrate the endeavour of the Hierarchy. By an unfortunate irony they resist the emergence of the Messiah they fervently yearn for every day of their lives! Unconscious of it all!

'We'll be watching like hawks. We'll ask urgent questions evaded until now, 'Why do human beings return disguised in pious clothing? What business is it of theirs to encroach on the progress of mankind? Do they not know that the world has changed since the days of the Golden Calf?

They pause to gaze at the light. They feel drained in mind and body. But the force that drives them mercilessly steers them on.

'The human energy field is an accurate video recorder, nothing is ever erased. Therefore no amount of fasting or praying will change things, resumes Levinson. Scores have to be settled by the actors of the karmic drama. It is futile to pray for things to change since the gods have nothing to do with it. Our destiny is of our own making, we alone can change it. 'Remember, ye are gods'. As gods we have the power to 'create' for good of ill. The responsibility for the perpetuation of the Jewish condition rests squarely on the shoulders of mankind; it is as much a state of mind as it is a biological reality. All forms of racial discrimination will disappear; they served their malign purpose, but are now redundant. Mankind is coming of age, the old tricks of the past are no longer appropriate.

Clara's dream

At breakfast Clara is lost in thought. Jeremy asks her if she had slept well, and as if waking up, she replies that she had a very strange dream still lingering

'Would you share it with us, we will try to shed some light.

'I have this dream at regular intervals, of all the recurrent dreams I have, this one is the most persistent. It is Saturday lunchtime; I arrive at the Rabbi's home where I am greeted warmly by his wife. I inform her that I have discarded all traces of religious loyalty and shed all tribal attachment. She smiles and invites me in. We walk into a room where the rabbi, seated at a table, looks through the window unaware of our presence, lost in thought. He is wearing a white shirt in the style worn in the 19th century, large sleeves and scarf-collar. He has no beard, no hat. I ask the rabbanite 'Is Rabbi Simeon having lunch with us? She invariably replies, 'Where he is, it does not matter any more, it is of no concern, it has no meaning now'.

Jeremy listening intently suggests,' She seems to be telling you that he is doing fine where he is and that the beliefs he held on Earth are now devoid of meaning for him, if not altogether forgotten. Indeed we are being urged to rethink the beliefs we accepted unquestioningly. We are being reminded that religion belongs to Earth; it was an attempt by earlier generations to make sense of their world. As an unsympathetic friend of mine put it 'it is a tissue of fancies, fantasies and fallacies, a cloud that obscures the vast expanse of the skies'. We must look at the world in a transparent light.

'Yes, I have arrived at this realisation, but last night's dream brings in a new element. The rabbi was, as in previous dreams, sitting by the window, looking out, unaware of his surroundings. The rabbanite was wearing a nun's habit, she uttered with a solemn look, 'the Shabbat meal has no longer any meaning, nothing matters any more. I saw my dead uncles, all learned rabbis back in Russia before the war, they were sitting round an empty dark room, faintly lit by candles, I went to my uncle Menahem, he was asleep, I looked around, they were all asleep. Alarmed, I questioned my escort who explained that my uncles felt betrayed because God was not there to greet them at the gates, nor the Messiah nor the Prophets. They lamented that their religious lives had come to nothing. A few guides or mentors present in the room were encouraging my uncles to wake up, 'Now is the time to leave the past behind and move on; this is no time for sleep, you must prepare for your next incarnation'. What they had held sacred was foreign to their new surroundings, it belongs to life on Earth they were told. They are now asleep, waiting for the Messiah, and they refuse to wake up until he comes to deliver Israel.'

'What a sad story, remarks Jeremy. Tales abound of people who refuse to adjust to their new world and go on clinging to what they were familiar with while on Earth They fall asleep, waiting for someone to deliver them.

'They may have to wait a long time. The universe never offered mankind the painless option of a saviour, but the harsh, lonely road of self-realisation, inserts Tara. Each one is his own saviour as Buddha taught.

'Right, emphasises Jeremy. Evolution, karma and reincarnation are the painful paths to salvation. It has taken humanity millions of years to get where we are today.

'As for the rabbanite, suggests Tara, she may have chosen the Jewish form to have children if she was a nun in former lives.

'What about those who have been captured in their sphere of influence, asked Clara with some anguish?

'Those captured in their orbit were foolish enough to be manipulated and accept entrapment and capitulation, snaps Levinson!

'Sure, reflects Jeremy, in the last analysis we choose those who mess up our lives! As long as we evade the in-dwelling Master silently waiting to inspire us, we shall fall pray to others. We need different gods at different times in our lives to satisfy the needs of the moment. In each incarnation we come back to discover new things and grapple with new ideas. Ideas are personalised into gods, so we worship gods, until we wake up to the realisation that they are a figment of our imagination.

'You see, says Levinson, in a thoughtful if somewhat polemical mood, ours is a world of incongruity. Nothing is quite what it seems. You have sincere people locked on a certain rung on the evolutionary ladder who expect all of us to be on that rung with them! Captured on the astral/emotional plane, they are retarding the progress of all Jews, indeed the progress of all, for there is one humanity and what affects one individual affects all. They feel a pious contempt for those who refuse to get stuck with them. They regard their own behaviour as the model we must all emulate.

'The genuine article, all others are fake, laughs Tara.

'Is this not the case with all of us who at one time played the religion game according to the rules while knowing nothing, notes Clara?

306

'Let us examine the rabbanite further, ponders Tara. She serves a people she claims to love. Is it not the same people she once cursed in the silence of the cloister for killing her god? In this incarnation she switched loyalty to serve the god of the people she held responsible for the death of her god.

'It makes sense, there you have a woman - this is a strong probability - who adored one god and pledged eternal odium to Jews in a former life, reflects Jeremy. In this life she decides to borrow a Jewish body to get enmeshed in Jewish life. There is a reversal of feelings. She now professes an unflinching love for Jews. This love she transports to the four corners of the world. It shows in her behaviour, her mode of dress, her ritual routines and ardent avowal of faith. She must implant her faith in those same Jews she blamed in former lives. Pure conjecture of course, yet a real probability.

'The god of love is now a dim memory. As a nun she assumed control over her mind and body. In this life, in her rabbanite role it is the dead rabbis who dictate from beyond the grave what she must do with her body.

'From autonomy to subjection. We have to experience all facets of life, notes Jeremy. This may be a loss or a gain, depending on your view point. In this life she came to learn what it's like not to own her own body.

Role reversal

'What we are discussing is the reversal of roles, reflects Levinson. Think of the atheist, think of the keyed up believer, they are the two sides of the same coin, and not just psychologically. One denies vigorously what the other affirms as vigorously: the existence of a god they know nothing about. The Jewish world is as much of the atheist as it is of the believer. The two poles are tilting this way or that way. The atheist is so resolute about the non-existence of god that he seems to be suffering from an inverted form of belief, building defences around himself, fighting and denying the very possibility. Some show a kind of evangelical passion in denying the existence of God.

'While the believer endeavours to believe, continues Clara. He struggles to uphold his shaky beliefs. Below the surface lurks the tormenting question: 'What am I doing? What if it is a figment of my imagination? Where is the truth in all this? What proof do I have, how do I know? I have no inner, immutable realisation; I don't even know what it is I believe in'!

'The atheist denies a faith that gnaws clandestinely and the believer denies a doubt that torments him furtively, rounds up Levinson. The religious is grappling with his impiety; the atheist is battling with his disallowed belief! Each travelling down the narrow path of the Jewish condition, experimenting with the opposite pole of what his past experience seems to impel him to do. Paradoxically, the atheist may be drawing closer to his soul, while the believer is ever more estranged from his soul by the rigidity of his piety. The atheist, often endowed with a searching mind and subtle feelings does not relate to the harsh god that is presented to him. No quite so with the believer who before this life may have found that the god resonated with his own nature.

'The cosmic Law of Attraction: 'like attracts like'.

Master Sananda on Solomon

Levinson and Clara decide it is time to find out about Solomon. A private meeting is arranged with Jeremy. The questions are fired at the Master after the initial greetings:

'What was the motive on the part of the Hierarchy in sending Solomon, with all his glory and glamour? To make social changes and resume Temple activity? To rekindle the cult of the Goddess, in spite of opposition?

'Solomon was a very dynamic being, as you would appreciate. He was someone who came into this life with a very strong vision. He foresaw in many ways the age that the human race is at present entering. And his mission, as he perceived it, was to do all he could to; first of all, make insurance policies for this time, to safeguard this time.

'The present?

'Yes, the present. He also laid down, principally in terms of energy matrices, patterns of energy. Using physical forms to hold those patterns of energy. What could be seen as 'keys' to open the awareness of humanity to the realisation of the vision he held. He was born into a position where for him to achieve prominence was natural and fairly easy so that he could focus on his core mission. You are quite right, he emphasised strongly the importance of female energy, on a general principle. The balancing of polarities would be that principle; he recognised that male energy in the world around him was becoming far too dominant, a threat to the maintaining and safeguarding of peace, really. And he thought to redress that balance in any way he could. In more esoteric ways, he formulated techniques for holding across thousands of years, these forms of energy I called 'keys' which are in the process of being re-awakened now.

Naturally he did not do this all by himself. He received much angelic help and guidance from the Higher Realms and there were places within the Temple where the energy was balanced to such an extent that it was possible for Higher Beings to manifest in quite clear forms. And so he was able to receive clear and strong guidance he could follow to lay down, to hide away for safety, those secrets he had been entrusted with for this time. This is the time those secrets or 'keys' are being re-discovered bit by bit. Principally at the moment in the form of energy connections which are being made, which are happening inwardly with people, but there may also be physical discoveries that are about to be made in a few years time, you will see!

'You mean scientific discoveries?

'I mean that some of the artefacts he hid the energy 'keys' in, may be re-discovered.'

The encounter ends at the moment a visitor is announced. A smartly dressed middle-aged man enters the room. A sense of awe descends upon them; they stare at him in silence.

'My name is Menahem; I am a lecturer at the university and a friend of Benzaccai. We often discuss his work which has played a part on the development of my ideas. For this reason he has entrusted me to bring you the next chapters of The Hebrew Gods.

'Where is he, asks Jeremy, is he safe?

'Oh, he is safe. He is staying with a family just outside Jerusalem. He asked me to bring you these papers, as you know they will be read to you and then returned to him for publication'. Menahem accepts an invitation to share the meal. Over a desert of grapes and figs the reading begins.

Rabbi Moses & Sanaka on King Solomon

Rabbi Moses is in a thoughtful and sombre mood. He is turning his attention to a topic that had preoccupied him years before. In his scholarly past, back in Vilna, he had endorsed the accepted version passed down. Not surprisingly he had disapproved of the rebellious attitude king Solomon had adopted. Solomon's position lay outside the narrow band of permitted experience. Moses was fascinated by this prestigious renegade who cared nothing about his god and dismissed the certainties of his time. Solomon had cast to the winds the core of Hebrew doctrine by introducing idolatry in the sacred Temple. One morning after meditation Sanaka, intuitively anticipating Moses request took him to the temple where a statue of Tara, the Goddess stood, glistening in the partial dimness of the room, lit up with oil lamps and candles which cast an unreal, dream-like glow on the face of the Goddess who radiates kindness and love.

Sanaka was observing Moses who showed no surprise, by now familiar with the curious decisions of his master. On returning to their study room, Moses emboldened by the experience in the temple utters:

'One aspect of polarity is diminished and the other enhanced.

'Equilibrium was disrupted. The Father stable, rigid, immovable, unchanging tipped the balance and the natural bond with Earth was dented. The Father as expression of man's growing sense of self was strengthening its hold. The natural order was dislocated. Primitive people lived in harmony with natural law; they saw Earth as a living being, a nurturing Mother. In his primeval simplicity man respected the world around him. The Hebrew, yielding to his rising self became estranged from the nurturing influence of Earth; his forceful god reflects his growing sense of selfhood. It is in the nature of the human self to separate, divide, isolate, and fragment.

'Solomon was aware of this, enquires Moses not yet convinced?

'Solomon stepped in to redress the balance. In rekindling the Goddess, he aimed to lessen the force of the lower self. The feminine is not just the natural opposite of the masculine. The feminine energy is also the intuitive, sensitive, creative aspect of the human mind, present in all of us. But there is a paradox, while the feminine is pictured as the instinctual, dark aspect of human nature; it is also pictured as the higher expression of the human being. Asherah is the nurturing, sensitive Mother. Asherah esoterically is the cosmic aspect of man's nature.

'Solomon was active in restoring the primeval balance? The light is dawning on me. It has nothing to do with belief or disbelief. It is more important, it filters through to the core of Creation, to the very meaning.

'Well done my son, smiles Sanaka with visible joy. Solomon was attempting to bring back on the stage of the human drama the forces that brought about the universe: the physical and the spiritual. Solomon was rekindling Moses' vision of an enlightened society, and his method was adapted to the time. Realising that such an elevated ideal was an unattainable goal, he settled for a more realistic alternative.

'Both were concerned with the progress of the people, with humanity, but exile jeopardise their intentions. What is the **role of exile?**

'Both were concerned with the progress, the liberation, the expansion of consciousness of the people. Instead they grappled with the growing power of the self, the assertive self that shaped the rigid code of behaviour you know so well. At the time of Solomon the triumphant self had a body of legislation to use as a buttress. The successful self enlisted the god-force to become firmly established. The course of enlightenment was submerged by the wave of ritualism and legality.

'How do I come in? Surely not to reinstate the feminine principle and lessen the masculine, enquires Moses anxiously? I have no wish to bring back the Goddess. He rebels against the very thought.

Sensing Moses' inherited aversion for the feminine principle, Sanaka replies:

'The feminine is an aspect of the Divine; the feminine is an aspect of yourself! The soul includes all; the soul unites all opposites. The soul selects the gender of its ego in any incarnation because the soul must experience all aspects of the feminine and of the masculine. In trivialising, in marginalizing the feminine you slight the Divine's vision for the world. The world was constructed around the primordial feminine and masculine principles and in excluding one you upset balance in the world. When in the future your scientists probe the atoms, they will find the primary opposites in the smallest particles of matter. You cannot imperil cosmic stability just because you are afraid of the feminine aspect in the world and in yourself!

'We know not of the soul choosing its gender, or choosing anything at all! Man we believe is thrown on the Planet for reasons that god alone knows. Man is the passive, unconscious recipient of his life. His life is inflicted on him without his having the right to know why. Man's life is foreign to him.

'And so the emphasis on the body and the bloodline! Man lives his life in a daze. His life is an extended dawn period, a promise that never materialises. In middle age he is an infant abiding by the Father's rules, conforming to the Father's will, fearful of the Father's s disapproval.

'A terrible predicament, sighs Moses.

'The central role women played in ancient society was a threat to the rise of male ascendancy. The importance of women was evident in the presence of the Goddess who loves and makes no demands. With the rise of patriarchy Mother Earth became a stranger to distrust, the same Earth that gives life and sustains life! The human body is made up of all the elements found in the earth. Earth is the womb that creates life. The nurturing, all-embracing Goddess was removed; in her place patriarchy erected a symbolic Tower of Babel to house the egotistical god of man.

'The struggle between love and fear, compassion and the rule of law, inclusiveness and prejudice, empathy and intolerance.

'Only the Initiates penetrate into the world of meaning, the rest make do with the shell. It is the shell you studied all your life, Moses.

'The Hebrew scholars have searched for unity, unity behind polarity.

'By eliminating polarity? Eliminating resolves nothing; only understanding resolves. To achieve unity you must transcend polarity, not by destroying it but by resolving it! Polarity is ultimately an illusion, a kind of ladder that man must climb in order to find reality beyond. Polarity, primordial purpose of Creation is dealt a severe blow by patriarchy. Paradoxically, as you disturb polarity, you reinforce polarity to a degree that was unknown in the ancient world: you divide space, time, matter, Planet and people into two neat categories, good and bad, holy and unholy and you erect a wall around your classifications.

'Duality is a reality, we did not invent it. We recognise its existence.

'With much creative imagination! In the beginning there was light and dark, man and woman, good and evil but this was not enough, you had to subdivide: holy / unholy, pure / impure, Jew / non-Jew, pious / impious, sacred / profane! Spiritual evolution was delayed but not lost. Man is growing in self-confidence: his intellectual competence, his capacity for love and his capability to take charge of his life are developing. He is learning to act responsibly, no longer will he look to an elusive god for direction, no longer will he look for enemies to blame either! It dawns on him that the root of suffering is embedded in him. Buddha taught that each man is responsible for his own suffering, except that the cause is unknown to him and may stretch back many life times, centuries, millennia even.

'All is not lost, says Moses with a sigh of relief. Mankind has found a way of circling around the added limitations.

'That's right! The human spirit is not defeated for ever; it finds a way of triumphing over adversity. Paradoxically, had it not been for your lasting fascination with the human ego, its fears, its dynamism, its artificial boundaries, its separative leaning, its intolerance, its fanaticism, Western civilisation may never have arisen. The self that shaped your law is in part responsible for one of the most brilliant civilisations the

Earth has known. Much good has come of it. You displaced the cosmic Soul for the god of selfhood, yet the search for the meaning of life, the quest for the nature of the universe and the longing for the spirit produced some of the most insightful philosophical theories and ingenious theological doctrines. It inspired music, painting, poetry, drama, architecture, all the beauty and wonder than man brought into existence.

'Should mankind regret or welcome the vast movement of civilisation?

'Welcome it of course! The Creator sustains this universe in order to expand his own light, this can only happen in polarity, only in space and time. Now you have been instrumental in fulfilling this purpose. In future, many scientists will be born among the Jewish people.

'To help or hinder the process?

'To help naturally, to make their unique contribution. And for the reasons just mentioned, your fascination with the world of matter, time and space.

'But Buddha stated that both Samsara and Maya make up the world of illusion? Must we contribute to prolong illusion?

'Remember that the cosmic Mind created the world of illusion, this universe of polarity, for his own classroom. You are ideally suited for the roles. It may seem a long detour back to unity, but man is evolving all the time and there is much learning along the way. The cosmic Mind and humanity are a team in this learning endeavour. God relies on humanity for this. Idle he certainly is not; he did not need the 7th day of rest! If indeed there is a 7th day it is to work not to rest!

'So there is no 1st day of Creation, no 7th day either as no one is resting. And God is at school on this Planet! Pure heresy!

'The truth is exhilarating don't you think, asks Sanaka laughing? In the end, it may be that your religious materialism has rerouted mankind back to the Source, back to the beginning.

'Is scientific enquiry the way back?

'Yes, science will signal and head the way back. Religion is bankrupt; it has deceived mankind, it failed to be the bridge it was intended to be. It is a mummified prehistoric giant that does not reflect the laws of the Universe.

'It was given by God at Sinai, mumbles Moses.

'No God ever was at Sinai.

'What of the deeper meaning?

'What of it? The Initiates of all generations have penetrated the world of meaning. Why did you muddle through with the coverings and the fantasies you built around those coverings?

'Is it my assignment to hinder their efforts?

'In part. Your assignment is thorny since you have embarked on the Path of Return. I know the agony you live through. This is the path each initiate, each disciple must tread, the path humanity is treading. You will go back to Vilna to tell them of the coming of the Kingdom of God.

'This has a biblical ring ...

'It has, chuckles Sanaka, not quite what they want to hear though! To bring to humanity knowledge of the reality of the Hierarchy, of the Divine Plan, of the coming Redeemer Lord Maitreya, of the all-encompassing presence of the Planetary Logos known as the Ancient of Days in your books. Most importantly it is to tell men that God is Love, that Maitreya is Love, that the Ancient of Days is Love, that the Hierarchy is Love! It means that the reign of fear is coming to an end. The materialism of isolation, fear, attachment, hostility, submission and authority is fading. This is your assignment!

'Why me? I am neither Krishna nor Buddha. This is too much!

'If not you who? You have been prepared over many incarnations for this mission. Science will rediscover what Buddha taught: the underlying oneness of all life and the conscious nature of the universe. Science will demonstrate that Maya - time and space - is an illusion, that matter can be reduced to minute bits of light, invisible atoms endowed with energy. They will uncover the universal energy which lies behind all the forces known to man.

'May I be so bold as to ask how you know this?

Smiling, Sanaka replies, 'not at all. First of all as you know I spent many years in Europe as part of my training, I studied at various universities. I travelled extensively and met some remarkable scientists and thinkers. In Tibet I studied with the Masters of Shamballa, this noble and erudite community whose knowledge of the physical and non-physical world is extensive. They are behind the great intellectual movements that come to the Earth.

'They are also the source of religious movements?

'They most certainly are. In the field of ideas, they are always influential, inspiring, stimulating, encouraging, always motivating. All ideas originate in the world of Ideas, the Ideal plane Plato refers to. They are received by the Hierarchy, analysed and sieved through before being released into the world of men. Nothing of what affect men is foreign to them.

Solomon by Sanaka

'Master Sanaka, how crucial were the Mysteries in Solomon's life?

'An interesting question, Moses. You are not idle in your quiet moments! First, I wish to dispel a myth your ancestors have cultivated, the Mysteries are not the product of primitive, idolatrous pagans. They are the Mysteries of life and of the cosmos and were imparted by the Hierarchy long ago to move mankind forward. Now to your question, the Mysteries celebrated the perfection of the Goddess.

'The Soul?

'Yes, the soul, the divine principle in man. Within Israel, the people worshipped the gods that gave them the solace they longed for. Solomon who shared this yearning devised a form of worship which satisfied the mood of the time.

'He was able to give expression to that inner need?

'That's right. Contrary to patriarchal belief, idolatry is not depraved; it grows out of the human soil. Attempts to block the idolatrous impulse trigger social unrest and emotional disquiet.

'If so it is the worship of the one god imposed from outside which is arbitrary and unnatural. Looking at our painful history who would doubt it? Who was Solomon, how was he able to express such a deep need?

'A king, but not any king. A Master sensitive to the mood of the time aligned himself with that desire, giving it expression and acceptance.

'He was a poet of love, passionate love, how can this be reconciled with his mission to enlighten?

'There is no contradiction. Solomon reinstates the Goddess, he also writes about passionate love, not human love, but the passionate longing for union with the soul. Solomon rekindles the Mysteries when he senses the Goddess. Not for Solomon the pious constraints and devout limitations which frustrate the soul in its journey towards the Light.

'He made his own rules, he transgressed every law.

'Every rabbinical law! He cared nought for man-made rules, he lived by cosmic Law. He lived on a different plane of existence, like you Moses; he would not be restrained by trifling human concern. He did not abide by marriage rules, if indeed there was such a thing! Marriage laws applied to women, not to men. Monogamy was potential, not actual; the religious powers dared not impose it on the men. Marriage was based on physical, social and above all survival concerns. Natural man would not tolerate monogamy. So the religious powers allowed additional wives, slave girls and concubines, a concession to man's natural urges, to prevent social strife.

'It is an oddity that a religion which intrudes on our intimacy should turn a blind eye to what amounts to sexual licence! The conviction is that god is present in the most intimate moments between man and wife!

'It is against this background of religious intolerance and indulgence to the flesh that Solomon stepped on a social stage in disarray. Sent out to restore equilibrium, play down religious power and curb clerical authority, he set out to weaken the patriarchal hold. His father, David had inaugurated a liberal climate in religious life. In one of the most repressive religious routine, religious diversity became part of the social fabric. Temples to foreign gods sprang up, religious tolerance was sanctioned. The 'chosen' people were becoming a more tolerant society!

'Why such preoccupation with woman?

'In ancient societies woman was priestess, prophet, healer, adviser, midwife, her role was crucial to the stability of the group. Woman is the mother of humanity. In the great Myths she is the feminine force, 'l'eternel feminin'. In Genesis Eve occupies central stage; she emerges out of a long sleep and questions. Patriarchy gets hold of the eternal myth and uses it to serve its own end; woman is devalued to make the case of patriarchy more convincing. Devotion to woman is banned by patriarchy. Yet woman lives on in the heart of man as a perfect ideal.

'This Solomon brings forth, this longing in the heart of man?

'Solomon is an inspired artist who restores the great Myths. In his poems and music he celebrates woman, life and love. The divine inspiration in man is feminine. When man salutes the feminine - the divine in him - his redemption will begin, he will journey consciously toward the Light. This is the theme of all great works of art: the hero goes into the wilderness in search of the eternal woman who will redeem him; he endures terrible trials along the way before he finds the Beloved. Orpheus journeys into the Underworld to find Eurydice, Tristan journeys in search of Iseult. Woman is the promise of Redemption, the promise of immortality.

'Art explores regions which ought to be the land of religion, notes Moses.

'The role of art is to express the mysteries of life which religion fails to do. Religion is bogged down into rules hostile to the soul of man. It has lost its way, if ever it had a way!

'They were given by god directly in 'bat kohl' or 'daughter of the Voice' to the rabbis who then translated the message into law.

'The God of Life never gave this law! It is 'the law that killeth' as the Master pointed out. How can Life be responsible for rules that imprison the spirit? God is interested in the journey of the soul through time and its eventual return. The God of Life is not interested in the game men play to ensnare the soul. So, the sacred feminine enters the Temple of Jerusalem and is reinstated in her former glory. Solomon was affirming the dignity of woman and her place in society. He was also introducing the notion of the soul to a people who lived in the shadow of Yahweh. The Goddess lives in the Temple of Shamballa as she does in the heart of all.

'Shall I have a glimpse of her?

'You will when you visit the Temple of the Masters. Union with the Goddess, union with the soul is now possible. With Solomon the soul as a vision of the Goddess enters man's life. Hope is dawning for humanity.

'Union with Yahweh was unthinkable, observes Moses. In our tradition god and man are two distinct entities, drawn to each other, but clearly different.

'It is a 'one looking up and the other looking down' type of relationship, remarks Sanaka, not the relationship of equals! Man and his gods belong to two conflicting worlds: matter and spirit are incompatible. With the Fall duality became ingrained. Patriarchy and monotheism anchored duality in human awareness. Solomon changes all that. Matter and spirit can unite; man can merge with the soul to achieve unity. Man can aspire to immortality. And having abandoned a Samsara god for the Goddess, Solomon also resolves duality; man can return to the One Reality. Solomon is infused with the spirit of the East.

'Not surprising, he came from Shamballa!

Solomon & Asherah

'Solomon loved Yahweh but he sacrificed and burnt incense on high places' wrote the biblical scribe. The 'high places' are the hills surrounding Jerusalem on which statues of the Goddess Asherah dominated the landscape. Even the Scriptures resort to self-deception: the Goddess lives in the heart of Solomon who is indifferent to the official god, Yahweh. The chronicler admits reluctantly: 'Solomon's heart was not whole with Yahweh his god'. Did Solomon, a Master of the Spiritual Hierarchy need Yahweh as his god? The rebellious Solomon disloyal to the ancestral deity followed in his father's footsteps. David lavished favours on the gods of the time to whom he built temples. The purists shrug it off as a temporary aberration. Aberration or inspired freedom? Solomon flattens prejudice and derides provincial outlook: he recognises other viewpoints.

'Not quite the democratic principles of Athens but getting there.

'It is! The celebrated king, guardian of tradition and pillar of the establishment, who rules by divine decree, unashamedly disregards the doctrine of the time, dismisses the conventional thinking of the day.

A silence follows in which Sanaka observes Moses.

'You look troubled, Moses my son.

'You read my soul, Master, I am reflecting on idolatry in ancient Israel where the people neglected Yahweh and worshipped strange gods. Even the great kings, David and Solomon built temples to foreign gods.

'Surely this is not a recent discovery, remarks Sanaka smiling with gentle irony. Remember also that affairs of state had something to do with it; there were social and international pressures. If building temples to Baal, Marduk or Asherah was necessary to ensure sound relations with neighbouring countries, so be it!

'I thought that integrity in religious matters was paramount, we died for it.

'So you did. Let us call to mind the story of Jacob. When Jacob set out to meet his brother Esau, he prepared for the encounter, he had two options, one was conciliation, the other war. So you see Jacob was behaving like a modern statesman. Is it new to you?

'No, I was well acquainted with it. But idolatry was regarded as an aberration and dismissed as such. The 'chosen' people of the true god could not be truly idolatrous! It was never seriously examined, but rather brushed over as a temporary anomaly not worthy of elaboration.

'Pity, replies Sanaka, aberrations have their reasons, if it was an aberration! But the religion of man behaves like man, dismissing things embarrassing, or things other than the semblance of the day. Had the law-makers analysed rather than dismiss, they would have made interesting discoveries. To dismiss is not only deceitful it is also damaging. To repress whole areas of our being is harmful. The human mind is a source of wonder deserving of respect, observation and study. All facets of the human mind, even the 'dark' corners merit respect. How can there be progress if entire facets of human nature are suppressed?

'Is it not what happens when the Tao is lost? When we no longer know that we are the Divine in human form walking the Earth, observes Moses now versed in the Wisdom.

'Absolutely, my son. When man forgets that he is the great Life walking the Earth than his humanity is diminished and his divinity forgotten. That is when rulers build rules to keep him under control, disempowered. The 'do & obey' is what the world is left with. But back to Solomon, tell me of your reflections.

'The great Temple was not to Yahweh dedicated, but to the Goddess Asherah or Esther in the Purim tale. The Hebrews never forgot the Goddess, she reappears under many guises. Yet at prayer we turn to the Temple unaware that it was dedicated to the Goddess and not to the god of patriarchy.

'The Goddess is alive and well, smiles Sanaka. Mankind has looked up to the heavens for help, guidance and protection and the Hierarchy have sent their ambassadors to remind man of his innate greatness. But man has a short memory; he soon reverts back to his old habit of seeing himself insignificant. The Beings who came from the Stars to inspire humanity became gods and the Egyptians built magnificent temples in alignment with the stars from which they came, Lyra, Orion, Sirius, and the Pleiades.

'The Hebrews who adopted cosmology - the science of the origins of the world - from Sumer and Egypt knew that it all started on the stars. The constellations are alluded to in a manner that does not distract from monotheism, the dominant idea of the time. We encounter the stars in the twelve sons of Jacob, the twelve Tribes, and the twelve loaves of bread in the Temple.

'That's right, continues Sanaka, the Hebrews turned to the advanced civilisations of Egypt, Sumer and Mesopotamia for knowledge. The gods of Egypt and Sumer visited

Earth long ago to teach mankind science, arts, morality, philosophy and crafts. The Masters who came from the stars taught that Maya the physical world if taken too seriously leads to disaster. They demonstrated that the nature of the universe is love and that progress for mankind is through love, understanding, conciliation and tolerance. Yet you insist on seeing Maya as truly real.

'Why love and compassion, why not knowledge, asks Moses, the scholar?

'Knowledge is of the intellect, it can get parched. Your profuse knowledge has not explained or removed suffering, it imparts nothing of your true nature, nor has it fostered self-reliance. It has not cultivated integration and wholeness. It has instead emasculated man by bullying him into submission. Disempowered man is cut off from the God within. It is not knowledge that created the universe, but the creative Life Force, the creative love energy. All over the enlightened world God has been identified with Love.

Moses feeling increasingly uneasy tries to redirect the conversation to a less distressing theme. 'Why revert to idolatry, is this a step forward?

'It depends on your point of view! In Maya all things exist in pairs, and as Buddha said to the fanatic who wanted to remove evil from the world, 'if you destroy evil, you destroy the world'. Maya is the world of duality, of good and evil, light and dark, masculine and feminine. Solomon sought to restore equilibrium since the cult of Yahweh was at odds with the cosmic order.

'Is this why when Elijah ordered the massacre of 400 priests of Baal who performed in Judea, he did not kill the priests of the Goddess Asherah?

'I think so, his swift response to the cult of Baal among his own people suggests he felt that equilibrium in society was overriding. So he had to compromise as all discerning rulers do. He also sensed that the people knew this intuitively; they needed the Goddess, the feminine principle to counter the rule of Yahweh. The people yearned for love not just harsh rule. Had he touched the Goddess, he would have triggered social unrest! A subtle political move!

'Or did he secretly sympathise with the people, enquires Moses? Did he know that the feminine principle must not be tempered with?

'As an ambassador of the Hierarchy he almost certainly did, but he also had to be a religious and political leader, a conflict of interests! He had to compromise all the way. Asherah was loved, whereas Yahweh had to be imposed; his rule was pledged by the priesthood. Yahweh the official god secures monotheism, the dominant doctrine of the day.

The friends have been quiet for a while, it is time for them to take a break to reflect and comment.

'Monotheism was a quantum leap in consciousness or so we believe, ponders Clara. Monotheism was a fake! The people indulged idolatry under the gaze of priests and prophets. That's not all, the kings picked by Yahweh the moment they sit on the throne turn to other gods! Blatant betrayal of the doctrine of the day.

'That's right. The people were moved by emotions, mumbles Levinson, they sought solace where they could find it, with the Goddess, the Mother. The Father had let them down, insensitive to their needs. The cult of Asherah was widespread inside and outside the land. It is striking that the cult of Yahweh foiled by the Kings and resisted by the people should have survived unquestioned for the twenty centuries of the present exile!

'I recently read that when exile became inevitable after the fall of Jerusalem the Rabbis sighed a sigh of relief, says Johansson.

'That's right, recalls Levinson. Idolatry, that thorn in the flesh of the priesthood, was finally going to be extracted. The suffering of exile would uproot idolatry. The extraordinary thing is that they were right! Monotheism was firmly anchored in exile, outside the Land. What a paradox, the obliteration of idolatry neither prophets nor clergy could pull off has been achieved through the suffering of the Christian exile!

Visit to the Knesset to Lobby an MP

Concerned for the safety of Benzaccai the friends head for the Knesset. Their intention is to enlist the assistance of a member of parliament. They secure an interview with a liberal MP known to sympathise with difficult cases; his negotiating skills have often proved invaluable.

The parliament building is a yellow stone structure that catches the golden glow of the morning light. It looks daunting standing alone on a hill off the city centre. Ancient Israel was never home to liberalism, free enquiry and secular ideas. Democracy was born in Athens, religious dictatorship in Jerusalem, the land where freedom of expression was damned as deviant. Yet it was also the land of religious insurgence, of idolatrous cults and heretical sects, swift to dissent against the state-imposed deity. In times of hardship the people would turn to any thing that might bring them solace. The more thinking knew that their ritualistic religion was not founded on ideas, on the lucid grasp of reality nor on rigorous reflection. Nor was it built on the intuitive vision of the inner Mysteries of being. It was not a religion of essence, but of form. As a religion of form it failed to grapple with the challenges of human existence. It failed to deal with the real issues faced by man in incarnation.

When the messianic dream was aborted by religious tyranny at the dawn of the new age, the people turned to their tradition in search of answers to their predicament and found the same naive dogmas, empty promises, shallow precepts and meaningless practices that never delivered. At such critical times they gazed at the void before them. No intelligent, realistic, applicable idea came to their rescue. They were alone, betrayed and desolate. The promised reward for their ritualistic efforts and diligent service never materialised. The enlightened Greeks and sophisticated Romans had encountered a people arrested in a lost age of juvenile expectations, broken dreams and stolen hopes.

The friends are standing before the symbol of democracy as they gaze at the giant Menorah. 'Democracy is alive and well in this building, remarks Levinson. After Meah Shearim it's a relief! In this building conflicting views clash across the political divide. Coalitions are formed, and unlikely alliances forged between political rivals. Democracy in action.

On entering the building they are asked to wait outside the MP's office. A moment later the MP appears and introduces himself, 'my name is David Nessim', what business brings you to me? He listens to their story with a look of genuine interest and says, 'Rumours surrounding the existence of a manuscript sent tremors to certain places. A few members stayed behind after the parliamentary session to discuss its implications. We sympathise with your plight but I cannot help you find or protect Benzaccai. If what I heard is true, the manuscript is a time bomb waiting to detonate.

'It has not detonated yet, replies Jeremy, the manuscript contains the hidden knowledge Moses could not deliver at the time. Revelation is limited, appropriate to the point of evolution of those it is given to. The people were insufficiently developed to grasp it then.

'And we are now, exclaims the MP! If only you knew!

'You are questioning the intelligence and the integrity of the people, continues Jeremy. I think you have a responsibility as an MP to bring this text to their awareness, they have waited long enough, don't you think?

'Do you want a full blown crisis in parliament and a civil war in the country?

'The manuscript speaks of love and light, neither produces civil wars!

'Love has yet to dawn on our collective consciousness. Besides, we cannot restrain our neighbours with love, we need force. And the manuscript, if it is authentic, could send the wrong signals to our enemies. We may as well abandon the land and drown in the sea!

'Rabbi Moses, the author does not question your right to this land.

'He does not have to, retorts Nessim. If our religious edifice stems from a misconception, the whole edifice collapses leaving us no alternative but to admit that it was a hoax!

'Quite the reverse, replies Jeremy, Rabbi Moses joined the Enlightenment Movement to explore new ideas. Liberated from the bonds that had stifled his originality, he was able to reflect on the Jewish condition in a new and creative way. He concluded that the only way forward for the Jews worldwide was to reclaim their ancestral land. They would have to fight for it rather than wait for an elusive Messiah. The Messiah is a metaphor for an enlightened age when human beings would take their destiny into their own hands, rather than rely on an absent god. Exactly what happened, he anticipated this time. Rather than fear him you should hail him as a national hero.

'And have riots on my hand?

'A minority may still live in a legendary past inhabited by space invaders, continues Jeremy. This minority eager to restore the mythological gods aim to establish a religious dictatorship. There is no turning back. You are one of the great democracies of the world. As a democracy you are making real Moses' dream of an enlightened society, you are creating it. Don't let the adversaries of Jewish emancipation and unification stand in the way, not now!

'A man sitting in a corner of the room gets up and strides towards them. He wears a skull cap and a short grey beard. He snaps with a sarcastic laughter:

'What liberal claptrap! Next you will ask us to work toward a rapprochement between Jews and Christians!

'Are you serious? In which century are you living? Have you heard of the 20th century, the post-religious century?

'I sure know! My family died in concentration camps, I know all about the 20th century, I know all about the cruelty of man to man, he snaps with blistering anger. Clara thinks, 'what he cannot do through reason he does through pity. Emotionalism wins the day!

'Not quite, exclaims Johansson. You don't know that the rapprochement came about on the bloody battlefields of the world? The war struck a blow to the civilisation of the gods from outer space. Western civilisation battered almost to oblivion emerged renewed. The near global destruction of mankind brought everyone to their senses.

'Spare me your profane arrogance, says the man who has now lost the initiative.

'Not yet. We live in post-religious societies eminent not for their bygone theology but for their respect of human rights. Their democratic principles are those of Buddha, Moses, Pericles and Christ. Democratic values and liberal ideals protect human rights. Rapprochement came not thought theological rambling, bigotry and fanaticism but through democratic principles.

'You are going too far, retorts the man visibly angry. Enough, take your leave!

'Not yet. Rapprochement between Christians and Jews is obsolete. Theology died on the battlefields of the world with all other tyrannies. The influence of the god-energy that governed the Planet exploded on those same battlefields. Modern man has outgrown the credulity of the past; he is climbing the ladder of evolution in his own body: from the lesser centres of fear, survival and tribalism down his spine to the higher centres of thought, reason and creativity. The climb is from matter to spirit, from ignorance to awareness. Evolution is not just of biology it is of consciousness and is irreversible. Rapprochement is of the plane of mind, not of the lesser plane of theological speculation.

Nessim has remained silent, observing and listening with a mocking grin resembling a smile. Is he enjoying the battle of words?

'I urge you to reconsider,' pleads Jeremy in an attempt to win Nessim to his point of view. The MP is immovable, his determination unsettling. The meeting comes to a close. Disappointed but not defeated the friends leave. 'A missed opportunity, bemoans Jeremy.

Grenade attack in a crowded street

The attack came in the morning rush hour when people were hurrying to work; children were on their way to school and housewives out shopping. The terrorists, members of an extremist group threw a grenade at the crowd, aiming at no one in particular, mindless of whom might be hurt, determined to cause maximum damage with minimum expenditure of energy and equipment. When confronted by a superior power, it is the psychological damage that is most effectual. The extremist group which carried out the attack rejected all peace negotiations, determined to sabotage all attempt at securing a peaceful settlement. Political radicals outside and religious radicals inside share a common goal: they shirk peace. One group claims its recently lost land, the other claims borders lost 2000 years ago. The grenade attack today on this Friday morning market, packed with shoppers preparing for the Shabbat injured several. People were screaming, calling for their loved ones, running in all directions, greatly distraught. Mercifully nobody was seriously hurt, but the psychological damage was immense. It is the kind of damage which fuels anger and fear. Groups hostile to peace on both sides of the divide ride the energies of fear.

Via Dolorosa & life after death

Clara and Levinson are strolling down Via Dolorosa. They walk enthralled by the images unfolding before their mind's eye. In dream-like mode they gaze at a sensitive man stumbling down this road, broken for responding to the suffering of humanity nailed on the cross of matter, while the multitude watch in dread and veneration, bearing witness to the cruelty of man.

Levinson breaks the spell, 'History repeats itself, there is a natural resistance to change, fear governs, any new idea, or even an old idea that resurfaces is a source of hostility. The noble ideas of the Essenes were ridiculed.

'The same noble ideas are resisted today by a few who cleave to separation and the mirage of genetic advantage. Steeped in the illusion they side with forces hostile to the unification of mankind.

'They agree on a single point: unification must be defended against! Their goal is to cling to archaic beliefs and bygone thought forms that have no foundation in reality.

'They are coming together in an unholy alliance to thwart the realisation of the cosmic Plan for the Planet. It's all so bizarre! The old foes are uniting to defend separation, fear and hatred.

'Long ago they assaulted Moses, today they sabotage peace treaties and dismiss international resolutions. The pagan practices Moses had expelled came swiftly back:

idolatry and rioting were the response to Moses' vision of a progressive society. To the keepers of the old energy the Essenes were bad news, just as Moses had been, same Brotherhood of Light too! There is nothing new under the sun!

'We are citizens of the Planet, indeed citizens the cosmos not just forlorn affiliates of a disoriented group which absconded from main stream humanity, choosing to flow against the natural drift of evolution. Our task as workers of the Hierarchy is to show the universal, timeless way of thinking, taught to mankind by the philosophers of classical Greece and before them by the Masters of the universe, Hermes, Seth, Ptah, Krishna, and Buddha.

'We are no heretics, more artists than rebels, simply suggesting a different way of looking at the world. We visited all continents, played a role in all cultures: we came to Lemuria and Atlantis, to Egypt and Greece. We reappeared among the Essenes 2000 years ago. We are always around at crucial times, at the dawn of a new age.

They perceive a thread running down the centuries. This slow and reflective walk down Via Dolorosa has a special significance for them; they were both unfairly disowned for questioning formal beliefs and values. They discarded attachment to ancient beliefs and loyalty to group preservation, but they care about their fellow men. Indeed they incarnated to be of service to mankind, to teach and to heal, to guide and to counsel, to offer light at the end of the tunnel. What irony! To be symbolically killed by a group which claimed to be 'holy'? They would not perpetuate the 'do & obey' and the 'go & multiply' as their ancestors had done. These mavericks made the diehards feel shallow, insecure, and aware of the flimsy nature of their beliefs. Those who choose world service do not need to make loud noises, wild statements and exuberant demonstrations; they simply want to 'be'! They value 'being' over 'doing'. Their presence is unsettling, it stirs something in people. It is the soul that has been touched, like the string of an instrument vibrates in the breeze. Their souls are being aroused from the timeless slumber. Sleeping Beauty waking up with a kiss!

'This Sleeping Beauty is not amused! In the film Ben Hur, the huge crowd of mourners line up the Via Dolorosa, this very walk. Two lepers, rising to the solemnity of this sombre walk, wake up to an inner truth and recover 'miraculously' from their illness. The dying girl now vibrant with health says something astonishing, 'I am no longer afraid, I know now that I am going to live for ever'. Striking insight by a girl from the people 'preoccupied with God'!

'I saw the film too. Until then we did not know of the existence of the soul.

'This sick girl, sent to the Desert to die a lingering death, had no window on a higher reality until that minute of realisation. The entire universe, so vast as to numb our thought, is also within us. The Egyptians and the Greeks knew this, we did not, we the people most 'preoccupied with God'!

Coming towards them smiling but restrained are Tara and Johansson. They greet each other with animation. They look uneasy.

'Something wrong, enquires Clara?

'Youths on the West Bank set fire to an Israeli flag. People throng the streets shouting abuse at soldiers and throwing stones, explains Tara.

'This cast a shadow on the restoration of peace, notes Levinson.

'The peace agreement collapsed months ago, reminds Clara, it was fragile, 'not enough' claimed one side, and 'too much' claimed the other.

'This beautiful city is blighted by human folly. Drenched in the illusion they believe that man can be the enemy of man! How is that possible when both house the I AM Presence? When both are animated by a soul which is a fragment of the All? When both are energized by the life force that fills the universe? Same I AM, same foundation, same source, and two enemies? This is the illusion Sananda alludes to.

'Nothing changes much, in the 19th century the French writer Renan wrote of the Jerusalem of 2000 years ago, 'Jerusalem was then what it is today, a city of pedantry, acrimony, disputes, hatreds and littleness of mind'.

On spirituality

'It feels almost unreal, strolling down the Via Dolorosa. This place has retained an imprint. The energies of that event permeate the atmosphere'.

Levinson inhales the warm still air. He senses something mysterious about the place, 'I have played with definitions, and not one approximates the reality of it. The devout like Atlas carry the world on their shoulders, to them spirituality is an activity, a ceaseless activity that must redeem the world! The more they 'do' the more spiritual they believe to be.

'Spirituality is yet to be discovered. Idolatry was the natural choice. Nothing inherently wrong with idolatry if it does not degenerate into tyranny. In fact idolatry tends to prevent tyranny as societies and cultures share the same gods. This sharing encourages tolerance and participation. Today we see something similar among liberal democracies. 'Democracy in religious matters was foreign to us. In imposing the ancient god they were serving their own interest! Astute politicians they closed the window to a higher reality, denying their reluctant flock the freedom to probe the world, the freedom to 'Know thyself' both as physical and cosmic beings. That's not spirituality, that's dictatorship.

'The priesthood had other reasons, not all conscious perhaps but compelling: the preservation of the ancestral god's plan for the world. Nothing to do with the Divine Plan to which we, the workers of the Hierarchy, are dedicated.

'To me spirituality has to do with the whole person. To be spiritual is to be whole; it is the opening of mind, emotions and soul to discovery. The human spirit is inquisitive, hungry for knowledge and experience. Spirituality is experiencing every facet of our being, stretching our mind inward into our inner worlds and outward through the sciences, forcing open the barriers.

'Spirituality is to know with reason and intuition that we are all interconnected, that we are one another! Each one can be likened to a cell in the body; in the healthy state man is aware that all systems work in accord. When health breaks down, this harmony is interrupted and cells, tissues and organs no longer collaborate to generate optimum health and well being. The body may be compared to a mechanical system. In such a system, the whole is greater than the sum of its parts. We are, I strongly feel, the parts that form a greater whole, and when a unit decides to go its way, it disrupts the subtle workings of the whole.

'Good analogy, no man is an island; we all take our being from the ocean of life, the cosmic life force. A dew drop may briefly be detached, but it will eventually return to the sea. Our separation is illusory; the life force that sustains us also holds the Planets, the galaxies, the blade of grass, the ear of corn, the cell, the molecule and the atom.

'Moses knew that, he was an Egyptian Initiate. These primary principles have been taught by the Hierarchy at each new cycle. Yet the doctrinaires still think in terms of blood line and selection, genetic advantage and chosen purpose, volatile myths that precipitated so much misery on the Planet. The ephemeral and illusory nature of things is the only reality they cling to. As the world caves in around them, the more desperately they hold on to the mirage.

Levinson and Clara are separated from the others by a crowd of tourists.

The world seen in a broken mirror

'Sauntering down this road infused with feeling and imbued with history, one stands at the crossroads of two worlds, the old world and the new world. Two irreconcilable views once met at this very point, the intersection of mind and matter. The entire cosmos did behold the clash of two visions. The collision of spirit and matter.

'The wisdom of the East insists that matter is the continuation of mind. There is no difference between the temporal and the permanent; the physical and the spiritual. It is the dualistic mind of man which divides, splits and fragments. Buddha explained that Samsara and Nirvana are one and the same: physical reality and spiritual reality are one and the same, but it is our 'deluded' mind that divorces them. We perceive the world as if through a broken mirror; the image is distorted, broken.

'That's why the Book of Genesis is a major source of confusion! It places undue emphasis on the creation of the physical world. But the true 'heresy' came later when the pundits set about to break things down further. They made a difficult situation more difficult as they climbed down the slippery slope of definition, explanation, distinction, differentiation and the world has continued to be split.

'Some seek gratification in dualities and sub-dualities.

'Cant' you see? They have caused all future generations to seeing the world broken up into fragments, to use your metaphor. Instead of looking at the one unified world through a transparent mirror, they broke the mirror into segments and have found nothing wrong with the cracked, warped images reflected back. They are delighted with the many fragments of images and find them not only attractive but absolutely true.

'They did not invent the dual world in which we live.

'You are right, they did not. But why emphasise division and separation when the purpose of creation is to return to the primeval unity?

'They are thrilled with their cracked view of the world and want all of us to see through the lens of their fragmented world. If we decline we are symbolically eliminated, like Rabbi Moses, like we were. Their flawed vision we must adopt and if we question we are doomed, we have a 'death' sentence hovering over our heads!

'Does this 'death' sentence worry you?

'Not in the least, I shrugged it off; I would have laughed it off had I not seen the implications lurking beyond my personal situation. I don't care about their curse; they know nothing about our cosmic stature, the enduring quality and nature of the soul, the existence of a Self that is imperishable. What concerns me is that they exert a significant influence over other minds, often young and impressionable around whom they weave their web. Further more, as they insist on their fragmented vision of the world, they perpetuate the sorry state of affairs humanity has known for aeons. To add insult to injury, those who fall into the trap may never recover. Liberation from redundant thought forms may take a long time. They keep mankind hooked on the ever-turning wheel of death and rebirth as Buddha said.

'The mind is like a vast expanse of pure sky. The true nature of the mind is limitless, self-determining, creative, a boundless expanse of radiance.

'A mind that forms an integral part of the cosmic Mind.

'That's right. Undeveloped people have this vastness for they share in the cosmic Mind, but theirs is obscured by a cloud formation. And for so long as the mind is darkened by the clouds of illusion and deluded thought patterns, humanity stumbles from one incarnation into another until the clouds lift, until men everywhere in one voice declare together, 'Enough is enough, no more obscurity, no more delusional thoughts. We reclaim the integrity of our mind, we want to behold its vastness and rediscover our essential nature. We hunt for the Holy Grail; we yearn to flow into the ocean of cosmic consciousness. We can dwell in eternity while still in temporality; we can be once again gods walking the Earth!'

'All human beings are our mothers' – a Buddhist meditation

'As I was ambling down Via Dolorosa, as I observed the man in prayers at the Wall, I recalled a Buddhist meditation. Tradition has it that it was given by Buddha; it is a reminder that all human beings are our mothers.

'Say that again!

'It is bizarre, I know. It goes like this, since it is impossible to look back to the beginning of our existence, it follows that we are ageless and we must have taken countless rebirths.

'Are you alluding to our humble beginnings as bacteria? Scientists are putting this date back even further, some 4 billions years!

'Just the duration of our human experience, we are of extreme antiquity, all of us. Humanity is extremely old; esoteric sources point to a very high figure. So if we have been revisiting Earth countless times, then we had many mothers. They are all around us today, the men, women and children we pass in the streets, our friends and enemies, the decent ones and the villains, the pious and the impious. As a result of the numerous karmic relationships we had with them in the past, some are more attractive than others, we like some while denigrating others. Our 'deluded' minds imagine that those in our groups who share the same prejudices and beliefs are our own kind, while others who do not voice the same slogans are our enemies!

'An interesting thought: these enemies may have been god-fearing in past generations and they who moved on. They shed the archaic mode of thinking either to adopt more deluded thought forms or embark on liberation!

'Exactly, that is why we should think each time we meet someone: 'This person is my mother'.

'And what if it is a man? He is not going to like it a bit, especially if he blesses his god three times a day for not having made him a woman!

'Too bad, a woman he was, countless of times and a woman he will be a few more times before he is through with his 'deluded' thinking!

'What is the point of it all, I don't see!

'When you imagine the other as having been your mother in a remote past, then you sober down, you see the futility of your conditioned response. You look at your enemy differently. You ask yourself, 'is the enemy across the border my enemy, or am I conditioned to see him as my enemy? He was once my mother!

'The entire script changes. The enemy is not an enemy after all. It's all a mirage, a trick of past karmic interaction. For this I was born.

'For what?

'To look at the world the right way up.

'Meditation and profound reflection are the tools to dissolve attachment and hatred. As we enter a new era, powerful frequencies stimulate the impulse to unification and cooperation. The triple evil of attachment, hatred and ignorance which has conditioned mankind for aeons is coming to an end, cosmic light is changing us. We are better able to discriminate between the real and the unreal, the true and the false, the rational and the irrational. We are becoming 'enlightened'!

'A stab in the ribs of patriarchy, a kick in the teeth of orthodoxy! It is throwing up in the air all that they spent thousands of years to erect, secure and shield. The man who prides himself of despising women, who praises his god for making him a man, the man who sees the other as his potential enemy is not going to be amused.

'He will be even less amused when he knows that each soul is sending out several fragments of itself to multiply its facets of experience. No time to waste for there is a lot of discovering, a lot of learning still to do.

'If each soul is segmenting into several individuals at the same time, the implications are incredible! It means that strangers we bump into in the street may share our soul. The soul clones itself?

'You could say that. The soul incarnates on Earth to explore the world and to explore itself. So it is possible that the enemy who is throwing stones at you from the other side of the fence may be a fragment of your own soul, another aspect of yourself! The individual behind barbed wires because he is of a different race, colour or creed may well share our very soul! Do you see? It means that we may be condemning one of our long-forgotten mothers to an unjust fate. It also means that as you confront your enemy, you realise that his is you, a fragment of you, that you are both aspects of the same entity, that you share the same soul! You could not be more intimately connected!

'Issues of culture, religious differences, biological inheritance and genetic advantage crumble into dust. We are juggling with chimeras. We are trying to capture moon beams in a jar! The jar is empty but we shove, argue, curse and threaten. We brandish books in support of our beliefs in culture, race and heredity. The soul must laugh silently in amusement and dismay.

'The soul laughs or weeps. The soul does not concern itself with gender, custom, prejudice, religious disparity, dogmas and race. The soul travels through time and space, unperturbed, untouched, unmoved by the noise and fury. The soul makes use of the race, gender, culture and dogmas it wishes to encounter at any point of its evolution, to learn, to grow, to experiment and … to discard!

'The implications for peace are immense. Who will ever look at the enemy pointing a gun and not silently comment: 'This one was my mother; he may even share my soul. How more closely related or more intimate can we possibly be?'

CHAPTER 6

RESURGENCE OF THE GODDESS - YIN, COSMIC FEMININE ENERGY

Love & Redemption - Promise of Immortality

'When the people of Earth can return to the love and worship of the beautiful Mother, the divine Mother, there will be a return to happiness. For the [light] *which shines forth from your Heart and reveals all mysteries, is the child of the great Mother and is born of love'.* (White Eagle)

CAPERNAUM - LAKE GALILEE

At the bend on the road, Capernaum! Images of beauty, of awakening, of new perception spring to mind.

'I sense that this town has special meaning for me, says Jeremy. In meditation I sometimes have flashbacks of people in ancient dress walking down cobbled streets, women carrying earth jars on their shoulders. I was here once; I shall walk down the streets and recognise all.

'If there is anything to recognise, says Johansson. Nothing stands still.

'Your memory is astonishing, says Clara, you remember the time before you came to Earth! What was it like? She is a thinker, not a visionary and she feels cheated when others have visual experiences in meditation.

'I was floating in space in a body of shimmering light and the call resounded out to infinity. I remember distinctly thinking, 'this is the opportunity I have been waiting for. What a challenge! This is it! That sounds like fun!'

'Fun indeed, says Clara caustic!

'I won't do it again though!

'I don't recall anything, it's a total blank, but I can't imagine thinking 'let's go down, its sounds like fun', remarks Levinson.

'They walk down the streets of Capernaum. Jeremy heads straight for the ruins. The very name has a magical ring, it evokes mystical images of a spiritual brotherhood teaching, working and living together. Little remains of the town except for the ruins enclosed in walls of black basalt. Buried for centuries it was excavated by Franciscan monks. The lake shimmers in the delicate light. Fishermen are casting their nets on the tranquil water; others are standing still in their boats angling leisurely, nonchalantly.

333

'We owe a debt to the Franciscan monks turned archaeologists who restored a lost biblical city, says Johansson. Son of a Danish parson, his relationship with Christianity has been a thorny one.

'There they are, exclaims Jeremy with uncharacteristic enthusiasm, the ruins of the houses I remember. I must have lived in one of these.

'Look at this, points Levinson in direction of the restored ruin of an elegant synagogue with Roman style façade and pillars of black and white marble. What a fine building, truly impressive!

'Some fervent theological debate this synagogue has heard, remarks Johansson, thoughtful. It may not be too far-fetched to figure that Christianity has its root in this building, at least in the form of passionate argument.

'This synagogue is too Roman, too pagan and too recent to be the house you describe, says Jeremy. The Romans were the occupying force and so their elegance, fine columns and marbles were probably resented by the people they subdued who saw just paganism in it.

Look at this 'pagan' image, a kind of male Mermaid, points Tara. Even mermaids are denied their feminine status.

They wait outside the imposing Roman synagogue for their messenger to deliver the next chapter. A smartly dressed woman emerges from the temple to greet them, 'I am Deborah, so good of you to meet me, she says with a sigh of relief. Would you step inside or do you prefer to enjoy the view? Did you have a pleasant journey, not too bumpy I hope?

'Everything was just fine, replies Jeremy reassuringly. It is getting late perhaps we should begin. It was most kind of you to come and meet us. Looking at this scroll of papers we shall be here all night.

'We may have to sleep under the stars by the lake. Have you brought sleeping bags?

'I like the idea of sleeping under the stars by the lake, replies Jeremy but we are staying at Kibbutz Ginnosar for a few days.

'I promised to deliver the next chapter of The Hebrew Gods. After leaving his teacher the Gaon de Vilna he joined the Hassidim and stumbled upon the revival of the Goddess. Shrouded in appropriate symbolism acceptable to the godly Hassidim'. She hands over a roll of papers and with a smile, 'I work with my husband, I share his interests, I am an archaeologist. Do you want me to read it, you may find his scribble difficult to decipher for he was translating in great haste while the soldiers waited for him downstairs.

Her attention shifts to the façade, 'look at the six-pointed Star, wrongly attributed to David. It is much more ancient, one of the oldest symbols known to man, the two entwined triangles pointing in opposite directions but meeting at the centre, symbolising man himself.

'I learned from my discarnate teacher that the Star of David is also the Star of Abraham. It has been in our possession for some time, says Clara.

'The soul pointing downward and the ego pointing upward, they meet right in the centre, the symbol of integrated man, where the ego comes into alignment with the soul, when it is illumined by the soul, explains Jeremy.

'A king of badge, continues Deborah with a cascading laughter, we take ideas, signs and symbols and claim they have been ours for ever.

'The star is the symbol of perfected man, man at one with himself, at one with the world, says Jeremy!

'The symbol of unity, teases Levinson, to us guardians of duality! An uncanny symbol! Yet it does not occur to us to craft unity. That is the challenge, 'Man has power on Earth to reverse the Fall's effects', a challenge we ignore. We shift it on the shoulders of a speculative messiah. No surprise the messiah never shows up.

'Somehow he never meets our specifications! We are in a quandary: we banish the Beings who can liberate us from our prison, yet we are unable to escape alone! 'The animal nature of man makes him resist seeing himself as the maker of his circumstances', quotes Clara. We are the makers of our reality, the originators of our experience, yet we deny our creative power, we clamour for a liberator!

'Quite, replies Deborah, we are the people of duality while claiming to be the people of unity. One god, one country, one people! All is unity, yet we perpetuate the ancient myth of the Tree of Knowledge of Good & Evil, that primeval symbol of duality. We distend because we adopt the human perspective, the human dimension, the human experience.

'Unity is wholeness, undivided reality, mumbles Jeremy.

'The Goddess culture fostered integration and wholeness, says Tara. This is by the way the definition of love. In contrast, the Father culture fosters separation, fragmentation, hostility and brokenness. The Father culture has captured the Planet.

'I fully agree. It's great to speak freely with like-minded friends. We exist in linear time, we indulge linear thinking, we live in one dimension only, resumes Deborah. Patriarchy has impoverished humanity. We exist beyond space and time but patriarchy made this a felony to the ancestral god. The Goddess energy was holistic, integrating, unifying. It respected and encouraged man's multi-layered nature. The Father's energy disputes our universal nature.

'The choice was made, perhaps not consciously, notes Clara. The Essenes sketched a new vision of the unity of all life and the meaning and purpose of human life. Theirs was a holistic view of existence; a universal vision that gave back to humanity its lost memory. The holistic vision of man's cosmic dimension was blasphemous... Man had to be kept flawed, sinful.

'I am writing a thesis entitled 'The Goddess in the Jewish Tradition', duality is of special interest to me, says Deborah.

'Quite, adds Tara, this is my field of interest too.

'As a subject of research it's fine, remarks a sceptical Johansson, but we are evolving beyond the pairs of opposites, as Master Sananda informs us, we are entering the state of Grace. Duality in conflict has been the Jewish experience; humanity has been shaped by it, restrained by it, imprisoned into it! Engrossed in duality by your culture, you should aim for synthesis, for unification, for the merging of the two in a meaningful whole.

'Jung's 'animus' and 'anima', suggests Jeremy? The male and female aspects in us fusing into a creative energy, an imaginative synthesis.

Deborah looks tense; a veil of sadness darkens her pale blue eyes. 'This set of opposites has a difficult ring for me. Did my husband tell you about our childless marriage?

'No, we never discuss private lives. We know he had a rough childhood.

'That's only half the story, she says in tears. You see, my first husband refused to grant me a 'bill of divorce', we are both remarried separately. Whereas he has 'legitimate' children, my children with my second husband would be under Jewish law considered illegitimate.

'How come, this is bizarre, says an indignant Tara!

'Under Jewish law my civil marriage is nil, I am still married to my former husband and therefore I am in an adulterous relationship.

'What are you saying, exclaims Clara, your first husband is legally remarried!

'According to rabbinical law, my husband is legally remarried, but because he refused to give me 'a bill of divorce' I cannot legally remarry. We had the secular marriage we both wanted, but it is not valid and so I am leading an 'immoral' life, that's the rabbinical position. We decided against having a family!

'What, exclaims Jeremy, you are not living in the Bronze Age!

'O yes we are! According to rabbinical law my children would be cursed to the 10th generation!

'And you believe it!

'What it means is that I would be bringing into the world a lineage of pariahs, a cast of 'untouchables'.

'Wait, exclaims Johansson, I don't get it; the religion that hinges around procreation is the same religion that decides you should remain childless?

'In effect, yes.

'And you went along with it; I know why your husband never talks about it!

'But things are changing, continues Deborah on a lighter note, my aim is the return of the Goddess. We have set up a group which meets every week for discussions, meditation and review of books on the Goddess. The Jewish predicament stems from the loss of the energy of love. The original sin is the loss of love.

'Love is the foundation stone of the universe, the ever-active, ever-present, ever-flowing, all encompassing, all-pervading life force, picks up Jeremy.

'We lost all this when patriarchy entered the stage of history and implanted itself. It has governed humanity; it has conditioned our actions and thoughts. Things do change, the creation of the State of Israel, for instance.

'I don't think that many will share your views, remarks Levinson.

'The State was formed from the ashes of the old world; it is the creation of modern man, of modern mind, insists Deborah. And modern man is now asserting his mind. Patriarchy and the reign of Yahweh in the world, particularly in the Western world were dealt a mighty blow in the apocalyptic 20th century. With the gradual decline of male culture and the waning of the Yahweh culture, love is making a return to this Planet. Yahweh demanded and nurtured fear; we are releasing his solid grip.

'Fear has had its day', sighs Clara who remembers her past of fear. Fear is still casting its ominous shadow over her. 'Fear at school, fear at home, fear inside me, fear outside, fear everywhere.

'And love is moving in, says Tara, about time too!

'Though the world appears in chaos, notes Jeremy.

'Chaos before order, destruction before reconstruction, disintegration before renewal, reminds Tara. The effect of the new waves of light reaching us.

'The fundamental law of the universe is love, underlines Jeremy. Patriarchy is fading away and with it the reign of fear. The intrepid challenge the Logos hurled into Creation: to emit particles of himself that would descend into matter and from the depth of matter- under pressure, darkness and tension - rise progressively back to the light, like a seed germinates in the dark earth into a plant that rises to the surface.

'Another analogy they use in the East, adds Tara is that of the lotus which has its roots in mud and rises above the water perfectly beautiful, unsullied.

'Why has it taken so long to discover this crucial cosmic law, asks Deborah?

'Because it is the most fundamental yet the most difficult law to rediscover. And as you know to break the primeval law – love - is the greatest sin.

'I found that out to my sorrow, moans Deborah.

'Others have too, notes Tara. It is not possible to plead ignorance in any court of law, human or cosmic. The law applies to all equally, and the suffering transgression precipitates forces us to learn and grow, this is the law of conscious evolution.

'We learned the hard way, we learned through fear, continues Deborah. Fear, nurtured by the clerics, is inflicted by the deity who relies on it. We have fed him on fear, fear is his food. Where fear reigns love is absent, just as night is the absence of day.

'Love and the Goddess disappeared when the stellar gods asserted their domination on the Planet, notes Levinson. The lonely, persecuted and sorrowful Jew is developing into a citizen of the Planet, he is on his way to becoming a citizen of the universe. Quite a leap in just one generation!

'Do you think that the gods and their human agents are going to observe in silence this giant leap and do nothing, asks Clara?

'You are right, replies Deborah. They are retreating but not quietly, with a resounding scream, a last clash of thunder. They will not depart in dignified silence.

'How are the broad-minded, rational, informed liberals among you speeding up the process, how do they view the final agony of the old order?

'By being who they are and by cultivating a wider awareness. It is not easy for modern, liberal, educated individuals in this age of knowledge and reason to influence a group arrested in the Bronze Age!

'They are the rational, liberal majority ushering in the Age of Man, as the 7th Ray of integration is entering human consciousness, concludes Jeremy.

'We agree on core issues, this is gratifying, delights Deborah. Now to Rabbi Moses' reflections on Monotheism, a topic of central interest since I am part of a movement working towards the overthrow of monotheism and its god. An extract from The Hebrew Gods.

The Goddess, the Cosmic Mother

'And the spirit of God moved upon the face of the waters' you read in Genesis. This symbolic image is edited by patriarchy to its visual, literal sense. In the graphic language of myth 'water' is the primal building block of the universe. 'Water', the feminine principle symbolises the soul, cosmic man. The universal Soul is the ocean of life in which we all live, move and have our being. What would patriarchy make of this, chuckles Sanaka?

'Patriarchy is not amused, replies Moses trying to match his Master's good humour. The Soul of the universe a Feminine force?

'And the spirit of God moved upon the face of the waters', repeats Sanaka. The feminine appears early in Genesis and hints at the union of the masculine with the feminine, God with the Goddess. She is the cosmic Mother who, energised by the cosmic Father brings forth all living beings. As the 'waters of Life' she stands for the visible universe. You recall the encounter with the Serpent. It is not Adam who discusses freedom, but Eve. And she is cursed for it! Being cursed for wanting to know, to participate, and to find out one's role in the scheme of things, in this visible universe? An aberration you might say! With the advent of patriarchy the search for truth is barred.

'That which is good can never originate from woman, notes Moses, woman is flawed, mindless and sinful, this is the official view.

'What a strange world you inhabit, a world in which woman is cursed by man and by god, where god curses man and where Nature, your Mother is cursed. Is this the wonderful universe God created or is it Hell?

'We prefer the things that originate in the mind, they are safe. We banished mythology because it is irrational; it comes from the depth of being.

'You prefer the things fashioned by the finite mind of man! You favour the temporal, the finite to the deathless and the timeless. You make do with the world of fiction rather than the Real.

'And we lost the Mother, we cut ourselves off from the 'waters of Life' of which we are an integral part, we chose instead to live as separate, lonesome units.

'Instead of living in the fullness of his being, man lives as a fragile, forlorn, lonely fragment of something he no longer knows. Such impoverishment!

'With the Fall we blamed Eve for the troubles of humanity.

'You blamed the 'waters of Life', the life-giving Mother, you blamed the soul of humanity! Absorbed in books conceived in the mind of men, you fail to sense the Goddess and the 'spirit of God' manifest in the universe.

'If the Goddess is the Mother of humanity, what role do the gods play?

'Well done Moses, you already answered your question, chortles Sanaka. The role they play is limited. Their boundaries are marked; the gods specialise in specific areas of activity. As expression of men, their role is specific. In spite of your efforts to make your deity the dominant one, he is as restricted as the others.

'What human attribute does he embody?

'The authoritarian, uncompromising, unforgiving, vengeful aspect of human nature: the self in its most forceful stance.

'Each social group has its own specific deity who embodies the character of that people?

'Exactly Moses, but we are covering old ground. The Goddess as the universal Mother is boundless, she encompasses, she includes, she embraces the whole of humanity. She does not discriminate on grounds of race, colour or creed. Specialised gods do.

'If I understand, the Goddess is the Mother of all life in the universe whereas the gods belong to human groups.

'You understand right, the Goddess is universal. The gods are localised, specialised, they are the property of specific groups and share the attributes of the groups they represent. With the gods emphasis is on the social and racial aspects. The Goddess rises above social groups and social limitations.

'Loyalty to a god is loyalty to a social form, mumbles Moses. As we herald the intolerant, inflexible nature of our god, we are in effect confessing our own human frailty!

The Myth of Monotheism - an archaeological site in Jerusalem

The friends are staying at Kibbutz Ginnosar and still pursuing Benzaccai who is nowhere to be found. A mysterious young man calls the next morning and asks to speak to Jeremy.

'How is Benzaccai, enquires Jeremy with a note of anxiety?

'Well, quite well. He has a message for you which will be delivered by Dr Isaac's wife.

'Who is Dr Isaac, asks Jeremy weary of chasing the elusive Benzaccai? Their hunt so far is leading nowhere. They have met many fascinating people, but this one is one too many for him.

'An archaeologist in charge of the excavation on the hills of Jerusalem. His wife works with him; she wishes to meet you at Capernaum in the church overlooking the lake. She will arrive in a military vehicle; no one will suspect her identity. The whole thing will pass for a routine patrol of the area.

'Discreetly in a military vehicle, laughs Jeremy? Yesterday it was Deborah meeting us in secret, today it is Dr Isaac's wife. This is not only needlessly convoluted, it is also exhausting. What about Deborah?

'You will continue reading from The Hebrew Gods together. I understand your weariness, says the young man with a confidence beyond his years. Benzaccai thinks that you might enjoy a day of excavation on the hills of Jerusalem. He is keen to offer you a variety of experiences.

'He certainly does that, laughs Jeremy! There is never a dull moment. We know where, now when?

'This evening at sunset .... He pauses for a moment and taking a long breath .... I have to talk to you'. He is nervous, bracing himself he begins, 'for years I have studied the esoteric wisdom of the East. I also devour works by scholars who have examined the Old Testament from a scientific perspective. This is an unusual interest, however a few who are of a liberal disposition support and encourage me.

'It is unusual for a soldier, remarks Jeremy.

'We have to defend our lives and our territory. I am a soldier through necessity not choice. My inclination is of a different nature, I study at the university. We do not choose to be soldiers.

'I disagree, you know from your study of Eastern wisdom that you come in this life well prepared, well rehearsed. Nothing is left to chance, you design the body you are going to inhabit, the circumstances and struggles you will have to confront, the people and situations you will encounter. You know because you write your personal drama before incarnating.

'Yes, of course, I know that but most people do not. They either claim that god is dead or they shout a belief in a singular god. The godly is no different from the ungodly; they are both unaware of universal law. God is another word for fate, everything is decided for them: body, parents, life circumstances, pain and joys are all arbitrarily determined by a god they distrusted long ago and continue to distrust. They are passive recipients of their god's liberality or miserliness.

'That's right each life event is decided, but decided by you not by a capricious god intent on messing up your life. The trickiest thing for us to grasp is that we choose! We choose all our life events, nothing is fated, nothing is predestined. Those with the victim instinct don't want to know!

'Violence is not just the curse of the world. We have our fair share of it in our family lives too, says Clara who remembers her disturbed family.

'That's right, the mayhem in your family, explains Jeremy came from your parents' response to their own karma and their ancestors' karma. They kept alive the pattern of emotional reaction. But they also brought with them the genetic memory of their blood line. So they had to grapple not only with their own obsessive thought forms, they also had to confront the fears and thought forms of their entire blood line! They lacked the insight and the method to deal with that burden. And so it all came crashing down on you! An opportunity for you to experience hatred, darkness and conflict. All utterly foreign to you who came from the world of light. You came to one of the darkest spot on the Planet to convert these negative energies into an energy form that would no longer harm, an energy that would benefit Earth.

'Thank you, you cleared the air, it is good to be reminded, says Clara.

'We come back to Earth in order to liberate our entire blood line, exclaims the young man? Have we not enough problems of our own?

'The cosmic workers working for the Hierarchy have to tackle both; they also have a redeeming function towards the Planet. Master Sananda explained that we are 'rescuers and leaders'. We visit the Planet at crucial moments in its history, usually at the start of a new age with a mandate to heal and to teach. Not an enviable destiny, I agree, smiles Jeremy.

That evening they were driven by the young soldier and his companion to Capernaum. Along the way they passed groups of Bedouins who stared in surprise. The friends felt uneasy; travelling with military escort was attracting attention. The journey unfolded without a hitch. They arrived at the Church when the sun was setting over the lake. The beauty was awe-inspiring. They contemplated the scene in wonderment.

'Let's wake from the magic of the moment; we have got work to do.

A young looking, attractive woman is standing at the entrance with two priests by her side. After the preliminary remarks Leah asks, 'are you wondering why me?'

'I no longer question anything, if this erratic journey has taught me anything it is the futility of questioning! Since you ask, why you, smiles Jeremy?

'I work on the site surrounding Jerusalem; we are excavating clay and stone figures of the Goddess who was worshipped in these parts before and during biblical times. God worship is fairly recent; Goddess worship on the other hand is very ancient. You met Deborah, we work together.

'Why the excavation of Goddess artefacts? And why now, asks Clara rather lukewarm on the whole project?

'If not now when, if not me who, smiles Leah paraphrasing Hillel. This is a time of revival for the Goddess, more to the point this is a time of revival for the people. Both have been separated for too long.

'What makes you think that the people want a resurgence of the Goddess, asks the sceptical Clara? Is this not a retrograde step? The phase of the Mother is but one phase in the evolution of humanity. Why go backward?

'There is more to it. The feminine principle is being rediscovered. It is a reclaiming of the feminine energy, a reintegration of the feminine idea among a people which has been dominated by the masculine ego.

'A rediscovery of one of the primordial principles, asks Clara reassured?

'The goddess has always been among us, discreetly veiled. We have always been influenced, we do not innovate, we borrow. With the 'invention' of agriculture and

343

writing, feminine energy began to wane. Specialisation had entered the human stage. Goddess culture recoiled from specialisation. Specialisation is limitation. Goddess energy embraced everything, aware that our world is filled with universal energy. Goddess energy emphasized fullness and union. It broadcast the unity of life and the worth of all life forms. Goddess culture was a holistic vision of a world in which universal energy permeates all things. All this was lost when the god-force seized power. Love vanished and the divine presence withdrew into pious books and selected buildings. Direct encounter with God was forbidden. It was done through official channels.

'It makes sense, patriarchal rule relies on authority, notes Tara.

'What you just said about the dawn of civilisation is interesting, takes up Johansson. The rise of monotheism ushers in linear thinking whereas goddess energy holds an intuitive, integrative vision of the world. Goddess culture nurtures the coalition of opposites: intellect and intuition, reason and sensitivity. Goddess nature transcends duality. God energy nurtures differences and promotes dualities. No marriage of opposites! God culture forbids all images.

'Why images, asks Clara? So critical was the diktat it was carved in stone!

'God energy banned the highest creative faculties in man, exclaims Jeremy the artist! Images spring from the intuitive faculty; all great artistic creation originates in the plane of intuition.

'And artistic creativity is not what patriarchy fosters, echoes Leah! It is impossible to control the creative impulse of an artist, a poet or a musician. Even the Church was unable to control Raphael, Leonardo or Michelangelo.

'Great art stems from the fusion of intellect and intuition, insists Jeremy. Linear thinking which relies on brain activity is more controllable. It sees from a specific angle, usually a narrow angle, not from a global perspective.

'What is the real problem, asks Tara who senses the answer?

'It is the imagination that shapes forbidden 'images'. And it is linear thinking that splits, fragments and ruptures, linear thinking that deconstructs. In holistic thinking all is one. Whole thinking connects, linear thinking disconnects, explains Johansson. Linear thinking is controllable, holistic thinking is not. Patriarchy seeks control. Patriarchy as agent of monotheism has to separate and disconnect. Patriarchy is lost in the illusion.

'That's why we are estranged from the soul - font of intuition and imagination, comments Levinson. With the rise of patriarchy soul qualities were exiled.

'And of course, thinking 'straight' means thinking what is approved, what is given, what one is told to think, inserts Clara.

'You understand now why it is so important to bring back the Goddess culture, smiles Leah exultant.

'There is more to Goddess culture than worship, says Clara with relief. It heralds a renewal for mankind. Liberated from the fetters of patriarchy, we'll be free to fuse intellect and intuition, love and reason. Free to receive and absorb the new Ray of Integration now reaching the Planet.

'Division belongs to patriarchy, unification is within view. The influence of the Ray of integration is being felt, notes Tara always keen to stab at patriarchy.

'Division is unpleasant to the more perceptive. Globalisation is a step toward assimilation. Assimilation, patriarchy's horror! Assimilation is inevitable, it must be hailed as a major force for progress, adds Clara.

'Goddess energy was veiled, repeats Leah. Robust monotheism barely disguised Goddess worship. Even the anointed kings fell for the Goddess. The Goddess has changed throughout history. The oldest image of the Goddess is the Shekhina present among the people in the Desert.

'A tangible Goddess in the life of a people who censures images and worships on the altar of an invisible god, remarks Jeremy!

'Quite a paradox, says Levinson. Sensitive to human suffering, she is modelled on Asherah, the Babylonian Goddess cherished by the Hebrews. As Leah mentioned, the Talmud records that the Goddess was present in the Desert, visible to all even the scoundrels who planned the downfall of Moses!

In Old Testament mythology, Yahweh like Baal lives in the clouds, but the Shekhina stays on Earth to assist man. The Talmud is saying that the Goddess is sensitive to the needs of man.

'The nurturing Mother, the ideal Woman, the sacred feminin among the most controlling patriarchal system, exclaims Tara!

'I would like you to come with me, suggests Leah.

'Where to, enquires Jeremy with a tinge of weariness in the voice. We are running around like headless chicken.

'We are on our way to the hills of Jerusalem to excavate a site recently discovered, a gold mine to us, of earthenware jars, vessels, jewels, statuettes, clay tablets, all priceless artefacts. Unearthed, these objects will give evidence of Goddess worship in biblical times. A fact recorded in the Talmud as a subversive act against state religion. Goddess culture was politically sensitive. A natural response from the people it was also a rebellion against religious dictatorship.

'So it was politically destabilising, says Jeremy.

'Yes', replies Dr Isaac now in sight, 'not the original intention though, people in those days were not political. They were impulsive, emotional and practical. They ignored tribal boundaries: gods traversed frontiers then as do new ideas or scientific findings today. Ancient gods were borrowed if they proved effective just as today we buy foreign products to enhance our life. All very pragmatic, very sensible. Gods who did not meet the specifications were dismissed, like Yahweh.

'And all that before the age of consumerism, teases Levinson?

'Well yes, they were very pragmatic in matter of worship; they went for what gave the best return.

They are driven up to the hills surrounding Jerusalem where they will join an excavation of clay figures of Asherah, the Goddess worshipped by Solomon who had pride of place in Temple. Isaacson drives the four-wheel car.

'The Goddess was central to the life of the people', he explains. They look down to the city below bathed in sunlight, the golden dome gleams in the light.

'Stunning, is it not? The Goddess was worshipped for hundreds of thousands of years and her demise did not dampen the regard people had for her. In fact, the more suppressed, the more she was loved.

'Only Asherah, asks Tara?

'Asherah was not the only one, there was Venus too. Men too adored the Goddess. However, biblical research indicates that the cult of Yahweh reaches back to the greatest antiquity. Yahweh is recorded in all ancient mythologies. Gods knew no frontiers; they travelled freely across geographical boundaries. The Sumerians, the people of Abraham, knew that Yahweh did not visit Earth alone but was one of three senior executives who landed on the Planet, so they revered Yahweh's father Anu and Yahweh's brother Enlil as well as Yahweh' s consort whose crucial role it was to carry the Adam in her womb.

'What made the Sumerians retain the memory of this distant event, they do not embellish, asks Levinson?

'The Sumerians were indebted to the Nefilim and their leader Yahweh, to whom they owed their brilliant civilisation. Thousands of years before the Greeks they had astronomy, medicine and a legal system which is the foundation of the Talmud. They also had mathematics, architecture, literature and crafts. They even knew that the Earth was round and revolved around the sun!

'Again why do the Sumerians adopt an almost liberal and secular attitude to their gods and we do not, insists Levinson?

'I can only suggest that we lacked the sophistication of the Sumerians; we always were literal, attached to the form of the narrative, replies Isaac. These tales were recorded in the psyche of humanity. We feared the god who 'made us' the god who shaped us in his image and who wanted us to be 'holy'. Holy means 'separate'. We have stood apart from the rest of humanity in glorious isolation. It is not easy to distance oneself and declare to a suspicious humanity: 'we are different, we are special. A nation of priests, we are morally as well as genetically better and we have to avoid contact with the outside world in order to remain pure'.

'You are a liberal scientist living in a secular state, says Jeremy, how do you feel about the cult of the masculine principle and the demise of the feminine?

'We have rectified the situation, balance is being restored. Women in our democracy have access to higher education and entrance to any career. As a secular people we no longer feel the need to believe in the god of our ancestors. We emphasise freedom of thought. I have a long-standing interest in the Goddess and when this excavation was approved I jumped at the opportunity to dig up a buried part of our history. We pride ourselves of having invented monotheism and even the most liberal among us see it as a momentous stride forward.

'The dream of unity lives on and the Goddess is fulfilling this dream. The longing to return to the primeval state of undifferentiated oneness, says Tara.

'Why is the idea of the one god so esteemed, asked Clara? It spells dictatorship in spiritual life!

'All other gods were eliminated; as in any dictatorship there is one viewpoint, no voice of dissent, replies Isaac. Theism, allegiance to a personalised god, has been outgrown. The despotism of theism is a major force behind our tragic history. The cataclysmic events in Europe put an end to it. If the 20th century taught us one lesson it is that reliance on an outer agency is a thing of the past. The god who ordered that 'we walk before him' and that we 'be holy unto him' was absent in our desperate hour of need. No voice broke through the clouds to alleviate our suffering. The sky was empty, the universe indifferent. Out of the silence came the revelation: god is immoral, irresponsible and unaccountable, we declare him incompetent'. God is well and truly irrelevant to our lives.

'From the ashes of the war, like the Phoenix, rose a new kind of Jew, a self- created man who takes his destiny into his own hands, expands Leah. We no longer pray to stay alive; we defend ourselves boldly and vigorously. We no longer pray for a few scraps of meat to put on the Shabbat table as we did in the ghettos of the past. We have a dynamic, modern economy. We no longer pray god to give us children, we have research laboratories specialising in genetics and fertility. I could go on and on.

'You are up against a strident and hostile group who regard you as outcasts, remarks Johansson, can you ever bridge the chasm between you?

'Yes, in time. We rely on education to open the minds of young people, they are the future. It may take another generation, but it will happen, replies Leah. Young people want to be part of this progressive movement, take their rightful place and make their contribution. Who wishes to be isolated and marginalized? We are up against deeply entrenched views and these rigid views condition every aspect of their lives. They refuse to let go!

'I remember long ago I too would not let go, I did not want to be proved wrong, the thought that I had wasted the best years of my life was simply intolerable, so I struggled on, desperately trying to deny reason. In the end, reason and evidence prevailed, says Clara.

'Yes, there is this fear, agrees Isaac, the fear to admit that one is wrong, but there is more. You see, they are unable to break the submissive mould, they refuse to shape a new vision, they are caught up in the passive model.

'Often the pliable subject who endures his defeated status becomes in turn an aggressor; I have seen this in my own family, remarks Clara.

'That's the point, says Isaac, subject mentality and aggressor mentality are the two sides of the same coin. They both stem from a lack of insight and inertia, from the failure to reflect. What is required is the surgeon knife to incise into the myths and remove the tumour of delusion. We need to engage in a transforming analysis.

'Well, I agree, says Levinson with relief. We always were objects of opprobrium. In Egypt we were relegated to the Nile delta. Legend has it that it was the same in Atlantis before the Flood. Same pattern always, the world rejects us and despises us. Surely some of the blame must lie with us. A sensitive issue for those who view their subjection as a mission.

'We have to find new ways of relating to the world, suggests Clara.

'When we find new ways of relating to ourselves, says Levinson, that is to say when we finally abandon our passive condition and have the courage to look at ourselves in a new and crude light that dispels deception.

A team of workers are digging close by. 'All this digging must be back-breaking, says a concerned Clara.

'It is, says Isaac, if you go to the make-shift museum, that mobile hut over there, you will find workers cleaning and indexing clay figurines and bits of pottery they are putting back together. This will not break your back!

'Archaeology made simple suits me just fine, mutters Clara.

Feminine energy enters the Temple

Cool lemonade is offered and after a short rest, Leah suggests they sit under a tree, away from the excavating team. 'From this vantage point we can look down across the hills and embrace the view of Jerusalem. A beautiful sight and a source of inspiration, sadly denied to Rabbi Moses. Let us go over there to this cluster of trees.

They settle under a tree; Leah draws from her bag the chapter on the Shekhina, the Hebrew Goddess who never left the Children of Israel, she hid discreetly behind the veil. But in 12th century Europe she re-emerges as Mother of the Jewish people. It is no accident that she surfaces at a critical time when Jews are victims of persecution during the Christian exile. Leah reads:

'The magnificent king Solomon built a magnificent Temple officially consecrated to Yahweh, begins Master Sanaka. Politics and religion fused, a great king was building a great temple to a great god. At least that was the official stance, but Solomon's views on politics and religion differed from the norm. As an astute politician he was endeavouring to appease and unite Mammon and God, the material world and the spiritual world. He intended to establish himself as a political and religious sovereign but on his own terms. Yahweh under Solomon's rule was discreetly replaced by the Goddess. The unspoken message was eloquent: Yahweh was irrelevant to the needs of the people, whereas he, Solomon was the new force for the age, the promise of renewal. The time of the Goddess had arrived; in fact it had never left. For too long the Hebrews had been held in thrall by the awesome deity and his forceful masculine attributes. Fear was Yahweh's most effective weapon, an inhibiting force that weaved a web in which they were caught like fish in a net. Fear contracts, shrinks, narrows, constricts and shrivels. Fear weakens the will and impoverishes the character. With fear unity is broken up into fragments and god is a potentially malign force to appease. Religious torment, dread of sin, feeling of aloneness and desertion, fear of God and longing for divine grace have spilt over time and space. European art, theology, philosophy and literature hinge around these issues.

'Viewed from this angle, this is not the formula for well-adjusted individuals, notes Moses. The rabbis were truly men of their generation.

'Right, they put their stamp on their times and on ours too. European thought finds its source in your tradition. Fallen man is racked with fear and riddled with sin. Tormented, disempowered and desolate he seeks salvation outside himself. In Christian thinking grace is granted by god, you get it or you don't! God saves or he does not! The biblical god is unreliable and capricious.

'But ... salvation, mutters Moses.

'What about it, challenges Sanaka? Who needs to be saved? You are your own saviour; no force in the world can save you. Is there a being in the universe powerful enough to save you?

'This is the reason why Solomon brings back the Goddess, erupts Tara who can no longer contain herself.

'I was just going to explode too, laughs a relieved Deborah. Solomon sensing the mood of the people gave them the goddess they longed for. The feminine force, the feminine grace was re-entering the Hebrew psyche. I see now why Solomon brought back the feminine qualities. He was redressing the balance. I now grasp the significance of Solomon's action. Mankind had been in a state of imbalance since the feminine was disqualified and removed from the cosmic equation.

'Polarity on which the world was built had been suspended, comments Isaac. The Hebrews were rewriting the script of Creation in trying to obliterate polarity. The irony is that in eliminating the feminine they were planting the seeds of social unrest as well as interfering with the psyche.

'Emotional turmoil and spiritual morass wrought by man, takes up Levinson a therapist who encounters this turbulence. Goddess energy fosters stability by fostering wholeness. Goddess energy values all aspects of our being, all expressions of who we are, nothing is discredited.

'A religious Jew should never seek Humanistic counselling, muses Clara. He would be unconsciously affirming Goddess qualities and denying his god's attributes. Psychoanalysis or Behaviourism would suit him better; they both deny whole aspects of our nature. I knew a rabbi who spent years in psychoanalysis, at the time I was stunned, not any more! He had intuitively turned to a method that grew out of the patriarchal and monotheistic soil.

'Patriarchy to establish itself must select and discard, notes Tara. Whole aspects of human nature must be removed or discredited, as Clara just said. I see more clearly now the roots of our modern disquiet.

'The world remains in equilibrium, continues Dr Isaac, at the inner and outer levels, for so long as both aspects of polarity function. Imagine, just imagine that a leading physicist decides that he hates the negative charge of the atom and that the atom from now will be positively charged? He would not last long in his job. We did just that, our ancestors messed about with natural law and got away with it! It spilled over the entire Planet.

'Let us return to Rabbi Moses, offers Leah. He speaks of the Shekhina and I have a special interest in the Goddess as you know'. The interrupted discourse by Sanaka resumes: 'to maintain balance both aspects of polarity must retain their equal and opposite values and importance. The Hebrews did away with polarity as Yahweh had wanted them to do long ago. On leaving his laboratory the first Adam was forbidden to taste 'the fruit of the Tree of Good and Evil'. The Tree of Knowledge was for the gods only. But man's natural curiosity saved him. He claimed his divine right to know both sides of things. Polarity was both the purpose behind Creation and the mechanism behind the workings of the universe. The priesthood elevated Yahweh, the masculine aspect, to great heights, inflating him beyond all measure. Yahweh, mirror reflection of man's self, became the Creator.

The Goddess Shekhina

'Moses, do tell me about the Shekhina.

'She is the Mother, explains Moses, she heals and comforts: 'He whose heart is broken and whose spirit is low and whose mouth rarely utters a word, the Shekhina walks with him every day.' She soothes nurtures and consoles.

'Like our Goddess Tara?

'Like Tara. After the destruction of the Temple, she follows her Children in exile. But there is a darker side to her nature. The Talmud tells us that she destroyed Sodom and Gomorrah and drowned the Egyptians in the sea.

'These terrible acts are attributed to the Mother Goddess, interrupts Sanaka?

'Acts of mass destruction were formerly attributed to Yahweh, but times were changing. The rabbis sensing the mood of a more ethical life had to polish the rough edges of the deity. They absolved Yahweh. He is now a just and moral god. These events are shoved on the Goddess.

Rabbi Moses continues his narration. 'Sanaka drew my attention to the fact that the Shekhina is a reflection of the rabbis' fear of women. In the ambiguous portrait they brush of the Mother they divulge their ambiguous attitude towards women. They brazenly debate the inferiority of women too stupid to study the Talmud, too irrational to comprehend. Worst still, the nurturing life-giving woman is in their eyes a source of corruption and damnation! This derogatory view of women was transferred to European society. To defeat femininity and reinforce masculine attributes, women were demoted to their reproductive function. This became the definition of a virtuous woman. The Rabbis failed to root out idolatry, thwarted by the mass of the people who continued to worship the Goddess. For 1000 years, from the time of Exodus to 400 BC, the Hebrews were idol worshippers with the rest of the ancient world. It was the Goddess not Yahweh that the people worshipped. And it was not the inscrutable god of Sinai who resided in the Temple of Solomon but a feminine figure, Asherah. The ancestral god was interfering with the way they perceived the world: ancient people valued diversity, to them all aspects of life were gifted with dignity and meaning. In contrast many aspects of life were tarnished and devalued by the rabbis.

The rabbis sighed a sigh of relief when the present exile brought to a close centuries of ingrained idolatry. Idolatry would be rooted out of Israel and for centuries it appears to be so. Exile would redeem the people; exile would heal 'the sickness of idolatry'. The cult of the Goddess was ended and Yahweh ruled supreme until the Middle Ages when Kabala appeared.

With the emergence of Kabala, the cult of the goddess was revived. Kabala rekindled the Goddess as Solomon had done centuries before. The Shekhina, renamed the Matronite reappeared as a loving Mother. The divine Mother buried in the depth of the Hebrew soul sprang back to life and was received with deep emotion. Claims to monotheism are denied by the evidence. Monotheism is a myth'.

'Sleeping Beauty awakes after a long sleep, notes Tara.

Shabbat – Master Sananda

Clara wishes to clarify conflicting facets of the Shabbat. Shabbat as a unit of time in the world we inhabit, Shabbat in the ancient world as the day offered to the god Saturn and Shabbat metamorphosed into a goddess in Medieval Europe. Shabbat as a goddess is embraced fervently by the Hassidic movement. Different cultural influences, different views of the world fused into one. Clara requests a meeting with Master Sananda which is graciously granted by Jeremy.

'Master Sananda, in Egypt the Hebrews borrowed a number of practices one of which they revere to this day is the Shabbat which the Egyptians celebrated. Shabbat is described as the 'Bride of God'. First, did the 7th day have a spiritual connection with the seven star systems that influenced Egyptian civilisation? Second, did it allude to the seven bodies of man? Third, did the Hebrews make up a link with Creation? I am going to digress a little here if I may. The Creation of the world, if it ever took place, is the material universe. Was their intention different from that of the Egyptians?

'The intention was broadly twofold. First, to hold a connection in consciousness with a particular form of energy which is underlying much of the experience of humanity on the Earth plane. One way of explaining is to describe it as the energy of the seven-pointed Star which comes from a particular dimension, a particular level of awareness which in turn can be seen as an appropriate aspiration for much of humanity. The seven-pointed star symbolises particular states of consciousness which are embedded within the spiritual body of humanity. Therefore, to create the division of a seven day

353

cycle keeps that resonance alive within the human energy matrix through time, through difficulty, through challenges, through darkness, through times of unknowing, stored within human consciousness, ready for a time when it can be more fully understood.

'The second aspect, continues Sananda, is more to do with the importance of the Day of Rest, the day devoted to spiritual practice, a recognition and emphasis of the importance of not getting lost in materiality and physicality; devoting a portion of your time to recognising your spiritual origins.

'The Hebrews are clearly aware of this second aspect, notes Clara. Ancient wisdom teaches that the Divine manifests as a Trinity, and then as Seven. Sumerian culture, the inspiration behind the Hebrew system had Anu, Enlil and Ea. The Hebrews selected Ea eliminating the other two.

'This selection was prompted by their recognition that Yahweh was truly their 'maker' and they owed him total allegiance. The notion of Trinity as well as expressing the three Divine attributes also symbolised the three dimensionality of the physical world. During their exile in Egypt, the Hebrews borrowed the 7th day for the reasons given. Seven as manifestation of the Divine was known and understood in Egypt. They knew of the existence of the seven Rays issued from the One primal Ray, of the main seven spiritual centres in the human subtle body; they consciously connected with the seven stars whose evolved beings had influenced Egyptian evolvement and shaped their culture.

'So the Hebrews stumbled upon the mystical Seven as expression of the Divine?

'They did not 'stumble' at all; they went down into Egypt precisely for that reason. Exile is no chance happening, exile is for your people what school is for the rest of humanity, a way of learning, of progressing, of letting go of old, stale, rigid ways of thinking and replace them by new ones, to soften their stiff energy fields, to 'enlighten' themselves, that is to say to let more light in'.

Monotheism & Idolatry - Master Sananda

'Master Sananda, I would like to expand on Sabbath, monotheism and idolatry. The Hebrews hold that monotheism is their greatest achievement. History shows that monotheism never took root, in spite of a resolute priesthood. They claim that it is a major step forward for mankind.

'I would not choose to describe it this way, no more than I would describe it as a step backward, replies the Master. In other words I do not want to evaluate it in this way. To appreciate its value, look at what is positive within it. I would say there is much that is positive in a monotheistic belief. It can assist people in recognising the oneness of all life. But equally, there is much that is positive in a polytheistic view, recognising, at least potentially, the sacredness of each separate form of life. And so each view offers a portion and a valuable portion of the greater Truth. And the Truth ultimately is made up of those lesser truths brought together. So the ultimate Truth of the nature of the Divine will contain, among other things, contradictions.

'Would you explain the nature of the Divine?

Sananda laughing softly replies, 'I probably could not, it is not possible to put the nature of the Divine into words. The words are not available, words are one small portion of experience and the divine contains all experience.

'Buddha, continues Clara, long before the age of Quantum physics recognised that we are sub-particles in a limitless energy field of cosmic consciousness he calls Emptiness. He enounced the famous phrase 'emptiness is form, form is emptiness'. As particles of cosmic energy, are we one with the cosmic field? In other words, can we perceive divine consciousness simply because we are particles of this infinite energy field?

'Yes, you are at once a tiny part and the whole simultaneously. In as much as you are a tiny part, you can glimpse the whole, and in as much as you are the whole, you can know yourself as the Divine, as cosmic consciousness.

'If each of us is a particle and the Divine at the same time, then what are we doing here? We come to Earth to gather knowledge and experience and relay back to cosmic consciousness. Why does the cosmic Mind need our personal experiences? If we are the totality of consciousness we are enlightened anyway. If we start with the premise that the Source is enlightened, then we are enlightened. What are we doing struggling on this miserable corner of the universe; it is not fun to be here!

'Yes in the sense that I refer to you as being the whole of cosmic consciousness! It is also true that you are already enlightened: at one level of your beingness you are a totally enlightened being. However, you have chosen to be in this particular place in the universe, this particular level of the universe to experience – and this is what so many of you find so difficult to understand - to experience limitations among other things. This is a good way of characterising the nature of life on the Earth plane. You are

355

unlimited beings playing at, exploring the idea of being limited, in order to discover more of yourselves during this process of exploration. Ultimately you are on Earth to grow, to become more alive. You have chosen, all of you, to do it in a paradoxical way, you have chosen to experience aliveness and vibrancy by feeling temporarily less alive, less vibrant, by feeling limited. It is the same kind of lesson you learn when you sit in a dark room for an hour then go out in the garden and are astonished by the light and colours, the fresh air and all those wonderful qualities. You see them afresh, by contrast. This would be one way of giving you a thumbnail sketch as to why you might choose to experience limitations'.

Yin, feminine energy

Rabbi Moses is looking into the sensitive issue of the feminine idea. Having migrated out of a patriarchal society in awe of an oppressive male deity, this issue arouses conflicting feelings. He approaches Master Sanaka who sensing his disquiet has come to him, 'What is troubling you Moses?

'The feminine principle, mutters Moses.

'Naturally, chuckles Sanaka. Let us investigate. The feminine principle is symbolically expressed as the soul. In biblical imagery the Father personifies the mind, the Mother depicts the soul. I detect some discomfort, Moses..... The soul, the feminine has had a hard time with your people. Eve in the biblical allegory is despised. The contempt in which the feminine is held does not change anything. It is important to remember what the soul stands for.

'It stands for unconditional love, freedom of expression, inquisitiveness, fearlessness, joy, compassion, replies Moses in haste.

'Yes it is, but are you ready for this? At one level of meaning the Father symbolises the human mind. Instead of despising the Mother for her 'stupidity, impurity and frivolity' he should celebrate her mysterious nature. The mind, this rational tool that has taken millions of years to evolve should not regard the soul which is unborn, timeless and infinite with disdain. To disown woman is to disown a vital aspect of one's being. Woman is the mother of humanity, how can she be despised! What is demeaning to woman is also demeaning to man, he is greatly impoverished.

'Put this way I lament my past ignorance. Born in the shadow of patriarchy I endorsed the values of patriarchy. Women were segregated. This may account for the anguish I experienced and could not explain.

'Your sensitive being was whispering something you did not want to hear. The mind is capable of a great many distortions. When the feminine was banished, the Father — figuratively the intellect - became sole ruler and as ruler it dictated its own terms; it set out to divide, separate, fragment and segregate. What makes you believe that you are unique and special?

'The fact that we were selected.

'Every individual is special; every person is the Divine in human form. You recognise this special quality in you while denying it to others. Now you see the fallacy of past delusion. You know that all humans revisit Earth countless of times in all kinds of garbs. Human beings who come back in the Hebrew garb have seen it all, done it all! They have all been in turn victims or aggressors down the ages. What makes you think that a person who was separative, self-absorbed, intolerant and fanatical yesterday is now a paragon of virtue? He borrows that body to be just as he was!

'This was difficult initially. We believe in one life, one single life. Belief in the single life is crucial to both monotheism and patriarchy. If a Jew knew that he had countless bodies over millions of years, his allegiance to the deity would be rather flimsy, even more flimsy than it already is.

'Or non-existent! The man in this new body is the man he was in his old body! Changing the body does not change the man. The self errs; it has to be illumined by the light of the soul. Even the Divine needs the feminine to create life! So the Mother and the Father beget the Son - the hidden Messiah. All three dwell in the chest of man. Disregard for woman blurts out the character of the man: uninspired, unevolved, unredeemed, and undeveloped. When man views woman as just a womb devoid of human and divine qualities, then how does he view himself? The diminishment of woman is the diminishment of man. When man denigrates a vital aspect of himself, he gives away his crude nature. He also unwittingly discloses the arrogant nature of the Father, the god made in his image. He has banished humility, love and empathy. The Father is hostile to kindness and sympathy, or in symbolic terms, the mind has not yet recognised the existence of the soul.

'I understand, admits Moses with sadness. We claim ownership of the Book of Genesis, yet we spurn the first verses, in the opening lines the Mother of humanity is found guilty. Eve is cursed, despised and downgraded. The pious scribe in all ignorance is cursing the human soul, cursing his own soul!

'You understand why the Hierarchy sent out Solomon to restore cosmic balance. To restore balance he had to reinstate the banished soul of humanity and give it pride of place in the centre of the Temple. The Goddess he placed in the purest part of the Temple, where she belongs. It is the soul that is put back at the centre of human life. The mind, the mortal self, has to step down and acknowledge the ascendancy of the soul. 'Solomon's heart was not wholly with his god', the rabbis lament! Solomon's heart was to reinstate the soul of humanity not to worship the mortal self!

The Rise of Patriarchy

'The rise of patriarchy and the demise of the Goddess bring about social change. Life no longer revolves around women, their natural affinity for the Earth cycles and their insight into the mystery of life. The banishment of the Goddess brings to an end the inclusive, sensitive mode of knowing which is essentially intuitive. The world of patriarchy is ordered and regimented. With the shift from intuitive knowing to controlled, regimented, disciplined outlook, humanity enters a new phase in its history. The controlled form of thinking dismisses images, dreams, intuitive insight and inspiration.

'One of the Ten Commandments forbids all images, notes Moses.

'Thus demonstrating the fear patriarchy had for intuition, inspiration and insight. These soul qualities are perceived as subversive.

'Subversive because they cannot be controlled, asks Moses?

'That's right, they are banned. More to the point it shows that the soul, infinite and timeless must step down to make space for the personality which is finite and ephemeral. Patriarchy is of this world and this world alone, it implants itself solidly and often aggressively into this dimension. Images, dreams, imagination and inspiration stem from the soul which is beyond their control. For that reason patriarchy must prohibit images and declare them idolatrous.

'Naturally, they are of feminine origin if they stem from the intuition!

358

'The feminine qualities of kindness, sensitivity, and feeling for nature, empathy and acceptance are driven underground. The masculine traits of authority, subjection, subservience, dependency, obedience, regulation and restraint take over. The feminine mode of relating to the world is discredited.

'I must interrupt the reading at this point, says Deborah. These reflections by Master Sanaka on feminine and masculine differences have infuriated me, I have to confess, but they also shed a raw light on an issue that was too emotional to discuss.

'I felt the same way, adds Tara, anger but also light.

'The rise of the new way of thinking – classifying, cataloguing, indexing, pigeonholing, separating, discriminating - had a long-term impact ponders Clara. Ritualistic religion has its source in it! Modern civilisation has its roots in it too. Anger but also illumination, for me too.

'The feminine mode went into decline, says Deborah, until now. Women are once again asserting their innate qualities and making their voices heard. Intelligent and educated, they demand that their rights be restored and the Goddess is emerging once again as feminine values are resurfacing.

'A new awareness is dawning as some people draw their imagery from Eastern thought: the duality of Yin and Yang confirms the cosmic equilibrium. Yin and Yang contain both the biology and the psychology of the masculine and feminine. Yang stands for 'left brain' or masculine aspect, linear, critical, fragmented and separative. Among the 'chosen people', left brain activity has been cultivated by the Talmudic passion for debate. Modern education is structured on this model, it stresses linear, analytical thinking, reflects Clara.

'While Yin stands for 'right brain' activity, the feminine aspect, butts in Tara, with its grasp of 'wholes', it has the holistic nature of the feminine awareness. This is something we must rediscover and reintroduce in our educational systems: lateral thinking, imagination and intuition are more important to our understanding of the world than modern education recognises.

'The rise of patriarchy and monotheism ushered in ethnic, social and religious intolerance, concludes Deborah. It promoted a religious system made by men and in which men do better. Patriarchy and monotheism acclaimed exclusiveness and separateness as norms, the two great evils that have plagued our people and are responsible for its lasting predicament.

Narcissism & group Identity

Deborah expands further the theme of her thesis. She is overjoyed to find such a receptive audience. She esteems their judgment and values their intelligence. 'There is more, she smiles waiting for an invitation to continue.

'We want to hear more, encourages Tara.

'Women fear their own femininity, resumes Deborah with renewed enthusiasm. The rabbis fear women's mysterious body and power. In their life-giving role women emulate the creative power of God. That's not all, women's fear of their femininity, men's fear of women's body are combined with their common fear of freedom. It is the fear of freedom that consolidated the rule of Yahweh on the world stage. Had women resisted their bondage and retaliated against their low standing they would have set us free!

'Women as saviours in a patriarchal society? Heresy, laughs Levinson.

'Capitulating to patriarchal propaganda, they surrendered their natural power. They chose to believe the fiction woven around their inferior nature. They had what it takes to 'save' mankind, to grasp the message of freedom the Essenes were presenting. They carried that message in the depth of their being. The majority of them still worshipped the Goddess. Many women had an altar in their homes dedicated to Venus. Yet the propaganda worked, had they not lost their poise they might have prevented the most terrible exile ever.

'Women preventing the present exile, laughs Levinson, decidedly not convinced. Try to tell that to patriarchal orthodoxy!

'I am not going to! Who will fracture the dam of prehistoric belief? It took an earthquake to bring down the walls of Jericho! An opportunity to stamp out our infantile Narcissism, the egotism Moses endeavoured to eradicate, was lost. They petrified under the all-seeing, all-menacing Father.

'Big Brother, Orwell's vision of a doomed future, notes Clara, I lived it.

'We are told that the shift from the Mother to the Father was an evolutionary necessity, suggest Jeremy. The Hebrews were on the same evolutionary path as the rest of humanity.

'Perhaps it is time to hit the road in the opposite direction, suggests Tara, an adept of the Goddess movement.

'I go along with this, replies Deborah. The grasp of 'wholes' was of woman, the fragmented grasp is the seal of patriarchal culture. In other words the shift was from wholeness to division, from universality to contraction, from altruism to narcissism. We abandoned the nurturing protection of the feminine energy; we dropped the subtle web of interconnections that unite us to humanity and the Planet. We swapped a universal view for a cramped view of the world.

'Furthermore, contributes Johansson who wrote his thesis on ancient cultures and religions, there is humanity - Goddess culture thrived on the principle of the oneness of humanity. Monotheistic patriarchy effectively hindered the progress of the whole of mankind, indeed the whole Planet. With a fractured ankle you cannot run, so a limping humanity has been hopping along ever since! Narcissus in the Greek myth admired his reflection in the water and fell in love with it. Seeing only himself, he lost touch with the world.

'You are writing my essay for me, laughs Deborah delighted with the response. The short-term opportunism of the rabbis in keeping women repressed delayed our collective emancipation by 2000 years.

Monotheism, Patriarchy & the Oedipus complex

Benzaccai's wife continues to talk about her thesis. Her interest has been growing in the course of her research. She asks if they would like to listen further. They do.

'I would like your honest opinion on it, because it is more than just an academic paper, I have developed with the thesis, I have discovered myself, I have expanded my thoughts as I was writing. It is as much a journey of self-discovery as it is academic research, a personal journey. I aim to challenge existing conditioned and outdated views that have kept us in a kind of parallel world ... one of the parallel dimensions science is postulating ...., or a kind of bubble, present but not quite present, real but unreal at the same time. Do you follow me? I want to pierce the bubble and let air in, let light in. I want to make a difference in the way we view the world, I want to inspire a desire for change.

'You have our full support, replies Jeremy. This is our life purpose too.

'In ancient society patriarchal rule coerces the son to abide by social rules laid down by the father. The mother perceived as 'impure' is demoted to a reproductive role and the son has to watch his mother downgraded. Torn between love for her, indignation at the way she is treated, fear of his father and greater fear of his father's god, he is caught up in an emotional whirlpool. Object of lust woman inspires aversion or is it desire?

'This aversion disguises a secret fear of the sensitive aspect in man; it is an unconscious rejection of intuitive life. But there is fear of the feminine in woman herself, notes Tara, compounded by a fear of the feminine in the world, the unconscious desire to eradicate this side of polarity. Patriarchy is at war with the feminine principle in the universe.

'Right, continues Deborah. Patriarchy has to design and implement strict rules that relegate women to an inferior role. Women are declared 'impure' and 'unclean', to be cleansed and purified by rituals designed by men. They are kept at bay so as not pollute 'sanctified' men. As a result love from her son and husband is discouraged as so many taboos surround her nature.

'This is fascinating, says Clara. The stage is set for every form of emotional and mental pain. Disconnection, fear, guilt, impurity, shame, self-disgust lurks behind much mental anguish. Advocates of these devastating traits we have unwittingly promoted emotional turmoil and social mayhem. Embedded in the human psyche they are the heritage of mankind. A new psychological science had to be invented to help man forgive himself an ease him back to wholeness.

'Not forgetting piety, adds Deborah.

'Why piety, asks Jeremy?

'Piety to reinforce the prejudices of one group, piety that edicts taboos to keep the other group subservient. Is this not discrimination in a minor key? Mystifying! We fear other people but we also fear Jewish women, we despise foreigners but we also despise Jewish women. We are at war not only with the world but with ourselves.

'The old system perpetuates the tyranny of the self. Illusion and self-deception we value, continues Clara. 'When the Tao is lost there is need for legality, morality and much pretence…'. When we lost the Way, long ago, we set up a stage on which to perform our 'passion' plays. We are conjurers; we deal in 'cloud castles', in mirages. Our currency is the unreal. That is our tragedy.

'Human beings, butts in Levinson, have been reincarnating for aeons to learn to discriminate between the real and the unreal, the true and the false and we can't see the wood for the trees! Human beings often reincarnate to replay past experiences. This replay is a chance to make sense of previous mistakes and choose a new outcome. Many are reluctant to learn from past mistakes, engrossed into the replay rather than in the understanding.

'What of the son, enquires Jeremy with interest?

'The son is on the rack, in conflict and in confusion, replies Deborah. The Oedipus complex arises out of fear, authority, guilt and prohibition. The son discouraged from loving an 'impure' mother develops a strong attachment to her. He also becomes dependent on her and this further hinders his emotional development. The crisis that gives rise to the Oedipus myth is acted out on a monotheistic stage where the social arrangement is stable, where the father' s power is secure and where the god who gives him that power is kept in awe. We have a strong triangle of forces in equilibrium: a rigid tribal system, a controlling father and a dictatorial god. Perfect recipe for stability and inertia, cohesion and stagnation, emotional turmoil and mental lethargy, social apathy and hidden resentment! This triangle of forces is potentially volatile; it detonated in our 20th century.

'No unrest in the walled up ghettos of the world, notes Clara.

'For so long as the 'triangle' was strong. The outside world was hostile and kept us confined within the walls. But more potent than the world was the insidious influence of the god-force which permeated our being, the very cells of our bodies, the DNA in our cells, comments Levinson.

'You hit the nail on the head! Our tradition is built on a triangular foundation of fear: man fear of woman, the son fear of the father and the father fear of his god. This pernicious triangle undermines our integrity and is source of inner dissonance and dissociation. It comes as no surprise that the model for the Oedipus myth, Akhenaton, was the first monotheistic Pharaoh of Egypt who banned the many gods and imposed his one god Aton.

'It is strange that fixation to the mother should arise in a society governed by men and dominated by a masculine god, says Jeremy. Quite a paradox. Is it an unconscious need to restore the balance that was lost, I wonder?

'Possibly, continues Deborah expanding further, but it will not come to light because we hide behind doctrine. The cloak of religious dogma shrouds the yearning for truth. And it should come as no surprise either that devout men deny their wives any courteous attention, refusing even to engage in polite conversation with them. The woman, object of sin, impurity and lust is also the embodiment of futility; she must not defile her husband who has to be pure for his god. There we have all the ingredients of psychological and emotional disturbance: a 'defiled' woman, a scornful man scared of the feminine and a dictatorial god who crafts taboos to keep them apart. What of the child in this recipe for disaster? Is it surprising that emotional distress is so pronounced in the Western world permeated as it is by the insidious presence of patriarchy and monotheism?

'The idealised woman adored in ancient times is no more, says Clara with guarded indignation.

'In biblical times a woman's reason for living was to ensure the perpetuation of the group. Her life then as now has meaning only in obedience to her husband and through him to his god. For as an inferior being, she relies on her husband to act as intermediary between her and his god. What gives dignity to her life is to serve. Her subservient role is rigidly legislated and enforced by tradition. Captive in the prison built for her she has internalised her inferiority, her natural 'stupidity' and her unworthiness.

'Women did internalise their inferiority and fake stupidity, repeats Clara.

'What is to be built on such shaky foundations when woman is fated to perpetuate the flesh, exclaims Deborah! Eve was dealt a fatal blow by patriarchy and monotheism. Woman fell from spirit to matter, from wholeness to fragmentation, from intuitive insight to ignorance. This is not progress, this is regression. Woman is no longer 'divinised', no longer idealised, no longer a being of love who creates harmony and peace, no longer one who inspires, unifies and redeems.

'I for one will oppose any attempt at evacuation to some distant planet if only on the ground of the subjection of women, says Clara with animation.

'All this will change when the Goddess makes her reappearance on the planetary stage. But the Goddess never left the Planet, reassures Tara! She has always guarded humanity, from Shamballa where she resides.

Women succumb to the 'Fall'

'These last few days have enhanced my thinking in ways I would never have thought possible, says Deborah. Women were denied their humanity and relegated to breeding.

We naively believed that god in his wisdom had picked us, his 'chosen people' to safeguard Torah. The events of the past few days force me to reappraise the whole thing. The role of women in Hebrew society has taken on a sinister tinge. A breeding programme was orchestrated in antiquity to ensure the future of a genetically enhanced people. Is it the sinister vision of an Orwell or the nightmare scenario of a Kafka? Neither, it's our prehistoric society which continues to this day its programme of genetic selection. Engineered selection that thwarts the forces of life.

'You are having a hand in evolution, notes Jeremy.

'We are forcing evolution in one sense and obstructing it in another, explains Clara. Throwing all our resources into survival we paralyse the higher impulse. In Maslow's 'pyramid of needs', when physical needs are satisfied we look to spiritual needs. We continue to invest all our energies into satisfying the lower needs, survival needs. What of our higher needs?

'Do you remember what transpires from the discussion on the Fall', enquires Deborah focussed on her subject. Not waiting for an answer she continues, 'there are two aspects to the Fall.

'Isn't one enough, interrupts Jeremy?

'The first concerns humanity, the other concerns women. The patriarchal system which defeated the Goddess and demoted women did so with the conspiracy of women. Starved of education, convinced of their innate incompetence, denied a mind, reminded that their bodies are impure and their emotions sinful, they regressed to a lost age that harks back to the myth of Genesis. Eve cursed by patriarchy and its god, loses her spiritual union with nature, her communion with all life, she is discouraged from asserting her own womanhood. This is the 'Fall' of woman.

'A return to the Goddess culture would change all this, agrees Tara. With a greater permissiveness women will rediscover their primeval power. Love will have a chance.

'How can we go back? Reverting to the primal state of union with the Mother would be a regressive step, a step that many neurotics take and that humanity has long outgrown. We are endeavouring to emerge from an age-long dependency to the Father, retorts Levinson.

'Not dependency to the Mother though, snaps Tara! It is the Father who restricts, restrains, fragments and separates. Disconnection leads to emotional turmoil and mental distress. To heal is to restore wholeness.

'To heal is to make whole, echoes Clara.

'The Father censures feelings, discredits individual thought and devalues personal experience, continues Deborah. We are forbidden our emotions, and our thoughts, yet nothing is more crucial than inner experience. We are denied an inner life. Patriarchy is not the recipe for mental health. The stern image of the Father would fade away in a less rigid set up.

'Buddha taught that the gods were stumbling blocks to man's emancipation. Zen Buddhism holds that to become free man must distance himself from his gods, adds Tara.

'Wholeness and integration the aim of healing arise from within, not from outside. To insist that redemption can only come from god is not only a denial of reality it is an anomaly, expands Deborah. It shows that we have never understood the fundamentals of living.

'I am not in favour of a return to any goddess, but I am in favour of the dissolution of the god-force which hovers over Western civilisation, argues Clara. Besides, we are getting there by a different route. We left long ago the mythical Garden of Eden, an allegory for 'whole' man conscious of his connection with the Divine and with the world. Man was truly 'perfect': the many dimensions of his being were known to him. With the Fall, he lost all: the memory of his multi-dimensionality dropped into his unconscious. This unconscious reservoir of knowledge is beginning to rise to the surface.

'Freud was the first to encourage the rediscovery of unconscious material to heal troubled minds, notes Tara.

'Yes, but I am talking about a different kind of unconscious material. It is the vast knowledge of man's identity; his cosmic nature. Cosmic waves of light are helping us remember and assist us in reclaiming our former fullness.

The Goddess

Long ago was matriarchy, continues Deborah. During the long period in which the Mother presided over human affairs, men worshipped the Goddess. Unconditional love she gave to all her children irrespective of their origins. Men were not judged and so they knew no fear.

'Sorry to interrupt, this is crucial for humanity, 'men knew no fear'. Fear prowls behind discord, antagonism and wars. Fear lurks behind most disease; there is a universal rise in tension, stress and anxiety. Even in this age in which we are rediscovering soul qualities, the Father does not relent.

'I take note, replies Deborah. They grew in a secure climate of love in which fear was absent. Never did the Mother place the mountain before her children with the thunderous clamour, 'Do and obey or the mountain will crush you'. They did not stifle their being in order to conform to tribal norms. They did not have to put up with tribal rules, stick to tribal values nor cave in to tribal bondage. Free from the prying eyes of Big Brother they were encouraged to simply 'be' without strings attached, free to experience the full range of feelings. How enriching and liberating to reject nothing, condemn nothing and respect everything. It is this fluidity that empowers. Free to live the moment that no synthetic belief tarnishes, the individual has no reason to repress whole aspects of his nature. Repression which psychoanalysis blames for our emotional distress was unknown to Goddess culture. Repression was the tool of patriarchy. Repression set in when the ruling power declared that feelings must be barred. There is repression when the individual is unable to acknowledge his feelings because he is programmed to disown them. He must distort his experience to make it fit preconceived ideas. Burdened by inherited thought patterns, he applies a petrified set of ideas to any encounter and so disfiguring the experience. He is conditioned to do so and as a result everything he experiences is untrue, unreal. His whole life is devoid of authenticity, it is a lie, a façade, a charade.

'A splendid analysis of influences on the evolution of mankind, says Jeremy.

'Thank you, I appreciate your attention and support, this means a lot to me, replies Deborah. I would like to conclude this section. As the Goddess soothed and consoled the heart of man, she ruled society and governed religious life. With the Mother toppled, patriarchy becomes the ruling force in society and religion.

'Patriarchy overthrows the Goddess and takes over the domination of Earth, but its goal is for ever thwarted, notes Tara.

'You are right. Patriarchy manipulates human perception and alters it irredeemably, so that from being a nurturing, supportive environment, the universe becomes threatening, arbitrary, and random. But man is reluctant to give up something that was so good. In spite of unremitting efforts to stamp out 'idolatry', the Goddess is tolerated because she is revered by the people who know that they are loved unconditionally. No demand, no competition, no fear, the mother loves regardless of success or failure. The people resonate with the Goddess; she is the imprisoned soul whispering in them. Yet they propitiate to the Father who choreographs their repetitive behaviour in which the soul is silent.

'So much for the naturalness, spontaneity and fluidity of life, laughs Clara.

'All of our experience is cast in that mould, a Pavlov type response to stimuli. Situations are new but our response is ancient. We meet the present with the calcified response of the past, the fossilised pattern of the past.

'The trouble is that this kind of conditioned response is linked to mental distress and emotional anguish. Patients with these symptoms are unable to experience life freely and genuinely, their perception has been warped. It is the task of therapists to disentangle the twisted strands, says Levinson.

'This conditioned behaviour is patriarchal in nature, continues Clara. The Father demands repetitive behaviour, automatic response. Spontaneity, fluidity, authenticity are discarded as deviant. Patriarchal conditioning distorts human perception and warps human experience.

'The Goddess is bringing back autonomy spontaneity, authenticity and personal responsibility, the pre-eminent qualities of the soul, says Tara.

'Absolutely, replies Deborah visibly elated. I delight in your comments. We don't even realise, it is so ingrained. There are a couple more points in my essay I must read out to you. Expiation and blood sacrifices are two main features of our tradition.

'Expiation for sins real or imaginary and blood offerings show that man has lost connection with the Infinite. In his distress he seeks approval and support from external forces; he is devoid of inner resources. The Mother does not promote guilt or shame nor does she exact atonement.

'The biblical god may forgive because he judges and condemns, she does not. As an aspect of the Divine, the Goddess does not forgive because she does not judge, mutters Clara who recalls the words of Sananda.

'The biblical injunctions 'Fear the lord your god', 'walk in the path of righteousness for the lord your god demands that you be holy', 'do not disobey, for the lord is quick to punish' are unknown in Goddess culture, continues Deborah. You know the story of Purim and the planned genocide of the Hebrews in exile. Their spiritual leader

Mordehai understood that only Esther could save them and she did. Extraordinary don't you think? Salvation came from Esther – the Goddess Ishtar!

'I must interrupt at this point, if I may, butts in Levinson. As a counsellor, I find the parallel between the biblical god and the Goddess significant. Underlying the psychology of Freud is the 'god of wrath'; sin and retribution lurk behind his theory in an ominous way. I am not suggesting that Freud enounces a psychology based on the old god; yet underlying the torment of mankind is the spectre of the energy of fear, alienation, betrayal, self-blame and self-loathing. Patriarchy, in suppressing whole areas of human experience, warps and distorts perception as was just said.

'Goddess knowledge is emerging with modern psychology, notes Clara always on Levinson's wavelength.

'Exactly, he replies. The energy of love - acceptance, tolerance, empathy and understanding - is reappearing in modern psychology and counselling. Judgment, retribution, expiation and sacrifice the pillars of the biblical world, are crashing down like the walls of Jericho. They infringe upon human integrity, violate the divine in man and foster mental distress.

'Paradoxically, psychoanalysis anchored in patriarchal culture is best suited to the 'godly' in spite of its determinism and because of it! Freedom is eminently the quality of the soul, the attribute of the Goddess and it is being rediscovered by modern psychology, says Levinson.

'I am grateful for the interruption; you have shed light from another angle, well worth it! This point will enhance my essay. I am reaching my conclusion in the form of a summary: 'In our patriarchal system, forlorn man deprived of the Mother lives in a frenzied whirl of religious rituals, acts of faith and acts of penitence. The more elusive god is, the more determined man is to reach out to him, and so the gap between them widens. God remains firmly 'out there' while 'deluded' man remains firmly grounded. Man in the 20th century has often preferred nihilism and atheism to frantic gyrations to a god he does not 'know'. This has given him a new sense of freedom and dignity.

'According to Sacred Teachings, the fall of humanity began from the time of the abasement of the Feminine Principle …. Woman should realise that she contains all forces…' writes Helena Roerich in her Letters, quotes Tara.

'Not surprising really, comments Clara, is not Eve the embodiment of the Feminine Principle? The fall of Eve is the fall of mankind.

'The 'abasement of the feminine principle' is more than the fall of woman, it has a cosmic significance, comments Jeremy. No rational physicist would suggest removing from the atom the negatively-charged particle; no sound astro-physicist would consider the possibility of a universe built on positively-charged particles to the exclusion of electrons. The entire fabric of the cosmos would collapse. Yet we do just that! The world was created around Yin and Yang but patriarchy played down the entire negatively-charged aspect of man, the 'negative' feminine force! 'Negative' is in no way derogatory.

'We are still doing it, exclaims Deborah! When a man says 'Thank god for not making me a woman' he is denigrating the fundamental principles of Creation.

'Were they trying to repeat the cataclysm of Atlantis, ponders Jeremy?

'One might think so. Could it be, as Eric Fromm suggests, that attachment to the Goddess - the Mother - represents one phase of development in the evolution of mankind which must be supplanted by that of the Father, enquires Johansson?

'Quite right! The Father phase follows that of the Mother, agrees Deborah, and monotheism is that phase, but remember that the Father phase of development must be displaced by yet another.

'The Son, points out Jeremy.

'The Son, confirms Johansson, symbolic form of the next phase of evolution. The Son asserts his individuality, claims his autonomy, and affirms his personal responsibility. The Son is now evolved, liberated from outside pressure, released from outside interference, free to make his life choices and as he does, he erodes and undermines the power of the Father. In esoteric terms, the god 'out there' begins to fade away while the god within rises in its power and radiance equipped to replace him.

'The decline of the Father parallels the rise of humanity, notes Tara.

'The emergence of the spirit, says Jeremy. The spirit that was suppressed reappears with its primordial features: love, empathy, gentleness, cooperation, tolerance, sympathy, equality and freedom.

'The demise of the Father opens the door to the re-emergence of soul in its cosmic and individual mode of expression, says Tara.

A woman rabbi in a patriarchal society?

'Clara, asks Johansson teasingly, ever thought of becoming a rabbi?

'What kind of a joke is that, retorts Clara not at all amused!

'No it's not. Long ago before you saw the light?

'Don't insult my common sense. Every thinking person knows that the old biblical system is essentially political. An exclusive men's club. A political-come-religious system in the despotic mode, 'do & obey' or death for dissent. A political system that brooks no departure from the norm, governed by a ruling elite dead for 2000 years! A one party rule.

'Things are changing, there are now women rabbis, notes Tara. Religious form is softening; a woman is best suited to soften, to smooth, to polish. Women rabbis can change things. They can transform the collective consciousness. They tend to be more 'liberal'.

"That's a joke, reacts Clara! So they offend reason and tradition, logic and belief! The super-orthodox offend reason; those of a more lukewarm or 'liberal' disposition affront both reason and faith! Ours is the oldest religious-come-political system, an all male bastion. To implant the dogma in the collective psyche they moulded a thought form that permeates all, Big Brother, an all-pervading presence. With a strong male deity the system was solidified for ever, never to be questioned. The deity who animates the political ideology is the manifestation of the unregenerate, unliberated human ego. How many emancipated Jews would identify with him?

'Not many I must admit, laughs Levinson.

'To think that women can break into this all-male fortress is naïve, continues Clara, why not try Fort Knox instead! Who is fooling who?

'Yet they do, notes Tara.

'They play the role, but who believes them? The collective instinct will find it hard to swallow. Will a woman rabbi polish and smooth the jagged edges of the male deity? Is she to impart some of her finer qualities? Will she redeem the human ego? The system rotates around the deity in his unrepentant form. Nothing has changed. To change is to destroy. 'Destroy' in the sense that the Hierarchy intends: to 'destroy' is to disperse the fossilised forms that obstruct the expansion of consciousness. To 'destroy' is to remove the forces that prevent man from knowing his own divine nature. To 'destroy' is to remove the blockages that obstruct the realisation of the divine Plan for the Planet and hold the soul of man in captivity. This is the long overdue 'destruction' planned and intended by the Hierarchy long ago. A woman rabbi is perpetuating a system which the Hierarchy has been working at 'destroying' for at least 2000 years and more!

Rabbi Moses explores his Jewishness

The journey of discovery was unfolding with no end in sight in spite of the expressed desire to go home. Benzaccai was more elusive than ever. They were tearing up and down the country looking for him, disappointed and disheartened. This search, meaningless to all accounts, was bearing fruit though they never seemed to reach their goal, something else was happening. Like the heroes of ancient myths who journey endlessly, never reaching their destination, they too were reaping the benefit of their travels. 'We are like Arjuna who wanders in search of some mysterious wisdom that will answer all his questions. Under the guidance of Krishna he discovers that he is on a journey of personal transformation once said Tara'. 'We are like the heroes of ancient myths who set sail in search of the elusive Holy Grail once said Clara'.

They decide to stay a while longer in spite of their weariness. They had to admit that their journey was neither meaningless nor aimless, they were going somewhere. But where? They only dimly sensed their destination. One morning a young man arrives with a letter from a Jewish doctor in Jericho, who explains that Benzaccai had stayed briefly at his house. He invites them for a meal that same day. Intrigued they accept. Another trip!

'My father has the next translated chapter from The Hebrew Gods. I am Joshua Delmar.

'May I ask what you are doing in Jericho, asks Jeremy? I don't want to pry …

'My father is a maverick. He came from Britain after qualifying. A sensitive person, he listened to his intuition and settled in a kibbutz that a few 'avant-garde' intellectuals and artists had established. They shared a common concern for the welfare of the less fortunate. As intuitive intellectuals they set out to establish a spiritual community.

'An unusual man indeed, says Jeremy. A spiritual community, I like that!

'Do you want to travel with me now, my car is spacious.

'We may as well'. They hurriedly pack. They were getting skilled at this game of hide-and-seek, of packing and unpacking at the drop of a hat! They did not want to leave Galilee, the lake, the sunsets, the trees. After what seemed an interminable and tiresome journey they finally arrive in Jericho. The doctor lives in a modest but comfortable area of the town.

'Dr Delmar greets them with joyous exuberance like long lost friends; they respond to his joy and feel his warmth. An unusual man indeed, he radiates kindliness and simplicity. Scented tea and cakes are served.

'What keeps you in Jericho, enquires Jeremy?

'The love of peace. When I first came to the land of my ancestors, I had a clear idea of what I wanted to do. I had just qualified as a doctor and wanted to offer my services, nothing more. But there was more, much more lurking under the threshold of consciousness, I sensed it but could not express it.

'How did you detect your real reason for coming here, asks Jeremy?

'It developed over the years, through study and deep reflection. A long gestation, he adds with laughter. A few intellectuals, artists, writers and professionals came to live and work together. Our intention was to offer an alternative way of life. Life could be lived differently, it was possible to transcend self-inflicted limitations, go beyond our ancestral pattern of thinking. Patriarchy had its day. We felt that times were changing and we had to respond to the changes, meet the new challenges headlong. We had a responsibility to the world. We could no longer walk in denial, no longer pretend. There was no place to hide; we had to face up to reality.

'A daring programme after centuries spent aimlessly wanderings into mists, mirages, rainbows and cloud castles, says Clara impressed.

'We were aware of that. Our goal was to foster unity.

'Not a mean task in this country, remarks Levinson.

'At times we wondered. But we refused to be browbeaten and defeated by the forces of conservatism, the forces of retrogression. These forces responsible for our catastrophic history were showing no sign of abating. You have to realise that the founders of Israel who came from a ravaged Europe were intent on creating a new world, a 'new man'. They had left behind the image of the battered Jew, archetypal victim of fate, cursed to wander aimlessly.

'The Flying Dutchman, inserts Clara!

'In a sense. What we were doing was in the spirit of the pioneers. These pioneers were the future of Israel, the future of humanity. A new human race was in the making, not a race distinguished by its skin colour or racial characteristics, but a human race sharing a

373

noble ideal of collaboration, assistance, understanding, equality, liberty and unity. This is the 'new' human race. Long ago we made fear our mental home. With fear come separation, hostility, distrust, aggression, conflict and death. Our negative outlook dispersed over the globe like nuclear fallout. Western civilisation founded on our worldview endorsed fear. Change is on the horizon; modern man is moving away from fear and claiming his natural birthright. This is the vision that the founding fathers of Israel held, the vision that is now being threatened by the forces of ritualism. This may be the most dangerous period in our history. Emancipation is a reality, but the self-styled prophets of today have other ideas.

'How did you all come together, asks Jeremy?

'From inside and outside Israel, idealists who like us visualised a better world. We realised that political and religious doctrines divide people. We were determined to bring people together, all people. This was a daring experiment. The diehards poured scorn on us and labelled us renegades. In their eyes we were the enemies of god!

'I am not surprised, smiles Clara, I am acquainted with their crude labelling.

'So am I, inserts Levinson. Self-styled prophets, spellbound by the letter of the law worship at the altar of division. Religious activists of all times, places and shades are much the same.

'Their knowledge ...wrong word, says Clara correcting herself, their pseudo-knowledge is mere opinion. There is more to knowledge than an artificial yardstick to gauge the world. True knowledge is derived from personal experience. Lacking the intuitive feel they make do with home-made brews. They resort to the lower frequency of fear which grounds them. Fear is to them desirable, they teach it in their schools where it is brewed with hope. In the words of the Sufi: 'Some need hope and fear; they are those who have had it prescribed for them'.

'I made Sufism my spiritual home, reveals Delmar with enthusiasm. I often quote this Sufi pearl of wisdom, 'What they took to be fundamentals are really worthless externals... And the casing which they think important the very barriers to their understanding'. Our predicament in a nutshell! What we believe to be the source of our survival is the source of our downfall.

'It keeps us anchored, 'prisoners of the Planet', notes Clara.

'The 'worthless externals', 'the casing' are to us absolute truth, we live and die for 'the very barriers to [our] understanding'. We imprison our progeny in these 'barriers', condemning them to the same captivity. Why keep the ancestral wound bleeding? The sincere seeker hunts for the essence, says Delmar, this is Sufism. True religion is the quest for the essence; this is why our religion is a lampoon of the real thing: it begins and ends with 'externals'. Our religion is not one of essence, but one of form. We are chasing a mirage, for the thing truly existent is Love, the essence of the universe. And as we discarded love in favour of fear we are for ever moving away from the essence. As the Sufi master El-Arabi explains it is the love of the Essential that makes man conscious, the love of phenomenon 'makes man unconscious of himself'. Our tradition keeps us 'unconscious'.

'It keeps us 'unconscious' because we it keeps us repeating like automatons, inserts Clara. Phenomena – things, forms, events and facts – deceive us; we are unable to see 'the spiritual purpose of phenomena'. We are duped by the externals. And so we go on living unconsciously.

'I agree, our distant ancestors made a solemn pledge to worship the 'god of wrath', replies Delmar. Why repeat endlessly their pledge? As we perpetuate the pledge we also perpetuate our disastrous fate. We keep the wound open, bleeding, festering. Instead of healing we induce more pain. We believe that we lost Paradise and that we are cursed for it! We believe what tradition conditions us to believe! The ancestors, in their simple assessment, resolved that to 'do & obey' would appease the 'god of wrath' and restore Paradise. All it takes is to mollify the idol and we shall be saved! How wrong they were! What they prescribed is the root of our perennial suffering, 'the casing which they think important the very barriers to their understanding'. Our moral obligation as thinking individuals is 'to break the mould', to smash the 'spell', we are dissolving the pledge.

'Paradise was never lost; we carry Paradise in our being if only we care to look for it, inserts Jeremy. The spirit in us lives in a state of Grace, if we care to find out. The Fall is of the Judeo-Christian tradition. The East does not have a history of the Fall. The Fall, Paradise Lost, Duality, the curse of man are illusions; they are useful learning tools. Where would we be without Michelangelo, Bach, Blake and other visionaries? They used the Fall to great effect. The world is all the richer for it.

'We are breaking the mould, we are lifting the spell, we are dispelling the ancestral curse that has forced us to live 'unconsciously', says Levinson. Jews everywhere are waking up from unconsciousness, like Sleeping Beauty. They no longer act unconsciously like

375

their ancestors did. In dissolving the spell they are healing themselves and healing the past.

'The ancestors passed their psychological damage to us. Chronic fear and pain impair neurological function, expands Delmar. Through time our brains have been rewired to register pain and to generate pain. The ancestral wound goes on festering. To heal in part means to reorganise the neural activity in our brains so that we no longer reactivate the ancestral pain.

'As Sananda explained we are entering the Age of Grace where we choose to learn not through pain but through joy. I am not acquainted with Sufism, says Jeremy, you obviously found in it what you were looking for.

'It is the Wisdom of the Ages, like Kabala. It's no coincidence that Moses de Leon who recorded Kabala lived in Spain among Sufis, so we can safely say that Kabala is Sufism under another name. My wife shared my views; she was an artist from France who longed for a new way of life, a new vision. We met in Jericho. We brought our children up as citizens of the Planet. Our fundamental belief was that by developing the entire person we could achieve unity.

'Not a timid project, smiles Jeremy, fascinated by the whole thing.

'Not a timid project, echoes the doctor. I guess we were looking for the magical number that would solve the riddle of the universe!

'A 'theory of everything', chuckles Levinson.

'Its equivalent in human terms. 'Left brain' expansion is what patriarchy set out to achieve knowingly or not. This is fine! It brought about the astonishing technological and scientific achievements of Western civilisation. The trouble with 'left brain' thinking is that it breaks up, cleaves, fractions, disjoins and disunites. Along the way, during the patriarchal age we lost sight of our 'right brain', the intuitive, creative, uniting, relating aspect of our nature.

'The feminine aspect of our nature, says Tara.

'You could say that, smiles Delmar.

'This is what brought you to Jericho, notes Clara with interest. Your search parallels mine, except that mine was a lonely uphill struggle.

'Ours was uphill too. I made Jericho my home in the firm belief that where there is the will-to-unity, hurdles can be overcome. Enough about me! I have the next chapter of The Hebrew Gods. I am fascinated by Benzaccai's work and ideas: the next frontier!

Delmar draws a bundle of papers from his desk. Declining Jeremy's offer to read the text, Delmar insists that he must read it himself, 'I have a hunch that this chapter is important for me'. The reading finally begins:

"Rabbi Moses was developing at a velocity that amazed and delighted Master Sanaka. As the old beliefs were crumbling, as he was releasing the thought forms that had oriented his life, he felt vulnerable like a child who starts out in life. At times he clutched at the past, hesitant to let go of the familiar certainties, the same certainties that had hoodwinked him. He visited temples, bathing in the soft glow and the scent of burning incense that lulled his trouble mind for a while. There he lost himself in the contemplation of the many images of Buddha and the Goddess, glimpsing beyond the form. He now trusted in his intuition to grasp the mystery of all that surrounded him. He was moving beyond the limited sense of self, experimenting with other dimensions of being, becoming aware of many realities at the same time. He set out on an inner journey that was to take him from restricted awareness to the realisation of his infinity. He was becoming multidimensional, limitless, timeless, and placeless. It was the epic journey which humanity was embarking upon, from physical reality to spiritual reality, from self to soul. What he had believed to be absolute truth was dissolving, his entire life seemed to have shattered into a myriad pieces. The ground under his feet was trembling and shock waves were still echoing within him, like a storm which subsides but still reverberates in the distance. Sensitive to the disquiet of Moses' mind, Sanaka asked him one morning to go out for a walk in the mountains. Surprised, Moses accepted in expectant mood. They quietly began climbing the snowy sides, embracing in a glance the mountains glittering in the early spring light. The peace was inescapable and Moses surrendered to it, he emerged from his troubled thoughts. Sanaka aware of the change coming over Moses began with an uncharacteristic bluntness:

'Spring is the season of renewal, of rebirth; some would call it 'resurrection'. Is it not what Passover is about? What applies to nature also applies to man. When man grasps that his religion fails to liberate him from suffering, he will emerge from the long winter of the soul. Religion lost its way into the dark regions of fear and has imprisoned man in those regions. But fear is an illusion and so is religion as you know it.

'What will be religion as yet unknown?

'It will be free-flowing, undefined and unrestricted, the free play of the soul.

'I agonised in one religion not to enter willingly into a new one, mutters Moses.

377

'Not the ritualistic religion that divides, but religion as union, as spiritual experience. Religion as the exploration of the mysterious, the unknown, the hidden. Religion as intuitive knowing, religion as the experiencing of other dimensions and realities. This is religion in its universal expression. The religion you know revolves around man as a physical unit. O I know! It speaks of heaven but with neither understanding nor conviction. As a student of the Wisdom you know these to be lesser goals, a way of appeasing human anxiety. Anxiety nourished by a religious form that separates man from his Self, from humanity and from the cosmos his natural home. Man gets the carrot along with the stick!

'So this is the religion in the making?

'Man alert to his developing mental faculty will rethink the notions he received unquestioningly. In a not so distant future, people will celebrate Buddha and Lord Maitreya.

'With respect, Master, I do not warm up to these impending changes. I am wary of religion, I feel threatened by it. I also grieve for the ancestors who believed and were deceived. I wonder if I shall ever release the pain.

'When you change your self image, when you no longer identify with who you think you are the pain will dissipate.

'What do you mean, Master?

'The pain will evaporate the moment you no longer equate with the identity you took at birth. You will heal when you no longer think, 'I was betrayed, I lost my family, I lost everything that gave meaning and substance to my life'. What you lost is only the mask, the illusion, the chimera. 'You', the real you is timeless and has nothing to do with your town, name, family, religion, racial group. 'You', the real you exists and move beyond time and space. 'You' are light and 'You' are love, the nature of the Divine. Your hereditary beliefs nourished the idea of you as a material form living in a material world. Behind the cloak of the man born in a certain place, at a certain time, in a certain group, is the real man. 'You' the cosmic being is not troubled by the limitations and restrictions imposed by birth and circumstances. Every day you are becoming your timeless Self.

'You read my mind that is why you brought me to the mountains.

Smiling warmly with a twinkle in his eyes, Sanaka replies, 'revelation came down from the mountain! The mountain symbolically stands for the higher Self, which is why

Moses went up the mountain; he rose to a higher plane of consciousness. From this height, the world below looks puny and the troubles of man recede.

'One feels even more insignificant in the mountains.

'You embrace the vastness of the landscape and you shed you earthly feeling of insignificance. You merge with it; it is no other than you. You and the world are one; you are this daunting mountain range! Your soul is the most insistent, insatiable and inquisitive 'thing' in the universe. Your soul has incarnated since time began to learn and grow and will continue to do so for as long as its needs to. Your soul came to Earth to explore the world and itself, to merge with the universe, to conquer all! Your soul wants to know all, to absorb all, to be all!

'You are leading me just where I am going! I am grappling with something I was unable to discuss, the identity of the Jew.

'I know, I was anticipating your question. It is not so much your identity but your acceptance of it. Until now you have struggled with it. The truth was eluding you. It is so tempting to profess with insincerity 'I am proud of who I am'. Why pretend? Pretence estranges man from his soul. Pretence destroys his integrity, his equilibrium. It is pretence that feeds his pain. When man seeks the truth about himself, he heals himself through spiritual growth. The truth is your truth.

'This is what I am trying to do, heal myself?

'And learn to love.

'When you resolve the past you will also love the identity that causes you so much pain.

'After I discard my identity, healing will ensue. It is quite a paradox.

'Not really, to heal is to understand, to understand is to love. And when you achieve this you will discard the past and assume your cosmic identity.

'What is a Jew? Who am I?

'At soul level you are a cosmic being transcending time and space, limitless and powerful'. He keeps silent for a moment embracing the peaks sparkling in the sunlight. He emerges from his contemplation; we may speak of the myth of the Jew. The accepted view is that the Jew is made by god for some specific purpose, the redemption of humanity! This doctrine has a number of inferences: first, God himself is a Jew, which is an absurd idea. Second, the Jew is a Jew because of his racial lineage, his birth makes him so. Nowhere is the Jew defined by the nature and quality of his soul. Instead he is defined by the nature and quality of his blood line! Third, god gives birth to a new soul each time someone is born. It means that each individual is tailor made and lives only once, he arrives in this world with no past and no future! So the Tsadiq was created perfect and never had to work for it!

'I see now! Common sense suggests that the villain was also created by god a villain and had no choice in the matter, says Moses. Is god so arbitrary?

'Well deduced Moses. And the last point, what happens to his soul when he leaves Earth? Hassidic doctrine reinterprets the esoteric facets of Hebrew tradition. It is in a sense Kabala made simple, this I say without disrespect.

'We must take some time out now, butts in Clara this is important to me, I am sorry to break the flow'. Almost imploring she turns to Jeremy 'could we have a short interlude in the form of a meeting with Sananda, I was intending to clarify some points regarding Hassidism, now is my chance!

'I suppose this can be arranged, laughs Jeremy. We are in for some probing questions! They sit in a circle, in a receptive mood.

'Master Sananda, begins Clara after the initial greeting, may I ask a few questions on the topic of Hassidic doctrine? I think I know the answers but I would like your seal of authority. One of the first claim hinges around the identity of the Baal Shem Tov. It is claimed that the soul of the Baal Shem was the global soul of all Jews. How can this be? 'Before I answer this question because of the way you phrase it asking for my seal of approval, allow me to remind you that you should not give up your own ability to discern, to discriminate and to disagree with the things I say, if that is appropriate. You should remind yourself always that I do not wish to be in a position of dictating to you truths which do not seem truths to you. Go with your own sense of this. That's just the preamble. Now, let us move to the question. Yes, I would broadly accept that, I would say there is a truth there.

'That one man can be the soul of so many?

'You see, in a sense, you are all One. So it is not so much that one man is exceptional in being the soul of many, but rather that one man is exceptional in being able and willing to endorse the fact and live the experience. There is a part of you which is in a sense and quite a real sense, the whole of the Jewish people. At one level the Jewish people is what you might describe as a group consciousness, an undifferentiated sea of consciousness which has particular characteristics. And all who experience some form of connection with the Jewish people will be tapping into that consciousness ... I am talking about collective consciousness. This consciousness will be within all those who participate in the Jewish condition, and to some extent it will ring true for many. Depending on the level you are experiencing yourself at, there is a change to the degree that this is true. So for some beings that will be very true, for others living at a slightly lower vibration it will not feel true or experienced as feeling true. But for all at some level, it is going to be true. What makes this particular being exceptional is the level of awareness rather than the nature of the connection.

'Thank you. The second core assumption of Hassidic doctrine states that there exist three basic souls in every Jew, the godly, the intellectual and the animal. Where does this leave the rest of humanity?

'I would say that this is just one manner of describing the way humans are made up. We can express it this way: the animal corresponds to your physical and emotional bodies, the intellectual equates with the mental body, the godly concurs with the spiritual body. This is one mode of describing the way people are composed or designed; it is universal and does not apply exclusively to the Jewish people. However there are ways in which this has a special resonance for the Jewish people. For instance, the way in which the Jewish people are made up – this is a generalisation there will be exceptions – those who have chosen to incarnate in Jewish form had tended to have within their energetic make up a strong strand of attraction to the divine, a strong strand of intellectuality and a strong acceptance of being human. These are quite common characteristics for the Jewish people in a way that is not quite so pronounced with non-Jews. I do not want to put too much emphasis because when you start to disentangle the incarnational journeys of all of you, you find that the picture is a good deal more complex than it appears on the surface. But nevertheless, if we accept that there is a Jewish identity, then to that extent, it can be seen as being constructed quite strongly out of these three elements in ways which differ from other peoples. For, to be sure, every human has within their energetic field always a strong and indissoluble bond with the divine, a mental body and a decision to experience physicality. These are present in all. But there is a kind of clumping together of strands of energy that is particularly marked in the Jewish consciousness along the lines these words suggest.

'This is particularly marked while they are in Jewish form but was it so marked in their energy field before they chose the Jewish frame?

'It is more marked in the manifestation in human form. This distinctive style of human form.

'The Jewish?

'Yes, the Jewish mould tends to be chosen by those with a particular interest in exploring those forms of consciousness, naturally enough. So you find that you can trace it back to the essential being.

'The soul already has these characteristics within itself?

'Indeed it has, but it becomes far more marked as the essential being begins to select those qualities that will make up his or her humanness. In other words, imagine the essential being as a very complex and beautiful three-dimensional pattern of energy very alive, constantly moving, deciding at some point to become human. Deciding that to become human as a Jew is going to give it the opportunity to study particular forms of energy and as it does, braiding or platting together unique characteristics of its own overall energy field to align them with what has been expressed as those three specific qualities, spirituality, intellectuality and physicality. So there is a kind of change of form as the spirit moves into matter.

'It sounds so beautiful the way you express it, like a work of art.

'It is indeed!

'Just like a dance, a ballet, it is poetic!

'Yes it is!

'Yet, for many who live the Jewish experience it is a Kafka-like nightmare! So unforgiving, so insensitive to the delicate nature of the soul! Agitation and despondency are endemic. It is the ugliness that hurts the most. Where is this beautiful work of art!

'It's there within all of you, within every human being and part of your journey in this life time is to learn to see it within yourself and within all others. Yes sometimes it is well disguised!' The encounter comes to an end.

They have listened in silent wonder. Finally, Delmar utters, 'there is no such thing as a Jew. The Jew is a myth, a mental creation to explain our strange situation and justify it. I know now what I always sensed. There is only mankind.

'Sananda, reminds Jeremy, said that throughout the universe countless beings marvel as they observe us resign ourselves to limitations, as we accept forgetfulness as an accelerated path to growth. As I see it the individual who partakes to the Jewish experience does this twice over. Levinson your turn!

'Why me? Do I have to read your mind too! Let's try to figure this out, first he forgets his exalted nature when he dons the human self as all humans do when they incarnate, but then he forgets it a second time, as a manner of speaking, as he slips into the Jewish garment.

'A double calamity, exclaims Clara.

'Why a calamity, it is their decision, says Levinson. Human beings choose the Jewish garb of their own free will; they are drawn to it by their temperament as outlined by Sananda. The belief that the deity dumps us on Earth is bankrupt. No entity in the universe has this power. We put ourselves on Earth to learn.

'Those who incarnate into the Jewish condition compound their problem, says Clara with melancholy'.

'Or may be not, replies Jeremy. It may be the shortest route to disentangle accumulated past karmic difficulties, purify energy fields and move on and up. Suffering is a cleansing fire.

'How? Can you clarify?

'Yes, the soul designs a Jewish persona to effect the resolution of past emotional, psychological and spiritual struggles and also to balance past karma. What religion does is to drop a curtain between man, his initial karmic intention and his ultimate goal. Beginning and end are hidden. Access to both is forbidden. One is in ignorance of these crucial existential features.

'Sananda did not raise the issue of Karmic balancing. Instead he speaks of the three forces that may motivate humans to incarnate into the Jewish mould, I quote: 'Within their energetic make up a strong strand of attraction to the divine, a strong strand of intellectuality and a strong acceptance of being human', reflects Delmar. Let's our imagination run wild, just suppose that the man in a Jewish persona was long ago in the sinister Inquisition? At some point he charts his next life on Earth, he writes the script, putting all the props together. He is not dumped on the Planet; he comes with a clear outline of the form his life will take and the nature of the learning he intends. He has a clear awareness of the painful experiences he will have, because he planned and designed them in advance. He knows that his forthcoming earthly experiences no matter how severe are crucial to his personal development. It is his inalienable right to know. The Declaration of Human Rights declares it so, the law of Karma dictates that it be so.

'It is a calamity to be born a Jew, to be sure, insists Clara stubbornly.

'Not necessarily, remarks Levinson, it has taken me decades to come to terms with my Jewishness. I admit that issues surrounding the meaning and purpose of life are made more difficult for the Jew because he is forbidden to know that he existed before and will exist long after this life. He is captive in a body of flesh and a body of dogmas that denies him awareness of his true identity. He is a Jew because he harbours his ancestors' genes, because he is of Jewish blood. It is biology that wins the day! The deity insists on the biological identity of the Jew.

'It is all too reductionist for me, says Clara. Man, this amazing multidimensional being is reduced to isolated parts! What a terrible price we must pay for illusory certainty. Humanity is entering the Age of the Soul, yet for us it is business as usual: we are organisms that must survive, but survive for what?

'Good point, replies Delmar! The body of rules is built around biological reality. So you see the problem of the Jew is magnified. Remember that the Jewish experience is humanity's problem: it is the Roman centurion, the medieval Crusader, the Inquisitor, dressing up, playing at being a Jew. It is an endless fancy dress ball in which we must play all the roles, wear all the masks, and appear under all disguises. But this role-play has a meaning.

'Your view is that man incarnates as a Jew to extend his range of perception, to expand, to develop?

'You heard Master Sananda, replies Delmar, a soul chooses the Jewish form for psychological reasons rather than to atone for past misdeeds. Karma is one aspect of it. I prefer to think of the individual clothed in Jewish garb as one who is inquisitive and wants to figure out what life is all about. One endowed with a strong inclination to worship, a strong desire to learn and a strong urge to be physical. It is not surprising that the wise Rabbis instituted marriage at the age of 18, they understood natural man. But it is surprising that the Pharisees of today impose chastity on those they mould to their specifications. On reflection, these neo-Pharisees probably were Puritans, Mormons or Quakers in an immediate past life, their physicality kept in check. Now in the Jewish frame their physicality can manifest.

'You are right, to stress that the Jew returns to Earth to repay karmic debts is perhaps an oversimplification, suggest Jeremy. The Jew is mankind searching for the way back to the forgotten Self. He is humanity in the process of becoming.

'You are an optimist, declares Levinson

I am a realist, insists Jeremy. Remember also what Sananda told us, that the Hierarchy time and again in the distant past resigned their distant role of guides and came down in a Jewish persona to help mankind evolve. They were prophets, kings, avatars, leaders. How many of the great Jewish scholars were members of the Hierarchy, I wonder?

CHAPTER 7

THE MYTH OF THE JEW

'Humanity has come from a number of different sources. There has been genetic input into the human race at different times in its history. The Jewish people was the recipient of a particular strand of DNA which contained particular types of information concerning the role to be played by those people who had this aspect of DNA within them. The safeguarding of this DNA strand took on the character of a goal. It offered the possibility of exerting a kind of stewardship over the rest of humanity. (Master Sananda)

JERICHO

Worship of selfhood

'It is ignorance that causes us to identify with the body, the ego, the senses or anything that is not the Self'. (Shankara)

The worship of the Father is woven with the worship of time, the Father exists in time. The Father, masculine energy, metes out retribution in response to sinful conduct, real or imagined. The Father is not amenable to clemency; emblematic of the masculine ego, he stands for sin and punishment. The Jew models himself on his god: he abides by Yang values and worships the unchanging Father archetype of time. Time-bound, the Jew is externally-stimulated; he abides by the rules of his group. His conduct is dictated by group norms since he also fears freedom. He yearns for approval and shares in the collective prejudices, attitudes and opinions. His self-image is inherited, constructed around the experiences and beliefs of people of the past. Living in an unsafe environment, he fears change; he fears anything that may upset his fragile world. As change is life, he fears life. Time-bound his fear of death is tangible: death gives rise to repellent ritual practices; he dreads death which he senses as final. Time-bound he is much occupied with the past – as the many rituals attached to the past demonstrate – and the future, a fantasized, unrealistic future. 'People like us, who believe in physics, know that the distinction between past, present and future is only a stubborn, persistent illusion', said Einstein. His religious practice revolves around past and future, but what of the present? His yearning for safety and security is palpable: wherever he is he seeks the comfort and reassurance of others in his group. He also needs social status to

386

appease his insecurity and establish his place firmly in his society. Fear of death, fear of the present, fear of insecurity and fear of freedom combine to give him a self-centred outlook on life; this narcissistic stance he shares with the group. Inevitably his point of view is inhibited, restricted to his situation in the society that shapes his beliefs about himself and the world. 'Materialistic-minded men who have no information of the Kingdom of God are mechanically engaged in the ritualistic discharge of prescribed duties and are inclined to satisfy the bygone forefathers and controlling demigods ...' The Jew is reliant on his group for his beliefs, values and direction. His conduct is dictated by the group, enforcer of tradition. Shankara states, 'It is ignorance that causes us to identify with the body, the ego, the senses or anything that is not the Self. Time-bound, the Jew does precisely that, he identifies with everything and anything that is not the Self! Time-conscious the Jew identifies with all that is not the timeless Self. He identifies with all things in time, fleeting, ephemeral, unreal, and non-existent. The 'Kingdom of God' the Bhaghavatam speaks of is the deathless, timeless Self in man. Time-bound Jew does not know of the existence of the timeless Self in him. When he does he will abandon group beliefs, attitudes, values and taboos since they relate to man who identifies with the self, the senses and all things in time. The Jew will know himself to be timeless. This new awareness will eradicate his fear of time, freedom and death.

Playing Roles

Beware of taking the clothes for realities. Clothes are not self-determining; it is the man that puts on various clothes'. (Gigen)

After a short break, mint tea and delicious almond cakes, Delmar is ready to resume the reading.

'Why am I a Jew, Master, asks Rabbi Moses bluntly?

'Because you wanted to, it's that simple.

'It has not been simple.

'It means that the choice your Self made was the right one, it does not mean that it was the simplest. Rather than choose an easy ride across idyllic countryside it chose instead the most difficult ride, across rough terrain and perilous territory. Explorers do travel to remote, inhospitable parts of the world; they prefer the ordeal of the desert or the perils of the jungle to the quiet life at home. You are an explorer, my son.

'But why a journey in the Jewish condition?

'To grapple with it, explore it, scrutinize all its facets, navigate its stormy waters. As a Light worker your task is to bring 'light'. Your mission was to bring the knowledge of the Source back to the Planet; to awaken your people to a higher form of awareness. You have come to transform humanity's experience from one of fear to one of love.

'Quite a mission, it takes my breath away, admits Moses!

'You were not born for an easy life, but no Jew ever is. It is the role you chose, I must emphasise this, you and you alone chose it. You are not a puppet on a string. Let go of the myths of the past.

'The past is clinging to me like a scab.

'When you let go, pain will dissolve away, suffering will vanish, the splits within you that prevent you from understanding will heal. You will know!

Human beings play roles like actors on a stage. Before incarnation they agree on the part they will play. Like actors back stage as they change costumes, one saying to the other: 'Yesterday you were King Lear, I was Macbeth, today we change roles, I am Macbeth and you are Lear and let see how we perform!' Children learn through playing roles. Yesterday's victim becomes today's foe. Foe and victim agree to swap roles. Humanity has been doing this since the dawn of time, since humanity at group level decided to adopt the Law of Karma and its implications. You dress up and act out a part. The greater the actor the more believable he makes his character, which is just fine on stage but not in incarnation. In incarnation the good 'actor' identifies enthusiastically with the character he plays. Fiction and reality get mixed up. His true identity fuses with that of the character and he no longer knows himself. But of course you know all about this, do you not, adds Sanaka with the ironic twinkle in his eyes and affectionate smile?

'I do, much to my sorrow.

'The soul before setting off on its next earthly adventure gathers its past roles and makes a listing of what was achieved and what remains to be done. It will, at some point, decide that some new exploration, new learning, new balancing is essential and starts to organise its next trip to Earth. The soul dreams up the entire plot, designs the stage props, writes the script, conjures up the characters, and decides on the blood line and environment to make the most of the learning experience. And so you come down in your chosen family, race, gender, religion, social and cultural background and you forget your initial intention. That's how it is! And as you forget your initial plan you allow the upbringing to mould the way you see yourself and make sense of your world. From creator of your own world, you become casualty of the world of others!

'From creator to casualty, that's quite a leap, mutters Moses!

'Man is in the universe just as the universe is in man, but few know this and fewer still want to know.

'They prefer to know that they are victims of angry gods, notes Moses! The cosmic Self must resign itself to being a victim of external, rampant forces.

'Enough to make you weep! You sob and beat your chests in devout penitence when you bow before the deity. Imagine what the cosmic Self is feeling? The divine majesty inside you having to kneel before a demigod! Loyalty to a tribe is far more important than reality. Man does not hesitate to trade the universe for a caste! People are so engrossed in the role they play, they are willing to kill or be killed for it. They no longer know the difference between the real and the unreal.

'How awful, says Moses. Humanity behaves like children.

'Buddha proposed an earth-shattering solution. He encouraged reasoned observation and intelligent reflection. Rather staggering for the time, not what formal religion normally advocates!

'Formal religion censures reflection and reason.

'He also urged to give up emotional attachment to conditions, milieu, circumstances, ideas, and opinions. The present situation is ephemeral, in force today gone tomorrow. He advised unbiased reasoning: why get passionate about environment, opinions and values? You incarnated countless times and each time you have adored a different god, dressed in a different persona and lived in a different milieu. As the embodiment of the cosmic Mind, Buddha taught that self-knowledge and self-mastery are the answer to man's predicament. Definitely not the emotions!

'The god a person adores today he may revile in his next life, reflects Moses. Today he kills those who do not believe in his god, next time he may kill those who do believe in it! Today he adores Yahweh next time he may revile Yahweh and mock his people.

'So why be inflexible about the belief of the moment when you know that in your next incarnation the god you idolise today will dispel into oblivion, you may even become its fiercest enemy.

'It is all pointless really!

'No, everything matters. What is meaningful and lasting is the learning you came to do. You chose this deity in order to learn how he compares and differs from all the other deities you have worshipped over countless incarnations. You learn to detect which minute aspect of the cosmic Mind you perceive in the god of the moment.

'Each time we adopt a new god or a new idea it is to discover a new aspect of the cosmic Mind?

'Right. Ultimately, the learning has to do with discovering who you truly are: you are that cosmic Mind! And you come back in incarnation to realise this.

'Passionate belief in a god or an idea is futile.

'You see, Moses, the standpoint must be one of rational detachment. Move away from the limited view of the self that you are today. Adopt a birds' eye view of the experience of being human and look down at your physical self that has certain racial and cultural characteristics. Silence your lower self and rise to the lofty Self, the part of you that transcends space and time and enables you to take a towering perspective of the human condition. When you fully equate with the role you play, you remain prisoner of the physical self. When you practice detachment, your restricted view of yourself and others falls off. All human beings are on Earth to play roles in order to learn what it is to be human and what it is to be divine. When you say, 'I am a Jew, I am chosen, my god is the only god, I alone have a soul, others are lesser beings', you confess a dismal ignorance of who you truly are, what man truly is and what life on Earth is all about! You shout to the world that you learned nothing over millions of years.

'Is it not rather a cruel game to play on mankind?

'If it is a game, then it is game played knowingly and deliberately by mankind for its own benefit. Furthermore, the rules of the game were laid down by collective humanity long ago. That's right, mankind as group consciousness decided on the rules of the game. No one imposed either the game or the rules; both were an intentional and resolute decision by humankind without any prompting or pressure from outside forces. We live in a universe in which freedom has full sway; so anyone who claims he knows better and tells you what to do is ignorant of universal Law.

[Jews] *constitute a unique and distinctly separated world centre of energy. The reason for this is that they represent the energy and the life of the previous solar system ... The 3rd Ray governed that system – active Intelligence – and also governs the Jewish race, if you bear in mind that that system was occupied with the divine aspects of matter only and with external conditions and that the Jews were the brightest product of that solar system'.* (Master DK)

Worship of the physical self – worship of an illusion

'What they took to be fundamentals are really worthless externals ... And the casing which they think important, the very barriers to their understanding'. (Sufi wisdom)

Is this the stable, enduring, permanent, independent and existent self religion and society insist we 'have'? Is it the 'self' we live for, die for and kill for? The self we invest an immense amount of energy, effort and resources to maintain in order to keep up appearances, bolster the group and retain our self-esteem and self-image intact?

The Jew defines himself in terms of 'existence': 'I am a Jew because I have Jewish blood in me'. Very simple, rather simplistic in fact, 'I am a Jew because biology tells me so. It is the genes and chromosomes in me that make me who I am'. What of 'essence'? Bronze Age man had no conception of an essence that endures and defies the corruption of the flesh.

What happens when we proclaim that we are an 'object'? An object occupies a certain space. With us it is a 'sacred' space with clearly delineated boundaries. We are fenced into that space, we must be separate our god says so; he insists that we live cut off from the rest. We are trapped inside our bodies, inside our group and inside our space. The outside world is irrelevant except that it also occupies space and is an implicit threat to the survival of our 'sacred' space and 'holy' body. We must at all times worship our 'pure' body. Our entire package of rituals revolves around the body, its purity and its saintliness.

A decaying, decomposing and disintegrating saintly body? Now an 'object' is independent; our god tells us that our selfhood is a guaranteed thing, an undeniable fact. We are self-sufficient, self-existent; our selfhood is intrinsic, untouchable. And because the self is an 'object' it endures. It has substance, it is stable. It is recognisable, 'I am a Jew because I have Jewish blood, I utter certain formulas and slogans, and I know that I am a descendent of Abraham. I depend on nothing external, I am separate, solid, enduring, predictable, recognised and labelled'.

391

Yet under the resounding sense of enduring, separate and unconnected identity, 'the individual is an innumerable swarm of disconnected impulses, thoughts, reactions, opinions and sensations which are triggered into activity by causes of which he is totally unaware'. But these 'disconnected' thoughts reactions and opinions are absolutely his; they originate within him and are totally independent of the external world or are they? Since he reacts emotionally rather than rationally he is not independent of the world; it is the world that activates his reactions and responses. He reacts in a pre-programmed way: he has been conditioned since childhood to feel, think and respond in line with a preset pattern imposed by the group which he has ingested. His response is the 'conditioned response' verified by Pavlov.

So much for the independence of the self, the 'I' we brandish to intimidate others or buy their unconditional acceptance. But this 'I' is a fabrication, made up of all kinds of bits and bobs; it is as real as a mirage. In the words of Aldous Huxley, 'I' affirms a separate and abiding me-substance, 'I am' denies the fact that all existence is relationship and change. 'I am', two tiny words, but what an enormity of untruth!'

As Guy Claxton explains, 'Though my nature is my own and exists independently ... paradoxically 'I' is instructed to set great store by what [others] say and think about me'. Others mark out the parameters of my behaviour, they decide what I can do and can think. My thinking is not mine at all, it is programmed into me. 'I' interpret 'my' nature in terms of other people's reactions to 'me' and their expectations of me. 'I' allow them to program into me instructions that set conditions for my 'worth'. 'I' is to regard my self through these evaluative goggles and to impose a forfeit, called 'loss of self-esteem' or 'guilt' when the self falls short of the standards'. Our definition of self depends on the outside world, we know who we are to the extend that the world tells us so, 'you are a Jew because your mother has Jewish genes in her, you are circumcised, you had your Bar Mitzvah, you eat matzoth at Easter and you fast at Yom Kippur'. What do these parameters and definitions share? They all are externals. None tells me 'who' I am, only 'what' I am. My sense of self revolves around biology, genetics, bodily integrity or the lack of it and external activities classified and approved by the group. My self-esteem is bound up with the group and their estimation of me. If they disapprove of me they can blot me out of the Book of Life! My self-image is determined by others since if they do not approve of me I am excluded, I am banished. Decisions surrounding our worth are based on externals, on things that are known, visible, tangible, solid, 'it denies the fact that all existence is relationship and change'. Everything depends on everything else.

They know not of our 'essence', concerned with what is perishable, impermanent, unreal, untrue and ephemeral.

But as mystics and Quantum physicists tell us matter is not solid, it is energy vibrating at a slow rhythm. Our thoughts and bodies are energy, so what of the boundaries, signs, programming, evaluations, externals and estimations? A puff of smoke! The entire universe is energy. Since all is energy, is a unit of 'Jewish' energy different from a unit of 'Christian' energy? Energy is energy; there is no superior or inferior energy. Can I be so foolish as to clamour the distinction of the unit of energy that 'I' am? Is a pebble on the beach superior to another pebble? Is a grain of sand different from another grain of sand?

Group character

'Master Sanaka, why are my people behaving in a specific way, why are they so very similar in temperament and emotional nature. Why do so few assert themselves?

'Two questions in one. First, there is the unique group character of all those who enter the condition. Naturally, the souls about to incarnate do a certain amount of research into the background of their choice. And as they learn, they take on those specific traits, indeed, they already have those traits or they would not be attracted to the Jewish condition in the first place! So they mould their persona to that of the group, this is the only way to fit in without too much strain and pain. Second, you are asking why, having moulded themselves to the group character, they do not break away from it. You see, things are more complex, they decide on the Jewish garb, the stage costume they will wear to experience the energy that prevails on Earth. So, they come down to find out what it is like to experience the boundaries of group life, the constraints of group rules and regulations, the restrictions of their way of life. Restrained by mental chains, captive in body and mind, how do you expect them to leap out?

'Yet this is what each person decides upon before incarnating?

'Indeed, but not every one is intellectually and spiritually gifted to feel solidarity with the whole of humanity. Earthlings are bound by custom, attitudes, prejudices and taboos which they take on board and assimilate. An earthling believes in his freedom yet he repeats what men dead centuries ago decreed for him, what the group has been reinforcing ever since. It's all done for him, all pre-digested, 'do and obey' but do not think, god will punish you and you will be plagued by guilt; you may end up in Hell too! Feeling imperilled in the depth of his being, tormented by guilt he does not question, he obeys, he renounces his divine faculty. It is easier this way, he does not offend the group, does not rock the boat, does not upset himself and does not have to stir out of his apathy. Thought is the third attribute of the Divine in the Trinity; it is by thought that God created the universe. 'Man was made in the image of God' what do you think this verse in Genesis mean?

'Why the fear of solidarity with humanity?

'Solidarity would defeat a doctrine constructed on blood purity and moral eminence. Someone from a specific bloodline imagines that because of his heredity he is also morally superior and must remain pure to lead humanity.

'The Jew's leadership role implies solidarity, notes Moses.

'Yes but purity implies separation. Is it not the command Yahweh made to Abraham? Permeated with the experience of the Fall, he makes himself the exponent and living symbol of the Fall. And the Fall is the blighting of Earth by an inflow of hostile forces. The Hebrew is alone on the Planet; he parted company with his fellow men long ago. He has kept his character through fear. Fear of the world, fear of himself, fear of dismissal by the group. Rejection by the group would intensify his aloneness and sense of alienation. He is in a sticky situation: his self-destructive behaviour is shaped by his dread of being forsaken by the group. So he remains in conditions he finds insufferable. Centuries of conditioning have implanted in him the belief of free-will. But he has no will, his will is quashed by superstition, he is only reacting to pressure.

'Man was made in the image of God', mutters Moses to himself.

'He is victim of his own fear. As you know fear is the opposite of love, as God is Love, fear is the opposite of God. He is truly in a sticky situation: he fears his god, yet it is this very fear that alienates him from his own soul and the Soul of the universe!

'He has ingested the dogmas of the past, but he has not reflected on their global implications, mumbles Moses. 'Man was made in the image of God'.

'When Will, Love, Thought - the divine Trinity - collapses, what is left of both God and man?

'What is to be done?

'May I remind you that you woke up to yourself when you were banished by your group, when you became a liability?

'How can I forget? Yet I shall for ever be grateful to them for giving me my life back. In rejecting me they assisted my search. The real 'me' was dormant; they helped me be born to who I am.

'That's right. The slumbering Self exists below the surface. You have to take your spiritual growth slowly or you would end up like Rabbi Akkiba's colleagues who, on beholding the Light went mad, it was too much for them. The buried knowledge of man's identity, his bond with the universal Self can gently be rekindled. Restraint is what earthlings have endured since they were interfered with by alien gods, and your people are no different. Except that you see this restraint as a sign of distinction; the rest of humanity agonises over it.

'You are saying that the character of the Jewish people was stamped into them? They 'do & obey' of their own free will or so they believe; yet they are only doing what they were made to do, unconsciously.

'Yes, each distinctive group in the world is fashioned this way. The leading elites buttress specific traits that set them apart, traits easily identifiable. Once ingested the collective character carves its own form. The group member adopts a certain mode of dress and bearing that give away his distinction and make known his moral primacy. This is the only way to endure through time. Any infraction to the rule, any deviation from the model would jeopardise the integrity of the group, its collective character and its survival. Some primitive groups are more intransigent than others when dealing with the 'deviants', other are more lenient. Had it not been for the extreme rigidity and oppressiveness of the rules and the way they were enforced you would have disappeared long ago.

'How can we transcend the restraining influence of group character that keeps individuals docile and apathetic through time?

'By doing what you have done! The mentally and spiritually evolved can tolerate the rejection of the group, for he has transcended the limits of his culture and is slowly rediscovering the forbidden knowledge.

'Forbidden knowledge?

'He rediscovers that he is a universal being who partakes in many dimensions at the same time. Knowledge of his essential unity with mankind, with the Planet, with the universe and with the Source. This forbidden knowledge lies dormant into the frame of man but is available to the spiritual seeker intent on finding it. He is the hero of all mythologies, alone and suffering but never daunted. As you know the search is sorrowful for the man who engages on the road of self-realisation. This is an enlightened, individual decision.

'What about the rest of mankind?

'Mankind at large is subject to the law of evolution and advances under the force of that law but this is done unconsciously. Because he identifies with his human self, man forgets from one incarnation to the next and so he keeps coming back. As long as man is defined by his group character and labelled by his group beliefs, he has to embody into a different group each time he revisits Earth. He remains undeveloped, unenlightened, unevolved, unredeemed, you might say unconscious because he does not know who he is. Encounter with the soul is the goal of evolution, the final destination.

'You are saying Master, that our reason for living is not to worship a god, not to engage in religious routine, not to be 'holy', not to 'do and obey' but to transcend separation and realise oneness?

'Absolutely. Prehistoric man had to 'do and obey' to secure the approval of his master. The serious seeker knows himself to be his own master. Union with the soul is union with all life. It is the realisation of the one life in a diversity of forms. Man has always been deceived by the multiplicity of forms. Concern with form is the field of religion and science. Concern with unity occupies spiritually evolved man. When he realises his unity with all life he becomes a citizen of the Planet, indeed a citizen of the cosmos!

Group consciousness

Delmar's wife comes into the room to tell her husband that a man has just been injured on a building site and needs urgent attention. He leaves immediately with the words, 'we shall resume the reading later'.

'My hunch is that Clara wants to clarify the points raised, teases Jeremy.

'Spot on, replies Clara, I accept the mocking invitation. I am perplexed by an account made by Djwahl Khul about group consciousness. He speaks of 'the maze of the three worlds of human evolution'.

'He may be referring to the three bodies that humanity has developed over its long evolutionary march, the physical, emotional and mental bodies, explains Jeremy. These three bodies correspond to three phases in human evolution.

'Humanity functions within all three realms, comments Levinson always in tune with Clara. Our people, in spite of their intellectual ability are latent, subdued by contrived beliefs. Engineered beliefs that mobilise faith while ruling out serious reflection. Conditioned to ingest beliefs which don't stand up to scrutiny, we live in denial. We fight reality and retreat into our fantasy world: 'we are the moral and spiritual guardians of mankind'. What evidence do we have in support of these outlandish beliefs? They don't measure up to reality. We are split between reality which we refuse and fantasy which we nurture. Reality demonstrates one thing and our imagination conjures up another. We live a split existence between reality we distort and fantasy we cultivate.

'Brilliant, says Clara but not quite what the Tibetan meant I think.

'I read the Tibetan's books, intervenes Johansson. I am acquainted with his ideas. According to the Tibetan, the Jew like all earthlings regards the world of phenomena as permanent, solid, unchangeable. Mortal man takes the world of form for reality.

'But physical reality is undeniable, says Jeremy.

'No one denies it, it is reliable enough: we did go to university to study external reality!

'Ancient Wisdom insists that the outer world is ephemeral and therefore unreal. The real lies beneath natural law and diversity.

'And you want Sananda to shed light at this point, smiles Jeremy. Let's start without delay. They sit quietly. Sananda greets the group and turns to Clara.

'Master Sananda, would you clarify the Tibetan's comment?' An encouraging smile is the reply. 'Reflecting on the origins of the "ancient and dire fate" of the Jewish people the Tibetan concludes that 'much that has happened to the Jews originated in their past history and in their pronounced attitude of separativeness and non-assimilability'. This is not the Jewish point of view! These attitudes are their distinguishing features; they take great pride in their 'separativeness' and 'non-assimilability', two vital clauses to their priestly function. Their leadership role dictates that they remain distinct, separate.

The Master has listened attentively, he smiles at the last remark. 'This strong sense of purpose and group consciousness so dominant among the Jewish race has been much less pronounced among other people and races. So, if for example you consider the Europeans as a race, they do not display and profess the same clarity of purpose; there is a good deal of scattered purpose for Europeans. In some way, the Jewish people are endorsing the stage of evolution that you, as individuals are experiencing at present, but they are doing it collectively as a people.

'The sense of group consciousness that embraces all humanity? The Jewish people are also experiencing group consciousness but it does not include humanity is that it?

'It is in a sense a courageous thing to do, but their global behaviour confronts us with a number of paradoxes. In many ways, they point the way to the future of humanity. The future looks to us [the Masters] to lie with all of you unfolding a mounting awareness of group consciousness, whereas at present you experience yourselves as being separate individuals. You display less of a strong feeling of group consciousness, but it is growing. The Jewish people, in contrast have sustained quite a strong sense of group consciousness but - and this is where the paradox comes in - what they are confronting now is the great challenge of letting go of that group identity in order to join the greater group identity of the entire human race.

'There is a paradox!

'There is indeed, echoes Sananda! Whereas, for many of the rest of humanity who have had less of a sense of racial, quasi-religious identity, it is easier to begin to experience themselves as part of the whole human group.

'They are beginning to realise that they are part of the human race!

'They are indeed! It can be more difficult for the Jewish people who are further along this path. A real paradox!

Suffering & the lower self - Master Chenrezig

'It is the love of the Essential that makes man conscious. The love of phenomenon makes man unconscious of himself'. (El-Arabi, Sufi scholar)

Dr Delmar returns looking pale and exhausted, 'the man will be alright, I thought I was going to lose him, he is young he will recover. Would you give me a few minutes for a shower'? He comes back a while later smiling and refreshed. 'I feel fine and keen to carry on with the reading'. The reading resumes.

Rabbi Moses is recounting an event. 'This morning I was awakened by a loud noise coming from the corridors. Surprised I stepped outside my room to investigate. The monks were walking down in some haste. The monastery normally so peaceful was buzzing.

'Do tell me what is going on?' A monk slowed down and without stopping said almost out of breath, 'Master Chenrezig is due to visit our monastery, it is a privilege, an honour, a unique way to gain merit, he will bring such good fortune and blessing to all of us. In his immense kindness he accepted our invitation'. My curiosity aroused, moments later I asked my Mentor about Master Chenrezig.

'He is one of the advanced Masters.

'Where does he come from?

'Shigatse, the city of light, dwelling place of the Masters who reside outside Shamballa.

'If he is enlightened what is he doing on the Planet, asks Moses bluntly? 'He pledged to return to Earth to guide mankind, this is what Bodhisattvas do. They suspend their own advanced evolution in order to steer mankind toward liberation. Master Chenrezig will lead the meditation and answer questions. You will be having a meeting with him.

'To be in his presence will be awe-inspiring enough!

The Master finally arrived with his retinue. A princely Tibetan with regal serenity and royal poise alighted from his carriage. Monks and abbots were lined up to greet him with the honours due to his dignity. His embraced them all in a sweeping glimpse. His glance came to a pause on Moses, he smiled and his face lit up. They were all overwhelmed by his august presence.

'He has in this brief glance read your quest and sensed your anguish, whispers Sanaka.

 Finally the moment came when he was summoned by the Tibetan Master: 'Tea will be served and as we drink we shall become acquainted.

The thought of having tea with such a being was daunting, Moses was about to decline the offer when the Master sensing his objection said with a reassuring smile, 'Your Master Sanaka is a sublime being; he too is an ambassador of Shamballa. Do sit down and let's have tea. He questions Moses about his life in Vilna, listening intently to the answers as if they revealed profound truths. Finally the Master has gathered the necessary information on Rabbi Moses, his karmic origins and his life purpose, most of which he perceived by simply observing Moses.

'Buddha states three barriers to reaching enlightenment, begins Master Chenrezig. He defines them as mental poisons that bar the path to union with the Self: attachment, hostility and ignorance. Ignorance is the root of all evil and so he urges his disciples to develop their own mind. Time and again he advises them not to accept his teachings out of faith but to test them against reason and experience 'do not rely upon the words but upon the meaning'. It is only on the basis of undeniable evidence that we should accept another's teachings, even that of Buddha who is the embodiment of cosmic Intelligence. Union with the Self is the ultimate goal of evolution. Everything that exists in the universe from the atom to the Solar System is the will of the cosmic Self to manifest in form.

'This is what my people believe Master.

'Not quite, replies Master Chenrezig with a smile. For you the universe is the handiwork of a Creator who hurled you into it for reasons you do not know. Your reason for living is to serve that being, but not to make sense of his Creation. Mechanical conformity is expected of you. The truth is that Universal Intelligence comprises all of us. So you see, in a sense and a real sense you are the Mind that created the world! Blasphemy to some, living truth to others! The groundwork of your religious credo is two-fold: first god created the world for you, his chosen people; second he created it for you to use as a workshop. This anomaly has not eluded the discerning Eastern mind. To you Creation has a dual aim, one to get you to earn your living by the sweat of your brow, the second to mollify your creator! It is all there in a nutshell: toil to meet the needs of your master-maker! Mere human opinion. Who benefits from all this, man slave-driven or god slave-driver? And what of Creation, is it just a factory, a workshop, a mill built for the specific purpose of producing man-made objects? The truth is not mere opinion but living reality. The universe exists to manifest the cosmic Mind of which man is a fragment. Fragment of the cosmic Mind, man is also paradoxically the whole. This is a reality that can be verified by reasoning and intuitive experience. Man gets attached to his opinions and ends up believing in them with tenacity.

'Master may I ask how this relates to the three mental poisons?

'Which poison comes to mind, smiles the Master?

'Ignorance or confusion.

'All three mental poisons spring from the human mind. Man sees the world along the lines of his social milieu. In other words, it is the past that dictates how we see and what we see. As man advances, his perception of himself and the world changes. It is logical to assume that animal-man living in the caves of long ago was very different from modern man who dwells in cities. Do challenge me on this.

'It is so perfectly rational, yet I never could think this through in my earlier life.

'How could you? You were held in an inert image of the world, unchanged for millennia. Those around you accepted the information given at Sinai literally. Their concrete mind does not discriminate between allegory and reality, the literal and the figurative, the myth and the fact. Your society is riddled with magical ideas. Concrete thinking and the magical approach have prevailed.

'We remain a primitive society because we cannot express rationally ideas and experiences; as a result we continue to use myth and magic. Ignorance, the mental poison that obstructs the progress of humanity is always lurking.

'Well thought through, Rabbi Moses. Mental poisons are forces that block the way to liberation. Man attached to the past is in bondage, petrified in the opinions of others. He absorbs opinions unconsciously; they get encrypted in the atoms of his body. He is in thraldom to his physical self oblivious to the need of his higher Self. Trapped in his unquestioning self and captive to the tyranny of his sense perception, he is unable to imagine the spiritual reality behind form. He believes the flimsy husks to be real.

'All the while, his silenced being struggles to set itself free through repeated incarnations. He has come back countless times to overcome the obstacles that lie in the way of his emancipation. Obstacles of his own making.

'Is this the reason why mankind suffers much and the Jewish people more?

'Yes, ignorance is at the root of suffering. Ignorance is the cause of attachment. Man in ignorance believes the physical self to be all and does not discriminate between his finite existence and his infinite Self. He thinks his mortal self to be real, and so he lines up with the three lower worlds, the physical, emotional and mental planes of existence. But the lower self is the source of all his suffering! Unaware that he is submerged in the world of illusion he repeats thoughtlessly: 'I am a man, I glorify god for not making me a woman; god created the world for me; I walk in holiness before my god; those who do not worship my god are lesser beings; I am truly special; I am holy, so I must keep separate from profane humanity'. This narcissistic opinion stretches back to prehistoric times. It is the bedrock of your creed and contains all three poisons held in suspension within man: attachment to his material form, attachment to his idea of god, attachment to his emotional life, attachment to his limited grasp of things. Hostility is observable too, hostility to woman, hostility to 'the other', running deep an insidious hostility to oneself.

'The poison of ignorance, mutters Moses.

'Man does not grasp his true nature and the true nature of all human beings. He is stunned by the form, the husk. In other words, he is immersed in 'the sea of matter'. The golden rule: you detect the Self in others to the extent that you detect the Self in yourself, this is cosmic Law. In denying the Self in others man denies his own Self. He is lost in the 'forest of delusion'.

'Thank you Lord for not making me a woman' is now embarrassing; I used to utter it daily. I never saw it this way!

'How could you, you were caught up in it! Eastern wisdom emphasises the vital role of mindfulness. Man can learn and progress only in mindfulness, when he is fully aware of the creative power of his thoughts, fully conscious of the significance of his actions. In other words when he is attentive and vigilant, when he accepts responsibility for the impact he has on the world. Articles of faith uttered mindlessly are a confession of ignorance; it is ignorance that fills human existence with pain and suffering; it is ignorance that keeps man hooked on the perpetual wheel of rebirth. Attachment to persistent thought forms is attachment to the lower nature of man. Attachment keeps him locked in duality. Attachment to the human form illustrates a fundamental imbalance: where is the spiritual man? It is attachment to your narrow view of the world and empathy with the three lower worlds that keeps you 'prisoners of the Planet'.

'I am disconcerted and amazed, in a few phrases you have shattered the world I knew and believed to be real. You have wiped out my entire life with just a few words!

'Yes, I know. The whirlwind in your spiritual body is saying it. The truth is painful, but less painful than random incarnations over millennia. To save a life a physician may have to cut into an abscess. I am only cutting into an illusion!

'I cannot begin to express my feelings. Attachment is at the root of all evil.

'Yes, it keeps man ensnared in the world of illusion; it has to be removed like a festered growth. The opposite of pain is non-attachment. Non-attachment is freedom from yearning, freedom from the pull of physicality, freedom from the urge to wander into the world of matter, emotion and desire. In Sumerian Scriptures, Yahweh is known as the 'god of the sea'. There is an irony in this, water symbolises material existence. Mankind has been submerged into the treacherous waters of material existence. When man emerges from 'the forest of delusion' and begins the gradual ascent toward the Self, liberation from the form that has kept him entranced will come.

'How will this liberation be noticed?

'Krishna answers you, 'When thy soul passes beyond the forest of delusion, thou shall no more regard what shall be taught or what has been taught'. Would you comment Krishna's statement?

'What is taught as absolute truth is born of the human mind and is not the truth at all. It is relative to the knowledge and point in evolution of the men who invented it. It must be approached analytically and dismissed if it does not satisfy reason and intuition. Buddha taught that all teachings must be approved by reason, experience and intuition. If they fail the test, they must be dismissed.

'This is what authentic Masters encourage, confirms Chenrezig. They urge discernment to liberate mankind from passive acceptance to the opinions of other. To ingest the narrow beliefs of others and soak up their biased views obstruct progress over time - in your case over thousands of years. It also precipitates intolerance, prejudice, conflict and wars. Mankind has been caught up on this merry-go-round for a very long time!

'No more learning, asks Moses concerned?

'Do not be alarmed! Learning will never end, remember that the cosmic Mind incarnates in the universe in order to learn, in order to expand his consciousness. Krishna alludes to the vast collection of ideas, words, assumptions about God and the world.

'Are they not the inevitable result of human advance, the very purpose of evolution?

'Indeed, but the intellect is a tool to learn about the world, it is not an end in itself. To the fearful and lonely self, this is indeed bad news. Krishna's words portend the demise of theology and the fall of the religion of man.

'The religion of man?

'The religion of the 'thou shall not' of 'an eye for an eye', of 'vengeance is mine'. A body of opinions and fanciful notions about God and the world. Krishna's words hint at the spiritual religion in the making, in the crucible of man's mind. It is not a religion given or 'revealed', but a religion that emerges out of man's spiritual realisation. It is the religion of meaning rather than form, of substance rather than appearances. It is about 'being' rather than 'doing', about man's infinite nature; his cosmic scale his limitless creative potential. Man as his own saviour, his own creator.

'All the teaching of the ages will be lost?

'Not necessarily, the soul will filter 'what has been taught' and retain what it deems useful. As the fog lifts, man recognises 'the forest of delusion'. Krishna elucidates the point further. What do you make of this, Moses?

'If I understand, Krishna is saying that 'traditional teachings' are man-made. They have kept man in ignorance of his true identity, of his vast mental powers; they have thwarted union with the Self, the ultimate purpose of life in incarnation. This statement is going to send shock waves among my group.

'A stark contrast to what they routinely believe to be true, smiles the Master. Further light is shed upon this vexed issue for those who indulge in 'traditional teachings'. What is the inherent flaw?

'Attachment naturally, replies Moses confidently. I know I was there! Intense attachment to those 'traditional teachings' as if life depends on them, as if the world hinges around them, as if God himself relies on them.

'Passion! But passion is of the emotional nature of man, the nature that keeps him 'prisoner of the Planet', submerged in the 'sea of matter'. Listen to these words of wisdom; I value your comments, Moses.

"Thirst for revealed objects' I am acquainted with. I spent my life trying to quench my 'thirst for revealed objects'. These 'revealed objects' were going to save me and save the world. Form is what has deceived mankind for ever.

'You are an authority on form, beams the Master with gentle irony. 'Thirst' for faltering ideas about God and misty images on the after-life pour out of man's mind in response to desire. While he sticks to his religious notions and 'thirsts' after them, he is not a Master, he is not 'freed from the bondage of rebirth', he is not free from suffering. Because suffering is of the self, the self that resists probing, that defies change. A most challenging task! Only through a serious examination of the past can you shed the burden of tradition that weighs you down, blocks your progress and nails you to the ground. Remember, this burden is not yours; it belongs to your ancestors. Then and only then can the healing begin. So suffering is suffering of the human self that refuses to accept change.

'May I interrupt Master, back home change is a denied possibility. They reject the very idea of change as sacrilegious. Change is seen as deviant, subversive, blasphemous. So they repeat the same routines of thinking and doing. Disheartened they pray for assistance.

'That's how suffering is perpetuated, sums up Master Chenrezig. The self falls prey to the three poisons Buddha denounced as the root of all suffering. The self forms attachment to roles; as a group you are attached to the roles you play. You are defined by your roles, moulded by them, governed by them, inhibited by them! Men in your society are proud of being men and with such attachment to gender and role there is the added perils of attachment to dogmas, opinions, prejudices, people and places. And when the path of life gets rough and you experience more pain, you petition a saviour to get you out of your troubles! Buddha showed the way to salvation, 'Be a lamp onto your own feet'. No one can save you but yourself.

'Is the way to salvation through devotion, good action and surrender?

'The way to salvation is by way of rigorous training of the mind, objective observation, philosophical reflection, self-knowledge and self-mastery. Buddha taught that when we no longer define ourselves by our body, desires, feelings, attachments, notions and beliefs we can then adopt a sound perspective on life. The path to liberation begins with the realisation that what we value so highly is ephemeral: race, family, gender, ideas, and creed. He said that 'all aggregate things decay'. What we value most is doomed. Everything we have created to express our identity festers and dies: our way of life, values, traditions, ideas about ourselves, beliefs about the world, in other words our cultures and our theologies. What does it all stem from?

'Attachment to the self which is transient, therefore unreal. Those things that are most ephemeral originate with the finite self; we gather them around us to remind us of who we are. There is a paradox, while these things remind us of who we are, they hide who we are! They are the cause of our suffering.

'Why, prods the Master?

'Because the things that express our identity keep up prisoners of an illusion. They prop up the transient nature of all things.

'You have some experience of this, smiles the Master with kind irony.

'I held to be true everything the rabbis, the community, the Talmud and my parents told me. For fifty years I lived by those principles, convinced that they were 'revealed' truth. I finally roused from my trancelike state to find that it all was a mirage. Nothing I had believed in had any substance, not even the god I prayed to. It was all unreal.

'A Master is one 'who has rid himself of thirst for either seen or revealed objects'. You Rabbi Moses could not quench your 'thirst for seen or revealed objects'. These 'objects' are of the senses, of the imagination, of the self that wants to assert itself. Buddha said, 'self-assertion is the cause of all sorrow', you found out sure enough!

'Is it inherently wrong to assert the self? It took man millions of years to emerge into selfhood.

'Excellent point. The self is only a stepping stone to the higher Self. For aeons mankind has equated with the self believing it to be permanent and real. Its noblest function is to lead us to the soul. The destiny of man is to progress from consciousness of the self to consciousness of the soul, but even the Self is a stepping stone to a higher consciousness, the Monad. This is the inevitable orientation of evolution. A perplexing adage sent a shock wave centuries ago, 'Except ye die ye shall not live'. An odd thing to say to people who identify unreservedly with physical conditions! And another enigmatic adage, 'I am the resurrection and the life'. This one is even more heretical. Blasphemer, shouted the priests! What was all the fuss about? What life is to be lost and what life is to be saved?

'The symbolic imagery hints to the self. The physical self has to surrender its power to the spiritual Self. Everything we value is of the self and must 'die' so that the Self can emerge. To die to the self is to be 'born' to the Self; this is the 'resurrection'. Everything we hold sacred, our body, religion, family, self, practices and doctrines, are all of the self. When the Self emerges, humanity will undergo a profound transformation.

'The Kingdom of Heaven is not going to fall from the sky, laughs the Master. And the worst peril of attachment?

'Attachment breeds intolerance, fanaticism, tribalism and hatred.

'Excellent deduction! Ignorance stems from illusion and illusion is the inability to discern the real form the unreal, the transitory from the permanent, the ephemeral from the eternal. The morbid dance with the three poisons.

'Is there a way out of this morbid dance?

'Reason and Love are the way out. A coherent man blends reason and love and acts in the world in a creative way. As man develops his spiritual 'centres', torpid, decaying attitudes will crumble. He will no longer react in fear. Fear has formed the backbone of your snarled history. A crisis is invariably responded to either in an outburst of indignation or in abject defeat. And three answers have been enduring favourites of yours: first, you are trained to react collectively, "A new crisis is upon us, we must have sinned, we have displeased god and we certainly deserve what comes to us. Let us repent, let us atone, god mistreats us, he assaults us, he injures us because he wants us perfect, we are his chosen children". So the first response is a complex one, self-deprecation and acceptance mixed with a feeling of specialness. The second response complements the first, "god punishes us because he loves us. He is the divine Father ferocious, brutal but loving". Do you discern the discrepancies?

'Reward and punishment, the stick and the carrot! God appears as loving Father and merciless judge, unreliable and unstable.

'Do you find anything defective about this argument?

'We project human characteristics onto the deity. He behaves like humans.

'Why must you esteem a god who is so human, so flawed, so irrational? What can you possibly expect of him? There is in your response a flaw you overlooked.

'God is perceived as a chastising father and a pitiless judge who metes out reward and punishment.

'You feel no disquiet that your god is locked in human roles? Is it not distasteful to your reason and moral sensitivity? Yet in spite of the harrowing evidence you do not see the tyrant you know him to be! You rebuild his image, you do some restoration work, you are artists as well as theologians!

'We are conditioned to seeing him this way.

'Experience shows that there is no certainty, no predictability in life and here enters your third enduring response to life crisis: you move away from the finite self of man and the finite self of your god and on to the finite self of humanity. Human beings are lesser, they have to be lesser or your whole edifice would collapse. You announce, 'the world is sinful and depraved, it is threatening our racial integrity, and we must keep separate in order to stay pure'. You brush the picture of a depraved humanity to contrast your own righteousness. Your triple answer is your triple poison: seclusion on the grounds of clannish superiority, specialness on the grounds of chosenness, separateness in order to justify your predicament and apportion blame outside. There is an internal logic in each and they hang together rather inevitably.

'The triple poison that plagues humanity is for us compounded by our unique triple poison: superiority, separateness and specialness.

'That's right. Quite a handful you might say.

'We are the moral and spiritual leaders of humanity, mumbles Moses.

'When thy soul passes beyond the forest of delusion, thou shall no more regard … what has been taught'. Now is the time to disregard what has been taught because you are in 'the bondage of rebirth'.

'We have an innate sense of responsibility towards humanity. We must do two things, lead humanity and retain our identity in order to carry out our duty effectively.

'This is coming to an end. This guiding role persists only in your imagination. Man is coming of age and needs no nanny to hold his hand. The Hierarchy is engaged in developing the mind of humanity, in raising consciousness.

'Our texts do not mention this.

'Do you not see it with your naked eye? In time of crisis, the real test is to resist using the past as licence for the present. The past is dead and gone, why prolong the past, repeat the past, nurture the past? The test is to avoid the pitfalls the mortal self puts in your path, it is to allow the higher Self to enter the debate and takes over, 'Except ye die ye shall not live'. To live is to live in the Self. The mortal self has led you from calamity to disaster, it is time to examine other modes of response, time to probe your being and recognise that you are more than your human self, much more. The Old Testament, altered over centuries, was woven around the finite self of your god and the finite self of man. In the absence of a sublime Self, the biblical writers assumed that both man and god were humans, all too humans! The test that confronts you today is to break free from the limitations of the finite self and recognise the reality of a sublime Self. The challenge is to escape the three poisons of specialness, superiority and separation, set against the backdrop of a malevolent universe. In a crisis, the ultimate test is to enlist the power of the higher Self. The natural tendency of the self is to repeat the ingrained habits of the past that bind you to physicality, fasten you to exile and lock you into suffering. In a crisis it is the higher Self that must be heard and take over.

The Three Illusions - Master Chenrezig

They drink tea in silence. The Master is deep in thought, attentive to the act of drinking; focussing on that simple act and Moses observes him intently. He admires the perfection of his features, the elegance of his bearing, the royal brow, and the luminosity of his presence. Sensing the gaze, the light seems to dim slightly as if the Master had modulated it to make Moses feel more at ease. He smiles, a sign that the conversation can proceed. Emboldened Moses says with distress, 'the three poisons that hold humanity down are heavy enough to bear. Is there no end to our predicament?

'Your predicament is of your own making. Your ancient texts given by the Hierarchy testify that man was created in God's image. What comes to mind when you read such a statement?

'Man is of divine origins; therefore he is God in potential.

'Interesting. But here you come to an abrupt end; you do not enlarge the point to its logical conclusion. If man resembles God, this means that he is endowed with God's faculties; surely even a child would figure this out! The primary faculty is the ability to think, to discriminate, to observe, to make sense of the world, to reason. You have used thought to conform, to bow out. You invented theologians to do the thinking for you and as a result you have endured great suffering. Those you appointed are just as fallible as you are, for they operate from the angle of the limited self. You trust them where you distrust yourselves and you are thrown from pillar to post, from disaster to calamity. 'The blind leading the blind' as the saying goes. Your assignment for this life, Rabbi Moses, is to open their mind to their predicament and show them the light at the end of the tunnel.

'A daunting prospect, how am I to show them the light when I am not fully out of the tunnel myself?

'For this task you were born, Rabbi Moses. Consciousness is well developed in man, what is undeveloped is inner consciousness. Man functions adequately in the outer world, not so well in the inner world. The inner realms are uncharted territories. Except for a few mystics, man is a stranger to the worlds he holds within. The material body holds the subtle body with its spiritual centres. These centres when accessed and developed will make him a Master of the universe! Man was designed by the 'creator gods', the Elohim, with great potentialities. Man belongs as much to the physical world as he does to other worlds and dimensions. He is so designed as to function both in inner and outer consciousness at once. His destiny is to become multi-dimensional, conscious of all dimensions, living in the past, present and future at once. You were born to make this contact, return to your world and herald a new awareness. Go and proclaim their true potential and invite them to sample their true power.

'Will they listen to me or curse me?

'What they do to you is no concern of yours. Remain at all times in touch with the inner realms, find the perfect equilibrium between the inner and outer worlds, and reside in the meeting point, your centre. Hold that central position and radiate love from that point of light. Your light will slowly dissolve the torpid energies that cloud their aura, dim their sensitivity, blur their consciousness and burden their subtle body as well as the Earth subtle body.

'It is the world that is in the dark, not them! They believe to be the saviours of humanity and they will brand me a blasphemer. All will be lost.

'No, you will anchor the light. You will initiate an awakening, outline your vision for a new world, and set the mood of change. You will do what the Essenes did 2000 years ago, far ahead of their time they planted the seeds of change. They painted the gentle and poetic image of the soul. They anchored the energy of love in your world. They repudiated judgment and punishment. They denounced as obsolete the vengeful god. Were they just anarchists, traitors set to offend the establishment?

'Not long ago I would have said 'yes'. Today my mental landscape is considerably enlarged. They were anchoring the qualities of the soul: love and compassion. They showed desperate people how to change the behaviour that brings about suffering. The ancestral idea – the god of wrath -was the font of their suffering. Suffering had its roots in fear. To eradicate suffering, love had to be restored.

'Rabbi Moses, you are a credit to Master Sanaka! Would you stretch your reasoning that bit further, smiles the Master encouragingly. You know that the alchemists were attempting to transmute base metal into gold. What is the 'base metal' the Essenes were attempting to transmute?

'The vengeful self. The aim of evolution is for the Self to subdue the lower nature. The transmutation of base metal is the transmutation of the lower self.

'Splendid! The Essenes did not succeed, the lower self prevailed and human suffering intensified.

'A lost opportunity!

'No effort to implant the light is ever lost; seeds germinate sooner or later, in your case later! Appointed by the Lord of the World, the Essenes came to anchor the energy of love and lift humanity to the next phase of its evolution.

'The human self does not give up and when it feels threatened it intensifies its hold, observes Moses with melancholy.

'To the three mental poisons which afflict humanity you added three more which form the bedrock of your orientation. The three core illusions: the first is the illusion of mission, the belief that you have an urgent task to perform, that yours is a significant destiny approved by your god and a messianic role that sets you apart. Inevitably there is an enlarged sense of self-importance not founded on reality. The idea of a Redeemer is ancient. The Messiah, as you call him, was anointed by Buddha twenty five centuries ago. Lord Maitreya has been preparing in Shamballa for the time when he will return to the world of men.

'The Messiah is a Tibetan, utters Moses, at once embarrassed by his remark.

'The great spiritual teachers who came to guide mankind down the ages emerged from Asia. Moses himself was a citizen of Shamballa and still dwells in the City of Light, as do your great prophets, Ascended Masters who work to advance the human condition.

'What is the second illusion Master?

'The second illusion derives from the first, exaggerated self-confidence. As 'chosen' people, you have the mission to salvage the world and as a result you are swollen with conceit. You are infallible! Pride locks you securely in the astral-emotional plane.

'I always thought that our world mission was noble and admirable.

'You no longer do! The work of the Hierarchy is to dissolve world illusion and raise mankind on to the mental plane, the next major step in evolution. Pride born of your belief in selection, chosenness, uniqueness and grand mission is arresting you on the plane of emotions. You along with humanity are being held captive of the world of illusion; you are steeped in the morass of the astral world of desire.

'Why humanity, I am still unclear about the relationship?

'Mankind is one unit, mankind and Earth are one. Man is made of earth, Earth is the great womb. Imagine each human being as a drop of water; each drops longs to reach the sea. Now imagine Earth as a drop of water longing to merge in the cosmic sea of life! The cosmic life force that holds the universe also feeds the diversity of forms. For so long as you focus on form and are oblivious to the life that animates the form, you will stumble over differences, diversity and multiplicity. Do you see the anomaly of such a position?

'I think so, replies Moses, the river of life cannot be interrupted, no drop of water is entitled to say to the other drops, 'I am special, the sea loves me more, I shall save you because I am better than you'. A drop is just a drop!

'Indeed Moses. Let us move on to the final illusion to which you are prone, I think that you have already guessed.

'Enlarged self-confidence inevitably leads to fanaticism, dogmatism and intolerance, suggests Moses.

'Right deduction, Rabbi Moses. If your point of view is the only valid one, if you never err then you feel entitled to disregard others. Are they not lesser than you? It is your sacred mission to guide them, scorn them or even dispense with them according to the moment. One belief, one scheme, one outlook, one conviction, one version of the truth! You are the elected keepers of absolute truth! Pride is always lurking and locks you up firmly on the astral plane of emotions.

'What is the answer to our predicament, asks Moses distraught?

'With the rest of humanity become engrossed in dissolving astral attachment and boldly set foot on the road that leads to the mental plane.

'For what purpose?

'The explicit recognition of the cosmic Plan! The Plan for the Planet is to be discerned by reason and intuition coalescing into unity. The grasp of the Plan come together with the grasp of the unity of all life, the meaning of evolution, the vision for the new Earth and the new Humanity. When the clouds of illusion dispel, the mind is refined and purified. Only then can you see the true nature of forms and their underlying unity. Truth is not hidden in dusty old books; it is all around you and inside you. This truth is accessible to you, to all of you when you search for it in the right places.

'What is it Master, they need to know.

'It is the meaning behind the form, the reality behind the allegory, the vision that illumines the form, the template, the fundamental nature, the Idea. This is what the Hierarchy and Moses imparted at Sinai.

'Lost! All lost! We perceive the form, the allusion, the heraldic sign, the mark, the seal, the outline, the motif. We play with the empty shell; we chucked out the pearl long ago.

'Your role, Moses is to return to Vilna for the task you have been entrusted with by the Hierarchy.

'Do clarify, Master.

'The focus of attention must shift from the emotional plane to the mental plane; this is the natural progression, the next phase as envisaged in the Plan of evolution. Men are captured on the plane of illusion; they long to be released. This is the work of the

Hierarchy and those who work with the Hierarchy, this is your task. The world of illusion must be dealt a blow in order to liberate man from the prison of the emotional plane.

'I sense a threat, Master Chenrezig.

'You sense right. If this is not done by men, then Earth herself will have to throw off the miasmas of the emotional plane which is suffocating her. The principles underlying religious and social life must change; if change does not come from reasoning men then it will be forced upon them. The time has come to think logically and to realise the imprudence of defunct beliefs, not just religious beliefs.

'I saw a mirage, a shifting cloud. But the truth hit me like a bolt of lightning. Authenticity is not an attribute of the self.

'In part this is true, however I advise you to avoid harsh judgment. The rate of evolution varies, it is not uniform. Human groups evolve at their own pace, and so the teachings that you now denounce had their time and place. They were designed for a specific group, at a specific moment in time, in a specific region of the globe. If the rabbis came back today they would be astounded to find that their teachings have been adhered to with such unconscious loyalty. Deep within you is the belief that the fount of truth is to be found within, in profound reflection and insightful meditation. This means an inward journey to the unlimited source of knowledge, rather than reliance on flawed outside information. The focus is distinctly inward bound.

Self & not-Self - Master Chenrezig

'Time to pause. We need to reflect on the encounter between the Tibetan Master and Moses. The divergent views of the Essenes and the rabbis demand clarification, suggests Levinson. The Essenes as ambassadors of Shamballa nurtured the doctrine of the soul while the rabbis, heirs to a dualist tradition fostered the doctrine of the self.

'A sound evaluation, approves Clara.

'A simple formula with volatile potential arises in the mind of the law-makers and crystallise into a basic tenet: 'I am a Jew, my god is the only god, and the world is created for me. I am everything'. Our own Tower of Babel throws its steeple into the sky. No other group in the ancient world ever enounced a formula with such far-reaching ramifications. This entrenched separatism bears the hallmark of a materialistic view of the world.

'Why materialistic, asks Jeremy?

'Because it emphasises separation, superiority and specialness, the three poisons elicited by the Tibetan Master.

'Interesting, says Tara but who the 'I' in your formula is.

'The ego struggling to assert itself with single-pointed resolve. This 'I' recognises no other reality but itself, no other truth but its own restricted version of it, no other existence than its finite, temporal nature. The ego broadcasts its separate, independent, divergent nature. Recorded in our collective consciousness, encoded in our genetic material it conditions our lives. Yet the self, focal point of the Talmud has no real independent existence. We change into a new ego in each incarnation. The ego has to adapt to the changing situation in our earthly lives, it is shaped by society and culture. To believe in the solidity of the ego is to believe in the solidity of a moon beam.

'The 'Word of God' written around an ego which does not exist!

'Let us return to the manuscript, says Jeremy.

The reading resumes with the compelling words of Master Chenrezig, 'Early humanity struggling to survive in a hostile environment was unaware of the reality of the hidden world. It took millions of years for animal-man to evolve. Early development was accelerated by the stellar visitors who came to Earth for a variety of reasons, not all altruistic. As repository of the timeless Wisdom we know the nature of the Self. The Upanishads show how the Self reveals itself in our lives in a poetic and enriching mode. The first Buddha many thousands years ago, enlightened mankind on the nature of man and the existence of the Self. To you, Moses, the next verse will ring even more true: 'Only the wise seeking the immortal amidst mortality turn their gaze away from the world and look inward - to find the Self'. Why Rabbi Moses?

'First, immortality is within our grasp. Second, we project the immortal out of the reach of man. We turn our desperate gaze to the world but the Self eludes us always. I know now why, because we search everywhere except where it can be found, man himself.

'Right comment, Rabbi Moses. Your people drifting and desolate engage in burnt offerings, invocations and lamentations to attract the immortal. While you atoned for imaginary sins and beseeched your deity 'out there', we looked inward to find the immortal; we had abandoned the gods of human imaginings. We sought union with the Self, with the Universe. You seek outside rather than inside a reality that always eludes you. Dazzled by form you buttress form, confused by diversity you accentuate diversity, and confounded by aloneness you intensify separateness. The Upanishads again:

'And see the One in the many. As long as you see diversity you will go from death to death. Cease this wandering and embrace your Oneness'. What do you make of this, Rabbi Moses?

'Diversity is an illusion of the senses. The mind translates what the senses convey along the line of a preset picture of the world. And the reward for delusion is a never ending cycle of death and rebirth. But this is fine for a mystical people like yours, Master, not for mine hoodwinked by diversity.

'Has it occurred to you that Nature in all its wonderful diversity is a mirage to mystify you so that you look beneath the form and discover the One? Listen to the Upanishads, 'This Self is the ultimate reality: That which was before creation and from which creation was born. Yet who sees this Self sees it resting in the hearts of all'. And you should take this injunction literally. The world was created by the Self. The Self is the ultimate Reality. But whereas to you the Creator resides outside his creation, to us the Self resides within creation and more to the point within the Heart of man.

'The Self is in man, the Self is man!

'Rabbi Moses you have just created the Universe'! With a tantalising laughter he adds, 'this alone would have you excommunicated, if you were not already 'blotted out of the book of life!'

'We have been tricked, can God delude man?

'Look upon it as a hide-and-seek game. The Self plays at hiding itself in order for you to find it. This is precisely what mankind has been doing for aeons. But there is a sting in the tail; the Self is not to be found outside but inside. And so humanity incarnates over and again, going back to the astral plane of deception and then coming back to the Earth plane of illusion.

'How long will it go on for, Moses enquires with a pain he cannot disguise?

'For as long as man plays the game. Each incarnation brings more pain but also more knowledge. And your people know about pain better than any other. 'Once the Self is known/ All sorrows end'. The tragedy of your people is the tragedy of all human beings, resistance to change.

'What has our evolution got to do with the world?

'You are right from your ancestral viewpoint because for you man exists in materialistic isolation. You picture yourselves as separate units, unrelated to other humans and unrelated to the universe and you overlook the Law which states that all sentient units are interrelated. What affects one necessarily affects the others. When you finally grasp the primary Law of the universe you will awake from your long sleep. Separation is an illusion. Imagine a grain of sand on a beach saying to another grain of sand, 'I am a better grain of sand than you, I am chosen by the beach, I must distance myself from you for fear that you defile me'. Indoctrination has crystallised your dream of chosenness. The outcome is inertia and smugness. Your actions affect all of us; your thoughts encroach on the entire Planet.

'Would you expand on this, Master?

'Human thought-forms affect the mental body of Earth, human emotions influence the emotional body of Earth. Earth is directly affected by our projected thoughts and emotions, remember that Earth is a sentient being. You have ignored the Law at your peril. Magical beliefs hark back to a remote past when primitive humans became conscious. Today the same illusive notions are a serious hurdle to your progress, to the progress of humanity and to the progress of the Planet. The interlocking of all life is the Law. Ignorance of the Law is at the root of all suffering! The cosmic life force animates all life forms; it is the same life in you as it is in plants and animals. Man contains all within himself, the animal, the vegetal and the mineral. To dismiss any life form as inferior is to dismiss the Life that animates all. Ignorance of cosmic Law is the root of all suffering.

'Because of the fluidity of the life force, when one part of the body hurts the whole body hurts?

'Right, there is one life; all forms of life are one. Answers are not in books covered in the dust of time. To find answers to the great questions of life, you must first let loose the bounds of religious dogma.

'Empowerment?

'The primary quality of the Self is power. Yet the mind-altering priests of old legislated to dis-empower you! Man stripped of his cosmic power has been sliding. He had to distrust himself, woman, Earth and even his god! He so distrusts his god that he has to dabble in persistent rituals to dodge his wrath.

'Ritual is the currency of appeasement. Freedom of enquiry is the answer.

'What else? How else can the Self be released from the bondage of the past? The Self of mankind is imprisoned by tradition, theology and authority. Dis-empowered man is at war with himself. Disabled man is at war with the world. Custom eggs you on, 'feel guilty', 'feel ashamed',' be resentful of others', above all 'be special'. What other creature in the world displays this insidious need to be what it is not?

'With soul power lost, love is also lost?

'The deity puts conditions to the love he gives, 'I will love you if and only if…'

Unloved by the Father, you are distrustful of love; love is an object to buy. You feel apprehensive: what is god going to do next. As a result you do not, cannot and must not love! Love is banished from your consciousness as the deity reminds you, 'I am the god of wrath' 'Vengeance is mine'. Love, the ultimate Reality is in a sense forbidden to you.

'It is becoming more thorny, more entangled, moans Moses.

'Conditional love, bedrock of tradition is fixed in humanity's memory. This flawed indoctrination you need to unlearn. To learn unconditional love is your ultimate challenge. The Bhagavad-Gita is categorical, 'When thy soul shall pass beyond the forest of delusion, thou shall no more regard what shall be taught or what has been taught'.

'All the belief, all the piety, all the learning, all the diligent ritual, all the words written are no more than a mirage, a rainbow, a cloud castle?

'What men hold sacred: tradition, practices and precepts, the Gita calls 'the forest of delusion'. The soul is lost in that forest and searching for the way out. The Gita has this to say about the liberation of the soul: 'When withdrawn from traditional teaching, thy Soul shall stand steadfast, firm in soul-vision. Then thou shall gain union with the Soul'.

'The Gita makes it clear that salvation is not to be found in tradition …

'… outside of it, continues Chenrezig, in freedom to observe, to question, to explore, to analyse, to grapple with the same haunting questions. There is no genuine help to expect from outside. Salvation can only come from within.

'Be a lamp onto your own feet', quotes Moses.

'That's right. The truth is never the property of the reckless that loses himself in 'the forest of delusion'. In the great myths and legends of the world, the hero goes out into the wilderness in search of the 'beloved' and his quest takes him to the edge of darkness. But nothing can deflect him; he is willing to die for his 'beloved'. He has one goal in life, to find the 'beloved', be it a mysterious sword, a magic wand or the mystical Holy Grail. Orpheus journeys into the Underworld in search of Eurydice, Tristan looks for Iseult, the Prince seeks Cinderella. The hero in all legends seeks out his Self!

'We alone seek nothing, blurts Moses.

'You have all the answers to the questions you never asked! As you feed on the same barren answers, the Self screams silently in captivity.

Delmar interrupts the reading, he looks sombre. They wait for him to speak.

The ancestral wound

'We are bound and gagged by pledges made ages ago by our ancestors, begins Delmar brooding. I just had this realisation, it hit me. In our daily prayers we pronounce, 'God of Abraham, Isaac and Jacob'. We utter these words with a deep sense of connection and purpose; they make us feel special, but are we? What happened? We bought into the ancestral pledge and we don't even know that we are in a secure prison!

'Archangel Michael explained that in healing myself I will heal the 'historic bloodline', inserts Clara. He meant that to heal our physiological, emotional and spiritual limitations would work back in time and heal the initial trauma, the initial pain. Remember what Sananda said about how the fear of Yahweh is stamped in the Jewish psyche? Not only have we inherited the initial wound we feel compelled to pass it on.

'Man has power on Earth to erase the Fall's effects', quotes Jeremy. Man can reverse the Fall - separation and duality. Man can reverse the energies of the Fall: fear, guilt, shame. This is what the Essenes came to teach, this is what the Archangel was reminding you. As a cosmic worker you came to 'reverse the Fall's effects' by absorbing the negative energies that prevailed in your background and transmute them. You may still have to heal your migraine which stems from the prevailing 'imbalance' of your bloodline. Heal yourself and you will heal the initial cause that you do not know, the initial trauma, the initial pledge made by the ancestors and recorded in your body.

'Think of the pact Abraham made with his god, muses Levinson. Why should it bind us today? Business contracts in the modern world are binding in a limited way; they do not involve our children. Yet our collective fate was sealed 4000 years ago! This is unnatural and quite frankly stupid! No curse inflicted on humanity has been made to last that long.

418

'This is not the full story, reflects Delmar. Pain, conflict, fear and their perpetual repetition are recorded in our cells. Research shows that people with intense memory recall may suffer from stunted growth. The brain is wired to register pain. Fear and thoughts of fear entertained over long periods may cause some form of brain damage, impair the ability of the brain to manufacture Serotonin, the 'feel good' chemical. As for the 'flight or fight' response, it is triggered by fear, yet with us the condition is chronic, it is passed down. So it makes alarming reading: the initial fear and the initial pledge made thousands of years ago affect our physiology, our brain chemistry, our neurological wiring and our psychology. When Abraham said 'Yes' to his god, he could never have predicted the immense damage his pledge would have on us: we are injured neurologically, physiologically, emotionally and physiologically.

'The physiology and neurology of an ancient pledge demonstrates the 'fallen' state of man, notes Clara. As guardians of the Fall, we are the most hurt by it. Not only do we preserve the Fall we also 'created' the god of the Fall, 'the god of wrath'. The primeval pledge has shaped the physiology, neurology and psychology of the man at war with himself, at war with life.

'Just as therapists help us dig up our private pledges and beliefs that make us ill, in order to change them, we can unearth the primeval agreements and review them. We have a moral obligation to renegotiate the ancestral pledge with 'the god of wrath', the human ego that lost its way back to the light, the human ego that lost its connection with the Soul. The ancestral belief of having been cast out of Paradise, of being cursed to a life of shame and pain is registered in our body; it can be healed. Why should our children be victims of a pledge that was made all those ages ago? The time has come for us all to disconnect from the past; the buck stops here.

'Things are changing and change is coming from social progress. Education and exposure to the world are altering the way we look at things, reflects Delmar. The old view of the world is changing. Gradually the Fall is being reversed in spite of the stubborn loyalty of the diehards. We are growing in self-awareness and this is bringing us into conflict with the restrictions of the ancient tribal contracts. We have kept alive the ancestral agreements unthinkingly. We are opening the windows of our mind to escape the prison of the past. We are emphatically refusing to live a meaningless existence which mirrors the meaningless existence of those who came before us. We bought unwittingly into a life of pain; pain which is recorded in our brain and physiological response. We have lived unconsciously. We are reclaiming our divine birthright to live in the fullness of our being. We will not settle for crippled existences. 'With the Fall enters the shadow self, a dark, painful aspect of our nature, notes Clara. The unconscious mind, receptacle of unwanted material associated with shame, fear and guilt, reaches out into the Underworld, the world of mythology. The pathological self is born. We have nurtured this self ever since. Our being was wounded by the primordial pledge; whole aspects of us are 'lost'. To heal is to bring to the light those 'lost' aspects. The Fall denotes a changed view of ourselves: from power to helplessness. The agreement Abraham made with his god under duress has wounded us and continues to wound our children.

The Hebrew 'occupied with god' - Master Chenrezig

'Master Chenrezig, what about the Creation of the world, if I may be so bold as to ask this question, begins Rabbi Moses?

'A tormenting question that divides opinion. This debate will intensify as science develops. Questions about the creation of the world, the origin of man or any other metaphysical opinion did not engage the interest of Buddha. He would not be drawn into theological debates that did not answer the fundamental question of life.

'The fundamental question of life, echoes Moses?

'The fundamental question for Buddha was the liberation of the mind.

'Is it not the question central to religion?

'Regrettably so! Theology made it the central question. Buddha sought to liberate humanity from the enthralment of theology. Theological questions he discarded as 'a thicket of views, a puppet show of views, a toil of views, a snare of views.'

'Why did he discard theological questions, they may be mere opinions but they have advanced man's thinking.

'You are right of course. But Buddha was essentially interested in finding the solution to human suffering. Theologies confuse more than they enlighten, they do not lead us to that 'unshakeable deliverance of the mind, the object of the holy life, its essence, its goal'. Metaphysical speculations distract us from the core subject, the 'deliverance of the mind'. It is the 'deliverance of the mind' that should mobilise our energy and galvanise us into action.

420

'The speculations Buddha dismissed as futile have occupied us for centuries. They are our reason for living and the pride of our scholars, notes Moses.

'To Buddha they are a distraction, another pretext from straying from the path of liberation. In humanity god must occupy man's thoughts at all time, or god might disappear! A primal echo of an age lost in the mist of time. When man is in prayer he makes god exist. To an infant an object no longer in view no longer exists. To man in his infancy to talk to god and about god is to keep god alive. You go on creating god!

'To the sophisticated theologian, god exists in transcendence; god is not a figment of the imagination of primitive man.

'Jeremy please, please implores Clara let's suspend the reading for a minute we have to discuss this.

'How could you wait so long without interrupting, laughs Jeremy? How about the rest of you?

'Fine by me, says Dr Delmar who looks to the others who nod in ascent.

'What is Master Chenrezig saying, asks Clara?

'He is saying that theologies leave man in the margin, they demote him to a minor role while god occupies central stage, reflects Delmar. I quote 'to man in his infancy to talk to god and about god is to keep god alive. You go on creating god'.

'This observation is now made by modern child psychologists. But what exactly does he mean, questions Johansson? 'You go on creating god'?

'It implies that man is in need of god, he must 'go on creating god' by talking about him and to him. Man in his infancy is unable to stand up without a prop, suggests Delmar. But if man needs to create god at all time, when does he create himself?

'He creates himself while creating his god, suggests Tara, a double whammy.

'Interesting. Are you saying that man exists only to the extent that he creates his god, asks Jeremy seriously?

'The answer may be simpler, replies Delmar, we are occupied with god, god is an enduring thought. Herodotus on his travels encountered a Hebrew community in Alexandria. He observed that they spent much time in theological argument. He remarked that no other people on Earth was so continuously 'occupied with god'.

'And that community was already Hellenised, snaps Clara!

'The more 'occupied with god' the more we fear god, remarks Delmar. Quite a paradox! Familiarity with god should generate love, it should liberate.

'To the modern mind, not so to the primitive psyche. Our psyche is nurtured when we 'are occupied with god'.

'A more pragmatic reason for this preoccupation with god, asks Tara?

'Man is 'occupied with god' because he is in Samsara, subject to the law of Karma, rooted in duality and because the god-image is interwoven with duality, with space, time, matter and gravity, rounds up Levinson.

Science & the Jewish mind – focus on the temporal world

'A professor of medicine encapsulates in a few words the ancestral mindset, says Delmar; he recounts how back in Vienna he was in charge of a prestigious medical unit: 'Then, my word was the word of God; I had co-workers who danced when I spoke'. All the ingredients are present: self-importance, self-enlargement, egotism, 'my word is the word of God' clamoured the rabbis of long ago with unshakable conviction. No longer is man rising to God; now God is descending to man, to pander and pamper, to endorse, and to condone. Worst still man is god in his own eyes!

'Not scientific facts people look for, science has let them down, it has given us everything we take for granted, but not the most important, moral direction, says Tara. Science is sterile from an ethical angle.

'Science is not religion, rectifies Delmar. Science investigates the physical world, it seeks facts and it relies on observation and deduction. Classical science is concerned with the discovery of the universal laws of nature. It is unfair to expect from science what religion has failed to give us.

'Even the science of mind, psychology leaves us searching for meaning and purpose, Tara remarks encouraged by the attention of the group.

'One of our most celebrated offspring, Freud unravelled the mystery of the human mind and made us aware of the existence of the unconscious, a vast repository of impulses and forces, expands Delmar. Yet this is only a fraction of the entire mind. Our tradition focuses on physical and social man, unsuspecting of other dimensions. We produce, proportionately, more scientists, doctors and lawyers than any other people. But again, they concern themselves with physical and temporal man, with the immutable laws of nature, with matter and energy. And when turning their attention to the human psyche, they focus on the variable part of the mind, the ego. Freud's scientific materialism, insistence on the authority of the father and on the driving force of the unconscious is the archetypal Hebrew: biological-psychological-social being determined by powerful forces, including the forces of his own unconscious. Man as perpetual casualty of outside influences over which he has no control.

'Freud would deny this, no doubt, notes Levinson. Unknowingly perhaps he stretched the grounds of our predicament. For the first time in our history the searching light penetrated into the recesses of the mind: our lives are driven by impulses, desires and emotions. He lived through the Nazi years where he witnessed the debacle such unconscious impulses, drives, desires and emotions can unleash. He had uncovered the true potential of the ego.

'How can we counter the ferocity of the ego?

'Dictators use coercion, oppression and indoctrination, replies Delmar. They channel man's irrational drives towards a grand nationalistic goal which mobilises the energy of the masses. What of man's aggressive tendency? They direct it towards a real or imaginary enemy. Irrational man is soothed; his instincts controlled by an external force. While his 'best' impulses are used for the benefit of the group. All is under control.

'It certainly rings true, agrees Clara. I saw this first hand, dislike, scorn, distrust were directed to 'others', our negative impulses, desires and emotions were projected onto them, while we kept for ourselves the noble traits. The Hassidim lavished the most fanciful qualities on to the Jew the object of their adoration; it was embarrassingly overdone.

'What goes for dictators also applies to the Hassidic group; they channel man's irrational emotions towards a noble group vision. What do they do with their hostile tendency? They direct it to the 'others' lesser humans, unclean and impure. Irrational man is appeased; his 'best' impulses are used for the benefit of the group while his negative traits are projected onto others.

'In our democratic societies, we use more subtle methods, the masses are lulled into a trance-like state under a constant bombardment of films, radio, televisions, newspapers and a powerful marketing machine, says Jeremy.

'Freud somehow rejects any intimation of a greater aspect of man, says Clara.

'How could he, replies Delmar? He was born in a society coming to terms with the fact of scientific thought, in a middle-class Jewish family itself waking up to the impact of modernity, in Vienna the city of imperial power, and as if all this was not enough, around him old world values were disintegrating and the great European empires were about to collapse. He encountered Darwin; with Darwin an age of materialist thought was being established.

'Nietzsche uttered the phrase that shaped a century: 'What I am saying, what I am predicting is nihilism', quotes Clara.

'In a sense we can say that Freud, Adler, Einstein and Oppenheimer were archetypal Jews, expands Delmar. Only we could bring forth men of genius bent on discovering more of the physical world, more of physical man.

'Careful with Einstein, he was as much a physicist as he was an intuitive!

'You see, continues Delmar grasping at the opportunity to raise issues of significance to him, they were continuing in the footsteps of their forefathers, the men who compiled the Talmud — a vast collection of laws, traditions, customs, superstitions, fables and legends - into a coherent structure. They too, were focusing their gaze on physical reality, debating issues they could not resolve. The dual view of the world threw its roots deep underground. It was given legitimacy by Newton to become the foundation stone of scientific thought.

'You could say that there was no intimation of a greater aspect of man, says his wife, the pull of opposites kept man earthbound.

'Things are changing, exults Delmar! The Hebrew view that had kept man earthbound was dealt a severe blow by modern physics. No messiah has appeared to flatten the derelict beliefs; science is doing it for us. Quantum physics inaugurates a new world of possibilities. It appears to bridge the gap between the physical and mental world. The immutable laws of classical physics echoed the immutable laws of monotheistic canon. Man was overlooked. Quantum physics brings in a new element, man. Man as observer affects sub-particles. Man is back on stage after having been banished backstage by monotheistic dogma.

'Quantum physics is restating in a scientific idiom Buddha's insight into the nature of the world, continues Tara. Buddha stated that the external world is not as immutable and unchangeable as our senses perceive it to be. The world exist because we believe it to exist, in other words, we as observers influence the world, we bring the world into existence.

'Fascinating, I want to find out more about Buddhism, says Delmar's wife.

'We will, says Delmar. I know of some distinguished psychologists and physicists who have drawn parallels between Buddhism and their disciplines. I now have to read them. Thank you for bringing all this to our attention.

'Buddha and Quantum physics cast a giant shadow over dogmatic religion, continues Levinson. The world is not just a giant machine with the god-force in absolute charge. The world responds to the presence of man and the thought of man. Man influences the world around him, he is not passive, and he is not irrelevant. Mechanistic religion maintains that we are the playthings of external forces. Not any more, from victim of fate to initiator of destiny! What a leap! When we grasp this, ritualistic religion will dissolve into oblivion.

'The findings of Quantum physics, Humanistic thinking and Buddhist philosophy have precipitated the Aquarian Age with its new vision of man, says Jeremy. Man is rediscovering his true nature, his identity and his connections with the universe and with all life. The blanket of ancient law had dimmed his inner light.

'Indeed, continues Delmar. Modern thinking opened wide a window onto a new reality, forcing a breach into the wall of Jericho, symbol of the archaic conditioning, the old world order. Pragmatic scientists are the true heirs to the biblical mind; they highlight the ancient determinism that the rabbis clothed into dogmas. Psychoanalysis states that we are determined by our unconscious drives and Behaviourism states that our behaviour determines us. Even empirical medicine reinforces biblical determinism with its belief that we are victims of disease. They want us to believe that we are the product of huge social and biological forces outside our control. We are dis-empowered by their determinism just as our Hebrew ancestors were dis-empowered by the god-force and his agents on the ground.

'That's right, says Levinson. As in biblical times we have to believe in forces outside our control, today it is psychology telling us that the unconscious mind is the driving force in us. In Hebrew mythology, it is the god-force who plays the role of the unconscious. He exposes us to guilt, remorse and shame. He is the ruthless judge and jury. He is the mythological projection of our inner tormentor. It is interesting to note that in Sumerian scriptures he is called 'Lord of the Sea', and his emblem is water. We know that water is the symbol of the unconscious!

'From the unconscious to the conscious, from the conscious to the super-conscious, this is the way of evolution; it is inescapable, inserts Jeremy.

'That is why biblical mythology must go, insists Clara, it solidified itself around the unconscious mind, it congealed around the emotional facets of the ego. As you summed up, the way of evolution is from the unconscious to the conscious, from the conscious to the super-conscious and we are entering this last phase. Debilitated by the biblical myth we just managed to reach self-consciousness and we got stuck there! The ancestral myth obstructs the path to soul-consciousness.

'The life current is enduring, blowing apart the form when it is obsolete, explains Jeremy. When form no longer serve the advance of man, it solidifies and stands in the way of the life stream like a dam; then it must be blown up to liberate the soul from the prison of the self. Obsolete belief, forms and methods must crumble away to enable us to venture into a new world of possibilities. This is happening now!

Resisting the liberation of the Jews

'We are enmeshed in an anomaly, begins Levinson with irritation. Appointed by the Hierarchy to transmute the destructive energies of the Father, we are the discreet workers of the one Humanity, yet we work in complete obscurity treading the Path quietly for fear of rousing self-righteous fury. Yet we work for them.

'I have lived with this anomaly, retorts Clara. The self-righteous may have been in a recent past the virulent Jew-haters. Now they are the virulent Jew-lovers, or are they?

'This is the way I see it too, snaps Levinson, Jew-haters yesterday, Jew-lovers today. The common thread 'virulent'! Rasping, trivializing, over critical, disparaging they are. In spite of their loud protestations it is not the welfare of the Jew they seem to have at heart. I believe that they care little about their fellow Jews and much more about the idol. It is the work of the idol they do. They are the uncivil 'civil servants' of the deity. They work at upholding his influence over the Planet. They are securing his civilisation. They are making sure that no change ever takes place. The cosmic workers of the Hierarchy are their enemies. They are the workers of the unchanging Father, the fierce guardians of the old world energy, the old Earth.

'I agree. As a doctor I believe it to be the great taboo of our time and one that must be exploded, notes Delmar. Our renewal hinges on it, our survival depends on it. What we are doing is give permission to an entire generation to express candidly their fear and malaise. Deep within is a secret loathing of our condition projecting as self-importance, brashness or grating devoutness. Only in the safe presence of the doctor or analyst do these suppressed feelings rise to the surface, troubled, tainted with shame and guilt!

'Jew-haters yesterday, Jew-lovers today! What about being anti-Jews next time around, or anti-something else, same merry-go-round! Their aim, as always is to prevent the emancipation of the Jews and thwart the liberation of both humanity and the Planet. In full unawareness.

Desire, root of suffering

'Interesting, mutters Delmar puzzled, a hand-written note by Benzaccai himself. He may have included it by mistake. Let us read it:

'Just as Earth has an astral energy field, man too has an astral energy field or 'body' with holds at its centre his emotions, desires, moods and feelings. The astral body is dynamic, controlling and tyrannical. It spurs us to action and governs our lives. We know it well; it perturbs our peace of mind, manipulates us through fear and throws us into mayhem. It lies at the meeting point between our instinctual nature and our higher aspirations. This body is central to Freud's theory as a powerful storehouse of emotional energy.

The astral body is the energy body responsible for the emotional distress so prevalent today. From the astral body desire springs. It is desire that moves us to action; action inspired by emotion. And there the drama fires up! Buddha taught that desire and the satisfaction of desire generates more suffering, more action and more desire; this never-ending cycle hooks us on the ever-turning wheel of rebirth. It is desire that binds us to the Father thought-form, fastens us to his pledges and threats, and hooks us to the dream of chosenness. We have been locked up in the astral plane from time immemorial. Liberation means liberation from the emotional plane. The process of liberation entails the process of healing. It is healing the past, resolving 'old world' issues that disable us, and dissolving 'old world' energy that lures us'.

'I can't make any sense of this, admits Delmar. I am not acquainted with all this esoteric material. It's all too arcane for my practical, empirical mind.

'I wonder why he included it under the Myth of the Jew, says Levinson?

'It is clear enough, says Clara, this arcane text which seems alien to the section is not alien at all. Benzaccai is saying something pertinent about the Jewish condition, indeed about the human condition as a whole.

'Be ye transformed by the renewal of your mind'

'Sanity entails the dissolution of the normal ego, that false self adjusted to our alienated social reality. (Dr Lang)

'What has desire to do with all this, enquires a perplexed Delmar?

'Desire is the stuff karma is made of. Desire is irrational, it stems from the astral body. It is desire that brings us back into incarnation. Our action is motivated by desire; desire wells up in us as greed, envy, self-grasping, selfishness and hostility. Desire makes us insatiable, uncontrollable; collectively we are prepared to go to war to appease desire. All of us have incarnated countless times. Religious canon rejects karma for a god who creates each one of us for the sole purpose of serving him. It was a clever PR exercise, but one fraught with difficulties. Why should god create us and then destroy us? And what about the rest of humanity?

'As a scientist I know that life began some 4 billions years ago with star dust that fell from the sky literally and that we evolved from bacteria.

'We have been revisiting Earth for millions of years in human form. It was reckless to reject karma and reincarnation, a grave disservice to our people and to mankind. Man is the sum total of all the thoughts, desires, actions and feelings that he accumulates and carries with him in all successive incarnations. This constitutes the karmic baggage he has to disentangle as he progresses through time. It is his karma that chains him up to the wheel of rebirth and keeps him 'prisoner of the Planet'.

'This is why as Sananda said 'part of the process of change is the process of healing' quotes Tara. Progress means change; so healing the past is imperative as well as healing the opaque 'old world' energies.

'The primeval Father-image and the Tower of Babel we erected around it is part of the 'old world' energies to disentangle and transmute, says Clara.

'In his paper Benzaccai alludes to the Solar Plexus, explains Jeremy, the emotional centre that keeps us clipped to the astral plane of emotion. It took millions of years to emerge from the density of matter into self-awareness and it has taken nearly as long to develop feelings and emotions. Now we are rising further up the ladder from emotions to mind, from feeling to reason. I am enouncing the law of evolution, Delmar!

'Evolution is individual as well as global, notes Delmar surprised? You push the theory of evolution a good deal further than Darwin did.

'That's right, replies Jeremy. Darwinian evolution is biological; what I am talking about is the evolution of consciousness. The vertical rise is from the emotional spring to action to the mental power to reason. The mind fosters criticism, discrimination and judgement. An objective mind discerns the real from the unreal, the permanent from the transient. A quantum leap in evolution! It has to do with the conversion of desire into reason, from the irrational life force to rational energy. We have been doing this since the birth of the scientific mind under the influence of the Hierarchy.

'For us the issue is critical, inserts Levinson. Some are still submerged in old world energy; coerced by the 'go & multiply'. They are arrested at the Root of tribalism situated at the base of the spine. And with the 'do & obey' they are arrested in the emotional centre, the Solar Plexus.

'Does it not apply to the whole of humanity, asks Delmar?

'To a lesser or greater extent it does, says Levinson. It governs our collective consciousness which has not changed much since Neolithic times. Do you realise that we are the only Neolithic people on Earth today to give intellectuals and scientist to the modern world?

'What is to be done, I am fascinated by this, smiles Delmar?

'We must operate a transfer of energy, explains Levinson. We must transfer the raw life force that animates the Root right up to the Head. In the Head the lower frequency of the Root-Desire is to be converted into a higher frequency: 'Be ye transformed by the renewal of your mind' urges the apostle Paul. The conversion of lower forces to higher energies is accompanied by a 'renewal of the mind', a conversion from a lesser viewpoint to an advanced viewpoint.

'Conscious evolution is very much 'vertical', it rises up the spine, says Delmar, I never thought of it in this graphic fashion.

'The phases of conscious evolution are recorded along the spine, explains Jeremy. Energy centres dotted along the spine open up in the course of evolution. Each centre declining in power as the next centre above it is activated and assumes control. It has taken man millions years to climb above the Root and Base chakras: centres of survival and reproduction around which his life revolved.

'Moses' intention was to lift his people vertically, suggests Clara. He did not succeed because astral desire was blocking the way to emancipation. The people were hooked to the dense energies that precipitated their predicament: belief, authority, dependency, powerlessness, defeatism, fatalism, aggressiveness and a bizarre blend of resentment and attachment to their deity. These traits were predominant in my family; I saw first hand their devastating effect. Attachment to the past prevents progress. Attachment to emotional response triggers mayhem and stifles soul life.

'Aggressiveness, enquires Delmar, we are the passive victims of fate?

'When the Hebrews left Egypt they were armed. They fought Amalek, they assaulted Moses and they forced their way into Canaan. They were not passive victims, reminds Levinson.

'Nothing much has changed. Both the uneducated masses and the 'informed' doctrinaires are caught up in the energy of desire and the need to experience the mirage conjured up by their emotional life, concludes Delmar who is embracing these new ideas with enthusiasm.

'Something else just struck me, exclaims Levinson. 'Be ye transformed by the renewal of your mind', is it not the call to Techouva? The secret meaning concealed in repentance? The rationale behind Yom Kippur, the day in which we fast in regret for past actions? It rings loud and clear now! Yom Kippur, repentance and 'be ye transformed' are one and the same! It is about the transformation of the limiting beliefs that keep us in thrall. It is a going inward. When the limiting beliefs about ourselves and the world come to the surface, it is time to forgive oneself and others. It is time to heal the past. It implies a reconnection with the neglected inner being, a move to a higher realisation. A move away from the mundane, the trite, the ordinary. From getting stuck in the past and its paralysing beliefs to moving into the present. Liberation!

'Nothing to do with pleading forgiveness from god, muses Delmar and all to do with personal release! As a doctor I see techouva as crucial to wellbeing: it is a rejection of old belief patterns that limit and cramp us, that stand in the way of self-fulfilment. Beliefs – other than group beliefs - that no longer serve us stand in the way of clarity and wellbeing. Techouva is no other than self-healing through inner scrutiny. As most illness springs from wrong beliefs, techouva has a major role to play in restoring health.

'When the TAO is lost ...'

'You are noted advocates of knowledge, says Sanaka, as a group you take great pride in knowledge, do you not Moses?

'We certainly do. Knowledge distinguishes us from the rest of humanity. We look down on other groups ruled by their animal nature. We are superior because of our intellectual faculty and our innate ability to lift our mind to god.

'You recap effectively, chuckles Sanaka who muses on the tricks man plays on himself! Your peculiarities always enlighten me. Knowledge is not an easy thing to discuss with the people who are master of all knowledge! What is knowledge?

Moses feels vulnerable under the penetrating gaze and the mirth of his Master. 'It has to do with understanding the world, he replies hesitantly.

'So the knowledge that fills the Talmud has to do with understanding the world, repeats Sanaka? I would not argue with this definition, he adds laughing gently. Knowledge revolves around human observation and experience and as such is detectable by the senses, it is recognisable. There is one overriding feature. ...

'That feature is intelligence. The use of the intellect, adds Moses in his element.

'Absolutely! Our observation has to be interpreted by the intellect. We agree so far, laughs Sanaka, decidedly in good humour. What is the intellect?

'The ability to make sense of what the senses receive. The ability to comprehend.

'You are half-way there! The intellect is of the personality, it is the tool for acquiring knowledge. In other words it is associated with the human self. Would you continue?

'The intellect relates to the world of the senses. It trades with the form.

'Right. Think of science, Moses, science makes use of the intellect, why?

'Science seeks to understand the physical universe, to unravel natural law; for instance, why does an apple detached from a tree fall to the ground?

'You are getting there Moses! The intellect, facet of the personality, deals with outer reality. Do go on!

'The intellect interprets what the senses receive. So the intellect deals with sense impression and the explanation of the sense impression.

'Indeed, the intellect has to do with perception and interpretation. These two words are crucial because perception and interpretation have governed your lives for thousands of years. You have accepted unquestioningly the interpretation of ancient man. Let's take an example closer to home, the Hebrew idea of man: the Talmud perceives man as naturally deviant, sinful and unruly; man's impulses must be curbed, his emotions tamed. Over time the rabbis have elaborated this doctrine of man, what is striking about it?

'It is verifiable. Perception and interpretation meet.

'We do not have this doctrine of man, chuckles Sanaka. Why?

'You view the nature of man differently.

'So perception and interpretation vary according to place and culture! Their image of man is part of a vast body of beliefs. They see man in the mirror of their beliefs.

'The way we see the world decides the way we see man. The world is corrupt, man is corrupt, woman is corrupt, Earth is corrupt, realises Moses.

'Exactly. The Fall tarnished your world. You impart this tarnished view to your children who in turn see the world tarnished. You see what others see!

'We see what we want to see! Nothing is real unless we make it so.

'Nothing is good or evil unless man makes it so. The world is corrupt because you are captive of the Fall. Yet man has the power to reverse the Fall's effects, says Sanaka.

'Nothing is true unless man makes it so.

'You create your own experience, your world, your circumstances: this is cosmic Law. The law-makers shaped the canon around their personal beliefs, attitudes and prejudices. They built a body of rules around their idea of man. Such was their perception and their interpretation of the outer world.... Man as material form is what they saw, the shell available to the senses. Now if the intellect is the gateway to perfect knowledge, how is it that we in the East do not share your view of man and of Nature?

'Why not? Why do you not perceive man as we do? After all man is man.

'The crucial question is 'what aspect of man do we look at? The Talmud sees man as a flawed being, finite, sinful, corrupt and perishable. The Talmud logically concluded that material man is not to be entrusted with his life direction.

'So this is what the intellect achieves?

'To know man you have to move beyond the intellect. The intellect informs us that man is a part of nature and the Talmud agrees. Long before the scientific age, the

Talmud adopts the stance of science: man is a material object, observable and interpretable. The totality of man!

'Man is mortal in a solid world. We need rules to control mortal man.

'Not what we perceive! Man is only pretending to be mortal and solid! All about man is supernatural even his mortal coil. The soul shapes the body; the soul animates the body, the soul, like an artist composes the life drama. The soul is all; the soul pervades the body as it pervades the universe!

'We are separated not just by land and sea but by millions of years of realisation! And we dismiss the East as idolatrous!

'Excellent, Moses. Two levels of evolution, the material and the spiritual.

'So the knowledge I gained with a diligence tinged with pride, touches only the material aspect of evolution, physical man, man in his selfhood? A respected Hebrew scholar I employed my life studying mortal man?

'Knowledge is not to be deplored, when wisely used it is transmuted into wisdom. Knowledge applied to the form is important, but limited.

'If wisdom is not concerned with the material envelope, it is concerned with the inner life, the meaning, the Platonic Idea behind the form, mutters Moses feeling gradually agitated.

'Sound deduction. Wisdom is not concerned with doctrines, dogmas and practices, but with the inner life that animates the form. Ritualism is foreign to wisdom. Wisdom evades the external, wisdom touches the life itself. This is the realm of great poets, artists and spiritual philosophers. The ritualistic deals with the form, its realm is the veils of illusion

'So ours is a body of knowledge that focuses on the form, the material aspect of evolution?

'Your attention on the form - of man and nature - heralds the scientific age. Your concrete worldview forestalls that of science. Not a negligible outcome! I know that the rabbis gave their opinions as 'revealed' wisdom and that their aim was spiritual. Yet all the while they were acting upon the physical world, they were men of their time! And so 'When the Tao is lost, there is need for morality, legality, knowledge and much pretence'. You recall this adage?

'The inner life, the spiritual germ, the fundamental nature, the core meaning have been lost, mumbles Moses distressed!

'Or never found! When perception of the 'whole' is lost, mankind must find ways of making up for the loss. Morality comes to the rescue as does legality. You know, morality is known only to man. At both ends of the spectrum morality is irrelevant; at one end the animal kingdom has no need for morality, instincts dictate their lives. At the other end, the Kingdom of the Masters is no longer concerned with it. They transcended morality when they transmuted duality. For them the astral plane has ceased to exist, they see beyond the veils of illusion. They know only the one primary life force that underlies all.

'We pride ourselves of our moral superiority. We gave moral principles to the world, we delight in them as a sign of our chosen status, moans Moses, with declining conviction. Are you saying, Master, that morality is an emotional concern that belongs to the astral world?

'Morality is concerned with 'right & wrong', 'good & evil'. These appeared when Duality appeared. This is well illustrated in the allegory of Adam, Eve, the Serpent and the Tree of Knowledge of Good & Evil. From that moment on certain actions were 'right' and others 'wrong'. Morality was born of the Fall.

'So our moral superiority is a fantasy?

'Not entirely. Morality is crucial when the Tao is lost. It is evident in your inventory of 'thou shall' and 'thou shall not'. You take this inventory seriously, and rightly so, for in the absence of the Tao, morality is the guiding light. When the Tao is lost, when the Way is lost, when the Whole is broken up morality is imperative. And when you finally awaken to the meaning behind the form, the essence disguised in form, morality will dissolve to be replaced by a higher consciousness.

'But morality is of the astral plane!

'Underpinning morality is duality: 'light & dark', 'good & evil', 'masculine & feminine'. To these elemental pairs you added a long list quite alien to the real world. Your additions reinforce your feeling of superiority, replies the Master with a gentle laughter. Your world is neatly split in two sections: one is desirable and must be bolstered; the other is not desirable and must be discouraged. So to keep the body clean, pure, separate and holy belongs to the 'good' side of your version of duality.

'Morality is of emotional/astral origin, mutters Moses in amazement.

'Do not forget that the sense of morality was first activated in Lemurian times, millions of years ago; when animal-man sensing his embryonic self was given basic rules to encourage the growth of self. The Masters gave the Lemurians basic rules to tame brutal physical appetites and keep their bodies clean.

'We are still occupied with the taming of our physical nature! We wash, we engage in marital routine, we select certain foods and discard others. We still do what Lemurian man did millions of years ago! Our religious routine hinges around cleanliness, purity and health, in short with the material side of evolution. Yet we have self-consciousness! 'You will have to answer this central question, Moses. For this your were born, for this you came to this monastery.

'So the same applies to legality, continues Moses in a flat tone.

'The same applies to legality, echoes Sanaka. Legality is vital to control man's lower nature and ensure a stable society. Absence of regulations would lead to lawlessness and a return to barbarism.

'And knowledge develops to mask the absence of the Tao?

'You are questioning the whole march of evolution, the whole movement of human progress! We just established that it is of the 'lower' mind. 'Lower' is not derogatory, the 'lower' mind perceives the world in a direct, linear manner, the higher Mind embraces the world in its 'wholeness', it perceives Reality. Do you see the major differences between knowledge and wisdom?

'Knowledge is divided up into branches, into fields of specialisation. But specialisation does not include, it excludes. Knowledge is selective.

'Excellent! As it attends to the material side of evolution, human knowledge leaves out the inner meaning, the Real, the 'whole'. The great artist and the mystic search beyond the form into the meaning'. A long pause follows in which Sanaka looks across the white peaks. Emerging from his contemplation, he says 'we have discussed the adage at length, that will be all for today.

'What of 'pretence', asks Moses with a tremor in the voice?

'Pretence, echoes Sanaka... Buddha used the analogy of the conjuror. Imagine a conjuror performing his tricks on the market place; he creates shadows and illusory forms which people believe to be real. 'Pretence' stands for the unreal, the make-believe, the illusory. When the Tao is lost, prior unity is lost; sense of the One life is lost. Myths and legends tell of a lost Golden Age. Man was made to believe that through diligent application of precepts and practices he would regain his lost Paradise.

'The purpose of religious routine is to guide man back to lost Paradise? To help him refine his lower nature, control his emotions, polish rough edges?

'You are as always right, smiles Sanaka. The diligent execution of practices will in time polish his nature, moderate his emotions and refine his mind. In other words the personality will develop. The benefit will be harvested in his future incarnations. But in this life time it is unlikely to lead him to liberation, unlikely to put him on the Path of Return.

'This is a severe blow, whispers Moses.

'It should not be! The way to liberation is through expansion of consciousness and unconditional love. You know this; it is carved in the Tablets: 'Love thy neighbour like thyself'. Love heals everything, love transforms everything. Love is the formula that brings Heaven on Earth. Love is the fabric of the universe, the very nature of the Logos. All exalted Beings in the universe are beings of Love.

'We know of love, yet we are not on the Path of Return!

'You read about love, you do not 'know' love! To 'know' love is to 'be' love! You proclaim love but defend methods that are opposed to love: separation, discrimination, selectiveness. Love is the very opposite.

'Expansion of consciousness! We devote our lives to study.

'Expansion of consciousness is neither esteemed nor cultivated. You spurn philosophy, you recoil from new ideas, and you reject science, humanities, music and the arts. For you and for the rest of humanity love is emotional rather than spiritual. You are permitted to love only your own kind, your own group. The unconditional love which governs the universe is to you very much subject to conditions!

'How can we arrive at unconditional love when our entire religious method is subject to conditions?

'With a major shift in consciousness: a steep climb from the Solar Plexus - abode of desire - to the Heart - temple of the I AM. A ritualistic life is just that, ritualistic! It may help refine coarse emotions and polish crude natures, but it is unlikely to do more. The path of appeasement is not the path of liberation, when you appease a Samsara god you stagnate in torpid waters.

'There is no hope, murmurs Moses in distress?

'There is much hope, a religious crisis is a moment, a chance of a new start, the possible gateway to liberation, you are writing a book about it, chuckles Sanaka! There is need for a sober examination, a collective self-analysis, a ruthless questioning. The urgent need to accept after 4000 years of self-deception that liberation is never thrown at man. Man earns his liberation through painful endeavour over countless incarnations. There is no entity 'out there' authorised to do it for him, cosmic Law forbids it. And when you implore the Messiah to appear in order to liberate you, you are simply requesting the most exalted Being to violate cosmic Law! Maitreya will not do it.

'Pretence suggests acting out, I know I was there! Competition creeps in.

'Competition is present. One must be more virtuous, more scholarly, more fervent; 'more holy than thou'. One must be seen to play the game better, 'I am unrivalled at this game, I am a fine actor. I am better than you at make-believe'!

'We are alone?

'Rabbi Moses you have to rise above 'what has been taught' and what 'will be taught' as Krishna urges you to do. Rise above the self to find the Master within. When you know love, 'what has been taught' that you took as absolute truth will dissolve. 'What has been taught' was nothing more than an allegorical enactment of an inner drama that you are about to bring to its denouement.

'A drama?

'The drama of the self in duality.

The god-force as the asserting self

The dissolution of the ego must be followed by the birth of a new kind of ego, the ego now being the servant of the Divine'. (Dr Lang)

Dr Delmar's wife has prepared a lavish meal. They move to the dining-room where they sit down to the succulent spread graciously cooked for them before returning to Delmar's office to resume the reading.

'The Old Testament, begins Clara is a symbolic text which cannot be read in its literal form, this both Sananda and Djwahl Khul emphasize.

'Its obsolescence is made clear by Sanaka, notes Delmar.

'The Tibetan speaks of a pending revelation, notes Tara.

'They also say that it will not necessitate the massive destruction of humanity and the Planet, clarifies Johansson. No Gog and Magog, no Armageddon. The doom-mongers will be disappointed! The imminent revelation is within us and around us. The coming revelation hints at the world of meaning behind the literal form, behind the fable. It is the spiritual core within all life forms. The biblical narrative has to be read as a giant allegory. No one ever told me this; I had to find out the hard way.

'I found out the hard way too, says Levinson with bitterness. It was taught to me in its outer form, to be grasped literally. The fable must be deciphered and the real meaning exposed. This is archaeology in a sense!

'Our god may stand as a metaphor for the evolution of man, mutters Delmar, a new idea to me.

'He is unlike the other stellar beings that came to Earth, explains Levinson. We are told that they came from various parts of the cosmos, to guide infant humanity. Many resorted to genetic manipulation to achieve this end. Their intention was to facilitate the progress of both man and Earth, for they were inspired by the principle of the Oneness of all life. Their plan was cosmic in scope; they aimed to lift the entire universe towards the resolution of polarity. In contrast the Nefilim work to secure and implement their self-interested programme.

'I was briefed by Benzaccai as to the origins of Yahweh, a fascinating character, the more I investigate, the more answers come to me, yet I look for more, mumbles Delmar. Who is Yahweh, Levinson you must have asked this question time and again?

'I have, it rings in my mind like a leitmotiv, it haunts me. What do you make of him, asks Levinson who throws the ball back into Delmar's court. Delmar must be given an opportunity to formulate his thoughts. He is at the vanguard of a movement crucial for the peace in the region.

Delmar is tentative; he has never before articulated his views. Gathering his thoughts and plucking up courage he begins: 'The symbolic representation of an inner drama, the drama of the self in duality', this phrase says it all. At one level he is a self-seeking personality out for his own gratification. At another level he is the projection of the collective psyche of an emasculated people. Traits offensive in humans are projected outside; somehow they don't look so bad in a god!

'We play out the drama of the self in our religious life, continues Levinson. Early Hebrew is increasingly aware of his rising self. With the Fall man begins to distrust nature, to fear nature. As he breaks away from nature Genesis gives him dominion over nature! We are reeling in the after-shocks of this catastrophic event. The intimate bond with Earth, the Mother is lost, while the flawed and fraught relationship with the Father becomes entrenched.

'The feminine aspect is lost, says Tara.

'It is lost, echoes Sarah Delmar who is just entering the room. 'May I join you; I am fascinated by the manuscript and want to know more, it is an Aladdin's cave. I live and work in Jericho too'. She is made welcome by all.

'More than that, it is the soul life in man and the Planet which is displaced by the mounting self. The self becomes its own authority, its own god. 'What has been taught is the representation of an inner drama, the drama of the self in duality', quotes Johansson.

'Some distortion creeps in, says Delmar. As a scientist it strikes me how self-absorbed man endows his god with the power to control natural laws and use them in his favour. His god can manipulate natural laws to serve the interest of man. An interesting twist in the relationship between man and nature. Nature must be mastered, exploited and utilised. Our scientific age! The foundation platform of Western civilisation! Man disconnected from nature, man wanting to control nature. The roots of science are in Genesis.

'Nature must be manipulated to make us feel less vulnerable, less lonely, continues Clara. 'Le silence the ces espaces infinis m'effraie' laments Pascal. Not surprisingly, he is the intellectual offspring of the biblical viewpoint.

'The story of the passage of the Red Sea and the fall of Jericho are two instances of man's mastery over nature, continues Delmar emboldened. The Red Sea opens up to permit a special group of human beings set apart from all others to pass, thus breaking the laws of nature. At Jericho, there is another infringement to natural law. Nothing is impossible to this people with a mission. Nature must bend. God created the laws of physics but he must also break them for this most special of people.

'Gratifying to the ego, but this is bound to have unpleasant repercussions, says his wife.

'It has, continues Delmar, alienated from his fellow men, biblical man is unmoved by their common humanity, he views them as lesser beings, he has set himself apart both from nature and from man.

'Later when he learns of the existence of the soul he applies the same stance, he simply denies it to others, expands Levinson. This stance has been bolstered by Hassidic doctrine which grants the Jew no less than five souls! The non-Jew has none! The violation of basic human rights has begun. Two hundred years ago, the soul was denied to African slaves; as lesser beings they could be sold, bought, tortured and killed.

'The natural cataclysms that strike the Planet at the time of Exodus are interpreted along similar lines by our history-shapers, explains Johansson. History as a discipline is born; we have a new 'science' made by those who triumph over their enemies and over nature. The deity becomes the liberator, a force for good, one who obliges nature to obey his command.

'But there is another facet, picks up Delmar; the liberator-god is not untouched by human affairs. He plunges into the thick of it; he takes side with his people against humanity. He is the god of physical law who plays with the forces of nature and turn these forces against mankind. He does not manipulate natural law to benefit mankind at large.

'Nietzsche answers, 'God degenerated to the contradiction of life, instead of being its transfiguration and eternal Yes! In God a declaration of hostility towards life, towards nature…' When god feels free to manipulate the laws of nature for his own end, trouble ensues. God becomes the enemy of life, the enemy of nature. This has been humanity's predicament since biblical times, expounds Johansson.

'In our god, the desire to protect his genetic material, reminds Clara.

'That's right, continues Delmar. The Egyptians are drowning, yet the devastation the Hebrews behold does not alarm them. Humanity is being destroyed before their very eyes and they praise their god, the women dance! So we have a complex picture: a god who has no regard for man and nature, lavishing his favours on a minority group at the expense of the many, a god of creation who violates the laws of creation!

'Nietzsche explains, 'A proud people need a God. It projects its joy in itself, its feeling of power onto a being one can thank for… Religion is a form of gratitude. One is grateful for oneself; for that one needs a God'.

'This picture illustrates the nature of man's growing ego, ferocious and inconsistent, says Levinson.

'What happened to the essential man, whispers Clara? Where is the sympathetic, compassionate, understanding Self? Our body of knowledge is an allegory for the relentless rise of the self, the 'allegorical enactment of the drama of the self in duality'. The tapestry of earthly and earthy man.

'Nietzsche touches the core, 'Formerly [Gods] represented a people, the strength of a people, everything aggressive and thirsting for power in the soul of a people... there is no other alternative for Gods: either they are the will to power – and so long as they are that they will be national Gods....'

'The compassionate Self is not for a people thirsting for power. The gods express 'everything aggressive and thirsting for power in the soul of a people'. The biblical gods are the gods of the Western world, mutters Delmar's wife!

The tyranny of the self

'Long ago in Lemuria, begins Sanaka, emerging from the darkness of matter, animal-man felt himself distinct from the herd. He had acquired a sense of 'self'. The self has been growing ever since. The self has assumed great power, becoming all there is. All violence, injustice, aggression and crimes have been committed by the self, for the self. The belief is that the self needs it. 'I', 'me' and 'mine' the ancient trumpet calls of humanity fill history books, mythologies and legends. They reverberate in your holy books: think of the legend of Cain & Abel, Isaac & Esau. Yet the 'self' that rules the world is unstable, unreliable and changes from moment to moment. Our thoughts, feelings and emotions fluctuate and have no more lasting quality than a cloud drifting in the sky. This outer self has from childhood ingested beliefs, attitudes, prejudices and notions presented to us by our society.

'Some of us do challenge these beliefs and prejudices, mumbles Moses.

'With much suffering! The self does not give in without a good fight! People live their lives never questioning beliefs about the self that were implanted in their impressionable mind. On the contrary we tend to reinforce them when we feel insecure or when they are disputed by the outside world. We fully identify with these beliefs. When you utter 'I am a Jew', these innocuous words open the gate to a flood of inherited beliefs, taboos, conjectures and attitudes. As the gate opens come hurtling down the pervasive presence of the deity, his intervention at Sinai, the endless wandering, the Holy Land, the prophets, the kings, the wars of attrition, the books of rules, the myriad of rituals to pacify the angry 'god' and to stay 'clean' for him.

'Is it not the purpose of life to remind ourselves that we are spiritual beings?

'Absolutely Moses! To be spiritual is to discern the real from the unreal, the true from the false. Discernment is crucial. To be spiritual is to know unflinchingly that he lower self is not the real you! The self is a working tool to act in the world. A farmer uses a plough and seeds in his field, but he knows that he is not the plough, the seeds or the field. He uses tools, he is not the tools! Only the insane would say 'I am the plough'!

'Yet this is the only tool we have to work in the world.

'It is not, we have a more sophisticated instrument in the intuitive mind. Prophets, great artists and musicians use the intuitive faculty. It is the gateway to the entire knowledge of the universe. More importantly, the 'self' we believe to be our true identity is not. Our true identity resides in the deathless Self, the enduring Self. With the lower self we come back into incarnation to play roles, to play the role of the Jew among others! When you say 'I am a Jew' you take this role to be all there is and the mortal self to be the real thing. You should be saying, 'I came back to Earth in this incarnation to play the role of the Jew on the stage of life, it is only a role, it is not real, I am only pretending'. You would not hoodwink yourself and others.

'Why pretend? What is the point of all this deception?

'All human beings in incarnation are pretending to be what they are. It is the soul which sends the self back to Earth on a journey of learning. You are in incarnation, all of you, because the soul wants you to progress on the Path.

'It all seems so pointless, sighs Moses.

'It is not, the 'game' started aeons ago with an explicit purpose. The Divine gambled on fragments of his essence being able to remember their true nature and return to him.

'The Divine incarnated in the darkness of matter to test himself! Heresy!

'Heresy to some. The nature of the Divine is love. The nature of the self is not. So … Moses, chuckles Sanaka tantalizingly.

'So the ultimate purpose of incarnation is to remember our true identity which is the Divine, which is love.

'Splendid my son, beams Sanaka. The purpose of incarnation is to learn to love. It is to become infused with the light of the soul; it is to merge with the soul. It is to emerge from the darkness of illusion to know yourself as the All.

'So when I say, 'I am a Jew' what I am saying unknowingly is that I am climbing the ladder of evolution, that my goal is not yet in sight, but that in some distant incarnation I shall arrive at my destination.

'Excellent summing up, Moses. You have to be very clear on this, the 'I' is not the real Self, it is a medley of ideas and beliefs that do not belong to the real you at all! Yet we cling to this self to bond with others, to develop a sense of identity. This self we fight for, torture for, kill for and are killed for is a creation of the human imagination. The beliefs fashioned by the religion-makers of all times and all lands are hammered in with every generation. And what happens? It all vanishes at death!

'What happens at death, asks Moses with anguish?

'At death the individual is projected back to the astral plane to be confronted with feelings of loss, betrayal and hurt. He is now in the astral-emotional plane of life after death. To deal with his overwhelming emotions he has to come back to Earth. He organises his return in a new setting, new land, new race, new gender, and new creed. Only to become ensnared in the beliefs, opinions, dogmas, fantasies and fallacies of his new society!

'When is this endless cycle of life death and rebirth going to end?

'When you all wake up! You are asleep on Earth, asleep after death, you come back to resolve your difficulties to fall asleep all over again!

'So being a Jew is not the ultimate, recaps Moses. It is only one small link in the long chain. The emotional burden with us from the moment we take our first breath vanishes without trace as we exhale our last breath.

'Your conclusion is accurate, Moses. The self is as transient as a mirage, as lasting as a rainbow, as real as a daydream. The self and its gods owe their existence to your need for stability, for authority and for certainty.

'In other words, self-deception, interrupts Moses.

'The mirage that lures the weary traveller lost in the Desert.

The Father, Satan & the self

Weary by a fruitless search for Benzaccai, Levinson and Clara sit quietly. The sun is setting in a glorious ball of orange light, the clouds reflects blues, yellows and pinks, the air is soft and warm, the moon already showing in the sky. All is peace and tranquillity, yet their mind is troubled. Clara, breaking suddenly the silence as if hit by a flash of lightning, 'The similarity between the activity of Satan and the god-force just struck me. They are present in concert in Genesis. Where the Serpent is, we are sure to find god. What was the Hierarchy's hidden message? What did they conceal in the strange encounters between the two leading cosmic players?

'An interesting flash of inspiration', smiles Levinson feeling weary and disheartened.

Trying to overcome his lassitude, 'what do you make of it?

'As I see it, they both target the erratic self. I remember how my parents, two halves of the same entity, united and blended their efforts. They never endowed us with mind or feeling, in my mother's eyes we were lumps of clay no breath of god had breathed life into. Satan the embodiment of negativity manipulates the self through shame, guilt, and blackmail. The intended aim is to inflict damage from within, so that the victim of malice becomes his own victim. It undermines emotional solidity and impairs the integrity of the self.

'Your parents understood the hidden meaning concealed in the text, chuckles Levinson sulkily. The arbitrators of the god-force use similar methods and the results are predictably the same; they too target the self which they manipulate through guilt, shame and fear.

'They grant us human dignity, concedes Clara. The myriad of rules safeguard our basic human rights.

'Exactly, they implement a certain respect for life. After all are they not fashioned in the image of their god, the god they claim to venerate? Yet they can't resist the temptation to manipulate other to the will of god...which is their own will. They bribe you into surrendering to him, using any means at their disposal, images of doom, prediction of gloom, discreet blackmail, implied threat of rejection, subtle warning of exclusion and isolation.

'Satan uses more subtle methods; he promises you the dominion of Earth.

'In exchange for obedience! He wants you to obey just the same! They both do, they rely on your capitulation, your fear, the fear that estranges you from your soul that alienates you from the cosmic Self.

'Satan is subtle; he invites us to desire, to discover, to experiment, to know. Buddha was offered the dominion of Earth, Faustus the pleasures of life. He appeals to our emotions as much as to our intellect. Satan is the self, crafty, manipulative, egoistic, materialistic, separative, and intelligent. Beyond desire and power, Satan urges us to look at the world and perceive it as a complex machine, separate from us, existing objectively. A machine in which we are remarkable only by our insignificance, a world empty of a directing Intelligence in which man suffers alone and is not permitted to know his place in the scheme of things.

'Any different from the idol?

'The idol starts off from the premise that man is frail, flawed and corrupt, so he must be coerced and manipulated. He must 'do & obey' that is his only reason for living, his only source of dignity and self-respect. Outside the 'do & obey', his life is meaningless and sterile. He exists not as a noble being for his own sake, but as an inferior creature designed to perform tasks. He must be organised, directed and dictated to.

'Our picture of the world supports the entire edifice of Western scientific and materialistic tradition. Man must be governed, controlled, directed and dictated to. These assumptions underlie not only our economic system but also the global marketing and advertising culture.

'That's right. Biblical man is split into two entities just as his world is split in two parts. Before the biblical period, the world was perceived in its holistic nature; the American Indians still view the world as a complete, integrated whole, as do the spiritual philosophies of India and Tibet.

'And it is this fragmented, broken picture of the world that forms the basis of Western scientific thought and method. The holistic vision of the past was swept away, probably as uncivilized superstition.

'Science moulded itself in the elemental dualities of spirit and matter fostered by its biblical origins. Like the biblical model science relies on the ability of the mind to use linear thinking, analysis, premise and reasoning.

'Analysis is a breaking, a splitting. Materialistic science parallels the religious materialism we are all familiar with. Science has its roots in the Fall; it relies on the separation of man from nature, of mind and matter. The physical world is the only reality we know, the 'do & obey' springs from it.

'With Quantum mechanics science has been shifting from objective observation - which excludes - to subjective observation, which includes. If 'old' science is outdated what of our old religious materialism which breaks up man and his Self, man and the Divine? If science is changing, our prehistoric tradition ought to begin the process of change, from dualism to holism, from materialism to spirituality.

'It is long overdue, but who will do it? The pseudo-rabbi spends a couple of years at Yeshiva to learn by rote countless rules on marriage practices, the rinsing of meat, the purification of women, the length of their fringe garments and countless activities of this sort which fill their heads to bursting. They measure their holiness by the amount of rules and rituals they have ingested and can regurgitate.

'You have a point there. They are godly to the extent that they deny the soul its impulse to explore and to know!

'The measure of godliness ought to be inclusion, understanding, tolerance and empathy! It should be the quest for the cosmic energy that underlies the whole of creation. The search for unity to enlighten us and to raise the vibrational frequency of the Planet.

'And all the while, the Self dispassionately observes this sorry state of affairs and uses it for its own purpose.

'The selfish Self, is that possible?

'The Self is concerned with the accumulation of experience. It descends into matter to learn. If it has to garble words of piety, stumble over rituals, boast imaginary feats, extol a god that is no god, so be it! If it has to wear a fur hat in high summer, fringes, belts, wigs, shawls and boxes on the brow, so be it. The Self retains what it needs after filtering the lot. After all, it is the Self that chose this state of affairs in the first place!

'I felt my soul laugh to itself; I heard my soul goad me. My soul went its own way regardless of the mayhem around it. It amuses itself at the performance of the human comedy.

'This is so true, when I look over my life; I trace effortlessly the journey of my soul, the satisfaction of its own agenda. It led me in spite of the mayhem surrounding me and my attempts at thwarting its design.

'Buddha taught that the true nature of the self is emptiness. Empty of existence.

'Empty of existence. Neither the Machiavellian effort from Satan nor the pious meddling by the deity makes the slightest indent. A puff of smoke, a cloud drifting across the sky!

'In Greek mythology, the sculptor Pygmalion carved a beautiful woman in stone and fell in love with it. Our ancestors carved their god from those qualities they envied but could not emulate and fell in love with him.

'They fell in terror of him! Love never entered the picture. Love is not a clause in the contract. Love is not part of the deal.

'As the Divine is love, so the Divine is absent from the deal!

The Jewish people keeper of mankind's memory

'What was Sananda saying when he enigmatically uttered that the Jews remembered what mankind had forgotten, asks Clara unexpectedly?

'I guess he hinted at the suppressed memory of the genetic manipulation of long ago by the god we have worshipped ever since, explains Levinson. Every day of their lives they remember! They sharpen their memory with the study of the revealed Book of Earth. They carry the memory of Earth with them down the ages. The revealed 'document' holds the memory of planetary events and cosmic events, to be deciphered.

'Is this the secret concealed in the perennial hatred of the Jew, enquires Jeremy, a touch uneasy at entering a debate foreign to him?

'The Jew is the man who knows too much! It sounds like a crime thriller, but it makes others feel troubled. They can account neither for their unease nor for their loathing of the Jew, says Levinson familiar with the subject.

'This is why the Jew had to die, wonders Jeremy?

'This is why the Jew had to live. You see, he holds the entire memory of the Planet and of mankind's impenetrable past.

'The Jew remembers the past, his noblest function as he sees it. The Book of the Earth is inflated with events, fables and allegories. It is impossible to disentangle fact from fiction, yet there is memory even if distorted by interpretation and the desire to magnify. We are confronted with an uncanny paradox: the Jew holds the memory of the Earth yet he cannot recall his identity, his origin or his destination! To compound the problem he is estranged from Earth the memory of which he carries deep inside him!

'A paradox indeed, notes Clara. He is the living memory of the history of humanity and the Earth. Those primordial events found their way into the caverns of humanity's unconscious. The Hebrew brings this unconscious material to consciousness. Normally, when repressed material emerges into consciousness the process of healing has begun. But where is the healing?

'No healing just yet, replies Johansson, an authority on ancient religions. I think that Sananda alludes to the strong attachment the Hebrews have for their genetic history. Interwoven with their genetic history is a deep sense of mission. Their assignment - as they perceive it - is to bring humanity under the flag of Yahweh through their long awaited Messiah, the Redeemer for all men. In short they seek to consolidate the kingdom of Yahweh on Earth.

'In modern idiom they seek to confirm and prove 'divine intelligence expressing itself in matter' through the laws of physics, remarks Jeremy, this view was given a knock by Quantum physics! The universe appears more as a giant thought than as a giant machine.

'And Buddha agrees, butts in Tara, 'With our thoughts we make the world'. Thought creates matter and events. The world is thought made visible.

'This is precisely what we, the workers of the Hierarchy came to fade out, exclaims Clara. We came to undermine the 'god of matter'. We came to thwart efforts at consolidating the materialistic stance. We infiltrated humanity to transmute those energies. Earth is the kingdom of the 'god of matter'; we want to change this. We came from all corners of the universe in response to the Hierarchy's call to release mankind from the shackles of the past and to assist the process of transformation. The old story of Creation has to be re-written to include man as creator not just as created.

'For the diehards there can be no new narrative, no new paradigm, no new myth of Creation, comments Levinson. It was all decided at Sinai for all time. The march of evolution has passed them by. The apocalyptic messianic times are projected onto a vague and distant future. In the meantime they are in possession of a doctrine so noble that it stands them apart as the most eminent and exalted people. Their greatness exists in their mind - 'with our thoughts we make the world' - but it does not stop them from imagining that they have a global moral and spiritual role to play.

'I like the idea of a workshop, says Clara joyously, she is keen to move on to something else. What issue do you propose we question Sananda about?

'What other than Genesis, chuckles Jeremy? We all need to know where Sananda stands on this issue. As a working title what about 'the Old Testament as the encoded record of the origins of time, space and matter?

CHAPTER 8

MATERIALISM OF THE OLD TESTAMENT

'The Old Testament is a secondary Scripture and its emphasis is material. The theme is the recovery of divine wisdom in the first solar system, which embodied that aspect of the Divine which is the active Intelligence expressing itself in matter'. (Master DK)

'The doctrine of causation ... is only applicable to a world of dualities and combinations ... As long as we are bound to a world of particulars we see causation and relativity everywhere. (D T Suzuki)

Worship of time, space, matter & causation

We have formulated our own views on the Old Testament, I think it is time to ask Sananda for further clarification, suggests Clara.

'Excellent idea, approves Levinson always keen to stretch further. Jeremy, could we have a session with Sananda?

'I think this can be arranged'. They sit quietly in a circle, eyes closed. Silence falls on the group. Sananda invites them to put their questions.

'Master Sananda, is the Old Testament genuine, asks Clara briskly?

'The Old Testament is, first of all as you hinted earlier, a document which has been worked over in places, it is not as it was originally received in all of itself, but some considerable portions are.

' Authentic?

'Authentic, yes.

'When you said 'received', received from whom?

'Right! This is what needs to be moved on to next. First of all bear in mind that there has been some doctoring, certainly in the later Books. Secondly, some of the text is genuinely, truly received from the higher sources of the universe, without getting too specific about the route it comes on. It is not exactly that the Source of All issued forth the Book of Genesis, not exactly; nevertheless, you can think of the Old Testament as being sanctioned by the Divine. Just as you do not receive electricity in your home directly from the power station, but stepped down through transmitters to usable voltage, so is the case with this kind of divine transmission, it is stepped down through intermediaries. But you are also presented with the question of interpretation: words

449

can be quite limiting, and so human interpretation has intervened over the years. Humans put their spin.

'You said that the Old Testament has elements of authenticity, presses Clara. Initially sanctioned by the Divine, it had to be stepped down through channels. Was one of the intention of the higher sources to strengthen a people already confident in itself, sure of its relative intellectual ability, certain of its genetic advantage? Or did they have something else in mind, a vision into future history, of the creation of some great civilisation perhaps? We know that Christianity and Western Civilisation developed from it.

Master Sananda replies with a gentle laughter, 'You will appreciate that the Divine takes a long view, there is certainly a long, far-reaching look into the future. It is also true that there was a wish to leave that document into safe-keeping; it was felt that the people who received it would safeguard it, that it would not be lost, if you like. The Divine speaks in many layers, this is an important point, words are quite limiting, they constitute a tiny portion of understanding. The Divine speaks in layers so that one group of people may take the surface meaning and another group may look beneath the surface to find a deeper meaning and benefit from this investigation, while another group will look deeper still and find yet more meaning. So the intention was to give each individual the kind of knowledge that would help him the most. And it is not always the case that people derive the greatest benefit from the first glance; the first glance may encourage them to take a second look and be led further in. So it also was designed to work in that way. In other words, for those to whom the Old Testament is a sacred book, there has been both the potential for a positive and a negative outcome, depending on the level of evolution those particular people reached at that time. The Divine teaches but does not enforce the lesson for you live on the Planet of free will.

'This document, continues Clara was sanctioned by the Divine before passing through various 'transformers'. It also has numerous layers of meaning. Is the Old Testament still relevant more than 3000 years on? We have progressed at an astonishing pace and the rate of progress has accelerated enormously in the last 200 years. Perhaps not in spiritual terms, but mentally we have moved forward hundreds of light years.

'Sure, inserts the Master.

'Do they have any significance today? Rituals and beliefs hark back to Neanderthal rather than to modern man, some are plain barbaric. At the dawn of the Christian era

450

the god-image changed. This mood of change was registered by the recalcitrant law-makers who had to redefine their idea of god. The concrete deity of the Desert was evolving into an abstract god remote in space and time. Modern humanity has evolved a probing mind. Do those teachings still mean anything or should we discard them and declare them obsolete?

'As you imply many were specific for the time and place in which they were first given. Unless you are willing to probe for the deeper meaning, you are not going to derive much benefit from a superficial reading. The surface reading is going to leave you with something very much fixed in time and place very unlike your modern society. So, the truth is still there to be found, but you need to use your own wisdom to discover it.

'What is its essence purpose, its core beingness, Clara asks using the Master's own terminology?

'It was first of all designed to function in a number of different levels, to have one essence, but with multiple expressions. This is the case with many religious texts designed to have a surface meaning or literal meaning and a deeper meaning. Part of the essence with this particular text, as with others, is to **awaken**. Through study, through deep inner quest and searching it becomes possible to find deeper truth. This is a very important aspect of its essence purpose. The Old Testament was also time-coded. So as well as having multiple layers of meanings at any one time, it also had different meanings at different times. For a while it acted as a handbook for living in a straightforward way. It then became, as time moved on – and this was built into its design - an image of your origins, your beginnings, what humanity came out of, a way of explaining Earth's past which in turn was designed to act as a jumping -off point for a new vision. Initially, that new vision came in the form of the New Testament, or at least that was one of the versions of what is possible; but actually its function is even wider.

'And of course, continues the Master, one of the essences of the Old Testament is that it should operate in a free-floating space in relationship to humanity. By this I mean that you are all free to form your own relationship with it. Now within this built-in freedom provision, there are complexities. As a result, some of you chose to feel bound to its words in one way or another, there are lots of ways of doing this. Some or you chose to throw that freedom away and this is a way of forming a relationship with it. But for others, it floats in their consciousness as an icon which has the power, to a degree, to awaken awareness within those who have consciousness of it. Again this has operated in a lot of different ways, because for some the impact of the presence of the energy of the Old Testament has been to seal off part of their consciousness. But now the predominant effect, and increasingly this will be so, is to open up a new level of awareness in the human race.

'So to summarise, the words that form the Old Testament were themselves drawn into existence around a core energy. You can think of this core energy as being like a magnet that draws to it the correct words to express this particular quality of energy in the physical world. The purpose of that core energy was to form one of the key structures of your reality, to become part of the electro-magnetic field of which your reality is formed, but for a limited period. Then, at the correct time, when certain triggers are touched, the energy transforms and begins to dissolve those very structures that it previously upheld. You could think of this as being to a degree, the energy input of that beingness you know of as Yahweh'.

The Old Testament by Djwahl Khul commented by Master Sananda

The Old Testament is a secondary Scripture and its emphasis is material. The theme is the recovery of Divine wisdom in the first solar system, which embodied that aspect of the divine which is the active intelligence expressing itself in matter'.

'Master Sananda I would like your comment on an enigmatic quote from Djwahl Khul. He defines the Old Testament in a manner that almost contradicts your evaluation of it: 'The Old Testament is a secondary Scripture and its emphasis is material. The theme is the recovery of Divine wisdom in the first solar system, which embodied that aspect of the divine which is the active intelligence expressing itself in matter'.

'Yes. He speaks of the Old Testament as a 'secondary' text from his point of view; for he would see the message of the New Testament as being more important to humanity at this crucial time and its particular qualities of energy as being more important in this age of change. I like that description of the Old Testament; I think it is rather good, laughs the Master. He is talking about important truths, but he is looking into the past into the nature – in symbolic terms, in encoded form, often hidden into the text, in ways that are not easy for you to decipher - of the history of humanity and of your Planet and how the life you are leading today came to have this particular type of form. It deals as

452

he said, with the history of your Solar System. But from his viewpoint, the point that he is making, history is history, it looks to the past, it is done with. It is interesting, even valuable, you can learn from it but it is the present which is most important.

'A persistent feature in the people I know is raptness in the past, enactment of the past, narrating of past events real or fictitious. The contemporary is marginalized if not altogether ignored. The focus on embroidered past events is to them the measure of their spirituality!

'It is one of the challenges many had to confront, comments the Master. There were other people who met the same challenge, the ancient Greeks for instance, who harked back to a Golden Age of their history. This happens to people who have some kind of memory within them of the way things used to be and when you look at the myths and stories of all the ancient peoples of the world, you will find this challenge for all of them. All of you, somehow, remember that there was a time when things were different; you have the memory of a Golden Age, a time when men and angels walked together, when Gods walked upon the Earth. All of you have these memories in your stories. And it can be a real challenge to strike a balance between keeping those memories alive so that they are not forgotten, while at the same time avoiding being so entrapped by them that you forget to be in the moment. It is essential that you remain free to find your way to creating again, creating anew those times that you have memories of. That has indeed been one of the challenges of the Jewish people they still wrestle with.

'Is it the right time to say to the Jewish people, 'the gods who walked the Earth long ago were not real gods, they were scientifically and technologically vastly superior to us, they were much more clever, but we have caught up with them we are now as clever as they were? When Yahweh was experimenting in the laboratories of Sumer, he was hailed as god, but now we have caught up with him, we have geneticists. I want to say to those who have plodded down the ages under the burden of the law, 'let go of the yoke. You have been slaves for too long, set yourselves free. You are just as clever as Yahweh and just as powerful and you have nothing to fear'. Now, am I justified in doing this, in saying to people 'I have this message for you'?

'One of the excellent qualities that a book has in your society is that it gives the author the freedom to say what he or she wants to say, replies Sananda. In your society, the book is then offered to anyone who wishes to share your thoughts; but it is not forced upon them. There is much to command in this way of doing things, in these kinds of areas. So, by all means communicate what is in your heart to transmit, that is excellent, but do not force it on others, it will not work. People will hear your message when they are ready to hear it. If they hear it prematurely, they will simply reject it and declare that you are a fool and a blasphemer - using insult and denigration as a defence mechanism. So that it is undoubtedly great for you to put your communication forth into the world, making it as much from your heart as possible. It will be your own unique contribution to the world but do not worry about the way it is received. Cast your seeds to the wind, some seeds will sprout and some will fall by the wayside and trust that this is the best way. After all, one of the things you do not wish to do is to force your views upon others in the manner that views were forced upon you! This has been one of your lessons in this life. So offer rather than force.'

CONCLUSION: A much 'chosen' people

'Legend has it that before Atlantis vanished in the ocean, Shamballa invested some effort and expectation in the pre-Hebrew group who lived on that lost continent. Esoteric wisdom teaches that it was the Manu who supervised the rescue of the family we know as Noah, begins Tara.

'How exact is the information? Sananda will confirm it or refute it, suggests Clara. But first why did Shamballa invest in them? What did the Manu and the Planetary Logos see in them: certain qualities of energy that would alter the course of evolution?

'The Hebrews are a much 'chosen' people, states Johansson. Chosen by Yahweh to carry his genes and implement his civilisation on the Planet, chosen by Shamballa to father the new human race post-Atlantis, much later chosen by the Hierarchy and Moses to bring forth a new age of enlightenment and finally chosen by the Essenes and their Master to initiate a new phase of progress for humanity, a new journey on the Path of Evolution, you might say.

'Yet all those 'chosen' episodes, crucial to human progress have not amounted to much for the people they were initially intended, observes Levinson. All those momentous developments which altered the course of history seem to have by-passed them. Failure of realisation or interpretation?

'Or failure to register facts for what they were, comments Clara. Yet the post-Atlantean humanity is dynamic, immensely creative and rapidly evolving out of the limitations of the past. Post-Atlantean humanity is shedding the old restricting view of itself. This constricting view cultivated by tradition and endorsed by culture is now fading away. Humanity is emerging out of the thought-forms that have kept it imprisoned.

'Moses had laid the foundations of the new awareness we are registering today, later Solomon inscribed the fundamentals principles in stone, wood and gold, adds Levinson. 'And it is candidly believed that Solomon built his Temple to the glory of Yahweh, laughs Clara! 'His heart was not wholly with Yahweh his god'. He offended everyone.

'Yet he was held in awe, inserts Johansson! He was a heretic but also a Master. A Master building a glorious temple to pay tribute to the 'god of matter'? To celebrate an extraterrestrial? To consolidate physical law?

Later they were able to secure a few moments with Sananda to put their questions, they sensed the significance of the event, though the exact reason eluded them. They sit in a charged silence. 'Welcome, do ask your questions, greets Sananda.

'Master Sananda, begins Clara, the question revolves around the historical origins of the Hebrews. More specifically it is about Noah's rescue. I realise that Noah cannot be the father of the Hebrew people whose origin is lost in prehistoric times. But Noah is the only 'historical' point of reference. Was Noah the father of the new humanity? Why did Shamballa invest so much in the descendents of Noah? What special qualities did the Hierarchy identify?

'Yes … you sense some hesitation … because this is one way of talking about that time. That narrative was not fully of this dimension, it belongs more to the world of myth than to history. If we talk about it in mythological terms, if we view this episode as a myth that tells the truth, then we would go along with that statement.

'That Noah was the father of humanity?

'Yes, replies the Master. The fall of Atlantis had been predicted and anticipated, many knew that it was going to happen and moved out into the world. This process of migration went on for a long time.

'It did not happen suddenly in one day and one night as Plato recounts?

'No, it took place over a very long period of time. Many Atlanteans escaped the Flood and spread out. Noah symbolises the experience of many people who went out into the world to start from scratch. They did so with a clear agenda, first to establish a new lineage, then to help with the survival of what existed before, this is symbolised by the animals in the Ark. Finally to salvage their knowledge and understanding. You ask about special qualities: you cannot quantify or qualify, because Jewishness is a quality of energy that can only be felt.

'The tale of the animals that went into the Ark two by two had to be read allegorically? Of course, the animals migrated; animals have migrated for millions of years without any help from man.

'Imagine, continues Sananda, that you wind back a film of history or pre-history in this case and project it on a screen, you are watching a newsreel of the Fall. You would see that the legend revolves around many groups of people, many families moving out in all directions across the world. The outward migration began centuries before the sinking of Atlantis. And the Noah story encapsulating a truth for humanity and formulated in a vivid form to be passed down through time, is a fascinating yarn. It is a good story people like to tell!

'The drawback, notes Clara, is that the story is believed literally to the smallest detail. They consume the words and dismiss the allegory.

'The downside, continues Sananda, is clearly literality, remember also that details get lost in the retelling and transcribing. Looking at it in a positive way, myths tell important truths about reality.

'If you were to reveal the Old Testament today and not when you did, if it was to be offered to humanity now, what form would it take, enquires Clara? Would it be presented in an allegorical form or would you go beyond the form to reveal the world of meaning?

'Different times require different approaches, replies Sananda.

'In a mythological or in a conceptual form, insists Clara?

'This process is happening now and you are involved in it. Truths are emerging into the consciousness of humanity and this process is occurring in different ways simultaneously, contributing to a fresh understanding.

'So no new Revelation, but a new understanding, a realisation that grows on its own soil, the consciousness of humanity. The Jewish people is a much 'chosen' people, the most 'chosen' people, insists Clara, who wants to explore further the initial question.

'It is part of their characteristic, explains Sananda, their gift to humanity to perceive themselves as 'chosen'. As if they were saying, 'we are all special'. This is their gift to humanity! However, they are in the process of coming to an understanding of that gift.

They are helping humanity to formulate, to visualise, to come to the realisation, 'you are all special'!

'They are passing from the 'we alone are special' to the 'the whole of humanity is special', a major shift in consciousness.

'Yes, continues Sananda. It takes a certain spirit to affirm 'we are special' and sustain this belief and commitment through time. In times of hardship, other people tended to say 'God has forsaken us, we are not special', but for a people to say 'we are special' is a gift to remind you all that you are special, that you can all hold your heads up.

'Again they were 'chosen' 2000 years ago, why?

'They were 'chosen' in part because they perceived themselves as special, replies the Master. In part it also relates to the land, that place on the Planet. The area around Jerusalem is an important energy point on the Planet. The two are related.

'Jerusalem is a challenged place; it is at the centre of much debate and much hostility. Is the dispute to be resolved by war or negotiation?

'We see Jerusalem as an extremely important place, replies Sananda, a gauge for raising the standard of humanity. For when all three religions are able to open up to one another, this will be a major landmark for humanity. It's not an easy task, and some are working diligently to make the outcome possible, to bring about a resolution. We do not envision a war. As for negotiation as you suggest, it has to go much further, it has to be fundamental. A profound change is required. It is about the opening of the Heart, it is about seeing the other as the brother and the sister. For the Jewish people it is the supreme challenge around the issue of attachment. They are presented with the dichotomy 'special' and 'non-special'. Specialness is their gift to everyone; they can give and teach specialness to all others. And so, not negotiation, it has to be fundamental, and this may take a little while.

'What about the state of Israel, were you, the Hierarchy, influential in bringing it about?

'Not in a straight and direct way. It would be inappropriate for us to interfere, if we are not invited to participate, we respect that decision. But, yes in the sense that we are all involved in the unfolding experience of Earth.'

The conversation comes to a close. 'Sananda alludes more than he discloses, begins Levinson, negotiation and war are no longer appropriate to solve the problems in the Middle East. What is required is a radical change in perception, the only solution to the political, social and religious problems of the region. He mentions the opening of the

Heart, this goes well beyond a gesture of good will, it has to do with a major shift in consciousness, a lifting into a new sensitivity, a new perception.

'As I see it, says Jeremy, the opening of the Heart esoterically points to a shift in human evolution. You are right, it sounds like a good idea to open the Heart, but it has nothing to do with good will, kindliness or generosity. It is of a different order, it is of the order of conscious evolution, focussed, calculated, designed evolution. Graphically it is a climb from the Solar Plexus, centre of human emotion to the Heart, seat of spiritual man. Something humanity has not fully grasped but which is enshrined in the Declaration of Human Rights. 'Liberty, Equality, Fraternity, slogan of the French Revolution.

'Sananda is making a point that might easily be overlooked, remarks Johansson. With reference to the Hierarchy's role in the creation of the modern state of Israel, he is implying, 'If you mean that 'we', the Hierarchy, were personally involved, the answer is in the negative. We were not directly involved; we will not take credit for it. If you mean 'we' collectively, the answer is in the affirmative, for we all participated in that creation, all of us on Planet Earth are creating the world, we all are co-creators. This is a Planetary participation, the collective effort of mankind'. But of course at this time of transformation for the Planet this participation goes beyond planetary creative action, it must involve the assistance, albeit invisible, of the entire universe.

PART TWO

NEGLECT OF SPIRITUAL LAW & THE HUMAN PREDICAMENT

DRAMA OF MAN IN THE TEMPORAL WORLD

'Relinquish the pride of mind which sees its way and its interpretations to be correct and true and others false and wrong. This is the way of separation. Adhere to the way of integration, which is of the soul and not of the mind'. (Master DK)

GALILEE

It was time to leave Jericho and Dr Delmar. In just a short time they had developed a real affection for this extraordinary man. They felt energised and enthused in his inspiring presence, his kind but probing eyes, his courage and the unusual nature of his work. They were especially impressed by the determination of one man to make the world a better place, to uproot ingrained attitudes in a most unassuming way. As they were driving toward Capernaum they talked about this strange and fascinating man, his ideas and his resolution to make a difference. Delmar is truly a man of peace and his countenance exudes peace.

A short ride along the shore of the Sea of Galilee a few miles from Capernaum is their destination. Kibbutz Ginnosar offers spacious accommodation, gracious hospitality and much appreciated comfort. They pause at the Museum of Man to brood over its 2000 year-old wooden boat, the kind of boat they may have used, all that time ago, when they lived on the shore of the Sea of Galilee among the Essene community. The well kept grounds are most inviting to the weary and much travelled group, the view of the lake and surrounding hills is irresistible. They are greeted by Joshua, a member of the kibbutz, assigned by Benzaccai to entrust the group with the next translated chapter of The Hebrew Gods. The text focuses on the nature of the deity, cosmic law, exile and suffering and is aptly entitled by Rabbi Moses 'Neglect of Cosmic Law & the Hebrew Predicament.

'My name is Joshua, smiles a charming man with a golden tan, deep blue eyes and greying hair. Welcome to Ginnosar your rooms are ready, if you wish to freshen up before dinner, you may do so, or you may prefer to enjoy the glorious sunset over the lake. As you know, I am Benzaccai's messenger, entrusted by him to give you the next chapter of the manuscript.

459

'The sunset definitely, replies Jeremy. They all acknowledge Jeremy's remarks with a **friendly nod.**

'What do you do for recreation, asks Clara, I heard that some kibbutzim have a dynamic cultural life'? He does not answer; silently he embraces the landscape with an expression of tenderness and reverence. Sensing his mood, Clara remarks, 'such beauty! One tends to think of Israel as a desert country. It is idyllic, so picturesque'.

'Yes, replies Joshua, this view compares favourably with the most famous in the world, your Lake District, for example. When you have soaked up the light, the peace and the radiant beauty you may go to Beit Gabriel, a relatively new kibbutz situated on the main road along the lake. Beit Gabriel is a cultural centre, with a concert hall. If this is your scene. Let me get you a leaflet from reception. He soon reappears with information. 'Well you are in luck, there is a concert tonight.

'The programme, asks Clara eagerly?

'Schubert's Lieder performed by a British pianist and a British singer. You will feel at home.

'Why not German musicians?

'No!

'We all reincarnate to play various roles. All human beings borrow a different garb in each incarnation. This role-swapping game has been played for millions of years; today a Jew, yesterday a Cossack, tomorrow a Peruvian, who knows? Scandalous and sacrilegious to you, but the law of reincarnation disregards human partiality, prejudices and aversions, explains Clara.

'The theory of reincarnation is not popular on these shore, snaps Joshua!

'What a pity, replies Johansson, it was on these shores that the theory of reincarnation was given to the world.

'Unpopular for reasons not difficult to figure out, reflects Levinson. Human beings who come to Earth to sample the Jewish condition have experimented with other conditions you disapprove of and will continue to do so until they are 'awakened'. The law of Karma – a cosmic Law -disregards our likes and dislikes.

'I am a pragmatist and a scientist, besides we are not in the East!

'Looking at it dispassionately we can identify a few points of convergence: fear and often disdain of the stranger, the materialism of separateness, of reverence to authority, law and order, of unquestioning obedience and a sense of grand purpose.

'The soul elegantly soars above the personality, divinely indifferent to the trifling squabbles of the ego. The little ego howls and roars to no avail, the soul has its own agenda. Passion and anger are of the ego. Passion and anger are unknown to the soul. 'To identify the similarities is the start of a positive change, expands Clara. What is required is a global movement of emancipation. To be on the defensive benefits no one. To keep alive the tattered and battered beliefs of the past solves nothing. To fuel adoration for a nature god is no longer a valid option since vanguard human beings have a well developed mind and are cultivating soul qualities.

The Age of Enlightenment Movement

'*Carlos Fuentes warned of a terrible approaching conflict between the 'essential activities of the human spirit – debate, humour, art – and a creed in which reality is dogmatically defined once and for all in a sacred text ... a sacred text is by definition, a completed and exclusive text. You can add nothing to it. It does not converse with anyone. It is its own loudspeaker'.* (Matthew d'Ancona, Sunday Telegraph)

The evening is soft and scented, the lake inflamed with the setting sun. They are walking silently by the lake, breathing in the energy of this magical place. Three men walk toward them. The man in the centre has a thoughtful and sensitive expression, he speaks first: 'We saw you in the dining room but waited for an opportune moment to have a word with you. We anticipated your arrival with some trepidation As you may have guessed we have an extract form The Hebrew Gods.

'It also means, says Jeremy that Benzaccai is nowhere to be found! He left just before we got here. Don't tell me I know! We have been chasing him for weeks and we are getting weary of this game of hide-and-seek.

'I understand your frustration, replies the man. Benzaccai has been entrusted with two unenviable tasks. A man of integrity he is aware of the opportunity presented to all of us by the manuscript. He also has a strong sense of loyalty to Rabbi Moses who endured much hardship to compose his manuscript. Benzaccai is unwavering about his 'mission' to bring Rabbi Moses' book to the attention of the world. This time the book will be known. As for Benzaccai he was taken to another kibbutz on his request, he is more concerned for the manuscript than for his own wellbeing.

'Thank you, we already feel at home, everyone is so kind and helpful. We share your esteem for Benzaccai, yet I cannot help but sense a shade of concern, notes Jeremy.

'Yes, you sense right. We are a small group of like-minded people who came together prompted by a sense of commitment and a feeling of disquiet. Subtle changes are being felt rather than observed. It is as if an invisible force was sapping our energy and scrambling our minds. The malaise is felt by many of us, academic, scientists, and humanists. Spurred by this unease, we set up a group to investigate the cause of the malaise. Our objectives are far-ranging.

'Why tell us all this, enquires Jeremy, why us?

'We spent several days with Benzaccai who introduced us to the manuscript and its content. What it conveyed had a familiar ring; it reinforced our views, for we had been thinking along Rabbi Moses' line for many years. During my students days I visited India, along with my two colleagues, Shemtov and BarYohai. We were in search of a spiritual philosophy of life. We stayed several months in a monastery where we were tutored in the art of meditation and the fundamentals of the spiritual wisdom. The knowledge of the East is phenomenal, a storehouse of the wisdom of the ages. Their spiritual development surpasses our wildest fantasies. For young idealists like us raised in traditional families which live by the unimaginative, dispiriting minutiae of the law, India was the sip of water given to the man dying from thirst in the desert! We had been conditioned to the ritualistic life and indoctrinated to the banal, prosaic, humdrum explanation that underpins it. We were flustered by the ritualised way of life that dulls the mind, stifles the creative impulse and deters the analytical yen. Our encounter with India was as much a spiritual awakening as it was a culture tremor. I fully endorse the phrase which so infuriated the rabbis of long ago about 'the law that killeth'.

'It most certainly does, I am the living proof of it, retorts Clara.

'I am too, snaps Levinson. Clara and I resurrected from the dead, and we were not dying a natural death either!

'It came in response to our silent appeal for inspiration and direction. We are a group of dedicated individuals from a variety of backgrounds but with a common purpose: to make a difference. While studying In the United States we encountered the New Age Movement which shares in many ways our concerns and goals. We discovered the works of Velikovsky, Sitchin, Kramer, and Jeremias among others.

'Quantum physics changed our view of the world, partakes Shemtov. We were scientists but we wanted to get away from the model proposed by Descartes of the separation of mind and matter. We grew up with stories of Creation which highlight the supremacy of matter and the inexorable nature of physical law. Determinism in life as in science was not for us, not after our spiritual journey to India. So we encountered Holism in science and we were hooked. Holism excludes nothing. Holism does away with determinism and duality; it includes everything, all aspects of human perception and experience.

'As Holistic scientists we were keen to draw from all sources, integrate all view points, assimilate all, contributes BarYohai. We blast-off into an unrelenting quest, spurred to expand our horizon and push the boundaries. We traced the Holistic movement through various disciplines, from medicine and psychology to physics. We also discovered the work of some of the great spiritual thinkers of our time.

'We are reading them too, nods Clara.

'We have much in common, says the man who finally introduces himself as Bendavid. We wish to discuss with you our commitment to a shift in consciousness. We seek to reorient our focal point. We aim to nothing less than a cultural revolution.

'As field workers for the Hierarchy, we are engaged in a similar journey, says Jeremy. How can we be of help, you seem to have a clear vision of what you want to achieve?

'The first aim is to give our mundane religious routine a spiritual orientation.

'A few of us disagree with this aim, corrects Shemtov, the physicist. We are secular, liberal intellectuals and the mere mention of a religion is offensive, it evokes the mental conditioning of an archaic age to which neither of us wishes to return.

'A spiritual philosophy of life' is a more pertinent depiction, rectifies Bendavid, a researcher of the civilisations of the ancient Near East. We are entering a new age in which heart and reason, spirit and matter are beginning to converge. We are leaving behind the Cartesian model which is the biblical view of the world: dualism. Descartes' view has shaped scientific thought. We are ushering in Holism in all fields of human endeavour.

'We are gathering around us, continues BarYohai, the biologist, individuals intent on manifesting the new ideal, those who can stretch their mind to the distant stars, their home of origins with their feet firmly on the ground, anchoring into physical reality the dreams they dream.

'How do you choose them, asks Jeremy?

'We don't. They choose themselves. They hear about our work and they come to us inspired by a vision that touches a deep chord in them.

'The realm of the intuition is the danger zone for patriarchy and monotheism, says Tara. The subtle mind is the uncontrollable factor which expresses itself in dreams, symbols and images. Inevitably these are a threat to authority.

'Those who survived the Manichean struggle of the 20the century ushered in a new world order, replies Bendavid. A new Jew emerged, Phoenix reborn of his ashes. From the devastation a new man was born. We are not going to let this new world and this new man be swept away by the thundering wave of regression.

'Dualism is at the core of their endeavour, steps in BarYohai, they want to reinstate division, separation, inferiority, impotency, obedience and authority, in other words they want to restore the old world as if the 20th century never happened.

'The physicist Feynman says of duality, 'If our small minds, for some convenience, divide this universe into parts – physics, biology, geology, astronomy, psychology – remember that nature does not know it! So let us put it all back together', quotes Shemtov.

'He echoes Chuang Tzu, 'Forget distinctions. Leap into the boundless and make it your home! Both the physicist and the mystic offer to abandon duality, says Tara.

'Again on the mind that sees difference, fragmentation, opposition and division - our dualistic minds - the physicist David Bohm says, 'What is needed is for man to give attention to his habit of fragmentary thought, to be aware of it, and thus bring it to an end. Man's approach to reality may then be whole, and so the response will be whole'. An invitation to wholeness, to unity. What we long for and work against with great application and zeal!

'The Fall, hence duality, is at the core of their enterprise, notes Levinson. It is the Fall they seek to intensify. It is the Fall's effects they consolidate: the separation, discord, fear and hostility humanity has engaged into. Yet duality for the mystic and the scientist is a mere 'shadow'.

'We are creating a new world in which collaboration, understanding, justice, equal opportunities and social concern are central, a world in which expansion of mind is paramount, pursues BarYohai. We are holding this new world in our embrace. We intend to thwart their capitulation to the earth-god.

'Do they not measure their piety with the yardstick of separation, continues Levinson? They frown with pious scorn at what is different. There is only one point of view, theirs. Their point of view is that of their god too! This is the way of the ego. We have been held in bondage by the ego since the Fall. Not surprising, they are the keepers of the Fall!

'The new Jew is defeating the self-interest of the ego, he measures his humanity with the yardstick of acceptance, understanding, integration, conciliation and inclusion, this is the way of the real man, says Shemtov.

'Djwahl Khul, resumes Johansson, is in complete agreement with you, 'Relinquish the pride of mind which sees its way and its interpretations to be correct and true and others false and wrong. This is the way of separation. Adhere to the way of integration, which is of the soul and not of the mind'.

'Encouraging endorsement.

'That's not all, he has more to say, 'For ages the soul has identified itself with the lower self and through the agency of that lower self has gained experience and acquired much knowledge. The time has come when that agency is 'no longer dear' to the soul and their respective positions are reversed'.

''their respective positions are reversed'', mumbles BarYohai.

'For aeons the soul has relied on the self – the ego - to gain experience and knowledge, explains Johansson. Now the soul is sufficiently evolved to declare that the self is 'no longer dear'. The roles are being reversed, the ego is gradually fading and the soul is taking over as the informing light. We are emerging out of the tyranny of the ego.

'In this case ritualistic religion, the religion of the ego is in trouble; it was made redundant by the soul itself! This is further evidence that we are moving in the right direction, notes Clara, I am thrilled.

'Fear is the hallmark of the self, and fear of freedom lies at the heart of any dictatorship, religious or political, notes Jeremy with reserve.

'Master Morya, informs Johansson, voices your concern: 'We are dissipating superstition, ignorance and fear. We are forging courage, will and knowledge. Every striving towards enlightenment is welcome. Every prejudice caused by ignorance is exposed'. I have these lines at heart.

'This sums up splendidly our goal, smiles Bendavid, thank you for bringing it to our attention. This phrase is going to be our flying banner!

'El Morya dwells in Shamballa the home of Buddha, inserts Tara. Buddha had the same goal. As embodiment of cosmic Intelligence, Buddha's goal was to enlighten the mind, dissipate superstition, ignorance and fear, and relinquish the ego.

'To the ritualist, enlightenment, courage, will and knowledge are offensive, states Clara. To the servants of the earth-god who love their 'Yoke' to 'be' is anathema. As loyal serfs they want to 'do'.

They nod in assent, free from constraint and formality, a bond has formed. They recognise each other as individuals on a similar life journey. They chat through the night. At dawn, exhilarated and exhausted they gaze at the rising sun. Filled with reverence they embrace the changing patterns of light, silently, reverently. A religious experience which requires no set prayer, no nature god, no self-immolation, no special garment, no rhythmic spin or whirl and none of the equipment of devotion. Finally, they make their way back to the kibbutz. Over the breakfast table, the friends promise to attend a meeting given by the Enlightenment Movement. They are due to make their first public appearance at the church in Capernaum.

The Age of Enlightenment Movement – their Manifesto

In the evening they go for a leisurely stroll by the lake to gaze at the setting sun. The next morning it is once again time to move on. Accompanied by Bendavid, Shemtov and BarYohai they set off for Capernaum. Early that evening people begin to arrive for the talk, and they keep arriving. Soon the church is filled and people are still coming; many have to stand. Bendavid begins by explaining the purpose of this meeting and the rationale behind the creation of their Movement. He speaks uninterrupted to a captive audience.

A man breaking the silence rises from his seat, 'I understand your ennui with the unchanging tradition, your irritation with the conditioning of the past, your desire to explore new horizons, but this puzzles me, what do you mean?

'This is a pertinent question. The best way to answer you is with a quote by an eminent Master, El Morya who said, "We are dissipating superstition, ignorance and fear. We are forging courage, will and knowledge. Every striving toward enlightenment is welcome. Every prejudice caused by ignorance is exposed'. This is our programme

'I wish to quote yet another eminent Master, encroaches Shemtov, 'For ages the soul has identified itself with the lower personal self ...The time has come when that agency is no longer dear to the soul'. From time immemorial the soul has allowed the personal self, the ego to take centre stage. Now this is changing, the soul is claiming centre stage. You understand. Time is ultimately an illusion as Einstein states, 'People like us, who believe in physics, know that the distinction between past, present and future is only a stubborn, persistent illusion'.

'The same eminent Master, continues BarYohai urges us to "Relinquish the pride of mind which sees its way and its interpretations to be correct and true and others false and wrong. This is the way of separation ....' The way of 'superstition, ignorance and fear', the way nurtured down the ages. You understand. And the physicist Heisenberg says about time and space that they are not quite what we think they are, 'The common words 'space' and 'time' refer to a structure of space and time that is actually an idealization and oversimplification'. Our religious worship focuses around space and time as if they were truly existent, when they are only an illusion.

'You are saying, articulates the man, that your programme presents several facets, first to do away with superstition and fear, I applaud this. Secondly to do away with prejudice, I also applaud this even more warmly.

'Your summary is sound, says Bendavid, you got the gist of it. Superstition, fear and prejudice are of the ego. Our aim is to stretch beyond the ego that shaped our beliefs, rules, dogmas, attitudes and prejudices. The way of separation is the way of the ego; the way of integration is the way of the soul. Surely this must ring a bell in all of you. We have been urged and ordered to be 'separate', to walk in holiness before the Lord, as Abraham was told to do by god. This is changing. The way of the ego is to be 'separate'; the way of the soul is to 'unite'. The mood of the soul is to uphold our common humanity.

'The self, the ego concocts ideas and interpretations, continues Shemtov. We had to believe that they emanated from God. How could they? Is it sensible to believe that God fosters separation, alienation and hostility?

'Our god does, replies the man.

'This is not the god we have in mind, declares Shemtov. The notions and interpretations the self conjures up have disastrous results. The way of the self leads to suffering. The Master sums up our aim, 'Adhere to the way of integration, which is of

467

the soul and not of the mind'. Our Movement promotes unification, alliance, understanding, conciliation, in other words we promote 'integration which is of the soul and not of the mind'.

'We are claiming back that which was taken from us, continues BarYohai, our divine identity! And as we do a new awareness is dawning. The opaque mantle of religious dogma shut out the light. For aeons the light was locked out, yet we were never cut off from it even in our darkest hour. The light resides in the sanctuary of the Heart in every human being.

Bendavid is relieved, he has the response he was hoping for, but did not expect, 'feel free to express your views. You have been silenced for too long. It may astound you to know that you created the universe, but you did, we all did. There is a great deal of unlearning to do; we have been conditioned to believe in our frailty, imperfection, sinfulness, iniquity, insignificance and inferiority. This unlearning may occupy the rest of your lives; I know it has occupied the best part of mine!

'Those of you aware of modern science know that man is not a detached onlooker, his observing influences the world around him. 'The universe is more a giant thought than a giant machine', quotes Shemtov. This divine thought deserves our exploring. The unravelling of the universe will also be your own unravelling. The universal Mind is hiding in matter and physical laws. It is up to us to lift the veil.

A man in the audience stands up, 'the pilpul which occupied my studious youth gave me much pride but caused a rift within myself.

'Now is the time to seal the rift, to integrate, the time to heal not only ourselves but the world around us, replies Bendavid. This may be a novel idea to you, to all of us, but we are an integral part of the world, though we deny it at our peril. What we do affects the rest of mankind and the Planet.

'Why, asks the man?

'Because we live in a field of energy, matter dissolves back into energy as Einstein said, replies Shemtov. Duality forms the pillars of our tradition; our ancestors looked at forms, things and appearances and took them to be real and substantial. The time has come to look beyond form, beyond duality. There is only one field of energy and everything is made of it, all forms, all beings, all life is made of it. This is what the physicist Eisenberg says of duality, 'We know that there is an ever-changing variety of phenomena appearing to our senses. Yet we believe that ultimately it should be possible to trace them back to some one principle'.

'The Self, the unborn indestructible principle of reality, undergoes modification through illusion (Maya) only and not in the real sense. Hence duality is not in the ultimate sense real', said the mystic Shankara, quotes Bendavid. Yet the entire edifice of our tradition is built around duality, it is not 'real'.

The audience shows no fatigue. Bendavid suggests a break. A man at the front shouts: 'We do not want a break, we want more. Do you hear me? I have been waiting all my life for this and despaired of finding it, I resigned myself to die in ignorance of it!

'We want more, shouts another man just as passionate, we have been waiting thousands of years to hear this and you want us to take a break? I want more on duality and unity.

'Alright, if you insist, replies Shemtov, this is what the physicist Max Planck has to say about duality, 'We always look for what is absolute behind what is relative, for the reality behind the appearance and for what abides behind what is transitory.'

'The transitory, the relative, the appearance that's for us, all that is duality and fragmentation, all that is a 'shadow', all that is 'illusion'! We exist in an illusion. We are master illusionists, exclaims a man at the front row!

'And the physicist David Bohm says, 'To be confused about what is different and what is not, is to be confused about everything'.

'He summed up our situation in the world, shouts the same man! 'Confused about everything' that's us!

BarYohai comes to the rescue of Shemtov, 'The plurality that we perceive is only an appearance; it is not real', said the physicists Schrödinger. Centuries before him the mystic Shankara said, 'Whatever you see as duality is unreal'.

'The plurality our tradition is built around is only an appearance, it is not real, paraphrases a woman sitting at the back.

'This is a unique moment in our history, says a woman, nothing like this has ever been heard since Moses came down from the mountain.

'You are giving us a glimpse of what might have been, says another woman moved to tears. Where have I been all my life? You just hint at my potential as a human being. The world has already changed in just a few minutes. When I came in the people in this church were ordinary, I felt nothing for them, I was indifferent. Now, I look around and I see them in a new way. With this new vision comes a feeling of love and wonder.

I sense in them the same dreams, the same potential and they all look so beautiful. They changed and I changed.

Encouraged by the response, Bendavid is going to speak his truth without toning down the boldness of his ideas, 'The split between spirit and matter triggered an age of religious materialism. You all know the telling features: intolerance hostility, distrust and contempt for the wisdom of others. In happier times, pagan man lived at peace with nature and in acceptance of the beliefs of others. Monotheism like a tidal wave swept across the world bringing with it the certainty that it is spot on to persecute those who don't share our views. The very attitude the Master denounces, 'the pride of mind which sees its way and its interpretations to be correct and true and others false and wrong. This is the way of separation....' This is the way of the ego and its god.

Bendavid takes a sip of water but sensing the eagerness of his audience continues, in spite of feeling tired and in need of a pause, 'The goal of evolution as envisioned by the Spiritual guardians of humanity is to bring into alignment the ego with the soul.

One man sitting at the front raises his hand. With a glance, Bendavid invites him to speak, 'Who are they to us those spiritual guardians?'

'They came to Earth aeons ago to guide mankind on the path of evolution, replies Jeremy. Their supreme Commander is mentioned in your books as the Ancient of Days. They dwell in Shamballa with Moses and the Messiah.

'Why don't we know about him?

'But you do, you know the texts! Moses certainly did, replies Shemtov. Moses received his mandate from Sanat Kumara, the Ancient of Days.

'Why don't we know about him, repeats the man stubbornly?

'I suppose, replies Bendavid, this has to do with the scribes who omitted or hid data relating to our true origin and nature.

'We would have progressed much earlier, instead of much later.

'Who knows, replies Bendavid? Perhaps we had to meander through the vast expanse of life, wander aimlessly through the sands of history, before finally awakening. We got bogged down in the superfluous and lost sight of the essential. In spite of our resistance to change, we have come a long way,

from idol-worship to self-direction.

'As a biologist, picks up BarYohai, I endorsed the 'inert' picture of the world, legacy of the Fall. As you know with the Fall mind and matter split. This view was confirmed by

Newton and has been with us since. Not any more, I now see the world as a living tapestry of living systems. Like us Earth is a dynamic being on an evolutionary journey. The enlightened Greeks knew this; they called Earth Gaia, the creative, nurturing, living, sentient organism. We were conceived in the womb of Earth, we are made of its chemical elements, its forces.

'Our bodies are composed of cells which communicate with each other, using chemicals and electrical signals, expands Shemtov. Our bodies are energy and information systems. Nothing is static, noting is solid. Life is energy in motion. Inertia is unknown except when the life current is blocked by wrong thinking and wrong feeling. When the life force is obstructed with inherited thought forms and negative beliefs, inertia sets in. When the life current is choked-up, split between soul and self is inevitable and disorder follows, it is the open door to disease, violence, aggression, misery. We do know!

'May I add, intervenes Levinson that the 'forces of opposition' have not stood by idly? They ignite every expression of intolerance, hate and confusion. They discourage any serious exploration of the world in science, philosophy and the arts. They thwart the exploration of our inner world too. They hinder the ethical ideals which are to benefit humanity. From the astral plane, they combat the mood of reconciliation. They are active incessantly; you can see them all around you. Bendavid you are an expert on Djwahl Khul would you take over?

Bendavid shuffles his notes to get the quotation, he finds it, 'Djwahl Khul outlines some of the techniques of the 'forces of opposition': 'They present half-truths, impute false motives, rake up past grievances and foretell imminent difficulties; they foster ancient prejudices and hatreds and emphasise religious and national differences. Racial and national emotions are fanned and nurtured by them..., sounds familiar?

'Too familiar shouts the first man and its getting worse!

'That's what Djwahl Khul says, 'This they will increasingly do ….. They will seek to offset the activities of the Hierarchy …. and to cloud the issues involved, to such a degree that the men and women of goodwill everywhere will be bewildered and will fail to see the clear outline of the situation or distinguish between what is true and what is false'. The Master wrote this during WW2. It rings as true today as it did then!

'That's more than true; we live in a fog, because of the fog we can't make out the true from the false. It must stop, shouts the stubborn man.

'In prehistoric times our 'maker' 'modified' primitive humans to work for him, not to discuss with him, chuckles BarYohai! Intelligence is a fairly recent intrusion. When Yahweh 'modified' our Sumerian ancestors, he improved Neanderthal who had only two parts to his brain: the reptilian and mammalian. The cortex developed much later. This is why the old religion fails to deliver satisfactory answers to life questions; it was never designed to tackle the crucial issues of life. It was designed to keep us clean, disease-free and reproductive, nothing more. The prescriptions given by Yahweh were adequate for Neanderthal not yet endowed with the cortex, the 'thinking' brain.

'Then it must go, snaps the stubborn man.

'It is holding on by a thread, playing hard at stirring up the lesser emotions, retorts another man. You summed them up. What does the Ancient of Days and his illustrious team stand for, what plan do they have for humanity. Can we know their intention? Or is it forbidden?

'I am coming to that. Yes, we do know the intention of the Hierarchy just as Moses did. Their intention is to give us once again the spiritual Law they gave Moses. I am not talking about 'do & obey', 'go & multiply' and the basic rules of clean living! The basic tenet of spiritual Law: all is gifted with the same life, no one is born to serve another, no one is inferior and no one is superior.

'So when we treat others like dirt we violate spiritual law, points out the same woman? We have always done it, it was defended, it was legal, god wanted it, the law authorized it!

'Nothing to be proud of, retorts Shemtov. Contempt for others is of the ego, the ego cut off from its soul, the ego cut off from cosmic Life. No more petitioning for prophets to show us the way either. This kind of infantile longing harks back to a long gone age.

'No Saviour, no teacher, no leader, exclaims the stubborn man?

'That's right, you are your own saviour, your own teacher and your own leader, this is what the Ancient of Days would impress upon you. The time has now come to forget what you have been conditioned to accept as true. There is much unlearning to do. Our fixation with 'chosenness' must be treated like any obsessive disorder, collective healing must be a priority.

'We are the 'chosen' people, shouts a young man, you want to destroy us, you want the end of us, are you the enemy?

'We want you to live, intervenes Bendavid, it is because we care passionately about what happens to all of us that we are doing this! 'The law that killeth' turned its back on spiritual Law; it was invented by the human ego; it has killed us because we were willing to let it. The basic tenet of spiritual Law is that all life forms are endowed with the same life. Given this definition - by the way Einstein gave a similar definition – do you still feel superior to all others? 'All is gifted with the same life'; the same life force flows in all, those of you who studied biology know this. What are you going to do about this, defy science and refute cosmic Law? That's what we have been doing: we have precipitated our tragic history. Our tragedy-laden history is no sign of chosenness, only a sign of ignorance.

'What will happen to us, shouts another man sitting at the back?

'Good question. You have been cut off from your inner being, from the Infinite and from the world. In order to be 'whole' again, in order to regain the lost Paradise you so lament, you will have to heal the rift inside you and then you will integrate back into humanity. Exciting don't you think? This is the new Revelation. And you know what? No messiah, no prophet is going to give it to you, you are going to discover it for yourself.

'We are discovering it for ourselves, responds dynamically the young woman!

'What of the chosen people, retorts the young man who will not be appeased.

'This is of the past. It's over! Spiritual Law states that all life forms originate in the one life Source, same origin, same life, same substance, we are one life. This is a statement of fact. Findings in genetics show that there is little difference between the DNA present in yeast, in bacteria and in man. We share the DNA of yeast and bacteria. Humiliating? No, sobering. If we are genetically similar to bacteria and yeast, can we still profess to be superior to other human beings? Think of all humans as pebbles on the beach; are not the pebbles all the same in form and composition?

'What is to become of our religion, shouts the young man?

''External' religion relies on formula, details, authority, threat, compulsion. The superstitious belief in the magical property of rituals is an insult to our intelligence. True religion springs from the soul in a spontaneous rousing, a longing for union, and an urge to pierce behind the veil. True religion hints at the invisible, the sublime, the unknown, the mysteries of being, the world of energy that lies just outside our senses. True religion has nothing to do with routine religion; it is a deep stirring, an intuitive knowing, an inner realisation, a personal experience. It rises from the depth of being, it does not come from outside, it is never imposed. 'External' religion belongs to the world bound to time. True religion belongs to the inner reality which is timeless. 'External' religion is a deception because it focuses on the physical form, on mortal man. The masses live in superstitious awe of it. Many use it as a crutch. A man with a broken leg uses a crutch; a man with good legs does not. We are broken we need that crutch. It is time to become 'whole' again. Freedom from religion as a crutch is the precondition to genuine progress.

'What are we going to put in its place, asks a woman genuinely concerned? Our external religion is all we have.

'Stop relying on outside agencies to lead you, ventures Jeremy. 'Be a light onto your own feet' urged Buddha. You have to take charge of your life and your destiny. The age of exalted prophets is over. Those who care for their own progress and the progress of the Planet emit a certain frequency of light which is picked up by the Spiritual Hierarchy. To assist in this awakening, thousands of cosmic beings are coming into incarnation. They form a bridge between humanity and Shamballa 'where the Will of God is known' and where the Masters hold the Divine Plan for humanity.

A man in the audience raises his hand: 'I am sorry to butt in but how do we go about it, it sounds too good to be true. Good things never happen to us. What is the method? How can we reach the Hierarchy? Are they going to tell us what to do?

'Definitely not, replies Shemtov! This is the very thing they would never do; it would breach cosmic Law and go against common sense. Einstein stated that matter is not solid, matter is energy. All the forms you see, your body and your thoughts, all are energy. Our body is an electro-chemical plant, our brain functions by sending electrical impulses. We all emit a certain frequency value, a certain rate of vibration, which can be picked up by the Hierarchy. Think of it in terms of a transistor radio, as you tune in to the right wavelength you get the station you want. The Masters can pick up these frequencies. Those of us who express the wish to progress are picked up.

'Do they approve of our religious fervour, do they value our piety, our diligence, asks a woman? Surely it must be a sign that we want to progress.

'Progress they value, intervenes Levinson. They do not encourage capitulation to dogma and fanatical diligence to details. They foster initiative, creativity, independence, autonomy, personal responsibility. When the Masters visited the Planet 2000 years ago, they emphasized the futility of religious exercise that keep us 'prisoners of the Planet', prisoners of natural law, Maya'. They spelt out the indignity of the 'do & obey'. Man, they explained, is not a slave to his gods, not a puppet in the hands of fate. Man is a noble and autonomous being capable of taking charge of his life. The worth of a man is never to be measured by 'what' he does but by 'who' he is. The 'doing' was right for Neolithic man terrified of his gods. The age of Pisces was a turning point for humanity, the 'old world' had run its term and the 'new world' was being birthed. That sealed the fate of our Neolithic mentality.

'And you know what, inserts Clara nothing has changed! We are caught up in the same Neolithic mentality. Same puppet show!

'Our religion we are so proud of is futile? We the holiest people on Earth, the most spiritual, the most moral! All this was an illusion, asks a woman?

''External' religion boosts our negative tendencies, resumes Bendavid. The priesthood manipulated us through our emotions, fear, guilt and shame. They abetted passivity, incited inertia and indolence. They conditioned us into believing that our purpose for living is to 'do & obey', 'go & multiply'. They advertised the power of the deity while broadcasting our powerlessness. It is difficult to govern rational beings, it is easier to steer irrational people. They made us powerless and the rules, dogmas and fables played on our emotions. They appealed to our lower nature. The way they manipulated their own people was similar to the manipulation of the masses that blighted the 20th century. They opened the way for our manipulative and exploitative 20th century. Stalinism and Fascism that swept over Europe in an apocalyptic wave of destruction have their root in the manipulation of long ago. All appeal to our human nature, all manipulate emotions, all seek to influence, and all rely on our unconscious assent.

'You look shocked, remarks BarYohai? You know that the 'father' of the unconscious was Freud. Man he said is victim of his unconscious impulses, instincts and irrational drives. These must be controlled to ensure a stable society. Our priesthood knew of the irrational nature of man long before Freud and they set out to control and manipulate it. Their programming was so effective that they still control us today, 2000 years on!

'There is a sinister aspect, picks up Shemtov. As we ingested the religious propaganda we came to believe in our special rights. We felt compelled and authorised to inflict our beliefs onto others. When we say 'We are right and the other is wrong', we see the

475

other as a lump of clay that must be reshaped to match our specifications, because we cannot tolerate his difference. In politics, we call this dictatorship. When we set out to change another we deprive him of his ability to reflect, to choose, to become, to be. In other words, we deny him his higher human faculties.

'I understand this. We have no right to impose our views on others, we have no right to manipulate others through emotions, and we have no right to regard them as irrational, sums up a young man. Now you have demolished the entire edifice, what is left?

'I am coming to this. The entire edifice has come tumbling down like a sand castle wiped away by the incoming tide. I can only reiterate that the conduct of our life must never be left to others. It must come under the direction of the inner being, the inner Master. We see only the outer man, not his karmic history or life purpose. We do not know why this person chose to come to Earth and it is foolhardy to assume that we can steer the other in our direction. It is unethical to manipulate him; it is immoral to mould him to our own opinion. It is irrational to impress our beliefs on him. What are beliefs? A belief is the subjective opinion of those who came before us. That's all it is, a view point, an angle. Beliefs are nothing more than human opinions, whatever their claim to divine inspiration!

'No outside interference, no outside direction, no outside leadership, says another man, what have we got left?

'There is a new tide of change coming in. Emotional man was manipulated through his emotions; he was told what to do; he received directives from outside. Things were done to him, forced upon him; he had no say, no voice, and no recourse action. He was living under a religious dictatorship. The man as envisioned by the Spiritual Hierarchy is very different. Nothing can be forced upon him, he has a say, he has a voice, he has a recourse action, nothing is done to him, he is under the direction of his inner Master. He is self-directed.

Shemtov observing his subdued audience decides to bring this meeting to a close. 'I want more, I am not leaving, retorts a grey-haired man, I am willing to spend the night here'. In one huge voice they clamour for more. 'Alright, tomorrow night, at the same time, gives in a weary but elated Shemtov.

A young man in the audience stands up and blurts out: 'The horrors of WW2 verified Nietzsche's insight that God is dead. God is dead, long live man! That people can still debate the possible existence of God after the cataclysm of WW2 confounds me! I am an atheist not because I want to, but because all the evidence suggests that I must be. I would prefer to be lulled into a false sense of security, have all my questions answered by some autocratic rabbis who don't know what they are talking about because their training is liturgical not philosophical.

'I endorse this, smiles BarYohai. I too went through a period of nihilism and atheism. It was one of the most enriching periods of my life. A necessary phase, a spiritual crisis to be appreciated rather than feared. Then I grew out of it, I had to move on.

'Why did the Hierarchy permit the devastation of the 20th century, they are the guardians of mankind after all, shouts a woman.

'Good question and a difficult one to answer, I shall put forward a few suggestions but you will have to do your own thinking if you are genuine about this. The old world system was corrupt, it revolved around imperial power, unfairness, colonialism, inequality, poverty for the masses, wealth and power concentrated in the hands of the few who owned and controlled everything. The world was their playground, they owned it. Imperial Europe had to crumble; it was a major stumbling block to the progress of mankind.

'To this end, the Shamballa force, the energy of Divine Will was released in its full destructive power and swept across the Planet, inserts Tara.

'What is this Shamballa force, asks a woman?

'Shamballa is the celestial Jerusalem that floats above the Gobi Desert and is home to the Masters, the Messiah and The Ancient of Days, explains Tara. Normally Divine Will is received by Shamballa and toned down by the Masters before being released safely into mankind. At the turn of the 20th century it was felt that the energy of Will had to be released directly into the world.

'Destruction for what, asks a young man?

'The old world had to dissolve to make way for the new world ideals of justice, freedom, equality, negotiation, collaboration, conciliation, sensible human relations and respect for human rights. The new world was to be born out of the ashes of the old. This is the perpetual cycle of life, symbolised by the mythical bird, the Phoenix which rises out of its ashes.

'We paid a terrible price, says a man.

'The whole of humanity paid a terrible price. No one escapes the cycle of life, death and resurrection, butts in Jeremy.

'The lesson is clear, inserts Clara, we must shed all things that keep us prisoners of dogma and look to our own inner resources. The truth, tells a Taoist poem can be only grasped this way: 'Close your eyes and you will see clearly. Cease to listen and you will hear truth'. Jung says that he who looks outside is asleep; he who looks within is awake. The Ancient of Days expressed the same idea when he said to us 'fear keeps you asleep, but when you let go of fear you wake up'. When we live in fear we live unconsciously. Truth lives in you and as long as you look outside for it, you can be sure never to find it! All we find outside is disappointment and pain.

'Fear is of the lower self, echoes Levinson, when we are in the grip of fear we are in the grip of the lower self. The lower self, the ego performs rituals to atone, to mollify, and to appease. Rituals are a response to fear. You see, the soul does not have a creed, dogmas and beliefs. The soul simply 'is'. The soul is concerned with 'being' not 'doing' and in the words of Plato, 'The true lover of knowledge is always striving after 'being'.'

'This has been our tragic plight, exclaims a man in the audience. We have always given in to the lower self, and this has been pressed upon us by our leading religious 'lights' down the centuries.

'It has. Fear has a strong hold and so we continue to sleep a disturbed sleep. Nothing wakes us up.

'We are waking up, you can bet on it, retorts the same man!

Worship of an illusion

The gods belong to the sphere of illusory separateness and mind-created projections ... But an illusion remains an illusion & thus is nothing at all'. (Carl Jung)

This exteriorization of God and the resulting devaluation of humankind's innate nature appears to be, according to the late mythologist Joseph Campbell, a uniquely "pathological mythology". (Larry Dossey, Healing Words)

On their return the friends are ready to delve into the next chapter of The Hebrew Gods. The successful talk at Capernaum enthused all. Bendavid is elated, 'As you know I was invited to read the next section of The Hebrew Gods by Benzaccai' s wife, before returning it to him at the earliest opportunity. The chapter is entitled 'Samsara god', a tantalising title!

Master Sanaka begins, 'Now is the time to turn our attention to Maya the world of space, time and matter, the physical reality in which man finds himself and which pervades the biblical text as it pervades your lives. The Gnostics of long ago admitted to the existence of two gods and two worlds.

'Duality is the pivotal shaft of the Old Testament, too. We have two gods, two creations, two worlds, two humanities, says Moses with lassitude.

'Yet you proclaim a severe monotheism! As man changes over time, his idea of god also changes. These changes manifest as the text develops through time. It was written down some 800 years after the events at Sinai and some 1500 years after Abraham. Inevitably the texts developed over time. In the ancient world the deity was an all too human being that man had to appease in order to survive, gain favours, defeat his neighbours and feel special. This view has dominated Hebrew thought ever since. The most lukewarm among you retain the awesome image of a vengeful, belligerent and capricious god. They may deny allegiance to the ancestral god but his image is engraved in their consciousness.

'We are still partial to the idea of a personal god no matter how invasive he may be, notes Moses. It makes us feel safe. Hassidism brings out the subjective, personal aspect of god. One Hassid rabbi said that it made him feel like a child asking his father to tuck him in to bed!

'To each his idea of god! Some need a rigid father to prolong their childhood. Over time the simple idea of a personal god grew into the universal idea of an impersonal force. The Hebrew still perceives his god as a being with inflated human qualities, warped human views and magnified human flaws.

'The idea of a personal god is central to our life, yet we also proclaim that he is an all-embracing force which transcends Creation. A contradiction?

'This needs to be resolved. A dogmatic, interfering, personal god cannot at the same time be an all-embracing divinely detached, divinely indifferent, divinely uninvolved being. The idea of a pervading life force belongs to Greek enlightenment. You, Moses will have to resolve this contradiction, this is your part of the Plan. The god-image has left an indelible imprint on your emotional lives. You are hostages to this controlling force which will either strike in anger or lavish favours on his 'chosen' few for no valid reason. No questioning because it raises the spectre of heresy. You are 'prisoners of the Planet' and through you humanity is in captivity.

'We have to suspend our reading and reflect a while to assimilate, suggests Tara, I need a respite.

'I welcome a breather, agrees BarYohai. This theme is important to me, I agonised over these issues long ago and this is my chance to explore them. I was plunged into this ambiguity. We hold on to the image of a human god, in spite of efforts from the rabbis to turn the god-force as Sanaka coins him into a 'divine' being they projected 'out there'. The tendency is so entrenched as to be imprinted in our DNA coding!

'And it almost certainly was, replies Shemtov. You don't think that the master biologist who genetically modified our Sumerian ancestors did so without a coherent blueprint. He had his master plan. We never recovered from those early influences; they were encoded and later cultivated. And we are told that the universe is love!

'Not all star systems are governed by love, as the history of the Jewish people verifies and confirms. It was not love that brought the Nefilim to Earth, but curiosity, self-interest, a yearning for power, notes Levinson. Their intention was clearly to set up a principality, a dominion on Earth. Our energy field displays our emotions. The gods not motivated by love would have needed a supply of human emotional energy as well as a source of manpower. Emotional energy and muscle power used as fuel.

'Is this the reason why tradition insists that god has everything except our fear; and fear is the thing he wants most, asks Clara?

'All despots need fear to stay in power, replies Levinson. You might say that it is the fuel that makes the wheels of absolute power turn.

'When asked about the nature and role of love, inserts Jeremy, the Masters are unanimous in their reply 'love is the ultimate binding force in the Cosmos, it is the law that governs all.'

'What are you saying, asks Clara?

'Anything other than love is an illusion, replies Jeremy. Our fundamental nature is love and anything other than love is unreal.

'It's obvious that not all the residents of the cosmos live by universal Law, admits Levinson, as our tradition demonstrates without inhibition. The god-image that occupies centre stage in Genesis clearly testifies to this.

'If the god of Genesis resists change, the universal Life Force in contrast is for ever changing, notes Jeremy. A difficult notion to grasp: the believer perceives his god as unchanging, static and absolute, yet at Sinai they witnessed great cosmic upheavals.

'The Baal Shemtov sensed this; he made a quantum leap when he stated that what is lacking in man is also lacking in God, explains BarYohai. He was saying that neither God nor man is static, that both are changing, both are evolving. He was exploding the long-held myth of an unchanging God.

'The god he envisioned is spot on, declares Jeremy, it was incredibly brave of him to confront deeply ingrained beliefs! The Creator manifested the universe to use as a laboratory for his own development. He emitted a myriad of 'bits' of his essence to go out in the cosmos and experiment with it. The idea of the universal Mind ever-evolving, ever-changing, ever-learning, ever-growing contrasts with the rudimentary idea of a static god. Like man the cosmic Mind needs to investigate his own essence and realise his potential, through the progress of all those 'bits', all of us. These 'bits' are fragments of his consciousness into form, each one pursuing its own goal. This is what Master Sananda taught us.

SAMSARA GOD

'God as the national controller took possession of man's mind and the Jehovah concept (as depicted in the Jewish dispensation) appeared'. (Master Djwahl Khul)

The personality & its gods

'Genesis registers the rise and expansion of the self. The self hurtling at an alarming velocity, devouring all in its trail; the self that admits no limitations, no restrictions; the self that breaks its banks like a swollen river after heavy rains. The gods are projection of the affirming self that will not be tamed. These projections are responsible for the Hebrew predicament, ponders Bendavid. The escalating self asserts its power in the image of the gods before falling victim to the thought-form it has created.

'And now we stumble on a paradox, notes Jeremy thoughtfully. In primordial times all is one, undifferentiated. Then the self emerges and we become separate, differentiated. The affirming self is a break from the primal unity, the prior unity in which all bathed. Yet this differentiation is crucial to the evolution of man.

'We begrudge differentiation, notes Clara, this is clearly evident in the allegory of Adam and Eve. How the ancestors bemoan lost unity! They must blame someone, so they curse Eve for corrupting the whole thing. They fail to grasp that it is a giant leap forward in evolution. And a paradox!

'But differentiation ushers in aloneness, suffering. We find ourselves alone in a hostile world, a random universe, notes Shemtov. The self has to protect itself from the world which it perceives as a threat. But here comes the paradox, the armoured self becomes over time an obstacle to progress. The ruling self obstructs evolution.

'An idea just hit me, exclaims Bendavid. We have the gods that we deserve!

'I am familiar with this idea, smiles Clara who has pondered over this issue for a considerable time.

'We have the gods that our mind can grasp or invoke, ruminates Tara. Primeval man living in an 'undifferentiated' state worships the Goddess, an uncomplicated, undemanding presence; he bathes in her motherly love. It is all so simple and natural. Then the self emerges, dynamic, anxious which demands gods that will satisfy its needs, gods that can reflect its own nature.

'A bit like Narcissus adoring his image in the water, notes Clara. A god who is the image of the self? So, early man looks at his god and falls in love with him not realising that he is falling in love with his own image reflected.

'Falling in love is hardly appropriate, laughs Shemtov, falling in fear might be more to the point.

'More to the point certainly, chuckles Clara, the tense, anxious self knows fear, fear that was unknown to the children of the Goddess. And it is fear that must curb its dark emotional urges, its instinctual drives. The rabbis knew that the grasping self is driven by instinctual forces that must be restrained. Fear was the weapon they used to restrain it. To put it another way, fear was the weapon of the deity.

'Evidence that we get the gods that we deserve, repeats Bendavid.

'Not exactly 'deserve', the gods do not fall from the sky! The gods we can conceive! We animate them, we activate them. The gods we cultivate reflect who we are. Today we call them 'ideologies', in a pre-cognitive age they were called 'gods'.

'There is more, explains Jeremy. We come back in incarnation with the ego-self we shaped over countless lives. We bring back the same thought forms, desire, emotions, potentials, attitudes and tendencies. Even before incarnation these mental forms have already made contact with similar mental forms across time and space. It is all a question of wave length. Thoughts tune in with other thoughts of the same frequency. We already are familiar with radio waves, with telephone and radio communications. There is another form of communication just as effective, just as powerful which works through space and across dimensions: the frequency of thought.

'You are saying that before birth we already know which god we are going to serve, asks Shemtov?

'The word 'god' is to be taken in the broad sense of the collection of beliefs, images and attitudes we come back in incarnation with, our personal baggage.

However gods do exist, this the Masters emphasise, replies Jeremy.

'Gods do exist, but gods are also the sum total of our unconscious emotions and drives, our thoughts, beliefs and attitudes, says Tara. In other words we bring back our personal gods.

'And we single out the biological group most likely to give us the gods we know. We pick the group that allows us to entertain its gods. There is mutual reinforcing.

'People select the god-force that matches their own disposition, continues Tara. After scouring the pantheon of all Earth gods they are drawn to those they resonate with. This is a choice that Buddha would not have made. The rationalist Buddha dispenses with gods altogether. He galvanises man to self-realisation through mastery of the mind. The intellectual and spiritual heirs to Krishna and Buddha need no gods, no authority, no leaders, no textbooks, no teachings, and no prayer houses.

'The intellectual heirs to Buddha and Yahweh are contemporary, yet millions of light years separate them, reflects Clara.

'So when you pass in the streets a relic from the past you may ask, 'tell me who your god is and I'll tell you who you are. The god you entertain is you'.

'You revere the self that Eve was cursed for birthing. The self responsible for humanity's predicament.

Genetic manipulation revisited

'Jeremy, declares Clara I need to speak with Sananda, can you arrange it?

'If you insist, laughs Jeremy. Do you ever take a breather, you are so driven! Alright let us start, Sananda is here, I sense his presence. Ask away Clara!

'Master Sananda, this is going to be a soliloquy more than a question. (A smile and a hand gesture invite her to proceed). The concept of god alters in recorded history. The personality of Yahweh changes from a virulent beginning at Sinai amidst cataclysmic events to the Talmud where he is depicted as benevolent. Times have changed, physical survival is not an issue, but religious survival is. The certainties of the past sound hollow, our history provides evidence that they never were accepted. As Pisces dawns those living under Roman occupation are asking probing questions. Dogmas are put to the acid test and are about to explode having failed the people lamentably. The people care nothing for doctrinal Judaism and go in search of solace outside, drawn to a variety of sects and cults. In desperation they switch allegiance from Yahweh to the gods who seem to hold a promise of consolation. Sinai god was threatening and terrifying, in contrast Talmud god emerges as distinctly more ethical and more sensitive to human suffering, traits which were not present in earlier times. Something else, the revised god is less human and more 'divine'. He even changes his name as he undergoes a personality change! How can we account for those changes, simply by virtue of the fact that societies evolve and therefore their concept of god inevitably changes? This is a long question, I know'.

Sananda has listened intently to Clara's soliloquy. He now replies, 'I would say that some of the early Jewish understanding of their gods was based upon memories of those beings who had been their genetic creators, genetic manipulators.

'Would you explain further, please?

'Yes, we go back a long way in time. Remember I talked about the particular quality of DNA present within the Jewish bloodline. Now those DNA qualities were placed there by beings from another part of the universe, beings who at that point in time appeared to mankind to be superior beings because they demonstrated skills that those humans they came in contact with did not have and did not understand. So, mixed in to the Jewish view of the divine were elements which contained ambiguous feelings. Feelings which mingled together gratitude with anger and resentment at having been in some way used. And those feelings combined together created the earlier view of who and what the divine presence on this Planet was. Later, I would say, there was really quite a conscious desire within an important strand of the rabbinic tradition you associate with the Talmud, to come to a more measured, less temporally-based, a more inward connection, a more considered view, a clearer understanding of the nature of the Divine. So in that sense there was indeed an evolution, but an evolution that had a particular quality attached to it: it was a deliberate letting go of what you can think of as historic memories, memories of having received a mixed treatment at the hands of very powerful beings.

'Were they the only ones to receive that treatment?'

'That group of alien beings were particularly interested in that specific racial strand.

'You mean the early Hebrews?

'Yes, the strand that was to become the Hebrews. But other extra-planetary groups of beings originating from various parts of the universe were interested in yet different racial strands. So there was a great deal of what in modern terms you call genetic manipulation of the human gene pool over thousands of years.

'Why were they interested in the gene pool of the various racial groups they found on the Planet - be it the Hebrew strand or any other? Were these extra-planetary groups benign in the first instance? Did they interfere with the human genetic makeup for benevolent reasons?

485

'In their own terms, yes. They wished to use the gene pool they found on Earth which had strong connections with themselves; it already had elements of their own genetic makeup. They saw - the extra-planetary group - had a mixed view of what later became the Jewish people, partly seeing them as their own children - for in some sense indeed they were - and partly seeing them as an interesting experiment, exploring another possible way of being. Some of it came out of an interest in the possibility of exerting power and control. But some of it was seen as an insurance policy: should something go wrong with their home gene pool they would have a place to come to. Some of it was indeed benign, simply a wish to understand more of life, which you can look upon as positive exploration. So quite a mixed motivation, and the way in which they behaved was also quite mixed. This experiment went on for many generations. And so there was a mixed experience of these beings who appeared from the sky in a god-like kind of way.

'Were they the Elohim spoken of in Genesis?

No these are not the Elohim, the Elohim have a considerably different role. We are talking about beings of a physical nature, much more of this level of being: beings who originated, in your terms, from a fairly near-by star system, who were just exploring what it is to have physical form, doing the best according to their own light, sometimes behaving in a benign way, sometimes succumbing to the temptations of power; if you like, showing off their power. Some of these things are reflected, not truly remembered, but reflected - in the same way that fairy stories reflect profound truth - in the Old Testament which reverberates a feeling of what God might be like. Those experiences got mixed in. This is one of the reasons why I said to you that in order to understand the text, it is important not to take things at face value, but to look deeply within. And to look deeply within the text, you have to look deeply within yourself; there is no other way of doing it.

'The memory of those earth-shattering events are recorded in our consciousness or even in our DNA, I think I understand this, replies Clara. Who are the Elohim who appear in Genesis?

'The Elohim are of the Divine, they are non-physical Beings who were given the responsibility for this particular bit of the universe, of creating the energy matrix, the underlying pattern of energy upon which your human form is built. They are Beings, highly evolved beings, who are coming into Creation at a stage very much prior to anything like the manipulation of the gene pool. They are of the non-physical side of Creation and as you rightly said, they are spoken of in the Bible.

'Their aim was benign. They were the Creator?

'Not 'the' Creator, but Creators yes, in the sense I gave you. They took specific qualities of Light, and if you like, wove them together to form particular patterns of Light which were the highest they could conceive of, and out of which it was possible, subsequently to create physicality. So we are talking about something with a great degree of abstraction, of a level considerably higher than the level of which I was speaking earlier. I was talking about technologically advanced physical beings from a near-by star who were using the same kind of experimental techniques that your geneticists are just beginning to learn to use, but theirs was considerably more involved.

'Are the Elohim the Brotherhood of Light?

'You can think of the Elohim as members of the Brotherhood, but there are other Beings who are also members of the Brotherhood. The Elohim are one group among many who make up the Brotherhood of Light.

'Do they have human form or are they pure spiritual Beings?

'They are pure spiritual Beings but they can manifest in human form and in some respect, it will not be stretching the point to say that you are the Elohim in physical form, because of the way I was talking.

'They are our Creators therefore we have some of their characteristics.

'Absolutely.

'Are they finite? They cannot be if they are pure spirits.

'They exist beyond space and time, they are not finite.

'Are they perfect in the sense that we understand perfection, fully realised.

'There are two broad meanings to perfection, in one sense they are perfect and they recognise their perfection, but they would be imperfect in the sense that they recognise the possibility of evolving to a higher state.

'They are fully enlightened then?

'They are fully enlightened but Light itself is capable of evolving'.

The encounter ends leaving Clara musing.

Yahweh, First Ray Ruler

Spare time is a rare luxury Levinson savours. In his quiet moments he is hard at work on a research paper he plans to publish, predictably entitled 'The Hebrew Gods'. This is an excerpt from it:

'The Sumerians Scriptures hold the key to understanding the Old Testament. Their engraved tablets and cylinders contain detailed information on the Annunaki, extra-terrestrial beings who came down from the stars some 300,000 years ago. Transferred to the Book of Genesis the Annunaki are renamed Nefilim. The carved tablets tell of vast projects the Annunaki undertook, their function in the 'creation' of the Adam and their active role in the development of the most advanced civilisation after Atlantis. The ancient Sumerians credit the Nefilim for their brilliant civilisation: they understood physics, cosmology, architecture, medicine, law, arts and crafts. The scientists of classical Greece travelled to Sumer in search of scientific information. Selected sections of this vast knowledge found their way into the Old Testament after being subjected to severe editing during the transfer. They were so condensed that their content has baffled scholars ever since. The texts had been purged of most of the relevant information that was crucial to the understanding of the original data.

The Hebrews trace their origins back to Abraham, a Sumerian of some social and political standing. Recent archaeological findings indicate that the biblical 'Revelation' on the origins of the Solar System, the creation of man, civil law, moral ruling, the Ten Commandments, dietary laws, marriage edicts and sexual rules originate in Sumer. The learned rabbis who compiled the Talmud over centuries knew where to find their source of inspiration!

The god whose energy, power and authority pervade the Old Testament is the leader of the Annunaki. Ancient Hebrews ascribed to their deity the awesome traits they feared and admired. Is he not the vengeful, jealous, wrathful god who expects absolute obedience? The capricious god who demands blood sacrifices, the punishing god who insists on the destruction of his enemies? To this day the most intense among his staunch followers entice you into an unequivocal capitulation. They mouth sensuously the enticing mantra, 'your reason for being, your purpose for living is to nullify yourself before the Holy Bless He Be!! 'Kadosh, Kadosh, Kadosh' reverberates down the ages. Yahweh is undeniably a 1st Ray ruler. His strong human qualities are plotted along the line of the 1st Ray of Power. All powerful rulers and dictators climb the ray of power.

The Tibetan explains that this ray manifests as the need for 'centralisation', 'uniqueness' and 'aloneness'. All the dictators of the 20th century display them. More tantalisingly we display them!

'What of 'centralisation'? The god-force occupies centre stage, all stems from that centre; all is controlled from the centre. This we endorsed with conviction and a strong sense of purpose. All human activity is drawn to the 'centre', all edicts emanate from the centre. The deity is both the pulling agent and the initiating force. 'Centralisation' is essential for the continuation of tradition; it ensures social cohesion, simplicity of organisation, clarity of direction. The 'central' figure is easily identifiable and never questioned. The guiding principles and precepts are recognised as emanating from that 'centre', registered and internalised by all. No judgment is permitted, no doubt expressed, no personal criticism vented, no intelligent questioning voiced. Centralisation of power as we have seen in the 20th century secures order by instilling fear and paralysing initiative. The people, centrally directed and controlled, cowering in fear, forbidden to make vital decisions vegetate in a drawn out childhood, an enforced childhood. The 'central' power is all-pervasive, all-knowing, and all-embracing. Yahweh might have served as blueprint for the 'Big Brother' model.

'What of 'uniqueness'? The uniqueness of the deity is matched only by the uniqueness of his chosen people, alone capable of understanding and perpetuating the plan of their leader. A 'unique' god requires a 'unique' people to execute his orders down the ages and secure his intentions.

'What of 'aloneness'? A group with the perilous mission to uphold a god's will-to-power is a lonely human group. No other people are entrusted to shoulder such a design, no other people are so doomed. These characteristics are clearly discernible in the personality of Yahweh and magnified in the people who serve him.

'What about the 'absorbing', 'isolating' and 'assimilating' qualities elicited by the Tibetan? These are the corollaries to the features of 'centralisation' 'uniqueness' and 'aloneness'. Everything is energetically drawn and sucked in by the central power which imbibes and ingests all. It absorbs that which it draws to itself and makes its own. The process of 'absorption' is coupled with that of 'isolation' and 'assimilation'. The first act of 'absorption' and 'assimilation' Hitler did was to invade Poland and other neighbouring countries. In depriving them of their freedom he was asserting himself and building the myth of the great Fatherland. After conquering Canaan our ancestors set out to build the myth of the people of destiny and launched ethnic wars. The 'greatness' of one group necessarily means loss of freedom, loss of innocence and loss of integrity for other groups. During the process of absorption and assimilation there is transformation. Reality is modified, cast in the ancient mould that remodels it to suit a preset format. The 1st Ray energy transforms all it touches and those who shelter under its canopy are mystified; they see the world as it was aeons ago. So they see no necessity to revise their narcissistic views. It is the world which must fit their preconceived ideas. 'We are the loyal Party members who tow the line, abiding unconditionally by Party rule. We have sensed the mood, grasped the intention and translated the will of the Leader. The Party faithful absorb his intention regardless of its impact on the rest of humanity. Our narcissistic viewpoint must prevail. The law is paramount, the will of the ruler irrevocable. This, the world witnessed in awe as Stalin, Hitler and Mussolini embarked on a programme of centralisation in which they set out to 'absorb', 'isolate' and 'assimilate'. Their plan of conquest was an affirmation of their 'uniqueness '. They were chosen for a great purpose! They saw themselves as men of destiny who sought to make their nations great again, leaders destined to rule the world and bend the will of men. This Yahweh did. And those who to this day accept as true his divinity continue to make the same affirmation and persist in confirming his 'centralised' power. And why not? The Yahweh-energy is ruling the world without sway. His civilisation founded on 'centralisation, uniqueness and isolation', on racial distinction, the right to rule, the right to oppress is in many parts of the world more potent today than at any other time in the history of the Planet. The dictatorship of Yahweh has served as model to all dictatorships in history.

There is another facet to the 1st Ray, 'destruction'! To absorb in order to dissolve. Ideas become fossilised into social, religious or political ideologies which cling. We tend to reject the new, we prefer the old. Ideologies and theories are used by the Hierarchy for so long as they inspire the imagination of man, stimulate his mental expansion and drive him along the path of conscious evolution. The Tibetan explains that the moment the form crystallises it becomes an impediment to human development. We have until now utilised the principle of 'absorbing' to hinder our progress, restrict our mental development and freeze into inertia. 'Absorbing' in order to understand, transform and change is the work of the cosmic workers who work for the Hierarchy. Master Sananda explains that the process of change has to do with the process of healing. To change the 'old world' energy into an energy form that is of benefit to all implies healing; there are aspect of the 'old world' that must be 'absorbed' into healing.

This is the Tibetan's view of our official god, 'God as the national controller took possession of man's mind, and the Jehovah concept (as depicted in the Jewish dispensation) appeared'. The idea of a 'national controller' who has power over all captured primitive imagination. Yahweh as local god who engages in all activities, oversees all functions and brooks no opposition was a new idea in the ancient world in which all gods had equal status, a world noted for its diversity and its tolerance. As 'national controller' – governor, superintendent, overseer - the deity takes charge of human affairs, social and political. He is the insidious Big Brother of our worst nightmares, the eye that sees all, penetrates all, and knows all!

'The civilisation the Nefilim gave to Sumer and through the Old Testament to modern humanity is founded on shared beliefs, on ethical rules of living but do not include knowledge of the inner worlds. There is a deletion of cosmic Law, as evidenced in the myth of the Tree of Knowledge. Adam is denied the right to grasp the meaning of polarity around which the world is constructed. The Tree stands figuratively for the world. He is starved of an intelligent understanding of the world in which he finds himself. The Adam emerging from unconsciousness is developing a rudimentary mind. He is dimly aware of the existence of dual opposites and the choices presented to him. But Yahweh has other ideas; he wants man not to know but to obey. Man is condemned to a state of arrested development.

'Doing' – a violation of the natural order?

'When the ego interferes in the rhythms of progress, there is so much doing! But nothing is done.' What do you make of Lao Tzu's enigmatic words, challenges Tara?

'A lot, replies Levinson! 'Doing' is the quintessence of life in our Judeo-Christian world, for the religiously-oriented man it is the measure of his capitulation to the will of the deity! 'Doing' is the purpose of existence. 'Doing' bonds with absence of reflection, this is beaten into the mind of Yeshiva boys. 'Doing' encapsulates the 'do as you are told' syndrome.

'They sensuously mouthed unconditional capitulation to the will of the idol. The slightest hint of intelligent questioning was abhorrent to them, a sign of heresy, of anarchy even, shudders Clara.

'And it is hammered into the brains of army recruits everywhere, coerced into becoming robots who 'do & obey' for maximum efficiency; as killing machines they must not think, just obey orders, continues Levinson. The way we train our armies in the world is contained in these two deadly words 'do & obey'. Is mindlessness spiritual? It is a violation of the natural order: we evolved a brain over millions of years but we are forbidden to use it. 'Doing' is a denial of evolution, a negation of progress. 'Doing' therefore goes against the natural rhythms of life. 'Doing' implies actions prompted by coercion. Force, intimidation and coercion are contrary to the divine order and a violation of human needs.

'Interesting, ponders Tara, Lao Tzu concludes with the enigmatic, 'All is done without doing'; when the ego no longer meddles with the flow of life, when action is in harmony with the life force then 'all is done without doing'. 'All is done' means going with the life flow to assist its movement, not to interfere with its natural rhythm.

"Do & obey' is inflicted on others by the ruling agencies, it does not emanate from the Source, inserts Jeremy. 'Doing' is Yang – the masculine ego - in it is the root of all coercion, greed and exploitation of man and of Earth's resources. Religion, politics, economics, education, medicine and the global economy are built on the same Yang foundations. Our institutions rooted in the capitalist system are Yang.

'Just as the Old Testament is Yang! When the rabbis clamour 'do & obey' as if it emanated from the Source, it is their own will-to-power they sanction, picks up Clara. The universe never demands, never controls, never dominates, never intimidates. The 'do & obey' appears to have divine sanction but it is no other than the human urge to rule and coerce.

'Look no further for the malignant roots of ownership, control and exploitation of man and Earth's resources, continues Jeremy. Our modern economy, our industrial base, our way of life revolve around these. 'Doing' is a licence to use and abuse. Many of our social values and attitudes have their roots in the detrimental diktat 'do'. It is a violation of the universal order when man's law abolishes cosmic Law, when Yang imposes itself with unrelenting force. Man's fixation with 'doing' is born of the will-to-power. 'When the Tao is lost...' integrity is lost. A return to sanity is imperative; it implies a transformation of our thoughts and behaviour and the dissolution of herd values and attitudes. A transformation along holistic lines: a quest for wholeness, integrity and integration.

'As women are enticed into economic activity, they donate their labour to enhance Yang, the masculine force, reflects Tara. They unwittingly invest their energies into reinforcing the 'old order'! Yet the mothers of humanity have in them what it takes to redeem the world. Lao Tzu adds in the same verse, 'The less we are compelled to take vested actions … until all is done without doing'. How are things 'done without doing'? I agree with Jeremy, with a return to sanity: collaboration between people and alliance with the forces of nature. 'All is done' in the natural flow of life, free from the interference of Yang, free from oppression, free from intimidation.

'That's alright but the god of the Western world is the Old Testament god who dictates 'do & obey', the god who exacts 'an eye for an eye', mutters Clara!

'You also know that the 20th century precipitated an apocalyptic conflagration between the forces of Light and the forces of Darkness, replies Jeremy! The forces of coercion and exploitation were considerably weakened throughout the world. Since then new institutions, new attitudes, new ideas have appeared. Advocates of the old world order are loud and disruptive but not effective.

And what of 'being'?

'The primary quality of the soul is creativity. And so insistence on 'doing' is denial of soul life. Denial of creativity is negation of the spirit in man, muses Tara. Emphasis has always been on 'doing' as if 'doing was salvation'. Right action as Buddha prescribed is required, but right action is not necessarily 'doing'.

'The Western ethos presents 'doing' as reason for living, notes Clara, as if this whirlwind of activity was the key to salvation. As Sananda insisted it is not doing but 'being' that liberates. There is a good reason for this; animal-man back in Lemuria was given rules of basic conduct to lift him out of his animal condition. We never forgot, 'doing' is programmed in our psyche, encoded in our genetic fabric, written in our books and studied with great diligence in religious schools. Fixation with 'doing' to achieve salvation reappears with Luther and his Protestant doctrine which gave rise to the familiar Protestant ethic of work. As if man was deserving of life only if he works like a beaver! This bizarre notion has filtered through the working-classes' code of living.

'Surprised? The working-classes are the beavers that made Western nations prosperous, the backbone of our liberal economies, notes Jeremy. 'Doing' was hammered into their soul by the ruling classes and their allies, the priests.

'Doing' aligns with the forces of separateness and materialism while 'being' aligns with freedom of the human soul and brotherhood, recalls Clara. Our world has always been tilted, unbalanced. When the force of materialism and the force of the soul reach a point of balance humanity will be redeemed as the Tibetan reminds us.

'Incorrect knowledge is based upon perception of the form and not upon the state of being, said Patanjali, quotes Tara.

'And as the Tibetan stated, 'The Old Testament is a secondary Scripture and its emphasis is material'. Its emphasis is on 'doing'. 'Doing' keeps us engrossed in the material necessities of life. 'Doing', ritualism and the ego are tied, reflects Levinson.

'Liberation comes from 'freedom of the soul and brotherhood', from being a channel of cosmic life. The ego obstructs the life flow and so death of the ego is crucial, 'Except ye die, ye shall not live'. To live in the world of form entirely - 'doing' - is to exclude the world of 'being', comments Jeremy. Ordinary man lives in the world of 'doing', while the Master lives in the world of 'being', he is Master of all universal laws.

'You recall how Buddha grappled with the Devil, inserts Tara. The Devil is the force that seeks to keep us hooked to the material world, the world of 'doing'. Evil is the force that obstructs the realisation of our Buddha nature.

Yahweh, Lord of Earth

They go for a walk along the lake. They choose to remain silent. They look at the light reflected in the water; they listen to all the sounds and take note of the colours. They focus on sensory impressions to re-connect with the outside world. An hour later they return to the kibbutz where Bendavid resumes the reading. Master Sanaka and Rabbi Moses are discussing the nature and function of Yahweh, leader of the Nefilim.

'You have to make a clear distinction between Ea, the Lord of Earth as he is known in Sumer and the Elohim, the 'creator Gods' who designed and created the body of energy of man that forms the basis of physicality, begins Sanaka.

'One group creates the essence of man and another other group alters his body, is it correct?

'Absolutely. Do you recall that the Dualists, that enigmatic group which claim to have the true Gospels, understood this? At the core of their doctrine is the existence of two gods, a good God who created the soul and Satan who created matter.

'Do you approve of this distinction? There appears to be some truth in their belief, replies Moses feeling uncomfortable with the subject.

'There is, the two stories of Creation in Genesis confirm their view, but it is only a fragmentary truth. Ultimately there is no God and no Satan, no good and no evil. All emanate from the one Source, all proceeds from the same Life Force.

'What of evil, we know it exists, who can deny it?

'Evil, like all else in our world is an illusion, it has no real existence. Evil is unevolved, undeveloped, uncultivated, unrefined, unredeemed, unconscious, unknowing energy. In other words evil is ignorance. Knowing dispels evil. As self-knowledge expands evil recedes: the inner barriers give way like a river breaks its banks after heavy rain. When man discovers intuitively and intellectually cosmic Law, he is enlightened. You see why evil is nonexistent? As man grows in self-knowledge his limitations and the hurdles put in his path by tradition dissolve. When he was living 'unconsciously' with the 'do & obey' he was asleep; now he is awake he no longer acts unconsciously, he claims his autonomy back.

'Adam means 'of Earth'. Both the Nefilim and the Elohim have a stake in this Earthling, remarks Moses.

'Genesis gives a strong hint concerning the nature of man and the nature of the experiment the Sumerian god embarked on. A casual reading reveals nothing; all it does is fill the reader with intense religious fervour and burning emotional zeal, the very obstacle to understanding! Sadly the devout are often arrested at that superficial reading. Yahweh creates an 'Earthling', a creature made 'of Earth'. Is this not tantalisingly materialistic? A powerful being the Sumerians call 'Lord of Earth' shapes a man 'of Earth' and you leave it at that! By the way the Sumerian god Ea becomes Yahweh when transposed in Genesis. You do not ask, like the Dualists have done, 'what is the true nature of man, is he just an animated lump of earth?' This explains why the Dualists rejected this undignified view of man. It is the soul of earthly man that interests them; it is the Soul of the universe they focus on!

The Sumerian texts speak of an 'Earthling' to tell him apart from the Nefilim, advanced beings who came to Earth from the stars.

'The Hebrew texts say that they were 'cast down', toppled over. It sounds like expulsion!

'The Nefilim came to Earth in their flying vessels, 'cast down'! They colonised Earth for gold and silver as well as for rare natural resources. They selected Earth as other colonising stellar groups had done. Earth enjoyed a privileged position in the Solar System. They brought with them a small number of Nefilim who were put to work in mining, digging and building. But the Nefilim workers grew weary and disgruntled. A rebellion ensued. This insurrection threatened the future of the vast colonisation project. The god Anu, father of Yahweh was concerned; he convened a meeting in which Yahweh was invited to speak. Yahweh's suggestion was to have far-reaching repercussions for mankind and for your people in particular: *While the Birth Goddess is present// Let her create a 'Primitive Worker'// Let him bear the yoke ... Let him carry the toil of the gods'.*

'Who is the birth goddess, why a primitive worker?

'She was Yahweh's consort. He needed a robust and obedient workforce, capable of hard work but not capable of thought. Primitive earthlings were plentiful; all that was required was to make them less crude, less brutal, less primitive, and more human.

'We still 'bear the yoke' and with immense pride, as a measure of our towering spirituality, says Moses! I have to go back to Vilna to tell them that their god had a consort?

'They unconsciously know, what about the Shekhina?

'And with these few words Ea changed the world, broods Moses! The Sumerian texts leave us under no doubt as to the intention of Ea and his associates. They created primitive man to work for them, to establish them on Earth and to secure their future civilisation. Why have we been denied this vital piece of information?

'You were denied nothing! Knowledge is available to who wants it, but it comes at a price. The quest for knowledge is a life long endeavour, one which requires endurance and sacrifice. Think of Arjuna and Buddha, think of the mythological hero. Your people were no Arjuna, no Orpheus, they settled for pseudo-knowledge given to them by those who had a vested interest in controlling them. And so collectively you surrendered your autonomy and the courage to take charge of your lives. You wanted to be controlled. You wanted to look up to the sky and plead, protest and moan. Suffering you endured, anything was better than the freedom to be and the freedom to become. Fear of freedom has been the inhibiting as well as the driving force.

'And Anu approved of Ea's suggestion? The 'primitive worker' was finally fashioned in clay, concludes Moses who is feeling increasingly uneasy.

'The gods voted in favour, continues Sanaka aware of Moses' disquiet. The new 'earthling' was to lift the toil from the shoulders of a dissatisfied and rebellious Nefilim workforce. 'Man shall be his name' decided the gods. The newly re-made man is put to work to tend the Garden. The implicit meaning, loud to the serious reader, is that Ea's intent was to appoint man as caretaker of the Planet. This view has been hammered in by tradition, you are the 'chosen' people, your reason for living is to 'serve' your god, you proudly wear the 'yoke', your ultimate purpose for living is to 'nullify' yourselves before your god! The god of Genesis who re-fashions existing earthling has no inclination for finer feelings, lofty ideals, intellectual goals or spiritual longings. You are under no illusion; the Garden is no Garden of Eden!

'I am well acquainted with this, sighs Moses. The words 'toil', 'yoke', 'work' reverberate throughout the Scriptures. Jewish tradition reiterates them with immense pride, they echo down the ages. The Jew bears the 'yoke'; he was created to 'serve' his god, to 'toil', to engage in constant 'Avodah'.

'This hurts you to the core, observes Sanaka. Man, limitless cosmic being created to incarnate the Divine, man whose body is a symbolic representation of the universe! Boundless and deathless man is by you relegated to the role of a meek servant, a docile slave to stellar visitors, who must wear the 'yoke' with pride. Man is owned by a foreign agency that operates him. The priesthood decline to set mankind free from the hold of the past, from the grasping embrace of the deity.

'An anomaly with serious implications, states Moses despondent. But this is not just an aberration.

'No it is not. Ancient Hebrew figured out that his most noble function was to 'do and obey'; his reason for living was to 'serve' beings from the stars who passed themselves for gods. The Garden of Eden was an open prison, Adam a docile slave and his god a slave-driver.

Yahweh in the Hassidic tradition

In the past Clara had mulled over the tenets of Hassidic doctrine. That morning at breakfast, when pressed to explain her sombre mood, she replies 'I was going through a difficult time, the 'dark night of the soul', reliving the past, a past blighted by my involvement with a Hassidic group. It comes back to haunt me every so often in spite of many years of meditation, learning and reflection. I was revisiting the past when I first met you. Jung would call that state a 'spiritual crisis'. Despondent I came to Jeremy's workshop.

'I know, says Jeremy calmly. You also received a substantial amount of healing that week-end.

'I had reached the lowest point of the arc. I began the slow ascent then. Last night again I had a troubled dream. I need a private encounter with Sananda to lift my spirit.

'This can be arranged, replies Jeremy always keen to soothe and assist. They sit in a circle, Jeremy enters into a receptive mood and they wait for Sananda to speak.

'Welcome please ask your question', rises the beautiful deep yet melodious voice of Jeremy.

'Master Sananda, I would like to return to a topic which still torments me. I had a hard time of it and though I left it behind, I am not yet free from it. One of the thorniest tenets of Hassidism hinges around the personality of Yahweh. It takes off in what appears to be a flight of the imagination. I quote:

'Yahweh refers to god the Infinite transcending creation. The one who is infinite who transcends time and space'. This strange statement ends with 'Yahweh is the divinity that brings all things into existence'.

Sananda with a chuckle, 'Just tell me where your difficulty lies with this?

Clara flustered by Sananda's chuckle mutters, 'we know that Yahweh was a being from a near-by star. Scientist and explorer he came to Earth to claim it as his principality. He also altered the genetic make up of primitive humans to gain control of the Planet. He may have passed for a god, he certainly was a god in the eyes of primitive humans, but he is not to be confused with the Creator, 'the Infinite transcending creation'. Yahweh and the Infinite are not one and the same. However Yahweh is the pervading influence in human consciousness and his energy permeates the Planet.

'Consider this for a moment, replies Sananda who has listened intently. You also transcend time and space, you also are divine, you also are a creator of reality. Now, this is not the way you usually see yourself. But in as much as you are an aspect of the Divine, so all things that are true of the Divine are also true of you, to a degree. Now, it is true that you are just one aspect of the All That Is, but nevertheless each one of you

- the single aspect that you are - also contains the whole. This is quite difficult to get your mind around: the part contains the whole. So therefore, there is in a sense, complete truth in what is being said about Yahweh. This being manifests forth divinity. These things are true. Also true, to some extent, is what you have been saying, that this being is not the entirety of the Divine, but an aspect of the Divine as you are; an aspect of the Divine who experienced himself as being more powerful than you experience yourself. In other words, this was a being who had abilities, skills, powers you do not yet recognise yourselves as having. At other levels of your being, you also have these same skills. So the whole thing becomes quite complicated to disentangle.

'However, continues Sananda, what I would say is that there is a degree of confusion in the statement made, in as much as Yahweh is being identified with the totality of the All That Is, where I would see this being as one manifestation of the All That Is, if you like, and I put inverted comas around this - with a gentle, almost imperceptible laughter - a 'local god' rather than the God of All. Again there are many different ways of seeing this and all of them will have some degree of truth. So for you who are experiencing pain around the whole issue of the nature of Jewishness, it is preferable to see the somewhat partial energy that was Yahweh to have an agenda which is not your agenda. Whereas for someone who sees Yahweh as a lens through which the All That Is may be seen, the perception is of a divine and pure energy. Both perceptions are aspects of the truth, neither is right, neither is wrong. They both have truth within them. So for you, it is a question of finding the truth that is most beneficial, the truth that helps you most to come to your own highest understanding, your own highest existence. You may find as you have already found in your life, that truth changes. What you hold to be true this week may not quite fit your feeling about the truth next week. Just as you felt strongly to be the truth, say 20 years ago, would not be exactly the same as what you hold to be true now. So the truth itself you might say, is an evolving energy, it changes as you change.

'Thank you for clarifying this difficult issue. I never quite saw it in terms of 'agenda'. Yahweh's agenda is one of ownership and control. My agenda is to bring ownership and control back into human hands. Is there no absolute truth or is it just truth as seen through our individual experience?

'If you were to look for absolute truth, concludes Sananda I would say let absolute truth be the sum of all truths and that all of you hold and indeed are an aspect of the truth, but together we, all of us, make the whole truth.'

Yahweh, the Hebrew predicament and the Messianic dream

'One day in the depth of winter, when the wind was howling in the mountains and snow was falling in a blizzard, the cold descended on the monastery enveloping it in an invisible shroud that even the monks disciplined to withstand such low temperatures found difficult to contend with. Moses was being initiated in the techniques of self-control but not yet fully adept at mastering such adverse weather conditions. After the dawn meditation, Sanaka walked to Moses and told him that he was now ready to discuss the nature of the god of the Western World.

'Shall we study in the library, asks Moses disconcerted by the sudden and unexpected decision?

'Right here in the meditation room, replies Sanaka smiling his radiant smile to lessen the impact, the tranquillity and light of this room will help you come to terms with a knotty issue.

The oil lamp is casting a softly shifting shadow on the statues of Buddha and Tara. Moses is focussing on the patterns of light and shade, serenely aware of living in the moment, a present which infuses him with a sense of calm. There is no past, no future, he simply is in the present, he is in eternity now. The flames of a fire being poked by a monk rise reassuring and warming. 'All is well, all is safe, all is just the way it should be thinks Moses.

'Move closer to the fire, invites Sanaka and while looking into the living fire listen and turn within to find the correspondence, to find the echo of what I am saying.

'The echo, enquires Moses?

'What I am about to say you already know'. Moses rises a questioning eyebrow which Sanaka detects, 'not intellectually perhaps, but the slumbering genius within already knows all, it has access to all. I am just refreshing your memory, he adds with a smile which dispels the gloom of the morning. You have been a scholar over many life times, so nothing of what you learn today is new to your knowing Self. If only man realised that he knows all, he would never again turn for succour or direction outside, he would simply move within his being where all is, where the All is.

'Man knows all, repeats Moses?

'Man is multidimensional, he participates in the physical and astral worlds to which he belongs and is strongly attached to; he also participates in the mental plane. Furthermore he also partakes to the inner planes where all knowledge is to be found. He can travel into the universe and withdraw information. It is easier to do this in an altered state of consciousness when the mind is more receptive to finer impressions. Ignorance of his true nature tempts man to fall into the hands of self-appointed controllers. He would spare himself much disappointment, disillusion and suffering if he admitted to the fact of his latent power.

'He has been conditioned to think of himself as flawed, inept and ignorant, notes Moses who remembers so well, he has been conditioned to expect salvation from outside.

'It was in the interest of monotheism and patriarchy to implant notions of limitation into the mind of man. Man is so much easier to control, then! Not surprisingly the 'one' god is the next theme to be discussed, we are lingering into monotheism, he smiles ironically. In the Hebrew myth, Yahweh is the secret name represented by the mysterious letters YHVH, so sacred that no one was permitted to utter it for fear of retribution, as you well know. The unpronounceable name was shrouded in mystery and dread of retribution.

'Anyone bold enough to utter the unutterable name was sure to receive the most severe punishment, people refrained for fear of being stoned to death, remarks Moses on familiar grounds now

'Some associate the name with an ancient volcano-god Yahoo. But Yahoo was also a name known in ancient Sumer. An apt name for in the Desert, the people did witness the strangest and most terrifying spectacle of mountains roaring, shaking and vomiting fire.

'The people were commanded to accept the Torah or resign themselves to being crushed by the mountain, this may be why, suggests Moses.

'In part, but what is the nature of this extraordinary god who by some incredible twist of fate endures not only as the controlling deity of the Hebrews but also as the less visible god of Christendom? He is presented as the creative energy of the universe, jealously protective of his immortality while denying it to humans. Adverse to darkness he passes for the 'god of light'.

'Did he not give rules of decent living to man, did he not 'create' man in his likeness? These surely justify his being called the 'god of light' and the 'creative force of the universe'. He can be credited for shedding light in the dark existence of primitive humans.

'You seem to miss a crucial point Rabbi Moses. The 'creative energy of the universe' expressing itself in matter is not Yahweh but Divine Intelligence. This essential fact is veiled to prompt man to observe the world and arrive at his own conclusion. As you rightly say this secondary deity did lift early man out of the unconsciousness of matter, so he may deserve the title of 'god of light'. What other key feature would justify the title 'god of light'?

'Light is consciousness, replies Moses unhesitatingly. As man develops a sense of selfhood, he finds himself thrust into the world of duality and into physical law...

'Animals also exist in Maya; they too are determined by physical law, Maya.

'But for man, expands Moses, the realisation that he has free-will and can affect the world around him is a possibility. Animals exist in Maya but they do not have choice. As man becomes conscious of himself and the world around him, he is able to make choices, since he is aware of duality. In other words he can create. In duality man becomes a creator or worlds.

'Inevitably, where there is possibility of choice there is duality, chuckles Sanaka. The primordial pair is good & evil. Primal inkling of good & evil conjures up in the mind of primitive man the god of good and the god of evil. Inevitably the god he projects outside of himself becomes the judge who deals out reward and punishment.

'... Mostly punishment, interrupts Moses, did he not send the Deluge to wipe out humanity? The Old Testament presents god as merciless, he neither forgets nor forgives. He sets out to annihilate Sodom and Gomorrah and plans the destruction of Nineveh. He does not hesitate to launch wars of attrition on his enemies. He was not swayed by moral scruples when the time came to eradicate humanity with the Deluge.

'Would primitive humans have grasped fine feelings like forgiveness and compassion? Would a god who displays the spiritual qualities of love, compassion and respect for life, interact with prehistoric man? Man is coherent, he can only identify with gods who exhibit qualities and emotions he is familiar with, Yahweh was just that being, perfectly suited to the times, mood and level of mental aspiration. As you see, a picture designed to satisfy the limited awareness of the times. In a more advanced era such a programme would appear distasteful if not plain immoral.

'Arbiter of good and evil, judge of the world, slayer of his enemies, besotted with his followers, lover of justice, I know the god of my ancestors!

'That is why you must resort to an external force to get you out of your predicament, remarks Sanaka! Your prophecy heralds a time when the world will be thrown upside down in mayhem, chaos and tumult. In the last hour when all is lost, a messiah will miraculously appear!

'Why do we insist on the coming of the Messiah, it never worked before?

'First, the Wisdom of the Ages presages a Redeemer for the end of this era, as mankind and Earth are to rise into a higher dimension of being. Second, his coming will herald a new era. A transformation in awareness: a breathtaking shift from a fractured world to the unbroken oneness of Light. This is written into the Divine Plan which is with the Hierarchy and is being regularly revised as mankind progresses. The problem is that you want a messiah made to your own specification, designed to suit your preconceived ideas of what a messiah should be and this will not happen. You want to keep things as they are, you want nothing to change, you want to stay in Maya, you want to stagnate in your present state of awareness but with a messiah to make things alright for you! You do nothing, he does all the work! A hero in shining armour.

'Where did it all go so wrong, asks Moses with deep sadness?

'As I see it, others might see it differently, the Father-image you have nurtured has driven you and humanity to the edge of the precipice. The cosmic Law that created the world, the creative energy which holds the world together is love. The All created the universe and man with his own substance which is love. Do you see Moses, my son?

'I think I do, an earth-shattering idea it is, the universe is not material, matter is not inert but sentient! I shall be burnt at the stake for that!

'You will not be the first one! So the universe is conscious and Earth is a sentient being. When man forgets his vital nature, in his despair he cries out to the gods that spring from his fears to save him. But the inherited god-images are powerless to save him. With each adversity you weep and lament and as nothing changes you revert back to the old god-forms which got you into trouble in the first place!

'And we go on petitioning a redeemer to get us out of trouble?

'Love transforms everything, clarifies Sanaka, it is the Law of the universe. Man ignores this cosmic law at his peril. This is what the Essenes tried to explain to the rabbis of Jerusalem who screamed 'blasphemy!' The Hierarchy are assisting the nativity of man, the Birth of a new consciousness - man's true nature is love and when mankind finally accepts it, the messianic age will have arrived.

'So we do not need a messiah, says Moses elatedly?

'When man nurtures the inner Son, when man embodies the cosmic Laws of love, compassion, tolerance, kindness and understanding, he will give birth to his inner messiah who will in turn attract out of Shamballa the cosmic Messiah, Lord Maitreya.

Group discussion

The dialogue between Master Sanaka and Rabbi Moses comes to an end. It stimulates the group to stretch it further. They fire their views, 'the god of Genesis is not different from other legendary gods the mythologies of the world are brimming with, sets in train Johansson. Yahweh represents the energetic creative and destructive force in the world. In India Shiva is the dynamic god of life and death. A god or an idea? A god or a projection? The boundaries are blurred. The ancients lived in an emotional world, they experienced the world through feeling; what they sensed they personified. Mythological gods embody human traits and human emotions. Love became Aphrodite. Fear became the god you know. The destructive mother energy became the goddess Kali.

'You are saying that we worship today ideas that the ancients could not grasp by thought, clarifies Clara.

'That's right, we continue to worship on the altar of gods-ideas and gods-emotions.

'That is why cosmic workers, all of us, came to the Planet, inserts Jeremy. We are here to reverse the trend. Humanity has been governed by the controlling emotions of fear, hostility, suspicion, hatred and attachment; all legacy of the past. We are here to denounce the materialism of the past and explode the gods-ideas. We came to awaken humanity to its true identity and nature. Fear is of the Fall. Fear is not of the Source. We came to 'reverse the Fall's effects'.

'Fear is of the Fall, the god of fear is of the Fall. We are here to awaken mankind to reality, echoes Clara as if day-dreaming.

'As a mythological figure the god of fear is no longer relevant, mutters Bendavid. He pervades our society, our world view, and our institutions. He is the only reality we have known since the Nefilim came to Earth, the reality humanity has had to grapple with. Humanity offers sacrifices on the altar of the god of fear.

"Offer sacrifices', echoes Shemtov? We abolished sacrifices long ago.

'So you think, retorts Bendavid! We sacrifice each and every generation to the god of our ancestors. Go over the course of your life: the moment you were born a fragment of your flesh was removed in his name, you were offered to him at puberty, you had to endorse a way of thinking and a mode of life in his name and you had to marry within the tribal cluster. Think of the wasted lives, think of the desolate marriages, think of the mismatches. Think of the gifted women with dreams and aspirations who enter wedlock with lesser individuals just because the men are circumcised? If that is not sacrifice what is? Were you ever free to do otherwise? Could you direct your life the way you wanted to? Slaves belong to their masters; they do not own their lives. Our lives are owned by external agencies. Some broadcast their servitude with pride; they exhibit the symbols of their bondage with ostentation, others feel embarrassed, many more discard it as we did.

'He is rapidly losing his influence, clarifies BarYohai, modern man is evolving toward the spiritual values that the Yahweh-idea does not embody: empathy, understanding, tolerance, justice, freedom, equality, unity, cooperation, collaboration, conciliation, all of which are spiritual ideals.

'On a planetary scale, agrees Jeremy, these values find expression as respect for the dignity of all men, the primacy of human rights and global collaboration. We accept the idea of the one humanity, 'the international community' as politicians label it. We also perceive the link between all kingdoms of Nature; we identify Earth as a living organism as did the enlightened Greeks who named her Gaia.

'These are the values taking root today as we enter the Age of Man; we are leaving behind the separation and prejudices of the past, says Tara.

'We are exiting the age of the gods, we are beginning to 'reverse the Fall's effects', savours Clara.

'But this transformation is not smooth, remarks Bendavid, the adversaries of universality are determined to thwart unification. Those who wave the Yahweh-idea as their banner have launched a crusade against change and they can barely conceal their hostility toward other Jews! What a paradox, the Yahweh-idea turning against itself!

'Some are so engrossed in this world that they visualize nothing other than limitations, separation, hostility and fragmentation, says Shemtov. They envisage nothing other than powerlessness, unthinking obedience to bygone notions and capitulation to archaic authority. Quantum physics has much to say on materialism or rather the end of materialism. The physicist Eddington expressed, 'That environment of space and time and matter, of light and colour and concrete things, which seems so vividly real to us ... has melted into a shadow'. All things that make up our belief system melt into unreality. We believe frantically in a shadow.

'All the mind's arbitrary conceptions of matter, phenomena ....and all conceptions and ideas relating to it are like a dream, a phantasm, a bubble, a shadow, said Buddha, quotes Tara.

'We must be the most fervent believers in the reality of matter, the reality of phenomena and the reality of our notions. Yet both Quantum physics and Buddha dismiss them as mere 'shadow', remarks Shemtov, because 'Ignorance apprehends its object as if it exists objectively'.

'The material world is the boundary of their sensibility, says Clara. Hence the passionate embrace in the tango of the 'do & obey'! The individual addicted to his 'yoke' knows of nothing resembling freedom of thought. The 'maker' who fashioned us to serve him is as alive and obeyed today as he was in prehistoric times.

'I would say 'more so'. It was just pointed out that in mythological times the ancients experienced the world through feeling, what they sensed they personified. Mythological gods embody human emotions. Yahweh embodies the tyranny of matter, suggests Shemtov.

'He has held humanity captive of physical reality, expands Levinson. I agree, he stands for materialism. Materialism relates to form - physical, religious, social, legal, and political. The inevitable outcome of which is separateness, distrust and hostility. Our dogmas capture with foresight the nature of the god-idea as the force inherent in matter. 'That the ancient god, archetype of the tyranny of matter, insists on his own immortality but denies it to man indicates that early man cannot envisage the continuation of life after death, suggests Johansson. Early man admits that he is of this world and this world alone!

'Is it not an indication that man regards matter eternal and himself mortal? He is aware of his own mortality as he projects immortality on to the god-idea, suggests Jeremy.

'This sounds credible, admits Levinson. In his daily prayers he utters with conviction - when he can marshal conviction - that his god is the god who created the world. The god he appeases and invokes is the god of the visible, tangible, material world. He offers his children on the altar of a force that sponsors materiality and denies the intrinsic wholeness of life. The god-idea personifies the Fall. As the 'creative' principle he stands for Maya, the world of illusion.

'That is why some of the principles that lie behind our culture are unreliable, comments Bendavid who has researched the subject. This accounts for much of the discontent and turmoil our society is going through. The god-idea is a vast ambiguity - human and superhuman, rational and irrational, constructive and destructive, moral and amoral, just and unjust. He is the product of human insecurity, ambivalence and inconsistency.

'You are saying, clarifies Clara that the god-idea is emblematic of the human self moved by contradictory feelings? As a result, the religion built around the god-idea is essentially dogmatic and intolerant. Intolerance and dogma are of the physical self, locked in temporality.

'What is surprising about that, questions Bendavid? Our gods, projections of our unconscious minds are subject to duality just as we are. Our gods, like us are enclosed in Maya, they move and act within the boundaries of physical reality. They do not transcend it, they succumb to it! Our gods are like us only more so! In time of crisis there is no help to expect from them, they flounder. Our history is a register of disasters in which god was conspicuous only by his absence: the great Flood and the sinking of Atlantis, the catastrophic events at Sinai and finally the annihilation of his Children during WW2. Where was he then?

'Yet we rely on them as if they were all powerful, notes Jeremy.

'Because we perceive ourselves as powerless, retorts Tara.

'There is a vital link missing in our tradition, the impact of science, explains Shemtov. Yahweh's culture is founded on scientific exploration. He prohibited intelligent questioning from his labour force, yet his civilisation emphasises the exploitation of the Earth resources. Genesis states that man was given dominion over the mineral, vegetable and animal kingdoms. There is also the strict rule of law. Dominion and law together form the basis for a scientific and technological society. The god we revere with uncritical acclaim was known in Sumer - the land where he had his scientific laboratories - as the giver of a mainly scientific culture. Yet, this aspect we discarded when we lifted Yahweh out of the Sumerian texts and implanted him in Genesis.

'Yet by a quirky twist of fate, ponders BarYohai, the 'nation of priests' failed to discern the essentially scientific orientation of its god. They overlook his scientific achievements for what they are. As they recount his divine exploits they adore the 'god', not the scientist. Occupied as they are with the deity's unusual worldly powers, they have discarded the study of physical law. The adoration of the god of matter takes precedence over the study of the material world. It is illogical.

A brief silence, then BarYohai continues with restrained indignation, 'the Hebrews shunned science in ancient Greece and Alexandria. To this day the pious do not permit their children to enjoy the benefits of a liberal and inclusive education, they deny their children the right to explore the world and gain knowledge. Yet their god was an accomplished scientist! His civilisation is of this world, it does not extend beyond physical reality.

Yahweh - a thought-form?

Rabbi Moses has postponed this burning question, as he dreads the answer. However, unable to contain his desire for the truth he approaches Sanaka. 'What is a thought form, Master, he asks with some foreboding?

'A thought form is an image which has no real existence. It is formed in the mind and energised by will and desire.

'It is short-lived in this case?

'Normally the image disperses and fades away when the mind focuses on another idea. You know the cosmic law 'energy follows thought'. When the mind single-pointedly focuses on an issue, the strength of the thought energises it and gives it form and a degree of existence, illusory as it is. When repeated, the image is fortified and gets entrenched. In India we have people who are capable of creating thought forms which take on a life of their own, almost like living creatures, they may be benign or malign depending on the initial intent. Normally thought forms have a limited life span, they depend for their prolongation on the force and nature of the thought.

'So humanity creates thought forms all the time, asks Moses in amazement?

'And this is a major problem. You see, thought is energy and it is indestructible. Negative, persistent thought forms live on and continue to haunt humanity. The most tenacious thought forms are the most repeated. They are kept alive by repetition. When people intensify the ideas of the past by repeating them, they reinforce the thought forms their ancestors created; energising them they keep them alive. When the thought form is of a loving, benevolent, beautiful nature it enriches the world.

So when the thought form is of a tyrannical deity who takes possession of the mind of men, this thought form continues to be stimulated. It stays alive.

'That's right, this is why it is so important to create thought forms which are not harmful to the Planet. The faithful through superstition and fear reinforce the thought forms of the past unaware of the workings of cosmic Law. The thought form of a potent deity nourished by the strong emotions of the devout endures; it lingers in the collective consciousness as indeed it has done. One tenacious thought form has dominated the world for a long time.

'How can we change this?

'By letting go of the old thought forms, by allowing them to die a natural death, by simply not feeding them! To survive thought forms require a constant supply of mental energy. Starve them of energy and they will dissipate! You were sent on this assignment to do just that! Fear is potent, it intensifies the thought form. Fear keeps man arrested at a point of perception well below his real potential. Fear handicaps the development of man's potential. So fear does two things, it feeds the thought form and delays man's progress. And humanity is not the wiser for it.

'If I understand man's fears feed the thought forms which have kept him entranced in this reality. They inhibit his mental progress because man lives in fear of the thought forms he creates and perpetuates. Only man can rescue himself by discarding the thought forms that keep him attached to the past and arrested at a lesser level of growth.

'Excellent Moses. Man can effect his own redemption by nurturing the nobler qualities of freedom, autonomy, creativity, individuality, meaning and purpose. These are liberating. This the Master meant when he uttered, 'Man hath the power to reverse the Fall's effects'. When man asserts his inner power, fear tends to disappear and the cause of fear vanishes.

'The cause of fear being his use of mental power to construct thought forms?

'In times of cataclysmic events, such as the sinking of Atlantis and the destruction of humanity, the few families who escaped the catastrophe reverted back to the cult of their primeval gods.

'Did Yahweh have something to do with both the destruction of Atlantis and the rescue of Noah?

'No, humanity had anticipated the fall of Atlantis, they knew that dark times were approaching, but it was Yahweh who received thanks for the rescue. You know with humans, someone has to be blamed and someone has to be praised! The time will come when an awakened humanity will see events for what they are.

'What are they?

'Events initiated by man himself, outcome of causes long forgotten. In the case of Atlantis, the forces of materialism were becoming increasingly dominant. Apart from the Masters walking among humans, few resisted the incoming forces of materialism. Humanity had lost its way. And so, it is not illogical to imagine that Noah's family may have built an altar to implore the god of their remote ancestors. The more persistent the evocation, the more energised the thought-form.

'What makes man implore, evoke and plead?

'Desire! From the lowest desire for bodily gratification to the highest desire for liberation, the whole spectrum. Thought forms are constructed with mental substance and are projected in the astral plane. Personal thought forms fade away when man focuses on another desire. But when thought forms are internalised by the group, they become considerably more resilient and more enduring. They are then implicitly believed by the group and this belief in turn gives the thought added energy. A merry-go-round.

'Succeeding generations are indoctrinated into them, convinced that they emanate from the Source, when all the time they emanate from man himself.

'Yes. Collective thought forms make up the 'Great Illusion'.

'Our governing thought forms can be traced a long way back to a few individuals? Although thoughts are normally fleeting, when they are internalised by a group and repeated endlessly they stabilise and endure. They become a force to reckon with. Would you explain how Yahweh may be said to be a thought form?

'As already said thoughts energised by desire and will become forceful thought forms of the astral plane. Thoughts are things, they are living forms. They have a life of their

510

own and can create to a degree. Every time someone contacts the god thought-form he boosts its potency. It has an enticing feel because it is man's idea of Yahweh not Yahweh himself. It can deceive, swerve and digress you as indeed it has done down the ages.

'What makes us prone to this kind of 'creations'?

'A 6th Ray emotional disposition mixed, in some cases, with a 1st Ray strong will personality. A potent blend.

The sum of all thought-forms make up the 'Great Illusion'

'Emotions construct thought forms, confirms Moses enquiringly. And I was led to believe that it was our spiritual aspiration that inspired our lives!

'That's right. Thought forms are always born of desire and as such they are the product of man' s emotional nature, his desire for protection, for safety, for survival, for domination and so on.

'So if I understand, the thought form we call Yahweh is a response of our collective desire and is born of our astral-emotional nature?

'Through time, it was felt that all was well as the people were being kept in fear of the deity. This took centuries to achieve, but it seemed to be working, at least in exile! But the leadership failed to realise that the thought form had whipped up the emotional life of their people. They worked hard at safeguarding the thought form accentuating its permanent and absolute nature. Motivated by the will-to-power, they buttressed the form. The form dilated to the point that it stifled soul life and dimmed its light.

'We have taken these factors as signs of our spiritual excellence.

'That is not all. The actions of one impinge on all, in line with the cosmic Law of the interdependence of all things. Each part affects the whole, no one is an island, and no one lives in isolation, contrary to belief. Through them it was the whole of humanity that was caught in this vast web. The dominant thought forms of the Western world were assembled and energised long ago. As mankind tend to function emotionally, the thought forms endure with great dynamism. Modern humanity has a decreasing need for the dominant thought forms of the past; it has outgrown this phase of development. Mankind is growing into self-determination. The thought form known as the Father, reflects man's limited perception. Modern man is disengaging from the thought forms that hastened suffering. Modern Hebrew with the rest of evolving humanity is claiming back what is rightfully his. He is sensing his own soul; he is discovering how to function as his soul. The thought forms that lulled him into surrender are being peeled away, they are falling off like a dead skin. 'Incorrect knowledge is based upon perception of the form and not upon the state of being' taught Patanjali.

'This applies to tangible forms and the forms we create with our mind?

'Absolutely. Let us consider a tangible form, a lion for instance. You know the form of a lion. What does the form suggest?

'Power, beauty, savagery, mastery, movement and stillness.

'Exactly. So a painter who toils with the idea of power and savagery, movement and stillness might draw the form of a lion. His idea becomes form and we visit museums to admire the form that his idea has taken. It is the 'idea', the 'core', the essence, the germ in the form that is the reality and as you know all beings be it a worm, a lion, a flower or a weed are evolving towards greater expression.

'Are you saying, Master that it is the 'core' hidden in the form and revealed by the form that is the crucial factor?

'It is the reality, the core 'idea' that shapes and dictates the form. The same applies to doctrines and theories; they too are ideas in form. The 'idea' of the creative power in the universe becomes the Father. It is easy to relate to the thought form of the 'Father' we all have a father, many have a painful memory of their fathers, too.

'We approximate, we translate the idea which is abstract into a form that we can handle.

'Exactly Moses. The soul, the Son, infiltrates reality. Only the soul has an all-encompassing grasp of the real, the 'idea'. At the heart of all things slumbers the essential 'atom', the life that shapes the form and sustains the form. I invite your comments.

'If the soul alone penetrates the essence of all things, thought forms created by generations, by nations, races and groups are unreal. They are framed by the human mind, not sensed by the soul. The idea of the Father is a human creation and as such it is unreal.

'Excellent Moses my son, I delight in your progress! As you pointed out thought forms created by all human groups add up to the 'Great Illusion', mighty structure that governs generations and entire nations.

'These thought forms moulded by the self and not by the soul have no real foundation. They are shadows; they have no more substance than rainbows.

'Man holds on to his creations, says Sanaka. The more illusory the form the more he tightens his grip. From the moment he creates it he is tied to it.

'I know, sighs Moses with mounting sadness, I too was hooked on a shadow, the more I felt despondent the more I was clinging to it; it was my salvation. It was in fact my downfall.

'And do you know why, asks Sanaka with understanding?

'The thought forms I was clinging to were the creation of the human ego, not of the soul. These thought forms were held together by the desperation of generations in the illusory hope that all would be well in the end.

'Why do they survive when they are only the figment of the imagination? As human creations they are transient and should melt away. But they are held together by man's emotional energy which feeds them. Thought forms need energy to survive, they cannot survive of their own.

'What is the way forward?

'A climb from emotional response to rational questioning. It is the soul which grasps the 'idea', the concealed life 'germ'. You recall how Michelangelo grasped the 'idea' of David in the stone. As man grows in reason and knowledge the mental pictures of his own imagination dissipate. The abstract mind relates to the soul. Rational man no longer feeds the images of the group or the nation. And the collective thought forms no longer have a hold on him.

Form, emotion and illusion

'I like the analogy with the dead skin falling off, interrupts Bendavid. Patriarchy, theology and dogma were the human response to the apocalyptic Age of the Ram. Tradition emphasised the irrational, the unproven; it kept mankind anchored in the astral which the Tibetan call 'glamour' or illusion.

'As workers of the Hierarchy we have the task to 'bring light into dark places' in the words of the Tibetan, says Jeremy. Our work is closely related to that of the Hierarchy who are involved in dissipating the astral/emotional plane of illusion. Humanity has been captive to its ability to shape the unreal. Our work in association with the Hierarchy is to dissolve the world of illusion.

'Form is illusion, as the Tibetan reminds us 'all illusions have a form of one kind or another', quotes Bendavid who read the Tibetan avidly.

'The form our people have been shackled with is the most persistent, the most intricate, the most obscure illusion, concludes Clara. The task of all who have chosen to incarnate in the Jewish condition is to dispel the grip of the world of illusion.

'The great avatars came to bring light, explains Tara. Light is a metaphor for wisdom and knowledge. The Egyptian god Hermes used 'light' when he taught in the Temples of Initiation. Krishna was the 'bringer of light' and Buddha is known as Lord of Light. Their task was to 'enlighten' mankind. They endeavoured to reawaken in man the memory of his limitless inner power and his role in his own salvation.

'Mankind has been lured by form for always, reflects Jeremy. Were Adam and Eve enlightened? Were they aware of the reality underlying the diversity of forms around them? It would seem not, they were dazzled by the world of form around them. As Eve opens her eyes to the fact of duality emotions creep in. Morality enters the human experience with good & evil, right & wrong. Moral choices sneak in and as Eve struggles to make sense of it all, she leaves us a legacy of desire, longing, fear and tension which continues to torment our lives and limit our horizon. Like Eve we have not as yet resolved the conflict of duality, nor have we realised that the whole thing is a mighty prank, a hoax the Divine played on himself and that we are party to it; we accepted to play the game. The Divine could not do it without us.

'That was not the way patriarchy saw it, replies Bendavid. Don't forget it is patriarchy which recounts the myth of Adam and Eve; it is patriarchy which curses Eve and imposes morality on the road to salvation. Patriarchy which harps on morality is deceived by the outer form of all things, believing them to be real and solid, unaware that underlying the diversity of forms is the one reality, unformed, uncreated, and intangible. Patriarchy in charge of the moral direction of mankind, its head buried in the sands, unable to see the wood for the trees; the blind leading the blind!

'Patriarchy will never resolve the conflict of duality, never lift the veil and will go on cursing Eve and upholding morality, concludes Clara. Look at the state of the world today! Chaos reigns in many regions of the Planet, not surprisingly they are governed by patriarchy, morality, duality and the Fall! But patriarchy and monotheism are exhaling their last breath. The last scream of the moribund, hence the mayhem everywhere copiously flaunted on our television screens. Back to Moses and Sanaka, I would like to hear more. The reading resumes.

'Sanaka touches on the issues of desire, longing and attachment, announces Bendavid who reads: 'Moses, what are the implications of duality, quite apart from seeing the world split in two halves, asks Sanaka with his luminous smile?

'I assume that with duality there is division and conflict, inevitably. The one has become two. A hint is given in the legend of Abel and Cain who symbolise good and evil. Cain must kill his brother, not realising that the destruction of one would precipitate the destruction of the other. The entire universe is built on duality, rejecting one half is recklessness said Buddha.

'Interesting, Moses, smiles Sanaka, you arrived at a brilliant realisation and you are not a scientist! There is more implied in the point you just made.

'You are teasing me Master.

'Look back on your religious life, to a feature of it.

'The preoccupation with duality amounts to an obsession. The world is neatly divided up in two portions. One half is superior and laudable, the other is not. We passionately hold on to the half we value, we are that half and we denigrate the other half. We impart to our half qualities and merits we deny the other half. I would say passion, attachment, longing, irrational perception not founded on verifiable evidence?

'Well analysed Moses. This is the stance of the adept who is a rationalist in as much as he analyses his observation and motives and refuses to be hoodwinked by emotions. Patanjali denounces attachment in the next Sutra, 'Non-attachment is freedom from longing for all objects of desire, earthly or traditional, here or hereafter'.

'Longing is the key, notes Moses. Emotional reactions keep us trapped in duality. The self becomes our jail keeper.

'Excellent Moses. Passion is of the self, passion is of the man trapped in Samsara, ensnared in Maya. On the other hand, the control of passion is of the Master. 'Passionless is the consciousness of being Master on the part of one who has rid himself of thirst for either seen of revealed objects'.

'We are a long way from this, laments Moses. Every verse, every ritual, every dogma, every precept induces more desire, generates more longing, arouses more passion. It is as if our ancestors wanted us entrapped in duality!

'They wanted you caught up in the world of belief, and belief is of the emotions, of the astral nature, the world of form. Form as we discussed earlier has no real purpose of itself, it is the idea it expresses that is the meaning. The purpose of the form is to force us to seek the underlying idea. With you it is the form that swallows up all.

'There is nothing other than form.

'You are the great builders of form, the great advocates of form. Your robust and enduring 'tradition' is made up of forms. Thought forms create the vast 'forest of delusion', erected by human notions about the nature of God, heaven, hell, the origins of the universe, the redeeming role of your people and so on.

'What causes men to identify with form almost to the exclusion of all else?

'We have discussed this. The soul came into incarnation millions of years ago to immerse itself into matter. Samsara and Maya were the controlling forces. The soul was imprisoned in what the philosopher, the theologian and the scientist grapple with. For a considerable time during the course of evolution the soul has equated with the world of form. Only a few initiates and mystics were and are able to go beyond form and enter the world of reality.

'Is advancing humanity better equipped to sense the world that lies beyond the senses?

'Paradoxically yes, the scientific method of investigation and rational enquiry will expand the mind and as men become more questioning, the old thought forms that have held mankind in captivity will begin to fall away. Theology, prejudice, fanaticism and religious belief unable to hold on to the vanishing thought forms on which they are built will gradually dissolve. This, the Bhagavad-Gita anticipates, 'When thy soul shall pass beyond the forest of delusion, thou shall no more regard what shall be taught or what has been taught'.

'Is all that is taught necessarily negative?

'No, what is negative is the reliance on words, these hold mankind in thraldom.

'So it is through the expansion of mind that contact with the soul is possible?

'Exactly. The Hierarchy is actively engaged in this project. The more advanced will expose the individuality, the atom of life or the soul within the form. The soul in the form is referred to as the Son of Mind. And mind is beckoning humanity. Humanity is poised to take a major Initiation.

'So science and philosophy will usher in the Age of Man, the Age of the Soul?

'Yes, does that surprise you? Should ignorance and bigotry take care of it? You know what Patanjali has to say about ignorance? 'Ignorance is the condition of confusing the permanent, the pure, the blissful with that which is impermanent, impure, painful'. Moses I invite your comments.

'Patanjali sums up the plight of the Jewish condition, indeed the plight of the human condition! The permanent is the Self, the deathless aspect of man, whereas the impermanent is the mortal self, the lower nature of man in incarnation.

'Quite right Moses, but do go on.

'Ignorance is the mode of perception that does not differentiate between the real and the unreal. Those who relate to Maya - matter, space and time - live in ignorance. They do not know the difference between the real and the unreal; they take appearances to be real.

'Excellent Moses. You summed up the plight of mankind! Are they entirely to blame for this?

'This goes a long way back to the decision of the soul to incarnate in matter to emerge out of it in the end. It goes further back still to the decision of the Source to incarnate in matter and struggle to return to the light in the end.

Again is Yahweh a thought-form?

'It is time we ask Sananda about the nature of Yahweh, suggests Clara, Jeremy could we have a moment with Sananda?

'I don't see why not, smiles Jeremy. Looking at the three guests, 'what about you, have you ever attended a channelling session?

'No, replies Bendavid, but we heard about channelling when we were in the United States and India and always wanted to sample it. This is our opportunity; please go ahead, we'll sit to the back and just experience.

They quiet down, Jeremy closes his eyes. All is silence. They wait for Sananda to speak: 'Welcome, begins Sananda, you may ask your question.

Clara is feeling uneasy at having been overheard. She realises that Sananda is in his own words 'always here'. She also knows that the Masters listen to group exchanges, because out of these discussions is emerging the 'new civilisation' as the Tibetan put it. Nevertheless she feels nervous, 'Master Sananda, is Yahweh a thought form hovering over the Planet or is he an integral part of the consciousness of humanity? A dynamic force within the collective psyche of humanity? I know that human beings, not just the

Jews, have strands of his DNA. Is he a thought form stalking humanity, more so the Jewish people? Has he acquired a living force of his own?

'More than that Yahweh 'is'! All gods exist as more than thought forms. They may primarily be experienced on the Earth plane as thought forms rather than real beings but nevertheless they all exist, in some dimension or other and certainly Yahweh exists as more than just a thought form. What is quite true and perhaps lies behind your question is the way in which a shared belied system among any group of people will tend to generate its own energy, which may or may not be closely related to the origins of that energy. In the same way that people know very little about the man Shakespeare, but every one has some idea about what Shakespeare was like. On a small scale this is the same sort of phenomenon.

'So if I understand, Yahweh exists as a living entity but he is also a thought form – an energy form - in the sense that he is constructed by the collective psyche. He was first perceived as a merciless god. But when the Planet returned to a more quiescent state and the threat of destruction was lifted, Yahweh was gradually perceived as more benevolent, less physical, more 'divine'. And since Talmudic times he has been increasingly built into that 'divine' being. He was acclaimed 'Lord of the World', he is hailed daily as the Holy Bless he Be.

'That's right'.

The meeting continues with more questions focussing on the nature of thought forms, a topic that fascinates Clara.

Yahweh & the Nefilim

'Our tradition has alienated us from Gaia the living Earth and distanced us from natural law, reflects BarYohai, the biologist. Gaia is a living organism. In Jewish tradition man exists almost independently of Earth, this is a fallacy, man is of Earth, he is made of all the elements and chemicals found on the Planet. Further more what affects Earth affects him, biologically all organisms are influenced by their environment. From time immemorial biology and environment have interacted, this principle lies behind the whole process of evolution. The Hebrew is no different, whatever his claims to the contrary. The world is 'split' into two parts: the first is the physical world with demonstrable laws, the world of scientific evidence that our tradition dismisses. The second is the metaphysical arena where oddballs know all the things that make God kick! But if we dismiss natural law, can we ever hope to know the mind of the originator of that law? Childish arrogance! We reject the scientific study of physical law preferring instead to lock our minds in 'revealed' texts!

'We do rather badly in both, replies Shemtov. What do we grasp of this revelation, the shell? In the end we know nothing. We have deciphered neither the secrets of nature nor the secrets encrypted in the 'revealed' texts. Only a few scholars, the select few, have ventured into the 'mysteries' and they have kept them secret, shielded from the masses! The masses were denied the real knowledge; they make do with the shell.

'To this day, snaps Bendavid, the faithful regurgitate the deeds of the Nefilim and mull over their achievement; this is their 'occupation', 'Avodah'. This 'occupation' overrides duty to country, economic activity, human relations and concern for the Planet. Collectively we esteem not the discovery of laws but their neglect.

'Ignorant of the universe yet subject to its laws, scornful of the world yet reliant on the world, mocking of the world yet casualties of the world, this is true piety! Ignorance is virtuous, notes Shemtov.

'Floating corks on stormy seas, virtuous, retorts Bendavid? Virtue to live and die at the hands of others? Virtue to expect the worst yet decline to prevent it? Virtue to evoke supernatural help yet insist on being powerless? An amazing paradox, we appeal to cosmic forces to make us extraordinary and indestructible yet our passivity makes us the most vulnerable, the most brittle, the most insecure, the most threatened group on Earth.

'As a scientist I see the tragic irony of it all, says BarYohai, the gods had vast knowledge of science and technology, they were master geneticists, explorers, engineers and builders. They used advanced weapons systems to defeat their opponents, weapons of such destructive potential that the Star War project is almost feeble in comparison. Yet the master scientists refused us the right to know! 'Thou shall not eat of the fruit of Knowledge of Good & Evil'. They were saying in effect, 'let us keep these inferior creatures, this slave labour force in the sleep of ignorance. They must never awake'.

'And they haven't, they are still asleep the sleep of ignorance, responds Clara. Regimentation, uniformity, servile practice, unthinking servitude are deemed virtuous. The ultimate in spirituality!

'Have they not come to realise that they are conditioned by fear? They have been around since Neolithic times, exclaims Tara?

'You may ask, replies Shemtov. Those who proudly wear the 'yoke' keep their children shielded from knowledge. Knowledge is an act of rebellion against the deity, knowledge is 'profane', scorned and defiled. They believe that the sun turns around the Earth; they recount the biblical legend of Joshua as undeniable proof! The irrefutable findings of astronomy are irrelevant!

'The Sumerians who received their civilisation from the Nefilim had a vast knowledge of astronomy and all other branches of science, reminds Clara.

'Tragic irony, grumbles Bendavid. The Old Testament is a condensed version of the Sumerian Scriptures. We have venerated the digest and discarded the original. We cast off the information to frolic with the fables! As a result of this confusion their children, deprived of an education, read stories. Deception and self-deception!

'The wavelength of piety beats the Yahweh-force into the energy field of Earth, injuring the Planet further. Earth was intended as a laboratory for the cosmic Mind to explore his own nature and the created world. As Sananda explained the All That Is incarnates in order to experience what it is like to be both 'Creator' and created', to ask questions and find out answers, comments Clara.

'World mythologies narrate mighty wars fought in the skies, begins Bendavid who has a special interest in ancient Near East civilisations. A cosmic Armageddon fought out in space between stellar civilisations. The Nefilim were probably involved in the primeval 'Star Wars'. If so were their motives altruistic or self-directed? Based on the Sumerian account, it would seem that survival and exploitation of Earth resources were their prime motives. I see the episode of the Serpent in a novel way. The Serpent, symbolic depiction of Wisdom, is 'personalised' to make man aware of his cosmic power.

'But the entwined serpent is also the symbol of the double-helix DNA and it is the symbol of medical science, adds BarYohai.

'I agree, replies Johansson delighted, I arrived at this. Like you I see the Serpent as the voice of reason against tyranny, as the light of knowledge against bigotry.

'Down the ages the Masters have come to advance human evolution. They visited Earth in ancient times to awaken primitive humanity. They gave the Old Testament to effect an 'awakening' as Master Sananda told us. The Nefilim encouraged apathy, inertia and stagnancy.

'We are externally-directed, notes Bendavid, we seek protection, we expect guidance, we demand direction, we want directives, we need to be told what to believe, what to do and how to do it. We expect the outside world to inform, command, direct, protect, judge and punish us. We gaze 'out there' as we long to be extricated from our predicament.

'And our predicament stems precisely from gazing 'out there', from being 'externally-directed', notes Clara. We are 'in' the world and 'of' the world. We are passive receivers and sorrowful recipients. And the world knows this.

'This is the opposite of Eastern Wisdom, remarks Tara. Buddha exhorted 'Be a light onto your own feet'. Krishna urged to quit relying on outside forces. Both endorsed self-reliance, self-knowledge, self-direction and self-mastery. In other words they encouraged man to be inwardly-directed. Then and only then can man achieve 'that unshakable deliverance of the mind, the object of the holy life, its essence, its goal.'

'Our tradition broadcasts the opposite, so our chances of becoming 'inwardly-directed' are remote. The new Pharisees who scour the world in search of 'lost' Jews want to keep us un-awakened a while longer, reflects Clara.

'It is the ego that plunges us into trouble, the ego that refuses to awaken, the ego that screams for external help. To get out of our misery we must look to the soul, our own guiding light, suggests Jeremy.

'We lack a spiritual philosophy of life, comments Bendavid, the spiritual philosopher. We have a blunt, spiritless, uninspired body of prescriptions. The paradox is that while ensuring our survival these have obstructed our progress. So we have an odd situation which defies natural law: survivalism but no evolution!

'Time is running out for the aficionados of the extraterrestrial gods, says Clara with relief. The universe is transmitting high frequencies of light charged with encoded information to help us remember who we were before the Fall. We are emerging from the dark ages of religious dogma which has paralysed us into capitulation.

Religious materialism

'The dead can not pray God', laments the Psalmist, 'Nothing that descends into the silence can pray God'. Strange statement from those loyal to the one god, the one variant of reality, the one fragment of the truth, ponders Sanaka. Why can the dead not pray God?

'Because they are dead! Death is final. Nothing survives physical termination; the ancestral god is the god of life, not death. His precepts and commands are for living life in physical form.

'And what about life in non-physical form, asks Sanaka? That was the age of David, the biblical age, one in which man was aware of mortality and the tyranny of form. An abyss separates man and god. David is grappling with a paradox: god is immortal, but man is mortal. Yet man is created in the image of god, is he not?

'God exists 'out there' not incarnate 'in all life forms'. Man's isolation is inescapable. The relationship is unequal and so man laments his earthly fate, his mortal condition.

'So man in material form can pray god, man in ordinary consciousness! What about man in a meditative state or in the dream state or in out -of-body state? In the inner silence he is free to examine the depth of his own being, encounter his spirit in the Temple 'not built by hands'. Within his body man holds the power, mystery and wonder of the entire universe! God stars and Planets all are present in infinitesimal form in man.

'God and Satan both lodge under the same sign, man. Man is the dwelling place of everything, it seems.

'He certainly is. Remember that man is made in the image of God and like God he is multifaceted. Duality is outside and inside man. All that exists outside man also exists within man. Talmudic literature - heroic metaphor for man's entrapment in physicality - exalts man in ordinary consciousness.

'I never looked at it in this light. So David reminds us that death is final, that we are doomed, that we are captured in matter and that there is no way out!

'Yes, but this limited view was dealt a severe blow. The invisible walls of the Talmud were exposed to three major assaults: the first breach was made by Moses de Leon with his Kabala. Medieval Spain was a ferment of spiritual life, a Golden Age of thought under the lead of the Sufis, brilliant scholars. They taught philosophy, mysticism, science, mathematics, poetry and the intellectual Jews of the time absorbed all this wealth. Kabala was the outcome.

'I thought that Kabala could be traced back to the Wisdom of the East.

'Certainly, continues Sanaka, there is only one Spiritual Law and it is given all over again at the beginning of each age, it feels original and novel because it appears in the idiom of the time. The Masters who revisit Earth do so to present afresh the Spiritual Law from which all religions branch out.

'The second breach to the absolute authority of the Talmud?

'…was made by the Baal Shem Tov, continues Sanaka. He did not try to conceal his simplicity; he also was a gifted psychic. Untrained in the spiritual method, he engaged in meditative feats with the startling outcome you know.

'In trance states, unguided, he wandered through the astral world where he claims to have seen the King of the World, or at least His throne. This 'vision' was muddled by claims of having talked to Lord Maitreya. The legend woven around the Baal claims that Maitreya revealed that He was about to return to Earth to save 'His People'! 'Buddha Maitreya coming back to save the few and dispose of the many, reacts Sanaka? These wild claims were ingested uncritically.

'He launched his followers on endless wanderings in search of Jewish souls to redeem.

'Or hoodwink! This unsophisticated man who meandered unguided in the astral world did grasp some profound truths though, reflects Sanaka. He caught a glimpse of the real being, he hinted at the deathless nature of man. He grasped a truth that was ground-breaking for the time: God needs man and God, like man, is evolving. God relies on man to learn and explore the world. These were revolutionary ideas…

'Too revolutionary for the followers of the Gaon of Vilna, replies Moses. Things changed after the initial period of exaltation. The initial vibrant mood faded away. His message of liberation drowned in the morass of the law tightening its noose around the masses.

'The Haskala movement caused the third breach in the walls of Talmudic law, continues Sanaka. Not surprisingly this progressive movement met with disapproval from all parties.

'Better the devil you know than the devil you don't' as the saying goes.

'Indeed, it was a brave attempt to unfetter the mind. They had the boldness to push away the boundaries that had kept their people prisoners of fear. Fear obstructs the flow of vital energy, fear imprisons, and fear inhibits human potential. Fear contracts, restrains and restricts.

'Fear of freedom is our governing characteristic.

Religious materialism - group discussion

'This dialogue calls for further probing, butts in Clara. The idea of a god separate from man, a god who denies man immortality, an unchanging god existing outside our Solar System who manipulates the laws of nature to defeat mankind to benefit the few, is the pivot of our tradition.

'A physical god who conversed with humans and walked among men, corrects Bendavid. At the time of the Deluge, his disappearance gave rise to the belief that he had become eternal. He had joined the ranks of the immortal gods.

'So a physical god becomes discarnate and immortal, says Shemtov. His negligence and cruelty endear him. Our creed is undignified if only because it negates man's reason and an innate sense of idealism and decency. It decries the advanced cultures which recognised the primacy of the soul, the ancient Egyptians, Essenes, Gnostics and Sufis. Our religious materialism will be evoked by future generations as one of humanity's more enduring aberrations, the worship of an illusion.

'Why not look upon it as a phase rather than an aberration, an important phase in the evolution of mankind, suggests Jeremy always reasonable.

'Our inherited materialism is being eroded by the realisation that matter is not as solid as it appears, replies the physicist Shemtov. The universe for Einstein was not a solid mass of dense matter, but a vast sea of pulsing energy, a 'field'; he arrived at this from two opposite avenues, the scientific theorising and the mystical insight.

'To grasp the nature of the world using scientific method is quite something, but to know it intuitively is something else, marvels Johansson.

'To the Buddhist the gods are barriers to liberation, contributes Tara. Buddha refused to be drawn into theological debate because it is of the intellect. The intellect is of the self and does not reflect personal experience, really knowing. Reality is to be grasped profoundly, directly and holistically. One experiences reality by going beyond the arguing mind. All the pretentious treatises on the nature of God joggle with words. A lot of hot air!

'Mystics and Quantum physicists explain that as we look deep inside matter we perceive it as it truly is, as energy vibrating, as light, living light, says Jeremy. Thought is an electrical impulse between brain cells. Our thoughts, ideas and concepts are electrical connections, energy connections.

'What are the implications for the work we do, asks Tara?

'If brain cells communicate by electrical signals, if thoughts are electrical pulses, indeed if life functions are electrical in nature, then where do we see differences, separation and opposites, replies Jeremy? The same applies to good and evil; one no longer sees them as a pair of opposites, but as expression of our mental activity, a force generated by the brain.

'Are you saying that thought and life itself are no more than electrical exchanges, this sounds like the deterministic science we are leaving behind, says Shemtov concerned!

'I am saying that thought, life and soul stem from the same field of energy, the original Word. 'In the beginning was the Word and the Word was with God and the Word was God'. This is no determinism. Figuratively God stands for pure creative energy. With the abstract 'Word' light came into existence. Light is the nature of the Divine and the building block of the universe. Light is energy.

'You got us worried for a moment, admits Shemtov.

'I am no materialist, laughs Jeremy. With the realisation that everything is energy then duality loses its power, it releases its grip on us. Duality, the axis around which the Judeo-Christian tradition revolves is dissolving. If everything is energy then duality is an illusion. Dualism, the theory that in any domain of reality there are two independent underlying principles – mind/matter, form/content - is a kind of optical illusion. Dualism is like a mirage in the desert, a rainbow after the storm, it has no reality. Realising the illusory nature of duality, it fades away. Dual pairs blend into unity, as two aspects of the same thing which are different only in our perception. Mystics have recognised that all is mind, all is consciousness, there is no matter, no duality, underlying all is the one undifferentiated unity.

'That's right, notes Shemtov, holistic science is advancing towards a unifying theory which will include all known energies, a 'theory of everything'.

'What applies to man and nature applies to the All too, muses Clara. If all life is energy pulsating, then it follows that the Originator of this life is energy. There is no physical god; the Logos is pure thought, pure energy. He is 'everything-ness' and 'nothingness' as Sananda put it.

'Sananda also said that figuratively the Father stands for the immobility and unchanging nature of the world, echoes Jeremy. The Hebrews ingested the views of the ancient world. These views were impressed upon them by the necessity of exile and the inevitability of the law of evolution.

'Exile is dictated by the law of Evolution, enquires BarYohai?

'Adversity, personal and collective, is dictated by evolution, explains Bendavid. The soul seeks to explore, to experience, to know, to grow, to evolve and to express itself. Both personality and soul look to the same outcome. Where there is reluctance to let the soul learn and grow, trouble ensues. One way of softening our hardened shell is exile. We hate it, curse it, bemoan it, yet we precipitate it.

'How all this links up to the Father, asks Tara who feels no attraction for the subject? She advocates the return of the Goddess.

'Stagnancy, solidity, immobility and an unchanging state of affair. This is what the Father-image symbolises, explains Levinson. The mythological Father is both matter and the creator of matter.

'It is bizarre, notes Shemtov, that having lived through the 'Plagues' of Egypt, the earthquake and volcanic eruption at Sinai we should go for a Father-idea that stands for the unchanging nature of the world. The world had changed; it had been turned upside down! Our ancestors witnessed the laws of physics being blown apart; they beheld the random nature of the universe. The universe was unstable and unpredictable. Earth has had a turbulent geological history. Yet we uphold a stable universe and a stable god!

'In pre-psychological times, that was 'magical' thinking, notes Johansson.

'The Sumerians were versed in astronomy and other sciences.

'Are you suggesting that for the Hebrews and other ancient people, God and nature are one, asks Clara?

'Egyptians and Sumerians were astronomers. They observed the elegant workings of the universe and inferred that the perfect laws of nature were divine, that an Intelligence was at work behind them. And so the idea of the Father and natural law fused.

'It seems that the Father has two personas, distinct yet complementary.

'That's right, continues Shemtov, for us the Father is the absolute master of the universe who manipulates the laws of nature to destroy his enemies and benefit the few. The trouble is that he also destroys his 'Children'. Be it blunder or intent, his unpredictable behaviour spells out insecurity for man. The universe is no longer a secure place founded on constant natural law. It is subject to the personal whims of a destructive god who in the process of destroying his enemies will also destroy his 'Children'.

'The Father is neither reliable nor predictable, says Clara. What about his other role?

'In his fatherly role the Father stands for patriarchy, says Bendavid. A male god implies a male social order. Immobility becomes a male_attribute reflected by the entire social group. So patriarchy as a social system must be bolstered to ensure its continuation, and the outlines between god, matter, creation and social order become blurred.

'A fascinating interpretation. I like it, says an elated Clara.

'It is. Things become more complicated as time goes on, continues Bendavid, the Tibetan stresses that the older a religious belief the more confusion and anomalies creep in. Time is no guarantee of authenticity, quite the opposite. We tend to pride ourselves of the great age of our religion, when we should feel troubled and sceptical precisely because of its great age.

'Quite right, replies Shemtov! Confusion sets in and the Father becomes the Creator. The Father in Hebrew mythology is changeless, unmoving, unwavering. He is the symbolic projection of the Hebrews' idea of matter. Matter appears solid, changeless and immutable. The solidity of matter is mirrored by the solidity of man.

'So now both the world and man are matter, concludes Clara!

'It was taken a step too far! An elegant and coherent cosmos that filled the ancients with wonderment is perceived as random and threatening by us. And with good reasons. At Sinai, Earth was thrown into convulsion and plunged into darkness. To bind together a motley array of individuals bent on revolt, the rulers devised measures to smooth the rough edges of a resentful people who wanted none of the noble unifying principles of Moses.

'We have now the vital missing link, says Clara always in search of the nucleus. To defend the idea of 'chosenness' and transmit the genetic fabric of the Nefilim, the deity was granted power of creation and destruction.

'The Yahoo of the mountain as the Ancients called him?

'Possibly, replies Shemtov. Many strands to bind together here. Fear is the binding agent. Patriarchy and monotheism were born, in part, of the same need to bind. They would bind the newly established society. One god, one creation, one social group, all binding together. This has all the appearance of unification, but only the appearance! Our dream of unity eludes us as ever. As both Creator and Father, the local god becomes the binding force that holds the universe in absence of consistent physical laws. It is coherent really

'This is a fascinating interpretation, comments Johansson. The idea of the Father became outmoded and was laid to rest by another idea better adapted to changing times. The universe hates immobility, so a new view of the world emerged 2000 years ago. The world for Buddha and the Essenes was not solid, immobile or unchanging. They knew the world to be energy vibrating at a slow rate, light solidified, thought made visible.

'What are the implications for us, asks Clara again?

'As the nature of matter changes, the nature of the Creator of matter must also change. The unchanging solid matter – the Father – is replaced by a fluid, evolving world – the Son, explains Johansson.

'Kafatos, a Quantum physicist, adopts a similar line of thought, expands Shemtov. He draws a parallel between particle physics and the ancient biblical allegory. The Father can be likened to the particle located in space and the Son to the wave that spreads outward. The Father symbolises the stability and inertia of matter. So we have stability and movement, inertia and fluidity. The dualism that has made up our reality is vanishing: in Quantum physics particle-wave exist simultaneously. Duality dissolves into unity.

'Stability and movement, inertia and fluidity exist at the same time. As with Einstein, this has implications for us, insists Clara. Are you saying that when polarity dissolves what is left is unity?

'You hit the nail on the head! The dissolution of dualism in physics leads the modern mystic Paul Brunton to quote the enigmatic phrase 'I and my Father are One', replies Jeremy.

'This phrase infuriated the rabbis of Jerusalem, they shouted 'blasphemy'.

'This phrase graphically challenged their view of reality, it was so unsettling that they resorted to violence, says Shemtov. The fusion of opposites - locked as they were in dualism - was unimaginable. So, 2000 years ago the priesthood violently rejected any attempt to integrate Father and Son, stagnancy and becoming, immobility and movement.

'The dream of unity was vanishing into the distance. A dream to be realised not by man's intelligent quest, but by supernatural intervention, concludes Bendavid. By defending at all costs our dualistic stance, we missed out - and the world with us - on the chance of achieving unity. The dream of unification was projected outside on to an elusive 'Messiah'. It will be his job to achieve unification, we shrugged off our responsibility.

'The resolution of duality is being effected by science and by humanity in its quest for integration, rounds up Jeremy. Dualism is better understood as mankind is moving beyond polarity. Progressive man is his own Messiah. We are in sight of the law of Grace.

'Law of Grace, enquires Bendavid?

'Grace is the resolution of polarity, the grasp of unity, the recognition that there is no 'good & evil', just a field of energy, a field of consciousness.

'When we break free from religion we shall know liberation, winds up Clara.

'A paradox, notes Shemtov. Religion has always evoked spirituality and liberation; I am not defending it, mind you!

'Religion was a phase like teething is a phase in a child development.

'A reality, notes Clara. I agree with Tara it is a phase of development and as such stands in the way of liberation. I think that it turned into stone to prevent man from discovering his true nature. Let's face it, when man moves into the inner worlds to experience his universality and the I AM Presence, does he need rituals?

'It was Jung who said 'Religion is a defence against the religious experience', quotes Johansson.

'I go along with that, throws in Clara, I know from personal experience that religion stands as a dam, a hurdle. Had I said 'I want to meditate to encounter my true Self and meet the I AM' to those who had all the truth, they would have branded me a heretic. What would the clerics do if we came face to face with our real Self and with our divine connection? They fear the spiritual experience as one fears the unknown. We gave our souls to religion, like Faustus gave his soul to Mephistopheles in exchange for trifling pleasure.

'This is why we need a dramatic shift in awareness, we need to change the thought-forms, metaphors, symbolic imagery, paradigm and archetypes that have held true but which are now obsolete. We aim for nothing less than a spiritual revolution, states Bendavid. This is what we, as a Movement stand for. Long ago we internalised the Father-image never realising that it is a metaphor for power, immobility, immutability, solidity, density and stability. We have ingested the image of the 'Children', expression of man's helplessness and mortality. Our entire tradition is built around these two evocative images.

'Is this not another way of presenting natural law, suggests Shemtov?

We can read the Old Testament from the angle of the laws of physics: particle-wave, Father-Son. A giant metaphor to explain the laws of nature.

'Now you are going to study Torah, laughs Bendavid!

The Elohim

'As we are probing the nature of the Samsara gods, I would like to ask Sananda some clarification, suggests Clara whose inquisitiveness cannot be appeased. Never satisfied with achieving a specific goal, she keeps pushing the boundaries further.

'I was wondering when, laughs Jeremy, you have been quiet for a long time.

'I fret when I am quiet, replies Clara in the same mood.

'They sit in a circle silent and at rest, waiting for Sananda to speak. Sananda invites Clara to put her question:

'Master Sananda, I would like to search the Hassidic mind. Hassidic doctrine defines the Elohim as an aspect of the Divine. In Genesis Yahweh and Elohim are used interchangeably. Elohim is used in the singular as one entity rather than as a group consciousness.

'Yes, says Sananda inviting further questioning.

'I quote 'Elohim is the power that makes the world appear as through it exists naturally, independently, by itself'.

' Hum!

'It is interesting, mutters Clara.

'It is, isn't it, laughs Sananda!

'Hassidic doctrine equates the Elohim with the immutable laws of nature? Why should it be the Elohim and not Yahweh, he is given every other role and function, why not this one?

'The Elohim were given a special role which was - to put it simply with some risk of oversimplification - the role of creating your particular reality, your bit of the universe, if you like. Yahweh's role lies within these boundaries. It is a different role, a more localised role. The statement about the Elohim would be more true of them than of Yahweh, although both have come to be seen as somewhat interchangeable. The original purpose was not to assimilate them, identify one with the other or have them merge into one. Indeed that is the reason why different names are used, because they are different beings. But overtime a certain amount of confusion and uncertainty has moved in and so a tendency to confound both the Elohim and Yahweh, to fuse them simply because they are seen as both forms of divine energy and so there is a tendency to lose the differentiation between the two.

'Did the Elohim have a hand in the creation of the universe or only in the creation of the 'beingness' of man?

'In a sense, yes, but it would perhaps be more true to your understanding to give them a role within the created universe, rather than as creators of the universe. In the form that is the Elohim they would not be seen as the creators of the cosmos. In other words, if you look at it in historical terms you would say that the universe was created first and then the Elohim came along as part of that Creation and in turn did some creating themselves. So if you were looking at it from a historical perspective, this would be a more accurate way of seeing it. But of course time itself is very much part of your particular experience, of your particular reality, your bit of the universe; time as you understand it anyway. And so we are talking about something which is beyond your particular universe in terms of your universe! It is like describing the sun as being like an orange. Yes, in some ways the sun is like an orange, but the analogy of the orange has severe limitations in describing what the sun is like!

'If I understand, we describe a cosmic reality using analogies, images and theories that apply only to our reality. This idea does not apply anywhere else in the universe, it is specific to Earth, it represents our level of understanding, our grasp of reality, it corresponds to our degree of evolution. As man advances, his ideas and images advance.

'Exactly.

'So the belief held by the doctrinaires that their Revelation is universal is flawed. The Old Testament has no relevance to the rest of the world and is very much a localised affair; for this reason it is irrelevant.

'Some would agree with this conclusion, other would not, for their gaze is very much turned to the past and they feel that because the revelation was sanctioned by the Divine and stepped down through intermediaries it is here to stay and cannot change, replies Sananda.

531

Samsara god

When thy soul shall pass beyond the forest of delusion, thou shall no more regard what shall be taught or what has been taught'. (Krishna)

The encounter with Sananda ended, reading resumes. The next chapter of The Hebrew Gods focuses on Samsara gods. Master Sanaka speaks: 'Extra-ordinary' man unaware of his soul becomes 'ordinary' man. He has fallen from being immortal to being mortal. He is now part of the natural order and subject to the laws of nature alongside the three lower kingdoms, the mineral, the vegetable and the animal. You are familiar with 'natural man'; smiles Sanaka ironically, tell me something about him.

'Natural man is subject to natural law. He does not transcend nature, he is part of nature, answers Moses feeling ill-at-ease.

'You miss a vital point, the Scriptures were given to 'natural man' to lift him above nature, continues Sanaka chuckling. What happened?

'To lift him above nature he was given rules of conduct, replies Moses, the conversation is becoming slippery.

'That's right, the moment he forgets his higher nature, man must be told what to do, he cannot be trusted. Fallen from immortality he is born sinful and his natural inclination is to do evil. So, the 'inspired' priesthood with its 'revealed' knowledge must dictate rules. And man no longer owns his mind and body. The plan that humbles man also invests in a god to keep 'ordinary' man under control. Man in his pitiful condition looks to the god he has conjured up and low-and-behold, what does he see? A god in his image: self-centred, wrathful, materialistic, unpredictable. A god not to tinker with. Ordinary man crafts an ordinary god endowed with ordinary human traits. To a Samsara man is born a Samsara god! Dazed, stunned, you fill your lives with drab, routine tasks. There is no time to confront the burning issues.

'What are the burning issues, asks Moses anticipating the response, yet wanting to hear it from the Master?

'Real issues such as, 'I am trying to discover the meaning of life? Do I sense the divine beauty in others or are they just lumps of flesh I despise? Have I taken my share of responsibility in the running of Creation or have I made the world more confused, more tangled, more ungainly for all? Have I stolen the joys of life from others because I wanted them to serve my god in the same desolate, dismal, insipid, prosaic manner? Is the world more ugly because of me?'

'That is only the first part?

'Our first Buddha came to guide mankind some 80,000 years ago. The last Buddha denounced the futility of religious practice; he taught that man alone is responsible for his salvation and no god can help him, why do you think he had no faith in the ability of the gods?

'Faith is not relevant to Buddha. Man has to progress by his own effort, he must rely on himself. Though Buddha recognised the existence of a gods' realm, he urged man to count on his own effort, not on external intervention.

'Why?

'Because for as long as he looks up to the gods man remains powerless, his development is arrested, he freezes in a pre-adult state in which his potentialities are never fulfilled.

'Excellent my son. Buddha realised that the gods are trapped in Samsara and need our help! Buddha was a contemporary of your religious reformers who waged total war against neighbouring lands. They thought their neighbours unworthy of life!' After a short silence, he turns briskly to Moses ..., tell me about God, you are the world experts on God, you have a special relationship with him. You know his mind better than you know your own minds!

Surprised and reticent Moses responds, words and images from the past flow, 'Hassidut is Divinity made comprehensible through human faculties. Hassidut brings the Godhead to perfect human comprehension'.

'Perfect comprehension of Divinity, chuckles Sanaka, with the human intellect, with the mortal self?

'Man can understand the 'intellect' of God and also the emotional attributes of God'.

'Understand the intellect of God and the emotions of God, chuckles Sanaka much to the embarrassment of Moses. This is news to me. The Masters of the Hierarchy understand neither the 'intellect' of God nor his emotions. I wonder if even the Elohim understand the intellect of God! Yet mortal man can gain 'perfect human comprehension of God'?

'At the end of time, when the Messiah comes, the aspect of Divinity which transcends nature will be revealed. This means that the name of God will be pronounced as it is written, continues Moses increasingly ill-at-ease.

'Interesting, tell me more, invites Sanaka much amused.

'Hava'ye - the Ineffable Divine name is unpronounceable. There are many names for God, but Hava'ye refers to God the Infinite, transcending Creation, the aspect of the Divine which brings everything into existence.

'Hava'ye is his name? He certainly has grown in stature since the days he walked in the Garden instructing Adam and Eve to 'go forth & multiply'! I wonder if the Sumerians would recognise their god!

'In the era of the Messiah, the name Hava'ye will be manifest throughout the entire world, continues Moses embarrassed.

'What muddle! Hassidut does not discriminate between the Infinite and a nature god yet it claims to have 'perfect human comprehension of God'? What derangement of the imagination turns a Samsara god into the Ineffable Creator?

'You did ask, mutters Moses.

'So his name will reverberate throughout the universe! The nature gods of India, Greece and Egypt were less flamboyant, less bold, and less arrogant. A nature god is a nature god! A nature god transcends nothing. A nature god is bound by the laws of nature.

Hassidic doctrine & the Samsara god – group discussion

'How about that, exclaims Clara! I did not know God had an intellect and even less that he had emotions! The next step of this unabashed romp? Hassidut is uniquely equipped to offer God psychotherapy to sort out his emotional problems!

'Amazing, inserts Jeremy. 'Hassidut is Divinity made comprehensible through human faculties'. Is Hassidut unadulterated Spiritual Law? If so how can it use the intellect, defective and inadequate to know the unknowable?

'More than that, remarks Bendavid, Hassidut claims to be the Source of that Law, the Creator!

'The arrogant stance of Hassidut is demolished by Quantum physics. Max Plank says about 'knowing' the universe, 'This world faces us with the impossibility of knowing it directly … It is a world whose nature cannot be comprehended by our human powers of mental conception.'

'Brahman is outside the range of any mental conception', quotes Bendavid, yet 'Hassidut is Divinity made comprehensible through human faculties'! Quantum physics and the Wisdom Knowledge of the enlightened East dismiss knowledge of the universe through mental powers, but the Hassid has absolute knowledge of Divinity and of the universe! It would be pathetic if it was not so serious, given that they implant this drivel in the mind of the Jews they seek to win over to their fantasy world.

'It gets better, exclaims Levinson, 'Hassidut brings the Godhead to perfect human comprehension'. 'Comprehension' is not good enough for the unabashed crowd-stirrer; it must be 'perfect'. A few aficionados who worship a Samsara god afflicted with human blemishes claim to know the mind of the Ineffable! They have 'perfect comprehension' of the Infinite!

'You share Sanaka's hilarity, notes Tara. The intellect is the instrument of the soul not the soul itself! Only the soul – fragment of the Divine – can apprehend the Divine, they are of the same nature, the same energy! Imagine a piece of chalk claiming to have 'perfect comprehension' of the mind of Einstein when he was writing his formulas!

'Meditation is the method used by spiritual seekers to by-pass human faculties, explains Shemtov. The intellect stands in the way of 'perfect comprehension' It is possible to sense the Divine through the intuitive, sensitive, holistic connection. Holism states that 'wholes' are greater than the sum of their parts. The intellect by its very nature is reductionist; it breaks down unity into parts. It is in the nature of the intellect to study the 'parts' and draw conclusion from that fragmentary, partial and disconnected approach.

'This fragmentary, partial and disconnected approach is that of the Talmudic tradition, echoes Bendavid. No holism for us, no perception of 'wholes', we break down the world into 'parts'. We are the originators of the intellectual line of attack and the scientific mode.

'The entire universe and everything in it is conceptually designated. The Sutras state that all these phenomena are designated by thoughts', quotes Tara. The same inevitably applies to 'absolute knowledge of the Divine', it is only an idea, it has no reality. Gen Lamrimpa goes on, 'The mere fact that something is conceptually designated does not necessarily indicate that it exists'.

'So Hassidut which breaks down the world has perfect comprehension of the 'Whole', exclaims Clara! Hassidut which deconstructs reality claims to know perfectly the totality! Everyone is entitled to flights of fancy, but with them the consequences are dire since they comb the world in search of unsuspecting Jews who may just fall for all that hocus-pocus!

'So Hassidut which claims to be 'Divinity made comprehensible through human faculties' is a non-starter, concludes Jeremy. The intellect conceptualises, it does not and can not apprehend Reality.

'All the mind's arbitrary conceptions of matter, phenomena and of all conceptions and ideas relating [to that] are like a dream, a phantasm, a bubble, a shadow' said Buddha, quotes Tara.

'What is the reality they apprehend, wonders Jeremy?

'A parallel reality! They are deceiving themselves. As they live 'a dream, a phantasm, a bubble, a shadow' they cause untold damage. Who will stop them?

Why does the Father pursue our elimination?

"If you forget the past, it will repeat itself" reminds Santayana, quotes Bendavid, an echo of the biblical behest, 'Remember Amalek'? Amalek and his warring horde attacked the Hebrews as they wandered aimlessly in the Desert, after losing their way.

'Potent symbolic meanings all around, notes Jeremy.

'And potent historical events, replies Bendavid who with his colleagues is well versed in the Scriptures. On three crucial moments in the history of the Planet, Yahweh sentenced us to near total annihilation. The first was the sinking of Atlantis documented in Genesis as the great Flood. The second at Sinai when the heaving, screeching, quaking Earth engulfed 98% of the Hebrews and more recently during World War 2, this you all know. Hence the perennial question 'why does Yahweh so persistently pursue our destruction?'

'Sanaka just said 'a nature god is a nature god! A nature god transcends nothing. A nature god is bound by the laws of nature', quotes Jeremy.

'Neither gods nor men transcend nature, replies Shemtov pensively. To revere a nature god is to revere matter. More to the point, to revere a nature god is to endorse our materiality.

'So the worship of matter is responsible for upheavals, asks Tara?

'The cataclysmic events may not have anything to do with gods or men, notes Jeremy. Why blame nature gods or natural man?

'You have a point, natural disasters are 'natural', why ascribe them to gods or men? The Planet has had a turbulent geological history, says BarYohai.

'When man gets entangled with Samsara gods, things get so muddled that he can't see his way out, the gods are blamed, man is blamed! Man caught up in Maya has lost his way back to the light, he strikes at all and sundry.

'Yet in his deluded state man claims to 'have perfect human comprehension of the Godhead', exclaims Clara. To each his thrill!

'The claims come from a sect vigorously anti-modernity, anti-liberalism, anti-knowledge, points out Levinson! A sect anchored in patriarchal authority and chained to things past. Yet they uphold the intellect as the royal road to 'know' God!

'They thrive on incongruity, replies Clara. This happens when mawkish religiosity governs, when intelligent enquiry is scorned, when any foggy notion is hailed as divinely inspired.

'A curious tendency I find disquieting, says Jeremy tentatively, of course I am an outsider, I lack the personal experience. This is what happens when human ideas take over; they must pass for divinely inspired. Whereas, when 'I & my Father are One' is known in experience, the ego is silenced.

'Figuratively the Father stands for the immutable nature of the universe; we know that the universe is energy. The Father also stands for transcendence. Man's true nature is cosmic energy, man is also transcendence as well as immanence, reflects Jeremy.

'I agree, remarks Shemtov. As I see it 'I & my Father are One' has nothing to do with any liturgical procedure. It has to do with the nature of thought, with the nature of energy. New physics explains that matter is energy in motion, that the entire universe is energy vibrating at a certain frequency. So thought is energy and just as it can create, it can also destroy. We have proved the workings of this primary law of physics throughout our tragic history. We are the living evidence of the law in action when the law has been ignored.

'I am going on a tangent here but this is also the domain of psycho-somatic medicine which recognises the role the mind plays in disease and in health, butts in Clara, a holistic therapist. This may seem alien to the topic at hand but it relates closely. We know that hypnosis and meditation can produce changes in our bodies. Directed thought can affect body cells. Thought which is energy can affect matter. 'I & my Father are One' as I see it means that we are gifted with the Father's awesome power to create. If I am One with the Father then 'I am the Father'! And so we all are the Father! This identity and affinity gives us the power to create. But it also gives us the power to destroy and this sadly humanity continues to do. More often than not we 'destroy' ourselves'; illnesses are evidence of this inclination. It was Jung who said that mental distress is a 'spiritual crisis'.

'So each crisis that marred our history was a 'spiritual crisis', an opportunity which the forces of life were throwing at us? If thought-energy can affect matter then a change in thinking would have mended our lives and restored our perception! We refuse to make the necessary changes that would extricate us from the clutches of illusion and suffering. 'We blow it every time! But there is something else, as we forget the awesome power of thought, we also forget our inherent capacity to self-create. We have taken to self-destroy instead!

'What have you forgotten, repeats Jeremy intently?

'We forgot that reality does not originate outside; it is generated in our electro-chemical brains, in the electrical activity of neurons, replies the physicist. It is futile to resist and resent the idea that the choices we make determine our life. We prefer to think that we are being manipulated by outside agencies.

'We create our own reality, quotes Jeremy. We create our own experience as Sananda tells us.

'With our thoughts we make the world', quotes Tara.

'We have been denied choice, snaps Bendavid. Choices are determined by others. To make choices is to affirm our innate creative abilities; these have been banned by tradition. But choices are determined by our point of evolution at any moment and not by outside agencies. We are back to our starting point: thoughts have the power to create just as they have the power to destroy. This is where we must start digging to get to the roots of our predicament. The thoughts of others have governed our lives down the ages with the destructive outcome we know.

'It is time we broadcast 'I and my Father are One'. Time we awaken to the realisation that it is the creative energy of thought that can transform our lives. Until now we have used the destructive energy of thought. We must effect a shift in consciousness, it is within our reach. There is nothing metaphysical about this, goes on Shemtov.

'The Masters encourage us to view a 'crisis as an opportunity', reminds Clara, in order to understand, to expand, to progress. What is evil? Evil is to have forgotten the lessons of the past that we never learnt because we refused to view a crisis as a possibility for change. If we regard a crisis as an act of fate rather than as an opportunity for change than we condemn the next generation to repeat the past. An act of love towards our children it is not!

'Evolution drives life inexorably. Ignorance of this inescapable law may be at the root of our predicament, reflects Bendavid. Arrested in the past, yearning for the past, we are resisting the forces of evolution and resisting the advance of humanity. So we linger in the past rather than focus on the present, we endorse redundant thought models, we reinforce inert notions, we bolster static thought-forms.

'Evolution of a peculiar kind, chuckles Clara. We perpetuate and expand the sweep of the Yahweh-force and we ensure the preservation of Yahweh's genetic material. These two factors may be our way of imagining evolution.

'I am not sure that the Hierarchy would agree with your definition of evolution, laughs Levinson. The Yahweh-force is definitely not what they seek to perpetuate and expand! It is this force that we, cosmic workers, came down to neutralise, undermine and dissolve.

'I am saying that we have our unique definition of evolution, replies Clara laughing. The fact that it does not correspond to the definition given by science, by the Hierarchy, by the Planetary Logos, by the universe, by the Divine or by humanity seems irrelevant, it is uniquely ours!

'Yahweh is more than a force that binds us in time, more than an adhesive that gives us cohesion, more than an admission of the materiality of man and the universe, more than a repository of genetic material. Yahweh is an idea, an ideology, a world-view, a way of thinking! This is what we are perpetuating, clarifies Bendavid.

'In so doing, intervenes BarYohai, we negate the forces of evolution built into life. In other words we infringe the law of the cosmos.

'Not what the doctrinaires want to hear, but certainly in conformity with cosmic Law, approves Levinson. The principle 'like attracts like' is universal and applies to the nature of our thoughts as it applies to all else. Going back to our original question 'why does the Father pursue our elimination' the answer is emerging into visibility: 'With our thoughts we make the world'.

'We are touching at reincarnation and the reasons that bring us back in a certain environment, spots Jeremy.

'It's all to do with the particular wavelength of our thoughts, the quality of our thoughts, comments the physicist. Those who are attached to inherited thought forms, attitudes and prejudices will find in the Jewish outlook their natural mental environment, like a fish its own water.

'This applies to the human race at large, replies Clara. Surroundings, family background, language, village, street, social group, country, all point to the real disposition of the individual, his temperament, his yearning, his desire, his needs, his natural attraction. The choice of environment can tell us a great deal about the forgotten past, the hidden disposition of the individual.

'The psychologists of the future will study these variables to sketch a true picture of the individual. They will use it to draft an inclusive healing programme, predicts Levinson. The healing of the future will take into account karmic development, natural inclinations, surrounding factors, family tendencies, group character, collective psychic inheritance and more.

'All this points to one certainty, there is no such thing as a Jew, confirms BarYohai. DNA and all biological events are common to the whole of humanity. The notion of biological differences is a myth being disproved in all the laboratories of the world.

'There is no such thing as a Jew, no more than there is an Eskimo, a Mongol or an Indian. In India they bathe in reincarnation culture, reminisces Bendavid. Those human beings preparing to return to Earth will choose events, people, situations and surroundings that feel familiar. They will be drawn to the frequency they resonate with, their own wavelength. So it is not fantastic to infer that they might have been Puritans or Mormons, Inquisitors, nuns or monks, crusaders, devotees to Shiva or Right-wing extremists.

'There is another question too terrible to ask, 'do we send out an inchoate evocation to the universe, asks Levinson boldly?

'You are walking on slippery ground. Be careful, warns Clara.

'I have thrown caution to the winds; I must ask the question that was never asked. We have had countless opportunities to curse our lives and our god. And so, given the power of thought, do we release unformed thoughts of self-destruction? There is much self-loathing, much hatred of life, much rage against the unjust god. Suicidal tendencies

540

among us are rampant. The distress that brings us to the analyst couch revolves around self-loathing, guilt and resentment.

'I agree, butts in Shemtov, is it possible that such thoughts floating in the unconscious are picked up by those on that particular wave-length? Thoughts are electrical signals, emotions are waves of energy, all mental activity is energy. Energy is never lost; it is received by those on that frequency range.

'We are locked in a paradox, admits BarYohai, in our collective consciousness we are jammed in the past, yet thought-energy is perpetually shooting out in ever widening ripples, seeking to bind itself to another thought-energy of the same frequency!

The Father as Nemesis

'I have delved into the mysteries of ancient myths; to decipher Hebrew mythology I had to explore other myths, begins Shemtov, the physicist. I notice a look of disbelief, what is surprising about that? All myths spring from a common origin, the form varies, the names differ but the hidden meaning is much the same. To make sense of what marred my youth and early adulthood, I came up with a few ideas I put forward to any potential reader for perusal. He may reject it with indignation, but before he does I urge him to read with an open mind. 'Physics is reflection on the divine Ideas of Creation, therefore physics is divine service' wrote the physicist Heisenberg. An echo of this in Eastern wisdom, 'Matter reveals itself to the realizing thought and to the subtilized senses as the figure and body of Spirit…' Matter and spirit, matter and thought are interchangeable. This was taught in the Mystery Schools of Atlantis, Egypt, India and Greece. 'Everything is essentially consciousness' uttered Shankara.

'The true nature of the universe is consciousness, 'The physical world is entirely abstract and without 'actuality' apart from its linkage to consciousness', enounced Eddington. Furthermore the world exists to the extent that we 'construct' it with our mind, 'Every man's world picture is and always remains a construct of his mind and cannot be proved to have any other existence' explained the physicist Schrödinger, confirming what Buddha had said, 'The objective world rises from the mind itself.'

'What about Genesis? We have spent thousands of years reading, learning, analysing, debating, arguing, writing and embroidering Creation, all a 'construction' of our mind, an abstraction, asks Clara?

'Eddington answers, 'The physical world is entirely abstract and without 'actuality' …
Going back to my initial idea, from time immemorial we have worshipped the god of
life and death. In his destructive persona he is Thanatos, the god of death, also known
as Shiva the originator of life and death. In his creative persona he is confused with the
Elohim, the 'creator Gods'. In his punitive persona he is Nemesis, the Greek goddess
of justice, an unforgiving judge. Freud understood well the god of his ancestors. The
death wish he observed, biologists are now identifying in the human DNA. The death
wish is prominent among us. I was struggling to understand the grip the idol has on us
and one day I had a eureka moment: he is the god of biological processes! Yahweh is
Shiva, Thanatos and Nemesis. He is a synthesis, he integrates the salient features of
most nature gods, absorbing, assimilating, and unifying them. Modern physics is
searching for a unifying theory, 'the theory of everything'. Yahweh was in pre-scientific
times a manifestation of 'the theory of everything', a unifying principle, all nature gods
blend in him. He is truly one!

The Slaying of the Father

Sarah and Maimon had to return to their university to attend a meeting. Two days later
they reappear and greet the group with warm emotion.

'I could not get away soon enough, says Sarah almost in tears. The meeting was so
tedious that somehow I had to escape at coffee breaks and meal times. The result of
my skiving is this paper I started on the Father, it is in its early stages but I would like
your comments'. A universal grunt of approval is the answer. Emboldened Sarah
begins, 'Of all ancient mythologies ours is the only one perhaps which fully endorses the
Father.

'Sorry to barge in, interrupts Levinson, but the Father was born in Lemuria a few
million years ago when the Masters taught animal-man how to take care of his body,
keep clean, eat clean foods, avoid behaving like a brute and recognise the Father in the
world around him.

'I take note, continues Sarah jotting down. In other folklores a special individual rises,
entrusted with the task of slaying the Father.

'Oedipus does the job efficiently, laughs Jeremy. He kills his oppressing father and
marries his mother! Quite a feat!

'This is no laughing matter, retorts Levinson. We have no hero to save us from the Father. Moses, hailed as the liberator, endorsed the Father.

'O but there is, butts in Maimon! What about the Messiah, isn't his primary role to liberate us? To free us from the tyranny of the Father?

'You know what happened don't' you, breaks in Jeremy? The triumph of the Father is the betrayal of the Son. The Son allegorically stands for the vital principle, the spirit in man. Are you referring to what happened 2000 years ago when the Essenes came to 'slay' the Father and replace him with the Son? They met with a tragic end.

'The 'death' of the Father is crucial to the emancipation of humanity, continues Sarah well pleased with the response. As already mentioned, Thanatos the god of Death obstructs our progress. In contrast the role of the Son – all of us – is to slay the Father who keeps us in his clutches. The Father, as you know, stands for that which is unchanging, calcified, fossilised. As he inflicts stagnation, he opposes life since life is ever-renewed, ever-changing, and ever-flowing. The Father is the barrage to the life stream.

'I know, I experienced that death, the most horrific of all deaths, inserts Clara. 'The dark night of the soul'. The horror of it haunts my dreams.

'Moses did not succeed, he secured the position of the Father instead of stabbing him, mutters Levinson clarifying his own thought.

'I recall Sananda's words, 'Through your own growth God also grows. So that God is at once the unchanging Father and the Son, changing and evolving'. Let us moderate our enthusiasm; I suggest we do as Sananda implies: integrate Father and Son, integrate the forces of stability and inertia with the dynamic forces of change. The integration of Father and Son is realised in us, in humanity.

'So humanity is the soil in which the realisation of the Father and the Son grows. This is coming to pass; we are in this age now! We are the engineers of this cosmic change, reflects Tara.

'Death to the ambassadors of Shamballa appointed to remove the forces of stagnation and inertia, exclaims Johansson hit by a realisation. The agents of the Father mocked the envoys of Shamballa on a mission to remove the Father. They were and still are the people of unchanging form, sentinels of the past that forgives nothing, the past that exacts its due.

'In Greek mythology, Theseus was the slayer of the Minotaur, that insatiable monster who fed on young virgins and young men, reminds Sarah.

'We finally 'killed' the Father, exclaims Clara!

'We have not! Heroes of myths go in search of a magic sword to slay the Monster and liberate the people of the kingdom, expands Sarah. Down the ages we have offered every generation on the altar of the Father. In the Greek tragedy, Oedipus kills his father and marries his mother. The myth reappears in the 20th century decoded by Freud: deep in the unconscious lurks hatred of the father. This suppressed hatred is the root of much distress and much illness. Oedipus kills his father, symbol of authority and tyranny. Not so the Hebrew myth which elevates the human father to the pinnacle of earthly greatness. Keeper of religious taboos and group values the father inflicts them on the child. He is keeper of the tribal order.

'Oedipus has the boldness to kill his father, inserts Clara. Virtuous slaying?

'Oedipus seeks to restore lost harmony, a primeval state of simplicity in the world, the father-oppressor has broken the natural order by separating mother and child, continues Sarah. A similar theme lies behind circumcision: the father-despot hurts the infant and separates mother and child. This may explain the strong attachment of the boy for his mother in our people. Symbolically Oedipus's union with his mother is a return to a world in which the Mother was revered, a pre-patriarchal age of nurturing, empathy, caring and compassion, an age which revered the Goddess. But patriarchy triumphs and Oedipus must flee for daring to restore primordial unity. The Father is the force that defies evolution. The Father, the masculine ego persists.

'Fascinating, says Jeremy. The elimination of the father is suggested by the world Saviours of the past.

'The father stands for the static, the rigid, the unchanging. 'Thou shall not' is the father's way of suppressing the natural impulse, continues Sarah. The father brings back home tribal rules and inflicts them on the child smothering the joy of life. Creative energy is suspended. The father obstructs the life current, the dynamic urge to life. The father stands for the tribal order, for the unchanging rules that bind individuals into a cohesive group but which suffocates soul life in the young. Soon the child learns to suppress his highest impulse; he is rewarded for his loyalty to tribal values. Who ever claimed that Abraham abolished human sacrifice?

'This can be done either in accordance with the Father's will or against his will. He may choose death for his children's sake' said the Master

With Krishna he approves of the removal of the father who impedes the growth of mankind. Now is the time for the Son to assert his presence and change the world. The Son, humanity.

'In the world of polarity the father and his god are a barrier to the natural flow of life, the impulse to life, inserts Jeremy. I see it as the primordial struggle between the forces of light and the forces of darkness. Ego and soul are engaged in a mortal combat. But Krishna, Buddha and the Essenes exist beyond polarity, beyond the social and tribal order. The father once removed, the life force resumes its normal flow and we begin to see the real picture.

'To return to Oedipus, the myth set the stage for the Jewish drama, resumes Sarah. It looms large in our lives and no effort was ever made to conceal it. It bolsters the entire biblical edifice. The Father symbolises the lifeless past, the Son is the dynamic present and the promise of a 'life more abundant'.

'Fascinating, repeats Jeremy. The myth of Oedipus is crucial to you. 'It is crucial to all of us, concludes Sarah. Myths tell stories of psychological events. In prehistoric times dangerous desires and emotions found expression that way, they became animated, personalised and deified. Today we use thoughts and emotions like tyranny, freedom, love, hate, and wrath. When early man sensed beauty, beauty became Venus, hatred became Cain, and tyranny became the Father.

'Reflecting back on Sananda's words, it suddenly hit me, says Jeremy! The Father is separate from humanity; man is estranged from the Father; there is an unbridgeable abyss between the two. The Father, remote from man makes demands and man must obey because man has lived in ignorance of his own nature, identity and power. In other words mankind has lived in unconsciousness. Whereas the changing and evolving Son is humanity itself; conscious humanity is assuming responsibility for its own direction. Two ages, two opposite viewpoints. The Judeo-Christian world is keeper of the first viewpoint, that of the separation between man and the universe. And the immense suffering that has ensued.

'Back to the old see-saw of polarity, Father versus Son, notes Tara pertinently. Polarity, illusion always!

'Right, this Sananda addresses with the words, 'So that God is at once the unchanging Father and Son, changing and evolving'. What Sananda alludes to is a fusion, a merging, an integration. The Age of Grace is precisely that, the assimilation of all polarities; the end of the biblical worldview that has prevailed. Grace is the opposite of the split reality of the old Hebrew world. From broken reality to unity.

Echo of the Father in Faustus's Mephisto

Levinson pursues his exploration of ancient myths and legends aware that they hold the answer to his life-long quest. That day the opera Faustus was being played on his portable radio. He had written an essay on Marlowe's 'Doctor Faustus' at university, fascinated by the metaphor. He had promised himself to return later to the strange story of the aging philosopher who on reaching the end of his existence is embittered at having missed so much out of life. To make up for lost time he signs a pact with Mephistopheles. But the enjoyment of life comes at a price. Mephisto must be paid with Faustus's soul. Reluctantly Faustus consents to the deal. Mephisto grants Faustus the pleasures of life in return for his abiding loyalty. He now 'owns' Faustus. He possesses the most important feature of man, his soul, his immortal Self. He owns the soul that makes Faustus a unique individual, a creative being, someone who, like God can create worlds. Faustus has given up his cosmic destiny in return for paltry pleasures. He is reduced to a mundane, pitiful, prosaic existence when he capitulates to Mephisto. Like Faustus we signed a pact with a cosmic force, partly real, partly figment of our imagination, in exchange for an elusive greatness and an illusory security. We signed with our blood. Freedom of the soul, creativity, power, greatness, and deathlessness we gave away. Docile we caved in to the 'do & obey' in exchange for a few pledges: the promise of security, safety, identity and racial advantage; most of it imaginary, most of it gratification, all illusory.

Echo of Yahweh in the god Mars

'Could Yahweh be our fashioned version of Mars? I have pondered over this for a few day, begins Levinson. The red Planet is named after Mars, the god of war. Make no mistake our ancestors were immersed in the same cultural waters; they personified not only mental events but astronomical events too! From an astronomical angle Mars is the red Planet. Psychologically the urge of Mars is to defend, attack, defeat and break up. Mars in cosmic terms is the expression of the masculine aspect of polarity. It is undeniable that Yahweh has attributes of Mars; he is the archetypal image of masculine energy in all its forcefulness, aggressiveness and defensiveness.

'Absolutely retorts Sarah, you left out paranoia. In his aggressive maleness, he is the god of patriarchy! He has hovered over our heads like the sword of Damocles. He has penetrated and manipulated our emotional life. He is encoded in our DNA. Our existence broadcasts his presence. He is the governing force on the Planet. We have integrated and internalised him to such an extent that we act as his self-appointed agents, meting out judgment and punishment on each other. In my practice I observe judgment and punishment on oneself, the god-force is kicking within us.

'They revel in their maleness, they split, segment, defy, deny and discard, reflects Maimon. They exaggerate the split, troubled with sexuality and gender. They live in a neatly split world where male-female polarity is taken to extreme, where sexuality is the subject of much regulation and taboos, tainted with fear, aversion and attraction. Polarity may be an illusion to the enlightened; to us it is the enduring reality.

'What is remarkable is that women defend and uphold the masculine energy: they preserve it in the home, they inflict its values and beliefs on their daughters and sons, inserts Clara. My mother was a ruthless defender of the Yahweh-energy; she ruled the roost with the rigid touch of a Luther, the inflexibility of a Mother Superior.

'Obsession with the male-female polarity is such that women are the fiercest guardians of patriarchy. They keep gender division and sexual taboos even more rigidly than men. Like the mythological Cerberus they guard the entrance to the Underworld, the dark world of emotional life, reflects Sarah.

'They devalue their daughters, suppress their aspirations, depress their spirit and smother their potential. Women, it seems are enemies of their own gender, they are the true servants of the god of war, replies Clara who remembers how her mother was the pitiless, unfeeling embodiment of the god-force. What muddle! Women loathing female polarity but guarding it with ferocious zeal! Women loathing male polarity and promoting it with resentment!

'The neat gender divide is not so neat after all, says Levinson.

'A hologram is a three-dimensional image formed by the interference of light beams from a light source. We live and move in a giant hologram in which each tiny part is an identical image of the larger picture. The larger image is repeated indefinitely. The god-force is a vast hologram and each one a smaller image of him, notes Sarah. A chilling thought. That is why healing is so vital for us and for the Planet.

'Now you see why the return of the Goddess is critical, retorts Tara?

'Quite, agrees Sarah. The goddess is making her presence felt all around in subtle ways. The Goddess seeks to bond, bridge, enlist, solve and unite. This happens to be the intention of the secular, liberal majority. The Goddess nurtures expansiveness, encourages inwardness, promotes the development of our potential. Whereas the urge of the god-force is to dispute, protest, argue, defeat and carve up; it is to prevent, thwart, deny and prohibit. Men and women feel bereft, wondering what their place in the world is. The unyielding taboos, the zealous disquiet with gender division lie behind some intractable emotional problems we have to treat in our practices. Women have to discover and accept their own femininity. Then the muddle, the tangle, the insecurity, the disorientation, the mayhem will dispel. What is crucial is a leap in realisation.

'Fixation with gender division and sexual taboos hark back to Lemurian times when animal-man was given basic rules of decent living, contributes Jeremy. With the new cosmic energies flowing on to the Planet the disquiet is deepening. Humanity is rising to a new level of awareness and women are responding to the turmoil by adopting masculine values. They compete with men in the work place where they embrace male values. It is mayhem all around!

'Women are claiming back their autonomy, their right to be, their right to do and to achieve, replies Clara. Order will emerge out of the turmoil.

Maimon announces that they are summoned back at the university, once again to attend a meeting. They promise to be back the following day.

The Father as archetype of 'old world' energy

'We came back to spend a few fascinating hours with you and enjoy a walk around the lake. We are expecting a call from the university, hopefully it won't come, but if it does we shall have to leave. We bring the next chapter of The Hebrew Gods; being inquisitive we stopped on the way to leaf through it, announces Maimon. Before you ask, we have not seen Benzaccai who is still in hiding somewhere in Jericho I believe. His wife gave us the translation and sends her love.

'We like having you, stay as long as you can, replies Jeremy graciously. Bendavid and his colleagues were called back home, they intend to come back within the next few days.

548

We shall meet and spend time together before we return to England. Failing that you will come to us, we are planning a big reunion in the Lake District. For a whole week we shall have workshops with Sananda and Sanat Kumara, lots of walks by the lake, fun, dance and lots of discussions!

'We look forward to it. That's settled then, replies Maimon assuredly. Sarah and I have been discussing an idea that sprang on our way here. The idea of the Father as archetype, no longer as an external reality.

'I am working on a similar idea, enthuses Levinson. A meeting of minds!

'We have always been kept in immobility, hoping, and waiting. And where there is pointless hope, hopelessness is sure to follow, says Sarah, I see this hopelessness in my patients all the time.

'Such steadfastness, remarks Jeremy, I would have given up long ago at the pointlessness of it all.

'That's the whole point. Is it faith driving us on inexorably, wonders Levinson? We longed for god to take charge, to get involved, to take us by the hand, to guide, to chastise, to praise. We have petitioned, pleaded, implored, hoped and waited ... in vain. We hoped and despaired, prayed and wept, powerless to do anything to change our lives.

'Many still do, inserts Clara. Nothing has changed.

'How can anything change? It is fear driving us inexorably, not faith, continues Maimon impassioned. The old fear. Remember Egypt? We implored god to take us out of bondage. Remember Sinai? We implored Moses to intercede in our favour to the god who was alien to us, the god we feared and could never love. We decided it was god's responsibility to get us out, give us water and see us through the cataclysms. When the hostile Amalek appeared, Moses had to tackle the enemy. Manna came down from the sky to feed us. Like little children we were powerless to act, powerless to make decision, totally dependent on the Father. All had to be done for us. When water and meat ran out, Moses was assaulted.

'It seems that faith has little to do with it, ponders Tara pertinently.

'That was 'old Earth' energy, we were dissociated from our innate ability to take charge, reflects Levinson. To take charge is seen as blasphemous. Not the sort of things children do.

'Thousand of years down the line the Hassidim carry the dark flame of helplessness. I was a maverick in their eyes. Disempowerment was the distinctive sign of spiritual distinction! I was definitely not of their 'madrega', their lofty spiritual height, recalls Clara.

'The reactionaries uphold the Fall's devastating effects, expands Levinson. Autonomy, personal responsibility, decision-making, discernment were removed. Immersed in 'old Earth' energy, they are submerged in the Fall and its effects. They see greatness in it.

'But the 'new Earth' energy was anchored in the Planet by the Essenes, informs Jeremy. They activated the demise of 'old Earth' energy. Love and light they gave. They gave back to humanity freedom and responsibility.

'You would think so, inserts Sarah. If love is the nature of the universe, our clerics wanted nothing to do with such potent energy. Think of it, they had fear that shrinks, contracts, diminishes, darkens, shrivels and withers! Who wants love when you can have human misery instead? As a result our brains are wired to experience pain, our physiological response is pathological and our emotional response erratic.

'That's right, replies Maimon. Fear is of the Fall, fear is of Maya and like Maya it is ultimately an illusion. We have lived in the world of illusion since the Fall. We still pray, fast, implore, beseech. We still demand to be taken care of; we still call on the Father who is deaf to our plea.

'Because we retain the mindset of the Fall. Our 'old god' is the god of the Flood, the god of the Fall. We are living the Flood, we are living the Fall. Our Torah reading revolves around the Fall and the god of the Fall. 'Old Earth' energy and 'old god' energy are inseparable, comments Levinson.

'Old Earth' energy relies on man's disempowerment, inserts Jeremy. The Essenes initiated the age of the soul, the age of empowerment. The Master insisted that man has the power to reverse the effects of the Fall. Man functioning as his soul is all-powerful. The Essenes were addressing a disabled flock: the blind, the lame, the infirm; these disabilities were as much actual as they were symbolic. They were given the new skills, the new knowledge that would heal them into wholeness. Man is a fragment of the Source, man shares all the gifts, all the abilities of the Source the Essenes told the lame, the blind and the infirm.

'Dangerous' powers, says Clara. Man would stay in the disabling 'old Earth' atmosphere. We rebuffed the new spiritual powers; we rejected the 'new Earth' energy. Fear was good enough for us.

'Not every one wants to be free or responsible, notes Tara aptly.

'All that is changing, the Masters are emerging and teaching us new spiritual skills. We are learning to be divine, cosmic and infinite, affirms Jeremy.

'People all over the world pray and wait, old habits die hard, expands Jeremy. Believers are infused with 'old Earth' energy and imbued with the sense of powerlessness. Spellbound in the Fall, they believe the old ways pertinent and 'old Earth' energy relevant. Ashes of the past! The 'new Earth' energy enables us to evoke our cosmic nature and reclaim our place in the universe. Those who pray and wait do little to heal the world; the balance of power is shifted on to their gods and demigods. In this 'new Earth' frequency we are aware of our direct connection with the Source. 'You are creators of your own reality' Sananda reminds us. As 'creators of reality' we are masters of our destiny. As 'creators of reality' we have responsibility to the Planet.

'With our thoughts we make the world', to take literally, quotes Tara.

'The human mind is a fragment of the cosmic Mind, pursues Jeremy. What the Source can do, we can do. The Source immanent in man gives us this power. The 'new Earth' energy reminds us of our divinity and power of creation. We co-create the world. We are learning with the Masters to rediscover our primordial power of creation. Just as we are part of the Creator, the Creator is part of us. We live in partnership.

'Adam Kadmon is no longer a Cabbalistic dream, notes Levinson.

'A mythical dream to the pious heretics, unless the 'old god' of 'old Earth' forces him on us with fire and brimstone, exclaims Clara! This is unlikely. When asked about the trend, Archangel Michael pictured a wonderful future for the Planet; he evoked the return of the Garden of Eden. This he meant literally.

COSMIC LAWS NEGLECTED

On Suffering. On Selfhood. On Freedom. On Heresy

'The wave, the foam, the eddy and the bubble are all essentially water. Similarly, the body and the ego are really nothing but pure consciousness. Everything is essentially consciousness'. (Shankara)

Maimon draws a few typed pages from his briefcase as they settle down to yet another encounter between Moses and Master Sanaka.

'Today I wish to discuss the role of the mind and the power of thought.

'With respect Master, we already discussed mind power when you elucidated the allegory of Creation, remarks Moses.

'Since all is thought as well as matter, then the debate on thought is never ending, chuckles Sanaka. As Buddha said, 'For the wise all 'things' are wiped away' and 'Fundamentally, there is no reality in external objects'. Before we journey into the rich fields of thought, let us clarify a few points. To speak of the mind is to imply autonomy. The mastery of thought renders man spiritually free and knowing. But the personality is unruly and demands rigorous training. Your religious leaders bemoan the unruly nature of their people yet they do not offer a mind-training method.

'Why is mind-training so important, apart from the satisfaction of being in control?

'Mastery of thought would render your Scriptures irrelevant. At one level, you would see the texts for what they are: form that keep you captive of the surface meaning; form that refuses to yield the symbol, the image, the Idea. You read the form and succumb to its influence. More importantly thought mastery would make you masters of your own lives. When you gain mastery over your mind you gain mastery over your life. For so long as you do not master your mind other people control you.

'What is the link with the obsolescence of the Scriptures? Thought is of man and the Scriptures were sanctioned by God before being imparted by the Spiritual Hierarchy.

'Sensible observation, Moses. The Scriptures emanate from the Hierarchy, in this sense they are of heavenly origin, but their interpretation is entirely human. The texts were taken hostage by the priesthood, the only educated class. Scribes and priesthood, the educated class, gave their interpretation to texts which were never intended to be read in their primary sense. The texts as given by the Hierarchy were by design cloaked in allegorical form since they concealed universal meaning. The intention of the Hierarchy was disregarded and the texts read in the literal mode.

'The literal mode is of limited appeal whereas the original texts as designed by the Hierarchy were of universal appeal. The hidden meaning to be deciphered concerned humanity at large.

'Indeed, but it was for humanity to decipher as the mind of man evolves, as man's awareness develops. The literal form obstructs the vision. As a result people have relied on the priests to clarify the mysterious verses but the meaning remained inaccessible. Man surrendered the responsibility to know, placing it squarely on the shoulders of the educated class and in so doing lost control of his direction. He has been reduced to living the life that others have traced out for him. In this context God's Plan for humanity is but a blurred dream, a faint memory lost in the mist of time, a corrupted version of the divine vision. The Scriptures are in reality a human creation.

'The prophets tried to do just that, they were the great rebels, those who dare to question kings and priests alike.

'Ambassadors of the Hierarchy they were misunderstood, far ahead of the limited intellectual grasp of their generation. What the Essenes were prevented from doing is gradually unfolding: the mind of man is progressing in accordance with the divine Plan. The emphasis on the part of the Hierarchy is on the development of the mind and this process will accelerate. Mankind is getting to its destination in spite of entrenched hostility to knowledge by those engrossed in the illusion, in Maya.

'It was all within the Plan, so mankind is following the map of evolution drawn up, notes Moses.

'The road inevitably leads back home. The Prodigal Son is returning to his Father's castle, even if he appears to have lost his way. You may recall Aesop's' fable in which a hare sets off on a race with a tortoise but is soon distracted. He gambols, prances, loiters, amuses himself and completely forgets the race. Mankind seems to have lost sight of its destination, yet in spite of the frolics it is somehow winding its way back. A vital step toward liberation would be to reclaim ownership of your body: most practices and taboos revolve around the body. The Masters taught animal-man in Lemuria, millions of years ago, how to take care of his body. This is long past, over and done with. Time to move on, time to move up from body to mind. An ascension, an initiation.

'This concerns a small section of humanity, observes Moses.

'This is so, but remember that no man is an island, the enlightened Greeks visualised mankind as rays of light emanating from the Central Sun, each ray inseparable from the Sun and inseparable from all the other rays. Alternatively visualise the countless pebbles on a beach, all together they make up the beach; just imagine that a few pebbles decide to break away 'we are special, we are the chosen ones, we do not belong to this beach, we are definitely of a superior kind'. Or imagine that a few of the countless cells that form the body decided to defect? The body would decline into disease and slide into death.

'So, what affects one part affects the whole, concludes Moses.

'Absolutely. Each thought affects the whole. Each thought has the power to destroy or to create. When released into the ether a thought ripples out in ever widening circles, reaches its target and does its work for good of ill. Also, the law of thought is further reinforced by the Law of Attraction, 'like attracts like'.

'So a thought according to this law goes out to meet another thought of the same kind, being attracted to it.

'Excellent, Moses. Thoughts are visible; they can take form where they are 'attracted' according to the Law of Attraction. Thoughts of love and compassion reach the highest realms while thoughts of fear and malice are captured by the astral plane. But thoughts also affect the person who emits them, positive thoughts enhance the quality of the subtle bodies, malign thoughts can be seen around the person as injurious patterns and stormy colours. Man is an open book for the whole universe to read, it is only man himself who does not know the effect his thoughts have on himself and the world around him. But the world is not blind; a human being is capable of sensing the quality of thought emitted by another. You intuitively know that a person or a place feels right. Equally some places and people release a negative energy that repels. The most sensitive individuals often feel ill in such thought atmospheres.

'If the nature of our thoughts decides everything, if follows that suffering is of man. It is not of god, it is not a sign of 'chosenness'.

'Suffering is not praised by the Masters of India. It is not virtuous to suffer. Your people were deceived into believing that suffering is a sign of selection, part of being chosen, of being special. The axiom is, 'you suffer because god loves you'. They romanticised suffering, they made suffering respectable. A questioning person would ask, 'how can a God of love inflict suffering?'

'But suffering is inevitable, it is an inherent part of the human condition, admits Moses. Suffering is a great teacher, is it not? It refines the character and filters the coarser aspects of the self.

'Suffering should lead to a refinement of the lower nature. Remember that the purpose of life is the 'death of the self', the dissolution of the ego into the soul so that the soul assumes leadership, so that man functions as his soul. Ultimately suffering leads to love as it refines the lower nature and awakens the spiritual centres. It is a cleansing, a purifying and a refining fire. When suffering has been used to accelerate the opening of the higher centres - Heart, Throat and Head - it has served its purpose. But does it always? And if not why?

'We tend to value suffering as a sign of selected status. I realise that we have failed to probe its meaning. We have endorsed it as a special privilege.

'Yet you bemoan suffering! Even if you see it as sign of selection you do not understand it! This is the inevitable outcome of man-made dogmas built on the shifting sand of belief rather than on the stable foundation of universal Law. Excuses are erected but they have no more solidity than a drifting band of clouds, and people continue to suffer and lament their misfortune. What do you infer Moses?

'It seems that suffering is the result of ignorance of cosmic Law rather than a sign of chosenness.

'Indeed, Moses. Man is in bondage to suffering. Suffering and ignorance are interchangeable and inseparable. Buddha explained suffering as product of man's ignorance. Suffering is the inevitable outcome of desire. Your doctrine which insists on attachment is conducive to suffering. It cultivates attachment to ancient opinions and interpretations obsolete the moment they were formulated. Attachment, as you know is one of the three mental poisons that bind man to suffering and traps him into Samsara. Attachment, aversion and confusion - the three mental poisons - are the root of all suffering. Samsara is the great hurdle man has to triumph over. This applies to humanity in general and to your people. How is it that your decision-makers made Samsara so respectable?

'They were in this world and of this world. At death man travelled to the Underworld. Life after death was not seriously contemplated. The crucial thing was physical life here on Earth and what one does with this life.

'Buddha emphasised the importance of this life and what one does with it!

'For Buddha it meant achieving liberation from Samsara. For us it means obedient service to the deity. Man's noblest aim is to serve his god, to bear the 'yoke'. We do not grasp that life on Earth is for man, not for god.

'Excellent analysis, Moses. You discarded the cosmic Law of Reincarnation as it did not fit in with your idea of finite life on Earth. The aim of repeated incarnations is to grow in realisation from servility to autonomy, from dependency to moral freedom. So, the purpose of reincarnation is to effect a transfer from the 'not-self' to the Self, from the mortal self to the deathless Self, from human-consciousness to soul-consciousness. This is not the phantasm of Eastern mystics, but the inescapable course of evolution.

'From human consciousness to divine consciousness, the ordained course? In the distant past I would have been stoned to death for this.

'Ideas not understood are seen as subversive and must be stamped out. Witches were burnt at the stake by religious fanatics who did not know that some people are gifted with more than just the ordinary senses, that their range of perception is much wider. But the bigots won the day!

'In ancient Israel dissidents were stoned to death, probably for the same reasons.

'The realisation that man is fenced in suffering by his own doing is the first step toward liberation. You live many lives in the present, since you are the sum of all your former personalities, you also move in different dimensions at the same time'. Sanaka is observing Moses very closely; playing on the element of surprise, 'there is no past, no future, only the Now. One basic belief you cling to is that you are restricted by space and time. In other words, you are trapped in Samsara and there is no avenue of escape!

'Is this not what religion is all about, to liberate us from Samsara?

'The religion of man focuses on the body; it keeps you rooted in Samsara. You are only aware of the part of you that is conscious, the ego which we call the 'not-Self'. The ego is conscious of itself, but the real you is conscious of itself, conscious of the multitude of incarnations you had, conscious of other lives lived in other worlds, of all the roles you have played since beginningless time, aware of other souls and conscious of other dimensions unknown to you. It is simply boundless, immeasurable, and unfathomable.

'Why have we been denied this basic right?

'Your ancestors did the best they could with the limited awareness they had. It is a matter of place, time and point of evolution.

'We resisted the emergence of soul-consciousness? So we are suffering because we are stuck in Samsara. And this is of our own choosing?

'The golden rule is: no god forced its will on you, no god inflicted on you your present existence! There never was at any time a power that imposed itself on you. The law of evolution dictates that you return to Earth time and again. The soul clothes itself in countless selves to learn, explore, know and grow. Your Self brushes aside your worldly constraints, profits from your earthly limitations and shrugs off notions of gender, race, colour and creed. You are a visitor to Earth, an observer, sent on an assignment to serve humanity. You are not a native of Earth, but a citizen of the universe, a cosmic being closely linked to the stars.

'I did not know intelligent life existed on the stars.

'You know remarkably little for a scholar who mastered the Scriptures, replies Sanaka with mirth. You recall the Twelve Tribes of Israel.

'I do, replies Moses now on familiar ground.

'The twelve constellations that have influenced the destiny of this Planet from time immemorial are recorded in your texts and personalised as all else.

'Why me?

'To fulfil your potential, expand in knowledge, serve humanity and heal the group you were born into.

'What is the purpose of life, Master Sanaka? Our eminent Rabbis pondered over this issue and came up with an answer that was consistent with their inherited wisdom: to serve god and lift the Earth.

'The question is which god? There is no god in the sense that you grew up to the word 'god'. The all-knowing, all-seeing deity set to ambush you belongs to the early days of human awareness. The Father was born in ancient Lemuria, millions of years ago, to keep ancient man within the bounds of basic, clean living.

'The Father is archaic?

'As the overseer whose role is to interfere, chastise and coerce he is past it. There is only the boundless cosmic Mind of which you are an integral part. As an aspect of the universal Mind you are cosmic in nature, you transcend physicality. So the purpose of

557

life can only be to fulfil yourself, to become who you truly are having realised your potential. Knowing the power of your soul, you become all-knowing. The purpose of soul return is to explore and utilize the divine faculties deposited in your being. Imagine your soul as a large diamond. You must first extract the rough diamond from the earth and then refine, cut and polish it. Realise all your potential.

'Back in Vilna it is anathema. To fulfil hidden potentials and develop abilities is not only profane, it is rebellious. I was struck off for less.

'In Vilna the point of view is consistent; if you are thrown to Earth to bear the 'yoke, to 'do & obey', keep the Planet in good order for the deity, the idea of self-realisation is anathema. Since when are 'yoke' bearing serfs expected to fulfil their potential? For your teachers self-fulfilment is an outrage because it detracts from the main issue which is to serve the deity. Anything that may endanger service to the god is blasphemous.

'So you want me to go back to Vilna, enter the synagogue and urge them to develop their potentials? They will throw me out and stone me!

'Some clarification is in order, I do not want you to go to Vilna, you want to go to Vilna! You planned this assignment long before this life. I have nothing to do with your decision, however I did agree to assist you and prepare you for the task. Now, your teachers in Vilna are coherent, their awareness is of a Samsara god and they act accordingly as their forefathers did before them. Their perspective has not changed, consistent with their inherited views.

'I don't stand a chance.

'You admit defeat before you try. All is mind; the universe came into being by the power of thought. You know that people change their mind, thoughts change. All it takes is a change of perspective, a transfer of pivot from a nature god to the cosmic Mind. Remember that you are a fragment from that Mind, you are that Mind.

'You want me to tell them that they are God. This is sacrilege.

'Not really, does not Genesis say that God made man in his image and likeness? Your teachers have explored this beautiful allegory in every letter and derivation to the last dot. If man is made in the image of God, it follows that he is God! You have a new equation, no longer do you see yourself as a puny human yoked to the plough of life staring at the god of fear, but the Creator in human form, coming down to explore the world and learn about it. There is room for everyone, for the scientist, the humanist, the artist, the philosopher, the priest, the nihilist, the dancer, the gambler, even for the crook, the vast tapestry of human diversity is spread out before you. The soul is creating and recreating itself tirelessly. The soul comes to Earth having set itself a specific mission which may take thousands of incarnations to accomplish. And so any obstruction to its natural flow is a crime against humanity and a crime against the One incarnate in human form.

'We have no awareness of a multi-facetted soul existing at many levels of being and in different dimensions simultaneously. We did not come across the idea of the soul designing a new persona to explore new horizons. But we do know about surroundings 'You have heard me often repeat 'you create your own reality'. We all are creators of the world around us. This idea would be dismissed as heresy and you as a blasphemer. It is all so simple!

'How can I get this idea across to victims of circumstances?

'They take action, they make decisions, they negotiate, they solve problems every day, they are not victims! A change of perspective is crucial, a transfer of attention is vital. If you imagine yourself helpless and hapless, if this image is hammered in you by others, then it lodges itself deep in your mind and you send out this image to the entire world. Thought travels; once a thought is released nothing can halt its trajectory. One day science will study thought and design instruments that can register thought. Thoughts are real, tangible, they can be seen, read and received.

'Are you saying Master that we project negative thoughts and that we are responsible for what comes back at us?

'It is shocking, I know. But when scientists in future explore the nature of thought this will be widely accepted. No one will deny the idea that it is the quality of our thoughts that make us who we are. It is the nature of our thoughts that determine the quality of our lives. Today they scream 'blasphemer', tomorrow they will accept it as they accept that breathing is vital to life.

'I must prepare myself for a rough ride! We hold that our suffering is either an act of god or the expression of humanity's wickedness, that we have nothing to do with it.

'The method is simple, when you project a cramped, trampled, flattened image of yourself, it winds its way to the astral plane where it resonates with similarly held views and images. The two visions band together and materialise as the malicious surroundings that fence you in. When you view your circumstances as existing separately of your mental activity, you are an object within it, rather than the agent that shapes it. You are the perpetual star-crossed, hapless group that has inspired derision since ancient Egypt.

'This is heresy', concludes Moses who is progressively grasping the spirit of Eastern enlightenment and expanding his own mental landscape. At times he feels hesitant and perplexed by the radical new ideas he finds daunting, at such times the old habitual mode of thought rears its head and obstructs his advance. He is a battle field on which the illusion of the past and the enlightenment of the present are wrestling. Reassuringly the Master continues, aware that only knowledge will allay Moses' inner turmoil, 'I greatly value knowledge though knowledge of itself is not the royal route to liberation. Knowledge needs inner experience, intuitive knowing. To know God perfectly with the intellect as the Hassidim claim is beyond their reach, since the intellect which is of this world cannot apprehend that which is beyond this world. The intellect generates ideas and opinions and ends up believing what it creates! 'All the mind's arbitrary conceptions of matter, phenomena and of all conditioning factors and all conceptions and ideas relating to [them] are like a dream, a phantasm, a bubble, a shadow', said Buddha.

'Intellect and soul do not belong together?

'The role of the intellect is to explore and make sense of the world, not to apprehend the Infinite. Knowledge is of the intellect, wisdom is of the soul and in meditation you touch the soul and access the higher Realms. But with you knowledge is perhaps as important as inner experience and this must be satisfied. You are a man of the mind as much as of the spirit. Some people function better at the level of mind and this must be recognised and honoured.

'Thank you Master, you always pick the right words at the right time. This is appreciated, I feel much relieved. May we return to heresy?

'A subject close to your heart, chuckles Sanaka! Heresy belongs to a certain place and a certain time. Heresy today will be the norm tomorrow. Remember Abraham and his reckless action in Sumer. The Sumerian Abraham could not face the new ideas of the time. The biblical text states that before leaving his homeland he destroyed the idols of the day. This was a political as well as a moral and social statement of disapproval. This was a blatant act of sacrilege.

'Yet we do not regard Abraham as a rebel.

'Indeed not, he is the founding father of the monotheistic movement. His heresy turned into the religious norm that has endured long after its intended term. In order to usher in the new order, the old order must crumble. When Judah Macchabee and his group of rebels planned an uprising against the Greek forces, he was held as the great hero of the fight against oppression, he was a thorn in the flesh of the Greeks though. Every new age gives a similar picture; the old world must disintegrate for the new world to be erected on the ashes of the old. The force driving mankind to its destiny is irrepressible, it is written into the Divine Plan. At some point in your historical past you came to a halt, you got stuck in the desert sands of time; you turned to stone like Lot's wife. The tragic paradox is that in order to escape from natural law you adopt a god who is bound by natural law, a god of nature!

The One Life - a biological perspective

'Mystics experience it, Masters teach it, and we talk about it: the One Life, what is it? The living cell holds the secret, begins BarYohai as if inspired by a muse. If the Creator is Life, then the tiny cell holds the secret of the universe!

'To see a world in a grain of sand/ And a heaven in a wild flower/ Hold infinity in the palm of your hand…' wrote Blake, quotes Johansson.

'He sensed the One Life, concurs BarYohai. In the pre-scientific past our insistence on separation and selection was a sign of intellectual paucity, moral inadequacy and spiritual scarcity. In the scientific present to cling to separation and selection spells out ignorance, inexcusable ignorance!

'Figuratively the Father stands for the immobility and unchanging nature of the world', quotes Clara. Why study physical laws when it is easier to worship the Father, god of physical laws?

'Good point, approves Shemtov. The Father stands for the inexorable laws of nature, the laws of physics, astronomy and cosmology. Is it the reason that prompts so many of us to study science? Instead of going to the synagogue we go to the laboratory, that's what I did. The chasm between the devout and the scientists is deceptive, they worship the same god!

'Therefore the Father and Samsara are one and the same, exclaims Clara!

'That's right, goes on BarYohai, why exert oneself in serious scientific study when the rituals designed to appease the Father – the god of physical law - require no expansion of mind, no academic endeavour, no intellectual rigour?

'Not to forget that physical law is also cosmic Law, inserts Jeremy. All laws emanate from Cosmic Consciousness.

'Indeed, picks up Shemtov. 'We always look for what is absolute behind what is relative, for the reality behind the appearance and for what abides behind what is transitory' said the physicist Max Planck. Unity pervades all, unity underlies all forms. Form is an illusion to the scientist and to the mystic alike.

'Whatever you see as duality is unreal, said Shankara, quotes Tara.

'The physicist Schrödinger said, 'The world is given but once. Nothing is reflected. The original and the mirror-image are identical. The world extended in time and space is but our representation'. He agrees with you Jeremy!

'As does Buddha, 'The fact is, there is only one world – there are not two worlds … People think there are two worlds by the activity of their own minds'. As Buddha said Samsara and Nirvana (the non-physical world) are one and the same. Duality is an illusion.

'Why unlock the secrets of Creation, goes on BarYohai, when a couple of verses in Genesis reveal the origins of the universe? Why look for solid knowledge when the opinions of our distant ancestors will do? Let's fall back on our Neolithic approach and call it 'kedusha', virtuous devotion!

'The triumph of ignorance virtuous, wonders Jeremy?

'The Father was presented to animal-man of Lemuria millions of years ago by the Masters, to keep them in obeisance of natural law and within the bounds of decent living, reminds Johansson.

'Going back to my initial idea, as a biologist I observe life at work, resumes BarYohai. Every cell consents to work for the benefit of the whole, man prefers to work for his own benefit. With living cells the motto is 'one for all', with man the motto is 'each man for himself'. While selfishness is alien to the cell it is the driving force in man. Selfishness in the cell becomes a cancer tumour. The cell will die to defend the integrity of the body, not many of us are prepared to die for our fellow men. Each cell communicates with every other cell. Declining to communicate is not an option for the cell, yet it is an option for man. Connection with humanity is foreign, for us godliness means disconnection! Cells adjust to the situation of the moment, in readiness to respond to new challenges; we are stuck in our prehistoric mentality and jammed up in rigid habits of behaviour. Cells know each other as equally important, we know ourselves as important and others as less so.

'Sananda stresses the interdependence of all things in the universe, of all living organisms, all ecological systems, inserts Jeremy.

'Interdependence is the rule, goes on BarYohai, for us it is not even the exception; we prefer proud separation and aloof disconnection! Although every cell is specialised (stomach cells, brain cells) they unite in ingenious ways, a person can adapt to severe cold or heat never experienced before yet survive or look at new objects never seen before yet make sense of them.

'The physicist David Bohm confirms this, 'An object does not have any 'intrinsic' properties belonging to itself alone; instead it shares all its properties mutually and indivisibly with the systems with which it interacts', quotes Shemtov. The key words are 'mutually' and 'indivisibly'. We are an anomaly.

'Nagarjuna said, 'Things derive their being and nature by mutual dependence and are nothing in themselves', quotes Tara.

'We should teach the mystery, beauty and wonder of living cells to children rather than fill their heads with dogmas of separation, disconnection and genetic advantage, all of which breach the laws of nature, suggests Clara. Learning the behaviour of cells they will learn the spiritual qualities we have disowned, qualities we scorn.

'I agree, approves BarYohai. Cells share a common genetic heritage; they know that they are essentially equal. Stomach cells are different from brain cells but in spite of their different function they know their common purpose and respect each other's integrity. Healthy cells never forget their common purpose or their common origin. When dis-ease sets in and the economy of the body fails, the cells work hard to restore normality, always striving towards the health of the whole, always in service to the whole.

'Archangel Michael told me that when there is balance within a person there can be no dis-ease, inserts Clara. In other words cells do not cause disease; it is our warped thinking that makes us ill, not our body.

'Another way of saying it: when we work with the laws of life we are in health, when we break the laws we are dis-eased, echoes Tara. When we break the laws we create an adverse karma which follows us from incarnation to incarnation and attract to us all manner of unpleasant situations and events

'In Sananda's words 'The true nature of the physical body is that it is a spiritual vehicle, it serves as a way of creating with light, it forms a bridge between this material world and the spiritual world', quotes Jeremy. The body is a spiritual instrument and the findings of biology confirm this.

'Sananda also said 'There are spiritual laws which are held within each human body. There is a spiritual structure within each human form'. Biology bears this out, notes Clara.

'When we deviate from the laws of life, when we fail our soul we get ill. Our cells know cosmic Law; we do not, echoes Johansson!

'Cells never choose to be outsiders, we do, adds BarYohai! The mystery of life is encrypted in the cell. It is perhaps the immune system which is the most staggering: cells rush in legions to defend the organism under attack; we have immune cells which remember invading organisms and ensure adequate response in future, the 'memory cells'.

'Amazing, exclaims Jeremy. In sacrificing itself for the whole, the cell is behaving in a truly spiritual manner! In working altruistically for the survival of the body, in communicating with other cells, in their adaptability, in their respect of other cells, in their inventiveness, they display the wonderful energy-qualities of realised cosmic Beings. The cell engages in unselfish service, self-sacrifice, acceptance, respect, originality, adaptability, generosity, group effort, cooperation, the very qualities of the soul!

'Cells demonstrate in action the altruistic idea of 'group consciousness', reflects Johansson. The emphasis on group effort and group purpose that the Masters are encouraging us to develop, that humanity is evolving into. The next phase in human evolution.

'The Masters tell us that each cell stores an atom of cosmic light, says Levinson. We worship the god of matter unaware that within each of the trillions of cells in our body resides cosmic Intelligence! We worship the tyrannical ego yet within each cell is an atom of the divine. God has a wonderful sense of humour!

'To quote Sananda again, the body 'is a way of manifesting light, it serves as a way of creating with light'. The body holds the primordial light of creation, comments Jeremy.

The flamboyant ego breaks universal Law but the humble cells in our bodies uphold divine Law.

'We have elaborated a vast network of principles and practices, dogmas and opinions that infringe divine Law, remarks Clara. We dispute them with smugness and derive much gratification from our squabbling, unaware that we are flouting spiritual Law! And the tiny cells in our bodies which behave according to cosmic law put us to shame!

'God is more present in my laboratory than he ever was in the synagogue, which for me was empty of his presence, rounds up BarYohai. The day is coming when biology will be taught in religious schools all over the world. No one can claim to be a believer yet ignore the spiritual behaviour of the cells inside a person, a flower, a tree or an insect! Man has forgotten spiritual law, the cells have not!

'You know now why the synagogue was empty of God's presence, remarks Levinson! The god-force that pervades the synagogue demands a response dissonant with the self-denying response of the cells, discordant with the love-energy the Masters embody. It is other than universal Law.

The Law of Karma

The reading from The Hebrew Gods resumes. Moses was studying in the library when

'Why Master, why the urgency, we already discussed karma?

'I want to emphasise the importance of karma. Karma is the ultimate law of the universe, the source of all other laws. It was not thrust upon mankind randomly by a capricious god bent on revenge. How do you envision karma?

'The biblical ruling of 'and eye for an eye' which means action and retribution, sin and atonement?

'A definition but a flawed one. At the simplest level karma is just that, action and its outcome. But let us start at the beginning. The game of life requires rules, all serious games have rules. At the highest level of group consciousness humanity settled on karma. It is the intelligent and equitable law that links an effect to its cause, even when the cause stretches back centuries. The law of 'cause and effect' applies to the physical kingdom just as it does to the human kingdom.

'Is the Law of Karma universal?

'It is. The entire universe is subject to the law of karma whereas not all stars and planets are subject to the law of gravity.

'It is the law that ensures justice?

'Not harsh justice, but sensible fairness. Behind karma is the Law of Harmony which stipulates that when we disrupt universal harmony, when we upset the cosmic order by our selfish actions, order has to be restored. The natural tendency in the universe as in man is the restoration of balance when balance has been disrupted.

'Is karma self-regulating?

'In a sense yes, when balance is disrupted, balance must be restored, this is a built-in tendency. In living things when disease strikes the body's healing forces come to the rescue to restore health. Health is the normal state of man, disease is not normal. Balance is the normal state and anything that thwarts balance is not normal.

'Karma has little to do with reward and punishment?

'Karma is a cosmic Law, it neither rewards nor punishes, it is impartial just as the law of gravity is impartial. But if you forget the Law, if you fall from a great height tragedy will ensue. As human beings we designed the Law of Karma in primordial times and we are in charge of it.

'We suffer it yet we are in charge of it?

'Karma seeks to restore balance when balance has been disrupted. If you break cosmic Law, if you disrupt cosmic balance then karma sets in. You set the law into motion, just as you set the law of gravity into motion when you throw yourself from the top of a mountain.

'We are in charge of karma, how is this possible? We administer reward and punishment.

'Strange as it may sound, we reward and punish ourselves! We administer the Law of Karma according to the way in which we either work with cosmic laws or infringe them. The mystical East endorsed this law aeons ago; it is deeply ingrained in us. In your world the idea of so much freedom and responsibility is almost unknown. You cling to the view that you are puppets on a string that a malign god holds to amuse himself at your expense.

'We reward and punish ourselves? How am I going to explain this law to my people back in Vilna?

'In much the same way that Newton explained the law of gravity. A cosmic law is a cosmic law; it is not open to debate. You do not haggle over a cosmic law. No sane person would say, 'I don't believe in the law of gravity'. Would you have persecuted Newton for finding out the law, as Galileo was for daring to say that Earth turns around the sun?

'Any infringement to the laws of the universe must be put right, muses Moses. 'An immutable law but a law that mankind set into motion in primordial times, a law that human beings administer. That's not easy to grasp! When you recognise the cosmic Law of Karma you will make a giant leap forward, not only your group but the whole of mankind.

''The one is the many, the many is the one', quotes Moses.

'Indeed, there is only one life. When a person gets in the way of the natural flow of life, he hurts all life. Equally when one progresses he benefits all life.

'This is what you want me to do?

'Yes, the time is approaching. Individual progress benefits all humanity, it also benefits the Planet. As you awaken, you awaken the whole of Creation. No person is an island, you may live isolated behind walls; the walls do not shield you, what you think and do affect the rest of the world. Thoughts travel and reach other thoughts of the same nature. Beautiful thoughts rise to the higher realms, negative thoughts and emotions stagnate and fester on the astral plane. You may shout your innocence, reality says it all. You may dupe your world but you will never dupe those who know the law of Karma.

'So no group can claim chosen status, no group can allege that their suffering are god-given as a sign of their holiness. People are who they are.

'Something else will infuriate them; the Law of Karma wipes out any allusion to a personal god. When you realize that you came to Earth of your own free will to restore balance and to progress, then the idea of a personal god becomes redundant. That is why Buddha rejected all higher authority and all dogma and why he was accused of being an atheist.

'Was Buddha an atheist?

'Buddha was not a theist. Theological debates were to Buddha 'a thicket of views, a puppet show of views, a toil of views, a snare of views'. The real issue for Buddha was the mental liberation of man, liberation from the shackles of illusion. The gods are powerless to help us; the gods swim in the ocean of Samsara like all humans.

'There is no help to expect?

'Not really, as Buddha told his disciples, 'Be a lamp onto your own feet'. You are very much alone and your liberation is your own responsibility.

'This is disquieting for those who rely on a higher authority and refuse to 'be a lamp onto [their] own feet', those who, the world over, 'do & obey' to pacify their gods and gain their favours.

'You are right. When they wake up to the fact of emptiness, impermanence, uncertainty and self-responsibility there will be no one to blame, no one to implore. When you remove authority and dogma, you also remove the habit of blaming someone else for your troubles. There is no one else.

'What befalls human beings is the resultant of the Law of Karma in action?

'You will no longer blame your god or mankind as you have done for centuries. Many are afraid of autonomy and responsibility; it's easier to find a scapegoat. Christians have done this for centuries, when things go wrong they find a scapegoat, your people! When people break cosmic Law, when they undermine cosmic balance, they alone must restore balance.

'So what is the future of religion as we know it in Europe?

'What do you think, Moses?

'It becomes superfluous. If we alone can restore the balance we have disturbed, then there is no act of god, no fate, no destiny, only human action.

Karma, the hand of destiny

'Right. It also follows that you have no need of temples in which to implore the gods to save you from the effects of your own actions!

'Misfortune is not an act of fate. Misfortune does not fall from the sky. Misfortune does not come from forces outside our control.

'We are not passive victims to misfortune; we are the agents of it!

'Under the Law of Karma, this is so. Misfortune is the result of events joining at a certain point in time. Imagine several brooks flowing towards the main river and merging at that point. We know that thoughts are things, once released they travel. They have the power to change, warp and destroy; they can make people sick, they can even kill. Malign individuals dart their thoughts like arrows to hit their intended victims.

'We are in the power of other people's thoughts?

'The thoughts released by humans fill the air, actively seeking their target. We can inflict harm on others effortlessly just by thinking harmful thoughts and darting them, but not without impunity. This is where the Law of Karma comes in. Some enjoy discharging malign thoughts that hurt others, but the thought travels back to the sender like a boomerang, if not in this life at some time in the future, but it will boomerang back at them. It may take moments, decades, centuries but it will travel back.

'So it does not pay to hurt others by thought or in any other way.

'We can wreak havoc with the lives of others and have a good time doing it, no one can prevent us. But as we do, we set into motion a sequence of events that will meet and lock at a point in time. The person suffering may be a good person in this life, but the law of Karma requires that he makes amends for his past thoughts and actions. Nobody knows about it, not even himself! He appears to be victim of fate and people commiserate. The thoughts he darted long ago have come back. This may have taken several centuries, several millennia, but they are back! There is no escaping Karma.

Neglect of Karma

'I stumbled upon a quote by the Dalai Lama I must read out to you'. They all nod in assent. 'When you believe in the connection between motivation and its effect, you will become more alert to the effects which your own actions have on yourself and others'.

'Interesting quote, approves Sarah, tell us more.

'The Dalai Lama's minimal and lucid definition of the law of Karma. Karma is the direct link between an action and its outcome, between a cause and its effect, goes on Levinson.

'It is the law of 'an eye for an eye', exclaims Shemtov, under a different name!

'It is more subtle than that, picks up Bendavid. An 'eye for and eye' is managed by an external force, be it the Sanhedrin judge or god. It is crude but well suited to Bronze Age disposition. The 'sinner' is guilty and must be punished. The crucial point is that he has nothing to do with the choice and gravity of the sentence. Punishment is inflicted on him. He is a victim and often takes a gloomy pleasure in it.

'They bare their soul in my practice, picks up Sarah. To revise their viewpoint goes against the grain, against the ancestral conditioning. Freedom frightens them. Yet there is no healing without acceptance of freedom.

'It seems to me that karma is retribution under any name you care to mention, notes BarYohai.

'Yes, but it is self-administered, corrects Jeremy. That's why if you are in the 'red', to use a banking metaphor, things may take a while to come into effect. Karma is very complex, it is justice in action. It is more than that, it involves learning. To know that your actions are wrong you have to evolve a moral sensitivity, an intellectual capacity, a philosophical aptitude. And this long process of mental expansion may take centuries, millennia of carefully planned incarnations.

'We all believe that action leaves us untouched, safe, expands Johansson back from a short retreat in a monastery. This narrow view does not take into account the Law of Karma. We emit low grade thoughts and negative emotions, we engage in mindless action and foolishly we assume that no one will ever know. How can anyone find out? Karma is at work diligently, patiently, exactly. Senseless action, malign thoughts and harmful emotions ripple out to find their intended target and wreak havoc.

'But as Sanaka explained, like a boomerang they come back to hit the agent who one day will have to face the music, says Levinson. There is no way of telling when; it may be in this lifetime or in some future incarnations. Accounts have to be settled sooner or later, often much later, so late that the sender has no way of knowing why he is confronted with that tribulation.

'The devout I knew would say, 'It is an act of god, we have to accept it, we must not question, we must not try to understand', says Clara.

'They run away from the crisis, analyses Sarah. Ascribing the crisis to their god they feel absolved, they feel good in a morbid way, they don't have to make sense of it, worse still they don't have to change their ways, just keep their heads buried in the sand! To write off life events as god's will and make their god liable, is a pietistic way of escaping the need to understand and to accept responsibility. In other words, to be free.

'Poor soul, we say in sympathy, acts out Clara who spent most of her life observing this phenomenon, such a nice person what has she done to deserve this?' We commiserate not knowing the facts, and who can ever know the facts. We conclude, 'God is unjust, life is nasty, there is no fairness.

'Could this be the reason why Western religion has eliminated karma and reincarnation from their entire agenda, asks Shemtov?

'Possibly, replies Jeremy, people do not want to think that a misdeed performed many lifetimes ago is coming back to haunt them, that now is the time to repay the overdraft with interest! They need consolation, they seek reassurance, 'God loves you, he is testing you as a mark of his appreciation'. I used to go to church with my parents when I was a kid and I often heard the priest say, 'You suffer now but the gates of Heaven will be wide open to receive you'. 'Chosen' by god you will be saved without question'.

'Everyone gets something out of this masquerade ball, continues Johansson, I too used to go to church when I was a kid, my father was the officiating parson. He used to thunder and roar, 'Rejoice you are the elect of God. We have a soul, we have a soul! We have been saved among all people, we are the elect, the Heavens are awaiting us'. The congregation was candidly reassured. He lost his faith towards the end.

'So Karma may be defined as the inevitable effect of a cause, the predictable outcome of a cause, spells out Shemtov, I am familiar with this in physics.

'That's right, explains Jeremy, it is inevitable but predictable? How can you predict what will happen to Attila the Hun, or Nero or Ivan the Terrible? When a person is aware that his actions have an effect on himself, on the people around him and on the Planet, he is also aware of his inescapable responsibility. The law of Karma ultimately has to do with responsibility. This is why it can only be self-administered. One has to grow into self-responsibility and also develop a sense of universal responsibility.

'Karma is widening as we define it, notes BarYohai in amazement. We started of with guilt and punishment, we moved on to conscious evolution and we are now tackling issues of responsibility, freedom, autonomy and authenticity. We kicked off with 'an eye for an eye' we are now touching at complex philosophical issues. Where is it going?

'It embraces the whole of the human condition at all levels of development, explains Jeremy. The problem is that the effect may show up years or life times after the cause was forgotten. The difficulty is immense, only enlightened beings are able to make this connection. For most people adversity in one life time cannot be traced back centuries and lifetimes earlier. As a result the individual or the group may feel deeply resentful toward fate or toward their gods. They carry the burden of pain but they lack the skills to make sense of it all.

'You mentioned an 'eye for an eye' Shemtov, continues Levinson.

The doctrine of Karma was raised by Moses when he uttered this heartfelt question, 'Why does the wicked thrive and the just languish in suffering?' As an Egyptian Initiate

Moses knew the answer, but the scribe did not, so he raised the ghost of the jealous god who chastises and rewards as he pleases. Fobbed off with this cop-out we have suffered much unnecessary pain.

'Karma provides answers to the tormenting question that has plagued mankind, notes Clara. I suspect that the scribe was too intellectually indolent and spiritually feeble to seek answer at source. Or it was calculated to instil fear in the heart of his folk. Perhaps the power in the land dictated it. His reasons might have been religious as well as political.

'Karma has to do with balance, this is what the Masters frequently remind us, explains Jeremy. You remember the old-fashioned scales? If you place a few apples on one tray of the scales, the tray tilts. To bring it back to its original position, it must be matched by its equal weight on the other tray. Karma is a constant balancing of forces between us and the world around us. When we disrupt the order of things, we precipitate a state of imbalance. Things become precarious for us and for others. Imbalance cannot be sustained indefinitely; the natural tendency built into all things is to strive towards equilibrium. In other words, karma is a natural law that regulates human behaviour and ensures that where balance is upset it must be restored. Karma is justice: unjust actions must be amended. Karma is balance: when imbalance occurs equilibrium must be restored. Karma is harmony: the natural flow of life streams towards a life-enhancing state.

'Segmentation, fragmentation, separation interfere with the spontaneous flow of life, obstruct natural law and defy cosmic law, rounds up Sarah, the therapist. This is clearly a life-threatening situation. Wrong actions disrupt the normal life current; they precipitate unrest, disquiet, and dis-ease. Karma by restoring balance also restores health. For some this may take a life time to grasp but then liberation is sweet indeed. From being split, from living a fragmented existence, we are made whole again; personality and soul are reunited, healing has occurred, truce at last!

'But the pain lingers for longer, notes Levinson. The trouble is that the majority swim in the collective pool, never wanting to know. They paddle in the brackish waters, in tune with the others, in their element.

'You are saying that the order to remain separate by our god and for our god was and is a diktat that contravenes cosmic Law, asks BarYohai?

'You are a biologist, smiles Clara. Imagine an influential religious figure instructing you to remove certain strands of DNA from a living cell, 'you must eliminate these strands of DNA they breach my decision to keep the people pure, holy and separate'. What would you respond?

'Nothing must interfere with the integrity of the living cell!

''The tooth for a tooth' code is redundant then, mumbles Shemtov?

'For many of us it is, for others it is as compelling today as it was in Neolithic times. We all are different, we all progress at a different pace, we all are at a different point on the ladder of evolution, replies Jeremy.

'For my teachers of long ago, the 'tooth for a tooth' code was the pinnacle of ethical accomplishment, the mountain top of moral realisation, the dizzy heights of spiritual achievement, admits Levinson.

'They did not find anything distasteful about it, asks Tara?

'They did not try to transcend the visceral 'tooth for a tooth', 'eye for an eye' response, enquires Jeremy?

'It is shocking to our modern sensitivity in an age of rational debate, liberal principles and human rights ideals, explains Levinson. The 'tooth for a tooth' was designed to subdue Bronze Age man, you also have to realise that the leaders were also men of their times! What does the 'tooth for a tooth' tenet tell us? It anchors us in physical reality as it confirms the limited scope of our ethical progress, highlights the narrow margins of our sensitivity, and shows the restrictions of our intellectual grasp.

'The 'tooth for a tooth' tenet is not to be taken too literally, corrects Bendavid, no one will pull your tooth out or pluck your eye out! But it shows in graphic form the type of legal system in place at the time, a system which promotes a violent response to misconduct. The Bronze Age legal charter does not offer rehabilitation, behaviour modification, education, moral guidance or clemency. It advocates violent retaliation.

'It endorses violence in response to violence, remarks Clara, it supports aggression in response to aggression. Blow for blow, force for force! Emphasis is on the physical nature of the action and the physical response to that action. Punishment is of a physical nature. Physical misdeed is met with physical retribution. We remain locked on the physical plane of action and reaction, cause and effect, crime and punishment.

'There must be another way, notes Sarah.

'There is another way, it was promoted by Buddha and the Essenes long ago but was too advanced for the times, explains Tara. Karma needs not be so brutal, so trivial or so mindless. It should not defeat, humiliate and demoralise the 'sinner'. All of us without exception through countless incarnations have committed heinous crimes and we come back to mend our ways, learn from past indiscretion and grow in moral stature. The 'tooth for a tooth' is the tenet of the tyrant who puts himself on a pedestal, showing off his perfection! Well I have news for him, he has 'sinned' in his countless incarnations and the fact that he is on Earth attests to his 'sinful' past. If he was perfect he would not walk the Earth with the rest of us. So harsh to others yet so lenient to himself!

'Having listened intently it is obvious that karma intelligently grasped has nothing to do with punishment. It has more to do with growth and self-realisation, with progress and emancipation, comments Bendavid. The crude 'tooth for a tooth' tenet benefits no one, least of all the 'sinner'.

'There is another way, a vertical climb into the mental sphere, reflects Tara, the Buddhist. The mental realm is the field of realisation, understanding and resolve to change. Karma finds its most effective expression on the mental plane. The return of balance is done consciously by the individual for the benefit of all.

'Healing has to do with self-knowledge, you are right it is of the mind, replies Sarah! Our Bronze Age code which advocates brutal retribution belongs to the mythological age that predates psychology. Our entire system predates the emergence of the rational mind, what are we lumbered with!

'We are lumbered with a pseudo-religious-come-legal system that sprang from the psyche of primitive man! A pre-psychological, pre-conceptual, pre-rational policy suited to the psyche of antediluvian man, replies Bendavid. We dance around it, we bow before it, and we sing to it, we revere it!

'The Essenes explained that love heals everything, notes Tara, by this they implied that violence breeds violence, punishment leads to resentment and unleashes more violence. Society finds itself caught up in crime and punishment. Some legal systems still abide by the 'tooth for a tooth' code, punishment must fit the crime. The more enlightened suggest rehabilitation and recovery.

'Of course, says Jeremy. Sin is of the lower nature, punishment of sin also stems from the lower nature. Sin and punishment are of the lower self. But there is another way; 'sin' could lead to the arousing of the higher spiritual centres in man. When a man no longer wishes to identify with his lower nature he is climbing to the abstract mind. This is what the Essenes meant when they taught that love heals everything. Love is the highest energy frequency in the universe. An energy conversion takes place, a transformation occurs. In the symbolic language of alchemy, base metal is transmuted into gold. The raw energy of the 'tooth for a tooth' is converted into a purer energy. The lower vibration is transmuted into a higher frequency that benefits all. The redeeming of the individual facilitates the redeeming of the Planet. Spiritual ascent of man encourages the spiritual ascent of the Planet.

'Karma is the law of progress; this is why karma is self-administered. Man has to grasp the futility of his actions and arrive at a sane realisation, reflects Shemtov. Man must grasp that he is the author of his destiny in order to avoid the same life-threatening pattern of behaviour. For as long as he projects his destiny outside himself, he is conditioned by unseen forces outside his control and he goes on bemoaning his unjust fate. We must let go of determinism.

'The Masters remind us repeatedly of our inherent autonomy and self responsibility, says Jeremy. There are no unseen powers or natural forces that decide our fate, and so there is no determinism. We are at all times makers of our destiny, 'creators of our reality'.

'There is light at the end of the tunnel, rejoices Shemtov. Physicists are searching for the 'theory of everything'. Consciousness lies at the core of our very own theory of everything. When we finally awaken to the realisation that man alone is responsible for what happens to him, that he alone has decided on this particular course of action, that he has selected his 'reward' or 'punishment', that he is the author of the fate he curses, we shall awaken.

'This is perhaps why so many thinking people turn away from tradition, notes Levinson. There is nothing that appeals to reason or even to common sense. For us atheism is still the best answer. It makes room for serious reflection.

'If god does not exist man can do anything, reckons one of the brothers Karamazov, reflects Johansson. This is absurd. If god does not exist, it is all the more crucial for man to take control of his life and liberate himself rather than extend his misery over a greater period of time. Buddha rejected the concept of god while urging man to set himself free.

'You recall the biblical curse 'the sins of the fathers are revisited on their children'. Quite apart from being downright immoral, it is also absurd. We have an ethical problem, remarks Bendavid. How can children suffer for crimes they did not commit? This simplistic view of the law of cause and effect is also illogical.

'Since the children repeat the behaviour of their fathers, they repeat the 'sins' of their fathers, reacts Sarah! I observe the workings of this law in my work. When we refuse to question the archaic notions of the past, when we anchor the same attitudes and prejudices, the same conviction, the same tribal values, when we endorse them unthinkingly before dumping them on our children then yes 'the sins of the fathers are revisited on their children'! No malevolent deity is cursing us, it is a self-inflicted curse!

'We reincarnate in order to be of service to others, redeem past misdeeds and change our mistaken view of the world, reflects Johansson. We come back to improve the nature of our relationship with god and with man.

'Interesting point 'our relationship with god', notes Clara, there is much to say about that! Our collective relationship with mankind infringes natural law and our relationship with God breaches cosmic Law!

Incarnation & Reincarnation

'What is the purpose of incarnation, Master?

'What is the purpose of incarnation, Moses, reflects back Sanaka?

'To attain liberation from the physical plane, from the illusion of Maya.

'I endorse your definition. Now you want my definition: the purpose of incarnation is to grasp the underlying nature of all things, the primary cause that lies beneath forms and events, it is to seek the Creator under the infinite diversity. It is to lift the veil that hides the Idea, the essence in all forms, the meaning behind the appearance. The form is symbolic.

'It is a game of 'hide and seek'? Is the Creator playing with us, is he saying 'Look for me, I am hiding so that you can find me, you want to find me and I need you to find me, we are playing this game together'. That's the way it is?

'In a sense this is true, God is hiding for man to find him, but it is more than a game of 'hide-and-seek', call it the game of evolution. In the beginning primitive man had to awaken from the darkness of matter and emerge into consciousness, before developing an emotional body and later a mental body.

'The purpose of incarnation, sums up Moses is to extract the nature of the form, the Ideas hidden in the form?

'Yes, the Idea, the soul-energy contained in the form.

'This applies to the animal kingdom as well?

'To the whole of Creation. The purpose of incarnation is to liberate the divine spark imprisoned in all things, the soul nature in all things, the germ of life.

'We languish on the surface and stagnate on the periphery! But there is a logic in this, admits Moses, we are custodians of dualism, keepers of time, guardians of the Fall. This is the Idea hidden behind the form which is the Old Testament. We are the wardens of Maya.

'Do you not find this courageous and even audacious on the part of your people, to be the guardians of the form? They long for the soul as much as any one else, but they were entrusted with the Book of the Fall, the Book of Duality. They agreed to be the memory of the nations and keep alive the origins of Samsara and Maya. Love and admire them for this, no other group has shown such sacrifice, such courage, such endurance. They are the custodians of form for the whole of mankind.

'I have to work on this one. Reality is just under the surface of things.

'The life force throbbing within forms is the ultimate reality.

'To attain this realisation we are tied to the ever turning cycle of birth and death?

'The diverse forms which appear real and solid are the veil behind which the Creator hides in order to be discovered. The Old Testament too is a veil behind which the Creator is waiting to be found.

'Why are forms illusions?

'They are illusions because they have no lasting existence, replies Sanaka, like a rainbow after the rain or a mirage which deceives the weary traveller in the desert. We notice the form which withers and dies but we do not see the soul-Idea that endures. The shell is expression of the Idea; the shell is not the Idea. The purpose of incarnation is to attain the realisation of the truth beneath the veil of form. You have to penetrate the unseen, sense the creative force at work in the cosmos.

'There can be no liberation until we sense the creative force at work in the cosmos? So it is rather pointless to live in expectation of a Redeemer.

'In a sense it is. No redeemer will negate the law of evolution. You recall what the Master told the Sadducee on the Last Judgment? When men rise from the dead they will be so much more evolved that they will 'neither marry, nor be given in marriage, but [will be] like angels in heaven'.

'When 'men are like angels in heaven' will they need a redeemer?

'Excellent Moses. No redeemer can alter the course of evolution. Man is his own liberator. When he is evolved enough to consciously create a body of light in which to move about 'like angels', he will no longer require a liberator.

'A new body, a 'light body'?

'Man is creating a new body other than the bodies he already has, the finer 'light body'. The physical body man gets from his mother. The substance he uses to fashion his 'light body' is his being. The Masters live and move in their 'light body'. The time is coming when man himself will live and move in his 'light body'.

'We have to forget about the liberator?

'O he will come, but not to liberate, this is the challenge for mankind! Man will already be liberated by his own endeavour. Long ago humanity could not grasp the complex ideas of personal responsibility, self-realisation, self-direction, self-knowledge and self-mastery. Child-man required the strict discipline of the 'do & obey'. Infant-man had to be inculcated, steered, chastised and frightened into obedience.

'What prevents mankind from achieving liberation?

'Good question. Attitudes, prejudices, dogmas, inherited beliefs, persistent thought forms keep mankind shackled to the Earth plane. Those who do not recognise that they are creators of their own experience, creators of their own destiny and who refute their undeniable freedom – those people are blown to the four corners of the Planet by the winds of karma.

'Hassidut is Divinity made comprehensible through human faculties. Hassidut brings the Godhead to perfect human comprehension'. This goes against reason and experience. It is the human faculties that keep us in illusion.

'The Truth itself ... can only be self-realised within one's own deepest consciousness' said Buddha. Definitely not with the intellect! And Shankara stated, 'Now you must realise that truth directly and immediately. Then only will your heart be free from any doubt'.

'Only personal experience will give us the truth, not what we read or argue over.

'You reach the universal within you, in the Heart, gateway to Reality. Buddha said, 'Transcendental intelligence rises when the intellectual mind reaches its limit. And if things are to be realised in their true and essential nature, its processes of thinking must be transcended by an appeal to some higher faculty of cognition'. What is this higher faculty?

'The intuition. The intuitive faculty is of the soul, only the soul can apprehend Reality because only the soul originates in Reality. So those who think that they can 'bring the Godhead to perfect human comprehension' do not know that God can only be apprehended by the soul, because only the soul can apprehend that which is of its own nature. They sleep the sleep of ignorance.

'Well thought through. 'Truth cannot be cut up into pieces and arranged in a system. The words can only be used as a figure of speech'. Words are only a reference, an insinuation; words hint, they allude, they do not disclose. You understand why poets and mystics use a symbolic language. The intellect relates to this world, the intellect is of the personality, it cannot apprehend that which lies beyond physical reality. It is not possible to 'know' the 'unknowable'. They belong to two different realities, different dimensions. You understand why theology is pointless, it is an intellectual exercise that aims to grasp that which it cannot grasp, it's like trying to catch moon beams!

'Humanity remains in suffering. Fate has nothing to do with it.

'Man invented 'fate' to make sense of his painful experience. It is the ego that initiates 'fate'. Realised Masters do not know 'fate' because they 'died' to the ego. Remember the Master urging Nicodemus to 'die' in order to live? Death of the ego means no suffering, no fate, and no illusion!

'What triggers the ego, what nourishes the ego?

'Attachment, aversion and confusion, the three mental poisons elicited by Buddha trigger and feed the ego. These keep human beings prisoners of the world of appearances, Maya.

'Attachment to any deeply-held view or belief?

'Attachment to principles, practices and dogmas mould human bondage. You take an opinion for Reality. An opinion is transient, it is of the personality. The purpose of reincarnation is to learn to discern the Real from the unreal. It is a journey from outer shell to essence, from outer form to Ideas, from effect to cause, from the objective to the subjective, from darkness to light. The long journey of the mythological hero.

'Master Sanaka, would you comment on the 'world of causes'? My people place 'causes' squarely on the shoulders of their god. To them it is blasphemous to envision that their world is of their own making, that the 'world of causes' is with them and not with some external force.

'Good question, my son. You see, the advanced civilisations of the universe do not live in the world of effects.

'Surely they too live in the world of effect, it is all around them!

'You are right but they are aware of creating the effects because they are aware of creating the causes that trigger these effects! Think of a ball, if you throw the ball hard against a branch of a tree, the branch will break. The cause, the throw of the ball, brings about an effect, the broken branch. There is no god and no fate involved, it is all of your own doing. Advanced beings in the cosmos are the conscious agents of the world in which they live; they know that they create their own reality.

'Their environment is literally 'their' world, their own creation.

'So is yours! The difference is that they know that thoughts create. They know that actions produce effects. Thoughts have their own driving force and ripple out in all directions. Sooner of later these thoughts will manifest. A thought will, in time, generate an effect. This is one of the major differences between the Master and the ordinary mortal, the Master is always conscious of the force of his thoughts and has total control over them, he lives in the 'world of causes'.

'The Master is aware of his creative power?

'Absolutely. He is aware of being a creator, like God he can create worlds. He is master of his thoughts precisely because he knows their power and their effects. He does not create causes, ordinary mortals create causes.

'Does he not, you do!

'You are right; I have to quality my answer. The Master has full control over his mind and generates only the effects he chooses to manifest. He is in control at all time; he knows the creative power of his mind.

'What if he ever had a bad thought?

'It is unlikely; he would not be a Master! A Master has achieved mastery. He functions as his soul. The Master has 'died' to the mortal self to be 'born' to his Self. You recall the powerful images of death and resurrection? Death of the self is a prerequisite to resurrection. The Master lives in the realm of causes even though he may still be encased in a physical body.

'You mentioned earlier how evolution can be expressed in terms of 'dimensions'.

'Yes, that is another way of looking at the same thing. In their physical bodies people function in the three lower worlds that make the physical dimension. But the initiate rises to higher dimensions. You are rising Moses my son!

'What are the characteristics of the higher dimensions?

'The Heart centre opens and love fills the entire chakra. The Heart is the gateway to other worlds and dimensions: the initiate is beginning to understand the nature of Reality; he knows that the universe is made of light. He also knows that the universe is love. He senses that this vast universe is sentient. He realises as he moves within his Heart the love that he is. As he enters the higher dimensions he becomes aware of his power of creation.

'You are teaching me to manifest?

'Exactly, you are co-creator with the Creator and with the Hierarchy. You could not revert back to the stage you were at before you came to India.

'Why? What mechanism is at work?

'Would you revert back to believing that matter is solid when you know that matter is light? Could you observe the Shabbat with conviction when you know that time is ultimately an illusion that you function in three time frames simultaneously, past present and future? Could you slip back to living in the world of effects when you are entering the world of causes? Could you revert back to identifying with your mortal self: your body, family, race, country, community and creed? Could you with candour utter the praise, 'Thank you O Lord for not making me a woman?'

'I could not.

'As co-creator with the Forces of Light you could not regress back to a phase you have transcended. The experiences of the vast majority of men are lived within these three worlds - physical, emotional and mental. Enmeshed in the lower worlds the usual response is always for more rules and regulations.

'They were intended to curb the lower nature, to ennoble, to humanise.

'This is true. In trying to subdue the lower nature you have suppressed your own vitality and depressed your spirit. While these rules have temporarily appeased your feeling of insecurity, their long term effect has been detrimental. How that Moses?

'Rules were intended to subdue the lower self with a view to lifting man to his higher Self, attempts Moses.

'Have they achieved this goal?

'They have not, control smothers the soul, stifles the life impulse.

'The impulse to do what exactly?

'To express our higher nature: to explore and expand, to experience joy, compassion and love, to embrace the whole of life.

'Precisely, Moses. Rules and regulations do the opposite; they have imprisoned and suffocated soul life. When the natural inclination is suppressed the soul withers. Understand that the soul – fragment of the Divine - incarnates in a body in order to explore the world and explore itself. Anything that stands in the way of this exploration transgresses Divine Law. Man is starved and the Divine is starved too.

'So man must learn every subject, experiment with everything in order to serve God? He must be an artist, a scientist and a humanist.

'Yes and much more besides, if he is serious about his own progress. If he is determined to evolve in order to benefit himself and the world. With ritualistic religion often the result is disquieting and contradictory, more laws bring a decrease in anxiety certainly but there is an increase in reliance on external forces, you become further anchored into the three lower worlds.

'So the development of science, literature, art and philosophy will encourage humanity to drop options that are not conducive to the expansion of mind and choose options that engage their full mental powers? Is that it?

'You have a way of darting at the heart of a question; I suppose this comes from your Talmudic skill, chuckles Sanaka. Advanced humanity is evolving to intuitive knowing, to reach the plane of Spirit. This of course is the aim of the divine Plan for humanity and man is evolution conscious of itself.

'Would you explain this last point,' man is evolution conscious of itself'.

'The impulse to evolve is encrypted in all life forms. A life form strives to attain its own intended perfection which exists in germ, in potential. In the lower worlds evolution is unconscious. Man is different, with him evolution is conscious, he strives in full knowledge of what it means to evolve.

'This lies behind reincarnation, the striving toward perfection, the conscious travail toward self-fulfilment.

'You see why it is crucial for earthlings to come back in incarnation time after time over millions of years, now in the body of a man, next time in the body of a woman, today with a white skin, tomorrow with a brown skin. You have to know all, experience all, explore all. Perfected man, liberated man is the sum total of all his previous experiences, his previous selves.

'This sounds exhilarating yet disquieting. Life flows on regardless of man's phantasms, beliefs and prejudices.

'Each incarnation brings change: personal beliefs, gender, race, creed, and skin colour – the form changes - the character within the form endures. The same 'man' inhabits a new body and confronts new circumstances. The implications are disturbing, 'what law shall I enforce next time around with the same consuming conviction, the same undaunted certainty, the same intolerance, the same intensity'?

'If the character remains the same why return in incarnation?

'Sound question. The individual longs to release the pain that escorts him life after life. So he designs a new situation which will rekindle the pain. He reawakens the pain in order to understand, to change, and to grow. Pain is, in the last analysis, pain of the ego which rejects change. So people come back to tackle their pain and when they experience the old pain they fail to make sense of it. They give in to despair, resentment and anger, they blame those around them, and they blame their gods.

'They will blame if no one explains to them the purpose of reincarnation.

'The purpose of reincarnation is explained again in every era, it was known in Atlantis, in ancient Egypt, in classical Greece, in India, in Tibet, in Mongolia and among the Indians of the New World. It emerged again 2000 years ago with the Essenes. You rejected it!

'We live in the world of phenomena. We grapple with the effects. What am I saying?

'The truth and it hurts! The causes may be lost in the remotest past but not so for the effects which stare at you. They are painful, what are you doing about it? Do you examine, probe and muse on the possible causes? No, you blame the world, your god, fate, any one, anything except yourselves.

'In the absence of a doctrine of reincarnation what else can we do, if not blame an unfair god or a blind fate? Ignorance is the root of all suffering.

'No one can plead ignorance of cosmic Law and get away with it. If you throw yourself from a rooftop and break your legs, would you get angry at the world because you forgot the law of gravity? It is your primary duty to learn about the world and yourself in order to lessen suffering and finally eliminate suffering. As you pointed out ignorance is the root of all suffering. It is the obligation of each human being to discover universal Law. Universal law states that every effect has a cause. What applies to nature also applies to man. The cause of man's suffering invariably lies within himself. He may dismiss it for ages and cycles but he will, in the end, have to confront it if he is serious about his progress. And so human beings drown in a world of effect having ignored the world of cause. The cause they project on to their god. The effects they grapple with. The result? They sink deeper into Maya.

Resurrection & the Last Judgment

'Would you give me a striking instance of the Law, Master?

'I don't think that you need it, replies Sanaka with a quiet laughter. You are the people who live in the world of effects.

'The laws of Karma and Reincarnation are indissoluble, are they not?

'As a Hebrew you know the law of Karma in action better than any one else on the Planet. Now I would like to veer off to an offshoot of the law of Reincarnation, the Resurrection. It will be best illustrated by a curious story recounted in the New Testament. Amazingly it demonstrates graphically the law by its very negativity.

'The Resurrection? This is not what I had in mind, Master.

'Bear with me, Moses. Once upon a time a group of Sadducees paid a visit to the Essene Master and put to him a convoluted question on the resurrection of the dead. I give you the gist of it: 'Rabbi, a woman marries in succession seven brothers. What will happen at the Last Judgment? Will the seven men resurrect and demand to marry her again all at the same time; will she be forced to live with seven husbands?' What a prospect! Can you imagine a woman having to share her bed with seven men at a time when humanity has reached a fine measure of moral sensitivity and spiritual awareness? At a time when humanity is loosening the bonds of physicality and rising to the plane of the mind, indeed to the plane of the soul? Could 'divine' law be so stupid? More to the point can human law be so stupid?

'I learned that the 'Luz' bone at the back of the head is unique. At the time of the Resurrection, a complete body will be built from this bone and so will the soul, explains Moses hesitantly.

'Whatever for? Each human being has had countless incarnations in human and pre-human bodies in his long odyssey, so which of the millions of 'Luz' bones will you choose from?

584

'They are being literal as always, sighs Moses with embarrassment.

'Indeed. The single most important event, the Day of Judgment, they envisage in physical, concrete terms. The moment the Prodigal Son returns home to his Father, the most exalted moment in the history of the Planet, a woman may have to marry seven brothers, because she was married to them thousands of years before! But that is not all, she indulged seven men in one life time, what about her previous incarnations? As you know she had countless incarnations like everybody else. Will she be commanded to marry a few millions men on the Day of Judgment?

'The law must not be read literally but figuratively.

'Indeed Moses, indeed. Archaic man comprehends the simple, the concrete. To these bizarre questions the Master replied bluntly: 'Are you not therefore mistaken, because you do not know the Scriptures or the power of God?' The Master chastised the Sadducees for their ignorance of cosmic Law.

'Are they talking about the same God?

'Probably not! The god the Sadducees glorify is a Samsara god bound by time and space. The God of the Hierarchy is the Consciousness that pervades the universe. That the dead will rise on the Last Day, the Sadducees take literally. They accept as true that the trillions of human beings who walked the Planet over millions of years will all rise. What a prospect! Can you imagine prehistoric men, early Lemurians rising to walk among us, barely human in appearance and nature, more like apes than men?

'Dust cannot reshape itself into human form, and what purpose will it serve anyway?

'Right Moses. What purpose will it serve, indeed? If this resurrection took place it would make a mockery of the entire Law of Evolution. The origins of man are humble, this your scientists will discover and your rabbis will deny robustly, the religious ego may resort to violence in its insecurity. But the Ambassador of Shamballa as he speaks to the Sadducees knows man's origins. He also knows the Law of Evolution which is being protected, inspired and promoted by Shamballa. The Law applies to the entire universe and is definitely not random, it is intelligent and directed.

'So what can we make of this strange story?

'If you understand even slightly the idea of evolution you know that the Sadducees understand nothing. At the Last Judgment when men rise from the dead they will be so advanced that they will 'neither marry, nor be given in marriage, but [will be] like angels in heaven'. This is the reply given by the Master of Shamballa. This is clear enough, is it not?

'The dead will not rise and there will be no Day of Judgment, exclaims Moses! This is quite clear now! The idea of the dead rising from the dust is bizarre: would God judge men who are 'like angels in heaven'? This is the goal of evolution, is it not, man revisiting Earth to make amends, to learn from past mistakes, to grow, to refine his nature, to polish rough angles, to expand his consciousness, to become 'like angels'? Is God going to judge the dry bones of prehistoric men who have returned into incarnations millions of times and continue to return in various skin colours, races and creeds?

'Well done Moses, my son. It is a joy to study with you; you are a credit to your people, indeed to humanity. Your evolution is a sound promise of progress for the Planet. Each man redeems himself and as he does he also redeems humanity. His thoughts radiate in all directions to touch everything and transform everything they touch.

'Did the Sadducees understand?

'Probably not, they wanted a literal and concrete answer and the reply propelled them to an unknown world. The Master and the Sadducees operate from two distinct planes of reference, two different worlds you might say. The Sadducees' question emanates from the physical plane while the Master's answer emanates from the mental and spiritual planes. One more point, I relinquished all religions, all dogmas, all beliefs, and all gods. I am an Initiate and have long transcended the illusion of Samsara. The Ambassador of the Hierarchy was forbidden to speak out, he who authorised the hand over of the Law to Moses! It was alright for him to authorise the Law at Sinai, but not alright to amend it, to adjust it, to adapt it to modern times. Everything evolves in the universe, including the cosmic Mind. The cosmos loathes immobility, all is life, all is movement, and all is change. The priesthood turned the Law into stone and mocked change. As life is change they also mocked life. As God is life, they also mocked God.

'You are saying Master that there is no resurrection of the dead but only of the living?

'Exactly. And not just any living but the living who have committed many life times to achieving liberation. This is the answer to Nicodemus, 'Except ye die, ye shall not live'. The resurrection is first a 'death'.

'Resurrection is not likely to fall on man like a hammer blow.

'Certainly not! It will grow from your own soil, your own being. Resurrection is liberation from the density of matter, from the pull of the lower nature, from the tyranny of the self. Resurrection is liberation from the confusion of Samsara, from the illusion of Maya. 'Except ye die, ye shall not live'.

'This runs counter to everything we stand for. Our tradition revolves around the created world.

'Well thought through, Moses. Every time you discover a new idea or examine a question and arrive at a satisfactory answer, you resurrect. Resurrection relates to expansion of consciousness.

'Resurrection has nothing to do with death and dying!

'Resurrection has to do with living! With freedom from illusion, 'And the truth shall set you free'. A journey from fear to love, from darkness to light, from illusion to Reality.

'Resurrection is to be understood symbolically not literally. The cosmic Mind is only interested in the resurrection of the living, summarises Moses.

'Moses, my son, laughs Sanaka you are being resurrected from the dead at this very moment!

Past, Present & Future

'While living in the present we are also living in two other time frames, begins the Master exploiting the element of surprise.

'As if the present was not difficult enough to contend with, groans Moses.

'We have been discussing the past and the present for quite sometime, what do you think karma is all about? The past brings us back and the present is intended to liberate us from the past. We return in the present to transmute the past. The future which is the resultant of past and present is in the making. So we are working on three time frames at the same time right now!

The past we created lingers into our present circumstances which we are forced to adjust to. The present shapes the future. If we live with the outcome of the past now and if the present is shaping the future, then we are timeless! We live in the past, present and future all at once!

'We abolished the past when we shed karma and reincarnation. The future we project on to external agencies. We are left with the present. Everything has to be decided in the present, remarks Moses.

'The timeless nature of man did not reach the land of 'revealed truth'. Essenes and enlightened Greeks reiterated cosmic Law; they taught that man is the aggregate of his past lives, the outcome of his former selves, a free and responsible agent who lives in the past, present and future simultaneously. He comes back countless times to make amend, refine his nature, polish his character, and progress on the road to self-realisation.

'What perplexed the Talmud writers? Was it sinful to think in terms of past, present and future? The Egyptians knew it and we descended into Egypt to learn spiritual Law from them.

'Is a self-initiated existence deviant, this is the question you are asking, Moses my son? Is the fact of the autonomy of the soul deviant?

'It was deviant to initiate one's life; it was deviant to proclaim the autonomy of the soul. If we admit to a self-initiated existence, this shows our freedom and the reality of the soul. In making a Samsara god all powerful we made ourselves powerless.

'Moses my son, your sorrow is the sorrow of humanity. Man threw 'out there' his divinely-given power and he is left to mourn his loss. He is convinced that he is a victim of fate when all the time he is a victim of his own illusion. That is why he comes back in the present to mend the past, but he repeats the past and transfers it into the future!

'Buddha hinted at a godless world in which man is free from 'divine' interference, says Moses. This is deviant, an insult to the monotheism we are so proud of having invented.

'An excellent comment Moses, do go on, this is interesting, chuckles Sanaka.

'If we accept that man chooses to revisit Earth then we have to admit to his inherent freedom and this freedom clashes with the traditional view of man governed by external, arbitrary forces. To us man is not free, he is a living mass of instincts and passions, he is driven by powerful desires that must be curbed. A deeply pessimistic view of man consistent with the time, the place, monotheism and patriarchy.

'I endorse this, Moses. You are saying that the foundation stone of monotheism and patriarchy is the unfreedom of man, that under these conditions man cannot be free or the whole edifice would collapse. The priesthood was holding tight to its negative view of man as a puppet on the strings of fate and they constructed the Talmud – impressive Tower of Babel – to put across their dark notion of man. What pessimism! What materialism! Feeble victim, flawed creature, man is impotent to change his fate. Redemption will come from the deity who may or may not grant it. Man is subject to the whims of external forces, forlorn in a random universe in which his god behaves in an unpredictable and often unethical manner.

'If I may sum up, Master, our life situation is of our own making, our past catches up with our present, the present hints at the future. When we handed over our innate freedom, we lost the memory of our boundless nature. We forgot that we exist in the past, present and future at once. To remedy we invented a god of destiny who has all the qualities we sacrificed. Is there hope for mankind?

'Much hope, Moses. The soul ever vigilant steers us in the direction of greater knowledge. The soul which exists beyond time has a cosmic landscape of past, present and future and arranges situations which will force us to adapt, change and progress. So that we come to realise that we are creators of our experience, instruments of our destiny.

'But the self defies the soul, the self resists change, the self opposed the emergence of the soul 2000 years ago.

'The self acting of itself will resist efforts from the soul. But the self enlightened by the soul will assimilate. The informed self is no longer the foe of the soul but the server of the soul. Those who claim that god fashions each one of you without a past betrays a profound ignorance of cosmic laws. Each human being is as old as the world, literally! Each incarnation choreographs its own dance, a ballet between past, present and future. The past precipitates the drama of now. The interplay between our past and our present is already showing glimpses of the future. We live in at least three dimensions - physical, astral and mental - just as we live in three time frames - past, present and future. And the priesthood want you to believe that you are powerless?

'Had the relentless march of the soul through time been recognised, our history would have taken a different turn

'And the history of mankind too, replies Sanaka. The decision of one affects all, there is but One life. Each individual influences humanity. To ignore the Law is to ignore the existence of the soul, the deathless nature of the soul.

'There is no hope?

'No, as long as man submits to an illusory fate. As victim of fate his progress is not conscious; it is imposed from outside by the combined Laws of Evolution, Attraction, Karma and Reincarnation.

'The perils of ignoring soul life are immeasurable, admits Moses. To recognise soul freedom is to be liberated. To deny soul freedom pushes liberation into an uncertain future. Liberation is no longer in our hands; it is imposed on us by external forces. A fate of our own making!

Ignorance breeds suffering

'Would you explain incarnation, Master?

'Different Masters offer different explanations. One suggests that the function of life in incarnation is to unravel the mystery of the universe, another to lift the veil and uncover the Reality that underpins physical reality, yet another will say that the purpose of life on Earth is to overcome Duality, another still will say that it is to perceive unity under the diversity, to uncover cosmic Consciousness under the form, or liberate the cosmic energy slumbering in matter. Do you find all these definitions bewildering?

'They appear bewildering, but on reflection they are not. They all are saying the same thing. What is your definition Master if I may be so bold …?

'As you pointed out all definitions are saying the same thing. Ultimately it is to learn to love for as you know the nature of the Divine is love, the nature of the universe is love, the essential nature of man is love. It follows that man reincarnates over aeons to uncover his true nature which is love. To turn into a realised being is not a one-off shot in the dark triggered by an arbitrary god. Realised beings are self-realised. No one does it for them; it is a conscious and deliberate decision. They are realised when they master the ego and all that the ego stands for. It takes vast time periods to spotlight the futility of man-made opinions and ideas, doctrines and dogmas, attitudes and prejudices. One of the many reasons we reincarnate is to uncover the cause of suffering. And as you know the source of suffering springs from man himself.

'Suffering is of the ego which refuses change.

'Suffering derives from aversion to change. Suffering springs from our attachment to derelict opinions and beliefs. Suffering arises from the materialism of separateness, the deadening force of authority, the paralysing effect of fear and the burden of the past. Somehow fear lies beneath all, fear permeates the entire being. Fear is a low-grade emotion which harks back to our animal past, so dark and opaque that it pulls you further down into Maya.

'But our tradition hammers in obedience to authority, upgrades fear as a virtue, nurtures attachment to the derelict opinions and beliefs of the past. The task is daunting.

'Buddha denounced the futility of separateness. Separateness breeds self-cherishing and self-grasping: 'I must be separate because I am special, I have a mission, I am chosen'. Buddha identified self-cherishing and self-grasping as the causes of suffering, karma and rebirth, do you see why?

'It is the ego that is clamouring. Man in his ignorance cherishes the ego and grasps at the ego as if it was truly existent, which it is not. The ego has no solidity, no reality, no permanence, the ego is an illusion. He resists the impulse of the soul which is to accept, to unite, to embrace, to include. He argues against cosmic Law.

'Excellent Moses. In separateness man is 'self-grasping': he believes his mortal self permanent and consistent, which it is not. In separateness man is self-cherishing: he cherishes his self, but the self is neither permanent nor consistent, so he cherishes a chimera. The only part of him which is boundless, timeless and deathless is his soul. Yet in separateness he disregards the nature of his soul. The ego demands separateness, the soul longs for unity, inclusion, understanding, empathy and sympathy. Conflicting aims! Human law requires that you flout universal Law. Buddha explained that it is self-grasping that keeps mankind chained to suffering, shackled to the wheel of rebirth and fastened to the rack of karma.

When the TAO is Lost

'Physical reality does not exist before us as an object of study but emerges from our consciousness during our changing experience within nature'. (Davenport)

'Every man's world picture is and always remains a construct of his mind and cannot be proved to have any other existence' (Schrödinger, physicist)

At the end of the section, Bendavid puts the bundle of translated papers down, 'We need to mull all this over and we also need a break. Let's go for a walk'. As they walk down to get a drink of cool lemonade, Bendavid unable to defer his thought explains, 'during the reading, words flashed through my mind, my teacher in India used to quote the famous phrase of Lao Tzu, 'When the Tao is lost, we need legality, morality, knowledge and much pretence'. I don't know why it came back just now but there is a connection.

'Self-grasping, self-cherishing, suffering, the Tao.....? You made the connection intuitively, try to make it rationally now, suggests Jeremy.

'Thanks for the backing, this concerns us all. In India at first I did not grasp the meaning, given the fact that I came from a strict patriarchal and monotheistic background, I respected legality, morality and I valued knowledge above all. Legality, morality and knowledge are the foundation stone of our way of life.

'It may be the reason why your teacher hammered it in, laughs Clara.

'How and when did you see the light, asks Tara?

'After months of arduous study and meditation.

'Give us the benefit of your insight; requests Johansson, I have not come across this phrase though I sense its meaning.

'The Tao symbolises the Self, the permanent nature of man, it also alludes to spiritual Law. The inner Self abides by universal Law.

'Say no more, butts in Tara, if the Tao relates to the higher Self, then everything else is of the lower self! All the rest is simply human interpretation, human opinion, human ideas. If the Tao is cosmic Law, the rest is human law.

'You hit the nail on the head, replies Bendavid, but you are a confirmed Buddhist! When spiritual Law is lost, human law takes over to multiply by division and go on multiplying uncontrollably. In prisons, there is a profusion of rules and regulations to keep prisoners restrained, to subdue their rebellious nature, to flatten and demoralise them. They must be coerced, threatened and even humiliated and degraded.

'They are stripped of their right to life and their right to death, interrupts Clara. Under Talmudic law, we have neither the right to live as free spirit nor the right to die as free spirit. Like prison inmates we are stripped of our personal responsibility and our divine autonomy. Any free spirit who refuses to conform is blacklisted.

'In a tyrannical system the individual is minor; it is the majority that counts. The survival of group principles, group purpose is paramount, continues Bendavid. All else must be sacrificed to group cohesiveness and continuation. The soul of the individual is muzzled, the price to pay to keep the idea of theism alive.

'We never lost the Tao because we never had the Tao, retorts Levinson!

'You hit the nail, exclaims Bendavid! This is the connection! Now is the time to find the Tao, we have been denied our divine birthright for too long.

'It is being rediscovered the world over, notes Jeremy. What do you think we are doing at this very moment? We are discussing the Tao. We are experiencing the Tao. The Tao was never lost. The Holistic movement in science, psychology, medicine, philosophy and ecology is ushering in a revival of the Tao. All is well.

'The many live in ignorance of the Tao, in ignorance of cosmic Law, locked up in the prison of human law, expands Bendavid. Man does not have to be muzzled, tied and restrained, as his Self he presents no threat. He is a threat when he yields to self-grasping and self-cherishing, so why did our law-weavers incarcerate man in the law of man? Why did they adopt the bleak view of their 'maker'? What a paradox! The law nurtures the self yet it suppresses the self. It inflates the self yet it demonises the self!

'You just answered your own angst-ridden question, responds Levinson. Our law-weavers adopted their 'maker's bleak view precisely because he was their 'maker'! There is a simple logic in this, if god thinks negatively about his creatures, he knows best. The flawed nature of man must be demonised, the way god sees it. Besides the deity is not reliable, he changes his mind; his moral disposition is in doubt after the Flood, the cataclysms in the Desert, the Exiles, the destruction of the Temple and crucially WW2. He waged terrible wars against his enemies, because they did not think like him and he abandons his Children in their darkest hour. All is confusion!

SUFFERING, EXILE & LIBERATION

'Liberation cannot be achieved except by the perception of the identity of the individual spirit with the Universal Spirit'. (Shankara)

Exile as an opportunity for transformation

'You must see exile as an opportunity for change, Rabbi Moses, an opportunity to heal.

'If to heal is to change then physicians are not needed.

'Excellent point Moses. True, in a perfect world they are not needed. But we live in an imperfect world in which man believes in many things, most of them questionable, unproven, unchallenged and confusing. He believes because he was instructed to. Under pressure from the group, with the fear of divine retribution hovering over his head, he capitulates. In caving in to the collective will he chooses the path of least resistance.

'Change will not come from the group which keeps him in a state of inertia and fear, reflects Moses.

'That's right. Change is forced from outside if man does not take the initiative. Change is unlikely where fear is woven into the fabric of the doctrine. Change is unlikely among people conditioned by fear and reliant on fear.

'To heal is to release all of these factors that keep man spellbound.

'There is more to it, man has so ingested the features of the group that they are part of his being, they stem from him as much as from outside.

'So how can he heal?

'To heal is to loosen your reliance on the things of the self, to let go of association with the self and with the material world. The self must release its grip. Suffering originates in the self which rebels against change, suffering stems from attachment to all that surrounds the self: beliefs, attitudes, prejudices, opinions, ideas and dogmas. For this reason see exile as an opportunity for transformation. To return to your point, physicians have no power to heal other than the power we give them.

'No physician can heal us?

'No physician can heal us unless we give ourselves permission to heal, that is to say until we are willing to let go of the past, let go of the strings that bind us to the past, until we let go of the illusions and attachments that thwart the healthy state.

'In the last analysis only man can heal himself?

'The true meaning of healing! The sick were miraculously healed when the Master uttered the magical words, 'Your sins are forgiven'. Was it really a miracle?

'In the light of what you just said, it was not. The sick were allowing healing to take place by letting go of the strings that bound them to the past. The Master knew this, they did not.

'The same applies to exile. Exile is a stern teacher that compels you to review your lives, opinions, beliefs, attitudes and prejudices, 'Be ye transformed by the renewal of your mind' said the disciple. To transform you by the renewing of the mind, in other words to heal you!

'Well, 4000 years of exile have not achieved much transformation.

'The forces of evolution are acting in concert to facilitate the progress of man.

'We have always viewed exile as god's retribution.

'On the Chosen people? On god's Children, laughs Sanaka!

'Exile is the cosmic response to our reluctance to change?

'Progress of one is progress of all. Equally, stagnation of one is stagnation of all. Everything a person does affect mankind and all life forms. A life equation you have ignored. You have lived in a sealed tank oblivious of the rest of the world. Exile is the force that pulls you out of the tank, out of your inertia. Exile is the force that brings you in contact with other cultures, other viewpoints. The aim is to expand your consciousness, to broaden your mind, to loosen up your energy fields, to learn, to grow.

'You rationalise exile when we emotionalise exile. We want to view it as a sign of our election, something that distinguishes us from the rest of the world.

'And it does just that! You wander aimlessly through time blown by the stormy winds of karma, oblivious to your inner power which alone can liberate you. When you finally let go of the self with its convictions and prejudices, its discriminations and attachments, you will awake. Exile is painful; it appears to be thrust upon you by a malign fate. But if you look from a higher perspective, it has a crucial role to play. Suffering is responsible for some of the greatest achievements in arts, literature, music and thought. Suffering forces us to seek answers and solutions. Suffering drives us in search of meaning and purpose. Suffering encourages us to let go of the illusory self. Suffering as an opportunity for change, to make a fresh start, to heal. When we finally realise that the source of suffering is the self, we go in search of the real Self like the mythological hero sets off on a journey of Self discovery.

'The land of darkness'

'Let us consider the various bodies of man, begins Sanaka. We examined the dimensions in space and time that man occupies at the same point. How do you picture the many-sided nature of man?

'As a many-sided being man exists simultaneously in the physical, etheric, astral and mental planes of experience just as he functions in the past, present and future. The more advanced also exist on the spiritual plane.

'Well done Moses, you have a sound grasp of the essential. Let us move into the finer dimensions, into man's other bodies. Spiritual religions are aware of the reality of multifaceted, deathless, boundless man. A ritualistic religion is of necessity aware mostly of the finite, limited, mortal nature of man.

'Why 'of necessity'?

'To endure, ritualistic religion relies on the fact of man's finite, limited and mortal nature. Man is more malleable, more pliable, more bendable, better disposed to be influenced by those in authority, but there is a downside to it'. Sanaka waits for Moses' response. He is not disappointed.

'Man is aware of his smallness so as a result he lacks inner resources, depth and solidity. He wants for a sensitive inner nature, an authentic spiritual disposition. He also tends to lack objectivity and a genuine interest in the world. Spiritual religions inspire man to know his deathless and boundless nature. Uninspired religions remind man of his irrational and corrupt nature. Spiritual religions rely on man's reason and essential goodness. Spiritless religions refute reason and deny man the right to make responsible life-changing choices.

'It is a joy to work with you my son. I am often tempted to call you 'my friend', but I prefer to think of you as my son, my spiritual son.

'This is making it all the more difficult for me to leave you and this wonderful monastery which I regard as my real home.

'You will be with us a while longer, Moses, I confess that I am not looking forward to giving up my son, smiles Sanaka with a touch of melancholy. I shall always be with you, distance is an illusion. We have been together before, we go back a long way you and I and we shall be together again in future. There is no room for sadness. Let us resume our study. Ancient cultures had personal experience of the sublime nature of man. They mapped out his complete constitution. They sketched the map of the seven subtle bodies: the etheric, astral, mental and spiritual vehicles each plunges in its own specific world. These interlinking bodies and their corresponding worlds make man multidimensional. Each body influences the others, the emotional body being the most unstable. The Egyptian high priests were well versed in the Ageless Wisdom, they knew of the esoteric anatomy of man. They were aware of the underlying Reality that underpins outer reality; they understood the workings of the mind. They knew how to heal both the body and the mind using advanced methods lost to your world. It is no surprise that they attracted the exalted biblical figures you revere to this day; their most illustrious Initiates include Abraham, Jacob, Joseph, Moses the son of Egypt, a priest-king in his own right.

'The Patriarchs and the Liberator of Israel, Initiates of Egypt!

'Inevitable fact. Where would the most influential beings of the past have found the education they needed if not in Egypt? Where else? Where would a contemporary intellectual find a scholarly environment if not in the universities of Vienna, Paris and Oxford among others?

'Yet we do not give Egypt credit for it, we refer to it instead as 'the land of darkness'. The land of materiality and evil.

'Darkness, chuckles Sanaka! It is in 'the land of darkness' that your Law-giver was born and educated and became an Initiate of the Temples of Wisdom. It is in 'the land of darkness' that your people came into existence socially, religiously and spiritually.

'It is embarrassing to think of Egypt as our spiritual country.

'Indeed it is, for a motley group of people who believe that they invented monotheism! The Egyptians knew the enduring quality of the soul, they knew about life after death. They understood that life is progress, that there is no sin only 'mistake' and that man can learn and grow. They knew that the purpose of life is to evolve from matter to spirit. They sensed the divine Plan of Creation: a life form must rise from its lowest state to its highest state; each form carries the cipher message of its own perfection, its own higher purpose, each striving toward that 'perfect' state.

'They knew that much?

'What went on in the Temples of Wisdom? What did Hermes teach in those Temples? What do you think the priest-kings, the Pharaohs, were taught and Moses himself?

'They knew that consciousness evolves over vast time periods?

'Intimately! They knew that progress is slow and requires many incarnations, they grasped that earthly life is a school. Their cultural achievement and spiritual awareness were signs of their insight in human evolution. They were a beacon for the entire civilised world.

'How come they were so far ahead of the rest of humanity?

'They owed their culture to those who fled the impending disaster in Atlantis. People began to migrate out of Atlantis centuries before the continent disappeared under the ocean and they went in search of suitable lands in which to salvage their civilisation and carve in stone their vast knowledge.

''The land of darkness' was host to the glorious civilisation of Atlantis?

'Indeed it was! They initiated the belief in a Redeemer Horus who was reborn every 2000 years period, under each successive sign of the zodiac. The idea of the Redeemer also appears in Sumer, land of a sophisticated culture.

'A Redeemer in Egypt, a Redeemer in Sumer?

'Beliefs and gods moved unchecked across lands. Enlightened times!

'The ancient world must have been wondrous, adept at exploring the many layers of reality it also had a universal outlook and respect for the ideas of others, mumbles Moses.

'The Goddess was widely revered in the ancient world. Exploration of the many layers of reality, a universal outlook and tolerance are not the distinguishing features of patriarchy! Do you see a parallel with the revolutionary events which took place in Europe a few years ago?

'The Revolution? I never saw a parallel until this very minute. 'Liberty, equality and fraternity' are the universal principles which affirm all men equal, all men free, all men brothers.

'Are these principles woven into your tradition? I think not. The 'one god' tenet is the foundation platform of the 'Ancient Regime' which has governed and trampled the people of Europe for centuries. One god, one king, one religion! The triumph of unity you might think. No, the triumph of tyranny!

'I always thought that our belief in the one god was the height of spiritual achievement!

'You thought what you were instructed to think! Was the French Revolution the dawn of the messianic age your texts predict asks Sanaka provokingly?

'Liberty, equality and fraternity? Decadence!

'The return of Horus anticipated for 4000 years? A return you obstruct, a return you avert, a return you defeat, asks Sanaka tantalisingly? The message you send out to the universe lacks coherence, it goes like this, 'We beseech you to send us the Saviour, but he must not come for if he does we shall deal with him effectively'. Or, 'We demand a Saviour who will not rock the boat, someone who will keep things just as they are'.

Prisoners of selfhood & prisoners of the Planet

'What is the meaning of 'prisoner of the Planet', asks Moses?

'Man is 'prisoner of the Planet' when he defines himself as his body. The body is composed of earth elements; the body is literally 'made of earth'.

'Adam was made of clay, 'made of earth'.

'The body is made of earth and after death it disintegrates back into its various elements. Man defines himself as his body when he says, 'I am made of earth', just as the verses of Genesis do. Some go all the way and affirm intrepidly, 'when I die it will be all over!' When man identifies with his material form he draws attention to his materiality. Some hold this view out of conviction, you are familiar with this!

'A few of us realise that religion has failed to meet the spiritual needs of man since it is embroiled in ritual practice and enmeshed in trivia. It fails to inform us of our true nature given that it gives emphasis to our physicality. Paradoxically futility breeds resolve, the more meaningless the ritualistic aspect, the more rigid people are. Futility is what thinking man is striving to overcome; futility is what ritualistic religion reinforces.

'This comes from identifying with the body. Rituals keep the body clean and people restrained in conformity. In other words, ritualism reduces man to identify with his physical self. Passionate belief often co-exists with passionate disbelief. The question of the resurrection of the body was debated yet unresolved in Talmudic times. You are a biblical scholar, tell me why?

'This has to do with the spectre of death I assume.

'You assume, Moses?

'What I took to be absolute truth is no more. I have had to rethink every dogma, every opinion, and every belief. Where I used to accept everything, now I accept nothing.

'Well done Moses, you are a living example of the adept according to Krishna, 'When thy soul passes beyond the forest of delusion, thou shall no more regard what shall be taught or what has been taught'. You have passed beyond the forest of delusion; you disregard what has been taught. You now rely on your judgment and discernment; you are your own Master.

'This would not amuse my old teachers; to them I am a renegade.

'You chose to Be! 'Doing' is the axis of your tradition. 'Doing' is pivotal to European civilisation. The surest way to serve mankind is through Being. Why does the image of the resurrection emerge with such intensity 2000 years ago?

'Impending death at the hand of the Romans triggers the argument. The promise of Redemption fails to materialise. Notions like 'chosenness' and 'world mission' now sound terribly hollow. The more thoughtful begin to ask questions. First the Greek occupation, then the Roman occupation, both prompt such debates. Tragedy galvanise people into thinking.

'You recall, my son, the story of the Pharisee priest Nicodemus who visited the Master and asked 'How can a man be born when he is old? Can he enter a second time into his mother's womb?'

'Nicodemus asks a valid question, literal, concrete, simple but honest.

'Perplexing by its very simplicity! Nicodemus lives in a concrete, literal but honest world! He knows of one birth when the child emerges from his mother's womb. He does not know that man has to recreate himself, reinvent himself, and give birth to himself every moment of his life. 'You must be born again' urges the Master. Nicodemus takes 'born' literally when it is meant figuratively. Words hide more than they reveal, and biblical texts are noted for their symbolic meaning, they were given long before the expansion of the rational, analytical mind.

'Nicodemus asks a pertinent question but does not grasp the answer.

'His background prevents him, replies Sanaka. Similarly when the Master encounters the learned Rabbis with the words, 'Before Abraham I Am', he unleashes a furore. The Rabbis take his words literally. Men of the 'real world', they deal with facts, they do not handle well symbols and metaphors, yet they lived in mythological times when all were conversant with symbolic imagery! Does this young maverick not know the fact? How can a young man be older than Abraham who died some 1500 years prior?

'We falter with the exact, we stumble over the literal, yet we live in a world of meaning, a world of symbols.

'The Master insists, 'Except ye die, ye shall not live'. Another tantalising idea, life in death? What is the Master saying? The Rabbis are confounded.

'Or death in life! Is he saying that many are dead while alive?

'Yes, do go on, this is interesting, Moses.

'To die to the illusion of the self? To be born to the inner reality which underpins outer reality? Whatever it is, it has nothing to do with the resurrection of the dead, more with the rebirth of the living.

'Yes Moses, to die to the illusion of the self, to Samsara. Man is prisoner of the Planet when he believes to be his body. Driven by moods, feelings, desires and fears, he knows no peace. It is the self that pulls man down, it is the self that perceives man as prey to forces, it is the self that keeps man 'prisoner of the Planet'. The great Beings of the past were tempted by the devil, Buddha was tempted by Mara under the Bodhi Tree. Temptation was an essential part of their testing. Mythological heroes and avatars had to grapple with demons and dragons and endure terrifying ordeals. The devil offered them dominion over Earth, power and riches. What are the texts telling us?

'They always triumphed over temptation.

'There is more. What are the forces at work? Do you believe that they had to grapple with demons and dragons?

'In the light of what you just said, I think it is their own demons they wrestled with, the temptation came from within, not from outside.

'You hit the nail on the head as always my son! They grappled with the self!

Karma, Reincarnation & the Jewish Condition

Clara waits for Jeremy to be in a joyful mood to approach him. He does not resist the request and she is able to secure a few moments with Master Sananda. The issues of karma, reincarnation and suffering are central to her reflection on the Jewish condition. The Master greets her and she begins:

'Master Sananda, karma and the Jewish tradition do not coincide. A group with a mission – a group that perceives itself as chosen for a purpose – cannot consent to the Law of Karma.

'I would not say so, no, replies the Master! Regardless whether individuals have had a belief in karma or not, I would say that it has been the predominant Law for humanity for a long while. Things are changing at present but the Law of Karma has operated for the whole of humanity whether they choose to believe in it or not.

'The Law of Karma seems to cancel out the goal of the Hebrews, insists Clara. The Law states that souls choose where they incarnate, in which context they will operate, while the Jewish point of view revolves around biological determinism. How do we reconcile freedom and determinism? How can the purity of a bloodline be guarded when souls are free to chase their own goals and are indifferent to race, colour, creed, gender or culture? Is it biological inevitability or soul autonomy?

'Several questions are involved here. First of all, sovereignty of the soul, yes you are quite right, a soul chooses to incarnate freely. But some individuals do not experience it that way, they retain between lives the illusion that they are not sovereign and to that extent, indeed they are deprived of freedom, for they deny it to themselves. In other words, between lives, individuals will reconnect with their 'being' to a greater of lesser degree. Some will be totally integrated with their souls and so they experience the process of reincarnation as expression of free-will. But others - who between incarnations do not reintegrate with their souls or do so to a small degree - may experience themselves as trapped on a cosmic treadmill, deprived of the freedom to choose the way in which they incarnate.

'The Buddhists have the image of the wheel of rebirth on which individuals are caught and which throws them back into incarnation, blown by the stormy winds of Karma for they have not taken the trouble in previous incarnations to enquire into the nature of life and death. How does the soul choose?

'A soul may freely choose - just for the sake of argument and this will be true of other races - to incarnate over and again into a Jewish body; this is somewhat an oversimplification. Just as a soul may choose to incarnate into a British body or a Chinese body over several lifetimes. Because both the biological make up and the environmental factors offer particular learning opportunities which the soul wishes to explore further, so that it is possible for someone to choose to incarnate down a particular genetic line for a number of lifetimes. Not that many choose that kind of a path, not over a long period of time … between five and ten incarnations following a widely-based genetic strand.

'I have a dread of repeating this life pattern. I never wish to incarnate in the Jewish garb ever again, the terror of it still haunts me. Unable to erase it, I have decided instead to remember it until the end of time! I intend to 'carve' it into the cosmic Archives, so that it is available to all. Those about to reincarnate must be informed.

'First, heal your fear! And you will have no need to repeat that experience ever again. This may seem perverse, but while fear remains - I am not suggesting that this will necessarily be the case – your soul may wish to give you another opportunity to heal that fear. Fear is simply love that has not yet shown itself as love, and since you are in essence a being of love, fear is an illusion. And one of your soul's wishes for you is that you become able to dissolve the illusion and to know the truth. Consequently, while a substantial fear remains of any particular state, your Self may feel that to experience that fear again is likely to be the most valuable gift that your soul can give you. You understand why healing your fear is your route away from needing to experience what you fear. It is quite a paradox!

The encounter between Master Sananda and Clara comes to a close.

Reincarnation & the Jewish Condition

'The time is soon approaching when it may no longer be appropriate to borrow the Jewish genetic form, when it no longer is perceived as a timely strategy, suggests Bendavid

'Why, asks Shemtov, human beings at all stages of development and from all creeds, races, nationalities, ethnic groups, colours and latitudes have revisited Earth in the Jewish garb since we emerged from the laboratories of the Nefilim somewhere in Sumer. What decides?

'The new awareness! Human beings coming back in the Jewish form may have felt secure in their choice. Secure in the sense that they would not be found out; but now the secret is out! The time is now when globally aware, socially responsible, progressive Jews the world over are asking serious questions. They no longer make do with the fables and fantasies of the past as their parents did. It is our role as cosmic workers to help them formulate the decisive questions.

'I agree, says Levinson, I have been thinking and writing along those lines for some time. The Jewish condition is humanity's problem. As you said the secret is out, there is no such thing as a Jew, only human beings borrowing the Jewish frame for reasons of their own. Our role is to help them identify their reasons. There is need for a serious method of investigation, a psycho-spiritual programme which would go to the heart of the matter. The method will borrow from Buddha, Freud, Jung and the 'new' psychologies. There is some unearthing to do. The whole of humanity will benefit; it is humanity which comes back in the Jewish form! There is no such thing as a 'chosen', Jew. The Jew is not hand-made by the gods in some remote heavenly laboratory. His purity, superiority and sanctity are myths which pump up his ego, keep him 'doing' without thinking or questioning. We almost certainly are the most deceived and self-deceived people that ever walked the Earth. The gulf between reality and fiction could not be wider.

603

'When people return in the Jewish form, suggests Clara, or in any other form, they have forgotten their prior incarnation, race, creed, gender, nationality and country. They leap into their new body, get engrossed in their new role and identify with the character they play so completely that they will die or kill for it.

'This is the point I am making, says Bendavid. Humanity is growing in awareness, in analytical ability, in questioning initiative and is increasingly receptive to innovative ideas. The intellectual climate approves of this sort of enquiry, this kind of questioning, it stimulates debate, it encourages scepticism. Never before has humanity, as a whole, been more receptive to the new mood, the new vision for the world. All these changes call into question the entrenched views of the past.

'Humanity is facing two fundamental choices which will determine its future, inserts Jeremy. The first is the unfamiliar path of Love and the higher consciousness which will usher in 'Heaven on Earth', an exhilarating age for mankind and the Planet. The second is the well known, well trodden, tried and tested path of Fear. Humanity has chosen this path.

'The Old Testament is the records library of the path of Fear, notes Clara. With fear come stagnation, apathy, inaction and entrapment in ossified thought forms, in pointless precepts and sterile practices. I should know I was there!

'This choice is even more crucial for our people who, from time immemorial, have wandered in defiance and denial along the path of fear, continues Bendavid. We embarked on the path of Fear and we decided to stay on it, no matter what. We deserve better, humanity deserves better. It is time to sample something new, time to give love a chance.

'What do you mean by love, enquires a sceptical Clara?

'Not the familiar drivel! By love I mean what my teacher in India meant: acceptance, respect, tolerance, collaboration, unity, equality, freedom, inclusiveness, the right for all to develop. These by the way are enshrined in the most advanced Constitutions of the world. In Israel, a few months ago, diehards banned women from using a mobile phone and relegated them to the back of buses. Why? Women in buses imperilled the sanctity of devout men! Discrimination against women in a modern democracy, that's not love, that's fear! The government, quick to respond, is building a giant wall to gratify our appetite for fear. It caters to our hunger for fear.

'To those who return in the Jewish form I would ask, 'why this choice, why now, questions Clara. The man indoctrinated in the myth of the 'chosen people' has long forgotten that he may have lived in the body of a Zulu, a Mongol, an Eskimo, a white Russian, a fascist Italian, an Inquisitor, a Centurion, a Crusader, one or all of these personas over time and many more besides. He needs to be reminded. As you know recalling forgotten events can be traumatic but also therapeutic.

'Each individual who embarks on this new life journey is faced with two choices: the first is to make amends and learn the beautiful qualities that suffering has taught our people. The second is to do nothing, stagnate in inertia, repeat the same old pattern, replies Levinson. This is the disquieting choice, the darker option.

'More of the same, what a prospect! Imprisoned in the thought forms of the past, conditioned by inherited prejudices and beliefs, the non-Jew, now in a Jewish body, is more himself than he ever was! Embracing the Jewish condition is the inevitable choice prompted by his temperament. For him, acting out the Jewish role, endorsing the Jewish persona is not a channel to emancipation; it is to stay just as he was. He fancies that the world will never know! The world knows now, retorts Bendavid!

'Do they dimly sense their prior intention, asks Shemtov? Do they return to play out the role they love and have no desire to change, be more of what they are regardless of their impact on the world?

'Sanaka has the answer, Shemtov, let me get the section'. Bendavid rifles through his papers, 'this is what Sanaka has to say, 'When you take liberties with another person, you are making a loud statement, you are saying, 'the other is less human, less godly, less worthy than me'. The intimation is that you are more precious in the eyes of God, in other words you are more God-like!

'Looking at it from a karmic perspective, the non-Jews who incarnate in the Jewish form do so in response to the cosmic Law of Attraction, 'like attracts like', rounds up Levinson. They decide on the Jewish genetic milieu to repeat the behaviour pattern they knew. As Master Sananda explained many humans do not know that they have an autonomous soul. So they tend to incarnate in groups which confirm and reinforce the beliefs that they are playthings in the hands of the blind forces of fate.

'From a spiritual perspective, human beings come back in the Jewish form to develop the beautiful spiritual qualities Sananda was talking about, says Tara.

'Looking at it from a scientific perspective, in this brave new world of globalisation, technological advance and the findings of archaeology and biology on the origins of life, it is old hat to think in terms of 'my group, my community, my party ideology, my religious belief', concludes BarYohai. Tribalism is of the past, now is the time to break down mental barriers and embrace humanity, expand our awareness, choose universalism. The next phase in our evolution.

Time or Timelessness

'Space and time … are names' (Nagarjuna)

'Maya is the all-inclusive effect which overwhelms a man who is immersed in materialism … Maya is an aspect of time – transitional, ephemeral, present …This connotes identification with form life. (Master DK)

'The moment has arrived to talk about time, says Master Sanaka one day after the early morning meditation. We have discussed the twin cosmic laws of Karma and Reincarnation, both inextricably bound to time as humans understand time. Allusion to one side of polarity brings in its opposite side. So allusion to time inevitably brings in timelessness.

'Eternity is now, we are in eternity in the present, utters Moses trying to convince himself.

Sanaka looks penetratingly at Moses with his radiant smile and sparkling eyes. 'Yes, we must talk about time now. Do you recall the phrase that flustered the Talmudists of long ago, 'Before Abraham was I Am'? This phrase sent a shock wave through the august assembly. In India we accept it as a fact. Why the dismay?

'They lived in the temporal world.

'Indeed Moses. 'Space and time … are names'. Rituals revolve around time; each ritual is set in time: you wear the leather straps in the morning; you rest on the 7th day and so on. The world was created with a 'Beginning', a reference to time; the Law was given at a set point in time. The entire Scriptures are set within the bounds of time. The learned rabbis went along with the reality of time and space, Maya. Even though they lived in a mythological world, in an uncanny way they anticipate the new rational age of philosophy and science with its concern for concrete knowledge, the credible, the explicable, the demonstrable, the provable, and the measurable. They related, unquestioningly, to external reality, unlike us in India who prefer the inner worlds, the worlds untouched by time. The doctors of the Law, divinely inspired, capable of making the mind of God intelligible to ordinary mortals, the moral guides of the world must have felt a sense of awe.

Worriedly Moses asks, 'what about time'? He wishes to move on.

'Moses, it has taken you thousands of years to ask the question, surely you can wait a few minutes for the answer! I am taking my time; I am following my line of thought. The law-makers luxuriated in theological dispute but the intellect cannot fathom the unfathomable. They were evading the real issue, the question central to human life 'who are we, why are we here?' Why?

'They lived in the temporal world; they were men of the moment. Physical reality was the only reality; they lived within the bounds of Creation, the world after the Fall, the world of plurality, of time and space. They were consistent. I know now why they lay the foundations of the present.

'You are right Moses. In The Upanishads we read, 'There are not many but only One. Who sees variety and not unity wanders from death to death'. They were men of this world! This is the root of your predicament. Man strides two worlds, the material and the spiritual. In order to know himself man must mobilise all of his resources: intellectual, emotional, intuitive and spiritual. Scholarly debates revolve around life conditions, mundane issues, social concerns, routine matters, not with the nature of man and the purpose of life. They trade in life conditions; they do not trade in the meaning of life. Buddha dismissed theistic disputes as 'a puppet show of views, a snare of views'. Rituals, theistic disputes relate to our mundane existence, they are of the finite self. To know the meaning of existence one has to plunge into the infinite Self. The tools are different since we are talking about two realities, the outer reality which is of the finite self and the inner reality which is of the infinite Self.

'We debate the central questions of life; we debate them at great length.

'You debate them! Debate is not what I have in mind. Higher reality is approached with the whole mind which includes reason and intuition. I am talking about the lifting of the veil of Maya, the lifting of the fogs of illusion, about soul life and soul purpose. Buddha uttered, 'The fact is, there is only one world – there are not two worlds... People think there are two worlds by the activity of their own minds'. Shankara echoes,

'Whatever you see as duality is unreal' said Shankara. Duality is an illusion; time and space are ultimately an illusion. There is no sacred time or profane time, no sacred space or profane space.

'It has nothing to do with sanctity, purity, godliness, mutters Moses dazed?

'Externals do not address the real issue, they are structured, undeviating, they slay soul impulse. Intuitive, genuine spiritual experience was unknown in some primitive societies and so it was forbidden. Primitive man was allowed to express himself within the permitted boundaries. Some experiences were permitted; others were outlawed as they were not essential to the survival of the group. Rules on hygiene, food, sexual conduct and behaviour were vital to survival and therefore strongly enforced. All else was a threat to authority. In a despotic society, respect for authority is paramount.

'It sounds like the 'ancient régime' before the French Revolution.

'It is! You recall the words 'the law that killeth'. The Law is the 'ancient régime'! It is just as despotic, patriarchal, authoritarian, inflexible, insensitive and unfair. The French 'ancient régime' had its roots in the old monotheistic religion. In the 'ancient regime' of the insensitive law, the rich were blessed, the sick doomed, women denied their humanness. Men alone could aspire to holiness, women were cursed: their impure body aligned them with the devil. The priesthood were operating from the standpoint of the mortal self, the only self they knew. Man was a material body and woman more so.

'What about time and timelessness, repeats Moses?

'We are talking about things in time; they shaped your controlling thought forms and governed your lives across the most turbulent historical times. Gigen uttered these striking words, 'Thinking that the words of the Masters embody … Wisdom, they treasure them in a most respectful manner. What a grave blunder they are committing. What kind of juice do they expect to come out of the old dried up bones?'

'This phrase will be inscribed on the walls of all schools of the future! We treasure the words of the past; we squeeze the old dried up bones in the frantic hope of extracting some juice. All we get is a handful of dust!

'My meandering is over, I am back on track, says Sanaka with a cheerful beam, back to the beginning, 'I Am before Abraham was': this is timelessness! To the temporal priesthood it is deviance. Their world was split between sacred time and profane time. To add insult to injury the sanctity of the Shabbat was trampled on; the healing of the sick on the Shabbat was a violation of sacred time. The sanctity of time prevails over the sanctity of the person! Worship on the altar of time brooked no breach. 'Why was healing the sick such an outrage, do you grasp the nature of the transgression?

'It upset the equilibrium; it threw away the polarities of Creation. The healing on 'sacred' time was intended to show that all time is the same. There is no sacred time and no profane time.

'Brilliant, my son. Duality pivotal to their world was shattered back into unity, this was an outrage. Their indignation was logical.

'Viewed from their perspective nothing had changed, the world had not been hit by a transforming flash. They were still under Roman occupation and their suffering was the same. Everything was the same.

'May be not! Everything had changed by a single decision, 'Man hath power to reverse the Fall's effects'. This is it! The end of sacred time and sacred space. The end of limitations and discrimination. The realisation that duality is an illusion which can be reversed by an act of will. Someone had declared that the illusion of duality had vanished, like a mirage vanishes or a rainbow! Lifting the fog of Maya would reveal Reality and bring an end to the conflict between sacred and profane which is the conflict between 'love & fear'. Because lurking in the shadows of the duality of sacred and profane is Fear. Fear lies in wait always. Fear removed there is only love.

'The world was saved?

'It might have been! The rabbis did not understand that all it takes to save the world is a change in perception.

'The chance of redemption was lost!

'Not entirely, humanity had to scramble, grapple, meander, dispute, argue, suffer, struggle and strive. But it never entirely lost sight of the goal, the vision of a better world. Buddha and the Master resolved duality, they came to Earth to show us how to do it. They lived and moved in timelessness and so the tormenting ring in the phrase: 'I Am before Abraham was'! Having overcome duality he was affirming something like this, 'I am a timeless being, as my soul I know no beginning and no end, I exist beyond space and time, you too exist beyond time and space, you too are timeless and boundless. I know it to be true from experience; I exist in time and in timelessness. I exist in space and beyond space at the same time. There is no sacred space and no sacred time. The entire universe is sacred space. Matter is primordial light solidified and we live in eternity now'. This was the hidden message in the transgression of the Shabbat and in the infuriating 'Before Abraham I Am.'

Belief or non-belief?

'Superstition and unbelief are both forms of unfreedom ... Both lack expansiveness, both lack inwardness and dare not come to themselves'. (Kierkegaard)

'Belief and non-belief are the two sides of the same coin, begins Sanaka. Belief is of the personality as is disbelief! To believe is to give in to the self which conjures up its gods. The self dreams up its own reality, the self is a conjurer. He who knows does not believe. Knowing rises above belief. Belief has kept mankind spellbound in the fabrications of the imagination. Man has been in bondage beguiled by the creations of his own mind.

'Hassidism has inflated belief, galvanized religious routine, energised devotees into deepening devotion while rousing an ardent desire to effect 'union'.

'It did all that. Remember also that Hassidism arose from a Christian culture and is rooted in that culture; it could never have taken roots anywhere else. Hassidism exemplifies the Piscean age; it has all the Piscean features: faith, belief, authority, devotion, credulity, enthusiasm, unquestioning acceptance, fervent adherence to the letter, capitulation to form and uncritical approval. It is the pinnacle of patriarchy and monotheism. What of the downside?

'Intolerance, prejudice, haughty separateness, sense of a spiritual purpose: 'God has entrusted me with a special mission'. Non-believers must be converted back into the ancient beliefs.

'The downside of the age of Pisces! The Piscean age is positioned along the line of the 6th Ray of cosmic energy and this ray is gradually fading out.

'To be replaced by the 7th Ray I presume?

'You presume right. As the influence of the 6th Ray is gradually waning and slowly receding, the 7th is rolling in and advancing. As one slowly ebbs away the other flows in. You observed the impact of the 7th Ray in Vilna.

'You are alluding to the echoes of the French Revolution?

'I am. It will take some time before the 7th Ray establishes itself; there is much resistance from the 6th Ray disciples. The Judeo-Christian belief structure, solidly anchored in the past, is resisting the incoming 7th Ray of unification, collaboration, cooperation, liberty, equality and fraternity.

'What about 'love thy neighbour like thyself', pivotal in both?

'So it is! How much love did you stumble over in Vilna, Vienna or Prague? 'Love thy neighbour' is definitely a good idea, I like it, chuckles Sanaka!

'If belief lurks behind the intolerance and fanaticism I encountered in Vilna, what is the solution?

'Knowing! To know intellectually and intuitively as Buddha makes clear, 'The Truth itself ... can only be self-realized within one's own deepest consciousness'. The truth is not 'out there', it is in you, since as Buddha elucidates, 'The external world is only a manifestation of the activities of the mind itself, and the mind grasps it as an external world simply because of its habit of false-reasoning.' To know through experience may be deviant to patriarchy, but there is no other way as Shankara said, 'Now you must realize that truth directly and immediately'.

'The world is not real?

'For Buddha who delved into the nature of things, 'All the mind's arbitrary conceptions of matter, phenomena ... conceptions and ideas relating to these are like a dream, a phantasm, a bubble, a shadow'. The believer believes the world to be objective, solid, tangible and real.

'Is the rejection of belief a step in the right direction?

'It can be. 'I do not believe' points to freedom of thought and a reflective disposition, but it stems from a similar mental operation. Disbelief is often as stubborn as belief with the same lack of desire to know. Some disbelieve when the time is ripe, when the social climate makes it acceptable. Others disbelieve after a long period of profound reflection. Belief and disbelief are of the personality. The finite mind has to formulate theories, ideas, dogmas and doctrines in order to make sense of the world, but they are not direct perception of the whole, they are fragments of the whole, splinters of the Truth. They are not intuitive apprehension of the Real; they do not embrace the Real. The Truth can only be apprehended by the subtle mind, the higher Self. When you link up with the Self, you utter in all authenticity and accuracy, 'I am the Truth', and at that level you also know the corollary, 'I am the Life'. Nothing doctrinal, liturgical or theological, just a personal realisation.

'These claims sent waves of alarm through the doctors of the Law. Words that were the epitome of sacrilege.

'Of course, law-makers have a deep conviction in their own power. With god on their side, they feel infallible. In the polarity of good and evil they alone occupy the side of good. The rabbis' allegiance was to their god, less so to their people. Decisions spring from that part of the mind that is inaccessible, so it is no more coherent to disbelieve than it is to believe. Remember that each one comes back into incarnation with a long past stretching back to the beginning of times. Each one carries a heavy luggage of buried memories, emotions, thought forms, beliefs, desire, aspirations and potentials, a vast reservoir of past lives. Is he freer when he believes than when he disbelieves?

'Are we governed by the past? What about the karmic burden of our bloodline, the karmic legacy of humanity and that of the Earth too?

'We carry all those too!

'Is our freedom an illusion? The Wisdom insists that we 'create our own reality', in other words man makes himself, man is his own creator. He defines himself by his existence, 'I make myself, therefore I am'.

'You are right as always. Buddha focussed on existence. It is through his existence - thoughts, feelings and actions - that man expresses his true nature, that he proves himself. Freedom is not an illusion, or else why should we return in incarnation? Coming back is a personal decision.

'If we come back burdened by our personal and collective past, are we free to believe or disbelieve? When do we know freedom?

'When you go beyond belief and disbelief. When you rise above the limitations of the lower mind, when you see through the eyes of the higher mind, the Self. Now that your personality is in alignment with the Self you know freedom from belief and disbelief. As I said earlier belief and disbelief stems from a similar mental operation. The believer accepts what the non-believer rejects; he affirms what the non-believer disclaims. One believes passionately what he does not know while the other disbelieves passionately what he does not know! It is all of the mind, all a creation of the mind. The lower self and the higher Self belong to two different orders of existence, two different dimensions of being.

'It does not matter really, belief or disbelief, it is all the same!

'That's right, the believer longs for insight as does the disbeliever, but they do it differently. The intelligent believer wants to unite with his god, the intelligent disbeliever longs for self-knowledge and self-realisation. They both seek the God within.

'Neither matters. The sublime is not of the personality.

'Right. Belief or non-belief, theism or atheism are equal and opposite, but strangely similar. They develop from the same mode of reckoning. They uphold separation, isolation and detachment. They dwell on the aloneness of man in an alien universe and separation between man and God.

'The separation between man and God is at the core?

'You see belief and non-belief have at their core the same aloneness and estrangement from the universe. This explains many things, not least the intolerance of the believers. They seek refuge in group character, group goals, ancestral customs, code of morals, set of dogmas, items of clothing all the things that hide our individuality, our true nature. The first thing prison guards do to prisoners is to deprive them of all the signs of selfhood. We dread above all being stripped off all the things that tell us who we are. This is why we define ourselves along visible, external markers: gender, race, family loyalty, group allegiance, religious allegiance. Yet these enveloping sheets are shrouding the truth of our being. 'When the Tao is lost there is need for morality ... '

'The answer then is to let go of the 'enveloping sheets' that tell us many things except 'the truth of our being', echoes Moses. The Talmud wove many such 'enveloping sheets', distinguishing symbols to separate us from all others: fringe garments, prayer shawls, beards, head dress, prayer box strapped around the arm along with the myriad of rituals. They made us feel so very special!

'When you let go of the props, when you 'drop it' as Buddha suggested, when you ditch the externals that cast a shadow on the light of the soul, then and only then you will know yourself to be the universe. Outer markers hide the real Self. Truth is not the product of intellectual guesswork and clever manipulation of words. Truth is not of the personality; that is why religion cannot reveal the Real; it may at best hint at its existence.

'Religion, it seems, is the font of man's dilemma rather than it resolution. It conceals the light rather than reveal the light; it obstructs the Way rather than point the Way. In the age to come, a new religion will emerge, notes Moses thoughtful. 'The new 'religion' will be the Timeless Wisdom presented afresh. It will displace the doctrinaire form of religion that has kept humanity restrained throughout patriarchal times. It will be the 'religion' of the soul finally liberated from the fetters of dogma, the manacles of doctrine, the shackles of fear, the irons of the 'do & obey'. This 'religion' will inevitably do away with belief; it will usher in 'knowing'.

'The religion I know is of the self. The coming religion will be of the soul.

'Religion as you know it masks rather than reveals because it is of the self. Man constructs religions and theories to explain the world around him. Nothing wrong in that, this is the reason why the Source incarnates. The universal Mind incarnates in us to experiment with all sorts of things, it is all learning material, not to be discredited. Hurdles surface when man gets attached to the form he has created: he believes it to be real and succumbs to it. In bondage to his own creation he feels compelled to push it down the throat of others! You know why Buddha denounced attachment as a primary mental poison that keeps man ensnared. As a result the thought forms created become part of the 'Great Illusion'. And all goes terribly wrong!

'Like David who wept 'My god, my god, why hast thou forsaken me'?

'Distraught you invoke the deity who has abandoned you and you plead, haggle, pledge, implore, weep, request and curse. The Judeo-Christian man feels deserted, forlorn and betrayed, but he goes on erecting potent thought forms that shore up the Great Illusion and enfold Earth in a shroud. You set aside a 'holy' day to atone for your sins. You beat your chests, weep and quarrel with the god you use as sticky resin to bond the brittle parts of a religion that was going to explain the world for you, give it meaning and purpose. You repent all manner of fanciful 'sins'; you remember all your 'sins' Rabbi Moses?

'I did repent all 'sins' I also added a list of my own. But that list did not include the one true sin, the sin of all sins: I had disregarded my cosmic Self for the illusion of identity.

'Anything that separates man from man is artificial, fictitious and fraudulent because there is no partition in the Oneness that holds all Creation. You recall the Sutra, 'Ignorance is the condition of confusing the permanent, the pure, the blissful - the Self - with that which is impermanent, impure, painful, the not-self'.

'The impermanent, the impure, the painful, the not-self is the bedrock of the religion of man and the mainstay of the human predicament. Our sin is the sin of ignorance, 'the condition of confusing' the real with the unreal. In the temple of the future, we shall repent the sins committed against the Self and against Oneness.

'Will you need to repent, chuckles Sanaka? When you 'know' what is there to repent? Knowing eradicates the 'condition of confusing' the real with the unreal!

The misunderstanding of Duality

'The law-shapers bemoan the loss of primeval innocence and unity, begins Sanaka. They blame woman for losing man's paradise. Knowledge of Duality they call 'original sin', carnal sin! Man, they insist was 'perfect' until Eve lured him into sin. Eve, they claim corrupted the world. The soul corrupting the world?

'Is it not what took place, enquires Moses with some apprehension?

'O it did take place! It is the grasp of it that is missing. Animal-man was not conscious of Duality; he knew what the rest of the animal world knew: how to survive. But late in the Lemurian period which spans a vast expanse of time, man developed a feeling of his nascent humanity. The moral sentiment was dawning. At that moment the Tree of Knowledge of Good & Evil appeared in the Garden. As with all mythological imagery the image of a tree with roots plunging deep into the Earth and branches rising into the sky must be understood symbolically.

'Why a tree, why not another image, asks Moses?

'The tree stands as a metaphor for man himself. Man is a tree; man also has a Tree concealed within his esoteric anatomy. Good and evil, right and wrong, virtuous and sinful, love and fear, these dual pairs entered the world stage two by two. Was it a sin to see the world as it was or appeared to be?

'This is what we bemoan?

'You bemoan the loss of innocence which you take for perfection! It is nothing of the sort. Animal-man loses his animal innocence not the perfection of the archetypal Adam as envisioned by the Elohim!

'To us, who believe in absolute Creation, Adam was in a state of perfection, he had to be or our entire edifice would collapse.

''He had to be'! Everything has to fit the opinion of the law-shapers! For all we know there was no absolute Creation, the world is being created in every moment. Perfect Adam was a vision in the great minds of the Elohim. There is only Adam in a state of becoming. Millions of years ago in Lemuria, animal-man, in graded steps, grew more enquiring. Animals do not ask questions about their world, man does. He looks at the world and tries to make sense of it. It is this newly acquired ability to ask questions that is symbolised by the image of the Tree of Knowledge. The whole thing is fraught with contradictions. There is a paradox; I invite you to suss it out.

'We understand it to be a retrograde step.

'Because you hold the image of an absolute Creation and a perfect Adam! It is your starting point which is flawed. To you man has been going downhill, to us man has been ascending! It is a giant stride from the unconsciousness of animal-man to the consciousness of 'modern' man trying out his embryonic mental faculty.

'We do not have the Wisdom of the Ages to inform our judgment and guide our action. The allegorical basis of our human condition, we misread.

'The stages of development are universal, first the animal phase, next the human phase and finally the spiritual phase. The Myth of Adam and Eve describes in pictorial form the great movement of evolution.

'So there is no woman to blame? If there is nothing to lament and no one to blame, where does that leave our entire tradition?

'You said it Moses. Humanity evolves very slowly, but it evolves. You are unfamiliar with this notion. To patriarchy there is absolute perfection or absolute wickedness. You are swayed by your fascination for dual pairs, good and evil, perfect and imperfect. The dawning of duality is engraved in your psyche. Do you detect the paradox?

'As I see it, Duality symbolised by the Tree of Knowledge is both Fall and Evolution. It is the loss of animal unconsciousness and the growth of individual consciousness. Should we grieve or rejoice?

'Rejoice naturally! Humanity is forging ahead in a loop; it will in future close the circle to regain unity once again.

'What is the way out?

'The perception of unity as we close the circle. Duality was a clever stratagem, a brilliant strategy to get mankind searching, longing, gazing, observing, enquiring, striving, and battling on. In his cosmic classroom the universal Mind needs to explore and ponder over duality. It must not be forgotten that duality is a learning, working tool. For man it means journeying down millions of years to arrive at the idea of duality before dismissing it! As the mind or man expands, he comes to understand the nature of duality and with the application of reason and intuition he is finally able to transcend it.

'The great Myth of Creation, a gamble! We were knocked over by this gamble. Millions of years to evolve into duality and millions more years to triumph over it!

'In their enthusiasm your ancestors failed to track the hidden intent, the veiled meaning, the Idea translated into form.

'Why?

'Many reasons. Fear of finding out that the truth does not match inherited beliefs. Fear of having to think originally, individually. Fear of change. Fear of being labelled heretics and blasphemers and as a result fear of being excluded as deviants. Fear of offending the deity and having to pay the penalty. Fear of having to take responsibility for one's direction. In other words fear of freedom.

'Fear, the central theme of our lives. Everything revolves around fear.

'It takes courage to confront the wrath of the deity and the guilty verdict of his agents on the ground. They had a limited grasp; those were mythological times, pre-rational times. A tragedy not only for you but also for humanity. You see, genuine knowledge emanates from the plane of Ideas. On that plane nothing is warped, nothing is despoiled; Ideas have all their integrity, their authenticity. Man not yet inspired, not yet inspirited, not yet informed, not yet enlightened by the soul endeavours to make sense of that which originates in the plane of Ideas, and trouble ensues.

'Their interpretations had their source on the highest planes: they heard unusual voices, they claimed supernatural intercession.

'They yearned for authenticity. They may have heard voices; they had guardian angels like all of us. They received guidance from their spirit guides. What you overlook is that spirit guides are not greatly different from us; we choose them for that reason. We have a similar life path; we may belong to the same Soul group.

'Master, you examine Duality and the Myth of Creation often. Why? 'Repetition is a sure way of learning. But you already know this, it is the method used in the Talmud, chuckles Sanaka. We meet on this one point!

'If repetition is a sure way of learning, would you go over the phases of evolution including the phase that Duality brings in.

'I am going to briefly identify two of the four phases of evolution. The fourth is the stage the Spiritual Hierarchy has attained, when evolved man becomes spiritual man. The soul finally emerges triumphant over the personality and walks the Earth in its full glory as did Buddha, Krishna and Lord Maitreya. These fully realised Beings have transcended human nature.

'We are not there yet, sighs Moses.

'Down the ages a few escaped the tyranny of the self and the prison of matter and have become enlightened, they are the 'Awakened'. You are on your way to joining their ranks, possibly the first rabbi in the history of humanity to do so!' After a reflective pause he adds, 'there was Moses of course, Abraham and Solomon but they already were drawn from the ranks of the Masters or later joined the Hierarchy'. After another pause, 'and the great Prophets.

'Why is that? We have produced many great 'Tsadiqqim'.

'Certainly, within the boundaries of your outlook. Within the conflict between matter and spirit, ego and soul. In other words within the limitations of duality. As custodians of the history of the Planet - the Old Testament - they also were custodians of duality.

'Custodians of boundaries?

'It was courageous to defer their liberation in order to defend the Revealed document. It was generous to donate future generations to the safeguard of that historical document. They had a sincere and profound sense of duty and responsibility. To keep alive the pledge, they had to be adamant about separation, uniqueness and selection. The fundamental unity beneath the diversity of forms eluded them. Even your great Maimonides faltered, though he was living among Sufi scholars. They remained Atlanteans in their consciousness, not realising that it was indeed a phase that had to be explored, resolved and transcended.

'If the biblical phase is the Atlantean phase, where does it stand in relation to the Spiritual Hierarchy, the ultimate that man can aspire to?

'Devotion and attachment to tradition, religious emotion, piety, faith, loyalty and service are the features. Modern humanity is rapidly progressing toward the age of Mind. The intellect, the scientific, the rational are being developed under the guidance of the Hierarchy. If the Atlantean phase is noted for its intuitive, emotional, non-rational nature, the present phase which will culminate in the Aquarian age will be eminent for its intellectual, scientific and rational achievements.

'How can reason and intellect lead to the final phase?

'It will lead to the recognition of soul qualities and principles.

'How can the mind blaze a trail to the soul. Are they not antagonistic?

619

'That's what you think! You are still the biblical scholar of duality, of Maya! The soul resides in the realm of pure Reason. There is nothing naïve and sentimental about the soul. With giant strides in intellectual development will come the realisation of the timeless principles of unification, inclusiveness, tolerance, liberty, brotherhood and equality for all. Humanity will not tolerate authoritarianism in religion or absolutism in government. Because man as his soul will be his one master, his own ruler.

'Paradoxes everywhere, mumbles Moses wearily. The personality cannot grasp the Infinite but man will rise to the plane of the soul with the use of reason and the intellect. I am mystified!

WHAT OF MOSES' DREAM OF SPIRITUAL TRANSFORMATION?

He who looks without, dreams
He who looks within, awakes'
(Carl Jung)

'We have looked 'without', begins Bendavid and found nothing to liberate us from suffering, from confusion and from the worship of a Samsara god. Yet we keep looking 'without', we perform, execute, ritualise, beseech, rebel, capitulate and implore the nature god who resides 'without'. The more disenchanted and disheartened we became, the more we looked 'without' in hope and in desperation. We implored the heavens, but no one came out of the clouds to show us how to alter our viewpoint, revise our orientation, modify our data, and check our map. Our compass proved unreliable, its range limited. Land was never in sight, we did not ride at anchor in any longed-for harbour. Tossed on the wild seas of life, we battled on in hope and despair. Without fail we looked to the heavens and turned to the 'inspired' leaders of the past, selected for the job of guiding us. The heavens were voiceless and the 'inspired' leaders mute. Never did we think about change.

'You hit the nail on the head, change is of the essence. As electro-magnetic units of life, as 'fields' of energy we are reborn every moment, inserts Jeremy. It is our mind that keeps us prisoners of the conditioning of the past, tied to the inherited thought pattern. It is all an illusion. We can break free from the illusion like an actor walks out of the theatre to resume his normal identity, 'free' from the character he incarnates on stage. We can be born again, sadly we choose to be born over an again in the same old mould. In essence we are pure consciousness; all that we believe is manufactured by us.

'Be ye transformed by the renewal of thy mind', quotes Tara.

'Absolutely, presses on Jeremy. The reality we live in is fabricated. We are making up this reality and getting stuck in it! Sanat Kumara said that as we create ourselves with our choices we also create the universe. He said that we are co-creators with the Divine, that we uphold the world around us. We 'create' the world. The world is not as As rigid as we think. It is more fluid, more elastic.

'Wonderful echoes of India, muses Bendavid. We create the world by our thought. So to insist that we are tied and bound by tradition is self-deception. It is a delusion, a hoax, a fantasy. We knew before incarnating that it was all a chimera, but early indoctrination and group conditioning made us believe that it was all true and real.

'More than that, reflects Clara. Past generations lacked our knowledge and sophistication but suffering ought to have galvanised them into digging an underground tunnel of escape, metaphorically speaking. Prisoners of war dig tunnels to flee their prison. They show great courage in refusing to endure their captivity. The human spirit rebels against incarceration, it is prepared to die for freedom. A prison is an insult to the spirit of man. Not one of our 'inspired' leaders helped us escape, quite the reverse, they forced us into inertia. On reflection it is more than self-deception, much more; it is an offence against the spirit in man.

'Arrested in the Atlantean phase of sentimental devotion, jammed in our primeval psyche, we are unaware of post-Flood reality, the growth of mind. And so we have no desire to probe, explore and know. We have to make the giant leap from the emotional to the conceptual, from the impulsive to the intellect, from the irrational to the rational, declares Levinson.

'Is the mental stage not as unreliable as the emotional stage you want us to leave behind, asks Tara pertinently?

'The mental stage is the next phase in evolution, of itself it may lead us into a lurch, but managed effectively it will inevitably show the way to the soul. This is the course of evolution, the orientation of progress, explains Jeremy.

'We see the world in line with what is registered in our minds, continues Bendavid. In other words it is the past that affects 'how' we see and 'what' we see. Past conditioning sieves through sense impression and selects. Say for instance you go by a beautiful building, you pose to admire it but it is a church and instead of admiration you feel horror, a conditioned response. Our reaction to the world is not candid and authentic; it is governed by the beliefs of our group rooted in your mind. It is your group attitudes which dictate whether you admire or disapprove, love or hate, respect or despise. Early experience decides the meaning we ascribe to the world: good and bad, right and wrong, fine and ugly are planted in the malleable soil of our minds in childhood and we go through life reacting, seldom questioning. Some take great pride in their conditioned response, they marvel at their own devoutness! We repeat the old warped, blinkered pattern, puppets on the string of antiquated beliefs. Our inherited beliefs are the dark caverns that hold us in captivity, monstrous mythological entities that feed on us, as many Minotaur of the collective psyche. Do you envision a way out?

'Other than exploding the old belief system, no! The situation seems hopeless, replies Shemtov, but of course there is expansion of mind with science, arts, humanities and philosophy. So we are getting there.

'This the Hierarchy is actively working at bringing about, confirms Jeremy. Education holds the key to the expansion of the mind. An 'enlightened' mind will lead the way to the soul. The realm of the soul is the realm of Ideas, the quest for universality, inspiration, sensitivity, intuitive knowing and perception of 'wholes'. The great and true artists of the world belong to that world.

'The end of duality, exclaims Clara I drink to that! The end of fragmentation, conflict and separation. The end of warring within men and between men. Integration in sight! The biblical gods are retreating after a protracted dominion of the Planet, domination of the Jewish people and through them of humanity.

'The way man sees the world depends on several things, comments BarYohai: his intellectual ability, his spiritual sensitivity and his ethical stance. Though we all are 'homo sapiens', individuals differ in their development; the body evolves with the mind; modern humans do not look like Neanderthal. It follows that as man advances, his perception of himself and the world changes. Animal-man living in the caves of long ago was very different from modern man who dwells in cities. Animal-man looked different, felt different and thought different if he was able to think at all!

'Our ancestors were cave-men, notes Shemtov, I never thought of it, yet scientifically it is undeniable. Travelling further back in time our remotest ancestors were non-humans!

'In a guided meditation we were taken to Shamballa by the Planetary Logos who invited us to meet our ancestors, says Clara, millions of them stretching back in time to our most humble beginning. We were reminded that some of them would be pre-humans. I allowed my imagination to roam free and travelled back a couple of billion years to the simple bacteria with which we share many of our DNA.

'Your first ancestor, a microbe. Was it thrilled to meet you, laughs Jeremy?

'I also met my parents, they were unchanged, I sensed a vague threat! My bacteria ancestor was quite harmless.

'We must teach the law of evolution in schools, the Darwinian version and the arcane account, states BarYohai, boldly, intently. The syllabuses will include the 'new' occult theory relating to our pre-human origins. We must shed our nurtured illusion about Creation. We must blend Creation and Evolution, include both. We believe the fantastic claim that Creation was for the Jew, pinnacle of the design, purpose of the whole Plan! Many of us persist in believing that our Solar System formed some 15 billions years ago was created for the sole purpose of planting a Jew in it.

'Or was it to plant a bacterium in it, that's how life on Earth started, laughs BarYohai.

'Seriously such credulity has no place among those rising to a higher plane of consciousness and entering the Age of Man, those who have identified the values and principles of the New Age and who already have an affinity with the 7th the Ray of Integration, declares Levinson.

'It takes countless generations to develop one quality, reminds Jeremy.

'One quality, exclaims Shemtov, just one quality?

'One quality which has taken millions of years to germinate! There is also the body; the body has evolved over time. As they developed that particular quality, the body changed, it improved. A finer mind requires a finer body. The crude body of Neanderthal could not accommodate our complex mind, remarks BarYohai, the biologist.

'I used to feel resentment toward my parents and their parents, confesses Bendavid. Now I feel sadness. This changes everything.

'In what way, asks Jeremy?

'We will manifest for them the vision that was encoded in their DNA. We are the final frontier. They have come to anchor in the harbour. Their protracted effort through the long darkness of time is coming to a head in need of completion. It is for us to conclude, to bring to a resolution. We project their vision of a better future into reality. All becomes possible. We are their concluding chapter.

'Awesome responsibility, shudders BarYohai. All those who came before us rely on us to bring their effort to fruition, to project that specific quality into reality, to fulfil their dream assuming that the grind and grime of life did not kill it. We are their hope of completion, of realisation. I feel deeply moved. I too was immersed in the old pattern, the old conditioning and though I came across the law of evolution I dismissed it at first not knowing what to do with it, it conflicted with the fantasy world I had inherited from my parents.

'How could you, asks Clara? The ancient attitudes and prejudices were stamped in our young minds. Many do not disentangle allegory from reality, the literal from the figurative, and the myth from the fact. Concrete thinking has prevailed in spite of the efforts of the Hierarchy to drive us forward. The Scriptures are a giant allegory. But like all allegories, they have to be decoded and translated into a form that makes sense for us now.

'Myths and fables are an asset to poets, painters and musicians; to us they are a disaster. It amazes me that an intellectually able people find it difficult to articulate ideas, make sense of experience and go beyond the concrete!

'Well thought through, teases Clara, you are making up for lost time! Attachment is of the ego, the root of all evil. Attachment to the old, fear of the new and ignorance of both! The mental poisons are lurking, obstructive forces that lie in the way of emancipation. Man attached to the past is calcified, he has turned into stone like Lot's wife who looked back, she would not leave the past, she would not move on.

'Is liberation possible, enquires Bendavid anxiously?

'While in bondage to the physical self, liberation will continue to elude us, bemoans Levinson. When we finally decide to read the Old Testament for what it truly is, we shall embark on the path of liberation. It is undoubtedly a treatise on the nature of the self, time, space and matter, duality and form. It is the treatise of the 3rd dimension, Maya, the world of illusion. When we finally grasp that everything around us is an illusion, that the self itself is an illusion, we shall be firmly set on the path of liberation. The Prodigal Son returning home to his Father! If we persist in seeing the Old Testament as a 'Revelation' we will continue to flounder. We will stay in the dark caverns of illusion, captive of the mythological creatures we conjured up.

'I agree, butts in Clara. A chronicle that describes duality, outlines the reality of Maya and illustrates their mode of manifestation is to be studied diligently, but it should never be idolised!

'What of the method, enquires Bendavid feeling tense?

'The method known in India, Tibet and to the Sufis, takes up Tara. Meditative training leads to liberation. First, meditation tames and calms the restless outer mind; through the practice of 'tranquil abiding' the agitated mind abates. With the mind at rest, the

625

negative aspects of man's nature diffuse; intruding, harmful thoughts and feelings disperse. These negative elements are like dark clouds which obscure the sky. Once the 'dark clouds' disperse, the inherent nature of mind is revealed which was until then hidden beneath the layers of agitation and fear. With the outer mind disciplined and under control, out of 'tranquil abiding' emerges clarity. The fog of separation and conflict disperse and we are left with 'clear seeing'. One of the greatest gifts Buddha made to mankind was his programme of graduated meditation.

''Clear seeing' means seeing through the fog of illusion, says Bendavid.

'That's right, seeing through the fog of illusion, explains Tara, you studied meditation in India? 'Clear seeing' offers an insight into our nature. The final stage comes when gifted with 'clear seeing' we plunge into the nature of Reality, the ocean of Life. Then is revealed our true Self, our Buddha nature untouched, unspoilt, radiant. No more suffering. We are transformed.

'We value suffering, it is sent for reasons we are forbidden to know, notes Shemtov. It is a sign of selection, of chosenness, of predilection.

'Suffering stems from man himself, never from the universe, comments Jeremy. Suffering stems from neglect of our true nature. When we ignore the prompting of the soul we fall into all the traps the ego places in our path. We do not change, we fall! We should regard suffering neither as an impediment nor as a virtue. Suffering is just suffering; it is neither a curse nor a blessing!

'Suffering is caused by a rift, a split, a dissociation, a dislocation, muses Clara. If suffering springs from the divided self, it follows that identification with the Higher Self will bring an end to suffering. This is liberation; this is the Messiah we have yearned for down the ages!

CODA

The friends are invited to attend a meeting at Kibbutz Ginnosar on the shore of Lake Galilee. Present will be all those who gave their time and effort to hand over the translated chapters of The Hebrew Gods. Prompted by a sense of responsibility they agree to meet in order to share their experiences of the manuscript, formulate comments and figure out ways of making its content known. The friends feel privileged to be invited. The founders of The Renaissance Movement and of the Age of Enlightenment are going to chair the meeting. The following text conveys in summary form the findings, views and hopes of the contributors. They decide to fuse their separate movements into a single unit that will reflect the aims and fundamental views of all. There is almost complete agreement. Bendavid acting as chairman for the Age of Enlightenment Movement addresses a small audience. Present are his colleagues, the founding members of the Renaissance Movement and the group from England

'We feel privileged to have met all of you, begins Bendavid. We have played the role of emissaries to Benzaccai in hiding, a role we enjoyed enormously for it brought us in contact with The Hebrew Gods, the unpublished manuscript of Rabbi Moses de Vilna. Without you acting as catalysts this would never have happened. We are indebted to you for assisting us in rekindling our loyalty to the Holistic movement and reaffirming our allegiance to the New Age principles which we discovered when touring India years ago. New Age principles are a re-statement of the Ageless Wisdom formulated in an idiom suitable to our modern minds. We set out to shape our own programme inspired by Holistic thought and the Timeless Wisdom. We have three major aims: the first is to lay the foundations for the return of Lord Maitreya, the next Buddha we heard so much about in India. We do not want a repeat of the failures of the past. We will identify the Messiah when the time comes. We missed the boat too many times before, why? Because we were reluctant to make the necessary adjustments: we could not let go of the Fall, duality, the ego, matter and the god of matter. How? With the dissolution of our tradition which stands in the way of the return of the Hierarchy; it also stands in the way of the return of Maitreya. We will hasten the resolution of the old Scriptures by bringing into being the meaning behind the form. For always we have been deflected by the form aspect; the literal husk has precipitated layers of flawed opinions that form a shield against the truth. Our second aim is to notify intelligent, educated, secular, liberal Jews all over the world that their viewpoint meets with the standards set by the Hierarchy and their agenda for the Planet. Liberal Jews are advancing on the path of liberation along the lines set by the Masters who guide the progress of mankind. Liberal Jews are collaborating with the forces of progress and helping by example the emancipation of the Jews world wide, the uplifting of humanity.

'Our third aim, picks up Sarah, is to design a Healing strategy. To heal is to change, 'Be ye transformed by the renewal of your minds'. This phrase is now our motto. The design and implementation of a radical programme of healing will occupy our attention for some time. We have gathered a strong team around us, clinical psychologists, philosophical counsellors, Jungian analysts. Several more, drawn from other disciplines but fascinated by our project have expressed the wish to get involved. We are shaping an inclusive programme around the unique nature of the Jewish condition. It will include karmic, philosophical, psychological and spiritual counselling to re-awaken the realisation of our nature, origin and destination.

'This is a joint effort. We, the whole of humanity, are members of the brotherhood of Life, all droplets of the Source, intervenes Johansson. We acknowledge that all human beings are our brothers, in line with the principle that 'there is neither Gentile nor Jew'. We all come back to Earth to play roles, all kind of roles, not all flattering. We also swap roles in each incarnation.

'The first crucial step is to shed the myths built around us by the weavers of myths, continues Maimon. We need to discharge the stale, torpid, persistent thought forms that have kept us spell-bound. And, if we are to be reintegrated into the human family, we must accept the fact that we too are actors in this planetary drama which started aeons ago and will end when we unearth the truth of our being.

'I have to say that I share all your views; may I ask why the emphasis is on healing, enquires Levinson?

'I thought this would be obvious especially to you Levinson, replies Sarah with friendly humour. You are right; there is much confusion around healing. Healing has nothing to do with going back to the way things were or with fixing malfunctioning parts. When things go wrong, people want to be healed back to the point they were before disease struck. This is not what healing is about. Paradoxically dis-ease plays a major part in healing. Dis-ease strikes when our thinking is stuck in the mud, when our emotions threaten to topple us. Dis-ease is an alarm bell to rethink everything, to get back to the centre, to return to 'sanity'. Dis-ease tells us to look at life afresh, to let go of the conditioning that entrapped past generations and is entrapping us. We are serving no one by repeating the past. We are denying our ancestors the fruit of their efforts and we arrest our own emancipation. And because we are the One Humanity, we are also arresting the liberation of all.

'But why healing, insists Clara.

'Healing is what we all are searching for, we have devoted our lives to it, explains Bendavid. Years ago I read voraciously modern humanistic and existentialist psychologists, I sought to 'create myself', to become the 'authentic' being that I truly was deep down. As I devoured the works of Frankl, Fromm, Maslow, May, Kierkegaard and Rogers among others, I was engaged in the turbulent quest for my own Self. I was healing the split, the rift, the fracture within me that had been forged by inherited conditioning. Our upbringing which revolves around separation triggers the split, the rift, the fracture, it cultivates dis-ease. It dawned on me that our fixation with 'doing' is at the root of our malaise. In order to heal we have to learn to 'be'. To 'be' is the new frontier, the shift to reunification with humanity.

'Reunification with humanity? What humanity will shout the doctrinaires? We are humanity, we are the pinnacle of Creation, we are the whole story! The rest is negligible, exclaims Clara. Forget the 'heathens', there is no hope for them!

'There is no hope for us, replies Bendavid, if we hold on to our warped views!

'Healing again! To change our warped views is the healing, stresses Sarah. To heal is to connect. It is because things were wrong from the start that dis-ease set in. The symptoms of our dis-ease are recorded in the Book of the Fall, chronicle of the calamities that befell our people. Dis-ease is the opposite of wholeness, of insight, of knowing and of union.

'Unwittingly we introduced dis-ease in the ancient world where the rift and separation we advocated was unknown, inserts Clara.

'Disease is a disconnection. To heal is to reconnect. In healing we reconnect body and soul, we also reconnect with the world, and we feel whole again. To heal is to love; it is the coming together of mind and body. To reconnect is an act of love, because love is unity and harmony. And the restoration of unity is what Creation is all about. Healing has to do with establishing a new balance, a new order, a new symmetry, defines Jeremy. 'I agree healing has nothing to do with going back to the past, to the way things were, continues Sarah the Jungian therapist. Healing has to do with the realisation that our thinking was flawed and in need of correction. Our thinking must change to enable the complex being we are to function in a unified manner. My aim is to bring our religious system to an end. Dis-ease stems from the ego warped by tradition and group pressure. Dis-ease strikes when we give in to collective myths, when we live by the ways of the world and the ways of tradition.

'Krishna warned against the constraints of society and religion, 'Those, whose wisdom has been led away by desire, resort to other gods, engaged in rite, constrained by their own nature', quotes Jeremy. Those led away by desire fall for the ways of the world.

Are they victims? Only of their compulsion to satisfy 'desire'. And desire is of the personality. So they give in to the ego when they follow the ways of the world: when 'they resort to other gods'.

'We do have a mission, that is the whole point, notes Shemtov.

'But who benefits from it, exclaims Maimon? The Jewish people? Certainly not! The world? Definitely not! I have sworn hostility to the derelict thinking that keeps us arrested in a defunct past. I do not disguise my aim which is the demise of the 'old world' religion and the creation of an enlightened State founded on the highest spiritual principles. Utopia!

'Cosmic workers, Essenes and Cathars are back to Earth to dissolve our archaic notions and heal the mayhem these notions have inflicted on our people, on humanity and on the Planet, states Clara.

'That's right, approves Johansson. To heal is to leave the past behind and engage fully in the present, it is to identify with the qualities of the soul, to reconnect with humanity, to tune in to the cosmic inside us. To heal is to restore unity. It has to be stated and restated. It is quite clear why healing occupies a central position in your rehabilitation plan.

'Yes, confirms Bendavid. Next on my list of aims is a new educational programme. We need a revolution in education. The spotlight will be the 'old world' Scriptural narrative which was adequate in the past but incongruous today. It will be commented directly by the Hierarchy who designed it and entrusted it to Moses. The words of the Master El Morya are carved in my mind, imprinted in our Manifesto: 'We are dissipating superstition, ignorance and fear. We are forging courage, will and knowledge. Every prejudice caused by ignorance is exposed'. This is our rallying call.

'Ambitious but not impossible, inserts Jeremy in a cheerful mood. The process has started and we are among the first to receive direct communication from the Hierarchy. Worldwide, cosmic workers are channelling the Masters.

Maimon is engaged in a struggle against religious dogmas and has embarked on the re-writing of the 'old world' Scriptures. He is not alone, a team of intellectuals have gathered around him to lend their support. 'The Scriptures are being interpreted from the perspective of comparative mythologies to draw out similarities. This is the first step. For too long this noble 'document' has stagnated in the hands of interpreters intellectually budding and spiritually nascent. Unable to make it intelligible they **adored** it instead, investing in that worship strong attachment, intense enthusiasm and inflexible loyalty. The age of radicalism in religion was born.

'The 'old world' Scriptures, continues Bendavid will be subjected to a scientific investigation. All scientific disciplines will play their roles. We are drawing specialists on climatology, archaeologists, language specialists, analysts of ancient mythologies, experts on volcanology and oceanography and more. It has been established that around 1300 BC a terrible catastrophe struck Earth.

'Exodus, the flight from Egypt, exclaims Clara!

'Researchers suggest that the eruption of the Krakatoa blotted out the sun for a long time. Earth was plunged into a nuclear winter, a great many died. Around that time the Santorini exploded. It was at that time that the Hebrews fled Egypt and began their wandering in the Desert. The columns of smoke and the flames were interpreted as 'miracles'. In their simplicity the Children believed that their god was sending flames to guide them during the night and smoke to guide them during the day! This version of events is read in religious circles and in synagogues today and believed implicitly. The story of this catastrophe is chronicled in Exodus. We need more science to dispel the myths of the past. We interpreted geological events as personal events, as emblems of our 'chosenness'! We prefer to ignore that the natural disasters annihilated almost all of our ancestors! It is estimated that 98% of Hebrews perished in the catastrophe. A mark of esteem from our fickle god?

'Next is the most thorny goal of all, open to all kinds of misreading, goes on Bendavid looking to his friends for encouragement. I aim to discourage mankind – with effective esoteric information - from embarking on the Jewish adventure. Mankind has to awaken to the fact of reincarnation and rediscover the freedom souls have in determining their future life. Many Jew-haters of yesterday may be the ardent Jews of today! All humans return to Earth to play roles and swap roles. The cultists, sectarians, zealots and radicals who intimidate us today may hide unsavoury pasts. Such memory is lodged in their energy field which is an open book to the entire universe!

'It is the quality of our thoughts that decides our next incarnation, nothing else. No capricious god dumps human beings on Earth for his amusement. It is man himself who makes this crucial choice influenced by his tendencies, his emotional state, his point in evolution and his personal beliefs about the world, comments Jeremy. In other words he chooses his next incarnation driven by his nature and the beliefs he has held over many incarnations. His choice of creed and culture, his religious extremism or his political radicalism are emblems of the beliefs he has held about the world for many life times, many centuries, millennia even. He dons the human garb time and again to reinforce those beliefs, or if he has evolved to sort things out and progress.

'He is in charge of his own spiritual growth and is relentlessly driven by the combined forces of karma and evolution, picks up Tara. The decision to reincarnate is too important to be left to a Samsara god. It entails more than our own progress, it involves the liberation of humanity and of Earth.

'What is happening now, continues Jeremy, is not only affecting the Planet, it is also affecting the Solar System and the entire galaxy. Planned on a universal scale, events are unfolding at the planetary level. Never before in Earth history has such concerted effort and focussed energy been at work toward a global purpose. All of this the result of a sequence of events carefully monitored and orchestrated by the cosmic Forces of Light, the Hierarchy and us the 'cosmic workers'.

'We have worked in concert drawing together and uniting the principal aims of our movements, says Bendavid. We are now able to enounce the essential features of our united Movement. The final outcome is a combined endeavour, a cohesive philosophy and a shared vision.

'The 'cosmic workers', including all of you, are collaborating with the Hierarchy to assist the evolution of humanity, expands Jeremy. The development of the human mind through intensive education is an essential feature gathering momentum. The royal avenue to the soul is not to be confused with the narrow corridor of 'good' actions and religious zeal. Expansion of mind is that royal road. Humanity is ascending the evolutionary ladder, rising out of the 6th Ray of devotion and climbing to the 'mind centres' of Heart, Throat and Head. The path followed by humanity in the Age of Pisces has been one of pious action, prayer and hope mingled with despair. Reward and punishment have been the two poles of religious life. This is no more; the age of Pisces is over. Time to move on!

'As Sananda said, picks up Clara, 'Part of the process of change is a process of healing. In order for the new to come into the world there are aspects of the old world to be healed, to be resolved'. Healing the 'old world' of Pisces and piety, bring to a close the 'old Earth' supremacy of the Yahweh-energy that has prevailed for ages and cycles. 'This may be misread, cautions Levinson.

'How? Mankind has been in serfdom to that energy. To heal has to do with 'awakening'. It is happening now; humanity is gradually emerging from a trance-like state assisted by the Hierarchy and their 'workers'. Humanity is shaking off the magic spell the Father placed on us. We have all been entranced by it. In the words of Sananda 'Figuratively the Father stands for the immobility and unchanging nature of the world'.

'Precisely, inserts Sarah. The Father who stands for the immutable laws of nature demands absolute obedience. No forgiveness for 'sin'. Punishment is swift and severe. The Father stands for sin and punishment. That was the 'old world'. In the 'new world' the Mother emerges who brings hope and the promise of redemption. Love and nurturing resurface in human consciousness. We see these changes in society and psychology. The new psychologies turn their back on the vengeful nature of the unconscious, the ruthless nature of matter. The qualities of the Mother are now discernible in world affairs, in widespread concern for the Planet and its inhabitants. Changes in society indicate that the forgiving Mother is among us.

'God as the national controller took possession of man's mind and the Jehovah concept appeared' said the Master DK, quotes Bendavid. Primitive man had urgent need of a 'national controller', a Big Brother image to keep him on the straight and narrow. We are still under the spell of that 'national controller'.

'I recall with a shudder the Father, symbolic image that stands for the inexorable laws of nature. The 'national controller 'embodied in the 'do & obey' and the 'thou shall not', I recall with horror, shivers Clara!

'As Sananda explained, the Planet is going through a time of transition, deep inner changes are occurring and these changes are acted out in people' s lives, recalls Jeremy. This is to ensure mankind's receptiveness to the reappearance of the Messiah, Maitreya, and the emergence of the Hierarchy. The Age of Aquarius is manifesting with a vast expansion of light. Uniting their efforts the 'cosmic workers' are clarifying the unfolding Plan and influencing the shaping of it.

'I would like to add a further two points to our programme as an amalgamated Movement. The first is the fact of our innate power of creation, quotes Maimon, 'You create your reality; you all are involved in reality creation. What you will be learning is to steer consciously this process of creation'. This is one core tenet of our Movement.

'The other is the admission that the Old Testament is a secondary Scripture [whose] emphasis is material' as Master DK states, picks up Bendavid. Physicality is less of a focal point, humanity has moved beyond survival. Advanced individuals are searching for the reality that lies beyond physicality. 'Incorrect knowledge is based upon perception of the form and not upon the state of being'. As worshippers of the Father - as disciples of Samsara - we have championed the 'perception of the form'. But what of 'the state of being'? The next frontier for us.

'So long as man has any regard for his corpse-like body, he is impure and suffers from his enemies as well as from birth, disease and death'. You recall this quote, asks Clara? We need to shift our gaze away from our 'corpse-like body' and the urgency of survival to 'the state of being'. This 'corpse-like body' is the axis around which our tradition revolves. What is there to retain?

'The Judeo-Christian religious literature which enshrines the 'old world' energy has shaped the experience of humanity. All this is changing and we are involved in this change. Healing has to do with that change, concludes Clara.

CONCLUSION - 'The Jews hold the key'

'There remains one more thing to do, I shall not rest until I have put the final question to Master Sananda, announces Clara.

'It was a question of time, laughs Jeremy! I will not rest either, I am sure!

'Do you think that Sananda will respond, asks Clara unsure?

'I think he will, laughs Jeremy who is decidedly in good spirits. The encounter begins. Without preamble Sananda invites Clara to put her question.

'I asked this question before; I would like to ask it again if I may?

'Yes, of course, replies Sananda graciously through his channel Jeremy.

'Are the Jewish people standing in the way of the unification of mankind?

'It would depend very much on your perspective, replies the Master. From one perspective you could see them as standing in the way of unification and from another perspective as the key that unlocks the door to unification. So you might look at the situation right now as being like this - this will be an analogy - you can see the Jewish people as being the key to the door of unification. The key at the moment is sitting in the keyhole but it is not turning the lock. So depending on your viewpoint, you might say they are blocking the way because the key is not turning just yet, or you might say they are prime movers in this drama and the key is about to turn! So that would be an analogy as to how you can see their position in two different ways, because of the remarkable persistence of their racial-spiritual vision, because of the way they have held that vision with such coherence over such a long period of time, in a way that no other large human groups has. There are small groups, some of the Aboriginal people also have this function, but they are much smaller and do not belong to your 20th century world, whereas the Jewish people belongs very much to the 20th century, they are very much of the modern age. So they are not unique in the persistence of the vision they hold, but it gives them a special role. Combined with a clarity of spiritual purpose is a sense of separateness which means that when they find a way to resolve that dilemma, that dichotomy within themselves, this in turn will produce a powerful effect on the rest of humanity'.

636

BIBLIOGRAPHY

*　　Direct communications with the Ascended Master Sananda.

*　　Initiations guided by the Ascended Master Sananda & the Planetary Logos.

AIVANHOV O. M,　Christmas & Easter in the Initiatic Tradition

Collection Izvor Prosveta, 1989

Know Thyself, Collection Izvor, Prosveta, 1995

You Are Gods , Collection Prosveta, 2002)

ALEXANDER, P,　The Ancient World to AD 300. The McMillan Co, 1968

BHAGAVAD GITA, KRISHNA' s Dialogues on the Soul

BOLEN, J. S,　Goddesses in Every Woman : A New Psychology of

Women. Harper & Row Publishers, 1984

BORDEAUX-SZEKELY, E, The Gospel of the Essenes,

CW Daniel &Co, 1996

BOWEN, J,　Correspondent & 'The Son of God', 2003

Investigative programmes shown on British Television

BRUNTON, P,　The Inner Reality. Rider & C0, London, 1970

The Secret Path. Rider & Co, London 1934

A Search in Secret India

The Spiritual Crisis of Man. Rider & Co, 1952

The Hidden Teaching Beyond Yoga

Century Paperback 1941, 1982

BUBER, M,　Tales of the Hassidim, Schocken Books, NY, 1961

CAMPBELL, J,　The Hero with a Thousand Faces, Fontana Press USA, 1949

CAPRA, F,　The Tao of Physics : An Exploration of

Modern Physics & Eastern Mysticism. Flamingo Books, 1975

CLAXTON, G,　The Heart of Buddhism, The Aquarian Press edition, 1992

CHOPRA, D,　The Book of Secrets, published by Rider, in Cygnus

Review 2004 Issue 11

COTTERELL, A,　A Dictionary of World Mythology Oxford University Press

DAVIES, PCW & BROWN, JR, The Ghost in the Atom, Cambridge University Press

(Conversations with leading Quantum physicists)

DHWAHL KHUL, in Alice Bailey's books. Published by Lucis Press

> Initiation Human & Solar
>
> The Reappearance of the Christ
>
> The Externalisation of the Hierarchy
>
> Glamour, a World Problem
>
> Problems of Humanity, 1969
>
> The Rays & the Initiations, 1960
>
> The Light of the Soul.
>
> A Paraphrase of the Yoga Sutras of Patanjali,1927 & 1965
>
> The Destiny of Nations 1945

FREKE, T & GANDY, P, The Jesus Mysteries, Thorsons, 1999

FROMM, E, 1957, Psychoanalysis & Zen Buddhism, Thorsons, 1995

GERBER, R, 2002. Vibrational Medicine for the 21st Century.

> A complete Guide to Energy Healing & Spiritual Transformation

GUIRDHAM, A, Theory of Disease: Neville Spearman London, 1957

> Exploration of the influence of Self, Race & Religion
>
> on Health
>
> Cosmic Factors in Disease, Duckworth & Co, 1963
>
> Man: Divine or Social, Vincent Stuart, London, 1960

HARMAN, W,   New Metaphysical Foundation of Modern Science,
Published by the Institute of Noetic Sciences 1994

HOWARD, M,   The Occult Conspiracy, 1989

HUMPHRIES, C,   The Search Within: A Course in Meditation,
Sheldon Press, 1977

JEREMIAS, A,   The Old Testament in the Light of the Ancient
East. Leipzig 1911

KAFATOS, M & KAFATOU, T, Looking in Seeing Out : Consciousness
& Cosmos, Quest Books, 1991

KAFATOS, M, The Conscious Universe: Part & Whole in Modern
Physical Theory, Springler - Verlag New York, 1990

LANE FOX, R, The Unauthorized Version

MAY, R,   Man's Search for Himself, Delta Books, 1953

MCDONALD-BAYNE, M, I Am the Life, Fowler & Co, London.

Beyond the Himalayas

MCFARLANE, T.J, Einstein & Buddha -The Parallel Sayings.

Ulysses Press 2002

MEUROIS-GIVAUDAN, D. Le Voyage à Shamballa – Un Pèlerinage vers Soi

MUKTANANDA, S, Play of Consciousness, Syda Foundation, NY, 1978

OKAWA, R, The Laws of the Sun, Element Books, 1994

(on the Myutram Civilization)

OYLE, I, The Healing Mind, Celestial Arts, California, 1979

OSMAN, A, Moses Pharaoh of Egypt. The Mystery of Akhenaton

Resolved, Grafton Books, 1990

PATAI, R, The Hebrew Goddess

The Jewish Mind

The Myth of the Jewish Race

PERRY, J, MINDWELD, A Cosmic Embrace, Amethyst Books, 1991

RAMACHARAKA Yogi, An Advanced Course in Yogi Philosophy, 1970

A Series of Lessons in Raja Yoga

RINPOCHE, S, The Tibetan Book of Living & Dying, Rider, 1992

ROERICH, N, Heart of Asia, 1929 & 1990, Inner Traditions, 1990

Shamballa – In Search of a New Era

SCHNEERSON, M, Rabbi, On the Essence of Hassidut, Kehot Publication, NY, 1978

SCHURE, E, Ramah & Moses

SHAH, I, The Way of the Sufi, Penguin Books, 1974

SITCHIN, Z, The 12th Planet, Avon Publishers, New York, 1978

STUBBS, T, An Ascension Handbook - Channelled from Master Serapis,

Oughten House Publishers

SMUTS, G Holism & Civilization, McMillan & Co, 1926

VELIKOVSKI, I, Ages in Chaos, 1973

Worlds in Collision, Abacus Books

WHITE EAGLE, Spiritual Unfoldment 3 - The Way to the Inner Mysteries, The

White Eagle Publishing Trust, 1987

Communication from the Master Sananda & the Planetary Logos, Sanat Kumara referred to in the Old Testament as The Ancient of Days and The Lord of the World

The Myth of Creation
Master Sananda
Zechariah Sitchin: The 12th Planet
Kramer: History Begins in Sumer
Omraam Mikhail Aivanhov: Christmas & Easter in the Initiatic Tradition

Shabbat
Master Sananda
Omraam Mikhail Aivanhov: Christmas & Easter in the Initiatic Tradition
'Jewish Law' - programme shown on British Television on 3/10/04
Master Sananda
The Planetary Logos, Sanat Kumara
Zechariah Sitchin: The 12th Planet

The Fall
Master Sananda
Elizabeth Bellhouse, originator of products that work on our subtle energy field - Newsletter Whitsun 2003

Job & the immorality of god
Robin Lane-Fox: The Un-authorised Version

The Flood & the Demise of Atlantis
Master Djwahl Khul: The Externalisation of the Hierarchy

Abraham & the Patriarchs
Master Sananda
Professor Jeremiah: The Old Testament in the Light of the Ancient East

Moses the Law Giver

Master Sananda

Edouard Schure : Ramah & Moses

Osman: Moses Pharaoh of Egypt

Exodus

P. Freke & P. Gandy :The Jesus Mysteries

Dr I. Velikovsky: Worlds in Collision & Ages in Chaos

Religion

Master Sananda

Prof. Jeremiah: The Old Testament in the Light of the Ancient East

Paul Brunton: The Inner Reality:

Mc Donald-Bayne: I Am the Life

Lewis Spence: The Occult Sciences in Atlantis (Aquarian Press, 1978)

Yahweh, god of the Old Testament

Master Sananda

Master Djwahl Khul

Zechariah Sitchin: The 12th Planet

The 'Miracles' at Sinai

Dr I. Velikovsky: 'Worlds in Collision' & 'Ages in Chaos'

The Goddess & Solomon

Master Sananda

Dr Raphael Patai: The Hebrew Goddess

Dr Eric Fromm: Psychoanalysis & Zen Buddhism

The Temple of Solomon & the Wailing Wall

'Horizon' Programme shown on British Television on 23/9/04

The Jew & the Jewish Mind

Master Sananda

Master Djwahl Khul

Dr Patai: The Jewish Mind

Circumcision

ROHEIM, Geza: The Eternal Ones of the Dream - in Joseph CAMPBELL 'The Hero with a Thousand Faces' (Fontana Press 1949 USA)

'Be ye transformed by the renewing of your mind'

O. M. Aivanhov: Christmas & Easter in the Initiatic Tradition

(for the story of Nicodemus, the Pharisee)

Titles that touch on the theme of extraterrestrial intervention and the genetic manipulation of early humanity:-

B. MARCINIAK   Bringers of the Dawn, Bear & Co Pub., 1999

J. ROBERTS   Seth Speaks – The Eternal Validity of the Soul, 1972

L. ROYAL   The Prysm of Lyra, Royal – Priest Research, Phoenix Arizona, 1992

S. STEVENSON   The Awakener, Gateway Books, 1997

TWILIGHT OF THE HEBREW GODS

Twilight of the Hebrew Gods has for subtitle 'Reflections on the End of the Jewish Condition in the Light of the Timeless Wisdom, the New Consciousness and modern Science. It follows and completes ***The Hebrew Gods.***

Twilight of the Hebrew Gods is an ensemble of Reflections on the prophesised dissolution of the biblical worldview manifestly authoritarian, monopolistic and materialistic. The biblical perspective – dominant aspect of our reality on the Earth plane - is being phased out. The 'old Earth' paradigm symbolises a phase of evolution enmeshed in the growth of the self and its repressive gods. Modern humanity is emerging out of this major but protracted chapter of its conscious evolution.

The first major breach was made by the Essenes 2000 years ago when they presented the deathless Soul to the beleaguered Pharisees. That attempt was later confirmed and secured by the creativity of the luminous Renaissance. Later still it was anchored by the spiritual insight of the Romantic Movement.

It is now left to progressive humanity to conclude the process of dissolution. And it is not a smooth process! A defensive and recalcitrant element is robustly holding on to the past, in so doing thwarting the efforts of the Spiritual Hierarchy who, on the inner planes, works tirelessly at fostering the advancement of mankind. This reactionary element is also frustrating the enterprise of the 'cosmic workers' who diligently work at transforming the stale, tired, clinging, lingering energies of the past. Lastly and crucially, this retrograde force is obstructing the realisation of the Divine Plan.

The primeval cosmic struggle between the Forces of Light and the Forces of Darkness – between the personality and the Soul – is being played out on the global stage.

PUBLISHER: LULU.COM

644

645

646

CPSIA information can be obtained at www.ICGtesting.com
Printed in the USA
BVOW02s1212250916

463208BV00001BA/110/P